D1417817

INTRODUCTORY PHILOSOPHY

INTRODUCTORY PHILOSOPHY

EDITED BY

FRANK TILLMAN

VASSAR COLLEGE

BERNARD BEROFSKY

UNIVERSITY OF MICHIGAN

JOHN O'CONNOR

VASSAR COLLEGE

Harper & Row, *Publishers*

NEW YORK, EVANSTON, AND LONDON

Library of Congress Catalog Card Number: 67-12552

D-R

CONTENTS

IV

EXPLANATION AND HUMAN ACTION

V

MORAL EVALUATION AND JUSTIFICATION

VI

POLITICAL PHILOSOPHY

VII

KNOWLEDGE, PERCEPTION, AND NECESSARY TRUTH

VIII

LANGUAGE AND MEANING

IX

GOD AND RELIGIOUS BELIEF

X

WORLD VIEWS AND PHILOSOPHICAL COMMITMENT

PREFACE

THIS BOOK is designed to acquaint the beginning student with philosophy—in particular to give him a sense of what a philosophical problem is and how it is generated. The readings will show him how a philosophical problem is related to other problems of philosophy, to problems in science, to society, and to ordinary ways of thinking. Finally, this book indicates how and to what extent a philosophical problem can be resolved or opened to further and more fruitful inquiry.

To all who have undertaken it, the teaching of introductory philosophy presents a number of persistent difficulties.

An advancement in philosophical learning is rarely attended by public pronouncement or acclaim. To all appearances philosophical problems remain perennial, leaving the impression that no progress can be made, since none has been made in 2000 years. The discouraged student or reader of philosophy finds it easy to abandon a problem too quickly. Yet philosophical problems have a great fluidity; through constant reformulation from radically different perspectives, each age simplifies, ramifies, and breaks forth with new insights toward partial solutions. For example, problems are refined to the point where they can be handed to specialists; just this has happened with physics, logic, and psychology, all of which were once part of philosophy. It is about to happen to semantics. This constitutes the best justification for philosophy occasionally to grow technical. As scientific learning develops, philosophy is in turn enriched. Advances in neurophysiology and computing machinery have provided fresh ways of reformulating some problems that cluster about the traditional conceptions of the relation of mind to body and man to nature. And so new areas of exploration are possible. Sometimes a more subtle advance is made by discovering the reasons why certain problems, as they stand, will not submit to any inquiry.

Philosophy is both a craft and a set of doctrines contributing to human learning. As a discipline, philosophy is so closely bound to the whole human scheme of things that the beginning student finds it difficult to mark what is peculiarly philosophical from what is not. The vocabulary of philosophy does not help very much, for it is far less technical than is supposed. The major issues of philosophy cannot be stated without making use of such ordinary terms as 'know,' 'believe,' 'good,' 'right,' and 'truth.' The student's impatience for a definition of philosophy may incline him to the view that philosophy is a set of abstract doctrines about man and the world, but he may miss the point that it is also an activity requiring skills.

Philosophical problems and concepts are themselves interdependent and mutually involved. Yet as problems they are frequently studied in isolation, so that it is difficult for the student to see what binds the whole cluster together. The time-worn categories of classification, such as epistemology, ethics, metaphysics, and philosophy of science, are sometimes actually barriers against insight. The discovery that a solution or fresh way of seeing one problem may have important conceptual bearing on a whole range of other problems leads us to look for a more flexible order or arrangement. Such problems as free will and moral responsibility, for example, cut across the whole philosophic landscape.

To reduce these difficulties and to provide an adequate introduction to philosophy, we have set before the student a constellation of brilliant and lucid writings drawn from the entire history of philosophy; we have tried to display its special skills: the way a problem can be unblocked by a new look from a different perspective, the way philosophy informs and is informed by the special sciences and other disciplines, and, finally, the way a study of philosophy may contribute to intelligent and responsible thinking in areas of practical concern.

To do this and to give a sense of the continuing enterprise of philosophy, we have tried to recreate a living dialogue by balancing one man's mind against another, one contemporary statement against a traditional one. We have, to some extent, modified the usual categories of classification, preferring instead ones that would display the growth of a philosophical problem and the variety of its impingements.

Each section of this book is built around a central question; each selection is part of a cluster of interrelated issues; and each section itself is part of a larger issue. A question treated in one section is reformulated in another, but from a different angle and with further and deeper ramifications. Frequently a question in one section is generated in a preceding section.

The book begins with the questions "What is man?" and "How is he like or unlike the rest of nature?" Section I, "Bodies, Minds, and Persons," starts with a dualistic account of man—man is both a mind and a body—and takes up the traditional and contemporary responses to dualism. Claims about the nature of man or mind lead naturally to questions concerning our way of knowing about ourselves and others. In Section II, then, the traditional questions concerning personal identity and knowledge of other minds are raised. In Sections III, "Determinism, Freedom, and Responsibility" and IV, "Explanation and Human Action," the original question "How is man like or unlike the rest of nature?" emerges in two new forms: "Is man free or determined?" and "Can we explain human actions in the same way as we explain physical events?" A discussion of these questions has direct bearing on considerations of responsibility and moral praise and blame, Section V, "Moral Evaluation and Justification," and on the discussion of the institution of legal and political obligation, Section VI, "Political Philosophy." In asking whether or not explanation of human behavior is essentially different from explanation of nonhuman behavior, we are drawn quite naturally to the general problem of knowledge: "What is the basis and scope of man's knowledge of himself and his world?" and "Is there any knowledge which is beyond dispute, a knowledge of things that must be so?" These problems are developed in Section VII, "Knowledge, Perception, and Necessary Truth." Questions about the extent and kinds of knowledge lead quickly to questions about meaning, "When are two words or sentences said to have the same meaning?" and to questions about the function of language, "What are the various forms of discourse and how are they appraised?" These questions are pursued in Section VIII, "Language and Meaning." Sections IX and X press questions of knowledge, meaning, and moral evaluation still further. Section IX, "God and Religious Belief," is devoted to man's knowledge of God and the questions of his ultimate commitment. Section X, "World Views and Philosophical Commitment," discusses the kind of knowledge, understanding, and guidance, if any, which philosophy contributes to the human enterprise.

Our thanks go to Mary O'Connor for her great help in the final stages of the preparations of the introductions. Our thanks also go to Alfred E. Prettyman, our editor at Harper & Row, for his advice and encouragement, both on matters of form and content. His interest and criticism, especially in the last stages of the work, were invaluable. Finally, we would like to thank Nina Hoffman, Tona Johnston, and Susan Leigh Smith for their assistance and interest.

FRANK TILLMAN
BERNARD BEROFSKY
JOHN O'CONNOR

January, 1967

INTRODUCTORY PHILOSOPHY

I

BODIES, MINDS, AND PERSONS

HE QUESTIONS "What is man?" and "How is he like or unlike the rest of nature?" have been asked ever since the dawn of self-consciousness. They are formulated and reformulated in every age. Recently, they have taken the following form: "Can a man's rational actions be explained in the same terms in which we explain physical occurrences?" "Are conscious states nothing but complex brain processes?" "Can a computer be 'conscious'?" These questions are disturbing to the degree that advances in neurophysiology and computer research, on the one hand, and new analyses of the philosophical concepts involved, on the other hand, threaten to displace the traditional conception of man.

One of the traditional answers to the question "What is man?" is that he is both a mind (or soul) and a body. Since, however, many things other than men are physical objects—bodies—it seems to be a man's mind that is unique to him. According to many traditional philosophers, then, man is unique in nature, and his uniqueness is marked by his mind and its conscious products, thought and intelligent action.

What is being challenged by these questions is the very distinction that all, or almost all, men and many philosophers make between themselves and the rest of nature. Any view that seeks to destroy this distinction is likely to be treated as an outrage. The existentialist philosophers have been most volatile in their reaction to any attempts to assimilate man as a person to man as an object of science. The French philosopher Jean-Paul Sartre expresses his outrage in this way:

> *If I am to be an object, a process, a pure phenomenon, then I am a fraud. And if scientific thought thus requires me to regard myself as a fraud, then science is not a boon to mankind, but a curse . . .*

Whether the answer to these new questions is a complicated "Yes" or a complicated "No," the questions themselves force us to re-examine the traditional conceptions of man.

Dualism

The view that man has a dual nature was expressed very early by the Platonic Socrates in Plato's dialogue *The Phaedo*. Socrates, imprisoned and awaiting execution, expresses the belief that what he really is, namely a soul, is capable of surviving the death of the body.

> *I cannot persuade Crito, my friends, that Socrates, who, now conversing and arranging the details of his argument, is really I: Crito thinks I am the one whom he will presently see as a corpse and asks how to bury me.*

Socrates here is saying that what Crito will bury is only Socrates' body. The real Socrates, he who is "conversing and arranging the details of his argument," is Socrates' soul (or psyche).

The word "soul" ("psyche") has not always been used to designate something in man that was capable of surviving death. "Psyche" originally meant breath; it was often used as a synonym for "life." To say that a being possessed a soul was simply another way of saying he was alive. The special use Plato made of the word was obviously attractive and so it was retained, but with elaborations.

Descartes (1596–1650) added two important features. (See the selection from Descartes' *Meditations* included in this section.)

First, he conceived of soul or mind as a substance that could exist entirely independently of body. A substance by definition is something which depends upon nothing else for existence. The conception of soul as a substance makes its detachability from body a conceptual necessity. As Descartes said:

> *Our soul is entirely independent of body and in consequence . . . it is not liable to die with it.*

The question of whether the soul survives the body in any interesting sense was hotly debated by clerics and laymen alike. If the soul survives the death of the body and retains its personal characteristics (memories, feelings, etc.) this would be very interesting to know. If, on the other hand, it loses its personal characteristics and becomes part of some general spiritual substance, as some have argued, this would be much less interesting. In his paper "Is Life After Death Possible?" (included in the selections), Curt Ducasse weighs the evidence offered by those who argue against personal survival. There he challenges an important assumption often made by those who argue against personal survival; viz., that the only real things are material things.

Descartes added a second feature to the conception of mind or soul. He said that mind, and only mind, was essentially a thing which thinks: "I notice," he said, "while I was trying to think everything false, it must be that I, who was thinking, was something." But "What am I?" His answer was

> *A thing which thinks. What is a thing which thinks? It is a thing which doubts, understands, affirms, denies, wills, refuses, which also imagines and feels.*

Thus, according to Descartes, the soul is an independent nonphysical substance whose being it is to think, imagine, feel, etc. But what it thinks, imagines, or feels is present only to one person, namely, the person designated by "I" whose experiences these are. These two additions were utterly decisive in determining the direction later philosophical work took and the problems that had to be solved in working out a coherent philosophy of man. The view that minds and bodies are independent substances generates a legion of difficulties known collectively as the mind-body problem. It is important to see how certain elements of Descartes' view lead to deep difficulties.

1. How, according to the view that minds and bodies are distinct substances, is it possible for a mind to cause a change in the body or vice versa? Consider some such action as moving a hand, or writing, or walking. How could something so rarified as a soul or mind produce the physical movements involved in such actions? And how could something happening to a body—for example, bumping into a table—produce something mental—for example, a feeling of pain? That is, how can a chunk of matter leave its impression on the soul? This picture of minds and bodies is reminiscent of what Gilbert Ryle has described as the doctrine of the "Ghost in the Machine." (See the selection entitled "Descartes' Myth" in this section.)

2. The first difficulty, that it is hard to see how minds and bodies—if conceived as two distinct substances—could have any causal effects on each other, suggests another problem. It seems that each mind is limited to its own purely *mental* world. How, then, is it possible for a mind to perceive anything *physical*, e.g. physical objects like tables and chairs? It would seem that it is not. Descartes had to prove the existence of God and then enlist His divine aid to help him out of his egocentric predicament. (See Part VII, on perception, for further discussion of this problem.)

3. Descartes provides a criterion for applying predicates to mind (or soul) and to body:

> *Everything that we discover in ourselves, which we see could also be in completely animate bodies, should be attributed only to our body; on the other hand, everything that is in us, which we could not conceive of as possibly belonging to a physical body should be attributed to our soul.* ("*Passions of the Soul*")

But, some have argued, these criteria do not apply to a large number of the predicates that we apply to ourselves. It is difficult to see how we should use the criterion to classify human actions such as walking, speaking, smiling, and other physical actions that seem to imply the presence of consciousness. None of these common human actions, it is said by some philosophers, are entirely mental or entirely physical. Only in wonderland can the grin be divorced from the cat. (See the selection entitled "Experience and the Subject" by John Dewey in this section.)

Responses to Dualism

Traditionally there were two kinds of reactions to dualism. One group of philosophers tried to maintain the natural distinctness of mind and body but at the same time tried to make intelligible their apparent relatedness. A second group of philosophers took a more radical approach by trying to reduce the two substances to one.

1. Philosophers of the first group all agreed that mind and body are irreducibly different but differ about the degree and kind of relatedness. In swift succession a number of proposals were presented, some employing fantastic machinery to make dualism work. First, Descartes himself elaborated on what seemed obvious to him, namely, that bodies and minds interact. He held that the point of their interaction was a small gland at the base of the brain (the pineal gland); there, what is purely physical is somehow converted into something mental, and vice versa. Descartes' account is strange; and it seems impossible to imagine what a satisfactory account of the interaction of two such logically distinct substances would be like. Another possibility is to suppose that all mental phenomena such as pain, pleasure, thought, are merely the by-products or epiphenomenal accompaniment of bodily changes. A twinge of experienced pain stands to the body like a shadow to a solid object. But it is still far from clear how these mental phenomena are caused. And epiphenomenalism does not account for what is at least the apparent effect of mental states on the body. Consider a third possibility. Since the mind is so intimately connected to the body, perhaps, as some philosophers reasoned, there is some more basic substance of which the mind and the body are aspects. But aspects of what? This solution of the mind-body problem depends on specifying some unknown substance which is neither mind nor body, but somehow more fundamental than either. And this no one has done successfully.

A more daring proposal is to suppose that instead of some causal interaction, the apparent relation between minds and bodies could be accounted for by imagining that the events in a person's mental history exactly coincide with events in his bodily history. What looks like interaction, then, is simply the simultaneous occurrence of events in two parallel histories. If God is said to be the original author of these parallel histories, then we have a doctrine that is called *pre-established harmony* (as if, as Leibniz [1646–1716] imagined the picture, two clocks were set in harmony so that one would show the hour on its face, the other by striking). If, instead, God intercedes from moment to moment, thereby directly causing every event in both series, we have a type of parallelism described as *occasionalism* and associated with Malebranche (1638–1715).

2. Such drastic attempts to bring mind and body into some relation make attractive a second and more radical view of man: man is not a dual substance, but a unity. This philosophical view is called *monism*. Traditional monism takes two forms: *idealism* and *materialism*.

An idealist, like Berkeley (see Section VII, "To Be Is to Be Perceived"), argues that the only substance is mental substance. What others call physical objects are really ideas. To exist is to be either a mind or an idea. Idealists have always disagreed about whether there are many minds or only one, but whatever the answer to this question is, the idealist would say that a man was only mind.

A materialist, e.g., Thomas Hobbes (1588–1679) or Baron d'Holbach (1723–1789), conceives of all the things we call "mental states"—willing, imagining, remembering—as material states and as explainable in terms of mechanical laws. For example, the phenomenon of imagination is nothing but the behavior of certain minute bodies that conform to the law of inertia. According to materialism, then, a mental state is really just a bodily state. (See the selection entitled "A Materialist Conception of Man" by Baron d'Holbach in this section.)

The idealist and materialist have simplified the problem of interaction by eliminating it. But both have the problem of saving and explaining the appearances. The idealist must account for the fact that the "physical" world appears to be independent of our perceptions and thoughts of it, and the materialist must account for the apparent difference between the qualities of experiences and the qualities of physical objects.

Recently the monism of idealism and materialism has taken different forms. Modern *phenomenalism* has almost replaced idealism in attempting to reduce physical objects to collections of sense-data. (See A. J. Ayer's "Sense Data and Physical Objects" in Section VII.) *Behaviorism* and *physicalism* have become the modern versions of materialism.

A radical behaviorism attempts to reduce all mental phenomena to bodily movements. The program has yet to be successfully carried out. One of the chief difficulties is that some of the terms that a behaviorist uses to describe human behavior, e.g., "response," seem to involve mental notions already. An adequate behaviorism would have to develop a set of purely physical terms which would be capable of describing all human behavior. This seems to be a difficult undertaking.

The attempt to work out a more modest behaviorism is the primary concern of Gilbert Ryle's selection ("Descartes' Myth"). Ryle tries to provide an analysis of psychological predicates in terms of behavior. His proposal is that terms such as "remembering," "thinking," and "hoping" do not have to be construed as the names of some kind of non-physical process going on inside a person, but all these terms may be interpreted as disposition terms. That is, to think is to be disposed to act in certain ways.

Another modern version of materialism, closer to Hobbes' original intentions, is presented by J. J. C. Smart in "Sensations and Brain Processes." Smart holds that the success of science makes it plausible to believe that something "mental,"—a sensation, for instance—is nothing over and above something physical—for example, a brain process. His chief concern is to show that there is nothing in principle impossible in this suggestion. He separates two senses of "same" as applied to words. Two words can mean the same thing: e.g., "bachelor" and "unmarried man"; or two words can stand for the same thing: e.g., "Morning Star" and "Evening Star." His claim is that while "sensation" and "brain process" do not, of course, mean the same thing, it is plausible to believe that they happen to refer to the same things. For this reason this view has come to be called the "Identity Theory." The contemporary physicalist must wait for the development of a more adequate theory of brain processes before he will be in a position to claim for certain that sensations are brain processes. In the meantime he must face objections from philosophers who wonder about the sense of identity or sameness that the physicalist is using, as well as objections based upon the fact that our language for speaking of human brain processes is, in some ways, quite different from our language for speaking about mental states.

Yet another attempt to deal with dualism is the work of John Dewey. (See the selection entitled "Experience and the Subject" in this section.) Dewey does not wish to reduce mind to matter or matter to mind. At the same time he rejects dualism on the grounds that mind does not designate a distinct substance different from matter. Events, including experiences, are intrinsically neither physical nor mental. Mental-physical and like distinctions are made in order to mark the different levels and character of events in their interaction. For example, to claim that a certain experience is *mine* is, among other things, to proclaim responsibility for its future consequences and not to specify an entity that owns the experience. Aristotle is often conceived as a natural predecessor of Dewey, for Aristotle too rejects the possibility that soul and matter can be separated from one another, conceiving of the soul rather as that which make the body what it is, i.e., a living body. (See the selection by Aristotle entitled "On the Soul" in this section.)

The following selections present in detail some of the views sketched above.

CERTAINTY, THE SELF, AND DUALISM

RENÉ DESCARTES

MEDITATION I

Of the things which may be brought within the sphere of the doubtful.

It is now some years since I detected how many were the false beliefs that I had from my earliest youth admitted as true, and how doubtful was everything I had since constructed on this basis; and from that time I was convinced that I must once for all seriously undertake to rid myself of all the opinions which I had formerly accepted, and commence to build anew from the foundation, if I wanted to establish any firm and permanent structure in the sciences. But as this enterprise appeared to be a very

These selections are taken from *Philosophical Works of Descartes*, translated by Elizabeth S. Haldane and G. R. T. Ross and reprinted by permission of the Cambridge University Press, New York.

great one, I waited until I had attained an age so mature that I could not hope that at any later date I should be better fitted to execute my design. This reason caused me to delay so long that I should feel that I was doing wrong were I to occupy in deliberation the time that yet remains to me for action. To-day, then, since very opportunely for the plan I have in view I have delivered my mind from every care [and am happily agitated by no passions] and since I have procured for myself an assured leisure in a peaceable retirement, I shall at last seriously and freely address myself to the general upheaval of all my former opinions.

Now for this object it is not necessary that I should show that all of these are false—I shall perhaps never arrive at this end. But inasmuch as reason already persuades me that I ought no less carefully to withhold my assent from matters which are not entirely certain and indubitable than from those which appear to me manifestly to be false, if I am able to find in each one some reason to doubt, this will suffice to justify my rejecting the whole. And for that end it will not be requisite that I should examine each in particular, which would be an endless undertaking; for owing to the fact that the destruction of the foundations of necessity brings with it the downfall of the rest of the edifice, I shall only in the first place attack those principles upon which all my former opinions rested.

All that up to the present time I have accepted as most true and certain I have learned either from the senses or through the senses; but it is sometimes proved to me that these senses are deceptive, and it is wiser not to trust entirely to any thing by which we have once been deceived.

But it may be that although the senses sometimes deceive us concerning things which are hardly perceptible, or very far away, there are yet many others to be met with as to which we cannot reasonably have any doubt, although we recognise them by their means. For example, there is the fact that I am here, seated by the fire, attired in a dressing gown, having this paper in my hands and other similar matters. And how could I deny that these hands and this body are mine, were it not perhaps that I compare myself to certain persons, devoid of sense, whose cerebella are so troubled and clouded by the violent vapours of black bile, that they constantly assure us that they think they are kings when they are really quite poor, or that they are clothed in purple when they are really without covering, or who imagine that they have an earthenware head or are nothing but pumpkins or are made of glass. But they are mad, and I should not be any the less insane were I to follow examples so extravagant.

At the same time I must remember that I am a man, and that consequently I am in the habit of sleeping, and in my dreams representing to myself the same things or sometimes even less probable things, than do those who are insane in their waking moments. How often has it happened to me that in the night I dreamt that I found myself in this particular place, that I was dressed and seated near the fire, whilst in reality I was lying undressed in bed! At this moment it does indeed seem to me that it is with eyes awake that I am looking at this paper; that this head which I move is not asleep, that it is deliberately and of set purpose that I extend my hand and perceive it; what happens in sleep does not appear so clear nor so distinct as does all this. But in thinking over this I remind myself that on many occasions I have in sleep been deceived by similar illusions, and in dwelling carefully on this reflection I see so manifestly that there are no certain indications by which we may clearly distinguish wakefulness from sleep that I am lost in astonishment. And my astonishment is such that it is almost capable of persuading me that I now dream.

Now let us assume that we are asleep and that all these particulars, e.g. that we open our eyes, shake our head, extend our hands, and so on, are but false delusions; and let us reflect that possibly neither our hands nor our whole body are such as they appear to us to be. At the same time we must at least confess that the things which are represented to us in sleep are like painted representations which can only have been formed as the counterparts of something real and true, and that in this way those general things at least, i.e. eyes, a head, hands, and a whole body, are not imaginary things, but things really existent. For, as a matter of fact, painters, even when they study with the greatest skill to represent sirens and satyrs by forms the most strange and extraordinary, cannot give them natures which are entirely new, but merely make a certain medley of the members of different animals; or if their imagination is extravagant enough to invent something so novel that nothing similar has ever before been seen, and that then their work represents a thing purely fictitious and absolutely false, it is certain all the same that the colours of which this is composed are necessarily real. And for the same reason, although these general things, to wit, [a body], eyes, a head, hands, and such like, may be imaginary, we are bound at the same time to confess that there are at least some other objects yet more simple and more universal, which are real and true; and of these just in the same way as with certain real colours, all these images of things which dwell in our thoughts, whether true and real or false and fantastic, are formed.

To such a class of things pertains corporeal nature in general, and its extension, the figure of extended things, their quantity or magnitude and number, as also the place in which they are, the time which measures their duration, and so on.

That is possibly why our reasoning is not unjust when we conclude from this that Physics, Astronomy, Medicine and all other sciences which have as their end the consideration of composite things, are very dubious and uncertain; but that Arithmetic, Geometry and other sciences of that kind which only treat of things that are very simple and very general, without taking great trouble to ascertain whether they are actually existent or not, contain some measure of certainty and an element of the indubitable. For whether I am awake or asleep, two and three together always form five, and the square can never have more than four sides, and it does not seem possible that truths so clear and apparent can be suspected of any falsity [or uncertainty].

Nevertheless I have long had fixed in my mind the belief that an all-powerful God existed by whom I have been created such as I am. But how do I know that He has not brought it to pass that there is no earth, no heaven, no extended body, no magnitude, no place, and that nevertheless [I possess the perceptions of all these things and that] they seem to me to exist just exactly as I now see them? And, besides, as I sometimes imagine that others deceive themselves in the things which they think they know best, how do I know that I am not deceived every time that I add two and three, or count the sides of a square, or judge of things yet simpler, if anything simpler can be imagined? But possibly God has not desired that I should be thus deceived, for He is said to be supremely good. If, however, it is contrary to His goodness to have made me such that I constantly deceive myself, it would also appear to be contrary to His goodness to permit me to be sometimes deceived, and nevertheless I cannot doubt that He does permit this.

There may indeed be those who would prefer to deny the existence of a God so powerful, rather than believe that all other things are uncertain. But let us not oppose them for the present, and grant that all that is here said of a God is a fable; nevertheless in whatever way they suppose that I have arrived at the state of being that I have reached—whether they attribute it to fate or to accident, or make out that it is by a continual succession of antecedents, or by some other method—since to err and deceive oneself is a defect, it is clear that the greater will be the probability of my being so imperfect as to deceive myself ever, as is the Author to whom they assign my origin the less powerful. To these reasons I have certainly nothing to reply, but at the end I feel constrained to confess that there is nothing in all that I formerly believed to be true, of which I cannot in some measure doubt, and that not merely through want of thought or through levity, but for reasons which are very powerful and maturely considered; so that henceforth I ought not the less carefully to refrain from giving credence to these opinions than to that which is manifestly false, if I desire to arrive at any certainty [in the sciences].

But it is not sufficient to have made these remarks, we must also be careful to keep them in mind. For these ancient and commonly held opinions still revert frequently to my mind, long and familiar custom having given them the right to occupy my mind against my inclination and rendered them almost masters of my belief; nor will I ever lose the habit of deferring to them or of placing my confidence in them, so long as I consider them as they really are, i.e. opinions in some measure doubtful, as I have just shown, and at the same time highly probable, so that there is much more reason to believe in than to deny them. That is why I consider that I shall not be acting amiss, if, taking of set purpose a contrary belief, I allow myself to be deceived, and for a certain time pretend that all these opinions are entirely false and imaginary, until at last, having thus balanced my former prejudices with my latter [so that they cannot divert my opinions more to one side than to the other], my judgment will no longer be dominated by bad usage or turned away from the right knowledge of the truth. For I am assured that there can be neither peril nor error in this course, and that I cannot at present yield too much to distrust, since I am not considering the question of action, but only of knowledge.

I shall then suppose, not that God who is supremely good and the fountain of truth, but some evil genius not less powerful than deceitful, has employed his whole energies in deceiving me; I shall consider that the heavens, the earth, colours, figures, sound, and all other external things are nought but the illusions and dreams of which this genius has availed himself in order to lay traps for my credulity; I shall consider myself as having no hands, no eyes, no flesh, no blood, nor any senses, yet falsely believing myself to possess all these things; I shall remain obstinately attached to this idea, and if by this means it is not in my power to arrive at the knowledge of any truth, I may at least do what is in my power [i.e. suspend my judgment], and with firm purpose avoid giving credence to any false thing, or being imposed upon by this arch deceiver, however powerful and deceptive he may be. But this task is a laborious one, and insensibly a certain lassitude leads me into the course of my ordinary life. And just as a captive who in sleep enjoys an imaginary liberty, when he begins to suspect that his liberty is but a dream, fears to awaken, and conspires with these agreeable illusions that the deception may be prolonged, so insensibly of my own accord I fall back into my former opinions, and I dread awakening from this slumber, lest the laborious wakefulness which would follow the tranquillity of this repose should have to be spent not in daylight, but in the excessive darkness of the difficulties which have just been discussed.

MEDITATION II

Of the Nature of the Human Mind; and that it is more easily known than the Body.

The Meditation of yesterday filled my mind with so many doubts that it is no longer in my power to forget them. And yet I do not see in what manner I can resolve them; and, just as if I had all of a sudden fallen into very deep water, I am so disconcerted that I can neither make certain of setting my feet on the bottom, nor can I swim and so support myself on the surface. I shall nevertheless make an effort and follow anew the same path as that on which I yesterday entered, i.e. I shall proceed by setting aside all that in which the least doubt could be supposed to exist, just as if I had discovered that it was absolutely false; and I shall ever follow in this road until I have met with something which is certain, or at least, if I can do nothing else, until I have learned for certain that there is nothing in the world that is certain. Archimedes, in order that he might draw the terrestial globe out of its place, and transport it elsewhere, demanded only that one point should be fixed and immoveable; in the same way I shall have the right to conceive high hopes if I am happy enough to discover one thing only which is certain and indubitable.

I suppose, then, that all the things that I see are false; I persuade myself that nothing has ever existed of all that my fallacious memory represents to me. I consider that I possess no senses; I imagine that body, figure, extension, movement and place are but the fictions of my mind. What, then, can be esteemed as true? Perhaps nothing at all, unless that there is nothing in the world that is certain.

But how can I know there is not something different from those things that I have just considered, of which one cannot have the slightest doubt? Is there not some God, or some other being by whatever name we call it, who puts these reflections into my mind? That is not necessary, for is it not possible that I am capable of producing them myself? I myself, am I not at least something? But I have already denied that I had senses and body. Yet I hesitate, for what follows from that? Am I so dependent on body and senses that I cannot exist without these? But I was persuaded that there was nothing in all the world, that there was no heaven, no earth, that there were no minds, nor any bodies: was I not then likewise persuaded that I did not exist? Not at all; of a surety I myself did exist since I persuaded myself of something [or merely because I thought of something]. But there is some deceiver or other, very powerful and very cunning, who ever employs his ingenuity in deceiving me. Then without doubt I exist also if he deceives me, and let him deceive me as much as he will, he can never cause me to be nothing so long as I think that I am something. So that after having reflected well and carefully examined all things, we must come to the definite conclusion that this proposition: I am, I exist, is necessarily true each time that I pronounce it, or that I mentally conceive it.

But I do not yet know clearly enough what I am, I who am certain that I am; and hence I must be careful to see that I do not imprudently take some other object in place of myself, and thus that I do not go astray in respect of this knowledge that I hold to be the most certain and most evident of all that I have formerly learned. That is why I shall now consider anew what I believed myself to be before I embarked upon these last reflections; and of my former opinions I shall withdraw all that might even in a small degree be invalidated by the reasons which I have just brought forward, in order that there may be nothing at all left beyond what is absolutely certain and indubitable.

What then did I formerly believe myself to be? Undoubtedly I believed myself to be a man. But what is a man? Shall I say a reasonable animal? Certainly not; for then I should have to inquire what an animal is, and what is reasonable; and thus from a single question I should insensibly fall into an infinitude of others more difficult; and I should not wish to waste the little time and leisure remaining to me in trying to unravel subtleties like these. But I shall rather stop here to consider the thoughts which of themselves spring up in my mind, and which were not inspired by anything beyond my own nature alone when I applied myself to the consideration of my being. In the first place, then, I considered myself as having a face, hands, arms, and all that system of members composed of bones and flesh as seen in a corpse which I designated by the name of body. In addition to this I considered that I was nourished, that I walked, that I felt, and that I thought, and I referred all these actions to the soul: but I did not stop to consider what the soul was, or if I did stop, I imagined that it was something extremely rare and subtle like a wind, a flame, or an ether, which was spread throughout my grosser parts. As to body I had no manner of doubt about its nature, but thought I had a very clear knowledge of it; and if I had desired to explain it according to the notions that I had then formed of it, I should have described it thus: By the body I understand all that which can be defined by a certain figure: something which can be confined in a certain place, and which can fill a given space in such a way that every other body will be excluded from it; which can be perceived either by touch, or by sight, or by hearing, or by taste, or by smell: which can be moved in many ways not, in truth, by itself, but by something which is foreign to it, by which it is touched [and from which it receives impressions]: for to have the power of self-movement, as also of feeling or of thinking, I did not consider to appertain to the nature of body: on the contrary, I was rather astonished to find that faculties similar to them existed in some bodies.

But what am I, now that I suppose that there is a certain genius which is extremely powerful, and, if I may say so, malicious, who employs all his powers in deceiving me? Can I affirm that I possess the least of all those things which I have just said pertain to the nature of body? I pause to consider, I revolve all these things in my mind, and I find none of which I can say that it pertains to me. It would be tedious to stop to enumerate them. Let us pass to the attributes of soul and see if there is any one which is in me? What of nutrition or walking [the first mentioned]? But if it is so that I have no body it is also true that I can neither walk nor take nourishment. Another attribute is sensation. But one cannot feel without body, and besides I have thought I perceived many things during sleep that I recognised in my waking moments as not having been experienced at all. What of thinking? I find here that thought is an attribute that belongs to me; it alone cannot be separated from me. I am, I exist, that is certain. But how often? Just when I think; for it might possibly be the case if I ceased entirely to think, that I should likewise cease altogether to exist. I do not now admit anything which is not necessarily true: to speak accurately I am not more than a thing which thinks, that is to say a mind or a soul, or an understanding, or a reason, which are terms whose significance was formerly unknown to me. I am, however, a real thing and really exist; but what thing? I have answered: a thing which thinks.

And what more? I shall exercise my imagination [in order to see if I am not something more]. I am not a collection of members which we call the human body: I am not a subtle air distributed through these members, I am not a wind, a fire, a vapour, a breath, nor anything at all which I can imagine or conceive; because I have assumed that all these were nothing. Without changing that supposition I find that I only leave myself certain of the fact that I am somewhat. But perhaps it is true that these same things which I supposed were non-existent because they are unknown to me, are really not different from the self which I know. I am not sure about this, I shall not dispute about it now; I can only give judgment on things that are known to me. I know that I exist, and I inquire what I am, I whom I know to exist. But it is very certain that the knowledge of my existence taken in its precise significance does not depend on things whose existence is not yet known to me; consequently it does not depend on those which I can feign in imagination. And indeed the very term *feign* in imagination* proves to me my error, for I really do this if I image myself a something, since to imagine is nothing else than to contemplate the figure or image of a corporeal thing. But I already know for certain that I am, and that it may be that all these images, and, speaking generally, all things that relate to the nature of body are nothing but dreams [and chimeras]. For this reason I see clearly that I have as little reason to say, 'I shall stimulate my imagination in order to know more distinctly what I am,' than if I were to say, 'I am now awake, and I perceive somewhat that is real and true: but because I do not yet perceive it distinctly enough, I shall go to sleep of express purpose, so that my dreams may represent the perception with greatest truth and evidence.' And, thus, I know for certain that nothing of all that I can understand by means of my imagination belongs to this knowledge which I have of myself, and that it is necessary to recall the mind from this mode of thought with the utmost diligence in order that it may be able to know its own nature with perfect distinctness.

But what then am I? A thing which thinks. What is a thing which thinks? It is a thing which doubts, understands, [conceives], affirms, denies, wills, refuses, which also imagines and feels.

Certainly it is no small matter if all these things pertain to my nature. But why should they not so pertain? Am I not that being who now doubts nearly everything, who nevertheless understands certain things, who affirms that one only is true, who denies all the others, who desires to know more, is averse from being deceived, who imagines many things, sometimes indeed despite his will, and who perceives many likewise, as by the intervention of the bodily organs? Is there nothing in all this which is as true as it is certain that I exist, even though I should always sleep and though he who has given me being employed all his ingenuity in deceiving me? Is there likewise any one of these attributes which can be distinguished from my thought, or which might be said to be separated from myself? For it is so evident of itself that it is I who doubts, who understands, and who desires, that there is no reason here to add anything to explain it. And I have certainly the power of imagining likewise; for although it may happen (as I formerly supposed) that none of the things which I imagine are true, nevertheless this power of imagining does not cease to be really in use, and it forms part of my thought. Finally, I am the same who feels, that is to say, who perceives certain things, as by the organs of sense, since in truth I see light, I hear noise, I feel heat. But it

* Or 'form an image' (effingo).

will be said that these phenomena are false and that I am dreaming. Let it be so; still it is at least quite certain that it seems to me that I see light, that I hear noise and that I feel heat. That cannot be false; properly speaking it is what is in me called feeling; and used in this precise sense that is no other thing than thinking.

From this time I begin to know what I am with a little more clearness and distinction than before; but nevertheless it still seems to me, and I cannot prevent myself from thinking, that corporeal things, whose images are framed by thought, which are tested by the senses, are much more distinctly known than that obscure part of me which does not come under the imagination. Although really it is very strange to say that I know and understand more distinctly these things whose existence seems to me dubious, which are unknown to me, and which do not belong to me, than others of the truth of which I am convinced, which are known to me and which pertain to my real nature, in a word, than myself. But I see clearly how the case stands: my mind loves to wander, and cannot yet suffer itself to be retained within the just limits of truth. Very good, let us once more give it the freest rein, so that, when afterwards we seize the proper occasion for pulling up, it may the more easily be regulated and controlled.

Let us begin by considering the commonest matters, those which we believe to be the most distinctly comprehended, to wit, the bodies which we touch and see; not indeed bodies in general, for these general ideas are usually a little more confused, but let us consider one body in particular. Let us take, for example, this piece of wax: it has been taken quite freshly from the hive, and it has not yet lost the sweetness of the honey which it contains; it still retains somewhat of the odour of the flowers from which it has been culled; its colour, its figure, its size are apparent; it is hard, cold, easily handled, and if you strike it with the finger, it will emit a sound. Finally all the things which are requisite to cause us distinctly to recognise a body, are met with in it. But notice that while I speak and approach the fire what remained of the taste is exhaled, the smell evaporates, the colour alters, the figure is destroyed, the size increases, it becomes liquid, it heats, scarcely can one handle it, and when one strikes it, no sound is emitted. Does the same wax remain after this change? We must confess that it remains; none would judge otherwise. What then did I know so distinctly in this piece of wax? It could certainly be nothing of all that the senses brought to my notice, since all these things which fall under taste, smell, sight, touch, and hearing, are found to be changed, and yet the same wax remains.

Perhaps it was what I now think, viz. that this wax was not that sweetness of honey, nor that agreeable scent of flowers, nor that particular whiteness, nor that figure, nor that sound, but simply a body which a little while before appeared to me as perceptible under these forms, and which is now perceptible under others. But what, precisely, is it that I imagine when I form such conceptions? Let us attentively consider this, and, abstracting from all that does not belong to the wax, let us see what remains. Certainly nothing remains excepting a certain extended thing which is flexible and movable. But what is the meaning of flexible and movable? Is it not that I imagine that this piece of wax being round is capable of becoming square and of passing from a square to a triangular figure? No, certainly it is not that, since I imagine it admits of an infinitude of similar changes, and I nevertheless do not know how to compass the infinitude by my imagination, and consequently this conception which I have of the wax is not brought about by the faculty of imagination. What now is this extension? Is it not also unknown? For it becomes greater when the wax is melted, greater when it is boiled, and greater still when the heat increases; and I should not conceive [clearly] according to truth what wax is, if I did not think that even this piece that we are considering is capable of receiving more variations in extension than I have ever imagined. We must then grant that I could not even understand through the imagination what this piece of wax is, and that it is my mind alone which perceives it. I say this piece of wax in particular, for as to wax in general it is yet clearer. But what is this piece of wax which cannot be understood excepting by the [understanding or] mind? It is certainly the same that I see, touch, imagine, and finally it is the same which I have always believed it to be from the beginning. But what must particularly be observed is that its perception is neither an act of vision, nor of touch, nor of imagination, and has never been such although it may have appeared formerly to be so, but only an intuition of the mind, which may be imperfect and confused as it was formerly, or clear and distinct as it is at present, according as my attention is more or less directed to the elements which are found in it, and of which it is composed.

Yet in the meantime I am greatly astonished when I consider [the great feebleness of mind] and its proneness to fall [insensibly] into error; for although without giving expression to my thoughts I consider all this in my own mind, words often impede me and I am almost deceived by the terms of ordinary language. For we say that we see the same wax, if it is present, and not that we simply judge that it is the same from its having the same colour and figure. From this I should conclude that I knew the wax by means of vision and not simply by the intuition of the mind; unless by chance I remember that, when looking from a window and saying I see men who pass in the street, I really do not see them, but infer that what I see is men, just as I say that I see wax. And yet what do I see from the window but hats and coats which may cover automatic machines? Yet I judge these to be men. And similarly solely by the faculty of judgment which rests in my mind, I comprehend that which I believed I saw with my eyes.

A man who makes it his aim to raise his knowledge above the common should be ashamed to derive the occasion for doubting from the forms of speech invented by the vulgar; I prefer to pass on and consider whether I had a more evident and perfect conception of what the wax was when I first perceived it, and when I believed I knew it by means of the external senses or at least by the common sense* as it is called, that is to say by the imaginative faculty, or whether my present conception is clearer now that I have most carefully examined what it is, and in what way it can be known. It would certainly be absurd to doubt as to this. For what was there in this first perception which was distinct? What was there which might not as well have been perceived by any of the animals? But when I distinguish the wax from its external forms, and when, just as if I had taken from it its vestments, I consider it quite naked, it is certain that although some error may still be found in my judgment, I can nevertheless not perceive it thus without a human mind.

But finally what shall I say of this mind, that is, of myself, for up to this point I do not admit in myself anything but mind? What then, I who seem to perceive this piece of wax so distinctly, do I not know myself, not only with much more truth and certainty, but also with much more distinctness and clearness? For if I judge that the wax is or exists from the fact that I see it, it certainly follows much more clearly that I am or that I exist myself from the fact that I see it. For it may be that what I see is not really wax, it may also be that I do not possess eyes with which to see anything; but it cannot be that when I see, or (for I no longer take account of the distinction) when I think I see, that I myself who think am nought. So if I judge that the wax exists from the fact that I touch it, the same thing will follow, to wit, that I am; and if I judge that my imagination, or some other cause, whatever it is, persuades me that the wax exists, I shall still conclude the same. And what I have here remarked of wax may be applied to all other things which are external to me [and which are met with outside of me]. And further, if the [notion or] perception of wax has seemed to me clearer and more distinct, not only after the sight or the touch, but also after many other causes have rendered it quite manifest to me, with how much more [evidence] and distinctness must it be said that I now know myself, since all the reasons which contribute to the knowledge of wax, or any other body whatever, are yet better proofs of the nature of my mind! And there are so many other things in the mind itself which may contribute to the elucidation of its nature, that those which depend on body such as these just mentioned, hardly merit being taken into account.

But finally here I am, having insensibly reverted to the point I desired, for, since it is now manifest to me that even bodies are not properly speaking known by the senses or by the faculty of imagination, but by the understanding only, and since they are not known from the fact that they are seen or touched, but only because they are understood, I see clearly that there is nothing which is easier for me to know than my mind. But because it is difficult to rid oneself so promptly of an opinion to which one was accustomed for so long, it will be well that I should halt a little at this point, so that by the length of my meditation I may more deeply imprint on my memory this new knowledge.

* Sensus communis.

MEDITATION VI

. . .

And first of all, because I know that all things which I apprehend clearly and distinctly can be created by God as I apprehend them, it suffices that I am able to apprehend one thing apart from another clearly and distinctly in order to be certain that the one is different from the other, since they may be made to exist in separation at least by the omnipotence of God; and it does not signify by what power this separation is made in order to compel me to judge them to be different: and, therefore, just because I know certainly that I exist, and that meanwhile I do not remark that any other thing necessarily pertains to my nature or essence, excepting that I am a thinking thing, I rightly conclude that my essence consists solely in the fact that I am a thinking thing [or a substance whose whole essence or nature is to think]. And although possibly (or rather certainly, as I shall say in a moment) I possess a body with which I am very intimately conjoined, yet because, on the one side, I have a clear and distinct idea of myself inasmuch as I am only a thinking and unextended thing, and as, on the other, I possess a distinct idea of body, inasmuch as it is only an extended and unthinking thing, it is certain that this I [that is to say, my soul by which I am what I am], is entirely and absolutely distinct from my body, and can exist without it.

. . .

DISCOURSE ON METHOD

. . . [It] will not seem strange to those, who, knowing how many different *automata* or moving machines can be made by the industry of man, without employing in so doing more than a very few parts in comparison with the great multitude of bones, muscles, nerves, arteries, veins, or other parts that are found in the body of each animal. From this aspect the body is regarded as a machine which, having been made by the hands of God, is incomparably better arranged, and possesses in itself movements which are much more admirable, than any of those which can be invented by man. Here I specially stopped to show that if there had been such machines, possessing the organs and outward form of a monkey or some other animal without reason, we should not have had any means of ascertaining that they were not of the same nature as those animals. On the other hand, if there were machines which bore a resemblance to our body and imitated our actions as far as it was morally possible to do so, we should always have two very certain tests by which to recognise that, for all that, they were not real men. The first is, that they could never use speech or other signs as we do when placing our thoughts on record for the benefit of others. For we can easily understand a machine's being constituted so that it can utter words, and even emit some responses to action on it of a corporeal kind, which brings about a change in its organs; for instance, if it is touched in a particular part it may ask what we wish to say to it; if in another part it may exclaim that it is being hurt, and so on. But it never happens that it arranges its speech in various ways, in order to reply appropriately to everything that may be said in its presence, as even the lowest type of man can do. And the second difference is, that although machines can perform certain things as well as or perhaps better than any of us can do, they infallibly fall short in others, by the which means we may discover that they did not act from knowledge, but only from the disposition of their organs. For while reason is a universal instrument which can serve for all contingencies, these organs have need of some special adaptation for every particular action. From this it follows that it is morally impossible that there should be sufficient diversity in any machine to allow it to act in all the events of life in the same way as our reason causes us to act.

By these two methods we may also recognise the difference that exists between men and brutes. For it is a very remarkable fact that there are none so depraved and stupid, without even excepting idiots, that they cannot arrange different words together, forming of them a statement by which they make known their thoughts; while, on the other hand, there is no other animal, however perfect and fortunately circumstanced it may be, which can do the same. It is not the want of organs that brings this to pass, for it is evident that magpies and parrots are able to utter words just like ourselves, and yet they cannot speak as we do, that is, so as to give evidence that they think of what they say. On the other hand, men who, being born deaf and dumb, are in the same degree, or even more than the brutes, destitute of the organs which serve the others for talking, are in the habit of themselves inventing certain signs by which they make themselves understood by those who, being usually in their company, have leisure to learn their language. And this does not merely show that the brutes have less reason than men, but that they have none at all, since it is clear that very little is required in order to be able to talk. And when we notice the inequality that exists between animals of the same species, as well as between men, and observe that some are more capable of receiving instruction than others, it is not credible that a monkey or a parrot, selected as the most perfect of its species, should not in these matters equal the stupidest child to be found, or at least a child whose mind is clouded, unless in the case of the brute the soul were of an entirely different nature from ours. And we ought not to confound speech with natural movements which betray passions and may be imitated by machines as well as be manifested by animals; nor must we think, as did some of the ancients, that brutes talk, although we do not understand their language. For if this were true, since they have many organs which are allied to our own, they could communicate their thoughts to us just as easily as to those of their own race. It is also a very remarkable fact that although there are many animals which exhibit more dexterity than we do in some of their actions, we at the same time observe that they do not manifest any dexterity at all in many others. Hence the fact that they do better than we do, does not prove that they are endowed with mind, for in this case they would have more reason than any of us, and would surpass us in all other things. It rather shows that they have no reason at all, and that it is nature which acts in them according to the disposition of their organs, just as a clock, which is only composed of wheels and weights is able to tell the hours and measure the time more correctly than we can do with all our wisdom.

I had described after this the rational soul and shown that it could not be in any way derived from the power of matter, like the other things of which I had spoken, but that it must be expressly created. I showed, too, that it is not sufficient that it should be lodged in the human body like a pilot in his ship, unless perhaps for the moving of its members, but that it is necessary that it should also be joined and united more closely to the body in order to have sensations and appetites similar to our own, and thus to form a true man. In conclusion, I have here enlarged a little on the subject of the soul, because it is one of the greatest importance. For next to the error of those who would deny God, which I think I have already sufficiently refuted, there is none which is more effectual in leading feeble spirits from the straight path of virtue, than to imagine that the soul of the brute is of the same nature as our own, and that in consequence, after this life we have nothing to fear or to hope for, any more than the flies and ants. As a matter of fact, when one comes to know how greatly they differ, we understand much better the reasons which go to prove that our soul is in its nature entirely independent of body, and in consequence that it is not liable to die with it. And then, inasmuch as we observe no other causes capable of destroying it, we are naturally inclined to judge that it is immortal.

THE PASSIONS OF THE SOUL

What the functions of the soul are.

After having thus considered all the functions which pertain to the body alone, it is easy to recognise that there is nothing in us which we ought to attribute to our soul excepting our thoughts, which are mainly of two sorts, the one being the actions of the soul, and the other its passions. Those which I call its actions are all our desires, because we find by experience that they proceed directly from our soul, and appear to depend on it alone: while, on the other hand, we may usually term one's passions all those kinds of perception or forms of knowledge which are found in us, because it is often not our soul which makes them what they are, and because it always receives them from the things which are represented by them.

Of the Will.

Our desires, again, are of two sorts, of which the one consists of the actions of the soul which terminate in the soul itself, as when we desire to love God, or generally speaking, apply our thoughts to some object which is not material; and the other of the actions which terminate in our body, as when from the simple fact that we have the desire to take a walk, it follows that our legs move and that we walk.

Of the Perceptions.

Our perceptions are also of two sorts, and the one have the soul as a cause and the other the body. Those which have the soul as a cause are the perceptions of our desires, and of all the imaginations or other thoughts which depend on them. For it is certain that we cannot desire anything without perceiving by the same means that we desire it; and, although in regard to our soul it is an action to desire something, we may say that it is also one of its passions to perceive that it desires. Yet because this perception and this will are really one and the same thing, the more noble always supplies the denomination, and thus we are not in the habit of calling it a passion, but only an action.

That the soul is united to all the portions of the body conjointly...

But in order to understand all these things more perfectly, we must know that the soul is really joined to the whole body, and that we cannot, properly speaking, say that it exists in any one of its parts to the exclusion of the others, because it is one and in some manner indivisible, owing to the disposition of its organs, which are so related to one another that when any one of them is removed, that renders the whole body defective; and because it is of a nature which has no relation to extension, nor dimensions, nor other properties of the matter of which the body is composed, but only to the whole conglomerate of its organs, as appears from the fact that we could not in any way conceive of the half or the third of a soul, nor of the space it occupies, and because it does not become smaller owing to the cutting off of some portion of the body, but separates itself from it entirely when the union of its assembled organs is dissolved.

That there is a small gland in the brain in which the soul exercises its functions more particularly than in the other parts...

It is likewise necessary to know that although the soul is joined to the whole body, there is yet in that a certain part in which it exercises its functions more particularly than in all the others; and it is usually believed that this part is the brain, or possibly the heart: the brain, because it is with it that the organs of sense are connected, and the heart because it is apparently in it that we experience the passions. But, in examining the matter with care, it seems as though I had clearly ascertained that the part of the body in which the soul exercises its functions immediately is in nowise the heart, nor the whole of the brain, but merely the most inward of all its parts, to wit, a certain very small gland which is situated in the middle of its substance and so suspended above the duct whereby the animal spirits in its anterior cavities have communication with those in the posterior, that the slightest movements which take place in it may alter very greatly the course of these spirits; and reciprocally that the smallest changes which occur in the course of the spirits may do much to change the movements of this gland.

How the soul and the body act on one another.

Let us then conceive here that the soul has its principal seat in the little gland which exists in the middle of the brain, from whence it radiates forth through all the remainder of the body by means of the animal spirits, nerves, and even the blood, which, participating in the impressions of the spirits, can carry them by the arteries into all the members. And recollecting what has been said above about the machine of our body, i.e. that the little filaments of our nerves are so distributed in all its parts, that on the occasion of the diverse movements which are there excited by sensible objects, they open in diverse ways the pores of the brain, which causes the animal spirits contained in these cavities to enter in diverse ways into the muscles, by which means they can move the members in all the different ways in which they are capable of being moved; and also that all the other causes which are capable of moving the spirits in diverse ways suffice to conduct them into diverse muscles; let us here add that the small gland which is the main seat of the soul is so suspended between the cavities which contain the spirits that it can be moved by them in as many different ways as there are sensible diversities in the object, but that it may also be moved in diverse ways by the soul, whose nature is such that it receives in itself as many diverse impressions, that is to say, that it possesses as many diverse perceptions as there are diverse movements in this gland. Reciprocally, likewise, the machine of the body is so formed that from the simple fact that this gland is diversely moved by the soul, or by such other cause, whatever it is, it thrusts the spirits which surround it towards the pores of the brain, which conduct them by the nerves into the muscles, by which means it causes them to move the limbs.

DESCARTES' MYTH

GILBERT RYLE

(1) *THE OFFICIAL DOCTRINE*

There is a doctrine about the nature and place of minds which is so prevalent among theorists and even among laymen that it deserves to be described as the official theory. Most philosophers, psychologists and religious teachers subscribe, with minor reservations, to its main articles and, although they admit certain theoretical difficulties in it, they tend to assume that these can be overcome without serious modifications being made to the architecture of the theory. It will be argued here that the central principles of the doctrine are unsound and conflict with the whole body of what we know about minds when we are not speculating about them.

The official doctrine, which hails chiefly from Descartes, is something like this. With the doubtful exceptions of idiots and infants in arms every human being has both a body and a mind. Some would prefer to say that every human being is both a body and a mind. His body and his mind are ordinarily harnessed together, but after the death of the body his mind may continue to exist and function.

Human bodies are in space and are subject to the mechanical laws which govern all other bodies in space. Bodily processes and states can be inspected by external observers. So a man's bodily life is as much a public affair as are the lives of animals and reptiles and even as the careers of trees, crystals and planets.

But minds are not in space, nor are their operations subject to mechanical laws. The workings of one mind are not witnessable by other observers; its career is private. Only I can take direct cognisance of the states and processes of my own mind. A person therefore lives through two collateral histories, one consisting of what happens in and to his body, the other consisting of what happens in and to his mind. The first is public, the second private. The events in the first history are events in the physical world, those in the second are events in the mental world.

It has been disputed whether a person does or can directly monitor all or only some of the episodes of his own private history; but, according to the official doctrine, of at least some of these episodes he has direct and

Reprinted from *The Concept of Mind*, London, 1949, pp. 11–24, with permission of the author and the publishers Hutchinson Publishing Group, Ltd., London, and Barnes & Noble, Inc., New York.

unchallengeable cognisance. In consciousness, self-consciousness and introspection he is directly and authentically apprised of the present states and operations of his mind. He may have great or small uncertainties about concurrent and adjacent episodes in the physical world, but he can have none about at least part of what is momentarily occupying his mind.

It is customary to express this bifurcation of his two lives and of his two worlds by saying that the things and events which belong to the physical world, including his own body, are external, while the workings of his own mind are internal. This antithesis of outer and inner is of course meant to be construed as a metaphor, since minds, not being in space, could not be described as being spatially inside anything else, or as having things going on spatially inside themselves. But relapses from this good intention are common and theorists are found speculating how stimuli, the physical sources of which are yards or miles outside a person's skin, can generate mental responses inside his skull, or how decisions framed inside his cranium can set going movements of his extremities.

Even when 'inner' and 'outer' are construed as metaphors, the problem how a person's mind and body influence one another is notoriously charged with theoretical difficulties. What the mind wills, the legs, arms and the tongue execute; what affects the ear and the eye has something to do with what the mind perceives; grimaces and smiles betray the mind's moods and bodily castigations lead, it is hoped, to moral improvement. But the actual transactions between the episodes of the private history and those of the public history remain mysterious, since by definition they can belong to neither series. They could not be reported among the happenings described in a person's autobiography of his inner life, but nor could they be reported among those described in some one else's biography of that person's overt career. They can be inspected neither by introspection nor by laboratory experiment. They are theoretical shuttlecocks which are forever being bandied from the physiologist back to the psychologist and from the psychologist back to the physiologist.

Underlying this partly metaphorical representation of the bifurcation of a person's two lives there is a seemingly more profound and philosophical assumption. It is assumed that there are two different kinds of existence or status. What exists or happens may have the status of physical existence, or it may have the status of mental existence. Somewhat as the faces of coins are either heads or tails, or somewhat as living creatures are either male or female, so, it is supposed, some existing is physical existing, other existing is mental existing. It is a necessary feature of what has physical existence that it is in space and time; it is a necessary feature of what has mental existence that it is in time but not in space. What has physical existence is composed of matter, or else is a function of matter; what has mental existence consists of consciousness, or else is a function of consciousness.

There is thus a polar opposition between mind and matter, an opposition which is often brought out as follows. Material objects are situated in a common field, known as 'space', and what happens to one body in one part of space is mechanically connected with what happens to other bodies in other parts of space. But mental happenings occur in insulated fields, known as 'minds', and there is, apart maybe from telepathy, no direct causal connection between what happens in one mind and what happens in another. Only through the medium of the public physical world can the mind of one person make a difference to the mind of another. The mind is its own place and in his inner life each of us lives the life of a ghostly Robinson Crusoe. People can see, hear and jolt one another's bodies, but they are irremediably blind and deaf to the workings of one another's minds and inoperative upon them.

What sort of knowledge can be secured of the workings of a mind? On the one side, according to the official theory, a person has direct knowledge of the best imaginable kind of the workings of his own mind. Mental states and processes are (or are normally) conscious states and processes, and the consciousness which irradiates them can engender no illusions and leaves the door open for no doubts. A person's present thinkings, feelings and willings, his perceivings, rememberings and imaginings are intrinsically 'phosphorescent'; their existence and their nature are inevitably betrayed to their owner. The inner life is a stream of consciousness of such a sort that it would be absurd to suggest that the mind whose life is that stream might be unaware of what is passing down it.

True, the evidence adduced recently by Freud seems to show that there exist channels tributary to this stream, which run hidden from their owner. People are actuated by impulses the existence of which they vigorously disavow; some of their thoughts differ from the thoughts which they acknowledge; and some of the actions which they think they will to perform they do not really will. They are thoroughly gulled by some of their own hypocrisies and they successfully ignore facts about their mental lives which on the official theory ought to be patent to them. Holders of the official theory tend, however, to maintain that anyhow in normal circumstances a person must be directly and authentically seized of the present state and workings of his own mind.

Besides being currently supplied with these alleged immediate data of consciousness, a person is also generally supposed to be able to exercise from time to time a special kind of perception, namely inner perception, or introspection. He can take a (non-optical) 'look' at what is passing in his mind. Not only can he view and scrutinize a flower through his sense of sight and listen to and discriminate the notes of a bell through his sense of hearing; he can also reflectively or introspectively watch, without any bodily organ of sense, the current episodes of his inner life. This self-observation is also commonly supposed to be immune from illusion, confusion or doubt. A mind's reports of its own affairs have a certainty superior to the best that is possessed by its reports of matters in the physical world. Sense-perceptions can, but consciousness and introspection cannot, be mistaken or confused.

On the other side, one person has no direct access of any sort to the events of the inner life of another. He cannot do better than make problematic inferences from the observed behaviour of the other person's body to the states of mind which, by analogy from his own conduct, he supposes to be signalised by that behaviour. Direct access to the workings of a mind is the privilege of that mind itself; in default of such privileged access, the workings of one mind are inevitably occult to everyone else. For the supposed arguments from bodily movements similar to their own to mental workings similar to their own would lack any possibility of observational corroboration. Not unnaturally, therefore, an adherent of the official theory finds it difficult to resist this consequence of his premisses, that he has no good reason to believe that there do exist minds other than his own. Even if he prefers to believe that to other human bodies there are harnessed minds not unlike his own, he cannot claim to be able to discover their individual characteristics, or the particular things that they undergo and do. Absolute solitude is on this showing the ineluctable destiny of the soul. Only our bodies can meet.

As a necessary corollary of this general scheme there is implicitly prescribed a special way of construing our ordinary concepts of mental powers and operations. The verbs, nouns and adjectives, with which in ordinary life we describe the wits, characters and higher-grade performances of the people with whom we have do, are required to be construed as signifying special episodes in their secret histories, or else as signifying tendencies for such episodes to occur. When someone is described as knowing, believing or guessing something, as hoping, dreading, intending or shirking something, as designing this or being amused at that, these verbs are supposed to denote the occurrence of specific modifications in his (to us) occult stream of consciousness. Only his own privileged access to this stream in direct awareness and introspection could provide authentic testimony that these mental-conduct verbs were correctly or incorrectly applied. The onlooker, be he teacher, critic, biographer or friend, can never assure himself that his comments have any vestige of truth. Yet it was just because we do in fact all know how to make such comments, make them with general correctness and correct them when they turn out to be confused or mistaken, that philosophers found it necessary to construct their theories of the nature and place of minds. Finding mental-conduct concepts being regularly and effectively used, they properly sought to fix their logical geography. But the logical geography officially recommended would entail that there could be no regular or effective use of these mental-conduct concepts in our descriptions of, and prescriptions for, other people's minds.

(2) *THE ABSURDITY OF THE OFFICIAL DOCTRINE*

Such in outline is the official theory. I shall often speak of it, with deliberate abusiveness, as 'the dogma of the Ghost in the Machine'. I hope to prove that it is entirely false, and false not in detail but in principle. It is not merely an assemblage of particular mistakes. It is one big mistake and a mistake of a special kind. It is, namely, a category-mistake. It represents the facts of mental life as if they belonged to one logical type or category (or range of types or categories), when they actually belong to another. The dogma is therefore a philosopher's myth. In attempting to explode the myth I shall probably be taken to be denying well-known facts about the mental life of human beings, and my plea that I aim at doing nothing more than rectify the logic of mental-conduct concepts will probably be disallowed as mere subterfuge.

I must first indicate what is meant by the phrase 'Category-mistake'. This I do in a series of illustrations.

A foreigner visiting Oxford or Cambridge for the first time is shown a number of colleges, libraries, playing fields, museums, scientific departments and administrative offices. He then asks 'But where is the university? I have seen where the members of the Colleges live, where the Registrar works, where the scientists experiment and the rest. But I have not yet seen the University in which reside and work the members of your University.' It has then to be explained to him that the University is not another collateral institution, some ulterior counterpart to the colleges, laboratories and offices which he has seen. The University is just the way in which all that he has already seen is organized. When they are seen and when their co-ordination is understood, the University has been seen. His mistake lay in his innocent assumption that it was correct to speak of Christ Church, the Bodleian Library, the Ashmolean Museum *and* the University, to speak, that is, as if 'the University' stood for an extra member of the class of which these other units are members. He was mistakenly allocating the University to the same category as that to which the other institutions belong.

The same mistake would be made by a child witnessing the march-past of a division, who, having had pointed out to him such and such battalions, batteries, squadrons, etc., asked when the division was going to appear. He would be supposing that a division was a counterpart to the units already seen, partly similar to them and partly unlike them. He would be shown his mistake by being told that in watching the battalions, batteries and squadrons marching past he had been watching the division marching past. The march-past was not a parade of battalions, batteries, squadrons *and* a division; it was a parade of the battalions, batteries and squadrons *of* a division.

One more illustration. A foreigner watching his first game of cricket learns what are the functions of the bowlers, the batsmen, the fielders, the umpires and the scorers. He then says 'But there is no one left on the field to contribute the famous element of team-spirit. I see who does the bowling, the batting and the wicket-keeping; but I do not see whose role it is to exercise *esprit de corps*.' Once more, it would have to be explained that he was looking for the wrong type of thing. Team-spirit is not another cricketing-operation supplementary to all of the other special tasks. It is, roughly, the keenness with which each of the special tasks is performed, and performing a task keenly is not performing two tasks.

Certainly exhibiting team-spirit is not the same thing as bowling or catching, but nor is it a third thing such that we can say that the bowler first bowls *and* then exhibits team-spirit or that a fielder is at a given moment *either* catching *or* displaying *esprit de corps*.

These illustrations of category-mistakes have a common feature which must be noticed. The mistakes were made by people who did not know how to wield the concepts *University*, *division* and *team-spirit*. Their puzzles arose from inability to use certain items in the English vocabulary.

The theoretically interesting category-mistakes are those made by people who are perfectly competent to apply concepts, at least in the situations with which they are familiar, but are still liable in their abstract thinking to allocate those concepts to logical types to which they do not belong. An instance of a mistake of this sort would be the following story. A student of politics has learned the main differences between the British, the French and the American Constitutions, and has learned also the differences and connections between the Cabinet, Parliament, the various Ministries, the Judicature and the Church of England. But he still becomes embarrassed when asked questions about the connections between the Church of England, the Home Office and the British Constitution. For while the Church and the Home Office are institutions, the British Constitution is not another institution in the same sense of that noun. So inter-institutional relations which can be asserted or denied to hold between the Church and the Home Office cannot be asserted or denied to hold between either of them and the British Constitution. 'The British Constitution' is not a term of the same logical type as 'the Home Office' and 'the Church of England'. In a partially similar way, John Doe may be a relative, a friend, an enemy or a stranger to Richard Roe; but he cannot be any of these things to the Average Taxpayer. He knows how to talk sense in certain sorts of discussions about the Average Taxpayer, but he is baffled to say why he could not come across him in the street as he can come across Richard Roe.

It is pertinent to our main subject to notice that, so long as the student of politics continues to think of the British Constitution as a counterpart to the other institutions, he will tend to describe it as a mysteriously occult institution; and so long as John Doe continues to think of the Average Taxpayer as a fellow-citizen, he will tend to think of him as an elusive insubstantial man, a ghost who is everywhere yet nowhere.

My destructive purpose is to show that a family of radical category-mistakes is the source of the double-life theory. The representation of a person as a ghost mysteriously ensconced in a machine derives from this argument. Because, as is true, a person's thinking, feeling and purposive doing cannot be described solely in the idioms of physics, chemistry and physiology, therefore they must be described in counterpart idioms. As the human body is a complex organised unit, so the human mind must be another complex organised unit, though one made of a different sort of stuff and with a different sort of structure. Or, again, as the human body, like any other parcel of matter, is a field of causes and effects, so the mind must be another field of causes and effects, though not (Heaven be praised) mechanical causes and effects.

(3) *THE ORIGIN OF THE CATEGORY-MISTAKE*

One of the chief intellectual origins of what I have yet to prove to be the Cartesian category-mistake seems to be this. When Galileo showed that his methods of scientific discovery were competent to provide a mechanical theory which should cover every occupant of space, Descartes found in himself two conflicting motives. As a man of scientific genius he could not but endorse the claims of mechanics, yet as a religious and moral man he could not accept, as Hobbes accepted, the discouraging rider to those claims, namely that human nature differs only in degree of complexity from clockwork. The mental could not be just a variety of the mechanical.

He and subsequent philosophers naturally but erroneously availed themselves of the following escape-route. Since mental-conduct words are not to be construed as signifying the occurrence of mechanical processes, they must be construed as signifying the occurrence of non-mechanical processes; since mechanical laws explain movements in space as the effects of other movements in space, other laws must explain some of the non-spatial workings of minds as the effects of other non-spatial workings of minds. The difference between the human behaviours which we describe as intelligent and those which we describe as unintelligent must be a difference in their causation; so, while some movements of human tongues and limbs are the effects of mechanical causes, others must be the effects of non-mechanical causes, i.e. some issue from movements of particles of matter, others from workings of the mind.

The differences between the physical and the mental were thus represented as differences inside the common framework of the categories of 'thing', 'stuff', 'attribute', 'state,' 'process', 'change', 'cause' and 'effect'. Minds are things, but different sorts of things from bodies; mental processes are causes and effects, but different sorts of causes and effects from bodily movements. And so on. Somewhat as the foreigner expected the University to be an extra edifice, rather like a college but also considerably different, so the repudiators of mechanism represented minds as extra centres of causal processes, rather like machines but also considerably different from them. Their theory was a para-mechanical hypothesis.

That this assumption was at the heart of the doctrine is shown by the fact that there was from the beginning felt to be a major theoretical difficulty in explaining how minds can influence and be influenced by bodies. How can a mental process, such as willing, cause spatial movements like the movements of the tongue? How can a physical change in the optic nerve have among its effects a mind's perception of a flash of light? This notorious crux by itself shows the logical mould into which

Descartes pressed his theory of the mind. It was the self-same mould into which he and Galileo set their mechanics. Still unwittingly adhering to the grammar of mechanics, he tried to avert disaster by describing minds in what was merely an obverse vocabulary. The workings of minds had to be described by the mere negatives of the specific descriptions given to bodies; they are not in space, they are not motions, they are not modifications of matter, they are not accessible to public observation. Minds are not bits of clockwork, they are just bits of not-clockwork.

As thus represented, minds are not merely ghosts harnessed to machines, they are themselves just spectral machines. Though the human body is an engine, it it not quite an ordinary engine, since some of its workings are governed by another engine inside it—this interior governor-engine being one of a very special sort. It is invisible, inaudible and it has no size or weight. It cannot be taken to bits and the laws it obeys are not those known to ordinary engineers. Nothing is known of how it governs the bodily engine.

A second major crux points the same moral. Since, according to the doctrine, minds belong to the same category as bodies and since bodies are rigidly governed by mechanical laws, it seemed to many theorists to follow that minds must be similarly governed by rigid non-mechanical laws. The physical world is a deterministic system, so the mental world must be a deterministic system. Bodies cannot help the modifications that they undergo, so minds cannot help pursuing the careers fixed for them. *Responsibility*, *choice*, *merit* and *demerit* are therefore inapplicable concepts—unless the compromise solution is adopted of saying that the laws governing mental processes, unlike those governing physical processes, have the congenial attribute of being only rather rigid. The problem of the Freedom of the Will was the problem how to reconcile the hypothesis that minds are to be described in terms drawn from the categories of mechanics with the knowledge that higher-grade human conduct is not of a piece with the behaviour of machines.

It is an historical curiosity that it was not noticed that the entire argument was broken-backed. Theorists correctly assumed that any sane man could already recognise the differences between, say, rational and non-rational utterances or between purposive and automatic behaviour. Else there would have been nothing requiring to be salved from mechanism. Yet the explanation given presupposed that one person could in principle never recognise the difference between the rational and the irrational utterances issuing from other human bodies, since he could never get access to the postulated immaterial causes of some of their utterances. Save for the doubtful exception of himself, he could never tell the difference between a man and a Robot. It would have to be conceded, for example, that, for all that we can tell, the inner lives of persons who are classed as idiots or lunatics are as rational as those of anyone else. Perhaps only their overt behaviour is disappointing; that is to say, perhaps 'idiots' are not really idiotic, or 'lunatics' lunatic. Perhaps, too, some of those who are classed as sane are really idiots. According to the theory, external observers could never know how the overt behaviour of others is correlated with their mental powers and processes and so they could never know or even plausibly conjecture whether their applications of mental-conduct concepts to these other people were correct or incorrect. It would then be hazardous or impossible for a man to claim sanity or logical consistency even for himself, since he would be debarred from comparing his own performances with those of others. In short, our characterisations of persons and their performances as intelligent, prudent and virtuous or as stupid, hypocritical and cowardly could never have been made, so the problem of providing a special causal hypothesis to serve as the basis of such diagnoses would never have arisen. The question, 'How do persons differ from machines?' arose just because everyone already knew how to apply mental-conduct concepts before the new causal hypothesis was introduced. This causal hypothesis could not therefore be the source of the criteria used in those applications. Nor, of course, has the causal hypothesis in any degree improved our handling of those criteria. We still distinguish good from bad arithmetic, politic from impolitic conduct and fertile from infertile imaginations in the ways in which Descartes himself distinguished them before and after he speculated how the applicability of these criteria was compatible with the principle of mechanical causation.

He had mistaken the logic of his problem. Instead of asking by what criteria intelligent behaviour is actually distinguished from non-intelligent behaviour, he asked 'Given that the principle of mechanical causation does not tell us the difference, what other causal principle will tell it us?' He realised that the problem was not one of mechanics and assumed that it must therefore be one of some counterpart to mechanics. Not unnaturally psychology is often cast for just this role.

When two terms belong to the same category, it is proper to construct conjunctive propositions embodying them. Thus a purchaser may say that he bought a left-hand glove and a right-hand glove, but not that he bought a left-hand glove, a right-hand glove and a pair of gloves. 'She came home in a flood of tears and a sedan-chair' is a well-known joke based on the absurdity of conjoining terms of different types. It would have been equally ridiculous to construct the disjunction 'She came home either in a flood or tears or else in a sedan-chair'. Now the dogma of the Ghost in the Machine does just this. It maintains that there exist both bodies and minds; that there occur physical processes and mental processes; that there are mechanical causes of corporeal movements and mental causes of corporeal movements. I shall argue that these and other analogous conjunctions are absurd; but, it must be noticed, the argument will not show that either of the illegitimately conjoined propositions is absurd in itself. I am not, for example, denying that there occur mental processes. Doing long division is a mental process and so is making a joke. But I am saying that the phrase 'there occur mental processes' does not mean the same sort of thing as 'there occur physical processes', and, therefore, that it makes no sense to conjoin or disjoin the two.

If my argument is successful, there will follow some interesting consequences. First, the hallowed contrast between Mind and Matter will be dissipated, but dissipated not by either of the equally hallowed absorptions of Mind by Matter or of Matter by Mind, but in quite a different way. For the seeming contrast of the two will be shown to be as illegitimate as would be the contrast of 'she came home in a flood of tears' and 'she came home in a sedan-chair'. The belief that there is a polar opposition between Mind and Matter is the belief that they are terms of the same logical type.

It will also follow that both Idealism and Materialism are answers to an improper question. The 'reduction' of the material world to mental states and processes, as well as the 'reduction' of mental states and processes to physical states and processes, presuppose the legitimacy of the disjunction 'Either there exist minds or there exist bodies (but not both)'. It would be like saying, 'Either she bought a left-hand and a right-hand glove or she bought a pair of gloves (but not both)'.

It is perfectly proper to say, in one logical tone of voice, that there exist minds and to say, in another logical tone of voice, that there exist bodies. But these expressions do not indicate two different species of existence, for 'existence' is not a generic word like 'coloured' or 'sexed'. They indicate two different senses of 'exist', somewhat as 'rising' has different senses in 'the tide is rising', 'hopes are rising', and 'the average age of death is rising'. A man would be thought to be making a poor joke who said that three things are now rising, namely the tide, hopes and the average age of death. It would be just as good or bad a joke to say that there exist prime numbers and Wednesdays and public opinions and navies; or that there exist both minds and bodies. In the succeeding chapters I try to prove that the official theory does rest on a batch of category-mistakes by showing that logically absurd corollaries follow from it. The exhibition of these absurdities will have the constructive effect of bringing out part of the correct logic of mental-conduct concepts.

(4) *HISTORICAL NOTE*

It would not be true to say that the official theory derives solely from Descartes' theories, or even from a more widespread anxiety about the implications of seventeenth century mechanism. Scholastic and Reformation theology had schooled the intellects of the scientists as well as of the laymen, philosophers and clerics of that age. Stoic-Augustinian theories of the will were embedded in the Calvinist doctrines of sin and grace; Platonic and Aristotelian theories of the intellect shaped the orthodox doctrines of the immortality of the soul. Descartes was reformulating already prevalent theological doctrines of the soul in the new syntax of Galileo. The theologian's privacy of conscience became the philosopher's privacy of consciousness, and what had been the bogy of Predestination reappeared as the bogy of Determinism.

It would also not be true to say that the two-worlds myth did no theoretical good. Myths often do a lot of theoretical good, while they are still new. One benefit bestowed by the para-mechanical myth was that it partly superannuated the then prevalent para-political myth. Minds and their Faculties had previously been described by analogies with political superiors and political subordinates. The idioms used were those of ruling, obeying, collaborating and rebelling. They survived and still survive in many ethical and some epistemological discussions. As, in physics, the new myth of occult Forces was a scientific improvement on the old myth of Final Causes, so, in anthropological and psychological theory, the new myth of hidden operations, impulses and agencies was an improvement on the old myth of dictations, deferences and disobediences.

IS LIFE AFTER DEATH POSSIBLE?

C. J. DUCASSE

The question whether human personality survives death is sometimes asserted to be one upon which reflection is futile. Only empirical evidence, it is said, can be relevant, since the question is purely one of fact.

But no question is purely one of fact until it is clearly understood; and this one is, on the contrary, ambiguous and replete with tacit assumptions. Until the ambiguities have been removed and the assumptions critically examined, we do not really know just what it is we want to know when we ask whether a life after death is possible. Nor, therefore, can we tell until then what bearing on this question various facts empirically known to us may have.

To clarify its meaning is chiefly what I now propose to attempt. I shall ask first why a future life is so generally desired and believed in. Then I shall state, as convincingly as I can in the time available, the arguments commonly advanced to prove that such a life is impossible. After that, I shall consider the logic of these arguments, and show that they quite fail to establish the impossibility. Next, the tacit but arbitrary assumption, which makes them nevertheless appear convincing, will be pointed out. And finally, I shall consider briefly a number of specific forms which a life after death might take, if there is one.

Let us turn to the first of these tasks.

This selection consists of portions of the Agnes E. and Constantine E. A. Foerster Lecture delivered at the University of California at Berkeley in May, 1947. It is here reprinted with the kind permission of Professor Ducasse and the Parapsychology Foundation.

WHY MAN DESIRES LIFE AFTER DEATH

To begin with, let us note that each of us here has been alive and conscious at all times in the past which he can remember. It is true that sometimes our bodies are in deep sleep, or made inert by anesthetics or injuries. But even at such times we do not experience unconsciousness in ourselves, for to experience it would mean being conscious of being unconscious, and this is a contradiction. The only experience of unconsciousness in ourselves we ever have is, not experience of total unconsciousness, but of unconsciousness *of this or that;* as when we report: "I am not conscious of any pain," or "of any bell-sound," or "of any difference between those two colors," etc. Nor do we ever experience unconsciousness in another person, but only the fact that, sometimes, some or all of the ordinary activities of his body cease to occur. That consciousness itself is extinguished at such times is thus only a hypothesis which we construct to account for certain changes in the behavior of another person's body or to explain in him or in ourselves the eventual lack of memories relating to the given period.

Being alive and conscious is thus, with all men, a lifelong experience and habit; and conscious life is therefore something they naturally—even if tacitly—expect to continue. As J. B. Pratt has pointed out, the child takes the continuity of life for granted. It is the fact of death that has to be taught him. But when he has learned it, and the idea of a future life is then put explicitly before his mind, it seems to him the most natural thing in the world.*

The witnessing of death, however, is a rare experience for most of us, and, because it breaks so sharply into our habits, it forces on us the question whether the mind, which until then was manifested by the body now dead, continues somehow to live on, or, on the contrary, has become totally extinct. This question is commonly phrased as concerning "the immortality of the soul," and immortality, strictly speaking, means survival forever. But assurance of survival for some considerable period—say a thousand, or even a hundred, years—would probably have almost as much present psychological value as would assurance of survival strictly forever. Most men would be troubled very little by the idea of extinction at so distant a time—even less troubled than is now a healthy and happy youth by the idea that he will die in fifty or sixty years. Therefore, it is survival for some time, rather than survival specifically forever, that I shall alone consider.

The craving for continued existence is very widespread. Even persons who believe that death means complete extinction of the individual's consciousness often find comfort in various substitute conceptions of survival. They may, for instance, dwell on the continuity of the indi-

* J. B. Pratt, *The Religious Consciousness,* p. 225.

vidual's germ plasm in his descendants. Or they find solace in the thought that, the past being indestructible, their individual life remains eternally an intrinsic part of the history of the world. Also—and more satisfying to one's craving for personal importance—there is the fact that since the acts of one's life have effects, and these in turn further effects, and so on, therefore what one has done goes on forever influencing remotely, and sometimes greatly, the course of future events.

Gratifying to one's vanity, too, is the prospect that, if the achievements of one's life have been great or even only conspicuous, or one's benefactions or evil deeds have been notable, one's name may not only be remembered by acquaintances and relatives for a little while, but may live on in recorded history. But evidently survival in any of these senses is but a consolation prize—but a thin substitute for the continuation of conscious individual life, which may not be a fact, but which most men crave nonetheless.

The roots of this craving are certain desires which death appears to frustrate. For some, the chief of these is for reunion with persons dearly loved. For others, whose lives have been wretched, it is the desire for another chance at the happiness they have missed. For others yet, it is desire for further opportunity to grow in ability, knowledge or character. Often, there is also the desire, already mentioned, to go on counting for something in the affairs of men. And again, a future life for oneself and others is often desired in order that the redressing of the many injustices of this life shall be possible. But it goes without saying that, although desires such as these are often sufficient to cause belief in a future life, they constitute no evidence at all that it is a fact.

In this connection, it may be well to point out that, although both the belief in survival and the belief in the existence of a god or gods are found in most religions, nevertheless there is no necessary connection between the two beliefs. No contradiction would be involved in supposing either that there is a God but no life after death or that there is a life after death but no God. The belief that there is a life after death may be tied to a religion, but it is no more intrinsically religious than would be a belief that there is life on the planet Mars. The after-death world, if it exists, is just another region or dimension of the universe.

But although belief in survival of death is natural and easy and has always been held in one form or another by a large majority of mankind, critical reflection quickly brings forth a number of apparently strong reasons to regard that belief as quite illusory. Let us now review them.

THE ARGUMENTS AGAINST SURVIVAL

There are, first of all, a number of facts which definitely suggest that both the existence and the nature of consciousness wholly depend on the presence of a functioning nervous system. It is pointed out, for example, that wherever consciousness is observed, it is found associated with a living and functioning body. Further, when the body dies, or the head is struck a heavy blow, or some anesthetic is administered, the familiar outward evidences of consciousness terminate, permanently or temporarily. Again, we know well that drugs of various kinds—alcohol, caffein, opium, heroin, and many others—cause specific changes at the time in the nature of a person's mental states. Also, by stimulating in appropriate ways the body's sense organs, corresponding states of consciousness—namely, the various kinds of sensations—can be caused at will. On the other hand, cutting a sensory nerve immediately eliminates a whole range of sensations.

Again, the contents of consciousness, the mental powers, or even the personality, are modified in characteristic ways when certain regions of the brain are destroyed by disease of injury or are disconnected from the rest by such an operation as prefrontal lobotomy. And that the nervous system is the indispensable basis of mind is further suggested by the fact that, in the evolutionary scale, the degree of intelligence of various species of animals keeps pace closely with the degree of development of their brain.

That continued existence of mind after death is impossible has been argued also on the basis of theoretical considerations. It has been contended, for instance, that what we call states of consciousness—or more particularly, ideas, sensations, volitions, feelings, and the like—are really nothing but the minute physical or chemical events which take place in the tissues of the brain. For, it is urged, it would be absurd to suppose that an idea or a volition, if it is not itself a material thing or process, could cause material effects such as contractions of muscles.

Moreover, it is maintained that the possibility of causation of a material event by an immaterial, mental cause is ruled out *a priori* by the principle of the conservation of energy; for such causation would mean that an additional quantity of energy suddenly pops into the nervous system out of nowhere.

Another conception of consciousness, which is more often met with today than the one just mentioned, but which also implies that consciousness cannot survive death, is that "consciousness" is only the name we give to certain types of behavior, which differentiate the higher animals from all other things in nature. According to this view, to say, for example, that an animal is conscious of a difference between two stimuli means nothing more than that it responds to each by different behavior. That is, the difference of *behavior* is what consciousness of difference between the stimuli *consists in;* and is not, as is commonly assumed, only the behavioral *sign* of something mental and not public, called "consciousness that the stimuli are different."

Or again, consciousness, of the typically human sort called thought, is identified with the typically human sort of behavior called speech; and this, again not in the sense that speech *expresses* or *manifests* something different from itself, called "thought," but in the sense that speech—

whether uttered or only whispered—*is* thought itself. And obviously, if thought, or any mental activity, is thus but some mode of behavior of the living body, the mind cannot possibly survive death.

Still another difficulty confronting the hypothesis of survival becomes evident when one imagines in some detail what survival would have to include in order to satisfy the desires which cause man to crave it. It would, of course, have to include persistence not alone of consciousness, but also of personality; that is, of the individual's character, acquired knowledge, cultural skills and interests, memories, and awareness of personal identity. But even this would not be enough, for what man desires is not bare survival, but to go on living in some objective way. And this means to go on meeting new situations and, by exerting himself to deal with them, to broaden and deepen his experience and develop his latent capacities.

But it is hard to imagine this possible without a body and an environment for it, upon which to act and from which to receive impressions. And, if a body and an environment were supposed, but not material and corruptible ones, then it is paradoxical to think that, under such radically different conditions, a given personality could persist.*

To take a crude but telling analogy, it is past belief that, if the body of any one of us were suddenly changed into that of a shark or an octopus, and placed in the ocean, his personality could, for more than a very short time, if at all, survive intact so radical a change of environment and of bodily form.

THE ARGUMENTS EXAMINED

Such, in brief, are the chief reasons commonly advanced for holding that survival is impossible. Scrutiny of them, however, will, I think, reveal that they are not as strong as they first seem and far from strong enough to show that there can be no life after death.

Let us consider first the assertion that "thought," or "consciousness," is but another name for subvocal speech, or for some other form of behavior, or for molecular processes in the tissues of the brain. As Paulsen and others have pointed out;**no evidence ever is or can be offered to support that assertion, because it is in fact but a disguised proposal to make the words "thought," "feeling," "sensation," "desire," and so on, denote facts quite different from those which these words are commonly employed to denote. To say that those words are but other names for certain chemical or behavioral events is as grossly arbitrary as it would be to say that "wood" is but another name for glass, or "potato" but another name for cabbage. What thought, desire, sensation, and other mental

* Cf. Gardner Murphy, "Difficulties Confronting the Survival Hypothesis," *Journal of the American Society for Psychical Research* for April, 1945, p. 72; Corliss Lamont, "The Illusion of Immortality" (New York, 1935), pp. 26 ff.

** F. Paulsen, "Introduction to Philosophy" (trans. by F. Thilly, 2d ed.), pp. 82–83.

states are like, each of us can observe directly by introspection; and what introspection reveals is that they do not in the least resemble muscular contraction, or glandular secretion, or any other known bodily events. No tampering with language can alter the observable fact that thinking is one thing and muttering quite another; that the feeling called anger has no resemblance to the bodily behavior which usually goes with it; or that an act of will is not in the least like anything we find when we open the skull and examine the brain. Certain mental events are doubtless connected in some way with certain bodily events, but they are not those bodily events themselves. The connection is not identity.

This being clear, let us next consider the arguments offered to show that mental processes, although not identical with bodily processes, nevertheless depend on them. We are told, for instance, that some head injuries, or anesthetics, totally extinguish consciousness for the time being. As already pointed out, however, the strict fact is only that the usual bodily signs of consciousness are then absent. But they are also absent when a person is asleep; and yet, at the same time, dreams, which are states of consciousness, may be occurring.

It is true that when the person concerned awakens, he often remembers his dreams, whereas the person that has been anesthetized or injured has usually no memories relating to the period of apparent blankness. But this could mean that his consciousness was, for the first time, dissociated from its ordinary channels of manifestation, as was reported of the co-conscious personalities of some of the patients of Dr. Morton Prince.* Moreover, it sometimes occurs that a person who has been in an accident reports lack of memories not only for the period during which his body was unresponsive but also for a period of several hours *before* the accident, during which he had given to his associates all the ordinary external signs of being conscious as usual.

But, more generally, if absence of memories relating to a given period proved unconsciousness for that period, this would force us to conclude that we were unconscious during the first few years of our lives, and indeed have been so most of the time since; for the fact is that we have no memories whatever of most of our days. That we were alive and conscious on any long past specific date is, with only a few exceptions, not something we actually remember, but only something which we infer must be true.

EVIDENCE FROM PSYCHICAL RESEARCH

Another argument advanced against survival was, it will be remembered, that death must extinguish the mind, since all manifestations of it then cease. But to assert that they invariably then cease is to ignore

* "My Life as a Dissociated Personality" (edited by Morton Prince; Boston: Badger).

altogether the considerable amount of evidence to the contrary, gathered over many years and carefully checked by the Society for Psychical Research. This evidence, which is of a variety of kinds, has been reviewed by Professor Gardner Murphy in an article published in the Journal of the Society.* He mentions first the numerous well-authenticated cases of apparition of a dead person to others as yet unaware that he had died or even been ill or in danger. The more strongly evidential cases of apparition are those in which the apparition conveys to the person who sees it specific facts until then secret. An example would be that of the apparition of a girl to her brother nine years after her death, with a conspicuous scratch on her cheek. Their mother then revealed to him that she herself had made that scratch accidentally while preparing her daughter's body for burial, but that she had then at once covered it with powder and never mentioned it to anyone.

Another famous case is that of a father whose apparition some time after death revealed to one of his sons the existence and location of an unsuspected second will, benefiting him, which was then found as indicated. Still another case would be the report by General Barter, then a subaltern in the British Army in India, of the apparition to him of a lieutenant he had not seen for two or three years. The lieutenant's apparition was riding a brown pony with black mane and tail. He was much stouter than at their last meeting, and, whereas formerly clean-shaven, he now wore a peculiar beard in the form of a fringe encircling his face. On inquiry the next day from a person who had known the lieutenant at the time he died, it turned out that he had indeed become very bloated before his death; that he had grown just such a beard while on the sick list; and that he had some time before bought and eventually ridden to death a pony of that very description.

Other striking instances are those of an apparition seen simultaneously by several persons. It is on record that an apparition of a child was perceived first by a dog, that the animal's rushing at it, loudly barking, interrupted the conversation of the seven persons present in the room, thus drawing their attention to the apparition, and that the latter then moved through the room for some fifteen seconds, followed by the barking dog.**

Another type of empirical evidence of survival consists of communications, purporting to come from the dead, made through the persons commonly called sensitives, mediums, or automatists. Some of the most remarkable of these communications were given by the celebrated American medium, Mrs. Piper, who for many years was studied by the Society for Psychical Research, London, with the most elaborate precautions against all possibility of fraud. Twice, particularly, the evidences of

* "An Outline of Survival Evidence," *Journal of the American Society for Psychical Research*, January, 1945.

** The documents obtained by the Society for Psychical Research concerning this case, that of the lieutenant's apparition, and that of the girl with the scratch, are reproduced in Sir Ernest Bennett's "Apparitions and Haunted Houses" (London: Faber and Faber, 1945), pp. 334–337, 28–35, and 145–150 respectively.

identity supplied by the dead persons who purportedly were thus communicating with the living were of the very kinds, and of the same precision and detail, which would ordinarily satisfy a living person of the identity of another living person with whom he was not able to communicate directly, but only through an intermediary, or by letter or telephone.*

Again, sometimes the same mark of identity of a dead person, or the same message from him, or complementary parts of one message, are obtained independently from two mediums in different parts of the world.

Of course, when facts of these kinds are recounted, as I have just done, only in abstract summary, they make little if any impression upon us. And the very word "medium" at once brings to our minds the innumerable instances of demonstrated fraud perpetrated by charlatans to extract money from the credulous bereaved. But the modes of trickery and sources of error, which immediately suggest themselves to us as easy, natural explanations of the seemingly extraordinary facts, suggest themselves just as quickly to the members of the research committees of the Society for Psychical Research. Usually, these men have had a good deal more experience than the rest of us with the tricks of conjurers and fraudulent mediums, and take against them precautions far more strict and ingenious than would occur to the average sceptic.**

But when, instead of stopping at summaries, one takes the trouble to study the detailed, original reports, it then becomes evident that they cannot all be just laughed off; for to accept the hypothesis of fraud or malobservation would often require more credulity than to accept the facts reported.

To *explain* those facts, however, is quite another thing, Only two hypotheses at all adequate to do so have yet been advanced. One is that the communications really come, as they purport to do, from persons who have died and have survived death. The other is the hypothesis of telepathy—that is, the supposition, itself startling enough, that the medium is able to gather information directly from the minds of others, and that this is the true source of the information communicated. To account for all the facts, however, this hypothesis has to be stretched very far, for some of them require us to suppose that the medium can tap the minds even of persons far away and quite unknown to him, and can tap even the subconscious part of their minds.

Diverse highly ingenious attempts have been made to devise conditions

* A summary of some of the most evidential facts may be found in the book by M. Sage, entitled "Mrs. Piper and the Society for Psychical Research" (New York: Scott-Thaw Co., 1904); others of them are related in some detail in Sir Oliver Lodge's "The Survival of Man," Sec. IV (New York: Moffat, Yard and Co., 1909) and in A. M. Robbins' "Both Sides of the Veil," Part II (Boston: Sherman, French, and Co., 1909). The fullest account is in the *Proceedings of the Society for Psychical Research.*

** Cf. H. Carrington, "The Physical Phenomena of Spiritualism, Fraudulent and Genuine" (Boston: Small, Maynard & Co., 1908).

that would rule out telepathy as a possible explanation of the communications received; but some of the most critical and best-documented investigators still hold that it has not yet been absolutely excluded. Hence, although some of the facts recorded by psychical research constitute, prima facie, strong empirical evidence of survival, they cannot be said to establish it beyond question. But they do show that we need to revise rather radically in some respects our ordinary ideas of what is and is not possible in nature.

CAN MENTAL STATES CAUSE BODILY EVENTS?

Let us now turn to another of the arguments against survival. That states of consciousness entirely depend on bodily processes, and therefore cannot continue when the latter have ceased, is proved, it is argued, by the fact that various states of consciousness—in particular, the several kinds of sensations—can be caused at will by appropriately stimulating the body.

Now, it is very true that sensations and some other mental states can be so caused; but we have just as good and abundant evidence that mental states can cause various bodily events. John Laird mentions, among others, the fact that merely willing to raise one's arm normally suffices to cause it to rise; that a hungry person's mouth is caused to water by the idea of food; that feelings of rage, fear or excitement cause digestion to stop; that anxiety causes changes in the quantity and quality of the milk of a nursing mother; that certain thoughts cause tears, pallor, blushing or fainting; and so on.* The evidence we have that the relation is one of cause and effect is exactly the same here as where bodily processes cause mental states.

It is said, of course, that to suppose something non-physical, such as thought, to be capable of causing motion of a physical object, such as the body, is absurd. But I submit that if the heterogeneity of mind and matter makes this absurd, then it makes equally absurd the causation of mental states by stimulation of the body. Yet no absurdity is commonly found in the assertion that cutting the skin causes a feeling of pain, or that alcohol, caffein, bromides, and other drugs, cause characteristic states of consciousness. As David Hume made clear long ago, no kind of causal connection is intrinsically absurd. Anything might cause anything; and only observation can tell us what in fact can cause what.

Somewhat similar remarks would apply to the allegation that the principle of the conservation of energy precludes the possibility of causation of a physical event by a mental event. For if it does, then it equally precludes causation in the converse direction, and this, of course, would leave us totally at a loss to explain the occurrence of sensations. But, as

* John Laird, "Our Minds and Their Bodies" (London, 1925), pp. 16–19.

Keeton and others have pointed out,* that energy is conserved is not something observation has revealed or could reveal, but only a postulate —a defining postulate for the notion of an "isolated physical system."

That is, conservation of energy is something one has to have if, but only if, one insists on conceiving the physical world as wholly self-contained, independent, isolated. And just because the metaphysics which the natural sciences tacitly assume does insist on so conceiving the physical world, this metaphysics compels them to save conservation by postulations *ad hoc* whenever dissipation of energy is what observation reveals. It postulates, for instance, that something else, which appears at such times but was not until then regarded as energy, is energy too, but it is then said, "in a different form."

Furthermore, as Broad has emphasized, all that the principle of conservation requires is that when a quantity Q of energy disappears at one place in the physical world an equal quantity of it should appear at some other place there. And the supposition that, in some cases, what causes it to disappear here and appear there is some mental event, such perhaps as a volition, does not violate at all the supposition that energy is conserved.**

A word, next, on the parallelism between the degree of development of the nervous systems of various animals and the degree of their intelligence. This is alleged to prove that the latter is the product of the former. But the facts lend themselves equally well to the supposition that, on the contrary, an obscurely felt need for greater intelligence in the circumstances the animal faced was what brought about the variations which eventually resulted in a more adequate nervous organization.

In the development of the individual, at all events, it seems clear that the specific, highly complex nerve connections which become established in the brain and cerebellum of, for instance, a skilled pianist are the results of his will over many years to acquire the skill.

We must not forget in this context that there is a converse, equally consistent with the facts, for the theory, called epiphenomenalism, that mental states are related to the brain much as the halo is to the saint, that is, as effects but never themselves as causes. The converse theory, which might be called hypophenomenalism, and which is pretty well that of Schopenhauer, is that the instruments which the various mechanisms of the body constitute are the objective products of obscure cravings for the corresponding powers; and, in particular, that the organization of the nervous system is the effect and material isomorph of the variety of mental functions exercised at a given level of animal or human existence.

* M. T. Keeton, "Some Ambiguities in the Theory of the Conservation of Energy," *Philosophy of Science*, Vol. 8, No. 3, July 1941.

** C. D. Broad, "The Mind and Its Place in Nature," pp. 103 ff.

THE INITIAL ASSUMPTION BEHIND THE ARGUMENTS AGAINST SURVIVAL

We have now scrutinized all but the last of the reasons mentioned earlier for rejecting the possibility of survival, and we have found them all logically weak. Before examining the one which remains, it will be useful for us to pause a moment and inquire why so many of the persons who advance those reasons nevertheless think them convincing.

It is, I believe, because these persons approach the question of survival with a certain unconscious metaphysical bias. It derives from a particular initial assumption which they tacitly make. It is that *to be real is to be material.* And to be material, of course, is to be some process or part of the perceptually public world, that is, of the world we all perceive by means of our so-called five senses.

Now the assumption that to be real is to be material is a useful and appropriate one for the purpose of investigating the material world and of operating upon it; and this purpose is a legitimate and frequent one. But those persons, and most of us, do not realize that the validity of that assumption is strictly relative to that specific purpose. Hence they, and most of us, continue making the assumption, and it continues to rule judgment, even when, as now, the purpose in view is a different one, for which the assumption is no longer useful or even congruous.

The point is all-imporant here and therefore worth stressing. Its essence is that the conception of the nature of reality that proposes to define the real as the material is not the expression of an observable fact to which everyone would have to bow, but is the expression only of a certain direction of interest on the part of the persons who so define reality—of interest, namely, which they have chosen to center wholly in the material, perceptually public world. This specialized interest is of course as legitimate as any other, but it automatically ignores all the facts, commonly called facts of mind, which only introspection reveals. And that specialized interest is what alone compels persons in its grip to employ the word "mind" to denote, instead of what it commonly does denote, something else altogether, namely, the public behavior of bodies that have minds.

Only so long as one's judgment is swayed unawares by that special interest do the logically weak arguments against the possibility of survival, which we have examined, seem strong.

It is possible, however, and just as legitimate, as well as more conducive to a fair view of our question, to center one's interest at the start on the facts of mind as introspectively observable, ranking them as most real in the sense that they are the facts the intrinsic nature of which we most directly experience, the facts which we most certainly know to exist; and moreover, that they are the facts without the experiencing of which we should not know any other facts whatever—such, for instance, as those of the material world.

The sort of perspective one gets from this point of view is what I propose now to sketch briefly. For one thing, the material world is then seen to be but one among other objects of our consciousness. Moreover, one becomes aware of the crucially important fact that it is an object postulated rather than strictly given. What this means may be made clearer by an example. Suppose that, perhaps in a restaurant we visit for the first time, an entire wall is occupied by a large mirror and we look into it without realizing that it is a mirror. We then perceive, in the part of space beyond it, various material objects, notwithstanding that in fact they have no existence there at all. A certain set of the vivid color images which we call visual sensations was all that was strictly given to us, and these we construed, automatically and instantaneously, but nonetheless erroneously, as signs or appearances of the existence of certain material objects at a certain place.

Again, and similarly, we perceive in our dreams various objects which at the time we take as physical but which eventually we come to believe were not so. And this eventual conclusion, let it be noted, is forced upon us not because we then detect that something, called "physical substance," was lacking in those objects, but only because we notice, as we did not at the time, that their behavior was erratic—incoherent with their ordinary one. That is, their appearance was a *mere* appearance, deceptive in the sense that it did not then predict truly, as ordinarily it does, their later appearances. This, it is important to notice, is the *only* way in which we ever discover that an object we perceive was not really physical, or was not the particular sort of physical object we judged it to be.

These two examples illustrate the fact that our perception of physical objects is sometimes erroneous. But the essential point is that, even when it is veridical instead of erroneous, *all* that is literally and directly given to our minds is still only *some set of sensations*. These, on a given occasion, may be only color sensations; but they often include also tactual sensations, sounds, odors, and so on. It is especially interesting, however, to remark here in passing that, with respect to almost all the many thousands of persons and other "physical" objects we have perceived in a lifetime, *vivid color images* were the only data our perceiving strictly had to go by; so that, if the truth should happen to have been that those objects, like ghosts or images in a mirror, were actually intangible—that is, were *only* color images—we should never have discovered that this was the fact. For all we *directly* know, it *may* have been the fact!

To perceive a physical object, then, instead of merely experiencing passively certain sensations (something which perhaps hardly ever occurs), is always to *interpret*, that is to *construe*, given sensations as signs of, and appearances to us of, a postulated something other than themselves, which we believe is causing them in us and is capable of causing in us others of specific kinds. We believe this because we believe that our sensations too must have some cause, and we find none for them among our other mental states.

Such a postulated extramental something we call "a physical object." We say that we observe physical objects, and this is true. But it is important for the present purpose to be clear that we "observe" them never in any more direct or literal manner than is constituted by the process of interpretive postulation just described—never, for example, in the wholly direct and literal manner in which we are able to observe our sensations themselves and our other mental states. . . .

ON THE SOUL

ARISTOTLE

BOOK II

I. The theories of the soul handed down by our predecessors have been sufficiently discussed; now we must return to our starting-point, and try to define what the soul is, and what account of it can be given which will be the most comprehensive. We describe one class of existing things as substance; and this we subdivide into three: (1) matter, which is in itself not any particular thing; (2) shape or form, in virtue of which it is called some particular thing, and (3) a compound of the two. Matter is then potentiality, while form is realization or actuality, but the word actuality is used in two senses, as is illustrated by the possession of knowledge and the exercise of it. Bodies seem to be pre-eminently substances, and most particularly those which are of natural origin; for these are the sources from which the rest are derived. But of natural bodies some have life and some have not; by life we mean the capacity for self-sustenance, growth, and decay. Every natural body, then, which possesses life must be substance, and substance of the class which is a compound. Since this —having life—is predicated of a body, the body cannot be the soul, for the body is not predicated of anything else, but rather has things predicated of it, and is therefore matter. So the soul must be substance in the sense of being the form of a natural body, which potentially has life. And substance in the sense of form is actuality. The soul, then, is the actuality of the kind of body we have described. But actuality has two senses, analogous to the possession of knowledge and the exercise of it. Clearly

Reprinted from *De Anima*, Book II, Chapter 1, Transl. W. S. Hett, Loeb Classical Library, by permission of Harvard University Press.

actuality in our present sense is analogous to the possession of knowledge; for, where there is a soul, there is both sleep and wakefulness, and wakefulness is analogous to the exercise of knowledge, sleep to its possession but not its exercise. Now in any one person the possession of knowledge, precedes its use. The soul may therefore be defined as the first actuality of a natural body potentially possessing life, and the body must be of a kind which possesses organs. (In plants also the parts are their organs, very simple ones, such as the leaf which covers the pod, and the pod which covers the seed; but the roots are analogous to the mouth, for both these absorb food.) If then one is to find a comprehensive definition which will apply to every soul, it is the first actuality of a natural body possessed of organs. So one can no more ask if the body and the soul are one than if the wax and the impression it receives are one, or speaking generally the matter of each thing and the form of which it is the matter; for admitting that the terms unity and existence are used in many senses, the paramount sense is that of actuality.

We have, then, given a general definition of what the soul is: it is substance expressed as form. It is this which makes a body what it is; supposing that instruments had a natural body, for instance an axe; the substance of the axe would be that which makes it an axe, and this would be its soul; suppose this removed, and it would no longer be an axe in the ordinary sense of the term. As it is, it remains an axe, because the soul is not the form of a body of this kind, but only of a natural body, which has in itself the power of movement and rest. We must therefore investigate the application of our definition to the parts of the body. If the eye were a living creature, its soul would be its power of seeing; for this is the substance of the eye expressed as form. But the eye is the matter of seeing, and if seeing were absent, there would be no eye, except in an equivocal sense, as for instance a stone or painted eye. Now we must apply what we have found true of the part to the whole living body. For the same relationship must hold good of the part to the part, and the whole of sensation to the whole body which feels, in so far as it does so. But it is not the body which has lost its soul, which has the capacity to live, but that which possesses its soul; so the seed and the fruit are potentially bodies of such a kind. Just as the cutting of the axe or the seeing of the eye is an actuality, so also is the waking state, and the soul is actuality in the same sense as the capacity of the eye for seeing, or of the instrument for doing its work. But the body is that which has a capacity for life; but just as the pupil and the power of seeing make an eye, so in the other case the soul and body make a living creature. It is quite clear, then, that neither the soul nor any parts of it, if it has parts, can be separated from the body, for the actuality of some animals belongs to the parts themselves. Not but what there is nothing to prevent some parts being separated, because they are not actualities of any body. It is also uncertain whether the soul as an actuality bears the same relation to the body as the sailor to the ship. This then in outline is a sufficient definition and sketch of the soul.

EXPERIENCE AND THE SUBJECT

JOHN DEWEY

As was remarked in the introductory chapter one can hardly use the term "experience" in philosophical discourse, but a critic rises to inquire "Whose experience?" The question is asked in adverse criticism. Its implication is that experience by its very nature is owned by some one; and that the ownership is such in kind that everything about experience is affected by a private and exclusive quality. The implication is as absurd as it would be to infer from the fact that houses are usually owned, are mine and yours and his, that possessive reference so permeates the properties of being a house that nothing intelligible can be said about the latter. It is obvious, however, that a house can be owned only when it has existence and properties independent of being owned. The quality of belonging to some one is not an all-absorbing maw in which independent properties and relations disappear to be digested into egohood. It is additive; it marks the assumption of a new relationship, in consequence of which the house, the common, ordinary, house, acquires new properties. It is subject to taxes; the owner has the right to exclude others from entering it; he enjoys certain privileges and immunities with respect to it and is also exposed to certain burdens and liabilities.

Substitute "experience" for "house," and no other word need be changed. Experience when it happens has the same dependence upon objective natural events, physical and social, as has the occurrence of a house. It has its own objective and definitive traits; these can be described without reference to a self, precisely as a house is of brick, has eight rooms, etc., irrespective of whom it belongs to. Nevertheless, just as for some purposes and with respect to some consequences, it is all important to note the added qualification of personal ownership of real property, so with "experience." In first instance and intent, it is not exact nor relevant to say "I experience" or "I think." "It" experiences or is experienced, "it" thinks or is thought, is a juster phrase. Experience, a serial course of affairs with their own characteristic properties and relationships, occurs, happens, and is what it is. Among and within these occurrences, not outside of them nor underlying them, are those events which are denominated selves. In some specifiable respects and for some specifiable consequences, these selves, capable of objective denotation just as are sticks, stones, and stars, assume the care and administration of certain objects and acts in experience. Just as in the case of the house, this

Reprinted from *Experience and Nature*, The Open Court Publishing Company, La Salle, Illinois, 1929, pp. 231–236, 258–262, 277–279, 303–305.

assumption of ownership brings with it further liabilities and assets, burdens and enjoyments.

To say in a significant way, "*I* think, believe, desire, instead of barely *it* is thought, believed, desired," is to accept and affirm a responsibility and to put forth a claim. It does not mean that the self is the source or author of the thought and affection nor its exclusive seat. It signifies that the self as a centred organization of energies identifies itself (in the sense of accepting their consequences) with a belief or sentiment of independent and external origination. The absurdity of any other conception appears upon examination of such affairs as are designated by "I do not believe" or "I do not like;" in them it is obvious that a relationship of incompatibility between two distinct and denoted objects is contained.

Authorship and liability look in two different ways, one to the past, the other to the future. Natural events—including social habits—originate thoughts and feelings. To say "*I* think, hope and love" is to say in effect that genesis is not the last word; instead of throwing the blame or the credit for the belief, affection and expectation upon nature, one's family, church, or state, one declares one's self to be henceforth a partner. An adoptive act is proclaimed in virtue of which one claims the benefit of future goods and admits liability for future ills flowing from the affair in question. Even in the most "individualistic" society some properties remain communal; and many things, like the bowels of the earth and the depths of the seas, are unowned by either group or person. The cogent line of defense of the institution of private property is that it promotes prudence, accountability, ingenuity and security, in the production and administration of commodities and resources which exist independently of the relationship of property. In like fashion, not all thoughts and emotions are owned either socially or personally; and either mode of appropriation has to be justified on the basis of distinctive consequences.

Analytic reflection shows that the ordinary conception of causation as a trait belonging to some one thing is the idea of responsibility read backward. The idea that some one thing, or any two or three things, are *the* cause of an occurrence is in effect an application of the idea of credit or blame—as in the Greek *αιτὶα*. There is nothing in nature that *belongs* absolutely and exclusively to anything else; belonging is always a matter of reference and distributive assignment, justified in any particular case as far as it works out well. Greek metaphysics and logic are dominated by the idea of inherent belonging and exclusion; another instance of naively reading the story of nature in language appropriate to human association. Modern science has liberated physical events from the domination of the notions of intrinsic belonging and exclusion, but it has retained the idea with exacerbated vigor in the case of psychological events. The elimination of the category from physics and its retention in psychology has provided a seeming scientific basis for the division between psychology and physics, and thereby for the egotism of modern philosophy. Much subjectivism is only a statement of the logical consequences of the doctrine sponsored by psychological "science" of the monopolistic possession of mental phenomena by a self; or, after the idea of an underlying spiritual substance became shaky, of the doctrine that mental events as such constitute all there is to selfhood. For the philosophical implications of the latter idea, as far as privacy, monopoly and exclusiveness of causation and belonging are concerned, are similar to those of the older dogma when it was applied to cosmic nature.

Enough, however, of negation. The positive consequence is an understanding of the shift of emphasis from the experienced, the objective subject-matter, the *what*, to the experiencing, the method of its course, the *how* of its changes. Such a shift occurs whenever the problem of control of production of consequences arises. As long as men are content to enjoy and suffer fire when it happens, fire is just an objective entity which is what it is. That it may be taken as a deity to be adored or propitiated, is evidence that its "whatness" is all there is to it. But when men come to the point of *making* fire, fire is not an essence, but a mode of natural phenomena, an order in change, a "how" of a historic sequence. The change from immediate use in enjoyment and suffering is equivalent to recognition of a method of procedure, and of the alliance of insight into method with possibility of control.

The development of the conception of experiencing as a distinctive operation is akin to the growth of the idea of fire-making out of direct experiences with fire. Fire is fire, inherently just what it is; but making fire is relational. It takes thought away from fire to the other things that help and prevent its occurrence. So with experience in the sense of things that are experienced; they are *what* they are. But their occurrence as experienced things is ascertained to be dependent upon attitudes and dispositions; the manner of their happening is found to be affected by the habits of an organic individual. Since myth and science concern the same objects in the same natural world, sun, moon, and stars, the difference between them cannot be determined exclusively on the basis of these natural objects. A differential has to be found in distinctive *ways* of experiencing natural objects; it is perceived that man is an emotional and imaginative as well as an observing and reasoning creature, and that different manners of experiencing affect the status of subject-matter experienced. Capacity to distinguish between the sun and moon of science and these same things as they figure in myth and cult depends upon capacity to distinguish different attitudes and dispositions of the subject; the heroes of legend and poetry are discriminated from historic characters when memory, imagination and idealizing emotion are taken into the reckoning. Again, it is discovered that the good of some objects is connected with one way of experiencing, namely appetite, while the acquisition of goodness by other objects is dependent upon the operation of reflection. In consequence, the experienced objects are differentiated as to their goodness, although good as an essence is unchanged.

. . .

That is to say, differences in qualities (feelings) of acts when employed as indications of acts performed and to be performed and as signs of their consequences, *mean* something. And they mean it directly; the meaning is had as their own character. Feelings make sense; as immediate meanings of events and objects, they are sensations, or, more properly, sensa. Without language, the qualities of organic action that are feelings are pains, pleasures, odors, colors, noises, tones, only potentially and proleptically. With language they are discriminated and identified. They are then "objectified;" they are immediate traits of things. This "objectification" is not a miraculous ejection from the organism or soul into external things, nor an illusory attribution of psychical entities to physical things. The qualities never were "in" the organism; they always were qualities of interactions in which both extra-organic things and organisms partake. When named, they enable identification and discrimination of things to take place as means in a further course of inclusive interaction. Hence they are as much qualities of the things engaged as of the organism. For purposes of control they may be referred specifically to either the thing or to the organism or to a specified structure of the organism. Thus color which turns out not to be a reliable sign of external events becomes a sign of, say, a defect in visual apparatus. The notion that sensory affections discriminate and identify themselves, apart from discourse, as being colors and sounds, etc., and thus *ipso facto* constitute certain elementary modes of knowledge, even though it be only knowledge of their own existence, is inherently so absurd that it would never have occurred to any one to entertain it, were it not for certain preconceptions about mind and knowledge. Sentiency in itself is anoetic; it exists as any immediate quality exists, but nevertheless it is an indispensable means of any noetic function.

For when, through language, sentience is taken up into a system of signs, when for example a certain quality of the active relationship of organism and environment is named hunger, it is seen as an organic demand for an extra-organic object. To term a quality "hunger," to name it, is to refer to an object, to food, to that which will satisfy it, towards which the active situation moves. Similarly, to name another quality "red," is to direct an interaction between an organism and a thing to some object which fulfills the demand or need of the situation. It requires but slight observation of mental growth of a child to note that organically conditioned qualities, including those special sense-organs, are discriminated only as they are employed to designate objects; red, for instance, as the property of a dress or toy. The difficulty in the way of identifying the qualities of acts conditioned by proprio-ceptor organs is notoriously enormous. They just merge in the general situation. If they entered into communication as shared means to social consequences they would acquire the same objective distinctiveness as do qualities conditioned by the extero-ceptor organs. On the other hand, the qualities of the latter are just shades of the general tone of situations until they are used, in language, as common or shared means to common ends. Then they are identified as traits of objects. The child has to learn through social intercourse that certain qualities of action mean greediness or anger or fear or rudeness; the case is not otherwise with those qualities which are identified as red, musical tone, a foul odor. The latter may have instigated nausea, and "red" may have excited uneasiness (as blood makes some persons faint); but discrimination of the nauseating object *as* foul odor, and of the excitation *as* red occurs only when they are designated as signs.

The qualities of situations in which organisms and surrounding conditions interact, when discriminated, make sense. Sense is distinct from feeling, for it has a recognized reference; it is the qualitative characteristic of something, not just a submerged unidentified quality or tone. Sense is also different from signification. The latter involves use of a quality as a sign or index of something else, as when the red of a light signifies danger and the need of bringing a moving locomotive to a stop. The sense of a thing, on the other hand, is an immediate and immanent meaning; it is meaning which is itself felt or directly had. When we are baffled by perplexing conditions, and finally hit upon a clew, and everything falls into place, the whole thing suddenly, as we say, "makes sense." In such a situation, the clew has signification in virtue of being an indication, a guide to interpretation. But the meaning of the *whole* situation as apprehended is sense. This idiomatic usage of the word sense is much nearer the empirical facts than is the ordinary restriction of the word in psychological literature to a single simple recognized quality, like sweet or red: the latter simply designates a case of *minimum* sense, deliberately limited for purposes of intellectual safety-first. Whenever a situation has this double function of meaning, namely signification and sense, mind, intellect is definitely present.

The distinction between physical, psycho-physical, and mental is thus one of levels of increasing complexity and intimacy of interaction among natural events. The idea that matter, life and mind represent separate kinds of Being is a doctrine that springs, as so many philosophic errors have sprung, from a substantiation of eventual functions. The fallacy converts consequences of interaction of events into causes of the occurrence of these consequences—a reduplication which is significant as to the *importance* of the functions, but which hopelessly confuses understanding of them. "Matter," or the physical, is a character of events when they occur at a certain level of interaction. It is not itself an event or existence; the notion that while "mind" denotes essence, "matter" denotes existence is superstition. It is more than a bare essence; for it is a property of a particular field of interacting events. But as it figures in *science* it is as much an essence, as is acceleration, or the square root of minus one; which meanings also express derivative characters of events in interaction. Consequently, while the theory that life, feeling and thought are never independent of physical events may be deemed materialism, it may also be considered just the opposite. For it is reasonable to believe that the most adequate definition of the basic traits of natural existence can be had only when its properties are most fully displayed—a condition which is met in the degree of the scope and intimacy of interactions realized.

• • •

The account which has been given will be repeated from a more analytic point of view, starting with evident empirical consideration. Every "mind" that we are empirically acquainted with is found in connection with some organized body. Every such body exists in a natural medium to which it sustains some adaptive connection: plants to air, water, sun, and animals to these things and also to plants. Without such connections, animals die; the "purest" mind would not continue without them. An animal can live only as long as it draws nutriment from its medium, finds there means of defence and ejects into it waste and superfluous products of its own making. Since no particular organism lasts forever, life in general goes on only as an organism reproduces itself; and the only place where it can reproduce itself is in the environment. In all higher forms reproduction is sexual; that is, it involves the meeting of two forms. The medium is thus one which contains similar and conjunctive forms. At every point and stage, accordingly, a living organism and its life processes involve a world or nature temporally and spatially "external" to itself but "internal" to its functions.

The only excuse for reciting such commonplaces is that traditional theories have separated life from nature, mind from organic life, and thereby created mysteries. Restore the connection, and the problem of how a mind can know an external world or even know that there is such a thing, is like the problem of how an animal eats things external to itself; it is the kind of problem that arises only if one assumes that a hibernating bear living off its own stored substance defines the normal procedure, ignoring moreover the question where the bear got its stored material. The problem of how one person knows the existence of other persons, is, when the relation of mind and life is genuinely perceived, like the problem of how one animal can associate with other animals, since other is other. A creature generated in a conjunctive union, dependent upon others (as are at least all higher forms) for perpetuation of its being, and carrying in its own structure the organs and marks of its intimate connection with others will know other creatures if it knows itself. Since both the inanimate and the human environment are involved in the functions of life, it is inevitable, if these functions evolve to the point of thinking and if thinking is naturally serial with biological functions, that it will have as the material of thought, even of its erratic imaginings, the events and connections of this environment. And if the animal succeeds in putting to use any of its thinkings as means of sustaining its functions, those thoughts will have the characters that define knowledge.

· · ·

While on the psycho-physical level, consciousness denotes the totality of actualized immediate qualitative differences, or "feelings," it denotes, upon the plane of mind, actualized apprehensions of meanings, that is, ideas. There is thus an obvious difference between mind and consciousness; meaning and an idea. Mind denotes the whole system of meanings as they are embodied in the workings of organic life; consciousness in a being with language denotes awareness or perception of meanings; it is the perception of actual events, whether past, contemporary or future, *in* their meanings, the having of actual ideas. The greater part of mind is only implicit in any conscious act or state; the field of mind—of operative meanings—is enormously wider than that of consciousness. Mind is contextual and persistent; consciousness is focal and transitive. Mind is, so to speak, structural, substantial; a constant background and foreground; perceptive consciousness is process, a series of heres and nows. Mind is a constant luminosity; consciousness intermittent, a series of flashes of varying intensities. Consciousness is, as it were, the occasional interception of messages continually transmitted, as a mechanical receiving device selects a few of the vibrations with which the air is filled and renders them audible.

The nature of awareness of meanings cannot be conveyed in speech. As with other immediate qualitative existences, words can only hint, point; the indication succeeding when it evokes an actual experience of the thing in question. Such words as apparency, conspicuousness, outstandingness, vividness, clearness, including of course their opposites vague, dim, confused, may assist the evocation. To denote the characteristics of mind a thoroughly different set of names must be used: organization, order, coherence. The relation of mind to consciousness may be partially suggested by saying that while mind as a system of meanings is subject to disorganization, disequilibration, perturbation, there is no sense in referring to a particular state of awareness *in its immediacy* as either organized or disturbed. An idea is just what it is when it occurs. To call it composed or perturbed is to compare one state with another, a comparison which by nature of the case can be made only indirectly on the basis of respective conditions and consequences. Emotional conditions do not *occur* as emotions, intrinsically defined as such; they occur as "tertiary" qualities of objects. Some cases of awareness or perception are designated "emotions" in retrospect or from without, as a child is instructed to term certain perceptual situations anger, or fear, or love, by way of informing him as to their consequences. Immediately, every perceptual awareness may be termed indifferently emotion, sensation, thought, desire: not that it *is* immediately any one of these things, or all of them combined, but that when it is taken in some *reference*, to conditions or to consequences or to both, it has, in that contextual reference, the distinctive properties of emotion, sensation, thought or desire.

The relation between mind and consciousness may be indicated by a familiar happening. When we read a book, we are immediately conscious of meanings that present themselves, and vanish. These meanings existentially occurring are *ideas*. But we are capable of getting ideas from what is read because of an organized system of meanings of which we are not at any one time completely aware. Our mathematical or political "mind" is the system of such meanings as possess and determine our particular apprehensions or ideas. There is, however, a continuum or spectrum between this containing system and the meanings which, being focal and urgent, are the ideas of the moment. There is a contextual field between the latter and those meanings which determine the habitual direction of our conscious thoughts and supply the organs for their formation. One great mistake in the orthodox psychological tradition is its exclusive preoccupation with sharp focalization to the neglect of the vague shading off from the foci into a field of increasing dimness.

A MATERIALIST CONCEPTION OF MAN

BARON D'HOLBACH

Man occupies a place amidst that crowd, that multitude of beings, of which nature is the assemblage. His essence, that is to say, the peculiar manner of existence by which he is distinguished from other beings, renders him susceptible of various modes of action; of a variety of motion; some of which are simple and visible, others concealed and complicated. His life itself is nothing more than a long series, a succession of necessary and connected motion, which operates perpetual and continual changes in his machine; which has for its principle either causes contained within himself—such as blood, nerves, fibres, flesh, bones, in short, the matter, as well solid as fluid, of which his whole, or his body, is composed; or those exterior causes, which by acting upon him, modify him diversely.

The beings of the human species, as well as all other beings, are susceptible of two sorts of motion: the one, that of the mass, by which an entire body, or some of its parts, are visibly transferred from one place to another; the other, internal and concealed, of some of which man is sensible, while some takes place without his knowledge, and is not even to be guessed at, but by the effect it outwardly produces. In a machine so extremely complex as man, formed by the combination of such a multiplicity of matter, so diversified in its properties, so different in its proportions, so varied in its modes of action, the motion necessarily becomes of the most complicated kind; its dullness, as well as its rapidity, frequently escapes the observation of those themselves, in whom it takes place.

Let us not then be surprised, if when man would account to himself for his existence, for his manner of acting, finding so many obstacles to encounter,—he invented such strange hypotheses to explain the concealed spring of his machine—if when this motion appeared to him to be differ-

Reprinted from *A System of Nature,* Part I, Chapter VI, London, 1884, first published 1770.

ent from that of other bodies, he conceived an idea that he moved and acted in a manner altogether distinct from the other beings in nature. He clearly perceived that his body, as well as different parts of it, did act; but frequently he was unable to discover what brought them into action—from whence he received the impulse; he then conjectured he contained within himself a moving principle, distinguished from his machine, which secretly gave an impulse to the springs which set this machine in motion; that moved him by its own natural energy; that consequently he acted according to laws totally distinct from those which regulated the motion of other beings: he was conscious of certain internal motion, which he could not help feeling; but how could he conceive, that this invisible motion was so frequently competent to produce such striking effects? How could he comprehend, that a fugitive idea, an imperceptible act of thought, was so frequently capacitated to bring his whole being into trouble and confusion? He fell into the belief, that he perceived within himself a substance distinguished from that self, endowed with a secret force, in which he supposed existed qualities distinctly differing from those, of either the visible causes that acted on his organs, or those organs themselves. He did not sufficiently understand, that the primitive causes which make a stone fall, or his arm move, are perhaps as difficult of comprehension, as arduous to be explained, as those internal impulses, of which his thought or his will are the effects. Thus, for want of meditating nature—of considering her under her true point of view—of remarking the conformity—of noticing the simultaneity, the unity of the motion of this fancied motive-power with that of his body—of his material organs—he conjectured he was not only a distinct being, but that he was set apart, with different energies, from all the other beings in nature; that he was of a more simple essence, having nothing in common with any thing by which he was surrounded; nothing that connected him with all that he beheld.

It is from thence has successively sprung his notions of *spirituality*, *immateriality*, *immortality;* in short, all those vague unmeaning words, he has invented by degrees, in order to subtilize and designate the attributes of the unknown power, which he believes he contains within himself, which he conjectures to be the concealed principle of all his visible actions: when man once imbibes an idea that he cannot comprehend, he meditates upon it until he has given it a complete personification: Thus he saw, or fancied he saw, the igneous matter pervade every thing; he conjectured that it was the only principle of life and activity, he proceeded to embody it, he gave it his own form, called it Jupiter, and ended by worshipping this image of his own creation, as the power from whom he derived every good he experienced, every evil he sustained. To crown the bold conjectures, he ventured to make of this internal motive-power, he supposed, that different from all other beings, even from the body that served to envelop it, it was not bound to undergo dissolution; that such was its perfect simplicity, that it could not be decomposed, nor even change its form; in short, that it was by its essence, exempted from those revolutions, to which he saw the body subjected, as well as all the compound beings with which nature is filled.

Thus man in his own ideas, became double; he looked upon himself, as a whole, composed by the inconceivable assemblage, of two different, two distinct natures; which have no point of analogy between themselves: he distinguished two substances in himself, one evidently submitted to the influence of gross beings, composed of coarse inert matter : this he called *body:*—the other, which he supposed to be simple, of a purer essence, was contemplated as acting from itself; giving motion to the body, with which it found itself so miraculously united: this he called *soul* or *spirit:* the functions of the one, he denominated *physical corporeal, material;* the functions of the other he styled *spiritual, intellectual.* Man, considered relatively to the first, was termed the *physical man;* viewed with relation to the last, he was designated the *moral man.*

These distinctions, although adopted by the greater number of the philosophers of the present day, are, nevertheless, only founded on gratuitous suppositions. Man has always believed, he remedied his ignorance of things, by invented words, to which he could never attach any true sense or meaning. He imagined he understood matter, its properties, its faculties, its resources, its different combinations, because he had a superficial glimpse of some of its qualities: he has, however, in reality, done nothing more than obscure the faint ideas he has been capacitated to form of this matter, by associating it with a substance much less intelligible than itself. It is thus, speculative man, in forming words, in multiplying beings, has only plunged himself into greater difficulties than those he endeavoured to avoid; and thereby placed obstacles to the progress of his knowledge: whenever he has been deficient of facts he has had recourse to conjecture, which he quickly changed into fancied realities. Thus, his imagination, no longer guided by experience, hurried on by his new ideas, was lost, without hope of return, in the labyrinth of an ideal, of an intellectual world, to which he had himself given birth; it was next to impossible to withdraw him from this delusion, to place him in the right road, of which nothing but experience can furnish him the clew. Nature points out to man, that in himself, as well as in all those objects which act upon him, there is never more than matter endowed with various properties, diversely modified; that acts, by reason of these properties: that man is an organized whole, composed of a variety of matter: that like all the other productions of nature, he follows general and known laws, as well as those laws or modes of action, which are peculiar to himself and unknown.

Thus, when it shall be inquired, what is man?

We say he is a material being organized after a peculiar manner; conformed to a certain mode of thinking, of feeling, capable of modification in certain modes peculiar to himself; to his organization, to that particular combination of matter which is found assembled in him.

If again, it be asked, what origin we give to beings of the human species?

We reply, that like all other beings, man is a production of nature, who resembles them in some respects, and finds himself submitted to the same laws; who differs from them in other respects, and follows particular laws, determined by the diversity of his conformation.

SENSATIONS AND BRAIN PROCESSES

J. J. C. SMART

This paper* takes its departure from arguments to be found in U. T. Place's "Is Consciousness a Brain Process?"** I have had the benefit of discussing Place's thesis in a good many universities in the United States and Australia, and I hope that the present paper answers objections to his thesis which Place has not considered and that it presents his thesis in a more nearly unobjectionable form. This paper is meant also to supplement the paper "The 'Mental' and the 'Physical,' " by H. Feigl,† which in part argues for a similar thesis to Place's.

Suppose that I report that I have at this moment a roundish, blurry-edged after-image which is yellowish towards its edge and is orange towards its center. What is it that I am reporting? One answer to this question might be that I am not reporting anything, that when I say that it looks to me as though there is a roundish yellowy-orange patch of light on the wall I am expressing some sort of *temptation*, the temptation to say that there *is* a roundish yellowy-orange patch on the wall (though I may know that there is not such a patch on the wall). This is perhaps Wittgenstein's view in the *Philosophical Investigations* (see §§ 367, 370). Similarly, when I "report" a pain, I am not really reporting anything (or, if you like, I am reporting in a queer sense of "reporting"), but am doing a sophisticated sort of wince. (See § 244: "The verbal expression of pain replaces crying and does not describe it." Nor does it describe anything else?)‡ I prefer most of the time to discuss an after-image rather than a

Reprinted from *Philosophy of Mind*, ed. Vere Chappell, by permission of the author, Prentice-Hall, and the editor of *Philosophical Review* in which the original version of this paper appeared.

* This is a very slightly revised version of a paper which was first published in the *Philosophical Review*, LXVIII (1959), 141–56. Since that date there have been criticisms of my paper by J. T. Stevenson, *Philosophical Review*, LXIX (1960), 505–10, to which I have replied in *Philosophical Review*, LXX (1961), 406–7, and by G. Pitcher and by W. D. Joske, *Australasian Journal of Philosophy*, XXXVIII (1960), 150–60, to which I have replied in the same volume of that journal, pp. 252–54.

** *British Journal of Psychology*, XLVII (1956), 44–50; reprinted in this volume, pp. 101–09 above. (Page references are to the reprint in this volume.)

† *Minnesota Studies in the Philosophy of Science*, Vol. II (Minneapolis: University of Minnesota Press, 1958), pp. 370–497.

‡ Some philosophers of my acquaintance, who have the advantage over me in having known Wittgenstein, would say that this interpretation of him is too

pain, because the word "pain" brings in something which is irrelevant to my purpose: the notion of "distress." I think that "he is in pain" entails "he is in distress," that is, that he is in a certain agitation-condition.* Similarly, to say "I am in pain" may be to do more than "replace pain behavior": it may be partly to report something, though this something is quite nonmysterious, being an agitation-condition, and so susceptible of behavioristic analysis. The suggestion I wish if possible to avoid is a different one, namely that "I am in pain" is a genuine report, and that what it reports is an irreducibly psychical something. And similarly the suggestion I wish to resist is also that to say "I have a yellowish-orange after-image" is to report something irreducibly psychical.

Why do I wish to resist this suggestion? Mainly because of Occam's razor. It seems to me that science is increasingly giving us a viewpoint whereby organisms are able to be seen as physicochemical mechanisms:** it seems that even the behavior of man himself will one day be explicable in mechanistic terms. There does seem to be, so far as science is concerned, nothing in the world but increasingly complex arrangements of physical constituents. All except for one place: in consciousness. That is, for a full description of what is going on in a man you would have to mention not only the physical processes in his tissues, glands, nervous system, and so forth, but also his states of consciousness: his visual, auditory and tactual sensations, his aches and pains. That these should be *correlated* with brain processes does not help, for to say that they are *correlated* is to say that they are something "over and above." You cannot correlate something with itself. You correlate footprints with burglars, but not Bill Sikes the burglar with Bill Sikes the burglar. So sensations, states of consciousness, do seem to be the one sort of thing left outside the physicalist picture, and for various reasons I just cannot believe that this can be so. That everything should be explicable in terms of physics (together of course with descriptions of the ways in which the parts are put together—roughly, biology is to physics as radio-engineering is to electromagnetism) except the occurrence of sensations seems to me to be frankly unbelievable. Such sensations would be "nomological danglers," to use Feigl's expression.† It is not often realized how odd would be the laws whereby these nomological danglers would dangle. It is sometimes asked, "Why can't there be psychophysical laws which are of a novel sort, just as the laws of electricity and magnetism were

---

behavioristic. However, it seems to me a very natural interpretation of his printed words, and whether or not it is Wittgenstein's real view it is certainly an interesting and important one. I wish to consider it here as a possible rival both to the "brain-process" thesis and to straight-out old-fashioned dualism.

* See Ryle, *The Concept of Mind* (London: Hutchinson's University Library, 1949), p. 93.

** On this point see Paul Oppenheim and Hilary Putnam, "Unity of Science as a Working Hypothesis," in *Minnesota Studies in the Philosophy of Science,* Vol. II (Minneapolis: University of Minnesota Press, 1958), pp. 3–36.

† Feigl, *op. cit.*, p. 428. Feigl uses the expression "nomological danglers" for the laws whereby the entities dangle: I have used the expression to refer to the dangling entities themselves.

novelties from the standpoint of Newtonian mechanics?" Certainly we are pretty sure in the future to come across new ultimate laws of a novel type, but I expect them to relate simple constituents: for example, whatever ultimate particles are then in vogue. I cannot believe that ultimate laws of nature could relate simple constituents to configurations consisting of perhaps billions of neurons (and goodness knows how many billion billions of ultimate particles) all put together for all the world as though their main purpose in life was to be a negative feedback mechanism of a complicated sort. Such ultimate laws would be like nothing so far known in science. They have a queer "smell" to them. I am just unable to believe in the nomological danglers themselves, or in the laws whereby they would dangle. If any philosophical arguments seemed to compel us to believe in such things, I would suspect a catch in the argument. In any case it is the object of this paper to show that there are no philosophical arguments which compel us to be dualists.

The above is largely a confession of faith, but it explains why I find Wittgenstein's position (as I construe it) so congenial. For on this view there are, in a sense, no sensations. A man is a vast arrangement of physical particles, but there are not, over and above this, sensations or states of consciousness. There are just behavioral facts about this vast mechanism, such as that it expresses a temptation (behavior disposition) to say "there is a yellowish-red patch on the wall" or that it goes through a sophisticated sort of wince, that is, says "I am in pain." Admittedly Wittgenstein says that though the sensation "is not a something," it is nevertheless "not a nothing either" (§ 304), but this need only mean that the word "ache" has a use. An ache is a thing, but only in the innocuous sense in which the plain man, in the first paragraph of Frege's *Foundations of Arithmetic*, answers the question "What is the number one?" by "a thing." It should be noted that when I assert that to say "I have a yellowish-orange after-image" is to express a temptation to assert the physical-object statement "There is a yellowish-orange patch on the wall," I mean that saying "I have a yellowish-orange after-image" is (partly) the exercise of the disposition* which is the temptation. It is not to *report* that I have the temptation, any more than is "I love you" normally a report that I love someone. Saying "I love you" is just part of the behavior which is the exercise of the disposition of loving someone.

Though for the reasons given above, I am very receptive to the above "expressive" account of sensation statements, I do not feel that it will quite do the trick. Maybe this is because I have not thought it out sufficiently, but it does seem to me as though, when a person says "I have an after-image," he *is* making a genuine report, and that when he says "I have a pain," he *is* doing more than "replace pain-behavior," and that

* Wittgenstein did not like the word "disposition." I am using it to put in a nutshell (and perhaps inaccurately) the view which I am attributing to Wittgenstein. I should like to repeat that I do not wish to claim that my interpretation of Wittgenstein is correct. Some of those who knew him do not interpret him in this way. It is merely a view which I find myself extracting from his printed words and which I think is important and worth discussing for its own sake.

"this more" is not just to say that he is in distress. I am not so sure, however, that to admit this is to admit that there are nonphysical correlates of brain processes. Why should not sensations just be brain processes of a certain sort? There are, of course, well-known (as well as lesser-known) philosophical objections to the view that reports of sensations are reports of brain-processes, but I shall try to argue that these arguments are by no means as cogent as is commonly thought to be the case.

Let me first try to state more accurately the thesis that sensations are brain-processes. It is not the thesis that, for example, "after-image" or "ache" means the same as "brain process of sort X" (where "X" is replaced by a description of a certain sort of brain process). It is that, in so far as "after-image" or "ache" is a report of a process, it is a report of a process that *happens to be* a brain process. It follows that the thesis does not claim that sensation statements can be *translated* into statements about brain processes.* Nor does it claim that the logic of a sensation statement is the same as that of a brain-process statement. All it claims is that in so far as a sensation statement is a report of something, that something is in fact a brain process. Sensations are nothing over and above brain processes. Nations are nothing "over and above" citizens, but this does not prevent the logic of nation statements being very different from the logic of citizen statements, nor does it insure the translatability of nation statements into citizen statements. (I do not, however, wish to assert that the relation of sensation statements to brain-process statements is very like that of nation statements to citizen statements. Nations do not just *happen to be* nothing over and above citizens, for example. I bring in the "nations" example merely to make a negative point: that the fact that the logic of A-statements is different from that of B-statements does not insure that A's are anything over and above B's.)

REMARKS ON IDENTITY

When I say that a sensation is a brain process or that lightning is an electric discharge, I am using "is" in the sense of strict identity. (Just as in the—in this case necessary—proposition "7 is identical with the smallest prime number greater than 5.") When I say that a sensation is a brain process or that lightning is an electric discharge I do not mean just that the sensation is somehow spatially or temporally continuous with the brain process or that the lightning is just spatially or temporally continuous with the discharge. When on the other hand I say that the successful general is the same person as the small boy who stole the apples I mean only that the successful general I see before me is a time slice** of

* See Place, *op. cit.*, p. 102, and Feigl, *op. cit.*, p. 390, near top.

** See J. H. Woodger, *Theory Construction,* International Encyclopedia of Unified Science, II, No. 5 (Chicago: University of Chicago Press, 1939), 38. I here permit myself to speak loosely. For warnings against possible ways of going wrong with this sort of talk, see my note "Spatialising Time," *Mind,* LXIV (1955), 239–41.

the same four-dimensional object of which the small boy stealing apples is an earlier time slice. However, the four-dimensional object which has the general-I-see-before-me for its late time slice is identical in the strict sense with the four-dimensional object which has the small-boy-stealing-apples for an early time slice. I distinguish these two senses of "is identical with" because I wish to make it clear that the brain-process doctrine asserts identity in the *strict* sense.

I shall now discuss various possible objections to the view that the processes reported in sensation statements are in fact processes in the brain. Most of us have met some of these objections in our first year as philosophy students. All the more reason to take a good look at them. Others of the objections will be more recondite and subtle.

Objection 1. Any illiterate peasant can talk perfectly well about his after-images, or how things look or feel to him, or about his aches and pains, and yet he may know nothing whatever about neurophysiology. A man may, like Aristotle, believe that the brain is an organ for cooling the body without any impairment of his ability to make true statements about his sensations. Hence the things we are talking about when we describe our sensations cannot be processes in the brain.

Reply. You might as well say that a nation of slugabeds, who never saw the Morning Star or knew of its existence, or who had never thought of the expression "the Morning Star," but who used the expression "the Evening Star" perfectly well, could not use this expression to refer to the same entity as we refer to (and describe as) "the Morning Star."*

You may object that the Morning Star is in a sense not the very same thing as the Evening Star, but only something spatiotemporally continuous with it. That is, you may say that the Morning Star is not the Evening Star in the strict sense of "identity" that I distinguished earlier.

There is, however, a more plausible example. Consider lightning.** Modern physical science tells us that lightning is a certain kind of electrical discharge due to ionization of clouds of water vapor in the atmosphere. This, it is now believed, is what the true nature of lightning is. Note that there are not two things: a flash of lightning and an electrical discharge. There is one thing, a flash of lightning, which is described scientifically as an electrical discharge to the earth from a cloud of ionized water molecules. The case is not at all like that of explaining a footprint by reference to a burglar. We say that what lightning really is, what its true nature as revealed by science is, is an electrical discharge. (It is not the true nature of a footprint to be a burglar.)

To forestall irrelevant objections, I should like to make it clear that by "lightning" I mean the publicly observable physical object, lightning, not a visual sense-datum of lightning. I say that the publicly observable physical object lightning is in fact the electrical discharge, not just a

* Cf. Feigl, *op. cit.*, p. 439.
** See Place, *op. cit.*, p. 106; also Feigl, op. cit., p. 438.

correlate of it. The sense-datum, or rather the having of the sense-datum, the "look" of lightning, may well in my view be a correlate of the electrical discharge. For in my view it is a brain state *caused* by the lightning. But we should no more confuse sensations of lightning with lightning than we confuse sensations of a table with the table.

In short, the reply to Objection 1 is that there can be contingent statements of the form "A is identical with B," and a person may well know that something is an A without knowing that it is a B. An illiterate peasant might well be able to talk about his sensations without knowing about his brain processes, just as he can talk about lightning though he knows nothing of electricity.

Objection 2. It is only a contingent fact (if it is a fact) that when we have a certain kind of sensation there is a certain kind of process in our brain. Indeed it is possible, though perhaps in the highest degree unlikely, that our present physiological theories will be as out of date as the ancient theory connecting mental processes with goings on in the heart. It follows that when we report a sensation we are not reporting a brain-process.

Reply. The objection certainly proves that when we say "I have an after-image" we cannot *mean* something of the form "I have such and such a brain-process." But this does not show that what we report (having an after-image) is not *in fact* a brain process. "I see lightning" does not *mean* "I see an electrical discharge." Indeed, it is logically possible (though highly unlikely) that the electrical discharge account of lightning might one day be given up. Again, "I see the Evening Star" does not *mean* the same as "I see the Morning Star," and yet "The Evening Star and the Morning Star are one and the same thing" is a contingent proposition. Possibly Objection 2 derives some of its apparent strength from a "Fido"-Fido theory of meaning. If the meaning of an expression were what the expression named, then of course it *would* follow from the fact that "sensation" and "brain-process" have different meanings that they cannot name one and the same thing.

*Objection 3.** Even if Objections 1 and 2 do not prove that sensations are something over and above brain-processes, they do prove that the qualities of sensations are something over and above the qualities of brain-processes. That is, it may be possible to get out of asserting the existence of irreducibly psychic processes, but not out of asserting the existence of irreducibly psychic *properties*. For suppose we identify the Morning Star with the Evening Star. Then there must be some properties which logically imply that of being the Morning Star, and quite distinct properties which entail that of being the Evening Star. Again, there must be some properties (for example, that of being a yellow flash) which are logically distinct from those in the physicalist story.

Indeed, it might be thought that the objection succeeds at one jump.

* I think this objection was first put to me by Professor Max Black. I think it is the most subtle of any of those I have considered, and the one which I am least confident of having satisfactorily met.

For consider the property of "being a yellow flash." It might seem that this property lies inevitably outside the physicalist framework within which I am trying to work (either by "yellow" being an objective emergent property of physical objects, or else by being a power to produce yellow sense-data, where "yellow," in this second instantiation of the word, refers to a purely phenomenal or introspectible quality). I must therefore digress for a moment and indicate how I deal with secondary qualities. I shall concentrate on color.

First of all, let me introduce the concept of a normal percipient. One person is more a normal percipient than another if he can make color discriminations that the other cannot. For example, if A can pick a lettuce leaf out of a heap of cabbage leaves, whereas B cannot though he can pick a lettuce leaf out of a heap of beetroot leaves, then A is more normal than B. (I am assuming that A and B are not given time to distinguish the leaves by their slight difference in shape, and so forth.) From the concept of "more normal than" it is easy to see how we can introduce the concept of "normal." Of course, Eskimos may make the finest discriminations at the blue end of the spectrum, Hottentots at the red end. In this case the concept of a normal percipient is a slightly idealized one, rather like that of "the mean sun" in astronomical chronology. There is no need to go into such subtleties now. I say that "This is red" means something roughly like "A normal percipient would not easily pick this out of a clump of geranium petals though he would pick it out of a clump of lettuce leaves." Of course it does not exactly mean this: a person might know the meaning of "red" without knowing anything about geraniums, or even about normal percipients. But the point is that a person can be *trained* to say "This is red" of objects which would not easily be picked out of geranium petals by a normal percipient, and so on. (Note that even a color-blind person can reasonably assert that something is red, though of course he needs to use another human being, not just himself, as his "color meter.") This account of secondary qualities explains their unimportance in physics. For obviously the discriminations and lack of discriminations made by a very complex neurophysiological mechanism are hardly likely to correspond to simple and nonarbitrary distinctions in nature.

I therefore elucidate colors as powers, in Locke's sense, to evoke certain sorts of discriminatory responses in human beings. They are also, of course, powers to cause sensations in human beings (an account still nearer Locke's). But these sensations, I am arguing, are identifiable with brain processes.

Now how do I get over the objection that a sensation can be identified with a brain process only if it has some phenomenal property, not possessed by brain processes, whereby one-half of the identification may be, so to speak, pinned down?

Reply. My suggestion is as follows. When a person says, "I see a yellowish-orange after-image," he is saying something like this: "*There is something going on which is like what is going on when* I have my eyes open, am awake, and there is an orange illuminated in good light in front of me, that is, when I really see an orange." (And there is no reason why a person should not say the same thing when he is having a veridical sense-datum, so long as we construe "like" in the last sentence in such a sense that something can be like itself.) Notice that the italicized words, namely "there is something going on which is like what is going on when," are all quasilogical or topic-neutral words. This explains why the ancient Greek peasant's reports about his sensations can be neutral between dualistic metaphysics or my materialistic metaphysics. It explains how sensations can be brain-processes and yet how a man who reports them need know nothing about brain-processes. For he reports them only very abstractly as "something going on which is like what is going on when. . . ." Similarly, a person may say "someone is in the room," thus reporting truly that the doctor is in the room, even though he has never heard of doctors. (There are not two people in the room: "someone" *and* the doctor.) This account of sensation statements also explains the singular elusiveness of "raw feels"—why no one seems to be able to pin any properties on them.* Raw feels, in my view, are colorless for the very same reason that *something* is colorless. This does not mean that sensations do not have plenty of properties, for if they are brain-processes they certainly have lots of neurological properties. It only means that in speaking of them as being like or unlike one another we need not know or mention these properties.

This, then, is how I would reply to Objection 3. The strength of my reply depends on the possibility of our being able to report that one thing is like another without being able to state the respect in which it is like. I do not see why this should not be so. If we think cybernetically about the nervous system we can envisage it as able to respond to certain likenesses of its internal processes without being able to do more. It would be easier to build a machine which would tell us, say on a punched tape, whether or not two objects were similar, than it would be to build a machine which would report wherein the similarities consisted.

Objection 4. The after-image is not in physical space. The brain-process is. So the after-image is not a brain-process.

Reply. This is an *ignoratio elenchi.* I am not arguing that the after-image is a brain-process, but that the experience of having an after-image is a brain-process. It is the *experience* which is reported in the introspective report. Similarly, if it is objected that the after-image is yellowy-orange, my reply is that it is the experience of seeing yellowy-orange that is being described, and this experience is not a yellowy-orange something. So to say that a brain-process cannot be yellowy-orange is not to say that a brain-process cannot in fact be the experience of having a yellowy-orange after-image. There is, in a sense, no such thing as an after-image or a sense-datum, though there is such a thing as the experience of having an image, and this experience is described indirectly in material object

* See B. A. Farrell, "Experience," *Mind,* LIX (1950), 170–98.

language, not in phenomenal language, for there is no such thing.* We describe the experience by saying, in effect, that it is like the experience we have when, for example, we really see a yellowy-orange patch on the wall. Trees and wallpaper can be green, but not the experience of seeing or imagining a tree or wallpaper. (Or if they are described as green or yellow this can only be in a derived sense.)

Objection 5. It would make sense to say of a molecular movement in the brain that it is swift or slow, straight or circular, but it makes no sense to say this of the experience of seeing something yellow.

Reply. So far we have not given sense to talk of experiences as swift or slow, straight or circular. But I am not claiming that "experience" and "brain-process" mean the same or even that they have the same logic. "Somebody" and "the doctor" do not have the same logic, but this does not lead us to suppose that talking about somebody telephoning is talking about someone over and above, say, the doctor. The ordinary man when he reports an experience is reporting that something is going on, but he leaves it open as to what sort of thing is going on, whether in a material solid medium or perhaps in some sort of gaseous medium, or even perhaps in some sort of nonspatial medium (if this makes sense). All that I am saying is that "experience" and "brain-process" may in fact refer to the same thing, and if so we may easily adopt a convention (which is not a change in our present rules for the use of experience words but an addition to them) whereby it would make sense to talk of an experience in terms appropriate to physical processes.

Objection 6. Sensations are private, brain processes are *public.* If I sincerely say, "I see a yellowish-orange after-image," and I am not making a verbal mistake, then I cannot be wrong. But I can be wrong about a brain-process. The scientist looking into my brain might be having an illusion. Moreover, it makes sense to say that two or more people are observing the same brain-process but not that two or more people are reporting the same inner experience.

Reply. This shows that the language of introspective reports has a different logic from the language of material processes. It is obvious that until the brain-process theory is much improved and widely accepted there will be no *criteria* for saying "Smith has an experience of such-and-such a sort" *except* Smith's introspective reports. So we have adopted a rule of language that (normally) what Smith says goes.

Objection 7. I can imagine myself turned to stone and yet having images, aches, pains, and so on.

Reply. I can imagine that the electrical theory of lightning is false, that

* Dr. J. R. Smythies claims that a sense-datum language could be taught independently of the material object language ("A Note on the Fallacy of the 'Phenomenological Fallacy,'" *British Journal of Psychology*, XLVIII [1957], 141–44). I am not so sure of this: there must be some public criteria for a person having got a rule wrong before we can teach him the rule. I suppose someone might *accidentally* learn color words by Dr. Smythies' procedure. I am not, of course, denying that we can learn a sense-datum language in the sense that we can learn to report our experience. Nor would Place deny it.

lightning is some sort of purely optical phenomenon. I can imagine that lightning is not an electrical discharge. I can imagine that the Evening Star is not the Morning Star. But it is. All the objection shows is that "experience" and "brain-process" do not have the same meaning. It does not show that an experience is not in fact a brain process.

This objection is perhaps much the same as one which can be summed up by the slogan: "What can be composed of nothing cannot be composed of anything."* The argument goes as follows: on the brain-process thesis the identity between the brain-process and the experience is a contingent one. So it is logically possible that there should be no brain-process, and no process of any other sort either (no heart process, no kidney process, no liver process). There would be the experience but no "corresponding" physiological process with which we might be able to identify it empirically.

I suspect that the objector is thinking of the experience as a ghostly entity. So it is composed of something, not of nothing, after all. On his view it is composed of ghost stuff, and on mine it is composed of brain stuff. Perhaps the counter-reply will be** that the experience is simple and uncompounded, and so it is not composed of anything after all. This seems to be a quibble, for, if it were taken seriously, the remark "What can be composed of nothing cannot be composed of anything" could be recast as an a priori argument against Democritus and atomism and for Descartes and infinite divisibility. And it seems odd that a question of this sort could be settled a priori. We must therefore construe the word "composed" in a very weak sense, which would allow us to say that even an indivisible atom is composed of something (namely, itself). The dualist cannot really say that an experience can be composed of nothing. For he holds that experiences are something over and above material processes, that is, that they are a sort of ghost stuff. (Or perhaps ripples in an underlying ghost stuff.) I say that the dualist's hypothesis is a perfectly intelligible one. But I say that experiences are not to be identified with ghost stuff but with brain stuff. This is another hypothesis, and in my view a very plausible one. The present argument cannot knock it down a priori.

Objection 8. The "beetle in the box" objection (see Wittgenstein, *Philosophical Investigations*, § 293). How could descriptions of experiences, if these are genuine reports, get a foothold in language? For any rule of language must have public criteria for its correct application.

Reply. The change from describing how things are to describing how we feel is just a change from uninhibitedly saying "this is so" to saying "this looks so." That is, when the naïve person might be tempted to say, "There is a patch of light on the wall which moves whenever I move my eyes" or "A pin is being stuck into me," we have learned how to resist this temptation and say "It *looks as though* there is a patch of light on the

* I owe this objection to Dr. C. B. Martin. I gather that he no longer wishes to maintain this objection, at any rate in its present form.

** Martin did not make this reply, but one of his students did.

wallpaper" or "It *feels as though* someone were sticking a pin into me." The introspective account tells us about the individual's state of consciousness in the same way way as does "I see a patch of light" or "I feel a pin being stuck into me": it differs from the corresponding perception statement in so far as it withdraws any claim about what is actually going on in the external world. From the point of view of the psychologist, the change from talking about the environment to talking about one's perceptual sensations is simply a matter of disinhibiting certain reactions. These are reactions which one normally suppresses because one has learned that in the prevailing circumstances they are unlikely to provide a good indication of the state of the environment.* To say that something looks green to me is simply to say that my experience is like the experience I get when I see something that really is green. In my reply to Objection 3, I pointed out the extreme openness or generality of statements which report experiences. This explains why there is no language of private qualities. (Just as "someone," unlike "the doctor," is a colorless word.)**

If it is asked what is the difference between those brain processes which, in my view, are experiences and those brain processes which are not, I can only reply that it is at present unknown. I have been tempted to conjecture that the difference may in part be that between perception and reception (in D. M. MacKay's terminology) and that the type of brain process which is an experience might be identifiable with MacKay's active "matching response."† This, however, cannot be the whole story, because sometimes I can perceive something unconsciously, as when I take a handkerchief out of a drawer without being aware that I am doing so. But at the very least, we can classify the brain processes which are experiences as those brain processes which are, or might have been, causal conditions of those pieces of verbal behavior which we call reports of immediate experience.

I have now considered a number of objections to the brain-process thesis. I wish now to conclude with some remarks on the logical status of the thesis itself. U. T. Place seems to hold that it is a straight-out scientific hypothesis.‡ If so, he is partly right and partly wrong. If the issue is between (say) a brain-process thesis and a heart thesis, or a liver thesis, or a kidney thesis, then the issue is a purely empirical one, and the verdict is overwhelmingly in favor of the brain. The right sorts of things don't go on in the heart, liver, or kidney, nor do these organs possess the right sort of complexity of structure. On the other hand, if the issue is between a

* I owe this point to Place, in correspondence.

** The "beetle in the box" objection is, *if it is sound*, an objection to *any* view, and in particular the Cartesian one, that introspective reports are genuine reports. So it is no objection to a weaker thesis that I would be concerned to uphold, namely, that if introspective reports of "experiences" are genuinely reports, then the things they are reports of are in fact brain processes.

† See his article "Towards an Information-Flow Model of Human Behaviour," *British Journal of Psychology*, XLVII (1956), 30–43.

‡ *Op. cit.* For a further discussion of this, in reply to the original version of the present paper, see Place's note "Materialism as a Scientific Hypothesis," *Philosophical Review*, LXIX (1960), 101–4.

brain-or-liver-or-kidney thesis (that is, some form of materialism) on the one hand and epiphenomenalism on the other hand, then the issue is not an empirical one. For there is no conceivable experiment which could decide between materialism and epiphenomenalism. This latter issue is not like the average straight-out empirical issue in science, but like the issue between the nineteenth-century English naturalist Philip Gosse* and the orthodox geologists and paleontologists of his day. According to Gosse, the earth was created about 4000 B.C. exactly as described in *Genesis*, with twisted rock strata, "evidence" of erosion, and so forth, and all sorts of fossils, all in their appropriate strata, just as if the usual evolutionist story had been true. Clearly this theory is in a sense irrefutable: no evidence can possibly tell against it. Let us ignore the theological setting in which Philip Gosse's hypothesis had been placed, thus ruling out objections of a theological kind, such as "what a queer God who would go to such elaborate lengths to deceive us." Let us suppose that it is held that the universe just *began* in 4004 B.C. with the intital conditions just everywhere as they were in 4004 B.C., and in particular that our own planet began with sediment in the rivers, eroded cliffs, fossils in the rocks, and so on. No scientist would ever entertain this as a serious hypothesis, consistent though it is with all possible evidence. The hypothesis offends against the principles of parsimony and simplicity. There would be far too many brute and inexplicable facts. Why are pterodactyl bones just as they are? No explanation in terms of the evolution of pterodactyls from earlier forms of life would any longer be possible. We would have millions of facts about the world as it was in 4004 B.C. that just have to be *accepted*.

The issue between the brain-process theory and epiphenomenalism seems to be of the above sort. (Assuming that a behavioristic reduction of introspective reports is not possible.) If it be agreed that there are no cogent philosophical arguments which force us into accepting dualism, and if the brain process theory and dualism are equally consistent with the facts, then the principles of parsimony and simplicity seem to me to decide overwhelmingly in favor of the brain-process theory. As I pointed out earlier, dualism involves a large number of irreducible psychophysical laws (whereby the "nomological danglers" dangle) of a queer sort, that just have to be taken on trust, and are just as difficult to swallow as the irreducible facts about the paleontology of the earth with which we are faced on Philip Gosse's theory.

* See the entertaining account of Gosse's book *Omphalos* by Martin Gardner in *Fads and Fallacies in the Name of Science*, 2nd ed. (New York: Dover, 1957), pp. 124–27.

Further Readings

DUALISM AND THE DISTINCTION BETWEEN THE MENTAL AND THE PHYSICAL

Broad, C. D., *The Mind and Its Place in Nature,* Routledge & Kegan Paul, London, 1925, chap. III.
Chisholm, Roderick M., "Sentences about Believing," *Proceedings of the Aristotelian Society,* Vol. LVI (1955–1956).
Ducasse, C. D., *Nature, Mind, and Death,* Open Court, La Salle, Ill., 1951.
Feigl, Herbert, "The 'Mental' and The 'Physical,'" H. Feigl and M. Scriven (eds.) *Minnesota Studies in Philosophy of Science,* Vol. II.
Flew, Antony (ed.), *Body, Mind, and Death,* Collier Books, New York, 1965.
Hook, Sidney (ed.), *Dimensions of Mind,* New York University Press, New York, 1960.
Laird, John, *Our Minds and Their Bodies,* Oxford University Press, London, 1925.
Lovejoy, Arthur O., *The Revolt Against Dualism,* Allen & Unwin, London, 1930.
Plato, *Phaedo,* trans. F. J. Church, Liberal Arts, New York, 1951.
Pratt, J. B., *Matter and Spirit,* Macmillan, New York, 1926.
Stout, G. F., *Mind and Matter,* Macmillan, New York, 1938.
Taylor, Richard, *Metaphysics,* Prentice-Hall, Englewood Cliffs, N.J., 1963, chaps. I and II.
Wisdom, *Problems of Mind and Matter,* Cambridge University Press, New York, 1934.
Vesey, G. N. A., (ed.), *Body and Mind,* Allen & Unwin, London, 1964.

THE POSSIBILITY OF SURVIVAL

Ducasse, C. J., *Nature, Mind, and Death,* Open Court, La Salle, Ill., 1951, Part IV.
Flew, Antony, *A New Approach to Psychical Research,* Watts, London, 1953.
Holmes, John Haynes, "Ten Reasons for Believing in Immortality," in Paul Edwards and Arthur Pap (eds.), *A Modern Introduction to Philosophy,* rev. ed., Free Press, New York, 1965.
Hume, David, *An Inquiry Concerning Human Understanding,* Liberal Arts, New York, 1955, ch. 11.
James, William, *Human Immortality,* Houghton Mifflin, Boston, 1898.
Lamont, Corliss, *The Illusion of Immortality,* Watts, London, 1935.
Martin, C. B., *Religious Belief,* Cornell University Press, Ithaca, New York, 1959, ch. 6.
Pringle-Pattison, A. Seth., *The Idea of Immortality,* Oxford University Press, Fair Lawn, N.J., 1922.
Russell, Bertrand, *Why I Am Not a Christian and Other Essays,* Allen & Unwin, London, 1957.
Taylor, A. E., *The Christian Hope of Immortality,* J. Baker, London, 1938.

BEHAVIORISM

Chappell, Vere (ed.), *Philosophy of Mind,* Prentice-Hall, Englewood Cliffs, N.J., 1962.
Farrell, B. A., "Experience," *Mind, 59* (1950), also in Chappell.
Hampshire, Stuart, "*The Concept of Mind,* by G. Ryle," *Mind, 59* (1950).
Hempel, C. G., "The Logical Analysis of Psychology," in H. Feigl and W. Sellars (eds.), *Readings in Philosophical Analysis,* Appleton-Century-Crofts, New York, 1949.
Hull, C. L., *Principles of Behavior,* Appleton-Century-Crofts, New York, 1943.
Price, H. H., "Some Objections to Behaviorism," in Hook (ed.), *Dimensions of Mind.*
Ryle, Gilbert, *The Concept of Mind,* Barnes and Noble, New York, 1949.
Scriven, Michael, "A Study of Radical Behaviorism," *Minnesota Studies in Philosophy of Science,* Vol. I.
Skinner, B. F., *Science and Human Behavior,* Macmillan, New York, 1953.
Tolman, E. C., *Behavior and Psychological Man,* University of California Press, Berkeley, 1951.
Watson, J. B., *Psychology from the Standpoint of a Behaviorist,* Lippincott, Philadelphia, 1919.
Whiteley, C. H., "Behaviorism," *Mind, 70* (1961).

Wisdom, J., "The Concept of Mind," *Proceedings of the Aristotelian Society* (1949–1950).

Ziff, Paul, "About Behaviorism," *Analysis, 18* (1957–1958), also in Chappell.

MATERIALISM, IDENTITY THEORY, AND BRAIN MECHANISMS

Anderson, Alan Ross (ed.), *Minds and Machines*, Prentice-Hall, Englewood Cliffs, N.J., 1964.

Brandt, Richard B., "Doubts About the Identity Theory," in Hook (ed.), *Dimensions of Mind*.

Hampshire, Stuart, *Philosophy of Mind*, Harper & Row, New York, 1966.

Hobbes, Thomas, *De Corpore*, (1655). *The English Works of Thomas Hobbes*, edited by W. Molesworth.

Kemeny, J. G., "Man Viewed as a Machine," *Scientific American, 192* (1955).

Lange, F. A., *History of Materialism*, Routledge & Kegan Paul, London, 1925.

Lucretius, *De Rerum Naturae*, Book III, trans. R. Latham, Penguin, Baltimore, 1951.

Malcolm, Norman, "Scientific Materialism and the Identity Theory," *Dialogue*, 1964.

Nagel, Thomas, "Physicalism," *Philosophical Review*, 1965.

Pitcher, George, "Sensations and Brain Processes," *Australasian Journal of Philosophy, 38* (1960).

Place, U. T., "Is Consciousness a Brain Process," *British Journal of Psychology, 47* (1956), also in Chappell.

Putnam, H., "Minds and Machines," in Hook (ed.), *Dimensions of Mind*.

Putnam, H., "Robots: Machines or Artificially Created Life," *Journal of Philosophy, 61* (1964), also in Hampshire.

Rorty, Richard, "Mind-Body Identity, Privacy and Categories," *Review of Metaphysics, 19* (1965), also in Hampshire, *Philosophy of Mind*.

Scriven, Michael, "The Mechanical Concept of Mind," *Mind, 62* (1953), also in Anderson.

Shaffer, Jerome, "Could Mental States Be Brain Processes?" *Journal of Philosophy, 58* (1961), also in Vesey.

Smart, J. J. C., "Further Remarks on Sensations and Brain Processes," *Philosophical Review*, 1961.

Smart, J. J. C., *Philosophy and Scientific Realism*, Routledge & Kegan Paul, London, 1963.

Turing, A. M., "Computing Machinery and Intelligence," *Mind, LIX* (1950), also in A. R. Anderson.

II

PERSONAL IDENTITY AND KNOWLEDGE OF OTHER MINDS

T IS NATURAL to assume that man is a composite of two things: a mind and a body. (This view is examined in detail in Section I.) Indeed the distinction between minds and bodies is reflected in a number of things that laymen and philosophers say. For example, we oppose the private to the public, what is subjective to what is objective, the inner to the outer, the way I know my own experience to the way I know your experience.

Although some or all of these expressions are very natural to us, an attempt to work out a complete and comprehensive account of what man is, which is based upon them, runs into serious obstacles. In addition to the mind-body problem (see Section I), there are a number of related problems which must be faced. Two of them, personal identity and knowledge of other minds, will be treated in this section.

Personal Identity

Suppose you see a person at a party who looks like a friend whom you have not seen for some time. His physical appearance leads you to think that he is your friend, but you are not sure. How can you be sure?

We might compare the person to a photograph of this friend, but most likely this would not be sufficient. People change as they grow older, and many photographs are—as we all have learned—not very accurate. If, however, we talk with the person and find ourselves reminiscing about old times, we would probably be convinced that this is our friend. If he can remember places we had visited together, friends we had in common, or similar touchstones, then our question would be answered. If, on the other hand, he had no recollection of such things, we would know we had made a mistake.

Notice that this suggests that personal identity lies in certain mental characteristics, in this case memory. We would judge that the person before us is the *same* person we travelled to Oshkosh with because he remembers going there with us. Can we conclude from this that the criterion of personal identity is fundamentally mental and not physical?

The problem of personal identity, then, is the problem of determining whether it is mental or physical characteristics (or perhaps both) which enable us to say that this person is the same person who was our friend.

This is not only a philosopher's problem. For example, in a court of law it is often necessary to determine whether or not the person on trial is the one who committed the crime. Then, too, an answer to the question of personal identity would be very helpful in answering questions about the possibility of survival after death: if what makes a person the *same* person from moment to moment is something physical, then it is hard to see how anyone could survive after the death of his body, since what survived would be something nonphysical. It could not, therefore, be the "same" person who was alive. Again, an answer to the question of personal identity would help in deciding whether what is called a "multiple personality" is possible. If, for example, the criterion of personal identity is mental, then it would seem possible that several persons could inhabit the same body, perhaps at the same time.

The problem of personal identity cannot be considered apart from the view one takes toward the nature of man. For a materialist there is no problem of personal identity over and above the problem of deciding, for example, that a certain physical object is the same as the one that was here before. For a materialist, disembodied survival would be a contradiction in terms. On the other hand, an idealist (one who believes that a man is something mental) would have the problem of determining when two minds were the same, i.e., were really one.

David Hume identified persons with their minds; but he faced a special problem of personal identity, because he identified minds with their ever-changing contents. A person, for Hume, is just a succession of impressions of love, hate, heat, cold. Hume's question is this: Are there any bonds among the separate impressions which would unite them and thus mark them as belonging to one particular person? If he can answer this question he can answer another question: What is it that distinguishes one person from another?

Some philosophers have expressed the view that Hume's question is mistaken. Hume's problem is to find some way of linking experiences together so that he may say that they constitute one person. These philosophers suggest that part of what we *mean* when we speak of an experience is that it is the experience of *some person.* Hence, there is no problem of trying to link experiences. To be an experience, these philosophers would say, is already to be an experience of some person.

Whether this view is correct or not, Hume's original question has led to a number of interesting proposals, none of which seems to be completely satisfactory. Immanuel Kant held the view that a person is just what is conscious of the numerical identity of itself at different times. So far from attempting to find the unity of mind among its contents, Kant contended that there could be no identifiable contents of a mind unless the unity of the self is presupposed. A point similar to Kant's is presented in very different ways in the selections by C. A. Campbell and Edmund Husserl. As Husserl expressed it:

> *It seems as if the elementary psychic fact is not thought, or this thought, or that thought, but* my *thought, every thought being owned. The universal fact is not that feelings and thoughts exist, but* "I *think*" *and* "I *feel.*"

He also developed a technique of phenomenological reflection, sometimes called the "transcendental phenomenological reduction," to reveal the hidden "I" that is presupposed in all consciousness. A brief description of the phenomenological technique precedes the Husserl selection.

Knowledge of Other Minds

It is perfectly natural to believe that I know about my own states of consciousness, my pains, anger, imaginings, by having them. I have some kind of direct awareness of them. But if this is so, how can I have knowledge of the mental states of others? It would seem that to know about them, I would have to have them. But I cannot. It appears, therefore, that I cannot have knowledge of the mental states of other people, that is, that I can never know when another person is in pain or is angry. This difficulty gives rise to the problem of other minds: How is it possible, if it is possible, to know that others are happy, unhappy, in pain, or angry?

1. Some philosophers have concluded that I cannot know what is in the mind of another. They accept, sometimes unhappily, the conclusion that I am forever cut off from the thoughts, feelings, and emotions of others. A philosopher who holds this view (which is sometimes called *solipsism*) would say that my knowledge of mental states and events is limited to my own mental states and events. (See the selection by W. T. Stace for a view of this sort.)

2. Other philosophers, however, refuse to accept this conclusion. They try to solve the problem of other minds by bridging the gap. One of the most familiar answers to the problem accepts the view that I know about my own mental states and events by having them, but goes on to say that I know the contents of other minds by analogy with my own case. For example, when I am in pain I have noticed that certain bodily movements, such as grimaces and winces, are constantly correlated with my experience of pain. When, therefore, I observe similar movements in others, I infer that they too are in pain. A philosopher who holds this view might reason this way: From my own case I know that my "pain-behavior" (grimaces, winces, etc.) is caused by my pain. Therefore, when I see

another person grimacing and wincing, I am entitled to say that his behavior is caused by his pain. In this way, I can come to know at least some of what another person feels or thinks.

This argument from analogy has been criticized on a number of grounds. One of the most persistent criticisms is that it rests on an inductive inference based upon a single case, namely my own. This, it is felt, is far too little in the way of evidence for such an important inference. Others have objected by saying that one can never test to find if other people have the same thing that I call pain, and this lack of verifiability renders the argument from analogy valueless.

3. A more radical view of the entire question was put forward by Ludwig Wittgenstein and elaborated by Norman Malcolm. Both the solipsist and the proponent of the argument from analogy accept the same formulation of the problem of other minds: I know my own mental states and events; how can I know the mental states and events of another person? Wittgenstein and Malcolm present a two-fold attack on this assumption.

First, consider the claim that I know my own mental states, e.g., my pains. They argue that whenever I claim to know something, there must be at least some possibility of my being wrong. Knowledge is contrasted with ignorance or being mistaken. But when I say that I am in pain, is there any room for doubt? Assuming I know what the word "pain" means, is there any possibility of my being mistaken? It seems not. But then what could it mean to say that I *know* I am in pain, except simply that I am in pain? Their claim is that the starting point for the problem of other minds —that I know my own mental states and events—is wrong. I don't know them. But I am not ignorant of them either. The concepts of knowing and not knowing don't apply here at all, just as being tall or short does not apply to rivers. If the problem of other minds arises because I am supposed to have superior knowledge of such things as my own pain states, then, in Wittgenstein's view, the problem should not arise. Knowledge and ignorance don't fit here. (In fact, Wittgenstein suggests that uttering "I am in pain" is really something like crying or groaning.)

Second, a major part of the solipsistic view is that my mental states are accessible only to me, while the contents of others' minds are hidden. This means not only that I can never know when another person is in pain, but also that I cannot even know what he means by the word "pain" (since I cannot know what he applies it to; what he calls "pain" I might call "itch"). However, it does seem that I know what *I* mean by words like "pain," even if these words form part of a language which is only mine, a kind of "private language." It is this possibility, the possibility of there being a private language, that Wittgenstein and Malcolm claim is incoherent. They argue as follows: For the word "pain" to have meaning to me, I must at least use it consistently. Suppose I feel something now and say that I have a pain. How do I know that this is the same kind of thing I called "pain" yesterday? Perhaps one would reply by saying that he remembers what he has decided to call pain, and what he has now feels like that, so it is pain. But how, Wittgenstein and Malcolm would ask, do you know that your memory is correct? Perhaps what you called "pain" yesterday you would call "tickle" today. One might say that at least it seems to be pain. But now there is no distinction between seeming to be in pain and being in pain. For a word to be part of a language it would seem necessary that there be a difference between thinking that you are using the word correctly and actually using it correctly. In the case of a private language, however, there appears to be no such distinction. Therefore, it is argued, since a "private language" fails to fulfill a necessary condition for something's being a language, there is—and can be—no such thing as a private language. Hence both the solipsist and the arguer from analogy are mistaken, for they begin by assuming the possibility of such a private language.

Wittgenstein goes on to indicate a positive view about our sensation language. It is, roughly, that we apply words like "pain" to other people on the basis of how they behave in certain circumstances. Since we have this method of telling when someone is in pain, we can use it to tell whether or not he has learned how to use such words. In this way, our sensation language is not private, since we can check up on each other's mastery of it.

This view has been quite influential in recent years. It has been the object of a number of serious criticisms. One of the most important of them doubts the validity of its premises about language. Other more general criticisms are about the value of studying language as a way of learning about the world (as Wittgenstein and many of his followers have done).

The selections presented here treat in detail a number of the positions discussed above and show the development of various lines of thought on these questions.

PERSONAL IDENTITY

DAVID HUME

There are some philosophers, who imagine we are every moment intimately conscious of what we call our SELF; that we feel its existence and its continuance in existence; and are certain, beyond the evidence of a demonstration, both of its perfect identity and simplicity. The strongest sensation, the most violent passion, say they, instead of distracting us from this view, only fix it the more intensely, and make us consider their influence on *self* either by their pain or pleasure. To attempt a farther

Reprinted from *A Treatise of Human Nature,* Book I, Part IV, Section 6, first published 1739 and 1740.

proof of this were to weaken its evidence; since no proof can be deriv'd from any fact, of which we are so intimately conscious; nor is there any thing, of which we can be certain, if we doubt of this.

Unluckily all these positive assertions are contrary to that very experience, which is pleaded for them, nor have we any idea of *self*, after the manner it is here explain'd. For from what impression cou'd this idea be deriv'd? This question 'tis impossible to answer without a manifest contradiction and absurdity; and yet 'tis a question, which must necessarily be answer'd, if we wou'd have the idea of self pass for clear and intelligible. It must be some one impression, that gives rise to every real idea. But self or person is not any one impression, but that to which our several impressions and ideas are suppos'd to have a reference. If any impression gives rise to the idea of self, that impression must continue invariably the same, thro' the whole course of our lives; since self is suppos'd to exist after that manner. But there is no impression constant and invariable. Pain and pleasure, grief and joy, passions and sensations succeed each other, and never all exist at the same time. It cannot, therefore, be from any of these impressions, or from any other, that the idea of self is deriv'd; and consequently there is no such idea.

But farther, what must become of all our particular perceptions upon this hypothesis? All these are different, and distinguishable, and separable from each other, and may be separatedly consider'd, and may exist separately, and have no need of any thing to support their existence. After what manner, therefore, do they belong to self; and how are they connected with it? For my part, when I enter most intimately into what I call *myself*, I always stumble on some particular perception or other, of heat or cold, light or shade, love or hatred, pain or pleasure. I never can catch *myself* at any time without a perception, and never can observe any thing but the perception. When my perceptions are remov'd for any time, as by sound sleep; so long am I insensible of *myself*, and may truly be said not to exist. And were all my perceptions remov'd by death, and cou'd I neither think, nor feel, nor see, nor love, nor hate after the dissolution of my body, I shou'd be entirely annihilated, nor do I conceive what is farther requisite to make me a perfect non-entity. If any one upon serious and unprejudic'd reflexion, thinks he has a different notion of *himself*, I must confess I can reason no longer with him. All I can allow him is, that he may be in the right as well as I, and that we are essentially different in this particular. He may, perhaps, perceive something simple and continu'd, which he calls *himself;* tho' I am certain there is no such principle in me.

But setting aside some metaphysicians of this kind, I may venture to affirm of the rest of mankind, that they are nothing but a bundle or collection of different perceptions, which succeed each other with an inconceivable rapidity, and are in a perpetual flux and movement. Our eyes cannot turn in their sockets without varying our perceptions. Our thought is still more variable than our sight; and all our other senses and faculties contribute to this change; nor is there any single power of the soul, which remains unalterably the same, perhaps for one moment. The mind is a kind of theatre, where several perceptions successively make their appearance; pass, re-pass, glide away, and mingle in an infinite variety of postures and situations. There is properly no *simplicity* in it at one time, nor *identity* in different; whatever natural propension we may have to imagine that simplicity and identity. The comparison of the theatre must not mislead us. They are the successive perceptions only, that constitute the mind; nor have we the most distant notion of the place, where these scenes are represented, or of the materials, of which it is compos'd.

What then gives us so great a propension to ascribe an identity to these successive perceptions, and to suppose ourselves possest of an invariable and uninterrupted existence thro' the whole course of our lives? In order to answer this question, we must distinguish betwixt personal identity, as it regards our thought or imagination, and as it regards our passions or the concern we take in ourselves. The first is our present subject; and to explain it perfectly we must take the matter pretty deep, and account for that identity, which we attribute to plants and animals; there being a great analogy betwixt it, and the identity of a self or person.

We have a distinct idea of an object, that remains invariable and uninterrupted thro' a suppos'd variation of time; and this idea we call that of *identity* or *sameness*. We have also a distinct idea of several different objects existing in succession, and connected together by a close relation; and this to an accurate view affords as perfect a notion of *diversity*, as if there was no manner of relation among the objects. But tho' these two ideas of identity, and a succession of related objects be in themselves perfectly distinct, and even contrary, yet 'tis certain, that in our common way of thinking they are generally confounded with each other. That action of the imagination, by which we consider the uninterrupted and invariable object, and that by which we reflect on the succession of related objects, are almost the same to the feeling, nor is there much more effort of thought requir'd in the latter case than in the former. The relation facilitates the transition of the mind from one object to another, and renders its passage as smooth as if it contemplated one continu'd object. This resemblance is the cause of the confusion and mistake, and makes us substitute the notion of identity, instead of that of related objects. However at one instant we may consider the related succession as variable or interrupted, we are sure the next to ascribe to it a perfect identity, and regard it as invariable and uninterrupted. Our propensity to this mistake is so great from the resemblance above-mention'd, that we fall into it before we are aware; and tho' we incessantly correct ourselves by reflexion, and return to a more accurate method of thinking, yet we cannot long sustain our philosophy, or take off this bias from the imagination. Our last resource is to yield to it, and boldly assert that these different related objects are in effect the same, however interrupted and variable. In order to justify to ourselves this absurdity, we often feign some new and unintelligible principle, that connects the objects together, and prevents their interruption or variation. Thus we feign the continu'd existence of the perceptions of our senses, to remove the interruption; and run into the notion of a *soul*, and *self*, and *substance*, to disguise the variation. But we may farther observe, that where we do not give rise to such a fiction, our propension to confound identity with relation is so great, that we are apt to imagine something unknown and mysterious, connecting the parts, beside their relation; and this I take to be the case with regard to the identity we ascribe to plants and vegetables. And even when this does not take place, we still feel a propensity to confound these ideas, tho' we are not able fully to satisfy ourselves in that particular, nor find any thing invariable and uninterrupted to justify our notion of identity.

Thus the controversy concerning identity is not merely a dispute of words. For when we attribute identity, in an improper sense, to variable or interrupted objects, our mistake is not confin'd to the expression, but is commonly attended with a fiction, either of something invariable and uninterrupted, or of something mysterious and inexplicable, or at least with a propensity to such fictions. What will suffice to prove this hypothesis to the satisfaction of every fair enquirer, is to shew from daily experience and observation, that the objects, which are variable or interrupted, and yet are suppos'd to continue the same, are such only as consist of a succession of parts, connected together by resemblance, contiguity, or causation. For as such a succession answers evidently to our notion of diversity, it can only be by mistake we ascribe to it an identity; and as the relation of parts, which leads us into this mistake, is really nothing but a quality, which produces an association of ideas, and an easy transition of the imagination from one to another, it can only be from the resemblance, which this act of the mind bears to that, by which we contemplate one continu'd object, that the error arises. Our chief business, then, must be to prove, that all objects, to which we ascribe identity, without observing their invariableness and uninterruptedness, are such as consist of a succession of related objects.

In order to this, suppose any mass of matter, of which the parts are contiguous and connected, to be plac'd before us; 'tis plain we must attribute a perfect identity to this mass, provided all the parts continue uninterruptedly and invariably the same, whatever motion or change of place we may observe either in the whole or in any of the parts. But supposing some very *small* or *inconsiderable* part to be added to the mass, or subtracted from it; tho' this absolutely destroys the identity of the whole, strictly speaking; yet as we seldom think so accurately, we scruple not to pronounce a mass of matter the same, where we find so trivial an alteration. The passage of the thought from the object before the change to the object after it, is so smooth and easy, that we scarce perceive the transition, and are apt to imagine, that 'tis nothing but a continu'd survey of the same object.

There is a very remarkable circumstance, that attends this experiment; which is, that tho' the change of any considerable part in a mass of matter destroys the identity of the whole, yet we must measure the greatness of the part, not absolutely, but by its *proportion* to the whole. The addition or diminution of a mountain wou'd not be sufficient to produce a diversity in a planet; tho' the change of a very few inches wou'd be able to destroy the identity of some bodies. 'Twill be impossible to account for this, but by reflecting that objects operate upon the mind, and break or interrupt the continuity of its actions not according to their real greatness, but according to their proportion to each other: And therefore, since this interruption makes an object cease to appear the same, it must be the uninterrupted progress of the thought, which constitutes the imperfect* identity.

This may be confirm'd by another phænomenon. A change in any considerable part of a body destroys its identity; but 'tis remarkable, that where the change is produc'd *gradually* and *insensibly* we are less apt to ascribe to it the same effect. The reason can plainly be no other, than that the mind, in following the successive changes of the body, feels an easy passage from the surveying its condition in one moment to the viewing of it in another, and at no particular time perceives any interruption in its actions. From which continu'd perception, it ascribes a continu'd existence and identity to the object.

But whatever precaution we may use in introducing the changes gradually, and making them proportionable to the whole, 'tis certain, that where the changes are at last observ'd to become considerable, we make a scruple of ascribing identity to such different objects. There is, however, another artifice, by which we may induce the imagination to advance a step farther; and that is, by producing a reference of the parts to each other, and a combination to some *common end* or purpose. A ship, of which a considerable part has been chang'd by frequent reparations, is still consider'd as the same; nor does the difference of the materials hinder us from ascribing an identity to it. The common end, in which the parts conspire, is the same under all their variations, and affords an easy transition of the imagination from one situation of the body to another.

But this is still more remarkable, when we add a *sympathy* of parts to their *common end*, and suppose that they bear to each other, the reciprocal relation of cause and effect in all their actions and operations. This is the case with all animals and vegetables; where not only the several parts have a reference to some general purpose, but also a mutual dependence on, and connexion with each other. The effect of so strong a relation is, that tho' every one must allow, that in a very few years both vegetables and animals endure a *total* change, yet we still attribute identity to them, while their form, size, and substance are entirely alter'd. An oak, that grows from a small plant to a large tree, is still the same oak; tho' there be not one particle of matter, or figure of its parts the same. An infant becomes a man, and is sometimes fat, sometimes lean, without any change in his identity.

We may also consider the two following phænomena, which are

* [Perfect?]

remarkable in their kind. The first is, that tho' we commonly be able to distinguish pretty exactly betwixt numerical and specific identity, yet it sometimes happens, that we confound them, and in our thinking and reasoning employ the one for the other. Thus a man, who hears a noise, that is frequently interrupted and renew'd, says, it is still the same noise; tho' 'tis evident the sounds have only a specific identity or resemblance, and there is nothing numerically the same, but the cause, which produc'd them. In like manner it may be said without breach of the propriety of language, that such a church, which was formerly of brick, fell to ruin, and that the parish rebuilt the same church of free-stone, and according to modern architecture. Here neither the form nor materials are the same, nor is there any thing common to the two objects, but their relation to the inhabitants of the parish; and yet this alone is sufficient to make us denominate them the same. But we must observe, that in these cases the first object is in a manner annihilated before the second comes into existence; by which means, we are never presented in any one point of time with the idea of difference and multiplicity; and for that reason are less scrupulous in calling them the same.

Secondly, We may remark, that tho' in a succession of related objects, it be in a manner requisite, that the change of parts be not sudden nor entire, in order to preserve the identity, yet where the objects are in their nature changeable and inconstant, we admit of a more sudden transition, than wou'd otherwise be consistent with that relation. Thus as the nature of a river consists in the motion and change of parts; tho' in less than four and twenty hours these be totally alter'd; this hinders not the river from continuing the same during several ages. What is natural and essential to any thing is, in a manner, expected; and what is expected makes less impression, and appears of less moment, than what is unusual and extraordinary. A considerable change of the former kind seems really less to the imagination, than the most trivial alteration of the latter; and by breaking less the continuity of the thought, has less influence in destroying the identity.

We now proceed to explain the nature of *personal identity*, which has become so great a question in philosophy, especially of late years in *England*, where all the abstruser sciences are study'd with a peculiar ardour and application. And here 'tis evident, the same method of reasoning must be continu'd, which has so successfully explain'd the identity of plants, and animals, and ships, and houses, and of all the compounded and changeable productions either of art or nature. The identity, which we ascribe to the mind of man, is only a fictitious one, and of a like kind with that which we ascribe to vegetables and animal bodies. It cannot, therefore, have a different origin, but must proceed from a like operation of the imagination upon like objects.

But lest this argument shou'd not convince the reader; tho' in my opinion perfectly decisive; let him weigh the following reasoning, which is still closer and more immediate. 'Tis evident, that the identity, which we attribute to the human mind, however perfect we may imagine it to be, is not able to run the several different perceptions into one, and make them lose their characters of distinction and difference, which are essential to them. 'Tis still true, that every distinct perception, which enters into the composition of the mind, is a distinct existence, and is different, and distinguishable, and separable from every other perception, either contemporary or successive. But, as, notwithstanding this distinction and separability, we suppose the whole train of perceptions to be united by identity, a question naturally arises concerning this relation of identity; whether it be something that really binds our several perceptions together, or only associates their ideas in the imagination. That is, in other words, whether in pronouncing concerning the identity of a person, we observe some real bond among his perceptions, or only feel one among the ideas we form of them. This question we might easily decide, if we wou'd recollect what has been already prov'd at large, that the understanding never observes any real connexion among objects, and that even the union of cause and effect, when strictly examin'd, resolves itself into a customary association of ideas. For from thence it evidently follows, that identity is nothing really belonging to these different perceptions, and uniting them together; but is merely a quality, which we attribute to them, because of the union of their ideas in the imagination, when we reflect upon them. Now the only qualities, which can give ideas an union in the imagination, are these three relations above-mention'd. These are the uniting principles in the ideal world, and without them every distinct object is separable by the mind, and may be separately consider'd, and appears not to have any more connexion with any other object, than if disjoin'd by the greatest difference and remoteness. 'Tis, therefore, on some of these three relations of resemblance, contiguity and causation, that identity depends; and as the very essence of these relations consists in their producing an easy transition of ideas; it follows, that our notions of personal identity, proceed entirely from the smooth and uninterrupted progress of the thought along a train of connected ideas, according to the principles above-explain'd.

The only question, therefore, which remains, is, by what relations this uninterrupted progress of our thought is produc'd, when we consider the successive existence of a mind or thinking person. And here 'tis evident we must confine ourselves to resemblance and causation, and must drop contiguity, which has little or no influence in the present case.

To begin with *resemblance;* suppose we cou'd see clearly into the breast of another, and observe that succession of perceptions, which constitutes his mind or thinking principle, and suppose that he always preserves the memory of a considerable part of past perceptions; 'tis evident that nothing cou'd more contribute to the bestowing a relation on this succession amidst all its variations. For what is the memory but a faculty, by which we raise up the images of past perceptions? And as an image necessarily resembles its object, must not the frequent placing of these resembling perceptions in the chain of thought, convey the imagination more easily from one link to another, and make the whole seem like the continuance of one object? In this particular, then, the memory not only discovers the identity, but also contributes to its production, by producing the relation of resemblance among the perceptions. The case is the same whether we consider ourselves or others.

As to *causation* we may observe, that the true idea of the human mind, is to consider it as a system of different perceptions or different existences, which are link'd together by the relation of cause and effect, and mutually produce, destroy, influence, and modify each other. Our impressions give rise to their correspondent ideas; and these ideas in their turn produce other impressions. One thought chaces another, and draws after it a third, by which it is expell'd in its turn. In this respect, I cannot compare the soul more properly to any thing than to a republic or commonwealth, in which the several members are united by the reciprocal ties of government and subordination, and give rise to other persons, who propagate the same republic in the incessant changes of its parts. And as the same individual republic may not only change its members, but also its laws and constitutions; in like manner the same person may vary his character and disposition, as well as his impressions and ideas, without losing his identity. Whatever changes he endures, his several parts are still connected by the relation of causation. And in this view our identity with regard to the passions serves to corroborate that with regard to the imagination, by the making our distant perceptions influence each other, and by giving us a present concern for our past or future pains or pleasures.

As memory alone acquaints us with the continuance and extent of this succession of perceptions, 'tis to be consider'd, upon that account chiefly, as the source of personal identity. Had we no memory, we never shou'd have any notion of causation, nor consequently of that chain of causes and effects, which constitute our self or person. But having once acquir'd this notion of causation from the memory, we can extend the same chain of causes, and consequently the identity of our persons beyond our memory, and can comprehend times, and circumstances, and actions, which we have entirely forgot, but suppose in general to have existed. For how few of our past actions are there, of which we have any memory? Who can tell me, for instance, what were his thoughts and actions on the first of *January* 1715, the 11th of *March* 1719, and the 3d of *August* 1733? Or will he affirm, because he has entirely forgot the incidents of these days, that the present self is not the same person with the self of that time; and by that means overturn all the most establish'd notions of personal identity? In this view, therefore, memory does not so much *produce* as *discover* personal identity, by shewing us the relation of cause and effect among our different perceptions. 'Twill be incumbent on those, who affirm that memory produces entirely our personal identity, to give a reason why we can thus extend our identity beyond our memory.

The whole of this doctrine leads us to a conclusion, which is of great importance in the present affair, *viz.* that all the nice and subtile questions concerning personal identity can never possibly be decided, and are to be regarded rather as grammatical than as philosophical difficulties. Identity depends on the relations of ideas; and these relations produce identity, by means of that easy transition they occasion. But as the relations, and the easiness of the transition may diminish by insensible degrees, we have no just standard, by which we can decide any dispute concerning the time, when they acquire or lose a title to the name of identity. All the disputes concerning the identity of connected objects are merely verbal, except so far as the relation of parts gives rise to some fiction or imaginary principle of union, as we have already observ'd.

What I have said concerning the first origin and uncertainty of our notion of identity, as apply'd to the human mind, may be extended with little or no variation to that of *simplicity*. An object, whose different co-existent parts are bound together by a close relation, operates upon the imagination after much the same manner as one perfectly simple and indivisible, and requires not a much greater stretch of thought in order to its conception. From this similarity of operation we attribute a simplicity to it, and feign a principle of union as the support of this simplicity, and the center of all the different parts and qualities of the object.

SELF-CONSCIOUSNESS AND SELF-IDENTITY

CHARLES ARTHUR CAMPBELL

. . .

2. Let us begin with a proposition the truth of which seems to me easily demonstrable within the context of our recent discussions; the proposition that the cognising subject is always in some degree aware of itself, or "self-conscious."

This, I think, can be seen to be yet another implication of the judgment-theory of cognition. All cognition involves judgment. All judgment involves reference to an "objective" reality which the judging mind is seeking to know. But an essential part of the meaning which "objective reality" carries for the judging mind is its independence of that mind. Hence a mind that is aware of itself as subject. It follows that all cognition implies in the cognising subject some degree of self-awareness.

It goes without saying that in very many cognitions the degree of self-awareness present is exceedingly small. But so, for that matter, in many cognitions, is the degree of awareness of an independent objective reality;

Reprinted from *On Selfhood and Godhood*, 1957, Lecture V, by permission of the author and publishers George Allen & Unwin Ltd., London and Humanities Press, New York.

and yet, as we saw earlier, there are cogent reasons for presuming it present, in however inexplicit a fashion, wherever anything which can strictly be called a cognition occurs. Hence if it be the case that "objectivity" defines itself, for the cognising mind, at least in part, by contrast with "subjectivity," we must, I think, conclude that cognition always involves some awareness, however, inexplicit, of the subject as subject.

3. But now what kind of a being is this "subject" of which there is consciousness in all cognition? Its most important, and at the same time its most perplexing, characteristic is that it is, for itself, somehow the *self-same* being throughout its different experiences; and the self-same being not merely in contemporaneous experiences, but in experiences far removed from one another in time. Thus I am conscious that I who am now thinking about a peculiarly intractable philosophical problem am the same being as I who am now feeling the room to be slightly on the warm side, and am *also* the same being as I who (as I remember) saw a rainbow yesterday. Indeed, "remembering" brings out in an especially striking manner the self's identity in difference. When we say "*I* remember that *I* saw a rainbow yesterday," we imply that the being who now remembers is identical with the being who saw the rainbow. The claim of the memory situation, a claim in the absence of which the situation ceases to be one of memory at all, is that the remember*ing* subject and the remember*ed* subject are somehow the *same* being in experiences that are different both temporally and qualitatively.

The difficulties in the way of attaching a clear meaning to the self-sameness of the subject in different apprehensions will engage us shortly. But we must first of all support by more formal argument the thesis that cognition of *any* kind—not merely in remembering—implies a subject conscious of its own identity in its different apprehensions.

4. The standard argument for this doctrine is so exceedingly well-worn as almost to require apology for its repetition, and I shall expound it in very summary fashion. It derives, of course, from Kant. What follows will perhaps serve as a sufficient reminder of its general character.

Cognition is never of an atomic simple. It is always of a related plurality *as* a related plurality. This is self-evident if all cognition involves judgment, for in all judgment there must be at least the differences of subject and predicate and the affirmation or denial of their union. But we need not invoke the judgment theory to establish our point. It is clear enough, on reflection, that an "object" which stands in no apprehended relation to other objects of our experience—"an atomic simple"—can have no significance for us, and is thus not an object of cognition at all. Even a "this" is, for cognition, a "this-not-that"; apart from its apprehended distinction from, and therefore relation to, a "that" it could not be cognised as "this." But it seems gratuitous to pursue further a point which has so often received classic expression in post-Kantian philosophy. The critic may be challenged to produce a single instance of cognition, or "meaningful apprehension," where the object does *not* consist in a related plurality.

What is cognised, then, is never bare A, but always A in some sort of relationship to B (C, D, etc.). But unless the subject to which B (C, D, etc.) is present is the same subject as that to which A is present, no relationship, obviously, could be apprehended between B (C, D, etc.) and A. To take the very familiar example of our cognition of succession in time, perhaps the most basic of all cognitions. If event B is cognised as sequent upon event A, clearly A must, in some form, be present to the same subject as that to which B is present. Otherwise A and B would simply fall apart into separate worlds of experience, and no discerned relationship—not even that of apartness, let alone that of temporal sequence—would be possible.

Does cognition imply not merely a subject identical in different cognitions, but a subject *conscious* of its identity in different cognitions? Some philosophers who are firmly persuaded of the subject's self-identity show a certain diffidence about pressing for the subject's consciousness of that identity. Nevertheless I would suggest that this must be pressed. For let us suppose that the subject, though in *fact* identical in two different apprehensions, is in no wise aware of its own identity in them. This subject, let us further suppose, has an apprehension of A, and then an apprehension of B. Now for an outside observer appraised, if that were possible, of the two apprehensions, A and B could be seen to be related, inasmuch as they could be seen both to be objects to the same subject. But for the *subject himself*, unaware (according to our supposition) that the self to whom B is present is the same being as the self to whom A was formerly present, the two apprehensions must fall apart into separate "worlds" just as surely and completely as though he, the self-same subject, were in fact *two different* subjects; and the discernment by him of any *relationship* between A and B (such as that of temporal sequence) must then become impossible. The *prius* of any discernment by the subject of a specific relation between A and B is surely that the subject is aware of A and B as having at least that general relationship to one another which consists in their both being objects for *him*, the one self. He must, in other words, be conscious of his own identity in the different apprehensions.

The point is apt to be as elusive as it is certainly important, and a further illustration may be helpful.

Suppose I hear Big Ben striking. A moment later I—the same subject—hear it striking again. Now is my being "the same subject" sufficient in itself to enable me to apprehend the second stroke *as* the second stroke, as *sequent upon* the first? Not, surely, unless by "the same subject" we *mean* a subject conscious of its self-sameness. I may be in so advanced a state of senility that my memory-span is no longer adequate to bridge the gulf between the two strokes, so that, having forgotten the first when I hear the second, I cannot relate the two to one another. It is a precondition of my apprehending the second stroke *as* the second stroke that I remember having heard the first. But then I do not "remember" having heard the first (and here is the crucial point) unless I am aware that it was

I, the being who now hears the second stroke, who heard the first stroke; unless, in other words, I am not merely the same subject, but also conscious of my self-sameness, in the two experiences.

It seems to me, therefore, that while the identity of the cognising subject is a necessary, it is not, without consciousness of that identity, a sufficient, condition of cognitive awareness.

5. The point we have now reached (retracing, for the most part, familiar lines of argument) is that all cognition implies a subject that is conscious of itself, and that this self of which we are conscious in cognition is a being which is identical with itself throughout—and in despite of—the diversity of its cognitions. But now our troubles begin. We are led by the argument, apparently, to posit a self which is something "over and above" its particular experiences; something that *has*, rather than *is*, its experiences, since its experiences are all different, while *it* somehow remains the same. It is, in short, what would usually be called a "substance" in some sense of that term, and as such it provokes in the modern mind an hostility which, to say truth, the history of philosophy has done much to justify. What, it will be asked, *is* this "I" that is supposed to remain the same, and in what does its sameness consist? By universal admission we never have any acquaintance with it by itself, but only as manifested in particular changing experiences. What possible meaning can we attach to an "I" as an identical "something" over and above these experiences? And our perplexities, it will be urged, by no means end there. If we try to conceive the self as an identical substance, how are we to reconcile with this all the phenomena of radical disunity made familiar to us by abnormal psychology, such as sudden drastic transformations of a self-personal character, not to speak of these strange cases of "multiple personality" in which the "one" self seems to divide up into two or more separate selves?

The difficulty of returning satisfactory answers to such questions has proved so formidable that the strong trend of philosophic opinion today is in the direction of relinquishing the notion of a "substantival" self altogether. The notion of a self of *some* sort, it is conceded, must be retained. We do mean something by the word "I"; and we do mean something when we refer to a variety of different experiences as all "my" experiences. But an interpretation must be found, it is urged, in terms of the particular knowable experiences themselves, not in terms of an "unknowable" something beyond them. Hence it has appeared to many to be the most promising procedure to search *within* the different experiences for some identical quality or, more hopefully, some common relationship, in virtue of which they come to be regarded as all experiences of "one self."

6. What then *is* this quality or relationship? That is just the trouble. I think it is fair to say that, while the great body of contemporary philosophical opinion favours the view that this is where the meaning of self-identity must be sought, there is no manner of agreement as to what the quality or relationship can be. Indeed, no one seems to have much confi-

dence even in the theory he himself proposes, but rather to be putting it forward tentatively as an hypothesis that is not wholly incredible, and is at any rate more credible than any form of substantival theory. As already hinted, some kind of common relationship, rather than some kind of identical quality, has been very generally taken to be the most hopeful thing to look for. But all the types of relationship between different experiences that are known to us in other contexts—similarity, causality, and the rest—seem open to obvious and crushing objections if we try to regard them as the basis of the mind's self-identity. Any one of them can exist between particular experiences without our having the slightest tendency to take these particular experiences to be all experiences of a single self.* It is, I think, not easy to dissent from the conclusion reached by Dr. Ewing after a critical survey of the several types of relationship that have been, or conceivably might be, suggested, viz. that "if we adopt a view of the self according to which its identity is constituted . . . by a relation between its experiences, it is probably best just to say that the relation is unique and indefinable.**

I do not, however, propose to take up time rehearsing the various relational theories *seriatim*, for the following reason. It seems to me that the whole project of seeking for the identity of the self in a relation of *whatever* kind, definable *or* indefinable, between members of a series or group of experiences, is fundamentally futile; indeed self-contradictory. For consider. What we are trying to account for is the identity of a self *not* for some *external observer*, but for the *self itself;* the identity of the self as *subject*, not its identity as an *object*—which the self, *qua* self, just is *not*. Now as a result of cognition of particular events and their inter-relationships we might come to regard as belonging to "one and the same" *object* events which exhibited a certain form of inter-relationship. Applied to mental events, there is some sense in saying that we might thereby arrive at the notion of an object-mind as an identical *it*. But it is the *subject*-mind, the identical "I" of *self*-consciousness, which we are trying to account for; and by the route suggested this is plainly impos-

* Mr. D. G. C. McNabb, in what is otherwise a most penetrating discussion of Hume's treatment of personal identity, seems to think that while such relations as similarity, causality, and spatial and temporal conjunction of perceptions will obviously not account for the kind of identity that belongs to a self, the relational theory may perhaps still be saved if we supplement these relations by another "empirically given relation which we may call co-presentation, which holds between any two or more perceptions which I am in a position to compare with one another". He confesses himself, indeed, not too happy about this solution, since "it looks very much as if it were an empirical fact that this relation is at least a three-term relation, involving at least two perceptions and something else, the mind to which they are presented and which is able to compare them". I suggest that "looks very much as if" is, to put it mildly, an understatement. If "co-presentation" is really "co-*presentation*", it is surely an analytic proposition that there is this "third term"; while if "co-presentation" means something else (which it has no right to mean), like "co-occurrence" of perceptions, it is plainly useless for the purpose in hand. It may be that the "third term" is, in Mr. McNabb's words, "a very curious kind of entity"; but this hardly seems adequate ground for denying an analytic proposition. (*David Hume, His Theory of Knowledge and Morality*, pp. 149–50.)

** *The Fundamental Questions of Philosophy*, p. 115. (Italics not in text.)

sible. For, as we have already seen, cognition of relationships, and indeed cognition of any kind whatsoever, *presupposes* an identical subject conscious of its own identity. It follows that the "relational" way of explaining self-identity can only be in terms which presuppose the very thing it is purporting to explain.

I suggest, then, that the attempt to find a form of relationship between different experiences which is sufficient to account for my regarding these experiences as "mine" is doomed to failure from the outset. There *is*, indeed, an apprehended relationship in virtue of which I call experiences "mine," but it is not a relationship of experiences to one another. It can, I think, only be stated as a relationship of experiences to *me*, an identical subject conscious of having or owning them; a relationship of "belonging to" which is unique and indefinable, but the apprehension of which is ingredient in all self-conscious experience. It is clear, however, that this relationship presupposes, and in no way constitutes, the identity of the self.

Still, the problem remains on our hands, "In what does self-identity consist?" The relational theory may be, and I think is, open to fatal objections; but so far nothing explicit has been said to show that the substantival account, the difficulties in which gave rise to the relational theory, is in any better case. Let us now look back, therefore, at the notion of the self as a substantival entity, distinguishable from its experiences, and, a little fortified by the apparent bankruptcy of the rival relational theory, consider whether it cannot be formulated in a way that escapes the objections usually thought to be conclusive against it.

7. Two preliminary points are worth making briefly. Critics of the substantival self seem to me a great deal too ready to assimilate it either to Locke's "unknowable substratum" of material things, or to Kant's "noumenal ego." This is, I think, unfortunate. It is by no means the case that the doctrine of the substantival self need take a form that lays it open to the objections to which Locke's and Kant's doctrines are notoriously exposed.

To take first the assimilation to Locke's unknowable substratum of material things, Berkeley has said perhaps all that needs to be said on the ineptitude of supposing that spiritual substance and material substance must stand or fall together. When Philonous in the Third Dialogue points out to Hylas that whereas I have no apprehension whatsoever of material substance, I yet "am conscious of my own being, and that I myself am not my ideas, but somewhat else, a thinking, active principle that perceives, knows, wills, and operates about ideas," he is indicating a *prima facie* difference in the epistemological status of spiritual substance and material substance respectively that is fundamental. Self-consciousness, it must be insisted, is a *fact*, a datum from which we have to *start*. And in self-consciousness the subject of which we are conscious is a subject which in some sense has, not is, its different experiences, and is identical with itself in its different experiences. Even if it were possible for self-consciousness to be illusory, its mere occurrence is enough to refute those who take the view that the notion of a substantival self is as "meaningless" as the notion of an unknowable substratum of material things. It is idle to deny that the former of these notions has any meaning for us if that *is* in fact what the self is for itself in self-conscious experience.

Very little more reflection is needed to see that the substantival self cannot be straightway identified with Kant's noumenal ego.

For Kant, it will be remembered, the subject self has its reality beyond the space-time world of mere phenomena; and while we can know in self-consciousness *that* it is, we can say nothing at all about *what* it is. Cognition of the character, the "what," of the self through introspection is not, for Kant, discernment of the nature of the self as *subject*—i.e. of its real nature *qua* self—but only of the self as *object*, which is a mere appearance in time of the timeless "real" self. Kant's noumenal ego is, from the point of view of theoretical cognition at any rate, as characterless as Locke's substratum of material things.

But the defender of the substantival self is under no obligation to accept Kant's views either about time or about what introspection can and cannot reveal to us. One may perfectly well agree with the argument from self-conscious experience to a distinguishable subject-self without being committed to any of the special arguments which led Kant to assert that we can have no theoretical knowledge of that self as it really is. I shall in a later lecture have to give some attention to the problem of the nature and status of introspection as a mode of knowledge, and I shall try to show there that it is a mistake to suppose that introspection cannot reveal real characteristics of the self *qua* self, that is to say, of the self in its functioning as a *subject*. Meantime I would merely point to the direct testimony of self-consciousness. When I am conscious that I who think *A* am the I who desires *B* and the I who feels the emotion *C*, I regard my "I" as manifesting *itself* in these operations of thinking, desiring and feeling: and as thus, so far, "characterised" by these operations. The subject self as apprehended in self-consciousness is in that sense always a determinate or characterised self. To deny that the self is *reducible to* its experiences is by no means to deny that the self manifests its real character (in whole or in part) *in and through* these experiences. The onus of proof lies upon those who wish to maintain that to the self as subject we can assign no determinate character at all.

• • •

PERSONAL IDENTITY AND INDIVIDUATION

B. A. O. WILLIAMS

There is a special problem about personal identity for two reasons. The first is self-consciousness—the fact that there seems to be a peculiar sense in which a man is conscious of his own identity. . . . The second reason is that a question of personal identity is evidently not answered merely by deciding the identity of a certain physical body. If I am asked whether the person in front of me is the same person as one uniquely present at place *a* at time *t*, I shall not necessarily be justified in answering "yes" merely because I am justified in saying that this human body is the same as that present at *a* at *t*. Identity of body is at least not a sufficient condition of personal identity, and other considerations, of personal characteristics and, above all, memory, must be invoked.

Some have held, further, that bodily identity is not a necessary condition of personal identity. This, however, is ambiguous, and yields either a weak or a strong thesis, depending on one's view of the necessity and sufficiency of the other conditions. The weaker thesis asserts merely that at least one case can be consistently constructed in which bodily identity fails, but in which the other conditions will be sufficient for an assertion of personal identity; even though there may be some other imaginable case in which, some other condition failing, bodily identity *is* a necessary condition of personal identity. The stronger thesis asserts that there is no conceivable situation in which bodily identity would be necessary, some other conditions being always both necessary and sufficient. I take it that Locke's theory* is an example of this latter type.

I shall try to show that bodily identity is always a necessary condition of personal identity, and hence that both theses fail. In this connexion I shall discuss in detail a case apparently favourable to the weaker thesis (Section 1).

. . .

In discussions of this subject, it is easy to fall into ways of speaking that suggest that 'bodily' and other considerations are easily divorced. I have

Reprinted in part from "Personal Identity and Individuation," *Proceedings of the Aristotelian Society* n.s. vol. LVII (1956–1957), extracts from pp. 229–244, by permission of the author and the editor of the Aristotelian Society.

* *Essay Concerning Human Understanding*, II, 27.

regrettably succumbed to this at some points, but I certainly do not believe that this easy divorce is possible; I hope that both the general tenor of my thesis and some more direct remarks on the subject (Section 2) will show why.

1. *Deciding another's identity.* Suppose someone undergoes a sudden and violent change of character. Formerly quiet, deferential, church-going and home-loving, he wakes up one morning and has become, and continues to be, loudmouthed, blasphemous and bullying. Here we might ask the question

(*a*) Is he the same person as he used to be?

There seem to be two troubles with the formulation of this question, at least as an *identity* question. The first is a doubt about the reference of the second 'he' if asked the question 'as *who* used to be?', we may well want to say 'this person', which answers the original question (*a*) for us. This is not a serious difficulty, and we can easily avoid it by rephrasing the question in some such way as

(*b*) Is this person the same as the person who went to sleep here last night?

We do not, however, *have* to rephrase the question in any such way; we can understand (*a*) perfectly well, and avoid paradox, because our use of personal pronouns and people's names is malleable. It is a reflection of our concept of 'a person' that some references to *him* cannot be understood as references to *his body* or to parts of it, and that others can; and that these two sorts of reference can readily occur in one statement ("He was embarrassed and went red.") In the case of (*a*), the continuity of reference for 'he' can be supplied by the admitted continuity of reference of 'his body', and the more fundamental identity question can be discussed in these terms without any serious puzzlement.

The second difficulty with (*a*) is that it is too readily translated into

(*c*) Is he the same sort of person as he used to be? or possibly
(*d*) Has he the same personality as he used to have?

But (*c*) and (*d*) are not identity questions in the required sense. For on any interpretation, 'sort of person', and on one interpretation, 'personality', are quality-terms, and we are merely asking whether the same subject now has different qualities, which is too easy to answer.

But this is only one interpretation of 'personality'. It corresponds interestingly to a loose sense of 'identity', which is found for instance in Mr. Nigel Dennis' novel *Cards of Identity*. There 'identity' is often used to mean 'a set of characteristics,' and 'giving someone an identity' means 'convincing someone that he is a certain sort of person'. It does not, however, only mean this; for Mr. Dennis' Identity Club do not stop at giving someone a new character—they give him a new background as well, and a local sponger is made by their persuasive methods not just into a submissive old-style butler, but into such a butler who used to be at sea and has deserted his wife.

We might feel that this was the point at which something specially uncanny was beginning to happen, and that this was the kind of anomalous example we were really looking for—the uncanniness of someone's acquiring a new past is connected with our increasing reluctance to describe the situation as one in which the same man has acquired a new set of qualities. Here we have one powerful motive for the introduction of memory. It can be put by saying that there are, or we can imagine, cases where we want to use some term like 'personality' in such a way that it is not a type-expression, meaning 'set of characteristics', but is a particular term meaning something like *individual* personality. It may seem that this particularity is attained by reference to memory—the possession of a particular past. Thus we are concerned here with cases more drastic than those in which for instance people say 'it has made a new man of him', or even 'he is not the same person as he used to be' in the sense suggested by a change of character; these cases we can too readily redescribe. Thus we may put our question in the barbarous form

(*e*) Is the (particular) personality he has now the same as the one he had before?

We must now see whether we can make sense, in terms of memory, of the idea of a particular personality; and whether there can be personal identity without bodily identity.

In doing this, two obvious but important features of memory have to be borne in mind.

(I) To say "A remembers x," without irony or inverted commas, is to imply that x really happened; in this respect 'remember' is parallel to 'know'.

(II) It does not follow from this, nor is it true, that all claims to remember, any more than all claims to know, are veridical; or, not everything one seems to remember is something one really remembers.

So much is obvious, although Locke* was forced to invoke the providence of God to deny the latter. These points have been emphasised by Prof. A. G. N. Flew in his discussion of Locke's views on personal identity.** In formulating Locke's thesis, however, Prof. Flew makes a mistake; for he offers Locke's thesis in the form "if X can remember Y's doing such-and-such, then X and Y are the same person." But this obviously will not do, even for Locke, for we constantly say things like "I remember my brother joining the army" without implying that I and my brother are the same person. So if we are to formulate such a criterion, it looks as though we have to say something like "if X remembers doing such-and-such, then he is the person who did that thing." But since "remembers doing" means "remembers himself doing", this is trivially tautologous, and moreover lends colour to Butler's famous objec-

* *loc. cit.* §13 He is speaking, however, only of the memories of actions.
** *Philosophy*, 1951.

tion that memory, so far from constituting personal identity, presupposed it. Hence the criterion should rather run: "if X claims to remember doing such-and-such. . . ." We must now ask how such a criterion might be used.

Suppose the man who underwent the radical change of character—let us call him Charles—claimed, when he woke up, to remember witnessing certain events and doing certain actions which earlier he did not claim to remember; and that under questioning he could not remember witnessing other events and doing other actions which earlier he did remember. Would this give us grounds for saying that he now was or had, in some particular sense, a different personality? An argument to show that it did gives us such grounds might be constructed on the following lines.

Any token event E, and any token action A, are by definition particulars. Moreover, the description "the man who did the action A" necessarily individuates some one person; for it is logically impossible that two persons should do the same *token* action.* In the case of events, it is possible that two persons should witness the same token event; but nevertheless the description "the man who witnessed E" may happen to individuate some one person, and "the man who witnessed E_1, E_2 . . . E_n" has a proportionately greater chance of so doing. Thus if our subject Charles now claims to remember doing certain actions A_1, A_2, etc., and witnessing certain events E_1, E_1, etc., which are themselves suitably identified, we have good grounds for saying that he is some particular person or has some particular personality.

Now by principle (II), we have no reason without corroborative evidence of some kind to believe Charles when he now claims to remember A or E; so we must set about checking. How are we to do this in the present case? Ordinarily if some person X claims to have witnessed E, and we wish to check this, we must find out whether there is any record, or anyone has any memory, of X's witnessing E. This is evidently inapplicable to the present case. For either the evidence shows that Charles was *bodily* present at E, or it does not. If it does, then Charles is remembering in the ordinary way, which is contrary to the hypothesis. If it does not, then there is no corroboration. Here we have a first important step. We are trying to prise apart "bodily" and "mental" criteria; but we find that the normal operation of one "mental" criterion involves the "bodily" one.

However, the situation may not be quite as desperate as this makes it appear. We can examine Charles' putative memories, and we may find that he can offer detailed information which there is no reason to believe

* This is to ignore the case of joint or co-operative actions. Thus when three persons A, B and C jointly fell a tree, it might be said that each of them has done the same action, that of felling the particular tree. But this would not be quite accurate. They have *all* felled the tree; what *each* of them has done is to share in the felling of the tree, or to have felled the tree with the help of the other two. When the variables implicit in this last expression are replaced with names, we obtain descriptions of token actions which indeed individuate; thus it is true of A, but not of B or C, that he is the man who felled the tree *with the help of B and C.*

he would ordinarily have known, and which strongly suggests the reports of an eye-witness of some particular events. What we can do with this information in the present case depends on a number of considerations. I shall now examine these, first in connexion with events, and then with actions. Events can in principle be witnessed by any number of persons, or by none. Some of the events which Charles claims to remember witnessing may be events of which we have other eye-witness accounts; others may be events which we believe to have occurred, though we do not know whether or not anyone witnessed them; others again may be events which we believe to have occurred, but which we believe no-one to have witnessed.

For all these, there is an hypothesis about—or, perhaps, description of—Charles' present condition which has nothing to do with a change of personality: the hypothesis of clairvoyance.* To describe Charles as clairvoyant is certainly not to advance very far towards an *explanation* of his condition; it amounts to little more than saying that he has come to know, by no means, what other people know by evidence. But so long as Charles claimed to remember events which were supposedly or certainly unwitnessed, such a description might be the best we could offer. We might do better than this, however, if the events Charles claimed to remember were witnessed; in this case we could begin to advance to the idea that Charles had a new identity, because we would have the chance of finding someone for him to be identical *with*. Thus if the events were witnessed, we might say that Charles was (now) identical with a witness of these events. This is ambiguous; it might mean that he was identical with anyone who witnessed the events, or with some particular person who witnessed the events. The former of these is no advance, since it comes to a roundabout way of saying that he claims to have witnessed the events, *i.e.* is possibly clairvoyant. The situation is different, however, if we can identify some one person who, it is plausible to suppose, witnessed all the events that Charles now claims to remember. That this should be possible is, indeed, a necessary condition of describing what has happened to Charles as *a change of identity;* I shall return to this point a little later.

. . .

Let us now go back to the case of Charles. We may suppose that our enquiry has turned out in the most favourable possible way, and that all the events he claims to have witnessed and all the actions he claims to have done point unanimously to the life-history of some one person in the past—for instance, Guy Fawkes. Not only do all Charles' memory-claims that can be checked fit the pattern of Fawkes' life as known to historians, but others that cannot be checked are plausible, provide explanations of unexplained facts, and soon. Are we to say that Charles is now Guy

* Together, of course, with the loss of his real memories.

Fawkes, that Guy Fawkes has come to life again in Charles' body, or some such thing?

Certainly the temptation to say something on this pattern is very strong. It is difficult to insist that we *couldn't* say that Charles (or sometime Charles) had become Guy Fawkes; this is certainly what the newspapers would say if they heard of it. But newspapers are prone to exaggeration, and this might be an exaggeration. For why shouldn't we say that Charles had, except for his body, become just like Guy Fawkes used to be; or perhaps that Charles clairvoyantly—*i.e.* mysteriously—knows all about Guy Fawkes and his *ambiance?* In answer to this, it will be argued that this is just what memory was introduced to rule out; granted that we need similar personal characteristics, skills, and so on as necessary conditions of the identification, the final—and, granted these others, sufficient—condition is provided by memories of seeing just *this*, and doing just *that*, and it is these that pick out a particular man. But perhaps this point is fundamentally a logical trick. Granted that in a certain context the expressions "the man who did A", "the man who saw E", do effectively individuate, it is logically impossible that two different persons should (correctly) remember being the man who did A or saw E; but it is not logically impossible that two different persons should *claim* to remember being this man, and this is the most we can get.

This last argument is meant to show only that we are not forced to accept the description of Charles' condition as his being identical with Guy Fawkes. I shall now put forward an argument to strengthen this contention and to suggest that we should not be justified in accepting this description. If it is logically possible that Charles should undergo the changes described, then it is logically possible that some other man should simultaneously undergo the same changes; *e.g.* that both Charles and his brother Robert should be found in this condition. What should we say in that case? They cannot both be Guy Fawkes; if they were, Guy Fawkes would be in two places at once, which is absurd. Moreover, if they were both identical with Guy Fawkes, they would be identical with each other, which is also absurd. Hence we could not say that they were both identical with Guy Fawkes. We might instead say that one of them was identical with Guy Fawkes, and that the other was just like him; but this would be an utterly vacuous manœuvre, since there would be *ex hypothesi* no principle determining which description was to apply to which. So it would be best, if anything, to say that both had mysteriously become like Guy Fawkes, clairvoyantly knew about him, or something like this. If this would be the best description of each of the two, why would it not be the best description of Charles if Charles alone were changed?

Perhaps this last rhetorical question too readily invites an answer. It might be said that there is a relevant difference between the case in which two persons are changed and the case in which only one is changed, the difference being just this difference in numbers; and that there is no guarantee that what we would say in one of these situations would be the same as what we would say in the other. In the more complicated situation our linguistic and conceptual resources would be taxed even more severely than in the simpler one, and we might not react to the demands in the same way. Moreover, there is a reason why we should not react in the same way. The standard form of an identity question is "Is this x the same x as that x which . . . ?", and in the simpler situation we are at least presented with just the materials for constructing such a question; but in the more complicated situation we are baffled even in asking the question, since both the transformed persons are equally good candidates for being its subject, and the question "Are these two x's the same (x?) as the x which . . . ?" is not a recognizable form of identity question. Thus, it might be argued, the fact that we could not speak of identity in the latter situation is no kind of proof that we could not do so in the former.

Certainly it is not a proof.* Yet the argument does indicate that to speak of identity in the simpler case would be at least quite vacuous. The point can be made clearer in the following way. In the case of material objects, we can draw a distinction between identity and exact similarity; it is clearly not the same to say that two men live in the same house, and that they live in exactly similar houses. This notion of identity is given to us primarily, though not completely, by the notion of spatio-temporal continuity. In the case of character, however, this distinction cannot be drawn, for to say that A and B have the same character is just to say that A's character is exactly similar to B's. Nor can this distinction be drawn in the case of memories—if you could say that two men had the same memories, this would be to say that their memories were exactly similar. There is, however, an extreme difficulty in saying these things about memories at all; it is unclear what it would mean to say that there were *two* men who had exactly similar, or the same, memories, since to call them real memories is to imply their correctness. Thus if we are to describe Charles' relations to Guy Fawkes in terms of *exact similarity* of everything except the body, we are going to have difficulty in finding a suitable description in these terms of his memory claims. We cannot say that he has the same memories as Guy Fawkes, as this is to imply, what we want to deny, that he really is Guy Fawkes; nor can we say that the memory claims he makes are the same as those made by Guy Fawkes, as we have little idea of what memory claims Fawkes in fact made, or indeed of how much he at various times remembered. All we actually know is that Charles' claims fit Fawkes' life.

These difficulties, in applying the concept of exact similarity in the matter of the supposed memories, are (I suspect) a motive for the thought that we *must* describe the situation in terms of identity. This is where the reduplicated situation of Charles and Robert gives some help. In that situation it is quite obvious that the idea of identity cannot be applied, and that we must fall back on similarity; and that one respect in which the trio are similar is—however we are to express it—that of

* I am grateful to Mr. P. F. Strawson for making this clear to me.

"memory". (If the situation sometimes occurred, we might find an expression; we might speak of "similarity of one's supposed past".) This eases the way for doing the same thing in the case of Charles alone, whose relation to Fawkes in his unique case is exactly the same as both his and Robert's in the reduplicated one. We can then say that Charles has the same character, and the same supposed past, as Fawkes; which is just the same as to say that they are in these respects exactly similar. This is not to say that they are identical at all. The only case in which identity and exact similarity could be distinguished, as we have just seen, is that of the body—"same body" and "exactly similar body" really do mark a difference. Thus I should claim that the omission of the body takes away all content from the idea of personal *identity*.*

I should like to make one last point about this example. This turns on the fact, mentioned before, that in order to describe Charles' change as a change of identity, we must be able to identify some one person who might plausibly be supposed to have seen and done all the things that Charles now claims to remember having seen and done; otherwise there would be nothing to pin down Charles' memory claims as other than random feats of clairvoyance. We succeeded in doing this, just by discovering that Charles' memory claims fitted Fawkes' life. This could be done only by knowing what Fawkes did, and what Fawkes did could be known only by reference to witnesses of Fawkes' activities, and these witnesses must have seen Fawkes' *body*. In order for their accounts to be connected into the history of one person, it is necessary to rely on the continuity of this body.

Now the fact that Fawkes is in this sense identified through his body does not rule out the possibility that Charles should later be identified with Fawkes without reference to a body; *i.e.* this fact does not rule out the weaker thesis about the non-necessity of bodies. To illustrate this, one might compare the case of someone's going to a crowded party, where he sees a girl who is very like all the other girls at the party except that she has red hair. This girl sings various songs and quarrels with the band; she is easily identified on each occasion by the colour of the hair. The man later meets a platinum blonde who recalls singing songs at a party and quarrelling with the band. He can identify her as the red-haired girl at the party, even though she has changed the colour of her hair in the meantime. There is an important difference, however, between this case and that of Fawkes. If the girl had remarkably changed the colour of her hair between songs and before the quarrel, identifying her at the various stages of the party would have been more difficult, but not in principle impossible; but if the Fawkes-personality changed bodies frequently, identification would become not just difficult but impossible. For the only other resource would be the memory criterion, and the operation of this would once more make exactly the same requirements. Hence it is a necessary condition of making the supposed identification on non-bodily grounds that at some stage identifications should be made on bodily

* I am indebted here, and elsewhere in this paper, to Mr. D. F. Pears.

grounds. Hence any claim that bodily considerations can be absolutely omitted from the criteria of personal identity must fail; *i.e.* these facts do rule out the stronger thesis.

2. *Some remarks on bodily interchange*. Anyone who believed that personalities could be identified without reference to bodies might be expected to make sense of the idea of bodily interchange; and anyone who thought that they might always be identified in this way would presumably require that for any two contemporaneous persons we should be able to make sense of the idea that their bodies should be interchanged. It is worth considering how far we can make sense of it, if we look at it closely.

Suppose a magician is hired to perform the old trick of making the emperor and the peasant become each other. He gets the emperor and the peasant in one room, with the emperor on his throne and the peasant in the corner, and then casts the spell. What will count as success? Clearly not that after the smoke has cleared the old emperor should be in the corner and the old peasant on the throne. That would be a rather boring trick. The requirement is presumably that the emperor's body, with the peasant's personality, should be on the throne, and the peasant's body, with the emperor's personality, in the corner. What does this mean? In particular, what has happened to the voices? The voice presumably ought to count as a bodily function; yet how would the peasant's gruff blasphemies be uttered in the emperor's cultivated tones, or the emperor's witticisms in the peasant's growl? A similar point holds for the features; the emperor's body might include the sort of face that just *could not* express the peasant's morose suspiciousness, the peasant's a face no expression of which could be taken for one of fastidious arrogance. These "could's" are not just empirical–such expressions on these features might be unthinkable.

The point need not be elaborated; I hope I have said enough to suggest that the concept of bodily interchange cannot be taken for granted, and that there are even logical limits to what we should be prepared to say in this direction. What these limits are, cannot be foreseen–one has to consider the cases, and for this one has to see the cases. The converse is also true, that it is difficult to tell in advance how far certain features may suddenly seem to express something quite unexpected. But there are limits, and when this is recognized, the idea of the interchange of personalities seems very odd. There might be something like a logical impossibility of the magician's trick's succeeding. However much of the emperor's past the sometime peasant now claimed to remember, the trick would not have succeeded if he could not satisfy the simpler requirement of being the same *sort* of person as the sometime emperor. Could he do this, if he could not smile royally? Still less, could he be the same person, if he could not smile the characteristic smile of the emperor?

These considerations are relevant to the present question in two ways. First, the stronger view about the identification implies that an interchange is always conceivable; but there are many cases in which it does not seem to be conceivable at all. Secondly, there is connected with this the deeper point, that when we are asked to distinguish a man's personality from his body, we do not really know what to distinguish from what. I take it that this was part of what Wittgenstein meant when he said that the best picture of the human soul was the human body.*

. . .

THE PHENOMENOLOGICAL APPROACH TO CONSCIOUSNESS

EDMUND HUSSERL

Edmund Husserl is credited with inventing a unique method in philosophy, sometimes called the "phenomenological method." Its purpose is to reveal the presupposition of ordinary technical thought and to study the structures of consciousness. One of the greatest difficulties in understanding Husserl's method is the language Husserl uses to describe it. He very often makes it appear highly esoteric and quite unrelated to anything in ordinary practice. Yet the first step, the development of a reflective attitude, is a perfectly ordinary practice which has been turned into a methodological device. What follows is a brief description of the method of phenomenology, which should be read before reading the section by Husserl.

When I am engaged in common commerce with the world, whatever I am involved in doing engages my attention almost entirely; while I am engaged, I have little opportunity to reflect on myself as engaged —whatever I am doing narrows my concern to what is immediately relevant to what engages me. If I am searching for a long, pointed red pencil I remember leaving on my desk, not only do I not reflect on myself as engaged in searching, but my field of vision is generally structured so that only long objects with the properties of being pointed and red stand out. And so it is with all practical task-oriented activities. But suppose in the course of looking for my pencil I become aware that my search is not successful. For the first time, I may be led to make my activity of searching itself an object of reflection. What I gave no notice to now *becomes prominent. I am now in the position of questioning what I was doing and how I was going about it. But, also, my world, once narrowed to just the awareness of red and pointed objects, may be expanded. Just this kind of wrenching myself away from my natural*

* *Philosophical Investigations*, II, iv.

involvement in the world is the ordinary counterpart of the preliminary step to the phenomenological method.

But between this ordinary approximation of disinterested reflection and a fully realized phenomenological attitude there are crucial differences.

1. I made searching itself an object of reflection in order to improve my search. No such practical end motivates phenomenological reflection. The attitude of disinterestedness is cultivated in order to let whatever appears present itself just as it appears. In ordinary circumstances, to have a pencil as the object of my search is also to believe in the existence of the pencil. But when I make searching the object of a phenomenological investigation, I am not trying to find the pencil, and I need not believe that a particular pencil exists. The act of searching remains phenomenologically interesting without such a belief. For I am now concerned with the question, "What is it for anything to be a case of searching?" rather than the questions, "Where is the object I am searching for?" or "Is this particular case a case of searching?" The latter are factual questions; the former is a question about meaning. This particular aspect of phenomenological investigation Husserl calls "bracketing" or "epoché"; in effect, it is a temporary suspension of belief in the existence of the objects of investigation.*

2. The suspension of belief in existence makes it possible to concentrate on an essential trait of searching, or for that matter, any cognitive or perceptual act like knowing, believing, or perceiving. Searching is object-directed in that searching is always searching for *something. But what is special to searching, in contrast to believing, is the belief in the object of search. It is a necessary truth that nothing is a case of searching unless the person searching believes in the existence of that for which he searches. This is hardly a profound insight. But it illustrates what Husserl calls "eidetic reduction" and shows why he distinguished pure phenomenology from phenomenological psychology. Phenomenology is pure in the sense that such studies are not dependent on empirical or statistical investigation. Just as I do not have to inspect a large number of cases of intersecting lines to see that a line can intersect another line at only one point in a plane, neither do I have to subject searching to an empirical study to know what is essential to it.*

3. There is yet another way phenomenological reflection differs from ordinary reflection. What is essential to all acts of consciousness is a directedness toward objects, a characteristic which Husserl, following the tradition, calls "intentionality". Although the act of searching differs from acts of consciousness in that searching requires the existence of the

* Husserl uses the technical term "phenomena" to designate whatever it is that presents itself. The name covers both perceptual and cognitive objects such as the objects of belief and knowledge. Thus, when Husserl uses perceptual verbs such as "see" or "inspect" he intends them to span both perceptual and cognitive uses. The sense of "seeing" phenomena is the sense of seeing something directly before us, the sense in which there is no room for doubt. Thus, our experiences of phenomena have a superior certainty which we do not associate with anything that is inferred or derived from experience.

object of search, these acts are on a par once we suspend belief in existence. Recall the example of searching; what becomes evident to me on phenomenological reflection was lost to me while I searched. While I was engaged in searching, what I saw was the world as *I structured it. What I did not see* was* that *I had structured it. I did not see that the world was invested with my intent, nor did I see that these figments of my intent had their source in me. When all consciousness is made the object of phenomenological inquiry, then every meaning-giving act and meant object comes within my purview, including the "I" to whom meaning is present and who is the source of meaning.*

The technique of phenomenological reduction provides a critical tool for revealing biases not only of ordinary task-related activities, but the seldom acknowledged beliefs and theories that are buried in all practical and theoretical disciplines.

From the phenomenological point of view, the attitude of scientific neutrality itself reveals its bias. A psychologist may scrutinize me with the hope that my behavior will eventually reveal regularities on the basis of which he may predict my future behavior. But to my phenomenological gaze the object of his study, my behavior, and the results of his investigations, regularities pertaining to me, are like artifacts from an alien culture.

Phenomenological investigation also purports to be constructive. In revealing the often unacknowledged assumptions of the special sciences, and in subjecting them to eidetic reduction, Husserl hoped to supply the rationally certain basis of all the sciences. And in studying lived experience, Husserl also hoped to reveal the simpler pre-verbal experiences and constructive principles which the mind uses to build up more complex concepts and operations.

THE THESIS OF THE NATURAL STANDPOINT AND ITS SUSPENSION

27. THE WORD OF THE NATURAL STANDPOINT: I AND MY WORLD ABOUT ME

Our first outlook upon life is that of natural human beings, imaging, judging, feeling, willing, "*from the natural standpoint.*" Let us make clear to ourselves what this means in the form of simple meditations which we can best carry on in the first person.

I am aware of a world, spread out in space endlessly, and in time becoming and become, without end. I am aware of it, that means, first of

Reprinted from *Ideas,* Part II, Chapter 3 by permission of Humanities Press, New York and George Allen & Unwin, Ltd., London.

* In the sense of "see" that spans both perceptual and cognitive objects called "phenomena."

all, I discover it immediately, intuitively, I experience it. Through sight, touch, hearing, etc., in the different ways of sensory perception, corporeal things somehow spatially distributed are *for me simply there*, in verbal or figurative sense "present," whether or not I pay them special attention by busying myself with them, considering, thinking, feeling, willing. Animal beings also, perhaps men, are immediately there for me; I look up, I see them, I hear them coming towards me, I grasp them by the hand; speaking with them, I understand immediately what they are sensing and thinking, the feelings that stir them, what they wish or will. They too are present as realities in my field of intuition, even when I pay them no attention. But it is not necessary that they and other objects likewise should be present precisely in my *field of perception*. For me real objects are there, definite, more or less familiar, agreeing with what is actually perceived without being themselves perceived or even intuitively present. I can let my attention wander from the writing-table I have just seen and observed, through the unseen portions of the room behind my back to the verandah, into the garden, to the children in the summer-house, and so forth, to all the objects concerning which I precisely "know" that they are there and yonder in my immediate co-perceived surroundings—a knowledge which has nothing of conceptual thinking in it, and first changes into clear intuiting with the bestowing of attention, and even then only partially and for the most part very imperfectly.

But not even with the added reach of this intuitively clear or dark, distinct or indistinct *co-present* margin, which forms a continuous ring around the actual field of perception, does that world exhaust itself which in every waking moment is in some conscious measure "present" before me. It reaches rather in a fixed order of being the limitless beyond. What is actually perceived, and what is more or less clearly co-present and determinate (to some extent at least), is partly pervaded, partly girt about with a *dimly apprehended depth or fringe of indeterminate reality*. I can pierce it with rays from the illuminating focus of attention with varying success. Determining representations, dim at first, then livelier, fetch me something out, a chain of such recollections takes shape, the circle of determinacy extends ever farther, and eventually so far that the connexion with the actual field of perception as the *immediate* environment is established. But in general the issue is a different one: an empty mist of dim indeterminacy gets studded over with intuitive possibilities or presumptions, and only the "form" of the world as "world" is foretokened. Moreover, the zone of indeterminacy is infinite. The misty horizon that can never be completely outlined remains necessarily there.

As it is with the world in its ordered being as a spatial present—the aspect I have so far been considering—so likewise is it with the world in respect to its *ordered being in the succession of time*. This world now present to me, and in every waking "now" obviously so, has its temporal horizon, infinite in both directions, its known and unknown, its intimately alive and its unalive past and future. Moving freely within the moment of experience which brings what is present into my intuitional grasp, I can follow up these connexions of the reality which immediately surrounds me. I can shift my standpoint in space and time, look this way and that, turn temporally forwards and backwards; I can provide for myself constantly new and more or less clear and meaningful perceptions and representations, and images also more or less clear, in which I make intuitable to myself whatever can possibly exist really or supposedly in the steadfast order of space and time.

In this way, when consciously awake, I find myself at all times, and without my ever being able to change this, set in relation to a world which, through its constant changes, remains one and ever the same. It is continually "present" for me, and I myself am a member of it. Therefore this world is not there for me as a mere *world of facts and affairs*, but, with the same immediacy, as a *world of values, a world of goods, a practical world*. Without further effort on my part I find the things before me furnished not only with the qualities that befit their positive nature, but with value-characters such as beautiful or ugly, agreeable or disagreeable, pleasant or unpleasant, and so forth. Things in their immediacy stand there as objects to be used, the "table" with its "books," the "glass to drink from," the "vase," the "piano," and so forth. These values and practicalities, they too belong to *the constitution of the "actually present" objects as such*, irrespective of my turning or not turning to consider them or indeed any other objects. The same considerations apply of course just as well to the men and beasts in my surroundings as to "mere things." They are my "friends" or my "foes," my "servants" or "superiors," strangers" or "relatives," and so forth.

28. THE "COGITO." MY NATURAL WORLD-ABOUT-ME AND THE IDEAL WORLDS-ABOUT-ME

It is then to this world, *the world in which I find myself and which is also my world-about-me*, that the complex forms of my manifold and shifting *spontaneities* of consciousness stand related: observing in the interests of research the bringing of meaning into conceptual form through description; comparing and distinguishing, collecting and counting, presupposing and inferring, the theorizing activity of consciousness, in short, in its different forms and stages. Related to it likewise are the diverse acts and states of sentiment and disapproval, joy and sorrow, desire and aversion, hope and fear, decision and action. All these, together with the sheer acts of the Ego, in which I become acquainted with the world as *immediately* given me, through spontaneous tendencies to turn towards it and to grasp it, are included under the one Cartesian expression: *Cogito*. In the natural urge of life I live continually in *this fundamental form of all "wakeful" living*, whether in addition I do or do not assert the *cogito*, and whether I am or am not "reflectively" concerned with the Ego and the *cogitare*. If I am so concerned, a new *cogito* has become livingly active, which for its part is not reflected upon, and so not objective for me.

I am present to myself continually as someone who perceives, represents, thinks, feels, desires, and so forth; and *for the most part* herein I find myself related in present experience to the fact-world which is constantly about me. But I am not always so related, not every *cogito* in which I live has for its *cogitatum* things, men, objects or contents of one kind or another. Perhaps I am busied with pure numbers and the laws they symbolize: nothing of this sort is present in the world about me, this world of "real fact." And yet the world of numbers also is there for me, as the field of objects with which I am arithmetically busied; while I am thus occupied some numbers or constructions of a numerical kind will be at the focus of vision, girt by an arithmetical horizon partly defined, partly not; not obviously this being-there-for-me, like the being there at all, is something very different from this. *The arithmetical world is there for me only when and so long as I occupy the arithmetical standpoint.* But the *natural* world, the world in the ordinary sense of the word, is *constantly there for me*, so long as I live naturally and look in its direction. I am then at the "*natural standpoint*," which is just another way of stating the same thing. And there is no need to modify these conclusions when I proceed to appropriate to myself the arithmetical world, and other similar "worlds," by adopting the corresponding standpoint. The natural world *still remains "present*," I am at the natural standpoint after as well as before, and in this respect *undisturbed by the adoption of new standpoints*. If my *cogito* is active *only* in the worlds proper to the new standpoints, the natural world remains unconsidered; it is now the background for my consciousness as act, but it is *not the encircling sphere within which an arithmetical world finds its true and proper place*. The two worlds are present together but *disconnected*, apart, that is, from their relation to the Ego, in virtue of which I can freely direct my glance or my acts to the one or to the other.

29. THE "OTHER" EGO-SUBJECT AND THE INTERSUBJECTIVE NATURAL WORLD-ABOUT-ME

Whatever holds good for me personally, also holds good, as I know, for all other men whom I find present in my world-about-me. Experiencing them as men, I understand and take them as Ego-subjects, units like myself, and related to their natural surroundings. But this in such wise that I apprehend the world-about-them and the world-about-me objectively as one and the same world, which differs in each case only through affecting consciousness differently. Each has his place whence he sees the things that are present, and each enjoys accordingly different appearances of the things. For each, again, the fields of perception and memory actually present are different, quite apart from the fact that even that which is here intersubjectively known in common is known in different ways, is differently apprehended, shows different grades of clearness, and so forth. Despite all this, we come to understandings with our neighbours, and set up in common an objective spatio-temporal fact-world as *the world about us that is there for us all, and to which we ourselves none the less belong.*

30. THE GENERAL THESIS OF THE NATURAL STANDPOINT

That which we have submitted towards the characterization of what is given to us from the natural standpoint, and thereby of the natural standpoint itself, was a piece of pure description *prior to all "theory."* In these studies we stand bodily aloof from all theories, and by "theories" we here mean anticipatory ideas of every kind. Only as facts of our environment, not as agencies for uniting facts validly together, do theories concern us at all. But we do not set ourselves the task of continuing the pure description and raising it to a systematically inclusive and exhaustive characterization of the data, in their full length and breadth, discoverable from the natural standpoint (or from any standpoint, we might add, that can be knit up with the same in a common consent). A task such as this can and must—as scientific—be undertaken, and it is one of extraordinary importance, although so far scarcely noticed. Here it is not ours to attempt. For us who are striving towards the entrance-gate of phenomenology all the necessary work in this direction has already been carried out; the few features pertaining to the natural standpoint which we need are of a quite general character, and have already figured in our descriptions, and been sufficiently *and fully clarified.* We even made a special point of securing this full measure of clearness.

We emphasize a most important point once again in the sentences that follow: I find continually present and standing over against me the one spatio-temporal fact-world to which I myself belong, as do all other men found in it and related in the same way to it. This "fact-world," as the world already tells us, I find to *be out there,* and also *take it just as it gives itself to me as something that exists out there.* All doubting and rejecting of the data of the natural world leaves standing the *general thesis of the natural standpoint.* "The" world is as fact-world always there; at the most it is at odd points "other" than I supposed, this or that under such names as "illusion," "hallucination," and the like, must be struck *out of it,* so to speak; but the "it" remains ever, in the sense of the general thesis, a world that has its being out there. To know it more comprehensively, more trustworthily, more perfectly than the naïve lore of experience is able to do, and to solve all the problems of scientific knowledge which offer themselves upon its ground, that is the goal of the *sciences of the natural standpoint.*

31. RADICAL ALTERATION OF THE NATURAL THESIS "DISCONNEXION," "BRACKETING"

Instead now of remaining at this standpoint, we propose to alter it radically. Our aim must be to convince ourselves of the possibility of this alteration on grounds of principle.

The General Thesis according to which the real world about me is at all times known not merely in a general way as something apprehended, but as a fact-world *that has its being out there*, does *not* consist of course *in an act proper*, in an articulated judgment *about existence*. It is and remains something all the time the standpoint is adopted, that is, it endures persisently during the whole course of our life of natural endeavour. What has been at any time perceived clearly, or obscurely made present, in short everything out of the world of nature through experience and prior to any thinking, bears in its totality and in all its articulated sections the character "present" "out there," a character which can function essentially as the ground of support for an explicit (predicative) existential judgment which is in agreement with the character it is grounded upon. If we express that same judgment, we know quite well that in so doing we have simply put into the form of a statement and grasped as a predication what already lay somehow in the original experience, or lay there as the character of something "present to one's hand."

We can treat the potential and unexpressed thesis exactly as we do the thesis of the explicit judgment. A procedure of this sort, *possible at any time*, is, for instance, *the attempt to doubt everything* which *Descartes*, with an entirely different end in view, with the purpose of setting up an absolutely indubitable sphere of Being, undertook to carry through. We link on here, but add directly and emphatically that this attempt to doubt everything should serve us *only as a device of method*, helping us to stress certain points which by its means, as though secluded in its essence, must be brought clearly to light.

The attempt to doubt everything has its place in the realm of our *perfect freedom*. We can *attempt to doubt* anything and everything, however convinced we may be concerning what we doubt, even though the evidence which seals our assurance is completely adequate.

Let us consider what is essentially involved in an act of this kind. He who attempts to doubt is attempting to doubt "Being" of some form or other, or it may be Being expanded into such predicative forms as "It is," "It is this or thus," and the like. The attempt does not affect the form of Being itself. He who doubts, for instance, whether an object, whose Being he does not doubt, is constituted in such and such a way doubts *the way it is constituted*. We can obviously transfer this way of speaking from the doubting to the *attempt* at doubting. It is clear that we cannot doubt the Being of anything, and in the same act of consciousness (under the unifying form of simultaneity) bring what is substantive to this Being under the terms of the Natural Thesis, and so confer upon it the character of "being actually there" (*vorhanden*). Or to put the same in another way: we cannot at once doubt and hold for certain one and the same quality of Being. It is likewise clear that the *attempt* to doubt any object of awareness in respect of it *being actually there necessarily conditions a certain suspension* (*Aufhebung*) *of the thesis;* and it is precisely this that interests us. It is not a transformation of the thesis into its antithesis, of positive into negative; it is also not a transformation into presumption, suggestion, indecision, doubt (in one or another sense of the word); such shifting indeed is not at our free pleasure. *Rather is it something quite unique. We do not abandon the thesis we have adopted, we make no change in our conviction,* which remains in itself what it is so long as we do not introduce new motives of judgment, which we precisely refrain from doing. And yet the thesis undergoes a modification—whilst remaining in itself what it is, *we set it as it were "out of action,"* we *"disconnect it," "bracket it."* It still remains there like the bracketed in the bracket, like the disconnected outside the connexional system. We can also say: The thesis is experience as lived (*Erlebnis*), *but we make "no use" of it,* and by that, of course, we do not indicate privation (as when we say of the ignorant that he makes no use of a certain thesis); in this case rather, as with all parallel expressions, we are dealing with indicators that point to a definite but *unique form of consciousness,* which clamps on to the original simple thesis (whether it actually or even predicatively *posits* existence or not), and transvalues it in a quite peculiar way. *This transvaluing is a concern of our full freedom, and is opposed to all cognitive attitudes* that would set themselves up as co-ordinate with the *thesis,* and yet within the unity of "simultaneity" remain incompatible with it, as indeed it is in general with all attitudes whatsoever in the strict sense of the word.

In *the attempt to doubt* applied to a thesis which, as we presuppose, is certain and tenaciously held, the "disconnexion" takes place in and with a modification of the antithesis, namely with the "*supposition*" (*Ansetzung*) *of Non-Being,* which is thus the partial basis of the attempt to doubt. With Descartes this is so markedly the case that one can say that his universal attempt at doubt is just an attempt at universal denial. We disregard this possibility here, we are not interested in every analytical component of the attempt to doubt, nor therefore in its exact and completely sufficing analysis. *We extract only the phenomenon of "bracketing" or "disconnection,"* which is obviously not limited to that of the attempt to doubt, although it can be detached from it with special ease, but can appear *in other contexts also,* and with no less ease *independently.* In relation to every thesis and wholly uncoerced we can use this *peculiar* ἐποχή, (*epokhe*—abstention), *a certain refraining from judgment which is compatible with the unshaken and unshakable because self-evidencing conviction of Truth.* The thesis is "put out of action," bracketed, it passes off into the modified status of a "bracketed thesis," and the judgment *simpliciter* into "*bracketed judgment.*"

Naturally one should not simply identify this consciousness with that of "mere supposal," that nymphs, for instance, are dancing in a ring; for thereby *no disconnecting* of a living conviction that goes on living takes place, although from another side the close relation of the two forms of consciousness lies clear. Again, we are not concerned here with supposal in the sense of "*assuming*" or *taking for granted,* which in the equivocal speech of current usage may also be expressed in the words: "I suppose (I make the assumption) that it is so and so."

Let us add further that nothing hinders us *from speaking bracketing correlatively* also, in respect of *an objectivity to be posited,* what ever be the region or category to which it belongs. What is meant in this case is that *every thesis related to this objectivity* must be *disconnected* and changed into its bracketed counterpart. On closer view, moreover, the "bracketing" image is from the outset better suited to the sphere of the object, just as the expression "to put out of action" better suits the sphere of the Act or of Consciousness.

32. THE PHENOMENOLOGICAL ἐποχή

We can now let the universal ἐποχή, (*epokhe*—abstention) in the sharply defined and novel sense we have given to it step into the place of the Cartesian attempt at universal doubt. But on good grounds we *limit* the universality of this ἐποχή. For were it as inclusive as it is in general capable of being, then since every thesis and every judgment can be modified freely to any extent, and every objectivity that we can judge or criticize can be bracketed, no field would be left over for unmodified judgments, to say nothing of a science. But our design is just to discover a new scientific domain, such as might be won precisely *through the method of bracketing,* though only through a definitely limited form of it.

The limiting consideration can be indicated in a word.

We put out of action the general thesis which belongs to the essence of the natural standpoint, we place in brackets whatever it includes respecting the nature of Being: *this entire natural world therefore* which is continually "there for us," "present to our hand," and will ever remain there, is a "fact-world" of which we continue to be conscious, even though it pleases us to put it in brackets.

If I do this, as I am fully free to do, I do *not* then *deny* this "world," as though I were a sophist, *I do not doubt that it is there* as though I were a sceptic; but I use the "phenomenological" ἐποχή, which *completely bars me from using any judgment that concerns spatio-temporal existence* (*Dasein*).

Thus *all sciences which relate to this natural world,* though they stand never so firm to me, though they fill me with wondering admiration, though I am far from any thought of objecting to them in the least degree, *I disconnect them all, I make absolutely no use of their standards, I do not appropriate a single one of the propositions that enter into their systems, even though their evidential value is perfect, I take none of them, no one of them serves me for a foundation*—so long, that is, as it is understood, in the way these scinces themselves understand it, as a truth *concerning the realities* of this world. *I may accept it only after I have placed it in the bracket.* That means: only in the modified consciousness of the judgment as it appears in disconnexion, and *not as it figures within the science as its proposition, a proposition which claims to be valid and whose validity I recognize and make use of.*

The ἐποχή here in question will not be confined with that which positivism demands, and against which, as we were compelled to admit, it is itself an offender. We are not concerned at present with removing the preconceptions which trouble the pure positivity (*Sachlichkeit*) of research, with the constituting of a science "free from theory" and "free from metaphysics" by bringing all the grounding back to the immediate data, nor with the means of reaching such ends, concerning whose value there is indeed no question. What *we* demand lies along another line. The whole world as placed within the nature-setting and presented in experience as real, taken completely "free from all theory," just as it is in reality experienced, and made clearly manifest in and through the linkings of our experiences, has now no validity for us, it must be set in brackets, untested indeed but also uncontested. Similarly all theories and sciences, positivistic or otherwise, which relate to this world, however good they may be, succumb to the same fate.

SOLIPSISM

W. T. STACE

. . .

It is evident that, however we may wish otherwise, we cannot, if we are honest, escape the conclusion that the initial position of every mind must be solipsistic. By this I do not mean that I shall remain in the belief that I alone exist. I think on the contrary that there is very good reason to believe in the existence of other minds. That is a question which I shall discuss in Chapter VIII. But in the meanwhile I assert that each of us must *begin* from within his own consciousness. Belief in other minds is not a datum.

That I am, to start with, only aware of *my own* thoughts and experiences, appears to be self-evident. Since it is the true beginning, it is clear that it cannot be an inference from anterior data, since in that case those anterior data would themselves constitute the beginning. We cannot *prove* the solipsist position in the sense of deducing it from some other position. But we can establish it by pointing out the given facts which *constitute* the position. This we have already to a large extent done, and nothing more is necessary here except once more to summarize those facts. They are as follows.

I cannot experience anything except *my own* experience. I can see my

Reprinted, with deletions, from *The Theory of Knowledge and Existence*, 1932, pp. 66–69, 102–103, 107–108, 174–175, 186–197, by permission of the Clarendon Press, Oxford.

red, but I can never see yours. I can feel a pain in my leg. But I can never feel the pain in your leg. I can feel my emotion, but not yours. Even if your anger infects me, so that I feel it in sympathy with you, it is yet, in so far as I feel it, *my* anger, not yours. I can never be you, nor you me. I cannot see through your eyes, nor you through mine. Even if you can telepathically transfer a mental state, say an image, from your mind to mine, yet, when I become aware of it, it is then *my* image and not yours. Even if, as some think, I can directly perceive your mind, without having to infer it from your body, still this perception of your mind will then be to me *my* perception, *my* experience.

All knowledge, all philosophy, must be based upon experience. And from whose experience can I begin except from my own? Whatever belief I hold on whatever subject must be either a datum of *my* consciousness or else an inference or mental construction which *I* base upon *my* data. If I accept a scientific belief on your authority, this belief must be an inference which *I* make from the sounds (words) I hear you utter, and from *my* belief in your repute as a scientific authority. Whatever I believe rests in the end upon the data of my own consciousness. Therefore all knowledge must have had its beginning in my own self-enclosed personal experience. This original solipsism is utterly unescapable except by prejudice or by refusing to see it. Philosophers blink the fact or gloss it over. But we shall begin here and loyally accept whatever results may follow.

. . .

Our starting-point is the given, along with its special and elementary concepts. And the given means for each individual his own given. My given is not your given. Nor am I yet aware of your given or even of your existence. The existence of other minds is not itself part of the given. It is a later discovery. And therefore each mind must be, at its starting-point, completely solitary. It is aware of its colour patches, its sounds, scents, and tastes. These are its aboriginal world. They come and go like the images in a dream. It is unaware of anything else. It has no knowledge of the existence of any other mind. It has no knowledge of the existence of external objects in so far as these differ from mere presentations.

. . .

How can I possibly know that my red resembles your red, or that any sensation of mine resembles any sensation of yours? Obviously there is only one way in which it could be proved, and that would be by comparing our sensations, e.g. my red with your red. But who is to perform this act of comparison? I can never see your red and you can never see mine. And a third party who might be impartial can see neither. It is clearly the same with all our experiences. I cannot feel the pain in your leg, and whether what you call pain is in any way similar to what I call pain I have no means of knowing. There is therefore no possibility of proving the similarity of our presentations. It is not an inference which follows from any of the data with which we started. Not only is it not demonstrable. It is not even a probable conclusion. It is not an inference of any kind.

I have no positive assurance that my red is not your blue, or that what is colour to me does not make on your mind an impression similar to my impression of sound. I have no positive assurance even that our two sets of presentations are in any way commensurable. Your presentations may be wholly inconceivable to me, and such as do not exist in my universe at all. It is a common reflection that we cannot conceive a new colour, a colour unlike any colour in the spectrum. It is quite possible that the whole of your presentations are as inconceivable to me as is a new colour. Even if this is so, it would not be a bar to communication and to the establishment between us of a common world, so long as our presentations, though dissimilar in content, *correspond* in order and relations.

. . .

My red and your red exist in different universes which are absolutely cut off from one another. The consciousness of each of us is a separate world. Not only is a comparison of our experiences in fact impossible, but it is difficult even to find any self-consistent meaning which can be attached to the idea of such a comparison. It is not merely a physical impossibility for me to see your red. If that were all, the difficulty might conceivably be some day overcome by the advance of psychological science. But the difficulty is a logical one. If I could see your red, your red would have become mine and, in so far as I saw it, ceased to be yours, and therefore the conditions of the comparison would have vanished. Or to put it in another way. Suppose that I could annihilate the barriers of personality and get into your mind and see your red. Yet it is still *I* who see it. And how do I know then that the red which I see is the same as the red which you see? I cannot know this so long as I remain I. In order to know it I must cease to be I and become you. But if my personality and yours are thus fused into one, then there are no longer two experiences to compare, and no relation of resemblance can be asserted.

The difficulty of finding an intelligible meaning for our first construction is thus very great. And such a meaning *cannot* be found so long as we attempt to express it in the form of a categorical judgement. So far, the solitary mind has made only categorical judgements. It has asserted 'This is red', 'This red is like (or unlike) that red', 'Red is different from green', and so on. But as soon as the mind enters upon its career of mental constructions a new form of judgement becomes necessary to express its new insights. It has to *invent* the hypothetical judgement. Let us see how this is.

To say that any two things, even when they are both within my own experience, are similar, implies either that a comparison has been made or at least that it might be, and that *if* it were made the alleged resemblance would be seen. '*A* is like *B*' means either '*A* and *B* have been compared and found alike', or it means 'If we compared *A* and *B* we should find them alike'. An assertion of similarity is necessarily relative to a possible act of comparison. Hence 'My red is like your red' means '*If* we could compare our reds we should find them similar'.

The condition, as we have seen, is actually an impossibility. We could not conceivably compare our reds. But the mind does not boggle at this difficulty. It swallows it because it suits its purposes to do so, because unless it does so, it will never be able to build up a common world and a society of minds.

. . .

It is difficult to believe that we have any direct apprehension of other minds. If we see a man lying on his bed with glassy eyes, absolutely motionless and with expressionless face, we do not know whether he is alive or dead. We have to ascertain whether he is warm or cold, whether his heart beats, whether he breathes. It may be that he is fully conscious all the while and is pretending to be dead. If we have any power of directly apprehending other minds without regard to their bodily behaviour, how is it that we do not detect the presence of a man's mind in such a case? How is it that we may be deceived and believe that his consciousness has gone out of existence? How is it that we have to examine his body to find out the truth?

I will leave that question to be answered as best it may, and will pass on to other points of view. It is said that we possess direct knowledge of the existence of other minds. What is meant here by the 'existence of minds'? Or more briefly, what is meant by 'minds'?

The object of this question is to clear the ground by getting rid of at least one possible misconception. By the existence of minds in this context we do *not* mean the existence of a transcendental ego, of a spiritual unity, or of a 'thinking substance'. The man in the street believes that both he and his fellows possess minds. But he has no knowledge of transcendental unities or thinking substances. He has never heard of these matters. Now what we are engaged in trying to find out is not how philosophers arrive at their metaphysical conceptions of the nature of personality. What we are trying to ascertain is how ordinary men and women know that their fellows have minds. The belief in the existence of foreign minds which we are studying is the ordinary everyday belief of plain men. And this has nothing to do with metaphysical theories of personality.

When Smith says that he believes that Jones possesses a mind substantially similar to his own, what is it that he actually means? Not that Jones is a transcendental ego, but simply that Jones thinks, perceives, feels, and wills. The belief in the existence of other minds, which is the subject of our discussion, means then simply the belief that other men—and animals too—have thoughts, feelings, perceptions, and volitions. It is, in short, belief in the empirical content of minds.

It follows that the question whether we can have direct knowledge of other minds means: can we have direct knowledge that other people perceive, feel, will, and think? And I can see no difference betwen this and the further question: can we directly perceive the thoughts, feelings, volitions, and percepts of other people? And the answer to this question is axiomatic. We cannot. I cannot see your red, feel your pain, or perceive the thought in your mind. My consciousness is absolutely cut off from your consciousness, and there is no view from one to the other.

. . .

We shall be forced back, therefore, upon some form of the theory of indirect or inferential knowledge. To see how it works out, we must go back to the beginning, to the solitary mind with which we started.

The solitary mind, then, is aware of itself, i.e. of its *activities* in thinking, feeling, willing, and is also aware of the group of presentations which is afterwards identified as its body. . . . I have an immediate view, through introspection, of my own thoughts, feelings, and volitions. They are *given*. They therefore belong, just as much as do our sense-data, to the ultimate certitudes on the basis of which we build up our knowledge. It would be palpably absurd to suggest that I can only know the contents of my own consciousness indirectly by way of inference from my knowledge of yours. We are entitled, then, to take our knowledge of ourselves as a logical starting-point, as an ultimate given fact of which we are certain.

The solitary mind is also immediately aware of the presentations which make up its own body. It is not aware of its body *as* a body. For it has not yet arrived at the stage in which it knows objects or 'things'. What it has before it is not a continuously existing independent object which could be called a body, but only a series of fleeting presentations. Among these presentations, of course, are those which afterwards go to make up its own body. My present point is only that these presentations are as certainly and immediately known to the solitary mind as are its own acts of consciousness. So that the logical beginnings from which the solitary mind starts on its journey to its knowledge of other minds are twofold: (1) its knowledge of itself, i.e. of its own acts of thinking, feeling, willing, &c.; and (2) its perception of those presentations which it afterwards separates out from other presentations and builds up into the object which it knows as its own body.

The next necessary step is the gathering together of these latter presentations into a single group and the association of this group with the consciousness of the solitary mind. There are, strictly speaking, two steps here, but they may be taken together. For the gathering of the presentations into a group and the association of that group with the mind both arise out of one and the same experience.

It will be clear to the reader that the grouping together of the presentations and their association with a mind are not originally given. We do not start with them. We have somehow to arrive at them. For the association of my body with my mind, or in other words the discovery that my hands and feet belong to me, and are not mere indifferent parts of the landscape, is not originally given. In the logical beginning my hand is merely a pinkish colour patch among all the others. If there happens to lie adjacent to it among my presentations a green patch which is actually a tree, there is no more reason for supposing that the pinkish patch is part of me or has any special connexion with me, than for supposing that the green patch is part of, or has a special connexion with, me. Thus in the beginning I am not aware of the existence of my body at all. The presentations which compose it are merely a portion of the general world of phantasms with which I am surrounded.

I become aware of my body in the end chiefly because it insists on accompanying me wherever I go. There is a group of presentations which I can never get rid of. It accompanies me about as a group, and so becomes associated in my mind with myself, i.e. with my thinking, feeling, willing self. It is true that when the light is turned out I can no longer see my hand. But I can touch it. Or, if that language is too advanced for the stage of the solitary mind, we should rather say that when the light is extinguished I have a tactile sensation which I soon come to associate with the visual sensation which has disappeared. It is true again that a local anaesthetic will destroy the sense of touch in the part affected. But I can still see the part (or, I still have an associated visual sensation). So that in spite of temporary and partial obliterations of some of the presentations of the group, it is still true that on the whole this group of presentations accompanies me about wherever I go in a manner which is not characteristic of other groups. The group of presentations which composes yonder tree, even though it grows opposite my study window, is a comparatively rare visitor to my life. It visits me only for a few hours each day, and it has only done so for the last two years since I came to live in this house. I never saw it before that. It is the same with all groups of presentations except the group which is my body. They are all temporary and infrequent visitors. My body is simply that portion of my presentations which forces itself always upon me.

Taking my body as a whole, moreover, it does not change its size as I move about, whereas everything else does. As I walk forwards, what is in front of me increases in magnitude as it draws nearer; while at the same time everything behind me dwindles as it recedes. My body alone remains roughly constant. It is true that my hands and feet vary in size slightly according as I bring them nearer to my eyes or push them away. But this variation is small and is rigidly confined within certain narrow limits. My hand never vanishes altogether in the remote blue sky as does the dwindling speck of a sky-lark. It is still true to say, in spite of minor variations, that the size of my body remains roughly constant whatever movements take place relatively between it and surrounding objects. This fact also helps to pick out from among all others the group of presentations which make up my body.

There is also another set of facts which assists in the process of picking out the presentations which compose my body and setting them apart as unique. When a pin is pushed into my leg I feel pain. When my leg is stroked I feel a sensation which I may account pleasurable. But when a pin is pushed into a tree I do not feel any pain. Nor do I receive any pleasurable sensation when the tree is stroked.

For these reasons, then, the various visual, tactile, and other presentations concerned first become thought of as a group instead of singly; and then this group becomes associated in my mind with *me* as a thinking, feeling being. It becomes 'my' body. I regularly associate the presence of the group of presentations with the presence of a mind, namely my own.

The next step is that I come to notice that there exist many groups of presentations which resemble the one which is my body. It is true that your body is unlike mine in the characteristics of which we have just been speaking. Your body does not accompany me about. It does not retain the same size whatever my movements relative to outside objects. I do not feel pain if a pin is stuck into it. But I can recognize it as like my body owing to its shape and colour, its general appearance and contour, its characteristic movements and postures, its special methods of behaviour, the sounds or cries which issue from it, and so on. These marks suffice to enable me to recognize the groups of presentations which are other people's bodies as similar to, and in the same class with, the group of presentations which is my own body.

It has been urged that primitive man, not having seen himself in a mirror, does not know the general appearance even of his own body, and therefore could not recognize other bodies as similar to it. It does not seem worth replying in detail to such a saltless argument, but I mention it since it has been put forward with apparent seriousness.* Apart from the existence of pools of water and other natural mirrors, it is surely obvious that we can see the whole of our bodies except our heads and back, and can explore our heads with our hands; and that in one way and another we should, even without mirrors, come to know our general appearance and its resemblance to the appearances of other persons. Will it be seriously contended that before the invention of mirrors every man went about quite unaware that his appearance resembled that of his fellows?

From this point the inference to the existence of other minds is quite simple, and proceeds much upon the well-known lines. The group of presentations which is my body is associated with my mind; and I come to think that its movements, gestures, and behaviour generally are caused by special kinds of mental content. When I am angry I hit out. In great pain I cry out. When I am frightened I sometimes run, sometimes turn pale and stand stock still. If I know a snake in my path to be poisonous, I

* For example, by Mr. C. C. J. Webb in the paper on 'Our Knowledge of One Another'.

make a detour to avoid it, or I pick up a stick and kill it. If I am amused I produce from my throat the peculiar kind of noise known as laughter. Now I also perceive around me other groups of presentations almost exactly like the one which I associate with my own mind. These groups behave in the same way as does mine. They laugh, cry out, run, smile, avoid snakes. Their general similarity of shape and colour, and their more remarkable similarities of behaviour suggest to me by analogy that with them are associated minds like mine, and that their behaviour is caused by fear, anger, amusement, knowledge–in general by a consciousness such as I myself possess. The inference to the existence of other minds is then complete.

The only way in which this differs from the usual form of the argument is that instead of bodies I have spoken of groups of presentations. For it must be remembered that we are still, when the argument begins, in the world of the solitary mind, and that in that world there are no permanent 'things', but only fleeting presentations. My body at that stage is no more than a group of such presentations. They go out of existence from time to time when I cease to be aware of them. But this will not prevent my recognizing the group as a group, and recognizing the similarities between groups on which the argument to the existence of other minds depends. For such recognition nothing more than the concepts of the given are required; and the concepts of the given are all within the reach of the solitary mind.

The ordinary form of the argument which bases it, not on groups of presentations, but on bodies conceived presumably in the ordinary way as permanent and independent objects, is in this respect faulty. For the recognition of a body as a permanent independent thing, as existing for example when no one is aware of it, is itself dependent, as we have abundantly shown, upon our knowledge of the existence of other minds. And therefore our knowledge of other minds cannot be an inference from our knowledge of permanent bodies. But it can be, and is, an inference from groups of presentations such as can be recognized by the solitary mind. The knowledge of other minds is logically prior to the knowledge of 'things'. Therefore the knowledge of other minds cannot be deduced from "things". But knowledge of other minds is not logically prior to presentations, since the latter are logical ultimates or givens. Therefore presentations may be used as premisses of the argument.

Of course these subtleties are necessary only to preserve the strict logical sequence. The logical order is as we have laid it down. Even if we assume that the actual or psychological development of our ideas has been moulded by logic, by the very argument which we have just been examining, still it is not of course necessary to think that the mind has actually followed out the argument in all these refinements. Whatever is the logical order, knowledge of the external world of things and knowledge of the existence of other minds have no doubt actually grown up together. If these facts are remembered and understood, there will be no necessity for us to continue to speak, with clumsy pedantry, of 'groups of presentations' instead of 'bodies'. We may for shortness equate our argument with the usual argument based simply upon the body and its behaviour.

. . .

It has to be admitted, of course, that the argument from bodily behaviour—the only genuinely logical argument which exists—does not yield certainty, but gives only a probable conclusion. This, as is well known, is true of all analogical reasoning. There is no means by which I can be absolutely *certain* that any mind exists except my own. It is *possible* that in addressing this book to my readers I am the victim of a complete delusion in supposing that they exist as conscious minds. It is possible that the whole universe is a dream of mine, and that all the other people in it are dream people. The contrary of this cannot be proved with absolute certainty. The argument by analogy from bodily behaviour goes as far as is possible towards proving the real existence of other minds. But it is a probable conclusion only.

But what of it? On the probable evidence before me I am prepared to believe. I am prepared to build up my universe on this basis. And one must remember that not only analogical, but all inductive reasoning, leads only to probability. After all, it is only probable that the sun will rise tomorrow. Yet no one ever lost a night's sleep over the uncertainty.

. . .

KNOWLEDGE OF OTHER MINDS

NORMAN MALCOLM

I

I believe that the argument from analogy for the existence of other minds still enjoys more credit than it deserves, and my first aim in this paper will be to show that it leads nowhere. J. S. Mill is one of many who have accepted the argument and I take his statement of it as representative. He puts to himself the question, "By what evidence do I know, or by what considerations am I led to believe, that there exist other sentient creatures; that the walking and speaking figures which I see and hear, have sensations and thoughts, or in other words, possess Minds?" His answer is the following:

Reprinted from the *Journal of Philosophy*, Vol. LV (1958), pp. 969–978 by permission of the author and editor and from *Knowledge and Certainty: Essays and Lectures*, © 1963 by permission of Prentice-Hall, Inc., Englewood Cliffs, N.J.

I conclude that other human beings have feelings like me, because, first, they have bodies like me, which I know, in my own case, to be the antecedent condition of feelings; and because, secondly, they exhibit the acts, and other outward signs, which in my own case I know by experience to be caused by feelings. I am conscious in myself of a series of facts connected by an uniform sequence, of which the beginning is modifications of my body, the middle is feelings, the end is outward demeanor. In the case of other human beings I have the evidence of my senses for the first and last links of the series, but not for the intermediate link. I find, however, that the sequence between the first and last is as regular and constant in those other cases as it is in mine. In my own case I know that the first link produces the last through the intermediate link, and could not produce it without. Experience, therefore, obliges me to conclude that there must be an intermediate link; which must either be the same in others as in myself, or a different one: I must either believe them to be alive, or to be automatons: and by believing them to be alive, that is, by supposing the link to be of the same nature as in the case of which I have experience, and which is in all other respects similar, I bring other human beings, as phenomena, under the same generalizations which I know by experience to be the true theory of my own existence.*

I shall pass by the possible objection that this would be very *weak* inductive reasoning, based as it is on the observation of a single instance. More interesting is the following point: Suppose this reasoning could yield a conclusion of the sort "It is probable that that human figure" (pointing at some person other than oneself) "has thoughts and feelings." Then there is a question as to whether this conclusion can *mean* anything to the philosopher who draws it, because there is a question as to whether the sentence "That human figure has thoughts and feelings" can mean anything to him. Why should this be a question? Because the assumption from which Mill starts is that he has *no criterion* for determining whether another "walking and speaking figure" does or does not have thoughts and feelings. If he had a criterion he could apply it, establishing with certainty that this or that human figure does or does not have feelings (for the only plausible criterion would lie in behavior and circumstances that are open to view), and there would be no call to resort to tenuous analogical reasoning that yields at best a probability. If Mill has no criterion for the existence of feelings other than his own then in that sense he does not understand the sentence "That human figure has feelings" and therefore does not understand the sentence "It is *probable* that that human figure has feelings."

There is a familiar inclination to make the following reply: "Although I have no criterion of verification still I *understand*, for example, the sentence 'He has a pain.' For I understand the meaning of 'I have a pain,' and 'He has a pain' means that he has the *same* thing I have when I have a pain." But this is a fruitless maneuver. If I do not know how to establish that someone has a pain then I do not know how to establish that he has the *same* as I have when I have a pain.** You cannot improve my under-

* J. S. Mill, *An Examination of Sir William Hamilton's Philosophy*, 6th edition (New York: Longmans, Green & Co., Inc. 1889), pp. 243–244.

** "It is no explanation to say: the supposition that he has a pain is simply the supposition that he has the same as I. For *that* part of the grammar is quite clear to

standing of "He has a pain" by this recourse to the notion of "the same," unless you give me a criterion for saying that someone *has* the same as I have. If you can do this you will have no use for the argument from analogy: and if you cannot then you do not understand the supposed conclusion of that argument. A philosopher who purports to rely on the analogical argument cannot, I think, escape this dilemma.

There have been various attempts to repair the argument from analogy. Mr. Stuart Hampshire has argued* that its validity as a method of inference can be established in the following way: Others sometimes infer that I am feeling giddy from my behavior. Now I have direct, non-inferential knowledge, says Hampshire, of my own feelings. So I can check inferences made about me against the facts, checking thereby the accuracy of the "methods" of inference.

> All that is required for testing the validity of any method of factual inference is that each one of us should sometimes be in a position to confront the conclusions of the doubtful method of inference with what is known by him to be true independently of the method of inference in question. Each one of us is certainly in this position in respect of our common methods of inference about the feelings of persons other than ourselves, in virtue of the fact that each one of us is constantly able to compare the results of this type of inference with what he knows to be true directly and non-inferentially; each one of us is in the position to make this testing comparison, whenever he is the designated subject of a statement about feelings and sensations. I, Hampshire, know by what sort of signs I may be misled in inferring Jones' and Smith's feelings, because I have implicitly noticed (though probably not formulated) where Jones, Smith and others generally go wrong in inferring my feelings. [*Op. cit.*, pp. 4–5.]

Presumably I can also note when the inferences of others about my feelings do not go wrong. Having ascertained the reliability of some inference-procedures I can use them myself, in a guarded way, to draw conclusions about the feelings of others, with a modest but justified confidence in the truth of those conclusions.

My first comment is that Hampshire has apparently forgotten the purpose of the argument from analogy, which is to provide some probability that "the walking and speaking figures which I see and hear, have sensations and thoughts" (Mill). For the reasoning that he describes involves the assumption that other human figures *do* have thoughts and sensations: for they are assumed to *make inferences* about me from *observations* of my behavior. But the philsophical problem of the existence of other minds *is* the problem of whether human figures other than oneself do, among other things, make observations, inferences, and assertions. Hampshire's supposed defense of the argument from analogy is an *ignoratio elenchi.*

If we struck from the reasoning described by Hampshire all assumption

---

me: that is, that one will say that the stove has the same experience as I, *if* one says: it is in pain and I am in pain" (Ludwig Wittgenstein, *Philosophical Investigations* (New York: The Macmillan Company, 1953), § 350).

* "The Analogy of Feeling," *Mind*, January, 1952, pp. 1–12.

of thoughts and sensations in others we should be left with something roughly like this: "When my behavior is such and such there come from nearby human figures the sounds 'He feels giddy.' And generally I do feel giddy at the time. Therefore when another human figure exhibits the same behavior and I say 'He feels giddy,' it is probable that he does feel giddy." But the reference here to the sentence-like sounds coming from other human bodies is irrelevant, since I must not assume that those sounds express inferences. Thus the reasoning becomes simply the classical argument from analogy: "When my behavior is such and such I feel giddy; so probably when another human figure behaves the same way he feels the same way." This argument, again, is caught in the dilemma about the criterion of the *same*.

The version of analogical reasoning offered by Professor H. H. Price* is more interesting. He suggests that "one's evidence for the existence of other minds is derived primarily from the understanding of language" (p. 429). His idea is that if another body gives forth noises one understands, like "There's the bus," and if these noises give one new information, this "provides some evidence that the foreign body which uttered the noises is animated by a mind like one's own. . . . Suppose I am often in its neighborhood, and it repeatedly produces utterances which I can understand, and which I then proceed to verify for myself. And suppose that this happens in many different kinds of situation. I think that my evidence for believing that this body is animated by a mind like my own would then become very strong" (p. 430). The body from which these informative sounds proceed need not be a human body. "If the rustling of the leaves of an oak formed intelligible words conveying new information to me, and if gorse-bushes made intelligible gestures, I should have evidence that the oak or the gorse-bush was animated by an intelligence like my own" (p. 436). Even if the intelligible and informative sounds did not proceed from a body they would provide evidence for the existence of a (disembodied) mind (p. 435).

Although differing sharply from the classical analogical argument, the reasoning presented by Price is still analogical in form: I know by introspection that when certain combinations of sounds come from me they are "symbols in acts of spontaneous thinking"; therefore similar combinations of sounds, not produced by me, "probably function as instruments to an act of spontaneous thinking, which in this case is not my own" (p. 446). Price says that the reasoning also provides an *explanation* of the otherwise mysterious occurrence of sounds which I understand but did not produce. He anticipates the objection that the hypothesis is nonsensical because unverifiable. "The hypothesis is a perfectly conceivable one," he says, "in the sense that I know very well what the world would have to be like if the hypothesis were true—what sorts of entities there must be in it, and what sorts of events must occur in them. I know from introspection what acts of thinking and perceiving are, and I

* "Our Evidence for the Existence of Other Minds," *Philosophy*, Vol. 13, 1938, pp. 425–456.

know what it is for such acts to be combined into the unity of a single mind . . ." (pp. 446–447).

I wish to argue against Price that no amount of intelligible sounds coming from an oak tree or a kitchen table could create any probability that it has sensations and thoughts. The question to be asked is: What would show that a tree or table *understands* the sounds that come from it? We can imagine that useful warnings, true descriptions and predictions, even "replies" to questions, should emanate from a tree, so that it came to be of enormous value to its owner. How should we establish that it understood those sentences? Should we "question" it? Suppose that the tree "said" that there was a vixen in the neighborhood, and we "asked" it "what is a vixen?," and it "replied," "A vixen is a female fox." It might go on to do as well for "female" and "fox." This performance might incline us to say that the tree understood the words, in contrast to the possible case in which it answered "I don't know" or did not answer at all. But would it show that the tree understood the words in the same sense that a person could understand them? With a person such a performance would create a presumption that he could make correct *applications* of the word in question: but not so with a tree. To see this point think of the normal teaching of words (e.g., "spoon," "dog," "red") to a child and how one decides whether he understands them. At a primitive stage of teaching one does not require or expect definitions, but rather that the child should *pick out* reds from blues, dogs from cats, spoons from forks. This involves his looking, pointing, reaching for and going to the right things and not the wrong ones. That a child says "red" when a red thing and "blue" when a blue thing is put before him, is indicative of a mastery of those words *only* in conjunction with the other activities of looking, pointing, trying to get, fetching and carrying. Try to suppose that he says the right words but looks at and reaches for the wrong things. Should we be tempted to say that he has mastered the use of those words? No, indeed. The disparity between words and behavior would make us say that he does not understand the words. In the case of a tree there could be no disparity between its words and its "behavior" because it is logically incapable of behavior of the relevant kind.

Since it has nothing like the human face and body it makes no sense to say of a tree, or an electronic computer, that it is looking or pointing at or fetching something. (Of course one can always *invent* a sense for these expressions.) Therefore it would make no sense to say that it did or did not understand the above words. Trees and computers cannot either pass or fail the tests that a child is put through. They cannot even take them. That an object was a source of intelligible sounds or other signs (no matter how sequential) would not be enough by itself to establish that it had thoughts or sensations. How informative sentences and valuable predictions could emanate from a gorse-bush might be a grave scientific problem, but the explanation could never be that the gorse-bush has a mind. Better no explanation than nonsense!

It might be thought that the above difficulty holds only for words whose meaning has a "perceptual content" and that if we imagined, for example, that our gorse-bush produced nothing but pure mathematical propositions we should be justified in attributing thought to it, although not sensation. But suppose there was a remarkable "calculating boy" who could give right answers to arithmetical problems but could not apply numerals to reality in empirical propositions, i.e., he could not *count* any objects. I believe that everyone would be reluctant to say that he *understood* the mathematical signs and truths that he produced. If he could count in the normal way there would not be this reluctance. And "counting in the normal way" involves looking, pointing, reaching, fetching, and so on. That is, it requires the human face and body, and human behavior—or something similar. Things which do not have the human form, or anything like it, not merely do not but *cannot* satisfy the criteria for thinking. I am trying to bring out part of what Wittgenstein meant when he said, "We only say of a human being and what is like one that it thinks" (*Investigations*, §360), and "The human body is the best picture of the human soul" (*ibid.*, p. 178).

I have not yet gone into the most fundamental error of the argument from analogy. It is present whether the argument is the classical one (the analogy between my body and other bodies) or Price's version (the analogy between my language and the noises and signs produced by other things). It is the mistaken assumption that *one learns from one's own case* what thinking, feeling, sensation are. Price gives expression to this assumption when he says: "I know from introspection what acts of thinking and perceiving are . . ." (*op. cit.*, p. 447). It is the most natural assumption for a philosopher to make and indeed seems at first to be the only possibility. Yet Wittgenstein has made us see that it leads first to solipsism and then to nonsense. I shall try to state as briefly as possible how it produces those results.

A philosopher who believes that one must learn what thinking, fear, or pain is "from one's own case," does not believe that the thing to be observed is one's behavior, but rather something "inward." He considers behavior to be related to the inward states and occurrences merely as an acompaniment or possibly an effect. He cannot regard behavior as a *criterion* of psychological phenomena: for if he did he would have no use for the analogical argument (as was said before) and also the priority given to "one's own case" would be pointless. He believes that he notes something in himself that he calls "thinking" or "fear" or "pain," and then he tries to infer the presence of the *same* in others. He should then deal with the question of what his criterion of the *same* in others is. This he cannot do because it is of the essence of his viewpoint to reject circumstances and behavior as a criterion of mental phenomena in others. And what else could serve as a criterion? He ought, therefore, to draw the conclusion that the notion of thinking, fear, or pain in others is in an important sense meaningless. He has no idea of what would count for or against it.* "That there should be thinking or pain other than my own is unintelligible," he ought to hold. This would be a rigorous solipsism, and a correct outcome of the assumption that one can know only from one's own case what the mental phenomena are. An equivalent way of putting it would be: "When I say 'I am in pain,' by 'pain' I mean a certain inward state. When I say '*He* is in pain,' by 'pain' I mean *behavior*. I cannot attribute pain to others *in the same sense* that I attribute it to myself."

Some philosophers before Wittgenstein may have seen the solipsistic result of starting from "one's own case." But I believe he is the first to have shown how that starting point destroys itself. This may be presented as follows: One supposes that one inwardly picks out something as thinking or pain and thereafter identifies it whenever it presents itself in the soul. But the question to be pressed is, Does one make *correct* identifications? The proponent of these "private" identifications has nothing to say here. He feels sure that he identifies correctly the occurrences in his soul; but feeling sure is no guarantee of being right. Indeed he has no idea of what being *right* could mean. He does not know how to distinguish between actually making correct identifications and being under the impression that he does. (See *Investigations*, §258–9.) Suppose that he identified the emotion of anxiety as the sensation of pain? Neither he nor anyone else could know about this "mistake." Perhaps he makes a mistake *every* time! Perhaps all of us do! We ought to see now that we are talking nonsense. We do not know what a *mistake* would be. We have no standard, no examples, no customary practice, with which to compare our inner recognitions. The inward identification cannot hit the bull's-eye, or miss it either, because there is no bull's-eye. When we see that the ideas of correct and incorrect have no application to the supposed inner identification, the latter notion loses its appearance of sense. Its collapse brings down both solipsism and the argument from analogy.

II

This destruction of the argument from analogy also destroys the *problem* for which it was supposed to provide a solution. A philosopher feels himself in a difficulty about other minds because he assumes that first of all he is acquainted with mental phenomena "from his own case." What troubles him is how to make the transition from his own case to the case of others. When his thinking is freed of the illusion of the priority of his own case, then he is able to look at the familiar facts and to acknowledge that the circumstances, behavior, and utterances of others actually are his *criteria* (not merely his evidence) for the existence of their mental states. Previously this had seemed impossible.

But now he is in danger of flying to the opposite extreme of behav-

* One reason why philosophers have not commonly drawn this conclusion may be, as Wittgenstein acutely suggests, that they assume that they have "an infallible paradigm of identity in the identity of a thing with itself" (*Investigations*, §215).

iorism, which errs by believing that through observation of one's own circumstances, behavior, and utterances one can find out that one is thinking or angry. The philosophy of "from one's own case" and behaviorism, though in a sense opposites, make the common assumption that the first-person, present-tense psychological statements are verified by self-observation. According to the "one's own case" philosophy the self-observation cannot be checked by others; according to behaviorism the self-observation would be by means of outward criteria that are available to all. The first position becomes unintelligible; the second is false for at least many kinds of psychological statements. We are forced to conclude that the first-person psychological statements are not (or hardly ever) verified by self-observation. It follows that they have no verification at all; for if they had a verification it would have to be by self-observation.

But if sentences like "My head aches" or "I wonder where she is" do not express observations then what do they do? What is the relation between my declaration that my head aches and the fact that my head aches, if the former is not the report of an observation? The perplexity about the existence of *other* minds has, as the result of criticism, turned into a perplexity about the meaning of one's own psychological sentences about oneself. At our starting point it was the sentence "*His* head aches" that posed a problem; but now it is the sentence "*My* head aches" that puzzles us.

One way in which this problem can be put is by the question, "How does *one know when to say* the words 'My head aches'?" The inclination to ask this question can be made acute by imagining a fantastic but not impossible case of a person who has survived to adult years without ever experiencing pain. He is given various sorts of injections to correct this condition, and on receiving one of these one day, he jumps and exclaims, "Now I feel pain!" One wants to ask, "How did he *recognize* the new sensation as a *pain?*"

Let us note that if the man gives an answer (e.g., "I knew it must be pain because of the way I jumped") then he proves by that very fact that he has not mastered the correct use of the words "I feel pain." They cannot be used to state a *conclusion.* In telling us *how* he did it he will convict himself of a misuse. Therefore the question "How did he recognize his sensation?" requests the impossible. The inclination to ask it is evidence of our inability to grasp the fact that the use of this psychological sentence has nothing to do with recognizing or identifying or observing a state of oneself.

The fact that this imagined case produces an especially strong temptation to ask the "How?" question shows that we have the idea that it must be more difficult to give the right name of one's sensation *the first time.* The implication would be that it is not so difficult *after* the first time. Why should this be? Are we thinking that then the man would have a paradigm of pain with which he could compare his sensations and so be in a position to know right off whether a certain sensation was or was not a pain? But the paradigm would be either something "outer" (behavior) or something "inner" (perhaps a memory impression of the sensation). If the former then he is misusing the first-person sentence. If the latter then the question of whether he compared *correctly* the present sensation with the inner paradigm of pain would be without sense. Thus the idea that the use of the first-person sentences can be governed by paradigms must be abandoned. It is another form of our insistent misconception of the first-person sentence as resting somehow on the identification of a psychological state.

These absurdities prove that we must conceive of the first-person psychological sentences in some entirely different light. Wittgenstein presents us with the suggestion (to which philosophers have not been sufficiently attentive) that the first-person sentences are to be thought of as similar to the natural non-verbal, behavioral expressions of psychological states. "My leg hurts," for example, is to be assimilated to crying, limping, holding one's leg. This is a bewildering comparison and one's first thought is that two sorts of things could not be more unlike. By saying the sentence one can make a *statement;* it has a *contradictory;* it is *true* or *false;* in saying it one *lies* or *tells the truth;* and so on. None of these things, exactly, can be said of crying, limping, holding one's leg. So how can there be any resemblance? But Wittgenstein knew this when he deliberately likened such a sentence to "the primitive, the natural, expressions" of pain, and said that it is "new pain-behavior" (*ibid.*, §244). Although my limits prevent my attempting it here, I think this analogy ought to be explored. For it has at least two important merits: first, it breaks the hold on us of the question "How does one *know when to say* 'My leg hurts'?" for in the light of the analogy this will be as nonsensical as the question "How does one know when to cry, limp, or hold one's leg?"; second, it explains how the utterance of a first-person psychological sentence by another person can have *importance* for us, although not as an identification—for in the light of the analogy it will have the same importance as the natural behavior which serves as our pre-verbal criterion of the psychological states of others.

Further Readings

Aune, Bruce, "The Problem of Other Minds," *Philosophical Review, 70* (1961).

Austin, J. L., "Other Minds," *Proceedings of the Aristotelian Society, Supplementary Vol. 20* (1946).

Ayer, A. J., "Can There Be a Private Language," *PASS, 28* (1954), also in Ayer, *The Concept of a Person and Other Essays*, Macmillan, London, 1963.

Ayer, A. J., "The Concept of a Person," in *The Concept of a Person and Other Essays*, Macmillan, London, 1963.

Ayer, A. J., "Our Knowledge of Other Minds," *Theoria* 1953, also in Ayer, *Philosophical Essays*, Macmillan, London, 1954, and in Gustafson.

Broad, C. D., *The Mind and Its Place in Nature*, Routledge & Kegan Paul, London, 1925, chaps. 6, 13, 14.

Broad, C. D., "Personal Identity and Survival," *Society for Psychical Research*, Society for London, 1958.

Butler, Joseph, Dissertation "Of Personal Identity," Appendix to *The Analogy of Religion*, Oxford University Press, Fair Lawn, N.J., 1896, vol. I.

Feigl, H., "Other Minds and the Ego-Centric Predicament," *Journal of Philosophy, 55* (1958).

Frondizi, R., "On the Nature of the Self," *Review of Metaphysics, 3* (1950).

Gallie, I., "Is the Self a Substance?" *Mind, 45* (1936).

Grice, H. P., "Personal Identity," *Mind, 50* (1941).

Gustafson, D. F. (ed.), *Essays in Philosophical Psychology*, Doubleday, Garden City, N.Y., 1964.

Hampshire, S., "The Analogy of Feeling," *Mind, 61* (1952).

Husserl, Edmund, *Cartesian Meditions*, Martinus Nijhoff, Hague, 1960.

Husserl, Edmund, *The Idea of Phenomenology*, Martinus Nijhoff, Hague, 1964.

James, William, *Principles of Psychology*, Holt, Rinehart & Winston, New York, 1890, vol. I, chaps. 9, 10.

Kant, Immanuel, *Critique of Pure Reason*, translated by Norman Kemp Smith, St. Martins, N.J., 1965, pp. 328–385. Macmillan, London.

Laird, John, *Problems of the Self*, Macmillan, London, 1917.

Lauer, Quentin, *Phenomenology*, Harper & Row, New York, 1965.

Locke, John, *An Essay Concerning Human Understanding*, Book II, Chapter 27, "Of Identity and Diversity."

Malcolm, Norman, "Wittgenstein's *Philosophical Investigations*," *Philosophical Review, 63* (1954), also in Chappell, *Philosophy of Mind*.

Malcolm, Norman, "The Privacy of Experience," A. Stroll (ed.), *Epistemology: New Essays*, Harper & Row, New York, 1967.

Martin, C. B., *Religious Belief*, Cornell University Press, Ithaca, N.Y., 1959, see chapter 6 "Life After Death."

Mellor, W. W., "Three Problems About Other Minds," *Mind, 56* (1956).

Merleau-Ponty, Maurice, *The Primacy of Perception*, Northern University Press, Evanston, Ill., 1964.

Mill, John Stuart, *An Examination of Sir William Hamilton's Philosophy*, Longmans, London, 1872, chap. 12.

Natanson, M., "The Empirical and Transcendental Ego," *For Roman Ingarden*, Martinus Nijhoff, Hague, 1949.

Paton, H. J., "The Idea of the Self," *University of California Publications in Philosophy, 8* (1926).

Paton, H. J., "Self-Identity," *In Defense of Reason*, Hutchinson, London, 1951.

Penelhum, Terrence, "Hume on Personal Identity," *Philosophical Review, 64* (1955).

Pitcher, George, *The Philosophy of Wittgenstein*, Prentice-Hall, N.J., 1964.

Pitcher, George, (ed.), Wittgenstein: *The Philosophical Investigation*, Doubleday, New York, 1966.

Price, H. H., "Our Evidence for the Existence of Other Minds," *Philosophy, 13* (1958).

Price, H. H., "Personal Identity and Survival," Society for Psychical Research, 1958.

Putnam, H., "Robots: Machines or Artificially Created Life," *Journal of Philosophy, 61* (1964), also in Hampshire *Philosophy of Mind*, Harper & Row, New York, 1966.

Reid, Thomas, *Essays on the Intellectual Powers of Man*, ed. and abridged by A. D. Woozley, Macmillan, London, 1941, Essays III and VI.

Sartre, Jean-Paul, *The Transcendence of the Ego*, Noonday Press, New York, 1957.

Shoemaker, Sidney, "Personal Identity and Memory," *Journal of Philosophy*, *56* (1959).

Shoemaker, Sidney, *Self-Knowledge and Self-Identity*, Cornell University Press, Ithaca, N.Y., 1963.

Stace, W. T., *Mysticism and Philosophy*, Lippincott, Philadelphia, 1960. Chapter entitled "The Problem of Objective Reference" reprinted in the present text in Section X, "God and Religious Belief."

Strawson, P. F., "Critical Notice of Wittgenstein's *Philosophical Investigations*," *Mind*, *63* (1954).

Strawson, P. F., *Individuals: An Essay in Descriptive Metaphysics*, Methuen, London, 1959, Chapter 3 "Persons."

Strawson, P. F., "Persons," in *Minnesota Studies in The Philosophy of Science*, Vol. II (eds.) Herbert Feigl, *et al.*, University of Minnesota Press, Minneapolis, 1958, also in Chappell and Gustafson.

Taylor, Richard, "The Stream of Thoughts *Versus* Mental Acts," *Philosophical Quarterly*, *13* (1963).

Tennant, F. R., *Philosophical Theology*, Cambridge University Press, London, 1930, vol. I, chaps. I, II.

Thomson, J. F., "The Argument from Analogy and our Knowledge of Other Minds," *Mind*, *60* (1951).

Wisdom, John, *Other Minds*, Blackwell, Oxford, 1952.

Wittgenstein, Ludwig, *The Blue and Brown Books*, Blackwell, Oxford, 1958, pp. 46–74.

Wittgenstein, Ludwig, *Philosophical Investigations*, Blackwell, Oxford, 1953, pp. 88e–104e.

(In addition to the preceding selections, see those listed under "Bodies, Minds, and Persons.")

III

DETERMINISM, FREEDOM, AND RESPONSIBILITY

CONSIDER an important decision you have had to make. You reflected at length, weighing each alternative in the light of considerations you believed to be relevant. You clearly felt the decision to be yours, one that *you* had to make. The alternatives were before you, and you were able to choose either one. After assessing reasons pro and con, you made your choice in full awareness of what you were doing, and you were prepared to take many of the consequences of this decision. For example, suppose someone charged you with having acted immorally on the grounds that your decision hurt a particular person. Then, assuming you had known beforehand that it would hurt the person, you would not say things like "It wasn't in my power to do anything else" or "It wasn't up to me." At any rate, should you say such things, you would not feel completely honest. You may try to excuse yourself in *other* ways, e.g., you may say that you had to hurt that person to spare the feelings of others. Or you may admit that you were wrong and even feel remorse, knowing quite well that you could have decided otherwise. You would, in short, accept responsibility for your decision.

It would be foolish to suggest that the above is an accurate description of all or even most cases of decision-making. But if you are prepared to accept this account for at least some of your decisions, then, like all or almost all human beings, you believe in "free will." (Some philosophers prefer to say that it is the decision, or the man who makes the decision, that is free.)

We may call this belief unreflective because it has not been tested in the light of various considerations philosophers have brought to bear. We shall reflect on this belief.

1

Let us consider a position called *determinism*. It is the belief that *all* events are governed by laws. (*Indeterminism,* on the other hand, is the belief that at least some events are *not* governed by laws.) The kind of law the determinist has in mind is not the kind of law passed by a legislature; it is rather a statement of the conditions under which events of a certain kind invariably occur. It can be formulated as follows: Whenever conditions of kind C obtain, then an event of kind E will occur. (There are also weaker laws called "statistical laws" which state that under conditions of kind C, an event of kind E will *probably* occur. The determinist is not interested in these. He claims that we can find laws which tell us what will *always* happen under certain conditions, not just what will *probably* happen.

Thus, for every event E that occurs, the determinist believes that there is a set of conditions C which determined or caused E to happen. Given the occurrence of C, the subsequent occurrence of E was inevitable. Likewise, the occurrence of C was determined by a set of conditions antecedent to it, and so on ad infinitum. That is, every event is determined by some law.

We do not know a good many of the laws that actually govern phenomena. It is the task of the scientist to discover them, and he often succeeds at this task. We are most familiar with the laws governing the behavior of nonliving things, but we are learning more and more about those governing the behavior of living things, including human beings.

We certainly do not know that determinism is true since we have not yet discovered the laws governing many phenomena. Determinists would say that the continued success of science is some ground for believing that laws govern all events, even if a shortage of time, intelligence, or effort, results in ultimate failure of the attempt to discover all those laws. Some philosophers would reply that the goal is so far from attainment in psychology and the social sciences that even if the belief in determinism is justified in the physical sphere, it is not justified in the human sphere.

The determinist says, however, that whether we have found them or not there are laws governing human actions and decisions. They might be one of three kinds:

(i) The laws may be what are called *genetic laws*, in which the conditions determining the decision are earlier events, experiences, reactions, and, possibly, earlier biological states and occurrences.

(ii) The laws might be what are called *structural laws*, in which the conditions for the decision involve some present psychological trait of the person making the decision. The conditions might include his desires, beliefs, character traits, personality traits, and goals.

(iii) The laws might be *physiological laws*, in which the conditions determining the decision might be complicated neurological or glandular states. Given such laws (if there are any), a physiologist could predict a man's decision from information about certain states of his body. His decision would not have been determined by his beliefs and desires (unless, of course, a man's beliefs and desires are just states of his body.)

We do not know if there are laws of any or all of these sorts governing every human decision and action. The determinist is one who believes there are. For a statement of determinism and some of its consequences see John Hospers, "What Means This Freedom?"

II

In the previous part we referred to the unreflective belief in free will, held by all, or almost all, men. We then discussed the philosophical belief in determinism, the view that all events (including human actions and decisions) are governed by laws. What is the relation betwen these beliefs? Do they conflict, or do they complement each other? Or are they totally independent of each other? Different answers which philosophers have proposed include the following:

A. *Incompatibilism.* According to this view, free will and determinism are incompatible. Philosophers who accept this position hold one of two views.
  (a) They accept determinism, that is, they believe that there is no such thing as free will. (Hospers, "What Means This Freedom?")
  (b) They reject determinism, that is, they hold that, as a matter of fact, there are at least *some* human decisions not governed by laws. This is the *libertarian* position. (Campbell, "In Defence of Free Will" and Merleau-Ponty, "Freedom and Consciousness.")

B. *Compatibilism.* According to this there is no conflict between free will and determinism. Rather, some say, they complement one another. Compatibilists then attempt to show why we feel there is a conflict. (David Hume, "Liberty and Necessity" and John Stuart Mill, "Freedom of the Will.")

C. *The Two-Level Theory.* According to this view, the beliefs in free will and determinism are independent. Human actions and decisions are not events which can be explained in terms of *causes.* The proper explanation of human actions and decisions is in terms of *reasons.* (See Richard Peters, "Actions and Explanation" and William Alston's discussion of his position in "Actions, Wants, and Causal Explanation.")

These positions will be examined in more detail.

A. The incompatibilist argues this way: If my decision was governed by *any* law, i.e., if it was determined, then there were conditions antecedent to the decision which rendered it inevitable. It matters little what those conditions might be. The decision was the necessary product of certain forces just as the output of a machine is the necessary product of the forces operating within it. Thus, the belief that one could have decided otherwise, that the alternatives before one were genuine ones, and that it was really up to the person to decide among them, was illusory. In other words, if every decision is determined, then free will is an illusion.

If free will is an illusion, then serious consequences follow. It would mean that no one ever can act or decide in a way different from that in which he does act or decide. This has consequences for our notion of responsibility. For example, consider the case of feelings of remorse and guilt. It is a fact that people do at times have these feelings. But if free will is an illusion, how can we feel guilt about something we did, for we could not have done otherwise. When we feel guilty about something, we do not merely feel bad about it in the way we feel bad about someone's death, even when we knew that the death was inevitable; we feel that *we* are to blame. This seems to imply that we could have acted otherwise. Others, too, may hold us responsible. But if there is no such thing as free will, it seems that no one ever could be responsible, for there would be no possibility of having acted otherwise. (Of course, we might hold people responsible even though they never are. It may be expedient to do so, perhaps because it will protect the lives of other people or help to rehabilitate the wrongdoer.)

As noted before, some philosophers who adopt this position of incompatibilism believe that there is no such thing as free will. Others, on the other hand, argue that free will is not an illusion for there are human decisions not determined by any law.

B. Compatibilists say that free will and determinism are not incompatible. They defend this with a number of arguments. Some say that far from there being a conflict between free will and determinism, a decision is free only when it is determined in a certain way. They argue this way: If freedom exists, then it is *our* decisions that are free. That is, a decision must be a decision of the person making it before we can say that it is free. But an undetermined decision is one that does not flow from the personality, character, and desires of the person making that decision. If it did, the decision would be determined. But surely, the argument goes, I identify myself with my desires and character, so that an undetermined decision is very much like a random happening, something that merely comes to pass, but is in no way an expression of *me*.

A libertarian, who accepts incompatibilism and believes in free will, would reject this argument. There is a sense, he would argue, in which *I* make a decision even when the decision is undetermined by any events in me or structural features of me. Moreover, there are decisions of this kind, and it is necessary that there be such in order for there to be free will.

Compatibilists would reply by saying that genuine freedom is not provided by the libertarian's mysterious "I" that is not identified with desires, beliefs, thoughts, and the like. Freedom, on the contrary, requires that my actions be determined by my desires and beliefs. Otherwise, as the argument presented before states, the action is in no legitimate sense mine.

One question which a compatibilist must discuss is, "Under what conditions is an action or decision free and under what conditions is it not free?" The compatibilist holds that an act that is free is also determined in some way. But most compatibilists would grant that *some* acts are determined in such a way that they are not free. The compatibilist must specify what sorts of laws are compatible with our decisions and actions being free.

For example, most compatibilists would say that if we do something because someone has a gun pointed at us, we are not acting freely. We are not normally held responsible for such actions. Similarly, if one acts from a compulsive drive, as a kleptomaniac does when he steals, we would say that he did not really decide to steal and that he was not responsible.

When we examine the three sorts of laws mentioned above—the genetic, the structural, and the physiological, it seems that the structural laws would be the most likely candidates for governing actions which are yet free. These laws mention the character, beliefs, and desires, of the person, and it is just these factors that we are inclined to cite in talking about a decision as the decision made by a particular person. As noted above, some philosophers feel that without some structural laws no decision could be free.

However, if the most plausible explanations of human actions turn out to be those using either genetic or physiological laws, the compatibilist position would seem less attractive. If, for example, our decisions are not determined by our character, desires, and beliefs, but rather by the way we were raised or by certain processes in our brain, then our feeling might well be that our decisions are not free. In both cases it appears that the decision-making process is irrelevant.

The one central advantage of structural laws is that the reasons you weigh when you deliberate appear in the laws as your desires and character traits. If you look at the structural law, you may say "Yes, that is why I decided in the way that I did; I wanted such and such." But if you decided as you did because of the character of your early relationship with your father or because of the conditioning you received at home, it appears that the deliberations in which you were engaged were quite irrelevant, were mere "epiphenomena" behind which the real forces were at work. If this feeling is present in the case of genetic laws, it is even stronger in the case of physiological ones. We may feel that our whole psychical life is but an interesting expression of physical forces which comprise the real determinants of our so-called "decisions."

The compatibilist must, therefore, be concerned to indicate a set of laws which show that human behavior is determined and yet free. The best candidate for this seems to be some sort of structural laws.

A more general defense of compatibilism takes this form: When we say that we could have acted otherwise, we really mean that if we had wanted to do something else, then we would have done so. This, it is argued, is compatible with determinism. All it says is that if a different condition, e.g., a different desire, had obtained, then a different course of action would have been chosen. This account is perfectly compatible with there being a law which explains the action.

C. The two-level position argues, as was noted, that we are confused if we search for the *causes* of human actions and decisions. Events have causes; even the movements of human bodies have causes. But human actions are not explained by citing causes; they are explained by citing *reasons*.

For example, my arm's rising is a physical event, and we can answer the question "Why did my arm go up?" by citing causes, i.e., physical conditions such as muscles tensing. But if you want to know why *I raised my arm*, you are asking for reasons and not for causes. The presentation of reasons is *not* the specification of antecedent conditions which caused the action to occur. If I say that I raised my arm in order to get the teacher's attention, I have given a reason which explains my action. Since, on this view, reasons are essentially different from causes, explaining human actions (which involves giving reasons) is essentially different from explaining events (which involves specifying causes). According to the proponents of this position, all traditional discussions of the free will problem suffer because they grant to the determinist the possibility that causal explanations can be given of human actions. Once it is seen that this is impossible, one will no longer be bothered by the traditional problem of the relation between free will and determinism.

The following selections have been chosen to illustrate the various views that have been discussed. They are arranged in such a way as to bring out the arguments for and against these positions and, therefore, serve to show the way in which philosophical discussion of important issues is carried on.

THE VOLUNTARY

ARISTOTLE

Virtue then is concerned with feelings and actions. But it is only voluntary feelings and actions for which praise and blame are given; those that are involuntary are condoned, and sometimes even pitied. Hence it seems to be necessary for the student of ethics to define the difference between the Voluntary and the Involuntary; and this will also be of service to the legislator in assigning rewards and punishments.

It is then generally held that actions are involuntary when done (*a*)

Reprinted from *Nicomachean Ethics*, Book III, Chapters 1–4, translated by H. Rackham, 1926, by permission of the publishers and the Loeb Classical Library, Harvard University Press, Cambridge, Mass.

under compulsion or (*b*) through ignorance; and that (*a*) an act is compulsory when its origin is from without, being of such a nature that the agent, or person compelled, contributes nothing to it: for example, when a ship's captain is carried somewhere by stress of weather, or by people who have him in their power. But there is some doubt about actions done through fear of a worse alternative, or for some noble object—as for instance if a tyrant having a man's parents and children in his power commands him to do something base, when if he complies their lives will be spared but if he refuses they will be put to death. It is open to question whether such actions are voluntary or involuntary. A somewhat similar case is when cargo is jettisoned in a storm; apart from circumstances, no one voluntarily throws away his property, but to save his own life and that of his shipmates any sane man would do so. Acts of this kind, then, are 'mixed' or composite; but they approximate rather to the voluntary class. For at the actual time when they are done they are chosen or willed; and the end or motive of an act varies with the occasion, so that the terms 'voluntary' and 'involuntary' should be used with reference to the time of action; now the actual deed in the cases in question is done voluntarily, for the origin of the movement of the parts of the body instrumental to the act lies in the agent; and when the origin of an action is in oneself, it is in one's own power to do it or not. Such acts therefore are voluntary, though perhaps involuntary apart from circumstances—for no one would choose to do any such action in and for itself.

Sometimes indeed men are actually praised for deeds of this 'mixed' class, namely when they submit to some disgrace or pain as the price of some great and noble object; though if they do so without any such motive they are blamed, since it is contemptible to submit to a great disgrace with no advantage or only a trifling one in view. In other cases again, such submission though not praised is condoned, when a man does something wrong through fear of penalties that impose too great a strain on human nature, and that no one could endure. Yet there seem to be some acts which a man cannot be compelled to do; and rather than do them he ought to submit to the most terrible death: for instance, we think it ridiculous that Alcmaeon in Euripides' play is compelled by certain threats to murder his mother! But it is sometimes difficult to decide how far we ought to go in choosing to do a given act rather than suffer a given penalty, or in enduring a given penalty rather than commit a given action; and it is still more difficult to abide by our decision when made, since in most of such dilemmas the penalty threatened is painful and the deed forced upon us dishonourable, which is why praise and blame are bestowed according as we do or do not yield to such compulsion.

What kind of actions then are to be called 'compulsory'? Used without qualification, perhaps this term applies to any case where the cause of the action lies in things outside the agent, and when the agent contributes nothing. But when actions intrinsically involuntary are yet in given circumstances deliberately chosen in preference to a given alternative, and when their origin lies in the agent, these actions are to be pronounced intrinsically involuntary but voluntary in the circumstances, and in preference to the alternative. They approximate however rather to the voluntary class, since conduct consists of particular things done, and the particular things done in the cases in question are voluntary. But it is not easy to lay down rules for deciding which of two alternatives is to be chosen, for particular cases differ widely.

To apply the term 'compulsory' to acts done for the sake of pleasure or for noble objects, on the plea that these exercise constraint on us from without, is to make every action compulsory. For (1) pleasure and nobility between them supply the motives of all actions whatsoever. Also (2) to act under compulsion and involuntarily is painful, but actions aiming at something pleasant or noble are pleasant. And (3) it is absurd to blame external things, instead of blaming ourselves for falling an easy prey to their attractions; or to take the credit of our noble deeds to ourselves, while putting the blame for our disgraceful ones upon the temptations of pleasure. It appears therefore that an act is compulsory when its origin is from outside, the person compelled contributing nothing to it.

(*a*) An act done through ignorance is in every case not voluntary, but it is involuntary only when it causes the agent pain and regret afterwards: since a man who has acted through ignorance and feels no compunction at all for what he has done, cannot indeed be said to have acted voluntarily, as he was not aware of his action, yet cannot be said to have acted involuntarily, as he is not sorry for it. Acts done through ignorance therefore fall into two classes: if the agent regrets the act, we think that he has acted involuntarily; if he does not regret it, to mark the distinction we may call him a 'non-voluntary' agent—for as the case is different it is better to give it a special name. Acting *through* ignorance however seems to be different from acting *in* ignorance; for when a man is drunk or in a rage, his actions are not thought to be done through ignorance but owing to one or other of the conditions mentioned, though he does act without knowing, and *in* ignorance. Now it is true that all wicked men are ignorant of what they ought to do and refrain from doing, and that this error is the cause of injustice and of vice in general. But the term 'involuntary' does not really apply to an action when the agent is ignorant of his true interests. For involuntary acts result not from ignorance displayed in moral choice (vice results from that sort of ignorance)—that is to say, they result not from general ignorance (because that is held to be blameworthy), but from particular ignorance, ignorance of the circumstances of the act and of the things affected by it; for in this case the act is pitied and forgiven, because he who acts in ignorance of any of these circumstances is an involuntary agent.

Perhaps then it will be as well to specify the nature and number of these circumstances. They are (1) the agent, (2) the act, (3) the thing that is affected by or is the sphere of the act; and sometimes also (4) the instrument, for instance, a tool with which the act is done, (5) the effect, for instance, saving a man's life, and (6) the manner, for instance, gently or violently.

Now no one, unless mad, could be ignorant of all these circumstances together; nor yet, obviously, of (1) the agent—for a man must know who he is himself. But a man may be ignorant of (2) what he is doing, as for instance when people say 'it slipped out while they were speaking,' or 'they were not aware that the matter was a secret,' as Aeschylus said of the Mysteries; or that 'they let it off when they only meant to show how it worked' as the prisoner pleaded in the catapult case. Again (3) a person might mistake his son for an enemy, as Merope does; or (4) mistake a sharp spear for one with a button on it, or a heavy stone for a pumice-stone; or (5) one might kill a man by giving him medicine with the intention of saving his life; or (6) in loose wrestling hit him a blow when meaning only to grip his hand. Ignorance therefore being possible in respect of all these circumstances of the act, one who has acted in ignorance of any of them is held to have acted involuntarily, and especially so if ignorant of the most important of them; and the most important of the circumstances seem to be the nature of the act itself and the effect it will produce.

Such then is the nature of the ignorance that justifies our speaking of an act as involuntary, given the further condition that the agent feels sorrow and regret for having committed it.

An involuntary action being one done under compulsion or through ignorance, a voluntary act would seem to be an act of which the origin lies in the agent, who knows the particular circumstances in which he is acting. For it is probably a mistake to say that acts caused by anger or by desire are involuntary. In the first place, (1) if we do so, we can no longer say that any of the lower animals act voluntarily, nor yet children. Then (2) are none of our actions that are caused by desire or anger voluntary, or are the noble ones voluntary and the base involuntary? Surely this is an absurd distinction when one person is the author of both. Yet perhaps it is strange to speak of feelings which it is right to aim at having as involuntary; but it is right to feel anger at some things, and also to feel desire for some things, for instance health, knowledge. Also (3) we think that involuntary actions are painful and actions that gratify desire pleasant. And again (4) what difference is there in respect of their involuntary character between wrong acts committed deliberately and wrong acts done in anger? Both are to be avoided; and also we think that the irrational feelings are just as much a part of human nature as the reason, so that the actions done from anger or desire also belong to the human being who does them. It is therefore strange to class these actions as involuntary.

Having defined voluntary and involuntary action, we next have to examine the nature of Choice. For this appears to be intimately connected with virtue, and to afford a surer test of character than do our actions.

Choice is manifestly a voluntary act. But the two terms are not synonymous, the latter being the wider. Children and the lower animals as well as men are capable of voluntary action, but not of choice. Also sudden acts may be termed voluntary, but they cannot be said to be done by choice.

Some identify Choice with (1) Desire, or (2) Passion, or (3) Wish, or (4) some form of Opinion. These views however appear to be mistaken.

(1) The irrational animals do not exercise choice, but they do feel desire, and also passion. Also a man of defective self-restraint acts from desire but not from choice, and on the contrary a self-restrained man acts from choice and not from desire. Again, desire can run counter to choice, but not desire to desire. And desire considers an object as pleasant or painful, choice does not.

(2) Still less is choice the same as passion. Acts done from passion seem very far from being done of deliberate choice.

(3) Again, choice is certainly not a wish, though they appear closely akin. Choice cannot have for its object impossibilities: if a man were to say he chose something impossible he would be thought a fool; but we can wish for things that are impossible, for instance immortality. Also we may wish for what cannot be secured by our own agency, for instance, that a particular actor or athlete may win; but no one chooses what does not rest with himself, but only what he thinks can be attained by his own act. Again, we wish rather for ends than for means, but choose the means to our end; for example, we wish to be healthy, but choose things to make us healthy; we wish to be happy, and that is the word we use in this connexion, but it would not be correct to say that we choose to be happy; since, speaking generally, choice seems to be concerned with things within our own control.

(4) Nor yet again can it be opinion. It seems that anything may be matter of opinion—we form opinions about what is eternal, or impossible, just as much as about what is within our power. Also we distinguish opinion by its truth or falsehood, not by its being good or bad, but choice is distinguished rather as being good or bad. Probably therefore nobody actually identifies choice with opinion in general. But neither is it the same as some particular opinion. For it is our choice of good or evil that determines our character, not our opinion about good or evil. And we choose to take or avoid some good or evil thing, but we opine what a thing is, or for whom it is advantageous, or how it is so: we do not exactly form an opinion to take or avoid a thing. Also we praise a choice rather for choosing the right thing, that is, for being correct, but an opinion for being true. And we choose only things that we absolutely know to be good, we opine things we do not quite certainly know to be true. Nor do the same persons appear to excel both at choosing and at forming opinions: some people seem to hold excellent opinions, but yet to choose wrongly from wickedness. That choice is preceded or accompanied by the formation of an opinion is immaterial, for that is not the point we are considering, but whether choice is the same thing as some form of opinion.

What then are the genus and differentia of Choice, inasmuch as it is not any of the things above mentioned? It manifestly belongs to the genus voluntary action; but not every voluntary act is chosen. Perhaps we may define it as voluntary action preceded by deliberation, since choice involves reasoning and some process of thought. Indeed previous deliberation seems to be implied by the very term προαιρετόν, which denotes something *chosen before* other things.

As for Deliberation, do people deliberate about everything—are all things possible objects of deliberation—or are there some things about which deliberation is impossible? The term "object of deliberation" presumably must not be taken to include things about which a fool or a madman might deliberate, but to mean what a sensible person would deliberate about.

Well then, nobody deliberates about things eternal, such as the order of the universe, or the incommensurability of the diagonal and the side of a square. Nor yet about things that change but follow a regular process, whether from necessity or by nature or through some other cause: such phenomena for instance as the solstices and the sunrise. Nor about irregular occurrences, such as droughts and rains. Nor about the results of chance, such as finding a hidden treasure. The reason* why we do not deliberate about these things is that none of them can be effected by our agency. We deliberate about things that are in our control and are attainable by action (which are in fact the only things that still remain to be considered; for Nature, Necessity, and Chance, with the addition of Intelligence and human agency generally, exhaust the generally accepted list of causes). But we do not deliberate about all human affairs without exception either: for example, no Lacedaemonian deliberates about the best form of government** for Scythia; but any particular group of men deliberates about the things attainable by its own actions. Also there is no room for deliberation about matters fully ascertained and completely formulated as sciences; such for instance as orthography, for we have no uncertainty as to how a word ought to be spelt. We deliberate about things in which our agency operates, but does not always produce uniform results; for instance about questions of medicine and of business; and we deliberate about navigation more than about athletic training, because it has been less completely reduced to a science; and similarly with other pursuits also. And we deliberate more about the arts than about the sciences, because we are more uncertain about them.

Deliberation then is employed in matters which, though subject to rules that generally hold good, are uncertain in their issue; or where the issue is indeterminate, and where, when the matter is important, we take others into our deliberations, distrusting our own capacity to decide.

And we deliberate not about ends, but about means. A doctor does not

* In the MSS. the words "The reason why . . . list of causes" come after "But we do not deliberate . . . Scythia."

** Or, "the best line of policy."

deliberate whether he is to cure his patient, nor an orator whether he is to convince his audience, nor a statesman whether he is to secure good government, nor does anyone else debate about the end of his profession or calling; they take some end for granted, and consider how and by what means it can be achieved. If they find that there are several means of achieving it, they proceed to consider which of these will attain it most easily and best. If there is only one means by which it can be accomplished, they ask how it is to be accomplished by that means, and by what means that means can itself be achieved, until they reach the first link in the chain of causes, which is the last in the order of discovery. (For when deliberating one seems in the procedure described to be pursuing an investigation or analysis that resembles the analysis of a figure in geometry—indeed it appears that though not all investigation is deliberation, for example, mathematical investigation is not, yet all deliberation is investigation—and the last step in the analysis seems to be the first step in the execution of the design.) Then, if they have come up against an impossibility, they abandon the project—for instance, if it requires money and money cannot be procured; but if on the other hand it proves to be something possible, they begin to act. By possible, I mean able to be performed by our agency—things we do through the agency of our friends counting in a sense as done by ourselves, since the origin of their action is in us.

(In practising an art) the question is at one moment what tools to use, and at another how to use them; and similarly in other spheres, we have to consider sometimes what means to employ, and sometimes how exactly given means are to be employed.

It appears therefore, as has been said, that a man is the origin of his actions, and that the province of deliberation is to discover actions within one's own power to perform; and all our actions aim at ends other than themselves. It follows that we do not deliberate about ends, but about means. Nor yet do we deliberate about particular facts, for instance, Is this object a loaf? or, Is this loaf properly baked? for these are matters of direct perception. Deliberation must stop at the particular fact, or it will go on *ad infinitum*.

The object of deliberation and the object of choice are the same, except that when a thing is chosen it has already been determined, since it is the thing already selected as the result of our deliberation that is chosen. For a man stops enquiring how he shall act as soon as he has carried back the origin of action to himself, and to the dominant part of himself, for it is this part that chooses. This may be illustrated by the ancient constitutions represented in Homer: the kings used to proclaim to the people the measures they had chosen to adopt.

As then the object of choice is something within our power which after deliberation we desire, Choice will be a deliberate desire of things in our powers; for we first deliberate, then select, and finally fix our desire according to the result of our deliberation.

Let this serve as a description in outline of Choice, and of the nature of its objects, and the fact that it deals with means and not ends.

Wishes, on the contrary, as was said above are for ends. But while some hold that what is wished for is the good, others think it is what appears to be good. Those however who say that what is wished for is the really good, are faced by the conclusion, that what a man who chooses his end wrongly wishes for is not really wished for at all; since if it is to be wished for, it must on their showing be good, whereas in the case assumed it may so happen that the man wishes for something bad. And those on the other hand who say that what appears good is wished for, are forced to admit that there is no such thing as that which is by nature wished for, but that what each man thinks to be good is wished for in his case; yet different, and it may be opposite, things appear good to different people.

As therefore neither of these views is satisfactory, perhaps we should say that what is wished for in the true and unqualified sense is the good, but that what appears good to each person is wished for by him; and accordingly that the good man wishes for what is truly wished for, the bad man for anything as it may happen (just as in the case of our bodies, a man of sound constitution finds really healthy food best for his health, but some other diet may be healthy for one who is delicate; and so with things bitter and sweet, hot, heavy, etc.). For the good man judges everything correctly; what things truly are, that they seem to him to be, in every department—for the noble and the pleasant have a special form corresponding to each of the faculties of our nature, and perhaps what chiefly distinguishes the good man is that he sees the truth in each kind, being himself as it were the standard and measure of the noble and pleasant. It appears to be pleasure that misleads the mass of mankind; for it seems to them to be a good, though it is not, so they choose what is pleasant as good and shun pain as evil.

FOREKNOWLEDGE AND FREE WILL

ST. AUGUSTINE

The manner in which Cicero addresses himself to the task of refuting the Stoics, shows that he did not think he could effect anything against them in argument unless he had first demolished divination.* And this he

Reprinted from St. Augustine, "The Freedom of the Will," in *The City of God*, translated and edited by Marcus Dods, Edinburgh House, London, 1892, Book V.

* *De Divinat.* ii.

attempts to accomplish by denying that there is any knowledge of future things, and maintains with all his might that there is no such knowledge either in God or man, and that there is no prediction of events. Thus he both denies the foreknowledge of God, and attempts by vain arguments, and by opposing to himself certain oracles very easy to be refuted, to overthrow all prophecy, even such as is clearer than the light (though even these oracles are not refuted by him).

But, in refuting these conjectures of the mathematicians, his argument is triumphant, because truly these are such as destroy and refute themselves. Nevertheless, they are far more tolerable who assert the fatal influence of the stars than they who deny the foreknowledge of future events. For, to confess that God exists, and at the same time to deny that He has foreknowledge of future things, is the most manifest folly. This Cicero himself saw, and therefore attempted to assert the doctrine embodied in the words of Scripture, "The fool hath said in his heart, There is no God."* That, however, he did not do in his own person, for he saw how odious and offensive such an opinion would be; and therefore in his book on the nature of the gods,** he makes Cotta dispute concerning this against the Stoics, and preferred to give his own opinion in favour of Lucilius Balbus, to whom he assigned the defense of the Stoical position, rather than in favour of Cotta, who maintained that no divinity exists. However, in his book on divination, he in his own person most openly opposes the doctrine of the prescience of future things. But all this he seems to do in order that he may not grant the doctrine of fate, and by so doing destroy free will. For he thinks that, the knowledge of future things being once conceded, fate follows as so necessary a consequence that it cannot be denied.

But, let these perplexing debatings and disputations of the philosophers go on as they may, we, in order that we may confess the most high and true God Himself, do confess His will, supreme power, and prescience. Neither let us be afraid lest, after all, we do not do by will that which we do by will, because He, whose foreknowledge is infallible, foreknew that we would do it. It was this which Cicero was afraid of, and therefore opposed foreknowledge. The Stoics also maintained that all things do not come to pass by necessity, although they contended that all things happen according to destiny. What is it, then, that Cicero feared in the prescience of future things? Doubtless it was this,—that if all future things have been foreknown, they will happen in the order in which they have been foreknown; and if they come to pass in this order, there is a certain order of things foreknown by God; and if a certain order of things, then a certain order of causes, for nothing can happen which is not preceded by some efficient cause. But if there is a certain order of causes according to which everything happens which does happen, then by fate, says he, all things happen which do happen. But if this be so, then is there nothing in our own power, and there is no such thing as freedom of will; and if we

* Ps. xiv. 1.
** Bk. iii.

grant that, says he, the whole economy of human life is subverted. In vain are laws enacted. In vain are reproaches, praises, chidings, exhortations had recourse to; and there is no justice whatever in the appointment of rewards for the good, and punishments for the wicked. And that consequences so disgraceful, and absurd, and pernicious to humanity may not follow, Cicero chooses to reject the foreknowledge of future things, and shuts up the religious mind to this alternative, to make choice between two things, either that something is in our own power, or that there is foreknowledge,—both of which cannot be true; but if the one is affirmed, the other is thereby denied. He therefore, like a truly great and wise man, and one who consulted very much and very skilfully for the good of humanity, of those two choose the freedom of the will, to confirm which he denied the foreknowledge of future things; and thus, wishing to make men free, he makes them sacrilegious. But the religious mind chooses both, confesses both, and maintains both by the faith of piety. But how so? says Cicero; for the knowledge of future things being granted, there follows a chain of consequences which ends in this, that there can be nothing depending on our own free wills. And further, if there is anything depending on our wills, we must go backwards by the same steps of reasoning till we arrive at the conclusion that there is no foreknowledge of future things. For we go backwards through all the steps in the following order:—If there is free will, all things do not happen according to fate; if all things do not happen according to fate, there is not a certain order of causes; and if there is not a certain order of causes, neither is there a certain order of things foreknown by God,—for things cannot come to pass except they are preceded by efficient causes,—but, if there is no fixed and certain order of causes foreknown by God, all things cannot be said to happen according as He foreknew that they would happen. And further, if it is not true that all things happen just as they have been foreknown by Him, there is not, says he, in God any foreknowledge of future events.

Now, against the sacrilegious and impious darings of reason, we assert both that God knows all things before they come to pass, and that we do by our free will whatsoever we know and feel to be done by us only because we will it. But that all things come to pass by fate, we do not say; nay we affirm that nothing comes to pass by fate; for we demonstrate that the name of fate, as it is wont to be used by those who speak of fate, meaning thereby the position of the stars at the time of each one's conception or birth, is an unmeaning word, for astrology itself is a delusion. But an order of causes in which the highest efficiency is attributed to the will of God, we neither deny nor do we designate it by the name of fate, unless, perhaps, we may understand fate to mean that which is spoken, deriving it from *fari*, to speak; for we cannot deny that it is written in the sacred Scriptures, "God hath spoken once; these two things have I heard, that power belongeth unto God. Also unto Thee, O God, belongeth mercy: for Thou wilt render unto every man according to his works."*

* Ps. lxii. 11, 12.

Now the expression, "Once hath He spoken," is to be understood as meaning "immovably," that is, unchangeably hath He spoken, inasmuch as He knows unchangeably all things which shall be, and all things which He will do. We might, then, use the word fate in the sense it bears when derived from *fari*, to speak, had it not already come to be understood in another sense, into which I am unwilling that the hearts of men should unconsciously slide. But it does not follow that, though there is for God a certain order of all causes, there must therefore be nothing depending on the free exercise of our own wills, for our wills themselves are included in that order of causes which is certain to God, and is embraced by His foreknowledge, for human wills are also causes of human actions; and He who foreknew all the causes of things would certainly among those causes not have been ignorant of our wills. For even that very concession which Cicero himself makes is enough to refute him in this argument. For what does it help him to say that nothing takes place without a cause, but that every cause is not fatal, there being a fortuitous cause, a natural cause, and a voluntary cause? It is sufficent that he confesses that whatever happens must be preceded by a cause. For we say that those causes which are called fortuitous are not a mere name for the absence of causes, but are only latent, and we attribute them either to the will of the true God, or to that of spirits of some kind or other. And as to natural causes, we by no means separate them from the will of Him who is the author and framer of all nature. But now as to voluntary causes. They are referable either to God, or to angels, or to men, or to animals of whatever description, if indeed those instinctive movements of animals devoid of reason, by which, in accordance with their own nature, they seek or shun various things, are to be called wills. And when I speak of the wills of angels, I mean either the wills of good angels, whom we call the angels of God, or of the wicked angels, whom we call the angels of the devil, or demons. Also by the wills of men I mean the wills either of the good or of the wicked. And from this we conclude that there are no efficient causes of all things which come to pass unless voluntary causes, that is, such as belong to that nature which is the spirit of life. For the air or wind is called spirit, but, inasmuch as it is a body, it is not the spirit of life. The spirit of life, therefore, which quickens all things, and is the creator of every body, and of every created spirit, is God Himself, the uncreated spirit. In His supreme will resides the power which acts on the wills of all created spirits, helping the good, judging the evil, controlling all, granting power to some, not granting it to others. For, as He is the creator of all natures, so also is He the bestower of all powers, not of all wills; for wicked wills are not from Him, being contrary to nature, which is from Him. As to bodies, they are more subject to wills: some to our wills, by which I mean the wills of all living mortal creatures, but more to the wills of men than of beasts. But all of them are most of all subject to the will of God, to whom all wills also are subject, since they have no power except what He has bestowed upon them. The cause of things, therefore, which makes but is not made, is God; but all other causes both make and are made. Such are all created spirits, and especially the rational. Material causes, therefore, which may rather be said to be made than to make, are not to be reckoned among efficient causes, because they can only do what the wills of spirits do by them. How, then, does an order of causes which is certain to the foreknowledge of God necessitate that there should be nothing which is dependent on our wills, when our wills themselves have a very important place in the order of causes? Cicero, then, contends with those who call this order of causes fatal, or rather designate this order itself by the name of fate; to which we have an abhorrence, especially on account of the word, which men have become accustomed to understand as meaning what is not true. But, whereas he denies that the order of all causes is most certain, and perfectly clear to the prescience of God, we detest his opinion more than the Stoics do. For he either denies that God exists,—which, indeed, in an assumed personage, he has laboured to do, in his book *De Natura Deorum*,—or if he confesses that He exists, but denies that He is prescient of future things, what is that but just "the fool saying in his heart there is no God"? For one who is not prescient of all future things is not God. Wherefore our wills also have just so much power as God willed and foreknew that they should have; and therefore whatever power they have, they have it within most certain limits; and whatever they are to do, they are most assuredly to do, for He whose foreknowledge is infallible foreknew that they would have the power to do it, and would do it. Wherefore, if I should choose to apply the name of fate to anything at all, I should rather say that fate belongs to the weaker of two parties, will to the stronger, who has the other in his power, than that the freedom of our will is excluded by that order of causes, which, by an unusual application of the word peculiar to themselves, the Stoics call *Fate*.

Wherefore, neither is that necessity to be feared, for dread of which the Stoics laboured to make such distinctions among the causes of things as should enable them to rescue certain things from the dominion of necessity, and to subject others to it. Among those things which they wished not to be subject to necessity they placed our wills, knowing that they would not be free if subjected to necessity. For if that is to be called *our necessity* which is not in our power, but even though we be unwilling, effects what it can effect,—as, for instance, the necessity of death,—it is manifest that our wills by which we live uprightly or wickedly are not under such a necessity; for we do many things which, if we were not willing, we should certainly not do. This is primarily true of the act of willing itself,—for if we will, it *is;* if we will not, it *is* not,—for we should not will if we were unwilling. But if we define necessity to be that according to which we say that it is necessary that anything be of such or such a nature, or be done in such and such a manner, I know not why we should have any dread of that necessity taking away the freedom of our will. For we do not put the life of God or the foreknowledge of God under necessity if we should say that it is necessary that God should live for ever, and foreknow all things; as neither is His power diminished when we say that He cannot die or fall into error,—for this is in such a way impossible to Him, that if it were possible for Him, He would be of less power. But assuredly He is rightly called omnipotent on account of His doing what He wills, not on account of His suffering what He wills not; for if that should befall Him, He would by no means be omnipotent. Wherefore, He cannot do some things for the very reason that He is omnipotent. So also, when we say that it is necessary that, when we will, we will by free choice, in so saying we both affirm what is true beyond doubt, and do not still subject our wills thereby to a necessity which destroys liberty. Our wills, therefore, *exist* as *wills*, and do themselves whatever we do by willing, and which would not be done if we were unwilling. But when any one suffers anything, being unwilling, by the will of another, even in that case will retains its essential validity,—we do not mean the will of the party who inflicts the suffering, for we resolve it into the power of God. For if a will should simply exist, but not be able to do what it wills, it would be overborne by a more powerful will. Nor would this be the case unless there had existed will, and that not the will of the other party, but the will of him who willed, but was not able to accomplish what he willed. Therefore, whatsoever a man suffers contrary to his own will, he ought not to attribute to the will of men, or of angels, or of any created spirit, but rather to His will who gives power to wills. It is not the case, therefore, that because God foreknew what would be in the power of our wills, there is for that reason nothing in the power of our wills. For he who foreknew this did not foreknow nothing. Moreover, if He who foreknew what would be in the power of our wills did not foreknow nothing, but something, assuredly, even though He did foreknow, there is something in the power of our wills. Therefore we are by no means compelled, either retaining the prescience of God, to take away the freedom of the will, or, retaining the freedom of the will, to deny that He is prescient of future things, which is impious. But we embrace both. We faithfully and sincerely confess both. The former, that we may believe well; the latter, that we may live well. For he lives ill who does not believe well concerning God. Wherefore, be it far from us, in order to maintain our freedom, to deny the prescience of Him by whose help we are or shall be free. Consequently, it is not in vain that laws are enacted, and that reproaches, exhortations, praises, and vituperations are had recourse to; for these also He foreknew, and they are of great avail, even as great as He foreknew that they would be of. Prayers, also, are of avail to procure those things which He foreknew that He would grant to those who offered them; and with justice have rewards been appointed for good deeds, and punishments for sins. For a man does not therefore sin because God foreknew that he would sin. Nay, it cannot be doubted but that it is the man himself who sins when he does sin, because He, whose foreknewledge is infallible, foreknew not that fate, or fortune, or something else would sin, but that the man himself would sin, who, if he wills not, sins not. But if he shall not will to sin, even this did God foreknow.

WHAT MEANS THIS FREEDOM?

JOHN HOSPERS

I am in agreement to a very large extent with the conclusions of Professor Edwards' paper, and am happy in these days of "soft determinism" to hear the other view so forcefully and fearlessly stated. As a preparation for developing my own views on the subject, I want to mention a factor that I think is of enormous importance and relevance: namely, unconscious motivation. There are many actions—not those of an insane person (however the term "insane" be defined), nor of a person ignorant of the effects of his action, nor ignorant of some relevant fact about the situation, nor in any obvious way mentally deranged—for which human beings in general and the courts in particular are inclined to hold the doer responsible, and for which, I would say, he should not be held responsible. The deed may be planned, it may be carried out in cold calculation, it may spring from the agent's character and be continuous with the rest of his behavior, and it may be perfectly true that he could have done differently *if* he had wanted to; nonetheless his behavior was brought about by unconscious conflicts developed in infancy, over which he had no control and of which (without training in psychiatry) he does not even have knowledge. He may even *think* he knows why he acted as he did, he may *think* he has conscious control over his actions, he may even *think* he is fully responsible for them; but he is not. Psychiatric casebooks provide hundreds of examples. The law and common sense, though puzzled sometimes by such cases, are gradually becoming aware that they exist; but at this early stage countless tragic blunders still occur because neither the law nor the public in general is aware of the genesis of criminal actions. The mother blames her daughter for choosing the wrong men as candidates for husbands; but though the daughter thinks she is choosing freely and spends a considerable amount of time "deciding" among them, the identification with her sick father, resulting from Oedipal fantasies in early childhood, prevents her from caring for any but sick men, twenty or thirty years older than herself. Blaming her is beside the point; she cannot help it, and she cannot change it. Countless criminal acts are thought out in great detail; yet the participants are (without their own knowledge) acting out fantasies, fears, and defenses from early childhood, over whose coming and going they have no conscious control.

Reprinted from John Hospers, "What Means This Freedom?" in *Determinism and Freedom in the Age of Modern Science,* edited by Sidney Hook, New York University Press, New York, 1961, pp. 126–142, by permission of the publishers and John Hospers.

Now, I am not saying that none of these persons should be in jails or asylums. Often society must be protected against them. Nor am I saying that people should cease the practices of blaming and praising, punishing and rewarding; in general these devices are justified by the results—although very often they have practically no effect; the deeds are done from inner compulsion, which is not lessened when the threat of punishment is great. I am only saying that frequently persons we think responsible are not properly to be called so; we mistakenly think them responsible because we assume they are like those in whom no unconscious drive (toward this type of behavior) is present, and that their behavior can be changed by reasoning, exhorting, or threatening.

I

I have said that these persons are not responsible. But what is the criterion for responsibility? Under precisely what conditions is a person to be held morally responsible for an action? Disregarding here those conditions that have to do with a person's *ignorance* of the situation or the effects of his action, let us concentrate on those having to do with his "inner state." There are several criteria that might be suggested:

1. The first idea that comes to mind is that responsibility is determined by the presence or absence of *premeditation*—the opposite of "premeditated" being, presumably, "unthinking" or "impulsive." But this will not do—both because some acts are not premeditated but responsible, and because some are premeditated and not responsible.

Many acts we call responsible can be as unthinking or impulsive as you please. If you rush across the street to help the victim of an automobile collision, you are (at least so we would ordinarily say) acting responsibly, but you did not do so out of premeditation; you saw the accident, you didn't think, you rushed to the scene without hesitation. It was like a reflex action. But you acted responsibly: unlike the knee jerk, the act was the result of past training and past thought about situations of this kind; that is why you ran to help instead of ignoring the incident or running away. When something done originally from conviction or training becomes habitual, it becomes *like* a reflex action. As Aristotle said, virtue should become second nature through habit: a virtuous act should be performed *as if* by instinct; this, far from detracting from its moral worth, testifies to one's mastery of the desired type of behavior; one does not have to make a moral effort each time it is repeated.

There are also premeditated acts for which, I would say, the person is not responsible. Premeditation, especially when it is so exaggerated as to issue in no action at all, can be the result of neurotic disturbance or what we sometimes call an emotional "block," which the person inherits from long-past situations. In Hamlet's revenge on his uncle (I use this example because it is familiar to all of us), there was no lack, but rather a surfeit, of premeditation; his actions were so exquisitely premeditated as to make Freud and Dr. Ernest Jones look more closely to find out what lay behind them. The very premeditation camouflaged unconscious motives of which Hamlet himself was not aware. I think this is an important point, since it seems that the courts often assume that premeditation is a criterion of responsibility. If failure to kill his uncle had been considered a crime, every court in the land would have convicted Hamlet. Again: a woman's decision to stay with her husband in spite of endless "mental cruelty" is, if she is the victim of an unconscious masochistic "will to punishment," one for which she is not responsible; she is the victim and not the agent, no matter how profound her conviction that she is the agent; she is caught in a masochistic web (of complicated genesis) dating back to babyhood, perhaps a repetition of a comparable situation involving her own parents, a repetition-compulsion that, as Freud said, goes "beyond the pleasure principle." Again: a criminal whose crime was carefully planned step by step is usually considered responsible, but as we shall see in later examples, the overwhelming impulse toward it, stemming from an unusually humiliating ego defeat in early childhood, was as compulsive as any can be.

2. Shall we say, then, that a person is not responsible for his act unless he can *defend it with reasons?* I am afraid that this criterion is no better than the previous one. First, intellectuals are usually better at giving reasons than nonintellectuals, and according to this criterion would be more responsible than persons acting from moral conviction not implemented by reasoning; yet it is very doubtful whether we should want to say that the latter are the more responsible. Second, the giving of reasons itself may be suspect. The reasons may be rationalizations camouflaging unconscious motives of which the agent knows nothing. Hamlet gave many reasons for not doing what he felt it was his duty to do: the time was not right, his uncle's soul might go to heaven, etc. His various "reasons" contradicted one another, and if an overpowering compulsion had not been present, the highly intellectual Hamlet would not have been taken in for a moment by these rationalizations. The real reason, the Oedipal conflict that made his uncle's crime the accomplishment of his own deepest desire, binding their fates into one and paralyzing him into inaction, was unconscious and of course unknown to him. One's intelligence and reasoning power do not enable one to escape from unconsciously motivated behavior; it only gives one greater facility in rationalizing that behavior; one's intelligence is simply used in the interest of the neurosis—it is pressed into service to justify with reasons what one does quite independently of the reasons.

If these two criteria are inadequate, let us seek others.

3. Shall we say that a person is responsible for his action unless it is the *result of unconscious forces* of which he knows nothing? Many psychoanalysts would probably accept this criterion. If it is not largely reflected in the language of responsibility as ordinarily used, this may be due to ignorance of fact: most people do not know that there are such things as unconscious motives and unconscious conflicts causing human beings to act. But it may be that if they did, perhaps they would refrain from holding persons responsible for certain actions.

I do not wish here to quarrel with this criterion of responsibility. I only want to point out the fact that if this criterion is employed a far greater number of actions will be excluded from the domain of responsibility than we might at first suppose. Whether we are neat or untidy, whether we are selfish or unselfish, whether we provoke scenes or avoid them, even whether we can exert our powers of will to change our behavior—all these may, and often do, have their source in our unconscious life.

4. Shall we say that a person is responsible for his act unless it is *compelled?* Here we are reminded of Aristotle's assertion (*Nicomachean Ethics*, Book III) that a person is responsible for his act except for reasons of either ignorance or compulsion. Ignorance is not part of our problem here (unless it is unconsciously induced ignorance of facts previously remembered and selectively forgotten—in which case the forgetting is again compulsive), but compulsion is. How will compulsion do as a criterion? The difficulty is to state just what it means. When we say an act is compelled in a psychological sense, our language is metaphorical—which is not to say that there is no point in it or that, properly interpreted, it is not true. Our actions are compelled in a literal sense if someone has us in chains or is controlling our bodily movements. When we say that the storm compelled us to jettison the cargo of the ship (Aristotle's example), we have a less literal sense of compulsion, for at least it is open to us to go down with the ship. When psychoanalysts say that a man was compelled by unconscious conflicts to wash his hands constantly, this is also not a literal use of "compel"; for nobody forced his hands under the tap. Still, it is a typical example of what psychologists call *compulsive* behavior: it has unconscious causes inaccessible to introspection, and moreover nothing can change it—it is as inevitable for him to do it as it would be if someone were forcing his hands under the tap. In this it is exactly like the action of a powerful external force; it is just as little within one's conscious control.

In its area of application this interpretation of responsibility comes to much the same as the previous one. And this area is very great indeed. For if we cannot be held responsible for the infantile situations (in which we were after all passive victims), then neither, it would seem, can we be held responsible for compulsive actions occurring in adulthood that are inevitable consequences of those infantile situations. And, psychiatrists and psychoanalysts tell us, actions fulfilling this description are characteristic of all people some of the time and some people most of the time. Their occurrence, once the infantile events have taken place, is inevitable, just as the explosion is inevitable once the fuse has been lighted; there is simply more "delayed action" in the psychological explosions than there is in the physical ones.

(I have not used the word "inevitable" here to mean "causally determined," for according to such a definition every event would be inevitable if one accepted the causal principle in some form or other; and probably nobody except certain philosophers uses "inevitable" in this sense. Rather, I use "inevitable" in its ordinary sense of "cannot be avoided." To the extent, therefore, that adult neurotic manifestations *can* be avoided, once the infantile patterns have become set, the assertion that they are inevitable is not true.)

5. There is still another criterion, which I prefer to the previous ones, by which a man's responsibility for an act can be measured: the degree to which that act can (or could have been) *changed by the use of reasons.* Suppose that the man who washes his hands constantly does so, he says, for hygienic reasons, believing that if he doesn't do so he will be poisoned by germs. We now convince him, on the best medical authority, that his belief is groundless. Now, the test of his responsibility is whether the changed belief will result in changed behavior. If it does not, as with the compulsive hand washer, he is not acting responsibly, but if it does, he is. It is not the *use* of reasons, but their *efficacy in changing behavior*, that is being made the criterion of responsibility. And clearly in neurotic cases no such change occurs; in fact, this is often made the defining characteristic of neurotic behavior: it is unchangeable by any rational considerations.

II

I have suggested these criteria to distinguish actions for which we can call the agent responsible from those for which we cannot. Even persons with extensive knowledge of psychiatry do not, I think, use any one of these criteria to the exclusion of the others; a conjunction of two or more may be used at once. But however they may be combined or selected in actual application, I believe we can make the distinction along some such lines as we have suggested.

But is there not still another possible meaning of "responsibility" that we have not yet mentioned? Even after we have made all the above distinctions, there remains a question in our minds whether we are, in the final analysis, *responsible for any of our actions at all.* The issue may be put this way: How can anyone be responsible for his actions, since they grow out of his character, which is shaped and molded and made what it is by influences—some hereditary, but most of them stemming from early parental environment—that were not of his own making or choosing? This question, I believe, still troubles many people who would agree to all the distinctions we have just made but still have the feeling that "this isn't all." They have the uneasy suspicion that there is a more ultimate sense, a "deeper" sense, in which we are *not* responsible for our actions, since we are not responsible for the character out of which those actions spring. . . .

Let us take as an example a criminal who, let us say, strangled several persons and is himself now condemned to die in the electric chair. Jury and public alike hold him fully responsible (at least they utter the words "he is responsible"), for the murders were planned down to the minutest detail, and the defendant tells the jury exactly how he planned them. But now we find out how it all came about; we learn of parents who rejected him from babyhood, of the childhood spent in one foster home after another, where it was always plain to him that he was not wanted; of the constantly frustrated early desire for affection, the hard shell of nonchalance and bitterness that he assumed to cover the painful and humiliating fact of being unwanted, and his subsequent attempts to heal these wounds to his shattered ego through defensive aggression.

> The criminal is the most passive person in this world, helpless as a baby in his motorically inexpressible fury. Not only does he try to wreak revenge on the mother of the earliest period of his babyhood; his criminality is based on the inner feeling of being incapable of making the mother even feel that the child seeks revenge on her. The situation is that of a dwarf trying to annoy a giant who superciliously refuses to see these attempts. . . . Because of his inner feeling of being a dwarf, the criminotic uses, so to speak, dynamite. Of that the giant must take cognizance. True, the "revenge" harms the avenger. He may be legally executed. However, the primary inner aim of forcing the giant to acknowledge the dwarf's fury is fulfilled.*

The poor victim is not conscious of the inner forces that exact from him this ghastly toll; he battles, he schemes, he revels in pseudo-aggression, he is miserable, but he does not know what works within him to produce these catastrophic acts of crime. His aggressive actions are the wriggling of a worm on a fisherman's hook. And if this is so, it seems difficult to say any longer, "He is responsible." Rather, we shall put him behind bars for the protection of society, but we shall no longer flatter our feeling of moral superiority by calling him personally responsible for what he did.

Let us suppose it were established that a man commits murder only if, sometime during the previous week, he has eaten a certain combination of foods—say, tuna fish salad at a meal also including peas, mushroom soup, and blueberry pie. What if we were to track down the factors common to all murders committed in this country during the last twenty years and found this factor present in all of them, and only in them? The example is of course empirically absurd; but may it not be that there is *some* combination of factors that regularly leads to homicide, factors such as are described in general terms in the above quotation? (Indeed the situation in the quotation is less fortunate than in our hypothetical example, for it is easy to avoid certain foods once we have been warned about them, but the situation of the infant is thrust on him; something has already happened to him once and for all, before he knows it has happened.) When such specific factors are discovered, won't they make it clear that it is foolish and pointless, as well as immoral, to hold human beings responsible for crimes? Or, if one prefers biological to psychological factors, suppose a neurologist is called in to testify at a murder trial and produces X-ray pictures of the brain of the criminal; anyone can see, he argues, that the *cella turcica* was already calcified at the age of nineteen; it should be a flexible bone, growing, enabling the gland to grow.** All the defendant's disorders might have resulted from this early calcification. Now, this particular explanation may be empirically false;

* Edmund Bergler, *The Basic Neurosis* (New York: Grune and Stratton, 1949), p. 305.

** Meyer Levin, *Compulsion* (New York: Simon and Schuster, 1956), p. 403.

but who can say that no such factors, far more complex, to be sure, exist?

When we know such things as these, we no longer feel so much tempted to say that the criminal is responsible for his crime; and we tend also (do we not?) to excuse him—not legally (we still confine him to prison) but morally; we no longer call him a monster or hold him personally responsible for what he did. Moreover, we do this in general, not merely in the case of crime: "You must excuse Grandmother for being irritable; she's really quite ill and is suffering some pain all the time." Or: "The dog always bites children after she's had a litter of pups; you can't blame her for it: she's not feeling well, and besides she naturally wants to defend them." "She's nervous and jumpy, but do excuse her: she has a severe glandular disturbance."

Let us note that the more *thoroughly* and *in detail* we know the causal factors leading a person to behave as he does, the more we tend to exempt him from responsibility. When we know nothing of the man except what we see him do, we say he is an ungrateful cad who expects much of other people and does nothing in return, and we are usually indignant. When we learn that his parents were the same way and, having no guilt feelings about this mode of behavior themselves, brought him up to be greedy and avaricious, we see that we could hardly expect him to have developed moral feelings in this direction. When we learn, in addition, that he is not aware of being ungrateful or selfish, but unconsciously represses the memory of events unfavorable to himself, we feel that the situation is unfortunate but "not really his fault." When we know that this behavior of his, which makes others angry, occurs more constantly when he feels tense or insecure, and that he now feels tense and insecure, and that relief from pressure will diminish it, then we tend to "feel sorry for the poor guy" and say he's more to be pitied than censured. We no longer want to say that he is personally responsible; we might rather blame nature or his parents for having given him an unfortunate constitution or temperament.

> In recent years a new form of punishment has been imposed on middle-aged and elderly parents. Their children, now in their twenties, thirties or even forties, present them with a modern grievance: "My analysis proves that *you* are responsible for my neurosis." Overawed by these authoritative statements, the poor tired parents fall easy victims to the newest variations on the scape-goat theory.
>
> In my opinion, this senseless cruelty—which disinters educational sins which had been buried for decades, and uses them as the basis for accusations which the victims cannot answer—is unjustified. Yes "the truth loves to be centrally located" (Melville), and few parents—since they are human—have been perfect. But granting their mistakes, they acted as *their* neurotic difficulties forced them to act. To turn the tables and declare the children not guilty because of the *impersonal* nature of their own neuroses, while at the same time the parents are *personally* blamed, is worse than illogical; it is profoundly unjust.*

And so, it would now appear, neither of the parties is responsible: "they acted as their neurotic difficulties forced them to act." The patients are

* Edmund Bergler, *The Superego* (New York: Grune and Stratton, 1952), p. 320.

not responsible for their neurotic manifestations, but then neither are the parents responsible for theirs; and so, of course, for their parents in turn, and theirs before them. It is the twentieth-century version of the family curse, the curse on the House of Atreus.

"But," a critic complains, "it's immoral to exonerate people indiscriminately in this way. I might have thought it fit to excuse somebody because he was born on the other side of the tracks, if I didn't know so many bank presidents who were also born on the other side of the tracks." Now, I submit that the most immoral thing in this situation is the critic's caricature of the conditions of the excuse. Nobody is excused merely because he was born on the other side of the tracks. But if he was born on the other side of the tracks *and* was a highly narcissistic infant to begin with *and* was repudiated or neglected by his parents *and* . . . (here we list a finite number of conditions), and if this complex of factors is *regularly* followed by certain behavior traits in adulthood, and moreover *unavoidably* so—that is, they occur no matter what he or anyone else tries to do—then we excuse him morally and say he is not responsible for his deed. If he is not responsible for *A*, a series of events occurring in his babyhood, then neither is he responsible for *B*, a series of things he does in adulthood, provided that *B* inevitably—that is, unavoidably—follows upon the occurrence of *A*. And according to psychiatrists and psychoanalysts, this often happens.

But one may still object that so far we have talked only about neurotic behavior. Isn't nonneurotic or normal or not unconsciously motivated (or whatever you want to call it) behavior still within the area of responsibility? There are reasons for answering "No" even here, for the normal person no more than the neurotic one has caused his own character, which makes him what he is. Granted that neurotics are not responsible for their behavior (that part of it which we call neurotic) because it stems from undigested infantile conflicts that they had no part in bringing about, and that are external to them just as surely as if their behavior had been forced on them by a malevolent deity (which is indeed one theory on the subject); but the so-called normal person is equally the product of causes in which his volition took no part. And if, unlike the neurotic's, his behavior is changeable by rational considerations, and if he has the will power to overcome the effects of an unfortunate early environment, this again is no credit to him; he is just lucky. If energy is available to him in a form in which it can be mobilized for constructive purposes, this is no credit to him, for this too is part of his psychic legacy. Those of us who can discipline ourselves and develop habits of concentration of purpose tend to blame those who cannot, and call them lazy and weak-willed; but what we fail to see is that they literally *cannot* do what we expect; if their psyches were structured like ours, they could, but as they are burdened with a tyrannical superego (to use psychoanalytic jargon for the moment), and a weak defenseless ego whose energies are constantly consumed in fighting endless charges of the superego, they simply cannot do it, and it is irrational to expect it of them. We cannot with justification blame them for their inability, any more than we can congratulate ourselves for our ability. This lesson is hard to learn, for we constantly and naïvely assume that other people are constructed as we ourselves are.

For example: A child raised under slum conditions, whose parents are socially ambitious and envy families with money, but who nevertheless squander the little they have on drink, may simply be unable in later life to mobilize a drive sufficient to overcome these early conditions. Common sense would expect that he would develop the virtue of thrift; he would make quite sure that he would never again endure the grinding poverty he had experienced as a child. But in fact it is not so: the exact conditions are too complex to be specified in detail here, but when certain conditions are fulfilled (concerning the subject's early life), he will always thereafter be a spendthrift, and no rational considerations will be able to change this. He will listen to the rational considerations and see the force of these, but they will not be able to change him, even if he tries; he cannot change his wasteful habits any more than he can lift the Empire State Building with his bare hands. We moralize and plead with him to be thrifty, but we do not see how strong, how utterly overpowering, and how constantly with him, is the opposite drive, which is so easily manageable with us. But he is possessed by the all-consuming, all-encompassing urge to make the world see that he belongs, that he has arrived, that he is just as well off as anyone else, that the awful humiliations were not real, that they never actually occurred, for isn't he now able to spend and spend? The humiliation must be blotted out; and conspicuous, fleshy, expensive, and wasteful buying will do this; it shows the world what the world must know! True, it is only for the moment; true, it is in the end self-defeating, for wasteful consumption is the best way to bring poverty back again; but the person with an overpowering drive to mend a lesion to his narcissism cannot resist the avalanche of that drive with his puny rational consideration. A man with his back against the wall and a gun at his throat doesn't think of what may happen ten years hence. (Consciously, of course, he knows nothing of this drive; all that appears to consciousness is its shattering effects; he knows only that he must keep on spending—not why—and that he is unable to resist.) He hasn't in him the psychic capacity, the energy to stem the tide of a drive that at that moment is all-powerful. We, seated comfortably away from this flood, sit in judgment on him and blame him and exhort him and criticize him; but he, carried along by the flood, cannot do otherwise than he does. He may fight with all the strength of which he is capable, but it is not enough. And we, who are rational enough at least to exonerate a man in a situation of "overpowering impulse" when we recognize it to be one, do not even recognize this as an example of it; and so, in addition to being swept away in the flood that childhood conditions rendered inevitable, he must also endure our lectures, our criticisms, and our moral excoriation.

But, one will say, he could have overcome his spendthrift tendencies;

some people do. Quite true: some people do. They are lucky. They have it in them to overcome early deficiencies by exerting great effort, and they are capable of exerting the effort. Some of us, luckier still, can overcome them with but little effort; and a few, the luckiest, haven't the deficiencies to overcome. It's all a matter of luck. The least lucky are those who can't overcome them, even with great effort, and those who haven't the ability to exert the effort.

But, one persists, it isn't a matter simply of luck; it *is* a matter of effort. Very well then, it's a matter of effort; without exerting the effort you may not overcome the deficiency. But whether or not you are the kind of person who has it in him to exert the effort is a matter of luck.

All this is well known to psychoanalysts. They can predict, from minimal cues that most of us don't notice, whether a person is going to turn out to be lucky or not. "The analyst," they say, "must be able to use the residue of the patient's unconscious guilt so as to remove the symptom or character trait that creates the guilt. The guilt must not only be present, but *available* for use, *mobilizable*. If it is used up (absorbed) in criminal activity, or in an excessive amount of self-damaging tendencies, then it cannot be used for therapeutic purposes, and the prognosis is negative." Not all philosophers will relish the analyst's way of putting the matter, but at least as a physician he can soon detect whether the patient is lucky or unlucky—and he knows that whichever it is, it *isn't the patient's fault*. The patient's conscious volition cannot remedy the deficiency. Even whether he will co-operate with the analyst is really out of the patient's hands: if he continually projects the denying-mother fantasy on the analyst and unconsciously identifies him always with the cruel, harsh forbidder of the nursery, thus frustrating any attempt at impersonal observation, the sessions are useless; yet if it happens that way, he can't help that either. That fatal projection is not under his control; whether it occurs or not depends on how his unconscious identifications have developed since his infancy. He can try, yes—but the ability to try enough for the therapy to have effect is also beyond his control; the capacity to try more than just so much is either there or it isn't—and either way "it's in the lap of the gods."

The position, then, is this: if we *can* overcome the effects of early environment, the ability to do so is itself a product of the early environment. We did not give ourselves this ability; and if we lack it we cannot be blamed for not having it. Sometimes, to be sure, moral exhortation brings out an ability that is there but not being used, and in this lies its *occasional* utility; but very often its use is pointless, because the ability is not there. The only thing that can overcome a desire, as Spinoza said, is a stronger contrary desire; and many times there simply is no wherewithal for producing a stronger contrary desire. Those of us who do have the wherewithal are lucky.

There is one possible practical advantage in remembering this. It may prevent us (unless we are compulsive blamers) from indulging in righteous indignation and committing the sin of spiritual pride, thanking God that we are not as this publican here. And it will protect from our useless moralizings those who are least equipped by nature for enduring them. As with responsibility, so with deserts. Someone commits a crime and is punished by the state; "he deserved it," we say self-righteously—as if we were moral and he immoral, when in fact we are lucky and he is unlucky—forgetting that there, but for the grace of God and a fortunate early environment, go we. Or, as Clarence Darrow said in his speech for the defense in the Loeb-Leopold case:

> I do not believe that people are in jail because they deserve to be. . . . I know what causes the emotional life. . . . I know it is practically left out of some. Without it they cannot act with the rest. They cannot feel the moral shocks which safeguard others. Is [this man] to blame that his machine is imperfect? Who is to blame? I do not know. I have never in my life been interested so much in fixing blame as I have in relieving people from blame. I am not wise enough to fix it.*

III

I want to make it quite clear that I have not been arguing for determinism. Though I find it difficult to give any sense to the term "indeterminism," because I do not know what it would be like to come across an uncaused event, let us grant indeterminists everything they want, at least in words—influences that suggest but do not constrain, a measure of acausality in an otherwise rigidly causal order, and so on—whatever these phrases may mean. With all this granted, exactly the same situation faces the indeterminist and the determinist; all we have been saying would still hold true. "Are our powers innate or acquired?"

> Suppose the powers are declared innate; then the villain may sensibly ask whether he is responsible for what he was born with. A negative reply is inevitable. Are they then acquired? Then the ability to acquire them—was *that* innate? or acquired? It is innate? Very well then. . . .**

The same fact remains—that we did not cause our characters, that the influences that made us what we are are influences over which we had no control and of whose very existence we had no knowledge at the time. This fact remains for "determinism" and "indeterminism" alike. And it is this fact to which I would appeal, not the specific tenets of traditional forms of "determinism," which seem to me, when analyzed, empirically empty.

"But," it may be asked, "isn't it your view that nothing ultimately *could* be other than it is? And isn't this deterministic? And isn't it deterministic if you say that human beings could never act otherwise than they do, and that their desires and temperaments could not, when you consider their antecedent conditions, be other than they are?"

I reply that all these charges rest on confusions.

1. To say that nothing *could* be other than it is, is, taken literally,

* Levin, *op. cit.*, pp. 439–40, 469.

** W. I. Matson, "The Irrelevance of Free-will to Moral Responsibility," *Mind*, LXV (October 1956), p. 495.

nonsense; and if taken as a way of saying something else, misleading and confusing. If you say, "I can't do it," this invites the question, "No? Not even if you want to?" "Can" and "could" are power words, used in the context of human action; when applied to nature they are merely anthropomorphic. "Could" has no application to nature—unless, of course, it is uttered in a theological context: one might say that God *could* have made things different. But with regard to inanimate nature "could" has no meaning. Or perhaps it is intended to mean that the order of nature is in some sense *necessary*. But in that case the sense of "necessary" must be specified. I know what "necessary" means when we are talking about propositions, but not when we are talking about the sequence of events in nature.

2. What of the charge that we could never have acted otherwise than we did? This, I submit, is simply not true. Here the exponents of Hume-Mill-Schlick-Ayer "soft determinism" are quite right. I could have gone to the opera today instead of coming here; that is, if certain conditions had been different, I should have gone. I could have done many other things instead of what I did, if some condition or other had been different, specifically if my desire had been different. I repeat that "could" is a power word, and "I could have done this" means approximately "I *should* have done this *if* I had wanted to." In this sense, all of us could often have done otherwise than we did. I would not want to say that I should have done differently even if *all* the conditions leading up to my action had been the same (this is generally not what we mean by "could" anyway); but to assert that I could have is empty, for if I *did* act different from the time before, we would automatically say that one or more of the conditions were different, whether we had independent evidence for this or not, thus rendering the assertion immune to empirical refutation. (Once again, the vacuousness of "determinism.")

3. Well, then, could we ever have, not acted, but *desired* otherwise than we did desire? This gets us once again to the heart of the matter we were discussing in the previous section. Russell said, "We can do as we please but we can't please as we please." But I am persuaded that even this statement conceals a fatal mistake. Let us follow the same analysis through. "I could have done *X*" means "I should have done *X* if I had wanted to." "I could have wanted *X*" by the same analysis would mean "I should have wanted *X* if I had wanted to"—which seems to make no sense at all. (What does Russell want? To please as he doesn't please?)

What does this show? It shows, I think, that the only meaningful context of "can" and "could have" is that of *action*. "Could have acted differently" makes sense; "could have desired differently," as we have just seen, does not. Because a word or phrase makes good sense in one context, let us not assume that it does so in another.

I conclude, then, with the following suggestion: that we operate on two levels of moral discourse, which we shouldn't confuse; one (let's call it the upper level) is that of actions; the other (the lower, or deeper, level) is that of the springs of action. Most moral talk occurs on the upper level. It is on this level that the Hume-Mill-Schlick-Ayer analysis of freedom fully applies. As we have just seen, "can" and "could" acquire their meaning on this level; so, I suspect, does "freedom." So does the distinction between compulsive and noncompulsive behavior, and among the senses of "responsibility," discussed in the first section of this paper, according to which we are responsible for some things and not for others. All these distinctions are perfectly valid on this level (or in this dimension) of moral discourse; and it is, after all, the usual one—we are practical beings interested in changing the course of human behavior, so it is natural enough that 99 per cent of our moral talk occurs here.

But when we descend to what I have called the lower level of moral discourse, as we occasionally do in thoughtful moments when there is no immediate need for action, then we must admit that we are ultimately the kind of persons we are because of conditions occurring outside us, over which we had no control. But while this is true, we should beware of extending the moral terminology we used on the other level to this one also. "Could" and "can," as we have seen, no longer have meaning here. "Right" and "wrong," which apply only to actions, have no meaning there either. I suspect that the same is true of "responsibility," for now that we have recalled often forgotten facts about our being the product of outside forces, we must ask in all seriousness what would be added by saying that we are not *responsible* for our own characters and temperaments. What would it mean even? Has it a significant opposite? What would it be like to be responsible for one's own character? What possible situation is describable by this phrase? Instead of saying that it is *false* that we are responsible for our own characters, I should prefer to say that the utterance is meaningless—meaningless in the sense that it describes no possible situation, though it *seems* to because the word "responsible" is the same one we used on the upper level, where it marks a real distinction. If this is so, the result is that *moral* terms—at least the terms "could have" and "responsible"—simply drop out on the lower level. What remains, shorn now of moral terminology, is the point we tried to bring out in Part II: whether or not we have personality disturbances, whether or not we have the ability to overcome deficiencies of early environment, is like the answer to the question whether or not we shall be struck down by a dread disease: "it's all a matter of luck." It is important to keep this in mind, for people almost always forget it, with consequences in human intolerance and unnecessary suffering that are incalculable.

LIBERTY AND NECESSITY

DAVID HUME

. . . It is universally acknowledged that there is a great uniformity among the actions of men, in all nations and ages, and that human nature remains still the same, in its principles and operations. The same motives always produce the same actions: The same events follow from the same causes. Ambition, avarice, self-love, vanity, friendship, generosity, public spirit: these passions, mixed in various degrees, and distributed through society, have been, from the beginning of the world, and still are, the source of all the actions and enterprises, which have ever been observed among mankind. Would you know the sentiments, inclinations, and course of life of the Greeks and Romans? Study well the temper and actions of the French and English: You cannot be much mistaken in transferring to the former *most* of the observations which you have made with regard to the latter. Mankind are so much the same, in all times and places, that history informs us of nothing new or strange in this particular. Its chief use is only to discover the constant and universal principles of human nature, by showing men in all varieties of circumstances and situations, and furnishing us with materials from which we may form our observations and become acquainted with the regular springs of human action and behaviour. . . .

Should a traveller, returning from a far country, bring us an account of men, wholly different from any with whom we were ever acquainted; men, who were entirely divested of avarice, ambition, or revenge; who knew no pleasure but friendship, generosity, and public spirit; we should immediately, from these circumstances, detect the falsehood, and prove him a liar, with the same certainty as if he had stuffed his narration with stories of centaurs and dragons, miracles and prodigies. And if we would explode any forgery in history, we cannot make use of a more convincing argument, than to prove, that the actions ascribed to any person are directly contrary to the course of nature, and that no human motives, in such circumstances, could ever induce him to such a conduct. . . .

We must not, however, expect that this uniformity of human actions should be carried to such a length as that all men, in the same circumstances, will always act precisely in the same manner, without making any allowance for the diversity of characters, prejudices, and opinions. Such a uniformity in every particular, is found in no part of nature. On the

Reprinted, with omissions, from *An Inquiry Concerning Human Understanding*, Section 8, 1748.

contrary, from observing the variety of conduct in different men, we are enabled to form a greater variety of maxims, which still suppose a degree of uniformity and regularity.

Are the manners of men different in different ages and countries? We learn thence the great force of custom and education, which mould the human mind from its infancy and form it into a fixed and established character. Is the behaviour and conduct of the one sex very unlike that of the other? Is it thence we become acquainted with the different characters which nature has impressed upon the sexes, and which she preserves with constancy and regularity? Are the actions of the same person much diversified in the different periods of his life, from infancy to old age? This affords room for many general observations concerning the gradual change of our sentiments and inclinations, and the different maxims which prevail in the different ages of human creatures. Even the characters, which are peculiar to each individual, have a uniformity in their influence; otherwise our acquaintance with the persons and our observation of their conduct could never teach us their dispositions, or serve to direct our behaviour with regard to them.

I grant it possible to find some actions, which seem to have no regular connexion with any known motives, and are exceptions to all the measures of conduct which have ever been established for the government of men. But if we would willingly know what judgement should be formed of such irregular and extraordinary actions, we may consider the sentiments commonly entertained with regard to those irregular events which appear in the course of nature, and the operations of external objects. All causes are not conjoined to their usual effects with like uniformity. An artificer, who handles only dead matter, may be disappointed of his aim, as well as the politician, who directs the conduct of sensible and intelligent agents.

The vulgar, who take things according to their first appearance, attribute the uncertainty of events to such an uncertainty in the causes as makes the latter often fail of their usual influence; though they meet with no impediment in their operation. But philosophers, observing that, almost in every part of nature, there is contained a vast variety of springs and principles, which are hid, by reason of their minuteness or remoteness, find, that it is at least possible the contrariety of events may not proceed from any contingency in the cause, but from the secret operation of contrary causes. This possibility is converted into certainty by farther observation, when they remark that, upon an exact scrutiny, a contrariety of effects always betrays a contrariety of causes, and proceeds from their mutual opposition. A peasant can give no better reason for the stopping of any clock or watch than to say that it does not commonly go right: But an artist easily perceives that the same force in the spring or pendulum has always the same influence on the wheels; but fails of its usual effect, perhaps by reason of a grain of dust, which puts a stop to the whole movement. From the observation of several parallel instances, philosophers form a maxim that the connexion between all causes and effects is equally necessary, and that its seeming uncertainty in some instances proceeds from the secret opposition of contrary causes.

Thus, for instance, in the human body, when the usual symptoms of health or sickness disappoint our expectation; when medicines operate not with their wonted powers; when irregular events follow from any particular cause; the philosopher and physician are not surprised at the matter, nor are ever tempted to deny, in general, the necessity and uniformity of those principles by which the animal economy is conducted. They know that a human body is a mighty complicated machine: That many secret powers lurk in it, which are altogether beyond our comprehension: That to us it must often appear very uncertain in its operations: And that therefore the irregular events, which outwardly discover themselves, can be no proof that the laws of nature are not observed with the greatest regularity in its internal operations and government.

The philosopher, if he be consistent, must apply the same reasoning to the actions and volitions of intelligent agents. The most irregular and unexpected resolutions of men may frequently be accounted for by those who know every particular circumstance of their character and situation. A person of an obliging disposition gives a peevish answer: But he has the toothache, or has not dined. A stupid fellow discovers an uncommon alacrity in his carriage: But he has met with a sudden piece of good fortune. Or even when an action, as sometimes happens, cannot be particularly accounted for, either by the person himself or by others; we know, in general, that the characters of men are, to a certain degree, inconstant and irregular. This is, in a manner, the constant character of human nature; though it be applicable, in a more particular manner, to some persons who have no fixed rule for their conduct, but proceed in a continued course of caprice and inconstancy. The internal principles and motives may operate in a uniform manner, notwithstanding these seeming irregularities; in the same manner as the winds, rain, clouds, and other variations of the weather are supposed to be governed by steady principles; though not easily discoverable by human sagacity and enquiry.

Thus it appears, not only that the conjunction between motives and voluntary actions is as regular and uniform as that between the cause and effect in any part of nature; but also that this regular conjunction has been universally acknowledged among mankind, and has never been the subject of dispute, either in philosophy or common life. Now, as it is from past experience that we draw all inferences concerning the future, and as we conclude that objects will always be conjoined together which we find to have always been conjoined; it may seem superfluous to prove that this experienced uniformity in human actions is a source whence we draw *inferences* concerning them. But in order to throw the argument into a greater variety of lights we shall also insist, though briefly, on this latter topic.

The mutual dependence of men is so great in all societies that scarce any human action is entirely complete in itself, or is performed without some reference to the actions of others, which are requisite to make it answer fully the intention of the agent. The poorest artificer, who labours alone, expects at least the protection of the magistrate, to ensure him the enjoyment of the fruits of his labour. He also expects that, when he carries his goods to market, and offers them at a reasonable price, he shall find purchasers, and shall be able, by the money he acquires, to engage others to supply him with those commodities which are requisite for his subsistence. In proportion as men extend their dealings, and render their intercourse with others more complicated, they always comprehend, in their schemes of life, a greater variety of voluntary actions, which they expect, from the proper motives, to co-operate with their own. In all these conclusions they take their measures from past experience, in the same manner as in their reasonings concerning external objects; and firmly believe that men, as well as all the elements, are to continue, in their operations, the same that they have ever found them. A manufacturer reckons upon the labour of his servants for the execution of any work as much as upon the tools which he employs, and would be equally surprised were his expectations disappointed. In short, this experimental inference and reasoning concerning the actions of others enters so much into human life, that no man, while awake, is ever a moment without employing it. Have we not reason, therefore, to affirm that all mankind have always agreed in the doctrine of necessity according to the foregoing definition and explication of it?

Nor have philosophers ever entertained a different opinion from the people in this particular. For, not to mention that almost every action of their life supposes that opinion, there are even few of the speculative parts of learning to which it is not essential. What would become of *history*, had we not a dependence on the veracity of the historian according to the experience which we have had of mankind? How could *politics* be a science, if laws and forms of government had not a uniform influence upon society? Where would be the foundation of *morals*, if particular characters had no certain or determinate power to produce particular sentiments, and if these sentiments had no constant operation on actions? And with what pretence could we employ our *criticism* upon any poet or polite author, if we could not pronounce the conduct and sentiments of his actors either natural or unnatural to such characters, and in such circumstances? It seems almost impossible, therefore, to engage either in science or action of any kind without acknowledging the doctrine of necessity, and this *inference* from motive to voluntary actions, from characters to conduct.

And indeed, when we consider how aptly *natural* and *moral* evidence link together, and form only one chain of argument, we shall make no scruple to allow that they are of the same nature, and derived from the same principles. A prisoner who has neither money nor interest, discovers the impossibility of his escape, as well when he considers the obstinacy of the gaoler, as the walls and bars with which he is surrounded; and, in all attempts for his freedom, chooses rather to work upon the stone and iron of the one, than upon the inflexible nature of the other. The same prisoner, when conducted to the scaffold, foresees his death as certainly from the constancy and fidelity of his guards, as from the operation of the axe or wheel. His mind runs along a certain train of ideas: The refusal of the soldiers to consent to his escape; the action of the executioner; the separation of the head and body; bleeding, convulsive motions, and death. Here is a connected chain of natural causes and voluntary actions; but the mind feels no difference between them in passing from one link to another: Nor is less certain of the future event than if it were connected with the objects present to the memory or senses, by a train of causes, cemented together by what we are pleased to call a *physical* necessity. The same experienced union has the same effect on the mind, whether the united objects be motives, volition, and actions; or figure and motion. We may change the name of things; but their nature and their operation on the understanding never change.

Were a man, whom I know to be honest and opulent, and with whom I live in intimate friendship, to come into my house, where I am surrounded with my servants, I rest assured that he is not to stab me before he leaves it in order to rob me of my silver standish; and I no more suspect this event than the falling of the house itself, which is new, and solidly built and founded.—*But he may have been seized with a sudden and unknown frenzy*.—So may a sudden earthquake arise, and shake and tumble my house about my ears. I shall therefore change the suppositions. I shall say that I know with certainty that he is not to put his hand into the fire and hold it there till it be consumed: And this event, I think I can foretell with the same assurance, as that, if he throw himself out at the window, and meet with no obstruction, he will not remain a moment suspended in the air. No suspicion of an unknown frenzy can give the least possibility to the former event, which is so contrary to all the known principles of human nature. A man who at noon leaves his purse full of gold on the pavement at Charing-Cross, may as well expect that it will fly away like a feather, as that he will find it untouched an hour after. Above one half of human reasonings contain inferences of a similar nature, attended with more or less degrees of certainty proportioned to our experience of the usual conduct of mankind in such particular situations. . . .

But to proceed in this reconciling project with regard to the question of liberty and necessity; the most contentious question of metaphysics, the most contentious science; it will not require many words to prove, that all mankind have ever agreed in the doctrine of liberty as well as in that of necessity, and that the whole dispute, in this respect also, has been hitherto merely verbal. For what is meant by liberty, when applied to voluntary actions? We cannot surely mean that actions have so little connexion with motives, inclinations, and circumstances, that one does not follow with a certain degree of uniformity from the other, and that one affords no inference by which we can conclude the existence of the other. For these are plain and acknowledged matters of fact. By liberty, then, we can only mean *a power of acting or not acting, according to the determinations of the will;* that is, if we choose to remain at rest, we may; if we choose to move, we also may. Now this hypothetical liberty is universally allowed to belong to every one who is not a prisoner and in chains. Here, then, is no subject of dispute. . . .

All laws being founded on rewards and punishments, it is supposed as a fundamental principle, that these motives have a regular and uniform influence on the mind, and both produce the good and prevent the evil actions. We may give to this influence what name we please; but, as it is usually conjoined with the action, it must be esteemed a *cause*, and be looked upon as an instance of that necessity, which we would here establish.

The only proper object of hatred or vengeance is a person or creature, endowed with thought and consciousness; and when any criminal or injurious actions excite that passion, it is only by their relation to the person, or connexion with him. Actions are, by their very nature, temporary and perishing; and where they proceed not from some *cause* in the character and disposition of the person who performed them, they can neither redound to his honour, if good; nor infamy, if evil. The actions themselves may be blameable; they may be contrary to all the rules of morality and religion: But the person is not answerable for them; and as they proceeded from nothing in him that is durable and constant, and leave nothing of that nature behind them, it is impossible he can, upon their account, become the object of punishment or vengeance. According to the principle, therefore, which denies necessity, and consequently causes, a man is as pure and untainted, after having committed the most horrid crime, as at the first moment of his birth, nor is his character anywise concerned in his actions, since they are not derived from it, and the wickedness of the one can never be used as a proof of the depravity of the other.

Men are not blamed for such actions as they perform ignorantly and casually, whatever may be the consequences. Why? but because the principles of these actions are only momentary, and terminate in them alone. Men are less blamed for such actions as they perform hastily and unpremeditately than for such as proceed from deliberation. For what reason? but because a hasty temper, though a constant cause or principle in the mind, operates only by intervals, and infects not the whole character. Again, repentance wipes off every crime, if attended with a reformation of life and manners. How is this to be accounted for? but by asserting that actions render a person criminal merely as they are proofs of criminal principles in the mind; and when, by an alteration of these principles, they cease to be just proofs, they likewise cease to be criminal. But, except upon the doctrine of necessity, they never were just proofs, and consequently never were criminal.

It will be equally easy to prove, and from the same arguments, that *liberty*, according to that definition above mentioned, in which all men agree, is also essential to morality, and that no human actions, where it is wanting, are susceptible of any moral qualities, or can be the objects either or approbation or dislike. For as actions are objects of our moral sentiment, so far only as they are indications of the internal character, passions, and affections; it is impossible that they can give rise either to praise or blame, where they proceed not from these principles, but are derived altogether from external violence. . . .

IN DEFENCE OF FREE WILL

C. A. CAMPBELL

Mighty issues turn, and turn directly, on the solution of the free will problem. It is in no way surprising that for centuries past it has exercised a fascination for thinkers both within and without the ranks of the professional philosophers that is probably not paralleled in the case of any of the other great problems of metaphysics.

. . . The present state of philosophical opinion on free will is, for certain definitely assignable reasons, profoundly unsatisfactory. In my judgement, a thoroughly perverse attitude to the whole problem has been created by the almost universal acquiescence in the view that free will in what is often called the "vulgar" sense is too obviously nonsensical a notion to deserve serious discussion. Free will in a more "refined" sense—which is apt to mean free will purged of all elements that may cause embarrassment to a Deterministic psychology or a Deterministic metaphysics—is, it is understood, a conception which may be defended by the philosopher without loss of caste. But in its "vulgar" sense, as maintained, for example, by the plain man, who clings to a belief in genuinely open possibilities, it is (we are told) a wild and even obnoxious delusion, long ago discredited for sober thinkers.

Now, as it happens, I myself firmly believe that free will, in something extremely like the "vulgar" sense, is a fact. And I am anxious to-day to do what I can, within the limits of a single lecture, to justify that belief. I propose therefore to develop a statement of the Libertarian's position which will try to make clear why he finds himself obliged to hold what he does hold, and to follow this up with a critical examination of the grounds most in vogue among philosophers for impugning this position. Considerations of time will, I fear, compel a somewhat close economy in my treatment of objections. But I shall hope to say enough to instigate a doubt in some minds concerning the validity of certain very fashionable objections whose authority is often taken to be virtually final. And if no

Reprinted from *In Defence of Free Will, An Inaugural Lecture* (1938), by permission of the author. Published by Jackson, Son and Co., Glasgow.

other good purpose is served, it will at least be of advantage if I can offer, in my positive statement, a target for the missiles of the critics more truly representative of Libertarianism than the targets at which they sometimes direct their fire—targets, I may add, upon which even the clumsiest of marksmen could hardly fail to register bull's eyes.

Let us begin by noting that the problem of free will gets its urgency for the ordinary educated man by reason of its close connection with the conception of moral responsibility. When we regard a man as morally responsible for an act, we regard him as a legitimate object of moral praise or blame in respect of it. But it seems plain that a man cannot be a legitimate object of moral praise or blame for an act unless in willing the act he is in some important sense a "free" agent. Evidently free will in some sense, therefore, is a precondition of moral responsibility. Without doubt it is the realisation that any threat to freedom is thus a threat to moral responsibility—with all that that implies—combined with the knowledge that there are a variety of considerations, philosophic, scientific, and theological, tending to place freedom in jeopardy, that gives to the problem of free will its perennial and universal appeal. And it is therefore in close connection with the question of the conditions of moral responsibility that any discussion of the problem must proceed, if it is not to be academic in the worst sense of the term.

We raise the question at once, therefore, what are the conditions, in respect of freedom, which must attach to an act in order to make it a morally responsible act? It seems to me that the fundamental conditions are two. I shall state them with all possible brevity, for we have a long road to travel.

The first condition is the universally recognised one that the act must be *self*-caused, *self*-determined. But it is important to accept this condition in its full rigour. The agent must be not merely *a* cause but the *sole* cause of that for which he is deemed morally responsible. If entities other than the self have also a causal influence upon an act, then that act is not one for which we can say without qualification that the *self* is morally responsible. If in respect of it we hold the self responsible at all, it can only be for some feature of the act—assuming the possibility of disengaging such a feature—of which the self *is* the sole cause. I do not see how this conclusion can be evaded. But it has awkward implications which have led not a few people to abandon the notion of individual moral responsibility altogether.

The first condition, however, is quite clearly not sufficient. It is possible to conceive an act of which the agent is the sole cause, but which is at the same time an act *necessitated* by the agent's nature. Some philosophers have contended, for example, that the act of Divine creation is an act which issues necessarily from the Divine nature. In the case of such an act, where the agent could not do otherwise than he did, we must all agree, I think, that it would be inept to say that he *ought* to have done otherwise and is thus morally blameworthy, or *ought not* to have done otherwise and is thus morally praiseworthy. It is perfectly true that we do sometimes hold a person morally responsible for an act, even when we believe that he, being what he now is, virtually could not do otherwise. But underlying that judgement is always the assumption that the person has *come* to be what he now is in virtue of past acts of will in which he *was* confronted by real alternatives, by genuinely open possibilities: and, strictly speaking, it is in respect of these *past* acts of his that we praise or blame the agent *now*. For ultimate analysis, the agent's power of alternative action would seem to be an inexpugnable condition of his liability to moral praise or blame, i.e. of his moral responsibility.

We may lay down, therefore, that an act is a "free" act in the sense required for moral responsibility only if the agent (*a*) is the sole cause of the act; and (*b*) could exert his causality in alternative ways. And it may be pointed out in passing that the acceptance of condition (*b*) implies the recognition of the inadequacy for moral freedom of mere "self-determination." The doctrine called "Self-determinism" is often contrasted by its advocates with mere Determinism on the one hand and Indeterminism on the other, and pronounced to be the one true gospel. I must insist, however, that if "Self-determinism" rejects condition (*b*), it cannot claim to be a doctrine of free will in the sense required to vindicate moral responsibility. The doctrine which demands, and asserts, the fulfillment of both conditions is the doctrine we call "Libertarianism." And it would in my opinion minister greatly to clarity if it were more widely recognised that for any doctrine which is not a species of Libertarianism to pose as a doctrine of "free will" is mere masquerade.

And now, the conditions of free will being defined in these general terms, we have to ask whether human beings are in fact capable of performing free acts; and if so, where precisely such acts are to be found. In order to prepare the way for an answer, it is desirable, I think, that we should get clear at once about the significance of a certain very familiar, but none the less formidable, criticism of free will which the Self-determinist as well as the Libertarian has to meet. This is the criticism which bases itself upon the facts of heredity on the one hand and of environment on the other. I may briefly summarise the criticism as follows.

Every historic self has an hereditary nature consisting of a group of inborn propensities, in range more or less common to the race, but specific to the individual in their respective strengths. With this equipment the self just *happens* to be born. Strictly speaking, it antedates the existence of the self proper, i.e. the existence of the self-conscious subject, and it is itself the effect of a series of causes leading back to indefinitely remote antiquity. It follows, therefore, that any of the self's choices that manifests the influence of his hereditary nature is not a choice of which *he*, the actual historic self, is the sole cause. The choice is determined, at least in part, by factors external to the self. The same thing holds good of "environment." Every self is born and bred in a particular physical and social environment, not of his own choosing, which plays upon him in innumerable ways, encouraging this propensity, discouraging that, and so on. Clearly any of the self's choices that manifests the influence of environmental factors is likewise a choice which is determined, at least in part, by factors external to the self. But if we thus grant, as seems inevitable, that heredity and environment are external influences, where shall we find a choice in the whole history of a self that is not subject to external influence? Surely we must admit that every particular act of choice bears the marks of the agent's hereditary nature and environmental nature; in which case a free act, in the sense of an act determined solely by the self, must be dismissed as a mere chimaera.

To this line of criticism the Self-determinist—T. H. Green is a typical example—has a stock reply. He urges that these factors, heredity and environment, are not, in so far as their operation in willing (and therefore in conduct proper) is concerned, "external" to the self at all. For the act of willing, when we analyse it, reveals itself to be in its nature such that no end can be willed save in so far as it is conceived by the self as a good for the self. A "native propensity" cannot function *as such* in willing. It can function only in so far as the self conceives its object as a good for the self. It follows that the self in willing is essentially *self*-determining; not moved from the outside, but moved always by its own conception of its own good. Inherited nature and environmental circumstance do play their part; but not as factors external to the self. They can function only in so far as their suggestions are, as it were, incorporated by the self in its conception of its own good. Consequently—so we are told—the threat to self-determination from the side of inheritance and environment disappears on an adequate analysis of the act of willing.

I am afraid, however, that this argument, though it contains important truth, cannot bear the heavy weight that is here imposed upon it. Let us grant that inheritance and environment can operate in willing only in the medium of the self's conception of its own good. But then let us ask, how is the self's conception of its own good constituted? Self-consciousness is required, of course: but mere self-conscious reflection *in vacuo* will not furnish the self with any conception of a personal good whatsoever. Obviously to answer the question in regard to any agent we are obliged to make reference to certain sheer external facts; viz. to the quality and strength of that person's inherited propensities, and to the nature of the influences that are brought to bear upon him from the side of environment. It seems certain, then, that the self's conception of its own good is influenced directly by its particular inheritance and environment. But to admit this surely involves the admission that external determination enters into choices. It may be true that the self's choices are always determined by its conception of its own good. But if what it conceives to be its own good is always dependent, at least partly, upon inheritance and environment, as external facts, then it is idle to deny that the self's choices are externally influenced likewise.

Indeed I cannot but regard the attempt to save self-determination by denying the externality of the influence of heredity and environment as a quite desperate expedient. It is significant that nobody really believes it in practice. The externality of these influences is taken for granted in our reflective practical judgements upon persons. On those occasions when we are in real earnest about giving a critical and considered estimate of a man's moral calibre—as, e.g. in any serious biographical study—we impose upon ourselves as a matter of course the duty of enquiring with scrupulous care into his hereditary propensities and environmental circumstances, with a view to discovering how far his conduct is influenced by these factors. And having traced these influences, we certainly do not regard the result as having no bearing on the question of the man's moral responsibility for his conduct. On the contrary, the very purpose of the enquiry is to enable us, by due appreciation of the *external* influences that affect his conduct, to gain as accurate a view as possible of that which can justly be attributed to the man's own *self*-determination. The allowances that we all of us do in practice make for hereditary and environmental influences in passing judgement on our fellows would be meaningless if we did not suppose these influences to be in a real sense "external" to the self.

Now the recognition of this externality is, of course, just as serious a matter for the Libertarian as for the Self-determinist. For the Libertarian, as we saw, accepts condition (*a*) no less wholeheartedly than the Self-determinist does: i.e. that an act is free only if it is determined by the self and nothing but the self. But though we have not been *directly* advancing our course by these recent considerations, we have been doing so indirectly, by narrowing and sharpening the issue. We know now that condition (*a*) is not fulfilled by any act in respect of which inheritance or environment exerts a causal influence. For that type of influence has been shown to be in a real sense external to the self. The free act of which we are in search has therefore got to be one into which influences of this kind do not enter at all.

Moreover, one encouraging portent has emerged in the course of our brief discussion. For we noticed that our reflective practical judgements on persons, while fully recognising the externality of the influence of heredity and environment, do nevertheless presuppose throughout that there *is something* in conduct which is genuinely self-determined; something which the agent contributes solely on his own initiative, unaffected by external influences; something for which, accordingly, he may justly be held morally responsible. That conviction may, of course, be a false one. But the fact of its wide-spread existence can hardly be without significance for our problem.

Let us proceed, then, by following up this clue. Let us ask, why do human beings so obstinately persist in believing that there is an indissoluble core of purely *self*-originated activity which even heredity and environment are powerless to affect? There can be little doubt, I think, of the answer in general terms. They do so, at bottom, because they feel certain of the existence of such activity from their immediate practical experience of themselves. Nor can there be in the end much doubt, I think, in what function of the self that activity is to be located. There seems to me to be one, and only one, function of the self with respect to which the agent can even pretend to have an assurance of that absolute self-origination which is here at issue. But to render precise the nature of that function is obviously of quite paramount importance: and we can do so, I think, only by way of a somewhat thorough analysis—which I now propose to attempt—of the experiential situation in which it occurs, viz. the situation of "moral temptation."

It is characteristic of that situation that in it I am aware of an end A which I believe to be morally right, and also of an end B, incompatible with A, towards which, in virtue of that system of conative dispositions which constitutes my "character" as so far formed, I entertain a strong desire. There may be, and perhaps must be, desiring elements in my nature which are directed to A also. But what gives to the situation its specific character as one of moral temptation is that the urge of our desiring nature towards the right end, A, is felt to be *relatively* weak. We are sure that if our desiring nature is permitted to issue directly in action, it is end B that we shall choose. That is what is meant by saying, as William James does, that end B is "in the line of least resistance" relatively to our conative dispositions. The expression is, of course, a metaphorical one, but it serves to describe, graphically enough, a situation of which we all have frequent experience, viz. where we recognise a specific end as that towards which the "set" of our desiring nature most strongly inclines us, and which we shall indubitably choose if no inhibiting factor intervenes.

But inhibiting factors, we should most of us say, *may* intervene: and that in two totally different ways which it is vital to distinguish clearly. The inhibiting factor may be of the nature of another desire (or aversion), which operates by changing the balance of the desiring situation. Though at one stage I desire B, which I believe to be wrong, more strongly than I desire A, which I believe to be right, it may happen that before action is taken I become aware of certain hitherto undiscerned consequences of A which I strongly desire, and the result may be that now not B but A presents itself to me as the end in the line of least resistance. Moral temptation is here overcome by the simple process of ceasing to be a moral temptation.

That is one way, and probably by far the commoner way, in which an inhibiting factor intervenes. But it is certainly not regarded by the self who is confronted by moral temptation as the *only* way. In such situations we all believe, rightly or wrongly, that even although B *continues* to be in the line of least resistance, even although, in other words, the situation remains one with the characteristic marks of moral temptation, we *can* nevertheless align ourselves with A. We can do so, we believe, because we have the power to introduce a new energy, to make what we call an "effort of will," whereby we are able to act contrary to the felt balance of mere desire, and to achieve the higher end despite the fact that it continues to be in the line of greater resistance relatively to our desiring nature. The self in practice believes that it has this power; and believes, moreover, that the decision rests solely with its self, here and now, whether this power be exerted or not.

Now the objective validity or otherwise of this belief is not at the moment in question. I am here merely pointing to its existence as a psychological fact. No amount of introspective analysis, so far as I can see, even tends to disprove that we do as a matter of fact believe, in situations of moral temptation, that it rests with our self absolutely to decide whether we exert the effort of will which will enable us to rise to duty, or whether we shall allow our desiring nature to take its course.

I have now to point out, further, how this act of moral decision, at least in the significance which it has for the agent himself, fulfils in full the two conditions which we found it necessary to lay down at the beginning for the kind of "free" act which moral responsibility presupposes.

For obviously it is, in the first place, an act which the agent believes he could perform in alternative ways. He believes that it is genuinely open to him to put forth effort—in varying degrees, if the situation admits of that—or withhold it altogether. And when he *has* decided—in whatever way—he remains convinced that these alternative courses were really open to him.

It is perhaps a little less obvious, but, I think, equally certain, that the agent believes the second condition to be fulfilled likewise, i.e. that the act of decision is determined *solely* by his self. It appears less obvious, because we all realise that formed character has a great deal to do with the choices that we make; and formed character is, without a doubt, partly dependent on the external factors of heredity and environment. But it is crucial here that we should not misunderstand the precise nature of the influence which formed character brings to bear upon the choices that constitute conduct. No one denies that it determines, at least largely, what things we desire, and again how greatly we desire them. It may thus fairly be said to determine the felt balance of desires in the situation of moral temptation. But all that that amounts to is that formed character prescribes the nature of the situation *within* which the act of moral decision takes place. It does not in the least follow that it has any influence whatsoever in determining the act of decision itself—the decision as to whether we shall exert effort or take the easy course of following the bent of our desiring nature: take, that is to say, the course which, in virtue of the determining influence of our character as so far formed, we feel to be in the line of least resistance.

When one appreciates this, one is perhaps better prepared to recognise the fact that the agent himself in the situation of moral temptation does not, and indeed could not, regard his formed character as having any influence whatever upon his act of decision as such. For the very nature of that decision, as it presents itself to him, is as to whether he will or will not permit his formed character to dictate his action. In other words, the agent distinguishes sharply between the self which makes the decision, and the self which, as formed character, determines not the decision but the situation within which the decision takes place. Rightly or wrongly, the agent believes that through his act of decision he can oppose and transcend his own formed character in the interest of duty. We are therefore obliged to say, I think, that the agent *cannot* regard his formed character as in any sense a determinant of the act of decision as such. The act is felt to be a genuinely creative act, originated by the self *ad hoc*, and by the self alone.

Here then, if my analysis is correct, in the function of moral decision in situations of moral temptation, we have an act of the self which at least *appears to the agent* to satisfy both of the conditions of freedom which we laid down at the beginning. The vital question now is, is this "appearance" true or false? Is the act of decision really what it appears to the agent to be, determined solely by the self, and capable of alternative forms of expression? If it is, then we have here a free act which serves as an adequate basis for moral responsibility. We shall be entitled to regard the agent as morally praiseworthy or morally blameworthy according as he decides to put forth effort or to let his desiring nature have its way. We shall be entitled, in short, to judge the agent as he most certainly judges himself in the situation of moral temptation. If, on the other hand, there is good reason to believe that the agent is the victim of illusion in supposing his act of decision to bear this character, then in my opinion the whole conception of moral responsibility must be jettisoned altogether. For it seems to me certain that there is no other function of the self that even looks as though it satisfied the required conditions of the free act.

Now in considering the claim to truth of this belief of our practical consciousness, we should begin by noting that the onus of proof rests upon the critic who rejects this belief. Until cogent evidence to the contrary is adduced, we are entitled to put our trust in a belief which is so deeply embedded in our experience as practical beings as to be, I venture to say, ineradicable from it. Anyone who doubts whether it is ineradicable may be invited to think himself imaginatively into a situation of moral temptation as we have above described it, and then to ask himself whether in that situation he finds it possible to *disbelieve* that his act of decision has the characteristics in question. I have no misgivings about the answer. It is possible to disbelieve only when we are thinking abstractly about the situation; not when we are living through it, either actually or in imagination. This fact certainly establishes a strong *prima facie* presumption in favour of the Libertarian position. Nevertheless I agree that we shall have to weigh carefully several criticisms of high authority before we can feel justified in asserting free will as an ultimate and unqualified truth.

Fortunately for our purpose, however, there are some lines of criticism which, although extremely influential in the recent past, may at the present time be legitimately ignored. We are not to-day confronted, for example, by any widely accepted system of metaphysic with implications directly hostile to free will. Only a decade or two ago one could hardly hope to gain a sympathetic hearing for a view which assigned an ultimate initiative to finite selves, unless one were prepared first to show reason for rejecting the dominant metaphysical doctrine that all things in the universe are the expression of a single Mind or Spirit. But the challenge so lately offered by monistic Idealism has in the present age little more significance than the challenge once offered by monistic Materialism.

Much the same thing holds good of the challenge from the side of physical science. Libertarianism is certainly inconsistent with a rigidly determinist theory of the physical world. It is idle to pretend that there can be open possibilities for psychical decision, while at the same time holding that the physical events in which such decisions manifest themselves are determined in accordance with irrevocable law. But whereas until a few years ago the weight of scientific authority was thrown overwhelmingly on the side of a universal determinism of physical phenomena, the situation has, as everybody knows, profoundly altered during the present century, more especially since the advent of Planck's Quantum Theory and Heisenberg's Principle of Uncertainty. Very few scientists to-day would seek to impugn free will on the ground of any supposed implications of the aims or achievements of physical science. I am not myself, I should perhaps add in passing, disposed to rest any part of the case against a universal physical determinism upon these recent dramatic developments of physical science. In my view there never were in the established results of physical science cogent reasons for believing that the apparently universal determinism of inorganic processes holds good also of the processes of the human body. The only inference I here wish to draw from the trend of present-day science is that it removes from any *contemporary* urgency the problem of meeting one particular type of objection to free will. And it is with the contemporary situation that I am in this paper anxious to deal.

I may turn at once, therefore, to lines of argument which do still enjoy a wide currency among anti-Libertarians. And I shall begin with one which, though it is a simple matter to show its irrelevance to the Libertarian doctrine as I have stated it, is so extremely popular that it cannot safely be ignored.

The charge made is that the Libertarian view is incompatible with the *predictability* of human conduct. For we do make rough predictions of people's conduct, on the basis of what we know of their character, every day of our lives, and there can be no doubt that the practice, within certain limits, is amply justified by results. Indeed if it were not so, social life would be reduced to sheer chaos. The close relationship between character and conduct which prediction postulates really seems to be about as certain as anything can be. But the Libertarian view, it is urged, by ascribing to the self a mysterious power of decision uncontrolled by character, and capable of issuing in acts inconsistent with character, denies that continuity between character and conduct upon which prediction depends. If Libertarianism is true, prediction is impossible. But prediction *is* possible, therefore Libertarianism is untrue.

My answer is that the Libertarian view is perfectly compatible with prediction within certain limits, and that there is no empirical evidence at all that prediction is in fact possible beyond these limits. The following considerations will, I think, make the point abundantly clear.

(1) There is no question, on our view, of a free will that can will just anything at all. The range of possible choices is limited by the agent's character in every case; for nothing can be an object of possible choice which is not suggested by either the agent's desires or his moral ideals, and these depend on "character" for us just as much as for our opponents. We have, indeed, explicitly recognised at an earlier stage that character determines the situation within which the act of moral decision takes place, although not the act of moral decision itself. This consideration obviously furnishes a broad basis for at least approximate predictions.

(2) There is *one* experiential situation, and *one only*, on our view, in which there is any possibility of the act of will not being in accordance with character; viz. the situation in which the course which formed character prescribes is a course in conflict with the agent's moral ideal: in other words, the situation of moral temptation. Now this is a situation of comparative rarity. Yet with respect to all other situations in life we are in full agreement with those who hold that conduct is the response of the agent's formed character to the given situation. Why should it not be so? There could be no reason, on our view any more than on another, for the agent even to consider deviating from the course which his formed character prescribes and he most strongly desires, *unless* that course is believed by him to be incompatible with what is right.

(3) Even within that one situation which is relevant to free will, our view can still recognise a certain basis for prediction. In that situation our character as so far formed prescribes a course opposed to duty, and an effort of will is required if we are to deviate from that course. But of course we are all aware that a greater effort of will is required in proportion to the degree in which we have to transcend our formed character in order to will the right. Such action is, as we say, "harder." But if action is "harder" in proportion as it involves deviation from formed character, it seems reasonable to suppose that, on the whole, action will be of rarer occurrence in that same proportion: though perhaps we may not say that at any level of deviation it becomes flatly impossible. It follows that even with respect to situations of moral temptation we may usefully employ our knowledge of the agent's character as a clue to prediction. It will be a clue of limited, but of by no means negligible, value. It will warrant us in predicting, e.g., of a person who has become enslaved to alcohol, that he is unlikely, even if fully aware of the moral evil of such slavery, to be successful immediately and completely in throwing off its shackles. Predictions of this kind we all make often enough in practice. And there seems no reason at all why a Libertarian doctrine should wish to question their validity.

Now when these three considerations are borne in mind, it becomes quite clear that the doctrine we are defending is compatible with a very substantial measure of predictability indeed. And I submit that there is not a jot of empirical evidence that any larger measure than this obtains in fact.

Let us pass on then to consider a much more interesting and, I think, more plausible criticism. It is constantly objected against the Libertarian doctrine that it is fundamentally *unintelligible*. Libertarianism holds that the act of moral decision is the *self's* act, and yet insists at the same time that it is not influenced by any of those determinate features in the self's nature which go to constitute its "character." But, it is asked, do not these two propositions contradict one another? Surely a *self*-determination which is determination by something other than the self's *character* is a contradiction in terms? What meaning is there in the conception of a "self" in abstraction from its "character"? If you really wish to maintain, it is urged, that the act of decision is not determined by the self's character, you ought to admit frankly that it is not determined by the *self* at all. But in that case, of course, you will not be advocating a freedom which lends any kind of support to moral responsibility; indeed very much the reverse.

Now this criticism, and all of its kind, seem to me to be the product of a simple, but extraordinarily pervasive, error: the error of confining one's self to the categories of the external observer in dealing with the actions of human agents. Let me explain.

It is perfectly true that the stand-point of the external observer, which we are obliged to adopt in dealing with physical processes, does not furnish us with even a glimmering of a notion of what can be meant by an entity which acts causally and yet not through any of the determinate features of its character. So far as we confine ourselves to external observation, I agree that this notion must seem to us pure nonsense. But then we are *not* obliged to confine ourselves to external observation in dealing with the human agent. Here, though here alone, we have the inestimable advantage of being able to apprehend operations from the *inside*, from the stand-point of *living experience*. But if we do adopt this internal stand-point—surely a proper stand-point, and one which we should be only too glad to adopt if we could in the case of other entities—the situation is entirely changed. We find that we not merely can, but constantly do, attach meaning to a causation which is the self's causation but is yet not exercised by the self's character. We have seen as much already in our analysis of the situation of moral temptation. When confronted by such a situation, we saw, we are certain that it lies with our *self* to decide whether we shall let our character as so far formed dictate our action or whether we shall by effort oppose its dictates and rise to duty. We are certain, in other words, that the act is *not* determined by our *character*, while we remain equally certain that the act *is* determined by our *self*.

Or look, for a further illustration (since the point we have to make here is of the very first importance for the whole free will controversy), to the experience of effortful willing itself, where the act of decision has found expression in the will to rise to duty. In such an experience we are certain that it is our self which makes the effort. But we are equally certain that the effort does not flow from that system of conative dispositions which we call our formed character; for the very function that the effort has for us is to enable us to act against the "line of least resistance," i.e. to act in a way *contrary* to that to which our formed character inclines us.

I conclude, therefore, that those who find the Libertarian doctrine of the self's causality in moral decision inherently unintelligible find it so simply because they restrict themselves, quite arbitrarily, to an inadequate stand-point: a stand-point from which, indeed, a genuinely creative activity, if it existed, never *could* be apprehended.

It will be understood, of course, that it is no part of my purpose to deny that the act of moral decision is in *one* sense "unintelligible." If by the "intelligibility" of an act we mean that it is capable, at least in principle, of being inferred as a consequence of a given ground, then naturally my view is that the act in question is "*un*intelligible." But that, presumably, is not the meaning of "intelligibility" in the critic's mind when he says that the Libertarian holds an "unintelligible" doctrine. If it were all he meant, he would merely be pointing out that Libertarianism is not compatible with Determinism! And that tautologous pronouncement would hardly deserve the title of "criticism." Yet, strangely enough, not all of the critics seem to be quite clear on this matter. The Libertarian often has the experience of being challenged by the critic to tell him *why*, on his view, the agent now decides to put forth moral effort and now decides not to, with the obviously intended implication that if the Libertarian cannot say "why" he should give up his theory. Such critics apparently fail to see that if the Libertarian *could* say why he would already have given up his theory! Obviously to demand "intelligibility" in this sense is simply to prejudge the whole issue in favour of Determinism. The sense in which the critic is entitled to demand intelligibility of our doctrine is simply this; he may demand that the kind of action which our doctrine imputes to human selves should not be, for ultimate analysis, meaningless. And in that sense, as I have already argued, our doctrine is perfectly intelligible.

Let us suppose, then, that the Determinist, confronted by the plain evidence of our practical self-consciousness, now recognises his obligation to give up the position that the Libertarian doctrine is without qualification "meaningless," and concedes that from the stand-point of our practical self-consciousness at any rate it is "meaningful." And let us ask what will be his next move. So far as I can see, his most likely move now will be to attack the value of that "internal" stand-point, contrasting it unfavourably, in respect of its claim to truth, with the rational, objective, stand-point of "pure philosophy." "I admit," he may tell us, "that there is begotten in the self, in the practical experience you refer to, a belief in a self-causality which is yet not a causality exercised through the self's character. But surely this must weigh but lightly in the balance against the proposition, which appeals to our reason with axiomatic certainty, that an act cannot be caused by a self if it has no ground in the determinate nature of that self. If the choice lies between either disbelieving that rational proposition, or dismissing the evidence of practical self-consciousness as illusion, it is the latter alternative which in my opinion any sane philosophy is bound to adopt."

But a very little reflection suffices to show that this position is in reality no improvement at all on that from which the critic has just fallen back. For it is evident that the proposition alleged to be axiomatic is axiomatic, at most, only to a reason which knows nothing of acts or events save as they present themselves to an external observer. It obviously is *not* axiomatic to a reason whose field of apprehension is broadened to include the data furnished by the direct experience of acting. In short, the proposition is axiomatic, at most, only to reason functioning *abstractly;* which most certainly cannot be identified with reason functioning *philosophically.*

What is required of the critic, of course, if he is to make good his case, is a reasoned justification of his cavalier attitude towards the testimony of practical self-consciousness. That is the primary desideratum. And the lack of it in the bulk of Determinist literature is in my opinion something of a scandal. Without it, the criticism we have just been examining is sheer dogmatism. It is, indeed, dogmatism of a peculiarly perverse kind. For the situation is, in effect, as follows. From our practical self-consciousness we gain a notion of a genuinely creative act—which might be defined as an act which nothing determines save the agent's doing of it. Of such a character is the act of moral decision as we experience it. But the critic says "No! This sort of thing cannot be. A person cannot without affront to reason be conceived to be the author of an act which bears, *ex hypothesi,* no intelligible relation to his character. A mere intuition of practical self-consciousness is the solitary prop of this fantastic notion, and surely that is quite incapable of bearing the weight that you would thrust upon it." Now observe the perversity! The critic says, excluding the evidence of practical self-consciousness, the notion makes nonsense. In other words, excluding the only evidence there ever *could* be for such a notion, the notion makes nonsense! For, of course, if there should be such a thing as creative activity, there is absolutely no other way save an intuition of practical self-consciousness in which we could become aware of it. Only from the inside, from the stand-point of the agent's living experience, can "activity" possibly be apprehended. So that what the critic is really doing is to condemn a notion as nonsensical on the ground that the only evidence for it is the only evidence there ever could be for it.

FREEDOM OF THE WILL

JOHN STUART MILL

Mill has just completed a discussion and defense of determinism or, as he calls it, necessitarianism. He has insisted that the evidence for it in the psychological sphere is convincing—our volitions are determined by antecedent causes. Although the selection that appears here concerns the argument from consciousness of Sir William Hamilton, the reader may consider Mill's critique as it applies to the appeal to consciousness of C. A. Campbell (preceding selection).

This argument from experience Sir W. Hamilton passes unnoticed, but urges, on the opposite side of the question, the argument from Consciousness. We are conscious, he affirms, either of our freedom, or at all events (it is odd that, on his theory, there should be any doubt) of something which implies freedom. If this is true, our internal consciousness tells us that we have a power, which the whole outward experience of the human race tells us that we never use. This is surely a very unfortunate predicament we are in, and a sore trial to the puzzled metaphysician. Philosophy is far from having so easy a business before her as our author thinks: the arbiter Consciousness is by no means invoked to turn the scale between two equally balanced difficulties; on the contrary, she has to sit in judgment between herself and a complete induction from experience. Consciousness, it will probably be said, is the best evidence; and so it would be, if we were always certain what is Consciousness. But while there are so many varying testimonies respecting this; when Sir W. Hamilton can himself say,* "many philosophers have attempted to establish, on the principles of common sense, propositions which are not original data of consciousness, while the original data of consciousness from which these propositions were derived, and to which they owed all their necessity and truth, these same philosophers were (strange to say) not disposed to admit;" when M. Cousin and nearly all Germany find the Infinite and the Absolute in Consciousness, Sir W. Hamilton thinking them utterly repugnant to it; when philosophers, for many generations, fancied that they had Abstract Ideas—that they could conceive a triangle which was neither equilateral, isosceles, nor scalene,** which Sir W.

Reprinted from *An Examination of Sir William Hamilton's Philosophy*, Volume II, chapter entitled "The Freedom of the Will," Holt, Rinehart and Winston, New York, 1874.

* Dissertations on Reid, p. 749.

** "Does it not require," says Locke (Essay on the Human Understanding, Book iv. chap. 7, sect. 9), "some pains and skill to form the general idea of a triangle (which yet is none of the most abstract, comprehensive and difficult?) for it must be

Hamilton and all other people now consider to be simply absurd; with all these conflicting opinions respecting the things to which Consciousness testifies, what is the perplexed inquirer to think? Does all philosophy end, as in our author's opinion Hume believed it to do, in a persistent contradiction between one of our mental faculties and another? We shall find, there is a solution, which relieves the human mind from this embarrassment: namely, that the question to which experience says yes, and that to which consciousness says no, are different questions.

Let us cross-examine the alleged testimony of consciousness. And, first, it is left in some uncertainty by Sir W. Hamilton whether Consciousness makes only one deliverance on the subject, or two: whether we are conscious only of moral responsibility, in which free-will is implied, or are directly conscious of free-will. In his Lectures, Sir W. Hamilton speaks only of the first. In the notes on Reid, which were written subsequently, he seems to affirm both, but the latter of the two in a doubtful and hesitating manner: so difficult, in reality, does he find it to ascertain with certainty what it is that Consciousness certifies. But as there are many who maintain with a confidence far greater than his, that we are directly conscious of free-will,* it is necessary to examine that question.

To be conscious of free-will, must mean, to be conscious, before I have decided, that I am able to decide either way. Exception may be taken *in limine* to the use of the word consciousness in such an application. Consciousness tells me what I do or feel. But what I am *able* to do, is not a subject of consciousness. Consciousness is not prophetic; we are conscious of what is, not of what will or can be. We never know that we are able to do a thing, except from having done it, or something equal and similar to it. We should not know that we were capable of action at all, if we had never acted. Having acted, we know, as far as that experience reaches, how we are able to act; and this knowledge, when it has become familiar, is often confounded with, and called by the name of, consciousness. But it does not derive any increase of authority from being misnamed; its truth is not supreme over, but depends on, experience. If our so-called con-

---

neither oblique nor rectangle, neither equilateral, equicrural, nor scalene; but all and none of these at once. In effect, it is something imperfect, that cannot exist; an idea wherein some parts of several different and inconsistent ideas are put together." Yet this union of contradictory elements such a philosopher as Locke was able to fancy that he conceived. I scarcely know a more striking example of the tendency of the human mind to believe that things can exist separately because they can be separately named; a tendency strong enough, in this case, to make a mind like Locke's believe itself to be conscious of that which by the laws of mind cannot be a subject of consciousness to any one.

* Mr. Mansel, among others, makes the assertion in the broadest form it is capable of, saying, "In every act of volition, I am fully conscious that I can at this moment act in either of two ways, and that, all the antecedent phenomena being precisely the same, I may determine one way to-day and another way to-morrow." (Prolegomena Logica, p. 152.) Yes, though the antecedent phenomena remain the same: but not if my judgment of the antecedent phenomena remains the same. If my conduct changes, either the external inducements or my estimate of them must have changed.

Mr. Mansel (as I have already observed) goes so far as to maintain that our immediate intuition of Power is given us by the ego producing its own volitions, not by its volitions producing bodily movements (pp. 139–140, and 151).

sciousness of what we are able to do is not borne out by experience, it is a delusion. It has no title to credence but as an interpretation of experience, and if it is a false interpretation, it must give way.*

* In answer to the statement that what I am *able* to do is not a subject of consciousness, Mr. Alexander says (pp. 22 *et seq.*), "Perhaps it is not; but what I *feel* I am able to do is surely a subject of consciousness. . . . As to 'consciousness is not prophetic, we are conscious of what is, not of what will or can be,' it seems enough to say that if we are conscious of a free force of volition continuously inherent in us, we are conscious of what *is*." If we can be conscious of a force, and can feel an ability, independently of any present or past exercise thereof, the fact has nothing similar or analogous in all the rest of our nature. We are not conscious of a muscular force continuously inherent in us. If we were born with a cataract, we are not conscious, previous to being couched, of our ability to see. We should not feel able to walk if we had never walked, nor to think if we had never thought. Ability and force are not real entities, which can be felt as present when no effect follows; they are abstract names for the happening of the effect on the occurrence of the needful conditions, or for our expectation of its happening. It is of course possible that this may be all wrong, and that there may be a concrete real thing called ability, of which consciousness discloses to us the positive existence in this one case, though there is no evidence of it in any other. But it is surely, to say the least, much more probable that we mistake for consciousness our habitual affirmation to ourselves of an acquired knowledge or belief. This very common mistake may have escaped the notice of Mr. Alexander, who (p. 23) considers knowledge to be the same thing as direct consciousness! but it is a possibility which it will not do to overlook, when one takes for one's standard (p. 25) the "general consciousness of the race;" especially if, with Mr. Alexander, one restricts "the race" to those who are not philosophers, on the ground that no philosopher "unless he be one of a thousand," can see or feel anything that is inconsistent with his preconceived opinion. If this be the normal effect of philosophy on the human mind; if, nine hundred and ninety-nine times against one, the effect of cultivating our power of mental discrimination is to pervert it; let us close our books, and accept Hodge as a better authority in metaphysics than Locke or Kant, and. I suppose, in astronomy than Newton. An appeal to consciousness, however, to be of any value, must be to those who have formed a habit of sifting their consciousness, and distinguishing what they perceive or feel from what they infer; to those who can be made to understand that they do not see the sun move: and, to have attained this power of criticising their own consciousness on metaphysical subjects, they must have reflected on those subjects, in a manner and degree which quite entitle any one to the name of a philosopher.

Mr. Alexander denies that the belief that I was free to act can possibly be tested by experience *à posteriori*, since experience only tells me the way in which I did act, and says nothing about my having been able to act otherwise. Mr. Alexander's idea of the conditions of proof by experience is not a very enlarged one. Suppose that my experience of myself afforded two undeniable cases, alike in all the mental and physical antecedents, in one of which cases I acted in one way, and in the other in the direct opposite: there would then be proof by experience that I had been able to act either in the one way or in the other. It is by experience of this sort I learn that I can act at all, viz., by finding that an event takes place or not, according as (other circumstances being the same) a volition of mine does or does not take place. But when this power of my volitions over my actions has become a familiar fact, the knowledge of it is so constantly present to my mind as to be popularly called, and habitually confounded with, consciousness. And the supposed power of myself over my volitions, which is termed Free-will, though it cannot be a fact of consciousness, yet if true, or even if believed, would similarly work itself into our inmost knowledge of ourselves, in such a manner as to be mistaken for consciousness.

It would hardly be worth while to notice a pretended inconsistency discovered by Mr. Alexander between what is here said, and my recognition in a former work of a "practical feeling of Free Will"—"a feeling of Moral Freedom which we are conscious of," if Mr. Alexander had not inferred from it that I "was at one time conscious" of what I now, for the convenience of my argument, deny to be a subject of consciousness. Mr. Alexander himself quotes the words in which I spoke of this

But this conviction, whether termed consciousness or only belief, that our will is free—what is it? Of what are we convinced? I am told that whether I decide to do or to abstain, I feel that I could have decided the other way. I ask my consciousness what I do feel, and I find, indeed, that I feel (or am convinced) that I could, and even should, have chosen the other course if I had preferred it, that is, if I had liked it better; but not that I could have chosen one course while I preferred the other. When I say preferred, I of course include with the thing itself, all that accompanies it. I know that I can, because I know that I often do, elect to do one thing, when I should have preferred another in itself, apart from its consequences, or from a moral law which it violates. And this preference for a thing in itself, abstractedly from its accompaniments, is often loosely described as preference for the thing. It is this unprecise mode of speech which makes it not seem absurd to say that I act in opposition to my preference; that I do one thing when I would rather do another; that my conscience prevails over my desires—as if conscience were not itself a desire—the desire to do right. Take any alternative: say to murder or not to murder. I am told, that if I elect to murder, I am conscious that I could have elected to abstain: but am I conscious that I could have abstained if my aversion to the crime, and my dread of its consequences, had been weaker than the temptation? If I elect to abstain: in what sense am I conscious that I could have elected to commit the crime? Only if I had desired to commit it with a desire stronger than my horror of murder; not with one less strong. When we think of ourselves hypothetically as having acted otherwise than we did, we always suppose a difference in the antecedents: we picture ourselves as having known something that we did not know, or not known something that we did know; which is a difference in the external inducements; or as having desired something, or disliked something, more or less than we did; which is a difference in the internal inducements.*

---

practical feeling of free-will as not one of free-will at all, in a sense implying the theory; and took pains to describe what it really is, expressly declaring our feeling of moral freedom to be a feeling of our being able to modify our own character *if we wish*. When I applied the words feeling and consciousness to this acquired knowledge, I did not use those terms in their strict psychological meaning, there being no necessity for doing so in that place; but, agreeably to popular usage, extended them to (what there is no appropriate scientific name for) the whole of our familiar and intimate knowledge concerning ourselves.

* Preferring, as he says, a homely instance, Mr. Alexander supposes (p. 29), that a man puts his finger to his nose, and asks, "Is not he conscious of being able to touch at will either the right side of his nose or the left? Having touched, let us say, the left side, is he not conscious he could have touched the right side had he so willed it, and conscious that he *could* have so willed, chosen, or preferred?" Mr. Alexander's *naïf* expectation that his opponent's answer will be different because of the futility of the example, reminds one of the *asinus Buridani*. I should, on the supposition which he makes, be aware (I will not say conscious) that I could have touched the right side had I so willed it; and aware that I could, and even should, have so willed, chosen, and preferred, if there had existed a sufficient inducement to make me do so, and not otherwise. If any one's consciousness tells him that he could have done so without an inducement, or in opposition to a stronger inducement, I venture to express my opinion, in words borrowed from Mr. Alexander, that it is not his "veritable consciousness." I will not imitate Mr. Alexander in calling it a "fraudulent substitute palmed upon him" by his philosophical system.

In refutation of this it is said, that in resisting a desire, I am conscious of making an effort; that after I have resisted, I have the remembrance of having made an effort; that "if the temptation was long continued, or if I have been resisting the strong will of another, I am as sensibly exhausted by that effort, as after any physical exertion I ever made:" and it is added, "If my volition is wholly determined by the strongest present desire, it will be decided without any effort. . . . When the greater weight goes down, and the lesser up, no effort is needed on the part of the scale."* It is implied in this argument, that in a battle between contrary impulses, the victory must always be decided in a moment; that the force which is really the strongest, and prevails ultimately, must prevail instantaneously. The fact is not quite thus even in inanimate nature: the hurricane does not level the house or blow down the tree without resistance; even the balance trembles, and the scales oscillate for a short time, when the difference of the weights is not considerable. Far less does victory come without a contest to the strongest of two moral, or even two vital forces, whose nature it is to be never fixed, but always flowing, quantities. In a struggle between passion, there is not a single instant in which there does not pass across the mind some thought, which adds strength to, or takes it from, one or the other of the contending powers. Unless one of them was, from the beginning, out of all proportion stronger than the other, some time must elapse before the balance adjusts itself between forces neither of which is for any two successive instants the same. During that interval the agent is in the peculiar mental and physical state which we call a conflict of feelings: and we all know that a conflict between strong feelings *is*, in an extraordinary degree, exhaustive of the nervous energies.** The consciousness of effort, which we are told of, is this state of conflict. The author I am quoting considers what he calls, I think improperly, an effort, to be only on one side, because he represents to himself the conflict as taking place between me and some foreign power, which I conquer, or by which I am overcome. But it is obvious that "I" am both parties in the contest; the conflict is between me and myself; between (for instance) me desiring a pleasure, and me dreading self-reproach. What causes Me, or, if you please, my Will, to be identified with one side rather than with the other, is that one of the Me's represents a more permanent state of my feelings than the other does. After the temptation has been yielded to, the desiring "I" will come to an end, but the conscience-stricken "I" may endure to the end of life.

I therefore dispute altogether that we are conscious of being able to act in opposition to the strongest present desire or aversion. The difference between a bad and a good man is not that the latter acts in opposition to his strongest desires; it is that his desire to do right, and his aversion to

* *The Battle of the Two Philosophies*, pp. 13, 14.

** The writer I quote says, "Balancing one motive against another is not willing but judging." The state of mind I am speaking of is by no means a state of judging. It is an emotional, not an intellectual state, and the judging may be finished before it commences. If there were any indispensable act of judging in this stage, it could only be judging which of the two pains or pleasures was the greatest: and to regard this as the operative force would be conceding the point in favour of Necessitarianism.

doing wrong, are strong enough to overcome, and in the case of perfect virtue, to silence, any other desire or aversion which may conflict with them. It is because this state of mind is possible to human nature, that human beings are capable of moral government: and moral education consists in subjecting them to the discipline which has most tendency to bring them into this state. The object of moral education is to educate the will: but the will can only be educated through the desires and aversions; by eradicating or weakening such of them as are likeliest to lead to evil; exalting to the highest pitch the desire of right conduct and the aversion to wrong; cultivating all other desires and aversions of which the ordinary operation is auxiliary to right, while discountenancing so immoderate an indulgence of them, as might render them too powerful to be overcome by the moral sentiment, when they chance to be in opposition to it. The other requisites are, a clear intellectual standard of right and wrong, that moral desire and aversion may act in the proper places and such general mental habits as shall prevent moral considerations from being forgotten or overlooked, in cases to which they are rightly applicable. . . .

FREEDOM AND CONSCIOUSNESS

MAURICE MERLEAU-PONTY

. . . It is clear that no causal relationship is conceivable between the subject and his body, his world or his society. Only at the cost of losing the basis of all my certainties can I question what is conveyed to me by my presence to myself. Now the moment I turn to myself in order to describe myself, I have a glimpse of an anonymous flux,* a comprehensive project in which there are so far no "states of consciousness," nor, *a fortiori*, qualifications of any sort. For myself I am neither "jealous," nor "inquisitive," nor "hunchbacked," nor "a civil servant." It is often a matter of surprise that the cripple or the invalid can put up with himself. The reason is that such people are not for themselves deformed or at death's door. Until the final coma, the dying man is inhabited by a consciousness, he is all that he sees, and enjoys this much of an outlet. Consciousness can never objectify itself into invalid-consciousness or cripple-consciousness, and even if the old man complains of his age or the cripple of his deformity, they can do so only by comparing themselves with others, or seeing themselves through the eyes of others, that is, by

Reprinted from *Phenomenology of Perception*, translated by Colin Smith, Routledge & Kegan Paul, London, and Humanities Press, New York, 1962, by permission of the publishers.

* In the sense in which, with Husserl, we have taken this word.

taking a statistical and objective view of themselves, so that such complaints are never absolutely genuine: when he is back in the heart of his own consciousness, each one of us feels beyond his limitations and thereupon resigns himself to them. They are the price which we automatically pay for being in the world, a formality which we take for granted. Hence we may speak disparagingly of our looks and still not want to change our face for another. No idiosyncrasy can, seemingly, be attached to the insuperable generality of consciousness, nor can any limit be set to this immeasurable power of escape. In order to be determined (in the two senses of that word) by an external factor, it is necessary that I should be a thing. Neither my freedom nor my universality can admit of any eclipse. It is inconceivable that I should be free in certain of my actions and determined in others: how should we understand a dormant freedom that gave full scope to determinism? And if it is assumed that it is snuffed out when it is not in action, how could it be rekindled? If *per impossible* I had once succeeded in *making myself into* a thing, how should I subsequently reconvert myself to consciousness? Once I am free, I am not to be counted among things, and I must then be uninterruptedly free. Once my actions cease to be mine, I shall never recover them, and if I lose my hold on the world, it will never be restored to me. It is equally inconceivable that my liberty should be attenuated; one cannot be to some extent free, and if, as is often said, motives incline me in a certain direction, one of two things happens: either they are strong enough to force me to act, in which case there is no freedom, or else they are not strong enough, and then freedom is complete, and as great in the worst torments as in the peace of one's home. We ought, therefore, to reject not only the idea of causality, but also that of motivation.* The alleged motive does not burden my decision; on the contrary my decision lends the motive its force. Everything that I "am" in virtue of nature or history—hunchbacked, handsome or Jewish—I never am completely for myself, as we have just explained: and I may well be these things for other people, nevertheless I remain free to posit another person as a consciousness whose views strike through to my very being, or on the other hand merely as an object. It is also true that this option is itself a form of constraint: if I am ugly, I have the choice between being an object of disapproval or disapproving of others. I am left free to be a masochist or a sadist, but not free to ignore others. But this dilemma, which is given as part of the human lot, is not one for me as pure consciousness: it is still I who cause the other to be for me, and who cause us both to be as members of mankind. Moreover, even if existence as a human being were imposed upon me, the manner alone being left to my choice, and considering this choice itself and ignoring the small number of forms it might take, it would still be a free choice. If it is said that my temperament inclines me particularly to either sadism or masochism, it is still merely a manner of speaking, for my temperament exists only for the

* See J. P. Sartre, *L'Être et le Néant*, pp. 508 ff. [see "Further Readings" at the end of this section for reference to an English translation, eds.].

second order knowledge that I gain about myself when I see myself as others see me, and in so far as I recognize it, confer value upon it, and in that sense, choose it. What misleads us on this, is that we often look for freedom in the voluntary deliberation which examines one motive after another and seems to opt for the weightiest or most convincing. In reality the deliberation follows the decision, and it is my secret decision which brings the motives to light, for it would be difficult to conceive what the force of a motive might be in the absence of a decision which it confirms or to which it runs counter. When I have abandoned a project, the motives which I thought held me to it suddenly lose their force and collapse. In order to resuscitate them, an effort is required on my part to reopen time and set me back to the moment preceding the making of the decision. Even while I am deliberating, already I find it an effort to suspend time's flow, and to keep open a situation which I feel is closed by a decision which is already there and which I am holding off. That is why it so often happens that after giving up a plan I experience a feeling of relief: "After all, I wasn't so very particular"; the debate was purely a matter of form, and the deliberation a mere parody, for I had decided against from the start.

We often see the weakness of the will brought forward as an argument against freedom. And indeed, although I can will myself to adopt a course of conduct and act the part of a warrior or a seducer, it is not within my power to be a warrior or seducer with ease and in a way that "comes naturally"; really to *be* one, that is. But neither should we seek freedom in the act of will, which is, in its very meaning, something short of an act. We have recourse to an act of will only in order to go against our true decision, and, as it were, for the purpose of proving our powerlessness. If we had really and truly made the conduct of the warrior or the seducer our own, then we should *be* one or the other. Even what are called obstacles to freedom are in reality deployed by it. An unclimbable rock face, a large or small, vertical or slanting rock, are things which have no meaning for anyone who is not intending to surmount them, for a subject whose projects do not carve out such determinate forms from the uniform mass of the *in itself* and cause an orientated world to arise—a significance in things. There is, then, ultimately nothing that can set limits to freedom, except those limits that freedom itself has set in the form of its various initiatives, so that the subject has simply the external world that he gives himself. . . .

The result, however, of this first reflection on freedom would appear to be to rule it out altogether. If indeed it is the case that our freedom is the same in all our actions, and even in our passions, if it is not to be measured in terms of our conduct, and if the slave displays freedom as much by living in fear as by breaking his chains, then it cannot be held that there is such a thing as *free action*, freedom being anterior to all actions. In any case it will not be possible to declare: "Here freedom makes its appearance," since free action, in order to be discernible, has to stand out against a background of life from which it is entirely, or almost entirely, absent. We may say in this case that it is everywhere, but equally nowhere. In the name of freedom we reject the idea of acquisition, since freedom has become a primordial acquisition and, as it were, our state of nature. Since we do not have to provide it, it is the gift granted to us of having no gift, it is the nature of consciousness which consists in having no nature, and in no case can it find external expression or a place in our life. The idea of action, therefore, disappears: nothing can pass from us to the world, since we are nothing that can be specified, and since the non-being which constitutes us could not possibly find its way into the world's plenum. There are merely intentions immediately followed by their effects, and we are very near to the Kantian idea of an intention which is tantamount to the act, which Scheler countered with the argument that the cripple who would like to be able to save a drowning man and the good swimmer who actually saves him do not have the same experience of autonomy. The very idea of choice vanishes, for to choose is to choose *something* in which freedom sees, at least for a moment, a symbol of itself. There is free choice only if freedom comes into play in its decision, and posits the situation chosen as a situation of freedom. A freedom which has no need to be exercised because it is already acquired could not commit itself in this way: it knows that the following instant will find it, come what may, just as free and just as indeterminate. The very notion of freedom demands that our decision should plunge into the future, that something should have been *done* by it, that the subsequent instant should benefit from its predecessor and, though not necessitated, should be at least required by it. If freedom is doing, it is necessary that what it does should not be immediately undone by a new freedom. Each instant, therefore, must not be a closed world; one instant must be able to commit its successors and, a decision once taken and action once begun, I must have something acquired at my disposal, I must benefit from my impetus, I must be inclined to carry on, and there must be a bent or propensity of the mind. It was Descartes who held that conservation demands a power as great as does creation; a view which implies a realistic notion of the instant. It is true that the instant is not a philosopher's fiction. It is the point at which one project is brought to fruition and another begun—the point at which my gaze is transferred from one end to another, it is the *Augen-Blick*. But this break in time cannot occur unless each of the two spans is of a piece. Consciousness, it is said, is, though not atomized into instants, at least haunted by the spectre of the instant which it is obliged continually to exorcise by a free act. We shall soon see that we have indeed always the power to interrupt, but it implies in any case a power to *begin*, for there would be no severance unless freedom had taken up its abode somewhere and were preparing to move it. Unless there are cycles of behaviour, open situations requiring a certain completion and capable of constituting a background to either a confirmatory or transformatory decision, we never experience freedom. The choice of an intelligible character is excluded, not only because there is no time anterior to time, but because choice presupposes a prior commitment and because the idea of an initial choice involves a contradiction. If freedom is to have *room** in which to move, if it is to be describable as freedom, there must be something to hold it away from its objectives, it must have a *field*, which means that there must be for it special possibilities, or realities which tend to cling to being. As J. P. Sartre himself observes, dreaming is incompatible with freedom because, in the realm of imagination, we have no sooner taken a certain significance as our goal than we already believe that we have intuitively brought it into being, in short, because there is no obstacle and nothing *to do*.** It is established that freedom is not to be confused with those abstract decisions of will at grips with motives or passions, for the classical conception of deliberation is relevant only to a freedom "in bad faith" which secretly harbours antagonistic motives without being prepared to act on them, and so itself manufactures the alleged proofs of its impotence. We can see, beneath these noisy debates and these fruitless efforts to "construct" us, the tacit decisions whereby we have marked out round ourselves the field of possibility, and it is true that nothing is done as long as we cling to these fixed points, and everything is easy as soon as we have weighed anchor. This is why our freedom is not to be sought in spurious discussion on the conflict between a style of life which we have no wish to reappraise and circumstances suggestive of another: the real choice is that between our whole character and our manner of being in the world. But either this total choice is never mentioned, since it is the silent upsurge of our being in the world, in which case it is not clear in what sense it could be said to be ours, since this freedom glides over itself and is the equivalent of a fate—or else our choice of ourselves is a genuine choice, a conversion involving our whole existence. In this case, however, there is presupposed a previous acquisition which the choice sets out to modify and it founds a new tradition: this leads us to ask whether the perpetual severance in terms of which we initially defined freedom is not simply the negative aspect of our universal commitment to a world, and whether our indifference to each determinate thing does not express merely our involvement in all; whether the ready-made freedom from which we started is not reducible to a power of initiative which cannot be transformed into *doing* without taking up the world as posited in some shape or form, and whether, in short, concrete and actual freedom is not to be found in this exchange. . . .

When I say that this rock is unclimbable, it is certain that this attribute, like that of being big or little, straight and oblique, and indeed like all attributes in general, can be conferred upon it only by the project of climbing it, and by a human presence. It is, therefore, freedom which brings into being the obstacles to freedom, so that the latter can be set over against it as its bounds. However, it is clear that, one and the same project being given, one rock will appear as an obstacle, and another, being more

* "avoir du champ"; in this sentence there is a play on the word "champ"—field [Translator's note].

** Sartre, *L'Être et le Néant*, p. 562.

negotiable, as a means. My freedom, then, does not so contrive it that this way there is an obstacle, and that way a way through, it arranges for there to be obstacles and ways through in general; it does not draw the particular outline of this world, but merely lays down its general structures. It may be objected that there is no difference; if my freedom conditions the structure of the "there is," that of the "here" and the "there," it is present wherever these structures arise. We cannot distinguish the quality of "obstacle" from the obstacle itself, and relate one to freedom and the other to the world in itself which, without freedom, would be merely an amorphous and unnameable mass. It is not, therefore, outside myself that I am able to find a limit to my freedom. But should I not find it in myself? We must indeed distinguish between my express intentions, for example the plan I now make to climb those mountains, and general intentions which evaluate the potentialities of my environment. Whether or not I have decided to climb them, these mountains appear high to me, because they exceed my body's power to take them in its stride, and, even if I have just read *Micromégas*, I cannot so contrive it that they are small for me. Underlying myself as a thinking subject, who am able to take my place at will on Sirius or on the earth's surface, there is, therefore, as it were a natural self which does not budge from its terrestrial situation and which constantly adumbrates absolute valuations. What is more, my projects as a thinking being are clearly modelled on the latter; if I elect to see things from the point of view of Sirius, it is still to my terrestrial experience that I must have recourse in order to do so; I may say, for example, that the Alps are *molehills*. In so far as I have hands, feet, a body, I sustain around me intentions which are not dependent upon my decisions and which affect my surroundings in a way which I do not choose. These intentions are general in a double sense: firstly in the sense that they constitute a system in which all possible objects are simultaneously included; if the mountain appears high and upright, the tree appears small and sloping; and furthermore in the sense that they are not of my own making, they originate from outside me, and I am not surprised to find them in all psycho-physical subjects organized as I am. Hence, as Gestalt psychology has shown, there are for me certain shapes which are particularly favoured, as they are for other men, and which are capable of giving rise to a psychological science and rigorous laws. The grouping of dots

.. ..

is always perceived as six pairs of dots with two millimetres between each pair, while one figure is always perceived as a cube, and another as a plane mosaic. It is as if, on the hither side of our judgement and our freedom, someone were assigning such and such a significance to such and such a given grouping. It is indeed true that perceptual structures do not always force themselves upon the observer; there are some which are ambiguous. But these reveal even more effectively the presence within us of spontaneous evaluation: for they are elusive shapes which suggest constantly changing meanings to us. Now a pure consciousness is capable of anything except being ignorant of its intentions, and an absolute freedom cannot choose itself as hesitant, since that amounts to allowing itself to be drawn in several directions, and since, the possibilities being *ex hypothesi* indebted to freedom for all the strength they have, the weight that freedom gives to one is thereby withdrawn from the rest. We *can* break up a shape by looking at it awry, but this too is because freedom uses the gaze along with its spontaneous evaluations. Without the latter, we would not have a world, that is, a collection of things which emerge from a background of formlessness by presenting themselves to our body as "to be touched," "to be taken," "to be climbed over." We should never be aware of adjusting ourselves to things and reaching them where they are, beyond us, but would be conscious only of restricting our thoughts to the immanent objects of our intentions, and we should not be in the world, ourselves implicated in the spectacle and, so to speak, intermingled with things, we should simply enjoy the spectacle of a universe. It is, therefore, true that there are no obstacles in themselves, but the self which qualifies them as such is not some acosmic subject; it runs ahead of itself in relation to things in order to confer upon them the form of things. . . .

This is true not only of an impersonal and, generally speaking, abstract function such as "external perception." There is something comparable present in all evaluations. It has been perceptively remarked that pain and fatigue can never be regarded as causes which "act" upon my liberty, and that, in so far as I may experience either at any given moment, they do not have their origin outside me, but always have a significance and express my attitude towards the world. Pain makes me give way and say what I ought to have kept to myself, fatigue makes me break my journey. We all know the moment at which we decide no longer to endure pain or fatigue, and when, simultaneously, they become intolerable in fact. Tiredness does not halt my companion because he likes the clamminess of his body, the heat of the road and the sun, in short, because he likes to feel himself in the midst of things, to feel their rays converging upon him, to be the cynosure of all this light, and an object of touch for the earth's crust. My own fatigue brings me to a halt because I dislike it, because I have chosen differently my manner of being in the world, because, for instance, I endeavour, not to be in nature, but rather to win the recognition of others. I am free in relation to fatigue to precisely the extent that I am free in relation to my being in the world, free to make my way by transforming it.* But here once more we must recognize a sort of sedimentation of our life: an attitude towards the world, when it has received frequent confirmation, acquires a favoured status for us. Yet since freedom does not tolerate any motive in its path, my habitual being in the world is at each moment equally precarious, and the complexes which I have allowed to develop over the years always remain equally soothing, and the free act can with no difficulty blow them sky-high. However, having built our life upon an inferiority complex which has

* Sartre, *L'Être et le Néant,* pp. 531 ff.

been operative for twenty years, it is not *probable* that we shall change. It is clear what a summary rationalism might say in reply to such a hybrid notion: there are no degrees of possibility; either the free act is no longer possible, or it is still possible, in which case freedom is complete. In short, "probable" is meaningless. It is a notion belonging to statistical thought, which is not thought at all, since it does not concern any particular thing actually existing, any moment of time, any concrete event. "It is improbable that Paul will give up writing bad books" means nothing, since Paul may well decide to write no more such books. The probable is everywhere and nowhere, a reified fiction, with only a psychological existence; it is not an ingredient of the world. And yet we have already met it a little while ago in the perceived *world*. The mountain is great or small to the extent that, as a perceived thing, it is to be found in the field of my possible actions, and in relation to a level which is not only that of my individual life, but that of "any man." Generality and probability are not fictions, but phenomena; we must therefore find a phenomenological basis for statistical thought. It belongs necessarily to a being which is fixed, situated and surrounded by things in the world. "It is improbable" that I should at this moment destroy an inferiority complex in which I have been content to live for twenty years. That means that I have committed myself to inferiority, that I have made it my abode, that this past, though not a fate, has at least a specific weight and is not a set of events over there, at a distance from me, but the atmosphere of my present. The rationalist's dilemma: either the free act is possible, or it is not—either the event originates in me or is imposed on me from outside, does not apply to our relations with the world and with our past. Our freedom does not destroy our situation, but gears itself to it: as long as we are alive, our situation is open, which implies both that it calls up specially favoured modes of resolution, and also that it is powerless to bring one into being by itself. . . .

ACTIONS AND CAUSAL EXPLANATION

RICHARD PETERS

(A) *'HIS REASON' EXPLANATIONS*

The over-riding aim of a scientist should be explanation. This sounds rather obvious, but it has many important consequences in relation to psychological theorizing. For the general question 'Why did Jones do that?' is capable of being asked and answered in a variety of different ways. The particular formula employed in asking the question usually dictates the sort of answer which is expected and which counts as an explanation.* The paradigm case of a human action is when something is done in order to bring about an end. So the usual way of explaining an action is to describe it as an action of a certain sort by indicating the end which Jones had in mind. We therefore ask the 'why' question in a more specific form. We ask what was his *reason* for doing that or what was the *point* of it, what *end* he had in mind. If we ask why Jones walked across the road, the obvious answer will be something like 'To buy tobacco'. Instead of saying this we could say 'because he wanted some tobacco'. This is, logically speaking, another way of giving the same sort of answer; for the answer 'to buy some tobacco' is only an explanation because we assume in Jones some sort of directive disposition—a general tendency to obtain and use tobacco (Peters, 1952).**

Even in this very simple sort of explanation in terms of a man's reason for doing something there are, as a matter of fact, concealed assumptions. We assume, for instance, that walking across the street is an efficient way of getting to the tobacconist. This counts as an explanation not simply because Jones envisaged walking across the street as a means to getting the tobacco but because it really is a means to getting it. We assume, too, that a man who has this information will act on it if he wants some tobacco. We assume that men are rational in that they will take means which lead to ends if they have the information and want the ends. 'His

Reprinted from *The Concept of Motivation*, Chapter 1, Section 1: a, b, c, Routledge & Kegan Paul, London, and Humanities Press, New York, 1958, by permission of the publishers and Richard Peters.

Professor Peters now thinks that, though the thesis in Section C about the impossibility of giving a mechanical type of causal explanation for human actions is still valid, the formulation of the arguments by which he attempted to show this is badly in need of revision.

* I am indebted to J. O. Urmson (1952) for some of these distinctions.

** 'Motives and Causes', *Proceedings of the Aristotelian Society*, Supp. 26 (1952), pp. 146–147.

reason' is an explanation in terms of what Popper (1945) calls 'the logic of the situation'.

But it is not only norms of efficiency and consistency that are implicit in the concept of 'his reason'. There are also norms or standards of social appropriateness. After all Jones might have crawled or run across the road. But 'to get some tobacco' would be a very odd answer to the question 'Why did Jones *run* across the road?' Yet running would be quite an efficient way of getting across the road. It would, however, be socially odd as a way of crossing the road to get some tobacco. *Man is a rule-following animal.* His actions are not simply directed towards ends; they also conform to social standards and conventions, and unlike a calculating machine he acts because of his knowledge of rules and objectives. For instance, we ascribe to people *traits* of character like honesty, punctuality, considerateness and meanness. Such terms do not, like ambition or hunger or sexual desire, indicate the sorts of goals that a man tends to pursue; rather they indicate the type of regulation that he imposes on his conduct whatever his goals may be. A man who is ruthless, selfish, punctual, considerate, persistent, and honest, does not have any particular goals; rather he pursues whatever goals he has in particular sorts of ways.

. . .

My reasons for stressing this rule-following purposive pattern into which we fit our common-sense explanations are twofold. In the first place I want to insist that most of our explanations are couched in terms of this model and our predictions of people's behaviour presuppose it. We know what the parson will do when he begins to walk towards the pulpit because we know the conventions regulating church services. And we can make such predictions without knowing anything about the *causes* of people's behaviour unless we include under 'causes' things like the parson's training and grasp of the rules, which are things of a different order from 'causes' in the sense of antecedent movements. Man in society is like a chess-player writ large. Requests for explanation are usually reflections of our ignorance about the particular rule or goal which is relevant to the behaviour in question. We usually know the general pattern but are unsure which part of it is relevant. Sometimes, of course, we are in the position of a free-thinker at a Roman Catholic mass. The question 'Why did X do that?' is then usually a request for an elucidation of the whole pattern of conventions. In explaining human actions we, like anthropologists, must all, in the first place be structuralists. Indeed I would go so far as to say that anthropology or sociology must be the basic sciences of human action in that they exhibit the systematic framework of norms and goals which are necessary to classify actions as being of a certain sort. They both—like classical economics—presuppose the purposive, rule-following model; in this respect they are quite unlike sciences which imply a mechanical model of explanation.

In the second place this rule-following purposive pattern of explanation must be sketched in some detail because a proper understanding of what is meant by a human action has very important logical consequences. It shows, for instance, as I shall argue, that human actions cannot be sufficiently explained in terms of causal concepts like 'colourless movements'. Indeed to claim that we are confronted with an action is *ipso facto* to rule out such mechanical explanations, as being sufficient.

(B) *'THE REASON' EXPLANATIONS*

But, of course, as psychologists will be the first to point out, people often invent reasons for doing things or delude themselves into thinking that the reasons they offer for their actions are operative reasons. We therefore often say of a man that *his* reason may have been x but *the* reason why he acted like that was y. For instance we might say that Jones said that he crossed the road in order to buy some tobacco but the reason why he did it was not really his desire for tobacco; it was sex. There was a pretty girl looking in the window of the tobacconist. This explanation may of course be erroneous. For instance a psychologist once told me that I delayed crossing the road to College because of an aversion to getting down to work. I replied, and I think more convincingly, that I stayed on the other side in order to look at the row of glistening cars drawn up opposite. But whether the explanation in question is correct or incorrect does not much matter; the point is that to speak of *the* reason why a person does something is different in that it is a way of calling attention to the law or assumed law that a given case actually falls under. *His* reason may coincide with *the* reason. *The* reason why Jones crossed the road might in fact be his desire for tobacco. He might also be aware that he wanted to inspect the girl at close quarters, but was concealing this by the camouflage of buying tobacco. This would then be his *real* reason. But whereas *his* reason—whether real or not—entails that a man is conscious of his objective, the reason why he did it does not.* *The* reason why he did it might well be sex or aversion to work; yet the individual might be quite unaware of pursuing or avoiding the relevant goals. And whereas to say that *he* had a reason for doing something is more or less to rule out a causal explanation, to give *the* reason why he did it is sometimes to subsume it under a law-like proposition of a causal kind. This is not necessarily so. For we can say that sex or aversion to work was *the*

* Hamlyn has pointed out to me the use of "the reason for his action" as well as "the reason why he did it". "The reason for" seems to be similar to "his reason" but to imply a coincidence between "his reason" and "the reason why he did it". I am not here concerned with the use of "reason" in the context of *justification* as when we say that a reason for giving up smoking is that it causes lung cancer. "His reason" and "the reason for" can be used in contexts both of justification and of explanation. Needless to say "the reason why he did it" is reserved for contexts of explanation with which I am here concerned.

reason why he did it and simply be insisting that a different directive disposition is being exercised. But *the* reason why he did it might also be that he was pushed or assailed by an attack of giddiness. These would be causal explanations which would rebut the suggestion that he had a reason for crossing the road. Causal explanations, in other words, can count as *the* reason why a person does something; but they are only one type of answer to the question 'What was *the* reason why he did it?'

(c) *CAUSAL EXPLANATIONS*

There are, however, other questions about particular goings on—I omit to say actions on purpose—to which answers in causal terms are appropriate. Instead of the omnibus question 'Why did Jones do that?' we often ask what made, drove, or possessed him to do it. These are usually cases of lapses from action or failure to act—when there is some kind of *deviation* from the purposive rule-following model, when people, as it were, get it wrong. This may be in respect of an efficiency norm—for example, when a person refuses to take the only quick route to his destination by underground train, or when he can't remember a well-known name when he is performing an introduction. Or the behaviour may go wrong in respect of a norm governing social appropriateness—as with a business man who runs to work when he is not late or a tutor who crawls round the room sniffing while listening to an undergraduate essay. Or behaviour may go wrong by being deflected towards a peculiar goal as with a married man who suddenly makes an advance to a choir boy. In such cases it is as if the man suffers something rather than does something. It is because things seem to be happening to him that it is appropriate to ask what made, drove, or possessed him to do that. The appropriate answer in such cases may be in terms of a causal theory.

These cases of particular goings-on which look like breakdowns of action are very similar to a whole class of general activities which seem to have no point or a very odd point—dreams, hallucinations, obsessions, anxieties, and perversions. In such cases the Greeks suggested that the gods intervene and take possession of the individual's mind. Very often recourse is made to crude physiological explanations. It was not till the advent of Freud that any systematic explanation of such goings-on was offered in psychological terms. Indeed Freud claimed in 1913 that the main contribution of psycho-analysis to general psychology was to link together and to give psychological explanations for happenings which had previously been left to physiology or to folk-lore. Many have claimed that Freud, by reclaiming these phenomena for psychology, was in fact extending the model of purposive rule-following behaviour to cover the unconscious. He showed, it is argued, that we have reasons for acts which were previously only explained in terms of causes. I shall argue later that this thesis is mistaken. Freud showed, perhaps, that the concept of 'wish' has a wider application than was previously thought. But his account of the working of the primary processes creaks with causality. In maintaining that in the unconscious there is no sense of causal or logical connexion he was *ipso facto* denying that the model of 'his reason', implying norms of efficiency and social appropriateness, was relevant. Freud, I shall argue, provides the classic case of giving quasi-causal explanations where causal explanations seem *prima facie* appropriate.

I shall also argue that Freud in fact only intended to explain by reference to unconscious mental processes cases where the purposive rule-following model breaks down or is inappropriate. He did not think—and often explicitly denied—that this sort of explanation can be appropriately given for everything—for cases where a man acts as well as for cases where something happens to a man. In this respect Freud was, from the point of view of my argument, on the side of the angels. For my case is not simply that causal explanations are otiose when we know the point of a person's action in that, life being short and time limited, we no longer feel inclined to ask 'why' once we have accommodated a piece of behaviour within the rule-following purposive model. It is also that if we are in fact confronted with a case of a genuine action (i.e. an act of doing something as opposed to suffering something), then causal explanations are *ipso facto* inappropriate as sufficient explanations. Indeed they may rule out rule-following purposive explanations. To ask what made Jones do something is at least to suggest that he had no good reason for doing it. Similarly to ascribe a point to his action is *ipso facto* to deny that it can be *sufficiently explained* in terms of causes, though, of course, there will be many causes in the sense of *necessary* conditions. A story can always be told about the underlying mechanisms; but this does not add up to a sufficient explanation, if it is an action that has to be explained.

To give a causal *explanation* of an event involves at least showing that other conditions being presumed unchanged a change in one variable is a *sufficient* condition for a change in another. In the mechanical conception of 'cause' it is also demanded that there should be spatial and temporal contiguity between the movements involved. Now the trouble about giving this sort of explanation of human actions is that we can never specify an action exhaustively in terms of movements of the body or within the body. (Hamlyn, 1953.)* It is therefore impossible to state sufficient conditions in terms of antecedent movements which may vary concomitantly with subsequent movements. 'Signing a contract', for instance, is a typical example of a human action. The movements involved are grouped together because they are seen by the agent to be efficient and appropriate means to an end. But it would be impossible to stipulate exhaustively what the movements *must* be. For if this is a case of a human action the agent must be presumed to be intelligent and he will, accordingly, vary his movements in a great variety of ways. He may hold the

* D. W. Hamlyn, "Behavior," *Philosophy*, 28 (1953), 132–145. Also in *Philosophy of Mind*, Vere Chappell (ed.), Prentice-Hall, Englewood Cliffs, N.J., 1962.

pen slightly differently, vary the size of his writing according to the space available, and so on, depending on the sort of ink, paper, and pen available. But provided that he produces a signature which conforms to rough and ready criteria—e.g., it must not be typed—more or less *any* movements will do. I suppose he could sign a contract by holding the pen between his toes. A very general range of movements could perhaps be specified, but no specific movements of the muscles, limbs, or nervous system, which *must* occur before it would be conceded that a contract had been signed. This is tantamount to saying that the concept of an action is inseparable from that of intelligence; for part of what we mean by "intelligence" is the ability to vary movements relative to a goal in a way which is appropriate to changes in the situation necessary to define it as a goal and in the conditions relevant to attaining it. So we could never give a sufficient explanation of an action in causal terms because we could never stipulate the movements which would have to count as dependent variables. A precise functional relationship could never be established. Of course, just as we could stipulate a general range of movements necessary to define signing a contract, so also we could lay down certain very general *necessary* conditions. We could, for instance, say that a man could not sign a contract unless he had a brain and nervous system. Such physiological knowledge *might* enable us to predict *bodily movements*. And *if* we had bridging laws to correlate such physiological findings with descriptions of actions we might *indirectly predict* actions. But we would *first* have to grasp concepts connected with action like 'knowing what we are doing' and 'grasp of means to an end'. As such concepts have no application at the level of mere movement, such predictions would not count as sufficient *explanations* of *actions*.

Furthermore, as I have already argued, general standards or rules are implicit in the concept of an action. We can therefore say that a man is doing something efficiently, correctly, and so on, if he knowingly varies what he does in accordance with changes in the situation conventionally singled out as the goal and the conditions perceived as relevant to attaining it. It only makes sense to talk of actions in this way, not of cases where something happens to a man. A man's action may break down because of a causal condition like a lesion in his brain. But all that can be said of such causal conditions is that they just occur. Movements *qua* movements are neither intelligent, efficient, nor correct. They only become so in the context of an action. There cannot therefore be a sufficient explanation of actions in causal terms because, as Popper has put it, there is a logical gulf between nature and convention. Statements implying norms and standards cannot be deduced from statements about mere movements which have no such normative implications. The contention that man is a rule-following animal must, if taken seriously, entail that the transition from nature to convention occurs wherever we try to give a sufficient explanation of human actions in causal terms. There is, however, no objection to such explanations of what *happens* to a man; for happenings cannot be characterized as intelligent or unintelligent, correct or incorrect, efficient or inefficient. *Prima facie* they are just occurrences. Perhaps Freud showed that some lapses and breakdowns may not be *just* occurrences. But this is another story. The point is that there is a *prima facie* case for treating them as such.

To make explicit the implications of my thesis for psychological theories: If the question is 'Why did Jones walk across the road?' a *sufficient* explanation can only be given in terms of the rule-following purposive model—if this is a case of an action rather than of something happening to him. Answers in terms of causal concepts like 'receptor impulses' and 'colourless movement', are either not explanations because they state not sufficient but only necessary conditions, or they are ways of denying that what has to be explained is a human action. If we ask 'Why did Jones *jump* while he was crossing the road?' it might be appropriate to say 'because of a twinge in his stomach' or 'because a car back-fired'. The stimulus-response sort of model would perhaps be appropriate and the causal type of explanation in terms of internal or external stimulation might be sufficient because the assumption might be that Jones was suffering something rather than performing an action. This sort of jump would then be quite different from the jump he might perform while competing in an athletic contest.

This is not to deny that causal explanations are *relevant* to human actions. It is only to deny that they are sufficient explanations of them. Causal theories have at least three jobs to do in this context. Firstly they can state *necessary* conditions for human actions to occur. Hebb's physiological speculations, for instance, might well provide a sketch of a typical class of necessary conditions.* But this does not mean that such speculations *explain* human actions. Secondly, as a corollary, they could show that some individual differences in performance are dependent on slight differences in such necessary conditions. Hebb's hypothesis of the relationship between the size of the association areas of the brain and the possibility of late learning would be such a hypothesis. Thirdly such theories could be used to give *sufficient* conditions for breakdowns in performance, as in the case of brain lesions, by indicating a necessary condition which was absent. Alternatively lapses and breakdowns could be explained by the postulation of special disrupting conditions—e.g. Freud's theory of the unconscious wish.

* D. O. Hebb, *The Organization of Behavior*, Wiley, New York, 1949.

WANTS, ACTIONS, AND CAUSAL EXPLANATION

WILLIAM P. ALSTON

The traditional problem of free will arises from an apparent conflict between the supposition that sometimes human beings act freely and can be held responsible for what they do, and the supposition that all human actions, along with all other happenings, are causally determined. In the immense literature which has grown up on this subject a great deal of attention has been given to the question of what it is to act freely and to be responsible, and the question of what causal determinism in general amounts to has been given a pretty thorough airing. But relatively little has been done to spell out what it would be for a human action in particular to be causally determined—what causal factors might possibly be involved and how they would have to be related to the action if they are to determine it. A few unspecific and unguarded references to "motives", "desires", "impulses", etc., are all that we usually get. Of late, however, philosophers have concentrated more heavily on this aspect of the problem, and the general tenor of the discussions has been that the idea that human actions are causally determined is fundamentally confused, and that we can see this when we look carefully at what a human action is and what causal determination is. For example:

> . . . if we are in fact confronted with a case of a genuine action (i.e., an act of doing something as opposed to suffering something), then causal explanations are *ipso facto* inappropriate.*

> Where we are concerned with causal explanations, with events of which the happenings in question are effects in accordance with some law of causality, to that extent we are not concerned with human actions at all but, at best, with bodily movements or happenings; and where we are concerned with explanations of human action, there causal factors and causal laws in the sense in which, for example, these terms are employed in the biological sciences are wholly irrelevant to the understanding we seek.**

I want to take issue with these views and, in the process of doing so, to explore some of the issues which arise when we try to imagine what causal determination of a human action might be.

I would suppose that here, as in other areas, causal determination of an

Published here for the first time with omissions by permission of William P. Alston.
* R. S. Peters, *The Concept of Motivation*, London: Routledge and Kegan Paul, 1958, p. 12.
** A. I. Melden, Free Action, London: Routledge and Kegan Paul, 1961, p. 184.

event would require the truth of certain general "lawlike" statements which would represent events of that sort as determinate functions of certain sorts of prior factors, so that by knowing the values of those factors in a given case one could predict just what form that kind of event would take.* Wherever there are such principles which permit such predictions, we may speak of the class of events in question as being causally determined. It seems obvious, at first glance, that one could not *show* that this is impossible with respect to actions; surely the idea that there are such true principles which have actions as the dependent variables represents an intelligible possibility. And yet this is what seems to be denied in the above quotations. I suggest that we look into the arguments which are given for this position. They can be usefully divided into those which do, and those which do not, proceed by a consideration of some particular sort of putative causal factor. We shall consider the latter first since, as we shall see, it very quickly collapses into the former.

I

Insofar as these authors give any reason for the *general* claim that no causal explanation of any sort can be given for actions, it amounts to saying (as in the above quotation from Melden) that any attempted causal explanation of an action will turn out to be only an explanation of a bodily movement, and that actions are not just bodily movements.

> To give a causal *explanation* of an event involves at least showing that other conditions being presumed unchanged a change in one variable is a sufficient condition for a change in another. . . . Now the trouble about giving this sort of explanation of human actions is that we can never specify an action exhaustively in terms of movements of the body or within the body.**

It must be admitted that actions are not identical with bodily movements or other physiological occurrences, not even the simplest actions. . . .

But what reason is there to suppose that an attempted causal explanation of actions could never get beyond explaining bodily movements? These philosophers have not arrived at their general thesis via a survey of all conceivable ways of attempting such explanations (vain aspiration!). I believe that a careful examination will reveal an implicit assumption that causal explanations (in any sense in which we have causal explanations in the natural sciences) always conform to a mechanistic pattern. This would mean explaining actions as the mechanical products either of inner physiological occurrences like neural impulses and muscular contractions

* There are well known difficulties involved in constructing a general criterion for "lawlike" statements, in contrast with other general statements. And there are further problems as to how simple the lawlike statements must be (and in what sense[s] of "simple") if they are to justify us in regarding events of a certain sort as causally determined. Since these problems are not special to causal determination of actions, I shall not even review them here and shall pretend that we can either solve them or can somehow continue to speak of lawlike statements and causal determination in the absence of a definitive solution.

** Peters, *op. cit.*, p. 12.

(the project criticized by Peters), or of volitions, desires, intentions and the like, construed as immaterial mental "pushes", "forces", or "impulses", (the project criticized by Melden). To dissipate this assumption, and with it the general claim that causal explanations can bear on movements, but not actions, it is sufficient to point out the logical possibility of causal explanations of other, non-mechanistic, sorts. And to defend that logical possibility is the chief task of this paper. But first we should scrutinize briefly the claim that actions cannot be explained in terms of such mechanistic models. Let us concentrate on the physiological model, since that is more of a live issue today than the "mental mechanism" model derived from the British empiricist tradition.

Why should we suppose that causal explanations of actions in physiological terms is impossible? Peters bases this thesis on the claim that actions, unlike bodily movements, contain a logical complexity not to be found in physiological states and processes.

> There cannot therefore be a sufficient explanation of actions in causal terms because, as Popper has put it, there is a logical gulf between nature and convention. Statements implying norms and standards cannot be deduced from statements about mere movements which have no such normative implications.*

If what I have said about actions is true, then there are many action terms which do carry implications about "norms and standards", and so it is impossible to *deduce* statements about actions from statements about "mere movements" or to translate the one type of statement into the other. Indeed we do not need to bring in norms and standards to make this point. All the sorts of conditions of application for action terms mentioned above, in addition to conditions specifying certain bodily movements, furnish reasons for this same conclusion. But in itself this does not show that actions cannot be causally explained in terms of physiological occurrences. To suppose it did would be to regress to a conception of causality on which the cause-effect relationship is a deducibility relationship or some other logical connection; or perhaps it would involve invoking the medieval principle that the cause must contain at least as much reality as the effect.

But it is true that if actions involve conditions of all the sorts mentioned above, it would be wildly implausible to suppose that they can receive a complete causal explanation in physiological terms. For to suppose that typing a letter could be so explained** would be to suppose that a certain brain state, e.g., is not only a sufficient causal condition of certain bodily movements, but also a sufficient causal condition of the presence of a typewriter with paper in it, and of the existence of a custom of sending letters in the society to which the man in question belongs. I am not sure whether such a causal connection is logically impossible. A reason for supposing that it is would be this. It does seem obvious that any specifiable brain state could be artificially produced by electrical

* Peters, *op. cit.*, p. 14.
** Peters, *op. cit.*, p. 14.

stimulation if our technology were sufficiently advanced. Suppose we carry this out in a completely bare room on a member of a culture in which letter writing is unknown. Could it be an empirical question as to whether this brain stimulation would cause a typewriter to materialize in the room and would suddenly introduce the institution of letter writing in the culture (or, alternatively, transport this chap, culturally, into another milieu). It is just barely conceivable, I suppose, that there is in fact a constant conjunction between a certain kind of brain state and the satisfaction of *all* the conditions that have to be satisfied for one to be writing a letter. But the above consideration casts considerable doubt on the supposition that such a regularity could have the counterfactual implications which it would have to have to be a causal connection.* But even if not logically impossible the suggestion is so wildly implausible as not to be taken seriously.

Nevertheless, it might be a sensible project to combine physiological factors with other sorts in causally explaining actions. Let's divide up the conditions which have to obtain if a given action is to be performed into those which are facts about the agent and those which are not. For typing a letter the former group would include making bodily movements which fall within a certain range, knowing a language, intending to produce a set of written sentence tokens of the language for the purpose of communicating with someone. The latter group would include the existence of a typewriter and paper in a certain connection with the agent's hands, the normal operation of this typewriter, and the existence of an institution of letter writing in the society. I would suppose that the highest aspiration a physiological theory could sensibly have would be the explanation of the former group of conditions. It could then form one segment of a total explanatory scheme which would have to bring in the determinants of the "external" conditions. If we look at the writings of people who want to approach psychology physiologically, e.g., D. O. Hebb, they do not seem to have grasped this point.** Their aspirations, when they are speaking programmatically, are pitched much higher. We might take the above as a rational reconstruction of their programme.

II

However interesting these possibilities, it is not with physiological schemes that I wish to concern myself. As noted earlier, quite apart from the considerations just advanced, one can rebut the claim that any attempted causal explanation of actions will turn out to be at best explanations of bodily movements by showing that one can envisage causal explanations of actions which are of a non-mechanistic sort. It would be of particular relevance to show that there are no logical bars to giving a causal explanation of actions in terms of such "intentional" factors as wants, beliefs, and perceptions. For such factors contain the

* e.g., if this brain state were produced in the conditions described, all the conditions necessary for writing a letter would be satisfied.

** D. O. Hebb, *The Organization of Behavior,* Wiley, New York, 1949.

same rich logical complexity as action terms. (Wanting to congratulate Jones on his appointment is, as Melden points out in detail, at least as complex logically as congratulating Jones on his appointment.) And so even Peters' gratuitous worry about a "logical gap" could be relieved. I wish to devote the rest of the paper to considering various reasons for supposing that such schemes are, in principle, impossible. Such a consideration will be of interest not only for the free will problem, where the thesis of causal determination of actions has often been put forward in such terms, but also for the strategy of theory construction in psychology, where schemes of this sort are among the alternative bases for theoretical thinking and experimentation.

. . .

III

The main bar to supposing that a causal theory of this sort is possible is the appearance of a logical connection between such factors as wants and the actions they are invoked to explain. It seems reasonable, at least it has seemed reasonable since Hume, to suppose that if A and B are logically connected they cannot be causally connected. And quite apart from facts about the use of the term "cause", it would seem that if wants and actions are logically connected, it would not be an *empirical* job to determine the way in which actions are a function of wants.

There are several different ways in which a logical connection might seem to be involved. For one thing it is claimed that when we "explain" an action by citing a want or intention, we are in fact simply giving a fuller description of the action, of what the person was doing; and that since the want or intention enters into the (full) description of the action, it cannot be causally related to it.

For instance, we might ask "Why did Jones walk across the room? Was it in order to put coal on the fire or out of politeness?" But this would not be a causal question. It would be a way of eliciting what sort of action it was.*

. . . on this supposition, the motive for the action is the cause of the action. This, however, is self-contradictory. As the alleged cause of the action, it cannot serve further to characterize the action. As motive it must—for it tells us what in fact the person was doing.**

Since a motive, in explaining an action, makes it clear what the action in question is, any description or account of the motive must of necessity involve a reference to an action being performed, and specifically to the kind of action that is thereby specified by the explanation given.†

*Peters, *op. cit.*, p. 55.

** Melden, *op. cit.*, p. 88.

† *Ibid.*, p. 90. These arguments, as well as others I shall be citing later, are specifically directed against the claim that the explanations of actions in terms of wants, etc., that we give in everyday discourse are causal explanations. *Although this is not the claim which I am defending,* these arguments are clearly relevant to that claim. For if wants, etc., are logically related to any action they might plausibly be brought in to explain, this fact would create just as much difficulty for the project of constructing a systematic causal theory of action in these terms, as it would for the attempt to interpret everyday explanations of actions in these terms as causal.

These arguments do not seem impressive to me, and this for two reasons. First, it is only in certain types of cases that we can be secure in going from an explanation in terms of want, etc., to an account of what the agent is doing. These are the cases in which the want or intention involved is a want or intention to do something which the agent is doing contemporaneously with the action being explained. Melden's chief example is of this sort: explaining the driver's raising his arm in terms of his intention to signal a turn. Signalling a turn is going on simultaneously with raising the arm, and, furthermore, in this situation raising the arm *is* signalling the turn. Other such cases would be explaining my writing a letter to Jones by saying that I wanted to invite him to visit us, explaining my leaving the room by saying that I wanted to avoid Smith, and explaining my laying down a certain card by saying that I did it in order to trump the trick. But there are many other cases in which we explain doing *A* in terms of a want or intention to do *B*, or a feeling that one has to do *B*, where *B* is not related to *A* in this way, but is a further action, which *A* is thought to lead to, or to put one in a position to perform. Thus I may explain getting up early by saying that I had to meet Jones at the airport, explain my getting out my tools by saying that I want to fix a door knob, or explain my walking down the hall by saying that I intend to have it out with my boss. In these cases the explanation does not "further characterize the action" or "make it clear *what* the action in question is", or even give us materials for such characterization. To say that I am getting up early because I want to meet Jones at the airport is not to imply that I *am* meeting Jones at the airport; nor is saying that I am getting out my tools because I want to fix a door knob to imply that I *am* fixing a door knob.

The second and more fundamental difficulty with this argument goes deeper and extends to all sorts of cases. Even where in explaining an action in terms of a want etc., we are providing, or at least providing materials for, a further description of what the agent is doing, this does not mean that explanans and explanandum are *logically* related in a way that would make a causal relationship impossible. Where, in answer to the question "Why are you leaving the party?", I reply, "I want to avoid Smith", I am, it is true, providing you with a further account of what I am doing at the moment, but that does not keep my wish to avoid Smith from being among the causal conditions of my leaving the party. What we must see is that in giving this explanation I am setting out to explain *the fact that I am leaving the party;* I am not setting out to explain *what I am doing at the moment*, taken in some all-inclusive sense, nor am I setting out to explain various other facts which also have to do with what I am doing at the moment, such as the fact that I am avoiding Smith, the fact that I am walking toward the front door, the fact that I am making a lot of noise, etc. We must not let the fact that *in this situation* leaving the party *is* avoiding Smith, or the fact that what I am doing at the moment can be correctly characterized both as leaving the party and as avoiding Smith, make us suppose that the task of explaining my leaving the party is the same as the task of explaining my avoiding Smith. And we should resist just as strongly the temptation to suppose that the job of explaining my leaving the party is a job of explaining what I am doing at the time (taken without further specification) or of explaining what is going on there and then. To give way to these tendencies would be to commit the elementary blunder of supposing that what we set out to explain is a slice of reality, a chunk of space-time in all its concreteness. If that were so, the way we characterize a chunk when we ask for an explanation of it would have no implications for *what* we are trying to explain. And, in the above situation, the questions "Why are you leaving the party?" and "Why are you avoiding Smith?" would turn out to be the *same* question! What we set out to explain is always *the fact that so-and-so*, an abstract aspect of a slice of reality, and so the aspect of the slice we pick out in order to specify our explanandum has a great bearing on what question we are trying to answer. If I set out to explain the fact that a person is given to compulsive hand-washing, there will be many other features of the events which count as cases of compulsive hand-washing, more specifically many other things that he is doing in compulsively washing his hands, which will not be adequately explained by my explanation of his compulsion, no matter how adequately that explanation does the job for which it was intended. Thus in washing his hands, the person may be destroying germs, seriously depleting the water supply, and affording amusement to his siblings. But my explanation will not also be an adequate explanation of the fact that he is doing all these things, though it should be if I were setting out simply to explain "what he is doing" on these occasions.

Once we see this point, we can see that even though what I am doing at the moment can be correctly characterized both as leaving the party and as avoiding Smith, it by no means follows that the fact that I want to avoid Smith is logically related to the fact that I am leaving the party, in such a way as to make it impossible that the first figures among the causal conditions of the second.

IV

There is a kind of putative logical involvement which does not disappear under scrutiny so quickly as this one. If one begins to try to imagine what sorts of principles would be involved in a Tolman-like theory,* it may seem that the connections between psychological states and actions specified by such principles would not be empirical principles at all (and so would not specify *causal* connections). Could it be an empirical discovery that wanting very much to do something would increase the likelihood of doing it; or that believing that doing something would lead to great injury to oneself, would engender a strong tendency not to do it?

* E. C. Tolman, "A Psychological Model", in T. Parsons and E. A. Shils, eds., *Toward a General Theory of Action*, Cambridge, Mass.: Harvard University Press, 1951.

Could we deny these principles without overturning our concepts of want, belief, etc.? But we must be careful not to pose the problem in terms which are too simple to make contact with the real issues.

Melden speaks of "the logical incoherence, and no mere violation of empirical fact, involved in the supposition that a person might never do what he wants to do or always do what he does not want to do."* Of course it is obvious that it is not logically, or even factually, necessary that a person always does what he wants to do, or even that he always tries to do what he wants to do. And it is certainly not logically true, though it might be true as a matter of fact, that people usually do what they want to do. But it does seem that there is something logically odd in the supposition that people never do what they want to do. And this would seem to make "If a person wants to do *x*, there is a considerable probability that he will do *x*" suspect as a candidate for a principle in an empirical theory relating psychological factors to actions. However, this particular logical involvement, assuming it does exist, does not seem particularly germane to our problem. For one thing, insofar as we are interested in causal determination from the standpoint of the free will problem, we are interested in deterministic, not probabilistic, principles. For another thing, any scheme which would be of interest to psychologists would include among the determinants of doing *x*, not wanting to do *x*, but rather wanting to do or have or be something else. The psychologist wants to get farther back in the causal chain than he would if he just traced doing *x* to wanting to do *x*. He will be more interested in seeing doing *x* as a function of a number of relatively generalized wants—for achievement, attention, approval, emotional stimulation, novelty, etc., plus various beliefs which relate these to specific types of actions and perceptions which relate them to the immediate situation—as in Tolman's scheme.

But analogous difficulties can be raised with respect to this more complicated sort of explanation. Suppose we think of explaining Smith's driving to town in terms not of his wanting to drive to town, but in terms of his wanting to go to a concert (or if we want something more general, of the sort actually considered by psychologists, his wanting the kind of emotional stimulation one receives from symphonic music) plus a belief that driving to town now is a necessary condition of his getting such stimulation (or, perhaps, a belief that driving to town would put him in the best possible position for getting such stimulation). It might be supposed that any general principle which would lie behind explaining the action in those terms would be logically true.

(1) Whenever any one wants to do *x* and believes that doing *y* will put him in the best possible position for doing *x*, he will do *y*.

However this will not stand up as such. It is not self-contradictory, or even logically odd, to suppose that Jones wants to go to the concert, believes that he can only go to the concert by driving to town, and yet does not drive to town. He might want more to stay home and read a

* Melden, *op. cit.*, p. 144.

book. Or he might have some work which he has to get done that evening. Or he might not have a car available. Or he might not be able to drive. Or he might have religious scruples against driving on Friday evening. Or the whole thing might have slipped his mind until it is too late. Or he may be too emotionally upset to go to the concert.

Of course, each time we think of something which would prevent the action actually being performed we can introduce something into the formula which excludes that interference. Presumably something like this is done when schemes such as Tolman's are excogitated. Thus we can construct the more complex principle:

> (2) Whenever A wants to do *x*, doesn't want to do anything incompatible with doing *x* more than he wants to do *x*, believes that doing *y* will put him in the best position for doing *x*, has both the capacity and opportunity for doing *y*, doesn't feel obliged to do anything incompatible with doing *x* or *y*, has no scruples against doing *x* or *y*, hasn't forgotten about doing *x*, is not too emotionally upset to do *x*, then he will do *y*.

It may well be that even this is not complex enough, but it is difficult to tell. What factors might prevent this complex antecedent from issuing in the consequent? Well, Smith's wife might strongly oppose his driving to town on the grounds that the roads were slippery, and in the face of this opposition Smith might abandon his project. But one could say that in this case he does have a stronger incompatible want—to avoid subjecting his wife to a great deal of worry. Perhaps his pride in some way interferes with his doing *y*. Is this to be counted as an incompatible want, or as a contrary scruple? Or is some separate category needed here? Although it is difficult to be sure at any point that we have a statement which is universally true and which would afford firm ground for prediction, it might well seem that the closer we get to such a statement the closer we get to a statement which is *logically* true. For it may seem that in filling out the statement we are simply reflecting on our use of the terms involved rather than appealing to empirical evidence. It would seem that I don't have to perform experiments to tell that having strong scruples against doing *y* might well prevent *y* from being performed, even though the other conditions are satisfied.

Before I go into the question of the logical status of (2) let me consider the following doubt as to the pertinence of this question to the philosophy of psychology. It may be thought that even if such principles as the above are logically true, or even analytic, this has no bearing on the status of the principles in a systematic psychological theory. For psychologists like Tolman are not employing the ordinary concepts of want, scruple, etc., but are constructing technical concepts which are only misleadingly expressed in these everyday terms. But this is not really a way out. The psychological theorist simply does not have the resources to get along without depending on the vague but rich content of these everyday concepts. He can attempt to refine them in various ways, introduce intersubjectively reliable indications and measures, and pare away this or that feature. But the state of the art is not such that he can straight out *define*, e.g., "motive" in terms of some measure like the thematic apperception test. If he tries to do so, he will be left high and dry with a methodologically pure concept which fails to connect interestingly with very many of the things with which he is seeking liaisons. And there is another reason why such isolation is unrealistic even as a goal. It is surely the case that in some way we do get real understanding of a person's action if we see that he did it because he wanted so and so. One would hope that psychology would, among other things, help us to understand better what kind of understanding this is and provide us with ways of acquiring more precise and more thoroughgoing understanding of this sort, rather than turning its back and talking about something else instead. (Indeed, as we shall see in a moment, Tolman himself, when elucidating his crucial concepts, explicitly indicates their close connection with commonsense concepts.)

To return to the question of the logical status of (2), if anyone thinks that any such principle is logically true, his grounds may simply be that its denial sounds "logically odd" or "deviant". But such a claim, however currently fashionable, provides at best a sandy foundation. Like its ill-fated predecessor, "I can't imagine (conceive, envisage) its not being so", it is notoriously difficult to distinguish at sight between different sources of the inability to conceive or of the odd sound. The fact that I can't form a conception of the agent not doing y when all the above conditions hold, *may* be due to logical features of the proposition, but it may also be due to deficiencies in my powers of conception or lack of imagination on my part. Similarly if it sounds very odd to me to say that all those conditions hold but nevertheless the chap doesn't do y, this may be because there is something logically defective about it, or it may be that (2) seems so obviously true, is borne out so pervasively by experience, that a suggestion that it might not hold falls strangely on the ears. (It certainly does sound odd to suggest that a bush might be in flames without being consumed.) And is it not rash to suppose that one can distinguish between these various sources of strangeness just by attending to the "quality" of the sound?

It is such deficiencies in the appeal to the immediate, whether of the older or the newer variety, that have led people to take a more discursive approach to the justification of claims to logical truth or falsity, and to attempt to justify such claims by appeal to formulations of the meanings of the terms involved. Thus L. J. Cohen, in an article entitled "Teleological Explanations",* claims that the following proposition is analytic.

(3) If an agent believes that y is contingent upon x, desires y, has no conflicting desires, and x is in his power, then he will probably do x.**

* Proceedings of the Aristotelian Society, New Series, Vol. LI, p. 264.

** Note that we have made the antecedent much simpler, without making the claim of analyticity wholly implausible, by having only the probability of doing x in the consequent.

Cohen's conviction that this statement is analytic is based on his conviction that "It is merely part of what is ordinarily meant by 'desire' "* and ". . . a desire of *x* entails a tendency to effect x under certain conditions."** Presumably this means that "*A* desires *x*" is to be analyzed in dispositional terms in such a way as to make a desire a disposition to perform certain actions under certain conditions. And such definitions, or sketches of such definitions, have been proposed from time to time. But just how is such a definition to go, and just how is it to ground the logical truth of (2)?

The heroic course would be to simply dump all the other components of the antecedent of (2) into a dispositional definition of "want".

> D1 *A* wants to do *x* = *df*. If *A* doesn't want to do anything incompatible with doing *x* more than he wants to do *x*, believes that doing *y* will put him in the best position for doing *x*, has both the capacity and the opportunity for doing *y*, doesn't feel obliged to do anything incompatible with doing *x* or *y*, has no scruples against doing *x* or *y*, hasn't forgotten about doing *x*, and is not too emotionally upset to do *x*, then he will do *y*.

Of course the first thing that leaps to the eye is the vicious circularity involved in including in the definiens not only "want", but also a specification of the particular want specified in the definiendum. But perhaps this could be remedied by first defining "*A* wants to do *x* at *t* more than he wants to do anything else at *t*", and then finding some way of defining the more general notion on the basis of that. Even so, there are many difficulties. It does seem incredible that we should have to drag in all the factors which might conceivably prevent a want from issuing into action into a specification of the meaning of the word "want". This would be a coherence theory of meaning with a vengeance. That would mean that we have to make our basic decisions about the shape of a theory of human action, e.g., decisions as to what major categories to use in sorting out the factors that can influence what a person does, before we could say what is meant by the terms for any one of these factors. Our disinclination to go along with this may be reinforced by the following considerations. Such a dispositional definition of "want" was brought in to dispel doubts about the logical truth of (2). But this particular definition could not be effective for that purpose because, since it exactly reproduces the content of (2), any doubts about the logical truth of (2) will automatically transfer to the claim that D1 is an adequate definition. Moreover, the fact that with respect to (2) one can quite reasonably wonder not only whether it is logically true but also whether it is true without exception for any reason whatever, D1 can hardly be an adequate statement of what we *mean* by "want". If it were, there could be no question as to whether cases might turn up in which all the conditions of (2) were satisfied but the agent did not do *y*. And it seems that such questions can sensibly be

* Loc. cit.
** Ibid., p. 265.

raised for any formula like (2) which can be constructed.

This may lead us to construct a much simpler dispositional definition of want, one which is not enmeshed in the details of (2) in fatal ways. We might try the following.

D2 *A* wants to do $x = df$. *A* has some tendency to do *x*.

Unfortunately it is possible for *A* to want very much to do *x* but to have no tendency at all to do *x*, at least in any ordinary sense of "tendency". This would be true, e.g., if doing *x* went against such firmly held principles that there was no real possibility of *A*'s doing it. What we need to express is the notion that the want substantially raises the probability of his doing *x*; that even though some contrary tendency may make it all but certain that he will not do *x*, still wanting to do *x* introduces a possible source of doubt which would not have been present otherwise. But we cannot, on pain of circularity, make our definiens read "The probability of *A* doing *x* is greater than it would be if he did not want to do *x*". However we can get substantially the same idea into the definition by introducting the notion of belief, as follows.

D3 *A* wants to do $x = df$. If *A* believes that doing *y* will put him in position to do *x*, he will be more likely to do *y* than he would have been without this belief.

One reason this cannot be taken seriously as a definition of "want" is that it fails to distinguish wanting to do *x* from, e.g., feeling obligated to do *x* or being under considerable pressure to do *x*. If the definiens is adequate for anything, it is rather some more general notion like "being motivated to do *x*", of which "wanting to do *x*" is one species. However this need not bother us, for even if this is true it could still be the case that the above definiens gives part of the meaning of "*A* wants to do *x*", in such a way that this would be entailed by "*A* wants to do *x*", and that might be enough for yielding the conclusion that (2) is logically true.*

But of course D3, even if it is a completely adequate definition, cannot yield that conclusion by itself. We can't have it both ways. We cut most of the detailed content of (2) out of the definition because otherwise it would have been too close to (2) to do us much good. But having suitably purged it, (2) cannot be simply analytic of "want". We shall have to bring in definitions of the other terms as well. And we are going to have different sorts of patterns for the definition of at least some of them. If we were to define each of the terms in (1) by a dispositional pattern involving some selection of the other factors, as, e.g.,

* It is worth noting that insofar as Tolman explicates his fundamental concepts, the explication takes a dispositional form. He says that a "need" is "to be defined in the last analysis as a readiness to get to and to manipulate in a consummatory fashion (or to get from) certain other types of objects." (p. 288) And he defines a belief, or a readiness or potentiality for expectation, as "a connection that makes a readiness to perceive and to behave in a certain way relative to one type of object (as end) give rise to a readiness to perceive and to behave in a certain way relative to certain other types of objects (as means)." (p. 293) Thus insofar as Tolman really means these as definitions, he is involved in any logical connections of needs and beliefs with actions that follow from this sort of definition in terms of behavioral dispositions.

D4 *A* is able to do $y = df$. If *A* wants to do *x* and believes that doing *y* will put him in the best position for doing *x*, he will probably do *y*.

D5 *A* has the opportunity of doing $y = df$. If *A* wants to do *y* and is able to do *y*, he will probably do *y*.

we should find ourselves rotating in a very small circle.

Of course other sorts of definitions might be found for some of the terms, which would then be used as a basis for dispositional definitions of the others. For example, belief might conceivably be defined in terms of perceptual thresholds. But until something like that is done, we could not begin to use a dispositional definition of "want" to ground a claim for logical truth for a formula like (2).* And it is worth noting that, quite apart from the aim to show that (2) is logically true, one could not use D3 for anything without having some idea of what the other factors are that influence action and how they are to be identified. For how am I to tell that a certain belief has or has not affected the probability of a certain action being performed? If I am to make use of anything other than observation of the relative frequency of the action in cases where the belief is and is not present (and unless both populations are both large and varied this result is not likely to be of much interest), I shall have to work against the background of some theory (at least a rough one) as to what factors influence action and how they interact in doing so. Otherwise I would have no reason to think in a particular instance that it is the acquisition of a certain belief that "tips the balance".

* This is in addition to the difficulty of deriving a deterministic principle from dispositional definitions in a probability form.

Further Readings

GENERAL

Books of General Interest

Adler, M. J., *The Idea of Freedom*, Doubleday, Garden City, N.Y. (2 vols.), 1958 and 1961.

Ofstad, Harold, *An Inquiry into the Freedom of Decision*, Norwegian Universities Press, Oslo, 1961.

Sidgwick, Henry, *The Methods of Ethics*, Macmillan, New York, 1907.

Original Collections

Hook, Sidney (ed.), *Determinism and Freedom in the Age of Modern Science*, Collier, New York, 1961.

Lehrer, Keith (ed.), *Freedom and Determinism*, Random House, New York, 1966.

Pears, D. F. (ed.), *Freedom and the Will*, St. Martin's, New York, 1963.

Anthologies

Berofsky, Bernard (ed.), *Free Will and Determinism*, Harper & Row, New York, 1966.

Morgenbesser, Sidney, and James Walsh (eds.), *Free Will*, Prentice-Hall, Englewood Cliffs, N.J., 1962.

Morris, Herbert (ed.), *Freedom and Responsibility*. Stanford University Press, Stanford, Calif., 1961.

LIBERTARIANISM AND INDETERMINISM

Berlin, Isaiah, *Historical Inevitability,* Oxford University Press, Fair Lawn, N.J., 1954.

Broad, C. D., *Determinism, Indeterminism, and Libertarianism*, Macmillan, New York, 1934, also in *Ethics and the History of Philosophy*, Humanities Press, New York, 1952, Berofsky, and Morgenbesser-Walsh.

Campbell, C. A., "Is Free-Will a Pseudo-Problem?" *Mind, 60* (1951), also in Berofsky, Morris.

Campbell, C. A., *Of Selfhood and Godhood*, Allen & Unwin, London, 1957.

Campbell, C. A., *Scepticism and Construction,* Allen & Unwin, London, 1931.

Eddington, Sir Arthur, *The Nature of the Physical World*, Macmillan, New York, 1928, ch. 14.

Eddington, Sir Arthur, *New Pathways in Science*, Cambridge University Press, New York, 1935, ch. 13.

Farrer, Austin, *The Freedom of the Will,* A. & C. Black, London, 1958.

James, William, "The Dilemma of Determinism," 1884, in *The Will to Believe and Other Essays,* Longmans, New York, 1931.

Kant, Immanuel, *The Critique of Practical Reason,* trans. Lewis White Beck, Liberal Arts, New York, 1956.

Kant, Immanuel, *Fundamental Principles of the Metaphysics of Morals,* trans. Thomas K. Abbott, Liberal Arts, New York, 1949.

Peirce, C. S., "The Doctrine of Necessity Examined," 1892, in M. R. Cohen (ed.), *Chance, Love and Logic,* Harcourt, Brace, New York, 1923, and in J. Buchler (ed.), *The Philosophy of Peirce,* Routledge & Kegan Paul, London, 1940.

Sartre, Jean-Paul, *Being and Nothingness,* trans. H. E. Barnes, Philosophical Library, New York, 1956 (selections in Berofsky, Morgenbesser-Walsh).

RECONCILIATIONISM AND ITS CRITICS

Austin, J. L., "Ifs and Cans," *Proceedings of the British Academy,* 1956, also in J. O. Urmson and G. J. Warnock (eds.), *Philosophical Papers,* Oxford University Press, New York, 1961, Berofsky, and Morris.

Ayer, A. J., "Freedom and Necessity," *Polemic, 5* (1946), also in *Philosophical Essays*, Macmillan, London, 1954.

Bradley, F. H., "The Vulgar Notion of Responsibility in Connection with the Theories of Free-Will and Necessity," in *Ethical Studies*, Oxford University Press, Fair Lawn, N.J., 1876.

Foot, Philippa, "Free Will as Involving Determinism," *Philosophical Review, 66* (1957), also in Berofsky, Morgenbesser-Walsh.

Hobbes, Thomas, *The Questions Concerning Liberty, Necessity, and Chance,* Andrew Crook, 1656 (selections in Morgenbesser-Walsh).

Mill, John Stuart, *A System of Logic,* Longmans, London, 1843, Book VI, chap. 2.

Moore, G. E., *Ethics*, Oxford University Press, Fair Lawn, N.J., 1912, chap. 6.

Nowell-Smith, P. H., *Ethics*, Penguin, Baltimore, 1954, chaps. 19 and 20.

Nowell-Smith, P. H., "Freewill and Moral Responsibility," *Mind, 57* (1948).

Nowell-Smith, P. H., "Ifs and Cans," *Theoria, 26* (1960), also in Berofsky.

Schlick, Moritz, *Problems of Ethics,* trans. D. Rynin, Prentice-Hall, Englewood Cliffs, N.J., 1939, ch. 10.

Stevenson, C. L., *Ethics and Language,* Yale University Press, New Haven, Conn., 1944, ch. 14.

Wilson, John, "Freedom and Compulsion," *Mind, 67* (1958).

ACTION THEORY

Bradley, M. C., "A Note on Mr. MacIntyre's *Determinism*," *Mind, 68* (1959), also in Berofsky.

Davidson, Donald, "Actions, Reasons, and Causes," *Journal of Philosophy, 60* (1963), also in Berofsky.

Ginet, Carl, "Can the Will be Caused?" *Philosophical Review, 71* (1962).

Hampshire, Stuart, *Freedom of the Individual,* Harper & Row, New York, 1965.

Hart, H. L. A., "The Ascription of Responsibility and Rights," in Antony Flew (ed.), *Essays in Logic and Language,* (First Series) Philosophical Library, New York, 1951.

MacIntyre, A. C., "Determinism," *Mind, 66* (1957), also in Berofsky.

MacKay, D. M., "On the Logical Indeterminacy of a Free Choice," *Mind, 69* (1960).

Melden, A. I., *Free Action,* Routledge & Kegan Paul, London, 1961.

Peters, R. S., *The Concept of Motivation*, Routledge & Kegan Paul, London, 1958.
Pears, David, "Predicting and Deciding," *Proceedings of the British Academy*, Oxford University Press, London, 1965.
Pears, David, "Are Reasons for Actions Causes?" A. Stroll (ed.), *Epistemology: New Essays*, Harper & Row, New York, 1967.
Taylor, Richard, "Deliberation and Foreknowledge," *American Philosophical Quarterly*, *1* (1964), also in Berofsky.

IV

EXPLANATION AND HUMAN ACTION

1

HERE ARE a number of kinds of things for which one can request explanations—events, the meanings of words, scientific laws, and kinship systems, to name a few. Although philosophers have been interested in the concept of explanation as it applies to each of them, their central concern has been with the explanation of events, including human actions. Admittedly, it is an open question how far conclusions drawn about the explanations of events can be extended to these other areas. We shall restrict our discussion to the explanation of events.

Given that philosophers are interested in the nature of knowledge, it is no surprise that they concern themselves with the concept of explanation. To know what happened is to know something but to explain why it happened, to render it intelligible, is to possess a deeper insight into the world. The philosopher wants to know, therefore, what it is that constitutes an explanation of an event.

The very form of this question, though, begs some of the most controversial questions in this area. Is there just one model for the explanation of *all* events? Is there just one kind of explanation for all kinds of events? Is human behavior to be explained in the same way that the behavior of molecules of gas is to be explained?

Those who answer this question affirmatively propound the so-called "deductive nomological" model of explanation as the universal standard. According to this standard, an event is explained when the sentence describing the event can be deduced from general laws together with sentences describing particular conditions. These particular conditions are sometimes called "the cause" or "the antecedent conditions." For example, to explain the fact that this water is boiling, one cites the fact that it has been heated to 100°C together with the general law that under standard conditions, the boiling point of all water is 100°C. (One may not *actually* cite the law if it assumed that one's audience knows it.) Notice that a person who gives this explanation could have predicted the event before he explained it if he had had the information beforehand. That is, if he knew the general law and the fact that the water was being heated to 100°C, he could have deduced and, therefore, predicted that the water would boil. (This view of explanation is represented by Hempel's "The Function of General Laws in History" included in this section.)

Numerous attacks on this model have been advanced in recent years. It has been claimed that the model is (1) not necessary for explanation; (2) not sufficient for explanation; (3) irrelevant to explanation; and (4) impossible as an account of explanation.

Some have been willing to concede the correctness of the model for the physical sciences, but reject its applicability to history and the social sciences. Some contemporary arguments that have been advanced for this view have roots in a conception of a scientific knowledge of man that received concentrated expression in the nineteenth and early twentieth centuries. The German term "verstehen" was frequently used by these advocates to designate the distinctive manner in which human behavior is understood. In the human sphere, it was contended, one must be able to share the state of mind of the person one wishes to understand. One must achieve an empathetic understanding that one does not require in the study of physical processes. Or one must "imaginatively reconstruct" the situation in which the person is involved in order to gain genuine insight, including insight into causal connections.

An objection frequently raised against this position is that it fails to distinguish two separate issues. It may very well be the case that the formulation of an hypothesis about human behavior requires or is aided by the ability to perform the operation of "verstehen." But even so, and even if the hypothesis is sufficiently confirmed to be accepted as a law, proponents of the deductive nomological model would say that the explanation itself is provided by the deduction of the sentence describing the behavior from general laws and sentences describing initial conditions. Thus, "verstehen" may be a valuable heuristic device, but it plays no role in the structure of the explanation proper. (For a discussion of the "verstehen" approach see the selection by Dray "Explaining and Justifying Actions" included in this section.)

Contemporary proponents of the distinctive character of explanation of human behavior do not advance views that belong to heuristics, although the arguments they employ are occasionally similar to the arguments of the advocates of "verstehen." We shall mention a few of these arguments.

1. To understand a physical event, one must, as the deductive nomological view insists, find a set of conditions which constitute the cause of that event. But prior to the event for which we seek an explanation, many events occur, and many conditions are present. For example, before the onslaught of Smith's stomachache, he had had three martinis, yelled at his wife, performed twenty situps, and scratched his ear (not all simultane-

ously). How do we decide which is the cause? Some, like the last, are obviously eliminable; further information is required to come to a decision. But any decision here, including the elimination of the last mentioned possibility, involves a tacit appeal to general laws. For example, if we say that Smith's stomach muscles are sufficiently strong so that the twenty situps cannot have been the cause we must be arguing from information about *similar kinds* of cases. Likewise, if we find that people who have digestive tracts like Smith's and who, like Smith, drink only infrequently, normally get stomachaches after consuming the amount of alcohol contained in three martinis, then we are more likely to choose the three martinis as the cause. Thus, the advocates of the deductive nomological view are correct in supposing that the isolation of the cause that is required for an explanation presupposes a general law that tells us what kinds of things occur under what conditions.

Proponents of the distinctive character of explanation of human behavior would say, however, that even though causal explanation presupposes a general law, explanation of human actions is not causal; for to understand a human action, one must know the reasons or motives that led the person to do what he did. Finding a reason, however, is not finding a cause:

(a) Causes are events antecedent to their effects. If I board the bus in order to get to the museum, that is, my reason for boarding the bus is that I want to get to the museum, what event antecedent to the boarding is my reason? Must I have consciously entertained the proposition "I want to get to the museum" as the bus was approaching? Clearly not. And if, perchance, I did entertain this proposition, did this entertaining produce the action of boarding the bus *in the same way* in which the impact of one billiard ball upon another produces motion in the latter?

(b) To say that C causes E is to say that there is a general law connecting C to E. But there is no general law connecting a reason to the action done for that reason. If Antony returned to Cleopatra in order to acquire the gold he needed to fight a war he believed essential to his political advancement, it is not possible to produce a general law, that is, a universal proposition that is true, testable, and nontrivial, that covers this case. Consider the following candidates for a general law connecting Antony's action and the reason for it. "All Roman generals go to Cleopatra to acquire gold when they need it to fight a war" is false. "All political figures who believe that an action is in their best interests will undertake that action" is no good for either (1) it is obviously false, or (2) its truth is maintained by deciding what a person believes is in his best interests on the basis of his action. That is, we either grant that it is false because political figures in fact do not always act in what they believe are their best interests, or we insist that it is true at the price of having to say that *whatever* a person does is what he believes is in his best interest. If we take the second alternative, then to say A did x because it was in his interest explains nothing. It is trivial because we have made it true by definition.

Suppose we try the following: "All people who (1) are political figures with personalities like Antony's, (2) are faced with the kind of dilemma in which Antony found himself, (3) believe that a successful war can extricate them from these difficulties, (4) do not have the money needed for this war and have no access to it in their own country, and (5) believe they can acquire the needed money from another country by feigning love for the leader of that country, will go to that leader in order to acquire the money."

Clearly, these philosophers would say, the above is no law. Besides being vague, it has been concocted so that it would be next to impossible to find another instance of what is supposed to be a *general* law.

So here is a case where we presumably *have* the explanation, but cannot find or construct a law that covers the case. On this basis, some have concluded that the deductive nomological model does not apply in the area of historical explanation, i.e., a general law is not necessary for historical explanation.

This first defense of the distinctive character of explanation of human action plays a central role in contemporary discussions of the problem of free will. It is alleged that the belief that there is no free will arises from the assumption that the model of explanation that is appropriate in the physical sphere applies as well in the human sphere. That is, on the basis of the deductive nomological model, we picture human behavior as governed by laws that tell us what human beings invariably do, given a knowledge of appropriate causes. But if this model does not apply in the human sphere, it has been argued, then there is no reason to believe that there is no free will. (For a further discussion, see Section III, "Determinism, Freedom, and Responsibility.")

Two further arguments against the applicability of the deductive nomological model to the explanation of human actions are as follows:

2. The deductive nomological model is deterministic. That is, the explanation of an event entails that the event is predictable from a knowledge of antecedent conditions. Explanation and prediction are, in effect, two sides of the same coin. Something is an explanation only if it could have served as a prediction, according to the model. Given these conditions, the event *invariably* occurs. But human behavior is not always—or there are no sufficient reasons for believing that it is always—deterministic. That is, it is not the case that all explainable behavior is predictable behavior. Thus, explanation of human behavior cannot always take the same form as explanation of nonhuman behavior. It may always be possible to find statistical laws for human behavior; i.e., laws that tell us that a human being will *probably* act in a certain way under given conditions, and these may suffice for explanatory purposes. But statistical laws are not deterministic laws. Again, debate on this issue has an important bearing on the free will issue.

3. Whether or not human behavior is deterministic, it has been argued that explanations which do not allow for prediction of the event explained are achieved in history and the genetic sciences, e.g., biology,

geology, the social sciences. In these sciences it is often thought to be enough to cite certain *necessary* conditions in order to explain. But one cannot predict an event just from a knowledge of necessary conditions. One cannot predict that Jones will play tennis tomorrow solely on the basis of the fact that Jones is not paralyzed.

Nor, of course, is it an adequate explanation of the fact that Jones plays tennis to cite the fact that he is not paralyzed. So not *any* necessary condition will do as an explanation. That is, since this view asserts that explanations are sometimes complete when they cite only necessary conditions, its advocates must specify which kinds of necessary conditions are legitimate explanations. The citing of certain necessary conditions is claimed to be explanatory when these conditions show a certain continuity of development in one direction or reveal the persistence of certain elements within a succession of events. For example, we understand why giraffes have survived, why there are giraffes in the twentieth century, by knowing that long necks are advantageous in various ways, e.g., food getting. Giraffe ancestors, therefore, had a greater chance of leaving descendants whose inherent variability allowed for further changes in the same general direction than of leaving descendants unable to develop in this direction. We, therefore, attain understanding in the way that this analysis describes. But no one is in a position to produce all the laws and antecedent conditions that would enable deduction of the sentence "There are giraffes in the twentieth century."

II

It is interesting to see this contemporary debate in relation to the work of Aristotle, the first philosopher to present a systematic theory of explanation. Aristotle lists four different ways to explain something and applies each to *all* things, human and nonhuman. Thus, to take the fourth explanatory factor or cause, both humans and nonhumans act for an end. But this mode of explanation (called "teleological") was almost completely eliminated by scientists from subsequent accounts of the physical world. The two questions this suggests are: (1) Is it possible to make do entirely with explanations in the nonhuman sphere that in no way suggest an end or goal? (2) Is it possible even to eliminate this mode of explanation (as well perhaps as Aristotle's second mode—the pattern or reason that the thing is what it is) in the human sphere? (See the selection by Aristotle entitled "Nature and Cause" included in this section.)

The deductive nomological theorists disagree with Aristotle, for they claim that there are not four different kinds of explanation, but only one. Thus, if explanation of human behavior is fundamentally the same as explanation of physical behavior, and if the latter is achieved without reference to ends or goals, then the former must be able to be achieved without reference to goals. The direction taken by this line of thought is strongly resisted by people like Dray.

If we suppose that at least many explanations are of the deductive nomological kind, then some interesting problems are raised when we ask the question: How do we know that some proposed explanation is true? Since the proposed explanation contains some statement that is supposed to be a law, then we must know that it really is a law, i.e., a true generalization. Now a law is a claim about a whole class of objects, e.g., *all* falling bodies, or *all* people with two blue-eyed parents; but we are only able to observe a part of each class. Hence, the claim that such statements are true involves an inference that the unobserved cases are like the observed ones. But how do we know that this is so?

Hume faced this problem (often called "the problem of induction") and apparently drew the perplexing conclusion that we have *no* right to make such inferences. This implies that we do not know any laws to be true. In fact, it involves the sweeping claim that we have no reason to accept any claim about some matter of fact that we cannot verify at the moment we make it. This extremely sceptical conclusion is ameliorated somewhat by Hume in the last part of the selection in this chapter. In order to see how, in general, one might avoid extreme scepticism, the reader will want to examine closely just what Hume does here. (See the selection by Hume entitled "Causality and Induction" included in this section.)

Regardless of whether or not the deductive nomological model is the universal standard, few would say that *no* explanations take this form. But we often feel that some explanations of this type are far better than others. Some seem to go deeper and really account for the phenomena in question, while others just classify the event under a more general heading. For example, suppose I wish to know why Jones has blue eyes. The answer I am given is that both Jones' parents have blue eyes, and there is a law that under these conditions, the children always have blue eyes. This tells me something, but I still may feel that I don't really know why Jones has blue eyes. Or I may express what bothers me by asking for an explanation of the law that was invoked to explain Jones' blue eyes.

If I am then presented with the genetic theory and learn that this trait is transmitted through genes and that people with blue eyes have only genes which produce blue eyes, I will feel much more satisfied. This does not mean that I will not want, in turn, an explanation of aspects of the genetic theory. But it does mean that the original question has received a satisfactory answer, and this was not the case prior to the time the genetic theory was introduced.

In the above example, the introduction of a theory into a domain where there are general laws illumines the entire domain. We see why the laws are what they are. The laws, which may simply be generalizations of what has been observed, are themselves explained. Theories often perform their explanatory functions by introducing terms like "gene" (biology), "electron" (physics), "magnetic field" (physics), and "unconscious" (psychology). Then, it would appear, the objects designated by these expressions must exist; if they do not, we are wrong in thinking that any genuine explanation has been achieved. But if we are forced to postulate the existence of entities like electrons and unconscious minds, then we must acknowledge that there are things in the world that are never directly experienced (seen, felt, heard, internally sensed). This perturbs many philosophers of an empiricistic cast who try to explain the concepts we use in describing the world in terms of notions drawn solely from sense experience.

Duhem grapples with two approaches to this problem. For him, science *explains* only if it postulates the existence of unobservables, even if this is embarrassing for empiricists. On this view, sometimes called "realism," science tells us about the real structure of things, and tells us, by reference to this structure, why the observable world behaves the way it does. (See the selection by Duhem entitled "Scientific Explanation" included in this section.)

The other approach that Duhem considers is that of construing scientific theories as not really explaining, but as *classifying*, observed regularities. We are not to take terms like "electron" as designating entities, but as devices for organizing, in as coherent and orderly a fashion as possible, the laws that describe observed regularities. Naturally, empiricists have often found this approach attractive.

The following selections present in detail some of the views sketched above.

NATURE AND CAUSE

PART I

ARISTOTLE

NATURE AND ART

Among beings, some are formed by nature, some by other causes.* Among those formed by nature, we may name animals** and their parts, plants, and the simple bodies (earth, fire, air, and water); all of these, together with beings like them, we call "formed by nature." Observation discloses how they differ from things not constituted by nature: each of them has *within itself* a beginning of movement and rest, whether the "movement" [or specific type of behavior] is a local motion, growth or decline, or a qualitative change. Such is not the case with things like beds and clothes: that is to say, to the extent that these come within the classification of "products of art", they do not have implanted within

Reprinted from *The Physics*, chapters 1 and 3, translated by Richard Hope, University of Nebraska Press, Lincoln, 1961, with permission of the publishers.

* ii.6.198a9,10. Cf. Plato *Timaeus* 30A,47E,52D,53B; *Philebus* 59; *Laws* x.886B–899D.

** *On the Parts of Animals* i. presents numerous parallels to *Physics* ii.

themselves any tendency to change; nevertheless, in so far as they happen to consist of stone or earth or a composite material, they do have such a beginning of movement and rest, but only in this respect. But even this circumstance gives evidence that the nature of a thing* is in some sense the factor which initiates movement and rest within that thing in which it is itself immediately, not incidentally, present. The reason for saying "not incidentally" may be illustrated by a physician who "incidentally" heals himself; but since even he cannot as a patient practice the medical art, physician and patient are usually two separate individuals, although under certain conditions the same individual may happen to be his own physician and his own patient. What applies to the restoration of a patient's health, applies also to the products of any other art: not one of them has the source of its own production within itself; rather is this source in an agent external to the product (as in the case of a house or of any other product of manual labor) or, when the thing happens incidentally to act upon itself, the source is in some distinct aspect of the product itself.

These remarks bring out what "nature" is. Accordingly, a thing may be said to "have a nature" if it has within itself the sort of "beginning" described: every such thing is a "primary being," since it is a "subject" [of change]; and a "nature" always involves a "subject" in which it inheres. Such things are also "according to nature." So, too, are their essential attributes; for example, the upward motion of fire neither *is* nor *has* a "nature" but happens "*by* nature" or, in other words, "*according to nature*." Thus we have explained what "nature" is and what it is to be "by nature" and to happen "according to nature." It would be ridiculous, however, to try to prove *that* nature is: it is obvious that there are many such natural beings; but to want to prove the obvious by what is not obvious shows inability to discriminate between what we can ascertain directly and what indirectly.** Yet as a man born blind may resort to reasoning to convince himself about colors, so this failing, too, is a possible one; but those who have it must be unthinkingly talking about words.†

Now, some hold that the nature of the primary being of natural beings is their proximate constituent by itself, apart from any arrangement of it: the nature of a bed,‡ they say, is wood and, of a statue, bronze. As Antiphon suggests, by way of giving a clue to this interpretation: bury a bed and let it rot until it gets enough power to send forth a shoot, this shoot would not be a bed but wood; hence, the bed's arrangement by convention and by art is only incidental to it, whereas its primary being is what remains continuously through its changing conditions! Moreover, suppose the relation between an object and its material to hold also

* *Metaphysics* v.4.

** "Knowing *that* our subject matter is, we inquire *what* it is." *Posterior Analytics* ii.1.89b34. With the approach of *Physics* ii.1, compare that of i.1.

† Thomas Aquinas (against Avicenna): "ignorantia principiorum moventium non impedit quin naturam esse sit per se notum."

‡ 192b19, 20.

between the material and something else (for example, between bronze or gold and water, between bronze or wood and earth, and so forth), then that element is the nature or primary being of the object! This is the reason why some declare earth, others fire or air or water, and still others some or all of these elements, to be the nature of beings. Whichever element or elements any of these men chooses, he puts it forward as the whole of a primary being, viewing all its other aspects as its modifications, states, or dispositions; any element, moreover, he contends, is eternal, since it cannot be transformed into anything else, and all other aspects of things he sets forth as coming and going an endless number of times. This, then, is one interpretation of "nature": the immediate persisting material of anything which has within itself a beginning of movement or change.

According to another interpretation, "nature" means "shape" or "form" as expressed in a definition. Analogously to the term "art," which relates to artistic skill and its products, the term "nature" relates to a natural process and its products. But since we do not ascribe the artistic character of an art object to a thing as long as it is only potentially, for example, a bed and has not yet received the actual form of a bed, a corresponding principle is to be maintained in the realm of things constituted by nature: what is potentially flesh or bone has not yet attained to its proper "nature" and is not properly a "natural" being as long as it has not assumed the definite form by means of which we define what flesh or bone is. On this interpretation, therefore, "nature" would be the form of anything which has within itself a beginning of movement, the form being not separable except in thought. To be sure, the being composed of both matter and form (for example, a man) is not *a* "nature," although it is [produced] "*by* nature";* yet, at any rate, form rather than material is "nature," since the term "nature" marks an actual being more appropriately than a potential one.

Again, man generates man. Because, on the other hand, a bed does not produce a bed, its "nature" is said to be not its pattern but wood: if the bed sprouted, we are told, what would come forth would not be another bed but wood. But even if this [pattern] is art, the shape [of man] is [his] nature, for man generates man.

Again, "nature" as genesis** is a process *towards* [the product's] "nature." By way of contrast, the attempt to heal is a process directed not to the "art" of healing but to a healthy state; the task of healing must start *from* the art of healing† instead of leading to it. But "nature" [as productive] is related to [the product's] "nature" in a different way: what grows out of something proceeds to something or "grows," not towards that from which it starts, but that towards which it tends. Hence, its final shape is its "nature." On the other hand, the "shape" or "nature"

* 192b32–193a1.
** Thomas Aquinas: "puta si natura dicatur nativitas."
† Thomas Aquinas: "actiones denominantur a principiis, passiones vero a terminis."

of anything has two meanings, for there is a sense in which even a "privation" is a "form." But whether or not there is a "privation" or a contrary [of the final form] in simple generation, we must consider later.

. . .

MATERIAL, FORMAL, EFFICIENT, AND FINAL EXPLANATION

On the basis of these distinctions, let us now examine what and how many sorts of explanatory factors there are. All inquiry aims at knowledge; but we cannot claim to know a subject matter until we have grasped the "why" of it, that is, its fundamental explanation. It must clearly, therefore, be our aim in the present inquiry to get knowledge of the first principles to which we may refer any problem in our exploration of generation and destruction and of any natural transformation.

"An explanatory factor," then,* means (1) from one point of view, the material constituent from which a thing comes; for example, the bronze of a statue, the silver of a cup, and their kinds. From another point of view, (2) the form or pattern of a thing, that is, the reason (and the kind of reason) which explains what it was to be that thing; for example, the factors in an octave are based on the ratio of two to one and, in general, on number. This kind of factor is found in the parts of a definition. Again, (3) the agent whereby a change or a state of rest is first produced; for example, an adviser is "responsible" for a plan, a father "causes" his child, and, in general, any maker "causes" what he makes, and any agent causes what it changes. Again, (4) the end or the where-for; so, when we take a walk for the sake of our health, and someone asks us why we are walking, we answer, "in order to be healthy," and thus we think we have explained our action. So any intermediate means to the end of a series of acts: for example, as means of health there are reducing, purging, drugs, instruments, and so forth; for all these are for an end, though they differ from one another in that some are instruments, and others are actions.

Since what we call an "explanatory factor" may be any one of these different aspects of a process, it follows not only that anything actually has several such factors which are not merely accidental differences of meaning (as both the sculptor's art and the bronze are needed to explain a statue as a statue, the bronze being its material, and the sculpturing, its agent), but it follows also that these factors are reciprocal: for example, exercise explains good health, and good health explains exercise; though they explain each other differently (good health as end, and exercise as means). And the same thing may explain contraries: for the same thing which by its presence explains a given fact is "blamed" by its absence

* The text of 194b23–195b21 is nearly identical with the text of *Metaphysics* v.2.

for the contrary fact; for example, a shipwreck is "caused" by the absence of the pilot, whose presence is responsible for the ship's safety.

All the factors here mentioned clearly fall under four varieties. From letters come syllables; from building materials come buildings; from fire, earth, and so forth, come bodies; from parts come wholes; and from assumptions come conclusions. The first factor in each of these pairs is the subject matter or the parts; the second is what it meant to be that particular whole, or synthesis, or form. A "cause" in the sense illustrated by a seed, a physician, an adviser, and any agent generally, is the factor whereby a change or state of being is initiated. Finally, there are the ends or the good of the others; for all the others tend toward what is best as toward their end. It makes no difference now whether we say "their good" or "their apparent good."*

These, then, are the kinds of explanatory factors. But they fall into many lesser varieties, which can also be summarized under a few heads. There are several ways in which explanatory factors explain, even when they are of the same general kind. Thus one factor is prior to another, which is posterior: for example, health is prior to both the physician and the technician; the octave is prior to the ratio of two to one and to number; and so always, the inclusive factor is prior to individual factors.

Then there are accidental factors of various kinds; for example, a statue is, we say, by Polyclitus, but it is also by a sculptor; the sculptor happens to be Polyclitus. And so the kind (sculptor) and the accidental (Polyclitus) it embraces are both factors in the statue; thus a man is responsible for the statue, and so is the more general species "animal"; for Polyclitus is a man, and man is an animal. These accidental factors are sometimes remote and sometimes proximate; for example, between Polyclitus in particular and man in general there would be such intermediate factors as "a white man" and "an artist."

Besides, any factor, whether essential or accidental, may be actually in operation or merely capable of acting: a house being built is the work of "builders," but more actually of the builder who is building it. The same is true of the things to which explanatory factors refer—they may be singled out or referred to more generally: for example, "this statue," or "a statue," or even more generally, "an image"; and "this bronze," or "of bronze," or, generally, "of matter"; and similarly with reference to the accidental factors.

Moreover, both accidental and essential factors may be combined: for example, instead of Polyclitus or the sculptor, we say "Polyclitus the sculptor." However, these varieties reduce to but six, each being taken either individually or collectively: the accidental factors (individual or collective); combined or separate factors; and actual or potential factors. There is another difference between them: the operating and individual causes exist and cease to exist simultaneously with their effects (for example, this man actually healing is correlative with this man who is now

* Thomas Aquinas: "quia quod apparet bonum non movet, nisi sub ratione boni."

being healed, and this actual builder, with this thing-being-now-built); but potentially they do not exist together (for the house and the builder do not perish with the act of building).

We must, however, always seek the "highest" [or "principal"] explanatory factor of each case, as in any other investigations [of "reasons why"]; for example, a man builds only because he is a builder, and a builder, only because he has mastered the builder's art, which is therefore the more primary factor; and so in all such cases. Again, generic effects go with generic explanatory factors (for example, a statue with a sculptor), particular effects go with particular explanatory factors (for example, this statue, with this sculptor); so, too, potential effects correspond precisely to potential factors, and things actualized, to factors actually operating.

Let this suffice, then, concerning types of explanatory factors and the ways in which they operate.

CAUSALITY AND INDUCTION

DAVID HUME

SCEPTICAL DOUBTS CONCERNING THE OPERATIONS OF THE UNDERSTANDING

PART I

All the objects of human reason or inquiry may naturally be divided into two kinds, to wit, *Relations of Ideas*, and *Matters of Fact*. Of the first kind are the sciences of Geometry, Algebra, and Arithmetic; and in short, every affirmation which is either intuitively or demonstratively certain. *That the square of the hypothenuse is equal to the square of the two sides*, is a proposition which expresses a relation between these figures. *That three times five is equal to the half of thirty*, expresses a relation between these numbers. Propositions of this kind are discoverable by the mere operation of thought, without dependence on what is anywhere existent in the universe. Though there never were a circle or triangle in nature, the truths demonstrated by Euclid would forever retain their certainty and evidence.

Matters of fact, which are the second objects of human reason, are not ascertained in the same manner; nor is our evidence of their truth, however great, of a like nature with the foregoing. The contrary of

Reprinted from *An Inquiry Concerning Human Understanding*, Sections 4 and 5, 1748.

every matter of fact is still possible; because it can never imply a contradiction, and is conceived by the mind with the same facility and distinctness, as if ever so conformable to reality. *That the sun will not rise tomorrow* is no less intelligible a proposition, and implies no more contradiction that the affirmation *that it will rise*. We should in vain, therefore, attempt to demonstrate its falsehood. Were it demonstratively false, it would imply a contradiction and could never be distinctly conceived by the mind.

It may, therefore, be a subject worthy of curiosity, to inquire what is the nature of that evidence which assures us of any real existence and matter of fact, beyond the present testimony of our senses, or the records of our memory. This part of philosophy, it is observable, has been little cultivated, either by the ancients or moderns; and, therefore, our doubts and errors, in the prosecution of so important an inquiry, may be the more excusable; while we march through such difficult paths without any guide or direction. They may even prove useful, by exciting curiosity, and destroying that implicit faith and security, which is the bane of all reasoning and free inquiry. The discovery of defects in the common philosophy, if any such there be, will not, I presume, be a discouragement, but rather an incitement, as is usual, to attempt something more full and satisfactory than has yet been proposed to the public.

All reasonings concerning matter of fact seem to be founded on the relation of *Cause and Effect*. By means of that relation alone we can go beyond the evidence of our memory and senses. If you were to ask a man why he believes any matter of fact which is absent; for instance, that his friend is in the country, or in France; he would give you a reason; and this reason would be some other fact; as a letter received from him, or the knowledge of his former resolutions and promises. A man finding a watch or any other machine in a desert island would conclude that there had once been men on that island. All our reasonings concerning fact are of the same nature. And here it is constantly supposed that there is a connection between the present fact and that which is inferred from it. Were there nothing to bind them together, the inference would be entirely precarious. The hearing of an articulate voice and rational discourse in the dark assures us of the presence of some person: Why? because these are the effects of the human make and fabric, and closely connected with it. If we anatomize all the other reasonings of this nature, we shall find that they are founded on the relation of cause and effect, and that this relation is either near or remote, direct or collateral. Heat and light are collateral effects of fire, and the one effect may justly be inferred from the other.

If we would satisfy ourselves, therefore, concerning the nature of that evidence, which assures us of matters of fact, we must inquire how we arrive at the knowledge of cause and effect.

I shall venture to affirm, as a general proposition, which admits of no exception, that the knowledge of this relation is not, in any instance, attained by reasonings *a priori;* but arises entirely from experience, when we find that any particular objects are constantly conjoined with each other. Let an object be presented to a man of ever so strong natural reason and abilities; if that object be entirely new to him, he will not be able, by the most accurate examination of its sensible qualities, to discover any of its causes or effects. Adam, though his rational faculties be supposed, at the very first, entirely perfect, could not have inferred from the fluidity and transparency of water that it would suffocate him, or from the light and warmth of fire that it would consume him. No object ever discovers, by the qualities which appear to the senses, either the causes which produced it, or the effects which will arise from it; nor can our reason, unassisted by experience, ever draw any inference concerning real existence and matter of fact.

This proposition, *that causes and effects are discoverable, not by reason but by experience*, will readily be admitted with regard to such objects as we remember to have once been altogether unknown to us, since we must be conscious of the utter inability, which we then lay under, of foretelling what would arise from them. Present two smooth pieces of marble to a man who has no tincture of natural philosophy; he will never discover that they will adhere together in such a manner as to require great force to separate them in a direct line, while they make so small a resistance to a lateral pressure. Such events, as bear little analogy to the common course of nature, are also readily confessed to be known only by experience; nor does any man imagine that the explosion of gunpowder, or the attraction of a loadstone, could ever be discovered by arguments *a priori*. In like manner, when an effect is supposed to depend upon an intricate machinery or secret structure of parts, we make no difficulty in attributing all our knowledge of it to experience. Who will assert that he can give the ultimate reason why milk or bread is proper nourishment for a man, not for a lion or a tiger?

But the same truth may not appear, at first sight, to have the same evidence with regard to events, which have become familiar to us from our first appearance in the world, which bear a close analogy to the whole course of nature, and which are supposed to depend on the simple qualities of objects, without any secret structure of parts. We are apt to imagine that we could discover these effects by the mere operation of our reason, without experience. We fancy, that were we brought on a sudden into this world, we could at first have inferred that one billiard ball would communicate motion to another upon impulse; and that we needed not to have waited for the event, in order to pronounce with certainty concerning it. Such is the influence of custom, that, where it is strongest, it not only covers our natural ignorance, but even conceals itself, and seems not to take place, merely because it is found in the highest degree.

But to convince us that all the laws of nature, and all the operations of bodies without exception, are known only by experience, the following reflections may, perhaps, suffice. Were any object presented to us, and were we required to pronounce concerning the effect which will result from it, without consulting past observation, after what manner, I beseech you, must the mind proceed in this operation? It must invent or imagine some event, which it ascribes to the object as its effect; and it is plain that this invention must be entirely arbitrary. The mind can never possibly find the effect in the supposed cause, by the most accurate scrutiny and examination. For the effect is totally different from the cause, and consequently can never be discovered in it. Motion in the second billiard ball is a quite distinct event from motion in the first; nor is there anything in the one to suggest the smallest hint of the other. A stone or piece of metal raised into the air, and left without any support, immediately falls: but to consider the matter *a priori*, is there anything we discover in this situation which can beget the idea of a downward, rather than an upward, or any other motion, in the stone or metal?

And as the first imagination or invention of a particular effect, in all natural operations, is arbitrary, where we consult not experience; so must we also esteem the supposed tie or connection between the cause and effect, which binds them together, and renders it impossible that any other effect could result from the operation of that cause. When I see, for instance, a billiard ball moving in a straight line towards another; even suppose motion in the second ball should by accident be suggested to me, as the result of their contact or impulse; may I not conceive, that a hundred different events might as well follow from that cause? May not both these balls remain at absolute rest? May not the first ball return in a straight line, or leap off from the second in any line or direction? All these suppositions are consistent and conceivable. Why then should we give preference to one, which is no more consistent or conceivable than the rest? All our reasonings *a priori* will never be able to show us any foundation for this preference.

In a word, then, every effect is a distinct event from its cause. It could not, therefore, be discovered in the cause, and the first invention or conception of it, *a priori*, must be entirely arbitrary. And even after it is suggested, the conjunction of it with the cause must appear equally arbitrary; since there are always many other effects, which, to reason, must seem fully as consistent and natural. In vain, therefore, should we pretend to determine any single event, or infer any cause or effect, without the assistance of observation and experience.

Hence, we may discover the reason why no philosopher, who is rational and modest, has ever pretended to assign the ultimate cause of any natural operation, or to show distinctly the action of that power, which produces any single effect in the universe. It is confessed that the utmost effort of human reason is to reduce the principles, productive of natural phenomena, to a greater simplicity, and to resolve the many particular effects into a few general causes by means of reasonings from analogy, experience, and observation. But as to the causes of these general causes, we should in vain attempt their discovery; nor shall we ever be able to satisfy ourselves by any particular explication of them. These ultimate springs and principles are totally shut up from human curiosity and inquiry. Elasticity, gravity, cohesion of parts, communication of motion by impulse—these are probably the ultimate causes and principles which we shall ever discover in nature; and we may esteem ourselves sufficiently happy, if, by accurate inquiry and reasoning, we can trace up the particular phenomena to, or near to, these general principles. The most perfect philosophy of the natural kind only staves off our ignorance a little longer: as perhaps the most perfect philosophy of the moral or metaphysical kind serves only to discover larger portions of it. Thus the observation of human blindness and weakness is the result of all philosophy, and meets us at every turn, in spite of our endeavors to elude or avoid it.

Nor is geometry, when taken into the assistance of natural philosophy, ever able to remedy this defect, or lead us into the knowledge of ultimate causes, by all that accuracy of reasoning for which it is so justly celebrated. Every part of mixed mathematics proceeds upon the supposition that certain laws are established by nature in her operations; and abstract reasonings are employed, either to assist experience in the discovery of these laws, or to determine their influence in particular instances, where it depends upon any precise degree of distance and quantity. Thus, it is a law of motion, discovered by experience, that the moment or force of any body in motion is in the compound ratio or proportion of its solid contents and its velocity; and consequently, that a small force may remove the greatest obstacle or raise the greatest weight, if, by any contrivance or machinery, we can increase the velocity of that force, so as to make it an overmatch for its antagonist. Geometry assists us in the application of this law, by giving us the just dimensions of all the parts and figures which can enter into any species of machine; but still the discovery of the law itself is owing merely to experience, and all the abstract reasonings in the world could never lead us one step towards the knowledge of it. When we reason *a priori,* and consider merely any object or cause as it appears to the mind, independent of all observation, it never could suggest to us the notion of any distinct object, such as its effect; much less, show us the inseparable and inviolable connection between them. A man must be very sagacious who could discover by reasoning that crystal is the effect of heat, and ice of cold, without being previously acquainted with the operation of these qualities.

PART II

But we have not yet attained any tolerable satisfaction with regard to the question first proposed. Each solution still gives rise to a new question as difficult as the foregoing, and leads us on to farther inquiries. When it is asked. *What is the nature of all our reasonings concerning matter of fact?* the proper answer seems to be, that they are founded on the relation of cause and effect. When again it is asked, *What is the foundation of all our reasonings and conclusions concerning that relation?* it may be replied in one word, Experience. But if we still carry on our sifting humor, and ask, *What is the foundation of all conclusions from experi-*

ence? this implies a new question, which may be of more difficult solution and explication. Philosophers, that give themselves airs of superior wisdom and sufficiency, have a hard task when they encounter persons of inquisitive dispositions, who push them from every corner to which they retreat, and who are sure at last to bring them to some dangerous dilemma. The best expedient to prevent this confusion is to be modest in our pretensions; and even to discover the difficulty ourselves before it is objected to us. By this means, we may make a kind of merit of our very ignorance.

I shall content myself, in this section, with an easy task, and shall pretend only to give a negative answer to the question here proposed. I say then, that, even after we have experience of the operations of cause and effect, our conclusions from that experience are *not* founded on reasoning, or any process of the understanding. This answer we must endeavor both to explain and to defend.

It must certainly be allowed that nature has kept us at a great distance from all her secrets, and has afforded us only the knowledge of a few superficial qualities of objects, while she conceals from us those powers and principles on which the influence of those objects entirely depends. Our senses inform us of the color, weight, and consistency of bread; but neither sense nor reason can ever inform us of those qualities which fit it for the nourishment and support of a human body. Sight or feeling conveys an idea of the actual motion of bodies; but as to that wonderful force or power, which would carry on a moving body forever in a continued change of place, and which bodies never lose but by communicating it to others; of this we cannot form the most distant conception. But notwithstanding this ignorance of natural powers and principles, we always presume, when we see like sensible qualities, that they have like secret powers, and expect that effects, similar to those which we have experienced, will follow from them. If a body of like color and consistency with that bread, which we have formerly eaten, be presented to us, we make no scruple of repeating the experiment, and foresee, with certainty, like nourishment and support. Now this is a process of the mind or thought, of which I would willingly know the foundation. It is allowed on all hands that there is no known connection between the sensible qualities and the secret powers; and consequently, that the mind is not led to form such a conclusion concerning their constant and regular conjunction, by anything which it knows of their nature. As to past *Experience*, it can be allowed to give *direct* and *certain* information of those precise objects only, and that precise period of time, which fell under its cognizance: but why this experience should be extended to future times, and to other objects, which for aught we know, may be only in appearance similar; this is the main question on which I would insist. The bread, which I formerly ate, nourished me; that is, a body of such sensible qualities was, at that time, endued with such secret powers: but does it follow, that other bread must also nourish me at another time, and that like sensible qualities must always be attended with like secret powers? The consequence seems nowise necessary. At least, it must be acknowledged that there is here a consequence drawn by the mind; that there is a certain step taken; a process of thought, and an inference, which wants to be explained. These two propositions are far from being the same; *I have found that such an object has always been attended with such an effect, and I foresee, that other objects, which are, in appearance, similar, will be attended with similar effects.* I shall allow, if you please, that the one proposition may justly be inferred from the other: I know, in fact, that it always is inferred. But if you insist that the inference is made by a chain of reasoning, I desire you to produce that reasoning. The connection between these propositions is not intuitive. There is required a medium, which may enable the mind to draw such an inference, if indeed it be drawn by reasoning and argument. What that medium is, I must confess, passes my comprehension; and it is incumbent on those to produce it, who assert that it really exists, and is the origin of all our conclusions concerning matter of fact.

This negative argument must certainly, in process of time, become altogether convincing, if many penetrating and able philosophers shall turn their inquiries this way and no one be ever able to discover any connecting proposition or intermediate step which supports the understanding in this conclusion. But as the question is yet new, every reader may not trust so far to his own penetration as to conclude, because an argument escapes his inquiry, that therefore it does not really exist. For this reason it may be requisite to venture upon a more difficult task; and, enumerating all the branches of human knowledge, endeavor to show that none of them can afford such an argument.

All reasonings may be divided into two kinds, namely, demonstrative reasoning, or that concerning relations of ideas, and moral reasoning, or that concerning matter of fact and existence. That there are no demonstrative arguments in the case seems evident; since it implies no contradiction that the course of nature may change, and that an object, seemingly like those which we have experienced, may be attended with different or contrary effects. May I not clearly and distinctly conceive that a body, falling from the clouds, and which, in all other respects, resembles snow, has yet the taste of salt or feeling of fire? Is there any more intelligible proposition than to affirm that all the trees will flourish in December and January, and decay in May and June? Now whatever is intelligible, and can be distinctly conceived, implies no contradiction, and can never be proved false by any demonstrative argument or abstract reasoning *a priori*.

If we be, therefore, engaged by arguments to put trust in past experience, and make it the standard of our future judgment, these arguments must be probable only, or such as regard matter of fact and real existence, according to the division above mentioned. But that there is no argument of this kind, must appear, if our explication of that species of reasoning be admitted as solid and satisfactory. We have said that all arguments concerning existence are founded on the relation of cause and effect; that our knowledge of that relation is derived entirely from experience; and that all our experimental conclusions proceed upon the supposition that the future will be conformable to the past. To endeavor, therefore, the proof of this last supposition by probable arguments, or arguments regarding existence, must be evidently going in a circle, and taking that for granted which is the very point in question.

In reality, all arguments from experience are founded on the similarity which we discover among natural objects, and by which we are induced to expect effects similar to those which we have found to follow from such objects. And though none but a fool or madman will ever pretend to dispute the authority of experience, or to reject that great guide of human life, it may surely be allowed a philosopher to have so much curiosity at least as to examine the principle of human nature, which gives this mighty authority to experience, and makes us draw advantage from that similarity which nature has placed among different objects. From causes which appear *similar* we expect similar effects. This is the sum of all our experimental conclusions. Now it seems evident that, if this conclusion were formed by reason, it would be as perfect at first, and upon one instance, as after ever so long a course of experience. But the case is far otherwise. Nothing so like as eggs; yet no one, on account of this appearing similarity, expects the same taste and relish in all of them. It is only after a long course of uniform experiments in any kind, that we attain a firm reliance and security with regard to a particular event. Now where is that process of reasoning which, from one instance, draws a conclusion so different from that which it infers from a hundred instances that are nowise different from that single one? This question I propose as much for the sake of information, as with an intention of raising difficulties. I cannot find, I cannot imagine any such reasoning. But I keep my mind still open to instruction, if anyone will vouchsafe to bestow it on me.

Should it be said that, from a number of uniform experiments, we *infer* a connection between the sensible qualities and the secret powers; this, I must confess, seems the same difficulty, couched in different terms. The question still recurs, on what process of argument this *inference* is founded? Where is the medium, the interposing ideas, which join propositions so very wide of each other? It is confessed that the color, consistency, and other sensible qualities of breed appear not, of themselves, to have any connection with the secret powers of nourishment and support. For otherwise we could infer these secret powers from the first appearance of these sensible qualities, without the aid of experience; contrary to the sentiment of all philosophers, and contrary to plain matter of fact. Here, then, is our natural state of ignorance with regard to the powers and influence of all objects. How is this remedied by experience? It only shows us a number of uniform effects resulting from certain objects, and teaches us that those particular objects, at that particular time, were endowed with such powers and forces. When a new object, endowed with similar sensible qualities, is produced, we expect similar powers and forces, and look for a like effect. From a body of like color and consistency with bread we expect like nourishment and support. But this surely is a step or progress of the mind, which wants to be explained. When a man says, *I have found, in all past instances, such sensible qualities conjoined with such secret powers:* and when he says, *Similar sensible qualities will always be conjoined with similar secret powers,* he is not guilty of a tautology, nor are these propositions in any respect the same. You say that the one proposition is an inference from the other. But you must confess that the inference is not intuitive; neither is it demonstrative: of what nature is it, then? To say it is experimental, is begging the question. For all inferences from experience suppose, as their foundation, that the future will resemble the past, and that similar powers will be conjoined with similar sensible qualities. If there be any suspicion that the course of nature may change, and that the past may be no rule for the future, all experience becomes useless, and can give rise to no inference or conclusion. It is impossible, therefore, that any arguments from experience can prove this resemblance of the past to the future; since all these arguments are founded on the supposition of that resemblance. Let the course of things be allowed hitherto ever so regular; that alone, without some new argument or inference, proves not that, for the future, it will continue so. In vain do you pretend to have learned the nature of bodies from your past experience. Their secret nature, and consequently all their effects and influence, may change, without any change in their sensible qualities. This happens sometimes, and with regard to some objects: why may it not happen always, and with regard to all objects? What logic, what process of argument secures you against this supposition? My practice, you say, refutes my doubts. But you mistake the purport of my question. As an agent, I am quite satisfied in the point; but as a philosopher, who has some share of curiosity, I will not say scepticism, I want to learn the foundation of this inference. No reading, no inquiry has yet been able to remove my difficulty, or give me satisfaction in a matter of such importance. Can I do better than propose the difficulty to the public, even though, perhaps, I have small hopes of obtaining a solution? We shall at least, by this means, be sensible of our ignorance, if we do not augment our knowledge.

I must confess that a man is guilty of unpardonable arrogance who concludes, because an argument has escaped his own investigation, that, therefore, it does not really exist. I must also confess that, though all the learned, for several ages, should have employed themselves in fruitless search upon any subject, it may still, perhaps, be rash to conclude positively that the subject must, therefore, pass all human comprehension. Even though we examine all the sources of our knowledge, and conclude them unfit for such a subject, there may still remain a suspicion that the enumeration is not complete, or the examination not accurate. But with regard to the present subject, there are some considerations which seem to remove all this accusation of arrogance or suspicion of mistake.

It is certain that the most ignorant and stupid peasants—nay, infants;

nay, even brute beasts—improve by experience, and learn the qualities of natural objects, by observing the effects which result from them. When a child has felt the sensation of pain from touching the flame of a candle, he will be careful not to put his hand near any candle; but will expect a similar effect from a cause which is similar in its sensible qualities and appearance. If you assert, therefore, that the understanding of the child is led into this conclusion by any process of argument or ratiocination, I may justly require you to produce that argument; nor have you any pretense to refuse so equitable a demand. You cannot say that the argument is abstruse, and may possibly escape your inquiry; since you confess that it is obvious to the capacity of a mere infant. If you hesitate, therefore, a moment, or if, after reflection, you produce any intricate or profound argument, you, in a manner, give up the question, and confess that it is not reasoning which engages us to suppose the past resembling the future, and to expect similar effects from causes which are, to appearance, similar. This is the proposition which I intended to enforce in the present section. If I be right, I pretend not to have made any mighty discovery. And if I be wrong, I must acknowledge myself to be, indeed, a very backward scholar; since I cannot now discover an argument which, it seems, was perfectly familiar to me long before I was out of my cradle.

SCEPTICAL SOLUTION OF THESE DOUBTS

PART I

The passion for philosophy, like that for religion, seems liable to this inconvenience, that, though it aims at the correction of our manners and extirpation of our vices, it may only serve, by imprudent management, to foster a predominant inclination, and push the mind, with more determined resolution, towards that side which already *draws* too much, by the bias and propensity of the natural temper. It is certain that, while we aspire to the magnanimous firmness of the philosophic sage, and endeavor to confine our pleasures altogether within our own minds, we may, at last, render our philosophy like that of Epictetus, and other *Stoics,* only a more refined system of selfishness, and reason ourselves out of all virtue as well as social enjoyment. While we study with attention the vanity of human life, and turn all our thoughts towards the empty and transitory nature of riches and honors, we are, perhaps, all the while flattering our natural indolence, which, hating the bustle of the world and drudgery of business, seeks a pretense of reason to give itself a full and uncontrolled indulgence. There is, however, one species of philosophy which seems little liable to this inconvenience, and that because it strikes in with no disorderly passion of the human mind, nor can mingle itself with any natural affection or propensity; and that is the Academic or Sceptical philosophy. The academics always talk of doubt and suspense of judgment, of danger in hasty determinations, of confining to very narrow bounds the inquiries of the understanding, and of renouncing all speculations which lie not within the limits of common life and practice. Nothing, therefore, can be more contrary than such a philosophy to the supine indolence of the mind, its rash arrogance, its lofty pretensions, and its superstitious credulity. Every passion is mortified by it, except the love of truth; and that passion never is, nor can be, carried to too high a degree. It is surprising, therefore, that this philosophy, which, in almost every instance, must be harmless and innocent, should be the subject of so much groundless reproach and obloquy. But, perhaps, the very circumstance which renders it so innocent is what chiefly exposes it to the public hatred and resentment. By flattering no irregular passion, it gains few partisans: by opposing so many vices and follies, it raises to itself abundance of enemies, who stigmatize it as libertine, profane, and irreligious.

Nor need we fear that this philosophy, while it endeavors to limit our inquiries to common life, should ever undermine the reasonings of common life, and carry its doubts so far as to destroy all action, as well as speculation. Nature will always maintain her rights, and prevail in the end over any abstract reasoning whatsoever. Though we should conclude, for instance, as in the foregoing section, that, in all reasonings from experience, there is a step taken by the mind which is not supported by any argument or process of the understanding; there is no danger that these reasonings, on which almost all knowledge depends, will ever be affected by such a discovery. If the mind be not engaged by argument to make this step, it must be induced by some other principle of equal weight and authority; and that principle will preserve its influence as long as human nature remains the same. What that principle is may well be worth the pains of inquiry.

Suppose a person, though endowed with the strongest faculties of reason and reflection, to be brought on a sudden into this world; he would, indeed, immediately observe a continual succession of objects, and one event following another; but he would not be able to discover anything farther. He would not, at first, by any reasoning, be able to reach the idea of cause and effect; since the particular powers, by which all natural operations are performed, never appear to the senses; nor is it reasonable to conclude, merely because one event, in one instance, precedes another, that therefore the one is the cause, the other the effect. Their conjunction may be arbitrary and casual. There may be no reason to infer the existence of one from the appearance of the other. And in a word, such a person, without more experience, could never employ his conjecture or reasoning concerning any matter of fact, or be assured of anything beyond what was immediately present to his memory and senses.

Suppose, again, that he has acquired more experience, and has lived so long in the world as to have observed familiar objects or events to be constantly conjoined together; what is the consequence of this experience? He immediately infers the existence of one object from the appearance of the other. Yet he has not, by all his experience, acquired any idea or knowledge of the secret power by which the one object produces the other; nor is it, by any process of reasoning, he is engaged to draw this inference. But still he finds himself determined to draw it: and though he should be convinced that his understanding has no part in the operation, he would nevertheless continue in the same course of thinking. There is some other principle which determines him to form such a conclusion.

This principle is Custom or Habit. For wherever the repetition of any particular act or operation produces a propensity to renew the same act or operation, without being impelled by any reasoning or process of the understanding, we always say that this propensity is the effect of *Custom*. By employing that word, we pretend not to have given the ultimate reason of such a propensity. We only point out a principle of human nature, which is universally acknowledged, and which is well known by its effects. Perhaps we can push our inquiries no farther, or pretend to give the cause of this cause; but must rest contented with it as the ultimate principle, which we can assign, of all our conclusions from experience. It is sufficient satisfaction that we can go so far, without repining at the narrowness of our faculties because they will carry us no farther. And it is certain we here advance a very intelligible proposition at least, if not a true one, when we assert that, after the constant conjunction of two objects—heat and flame, for instance, weight and solidity—we are determined by custom alone to expect the one from the appearance of the other. This hypothesis seems even the only one which explains the difficulty, why we draw, from a thousand instances, an inference which we are not able to draw from one instance that is, in no respect, different from them. Reason is incapable of any such variation. The conclusions which it draws from considering one circle are the same which it would form upon surveying all the circles in the universe. But no man, having seen only one body move after being impelled by another, could infer that every other body will move after a like impulse. All inferences from experience, therefore, are effects of custom, not of reasoning.

Custom, then, is the great guide of human life. It is that principle alone which renders our experience useful to us, and makes us expect, for the future, a similar train of events with those which have appeared in the past. Without the influence of custom, we should be entirely ignorant of every matter of fact beyond what is immediately present to the memory and senses. We should never know how to adjust means to ends, or to employ our natural powers in the production of any effect. There would be an end at once of all action, as well as of the chief part of speculation.

But here it may be proper to remark that, though our conclusions from experience carry us beyond our memory and senses, and assure us of matters of fact which happened in the most distant places and most remote ages, yet some fact must always be present to the senses or memory, from which we may first proceed in drawing these conclusions.

A man, who should find in a desert country the remains of pompous buildings, would conclude that the country had, in ancient times, been cultivated by civilized inhabitants; but did nothing of this nature occur to him, he could never form such an inference. We learn the events of former ages from history; but then we must peruse the volumes in which this instruction is contained, and thence carry up our inferences from one testimony to another, till we arrive at the eyewitnesses and spectators of these distant events. In a word, if we proceed not upon some fact, present to the memory or senses, our reasonings would be merely hypothetical; and however the particular links might be connected with each other, the whole chain of inferences would have nothing to support it, nor could we ever, by its means, arrive at the knowledge of any real existence. If I ask why you believe any particular matter of fact which you relate, you must tell me some reason; and this reason will be some other fact connected with it. But as you cannot proceed after this manner, *in infinitum*, you must at last terminate in some fact which is present to your memory or senses; or must allow that your belief is entirely without foundation.

What, then, is the conclusion of the whole matter? A simple one; though, it must be confessed, pretty remote from the common theories of philosophy. All belief of matter of fact or real existence is derived merely from some object, present to the memory or senses, and a customary conjunction between that and some other object. Or in other words; having found, in many instances, that any two kinds of objects—flame and heat, snow and cold—have always been conjoined together; if flame or snow be presented anew to the senses, the mind is carried by custom to expect heat or cold, and to *believe* that such a quality does exist and will discover itself upon a nearer approach. This belief is the necessary result of placing the mind in such circumstances. It is an operation of the soul, when we are so situated, as unavoidable as to feel the passion of love, when we receive benefits; or hatred, when we meet with injuries. All these operations are a species of natural instincts, which no reasoning or process of the thought and understanding is able either to produce or to prevent.

SCIENTIFIC EXPLANATION

PIERRE DUHEM

PHYSICAL THEORY AND METAPHYSICAL EXPLANATION

PHYSICAL THEORY CONSIDERED AS EXPLANATION

The first question we should face is: What is the aim of a physical theory? To this question diverse answers have been made, but all of them may be reduced to two main principles:

"A physical theory," certain logicians have replied, "has for its object the *explanation* of a group of laws experimentally established."

"A physical theory," other thinkers have said, "is an abstract system whose aim is to *summarize* and *classify logically* a group of experimental laws without claiming to explain these laws."

We are going to examine these two answers one after the other, and weigh the reasons for accepting or rejecting each of them. We begin with the first, which regards a physical theory as an explanation.

But, first, what is an explanation?

To explain (explicate, *explicare*) is to strip reality of the appearances covering it like a veil, in order to see the bare reality itself.

The observation of physical phenomena does not put us into relation with the reality hidden under the sensible appearances, but enables us to apprehend the sensible appearances themselves in a particular and concrete form. Besides, experimental laws do not have material reality for their object, but deal with these sensible appearances, taken, it is true, in an abstract and general form. Removing or tearing away the veil from these sensible appearances, theory proceeds into and underneath them, and seeks what is really in bodies.

For example, string or wind instruments have produced sounds to which we have listened closely and which we have heard become stronger or weaker, higher or lower, in a thousand nuances productive in us of auditory sensations and musical emotions; such are the acoustic facts.

These particular and concrete sensations have been elaborated by our intelligence, following the laws by which it functions, and have provided

Reprinted, with deletions, from *The Aim and Structure of Physical Theory*, Chapters 1 and 2, translated by Philip P. Wiener, Princeton University Press, 1954, by permission of the publisher.

us with such general and abstract notions as intensity, pitch, octave, perfect major or minor chord, timbre, etc. The experimental laws of acoustics aim at the enunciation of fixed relations among these and other equally abstract and general notions. A law, for example, teaches us what relation exists between the dimensions of two strings of the same metal which yield two sounds of the same pitch or two sounds an octave apart.

But these abstract notions—sound intensity, pitch, timbre, etc.—depict to our reason no more than the general characteristics of our sound perceptions; these notions get us to know sound as it is in relation to us, not as it is by itself in sounding bodies. This reality whose external veil alone appears in our sensations is made known to us by theories of acoustics. The latter are to teach us that where our perceptions grasp only that appearance we call sound, there is in reality a very small and very rapid periodic motion; that intensity and pitch are only external aspects of the amplitude and frequency of this motion; and that timbre is the apparent manifestation of the real structure of this motion, the complex sensation which results from the diverse vibratory motions into which we can analyze it. Acoustic theories are therefore explanations.

The explanation which acoustic theories give of experimental laws governing sound claims to give us certainty; it can in a great many cases make us see with our own eyes the motions to which it attributes these phenomena, and feel them with our fingers.

Most often we find that physical theory cannot attain that degree of perfection; it cannot offer itself as a *certain* explanation of sensible appearances, for it cannot render accessible to the senses the reality it proclaims as residing underneath those appearances. It is then content with proving that all our perceptions are produced *as if* the reality were what it asserts; such a theory is a hypothetical explanation.

Let us, for example, take the set of phenomena observed with the sense of sight. The rational analysis of these phenomena leads us to conceive certain abstract and general notions expressing the properties we come across in every perception of light: a simple or complex color, brightness, etc. Experimental laws of optics make us acquainted with fixed relations among these abstract and general notions as well as among other analogous notions. One law, for instance, connects the intensity of yellow light reflected by a thin plate with the thickness of the plate and the angle of incidence of the rays which illuminate it.

Of these experimental laws the vibratory theory of light gives a hypothetical explanation. It supposes that all the bodies we see, feel, or weigh are immersed in an imponderable, unobservable medium called the ether. To this ether certain mechanical properties are attributed; the theory states that all simple light is a transverse vibration, very small and very rapid, of this ether, and that the frequency and amplitude of this vibration characterize the color of this light and its brightness; and, without enabling us to perceive the ether, without putting us in a position to observe directly the back-and-forth motion of light vibration, the theory tries to prove that its postulates entail consequences agreeing at every point with the laws furnished by experimental optics.

ACCORDING TO THE FOREGOING OPINION, THEORETICAL PHYSICS IS SUBORDINATE TO METAPHYSICS

When a physical theory is taken as an explanation, its goal is not reached until every sensible appearance has been removed in order to grasp the physical reality. For example, Newton's research on the dispersion of light has taught us to decompose the sensation we experience of light emanating from the sun; his experiments have shown us that this light is complex and resolvable into a certain number of simpler light phenomena, each associated with a determinate and invariable color. But these simple or monochromatic light data are abstract and general representations of certain sensations; they are sensible appearances, and we have only dissociated a complicated appearance into other simpler appearances. But we have not reached the real thing, we have not given an explanation of the color effects, we have not constructed an optical theory.

Thus, it follows that in order to judge whether a set of propositions constitutes a physical theory or not, we must inquire whether the notions connecting these propositions express, in an abstract and general form, the elements which really go to make up material things, or merely represent the universal properties perceived.

For such an inquiry to make sense or to be at all possible, we must first of all regard as certain the following affirmation: Under the sensible appearances, which are revealed in our perceptions, there is a reality distinct from these appearances.

This point granted, and without it the search for a physical explanation could not be conceived, it is impossible to recognize having reached such an explanation until we have answered this next question: What is the nature of the elements which constitute material reality?

Now these two questions—Does there exist a material reality distinct from sensible appearances? and What is the nature of this reality?—do not have their source in experimental method, which is acquainted only with sensible appearances and can discover nothing beyond them. The resolution of these questions transcends the methods used by physics; it is the object of metaphysics.

Therefore, *if the aim of physical theories is to explain experimental laws, theoretical physics is not an autonomous science; it is subordinate to metaphysics.*

• • •

PHYSICAL THEORY AND NATURAL CLASSIFICATION

WHAT IS THE TRUE NATURE OF A PHYSICAL THEORY AND THE OPERATIONS CONSTITUTING IT?

While we regard a physical theory as a hypothetical explanation of material reality, we make it dependent on metaphysics. In that way, far from giving it a form to which the greatest number of minds can give their assent, we limit its acceptance to those who acknowledge the philosophy it insists on. But even they cannot be entirely satisfied with this theory since it does not draw all its principles from the metaphysical doctrine from which it is claimed to be derived.

These thoughts, discussed in the preceding chapter, lead us quite naturally to ask the following two questions:

Could we not assign an aim to physical theory that would render it *autonomous?* Based on principles which do not arise from any metaphysical doctrine, physical theory might be judged in its own terms without including the opinions of physicists who depend on the philosophical schools to which they may belong.

Could we not conceive a method which might be *sufficient* for the construction of a physical theory? Consistent with its own definition the theory would employ no principle and have no recourse to any procedure which it could not legitimately use.

We intend to concentrate on this aim and this method, and to study both.

Let us posit right now a definition of physical theory; the sequel of this book will clarify it and will develop its complete content: A physical theory is not an explanation. It is a system of mathematical propositions, deduced from a small number of principles, which aim to represent as simply, as completely, and as exactly as possible a set of experimental laws.

In order to start making this definition somewhat more precise, let us characterize the four successive operations through which a physical theory is formed:

1. Among the physical properties which we set ourselves to represent we select those we regard as simple properties, so that the others will supposedly be groupings or combinations of them. We make them correspond to a certain group of mathematical symbols, numbers, and magnitudes, through appropriate methods of measurement. These mathematical symbols have no connection of an intrinsic nature with the properties they represent; they bear to the latter only the relation of sign to thing signified. Through methods of measurement we can make each state of a physical property correspond to a value of the representative symbol, and vice versa.

2. We connect the different sorts of magnitudes, thus introduced, by means of a small number of propositions which will serve as principles in our deductions. These principles may be called "hypotheses" in the etymological sense of the word for they are truly the grounds on which the theory will be built; but they do not claim in any manner to state real relations among the real properties of bodies. These hypotheses may then be formulated in an arbitrary way. The only absolutely impassable barrier which limits this arbitrariness is logical contradiction either among the terms of the same hypothesis or among the various hypotheses of the same theory.

3. The diverse principles or hypotheses of a theory are combined together according to the rules of mathematical analysis. The requirements of algebraic logic are the only ones which the theorist has to satisfy in the course of this development. The magnitudes on which his calculations bear are not claimed to be physical realities, and the principles he employs in his deductions are not given as stating real relations among those realities; therefore it matters little whether the operations he performs do or do not correspond to real or conceivable physical transformations. All that one has the right to demand of him is that his syllogisms be valid and his calculations accurate.

4. The various consequences thus drawn from the hypotheses may be translated into as many judgments bearing on the physical properties of the bodies. The methods appropriate for defining and measuring these physical properties are like the vocabulary and key permitting one to make this translation. These judgments are compared with the experimental laws which the theory is intended to represent. If they agree with these laws to the degree of approximation corresponding to the measuring procedures employed, the theory has attained its goal, and is said to be a good theory; if not, it is a bad theory, and it must be modified or rejected.

Thus a true theory is not a theory which gives an explanation of physical appearances in conformity with reality; it is a theory which represents in a satisfactory manner a group of experimental laws. A false theory is not an attempt at an explanation based on assumptions contrary to reality; it is a group of propositions which do not agree with the experimental laws. *Agreement with experiment is the sole criterion of truth for a physical theory.*

The definition we have just outlined distinguishes four fundamental operations in a physical theory: (1) the definition and measurement of physical magnitudes; (2) the selection of hypotheses; (3) the mathematical development of the theory; (4) the comparison of the theory with experiment.

Each one of these operations will occupy us in detail as we proceed with this book, for each of them presents difficulties calling for minute analysis. But right now it is possible for us to answer a few questions and to refute a few objections raised by the present definition of physical theory.

WHAT IS THE UTILITY OF A PHYSICAL THEORY? THEORY CONSIDERED AS AN ECONOMY OF THOUGHT

And first, of what use is such a theory?

Concerning the very nature of things, or the realities hidden under the phenomena we are studying, a theory conceived on the plan we have just drawn teaches us absolutely nothing, and does not claim to teach us anything. Of what use is it, then? What do physicists gain by replacing the laws which experimental method furnishes directly with a system of mathematical propositions representing those laws?

First of all, instead of a great number of laws offering themselves as independent of one another, each having to be learnt and remembered on its own account, physical theory substitutes a very small number of propositions, viz., fundamental hypotheses. The hypotheses once known, mathematical deduction permits us with complete confidence to call to mind all the physical laws without omission or repetition. Such condensing of a multitude of laws into a small number of principles affords enormous relief to the human mind, which might not be able without such an artifice to store up the new wealth it acquires daily.

The reduction of physical laws to theories thus contributes to that "intellectual economy" in which Ernst Mach sees the goal and directing principle of science.*

The experimental law itself already represented a first intellectual economy. The human mind had been facing an enormous number of concrete facts, each complicated by a multitude of details of all sorts; no man could have embraced and retained a knowledge of all these facts; none could have communicated this knowledge to his fellows. Abstraction entered the scene. It brought about the removal of everything private or individual from these facts, extracting from their total only what was general in them or common to them, and in place of this cumbersome mass of facts it has substituted a single proposition, occupying little of one's memory and easy to convey through instruction: it has formulated a physical law.

"Thus, instead of noting individual cases of light-refraction, we can mentally reconstruct all present and future cases, if we know that the incident ray, the refracted ray, and the perpendicular lie in the same plane and that $\sin i/\sin r = n$. Here, instead of the numberless cases of refraction in different combinations of matter and under all different angles of incidence, we have simply to note the rule above stated and the values of n—which is much easier. The economical purpose here is unmistakable."**

* E. Mach, "Die ökonomische Natur der physikalischen Forschung," *Populärwissenschaftliche Vorlesungen* (3rd ed.; Leipzig, 1903), Ch. XIII, p. 215.

** E. Mach, *La Mécanique* . . ., p. 453. (Translator's note: Translated in *The Science of Mechanics* . . ., p. 485.)

(Translator's note: Translated by T. J. McCormack, "The Economical Nature of

The economy achieved by the substitution of the law for the concrete facts is redoubled by the mind when it condenses experimental laws into theories. What the law of refraction is to the innumerable facts of refraction, optical theory is to the infinitely varied laws of light phenomena.

Among the effects of light only a very small number had been reduced to laws by the ancients; the only laws of optics they knew were the law of the rectilinear propagation of light and the laws of reflection. This meager contingent was reinforced in Descartes' time by the law of refraction. An optics so slim could do without theory; it was easy to study and teach each law by itself.

Today, on the contrary, how can a physicist who wishes to study optics, as we know it, acquire even a superficial knowledge of this enormous domain without the aid of a theory? Consider the effects of simple refraction, of double refraction by uniaxial or biaxial crystals, of reflection on isotropic or crystalline media, of interference, of diffraction, of polarization by reflection and by simple or double refraction, of chromatic polarization, of rotary polarization, etc. Each one of these large categories of phenomena may occasion the statement of a large number of experimental laws whose number and complication would frighten the most capable and retentive memory.

Optical theory supervenes, takes possession of these laws, and condenses them into a small number of principles. From these principles we can always, through regular and sure calculation, extract the law we wish to use. It is no longer necessary, therefore, to keep watch over the knowledge of all these laws; the knowledge of the principles on which they rest is sufficient.

This example enables us to take firm hold of the way the physical sciences progress. The experimenter constantly brings to light facts hitherto unsuspected and formulates new laws, and the theorist constantly makes it possible to store up these acquisitions by imagining more condensed representations, more economical systems. The development of physics incites a continual struggle between "nature that does not tire of providing" and reason that does not wish "to tire of conceiving."

THEORY CONSIDERED AS CLASSIFICATION

Theory is not solely an economical representation of experimental laws; it is also a *classification* of these laws.

Experimental physics supplies us with laws all lumped together and, so to speak, on the same plane, without partitioning them into groups of laws united by a kind of family tie. Very often quite accidental causes or

Physical Research," Mach's *Popular Scientific Lectures* [3rd ed.; La Salle, Ill.: Open Court, 1907], Ch. XIII.)

See also E. Mach, *La Mécanique; exposé historique et critique de son développement* (Paris, 1904), Ch. IV, Sec. 4: "La Science comme économie de la pensée," p. 449. (Translator's note: Translated from the German 2nd ed. by T. J. McCormack, *The Science of Mechanics: a Critical and Historical Account of Its Development* [Open Court, 1902], Ch. IV, Sec. iv: "The Economy of Science," pp. 481–494.)

rather superficial analogies have led observers in their research to bring together different laws. Newton put into the same work the laws of the dispersion of light crossing a prism and the laws of the colors adorning a soap bubble, simply because of the colors that strike the eye in these two sorts of phenomena.

On the other hand, theory, by developing the numerous ramifications of the deductive reasoning which connects principles to experimental laws, establishes an order and a classification among these laws. It brings some laws together, closely arranged in the same group; it separates some of the others by placing them in two groups very far apart. Theory gives, so to speak, the table of contents and the chapter headings under which the science to be studied will be methodically divided, and it indicates the laws which are to be arranged under each of these chapters.

Thus, alongside the laws which govern the spectrum formed by a prism it arranges the laws governing the colors of the rainbow; but the laws according to which the colors of Newton's rings are ordered go elsewhere to join the laws of fringes discovered by Young and Fresnel; still in another category, the elegant coloration analyzed by Grimaldi is considered related to the diffraction spectra produced by Fraunhofer. The laws of all these phenomena, whose striking colors lead to their confusion in the eyes of the simple observer, are, thanks to the efforts of the theorist, classified and ordered.

These classifications make knowledge convenient to use and safe to apply. Consider those utility cabinets where tools for the same purpose lie side by side, and where partitions logically separate instruments not designed for the same task: the worker's hand quickly grasps, without fumbling or mistake, the tool needed. Thanks to theory, the physicist finds with certitude, and without omitting anything useful or using anything superfluous, the laws which may help him solve a given problem.

Order, wherever it reigns, brings beauty with it. Theory not only renders the group of physical laws it represents easier to handle, more convenient, and more useful, but also more beautiful.

It is impossible to follow the march of one of the great theories of physics, to see it unroll majestically its regular deductions starting from initial hypotheses, to see its consequences represent a multitude of experimental laws down to the smallest detail, without being charmed by the beauty of such a construction, without feeling keenly that such a creation of the human mind is truly a work of art.

A THEORY TENDS TO BE TRANSFORMED INTO A NATURAL CLASSIFICATION*

This esthetic emotion is not the only reaction that is produced by a theory arriving at a high degree of perfection. It persuades us also to see a natural classification in a theory.

* We have already noted natural classification as the ideal form toward which physical theory tends in "L'Ecole anglaise et les théories physiques," Art. 6, *Revue des questions scientifiques*, October 1893.

Now first, what is a natural classification? For example, what does a naturalist mean in proposing a natural classification of vertebrates?

The classification he has imagined is a group of intellectual operations not referring to concrete individuals but to abstractions, species; these species are arranged in groups, the more particular under the more general. In order to form these groups the naturalist considers the diverse organs—vertebral column, cranium, heart, digestive tube, lungs, swim-bladder—not in the particular and concrete forms they assume in each individual, but in the abstract, general, schematic forms which fit all the species of the same group. Among these organs thus transfigured by abstraction he establishes comparisons, and notes analogies and differences; for example, he declares the swim-bladder of fish analogous to the lung of vertebrates. These homologies are purely ideal connections, not referring to real organs but to generalized and simplified conceptions formed in the mind of the naturalist; the classification is only a synoptic table which summarizes all these comparisons.

When the zoologist asserts that such a classification is natural, he means that those ideal connections established by his reason among abstract conceptions correspond to real relations among the associated creatures brought together and embodied in his abstractions. For example, he means that the more or less striking resemblances which he has noted among various species are the index of a more or less close blood-relationship, properly speaking, among the individuals composing these species; that the cascades through which he translates the subordination of classes, of orders, of families, and of genera reproduce the genealogical tree in which the various vertebrates are branched out from the same trunk and root. These relations of real family affiliation can be established only by comparative anatomy; to grasp them in themselves and put them in evidence is the business of physiology and of paleontology. However, when he contemplates the order which his methods of comparison introduce into the confused multitude of animals, the anatomist cannot assert these relations, the proof of which transcends his methods. And if physiology and paleontology should someday demonstrate to him that the relationship imagined by him cannot be, that the evolutionist hypothesis is controverted, he would continue to believe that the plan drawn by his classification depicts real relations among animals; he would admit being deceived about the nature of these relations but not about their existence.

The neat way in which each experimental law finds its place in the classification created by the physicist and the brilliant clarity imparted to this group of laws so perfectly ordered persuade us in an overwhelming manner that such a classification is not purely artificial, that such an order does not result from a purely arbitrary grouping imposed on laws by an ingenious organizer. Without being able to explain our conviction, but also without being able to get rid of it, we see in the exact ordering of this system the mark by which a natural classification is recognized. Without claiming to explain the reality hiding under the phenomena whose laws we group, we feel that the groupings established by our theory correspond to real affinities among the things themselves.

The physicist who sees in every theory an explanation is convinced that he has grasped in light vibration the proper and intimate basis of the quality which our senses reveal in the form of light and color; he believes in an ether, a body whose parts are excited by this vibration into a rapid to-and-fro motion.

Of course, we do not share these illusions. When, in the course of an optical theory, we talk about luminous vibration, we no longer think of a real to-and-fro motion of a real body; we imagine only an abstract magnitude, i.e., a pure, geometrical expression. It is a periodically variable length which helps us state the hypotheses of optics, and to regain by regular calculations the experimental laws governing light. This vibration is to our mind a *representation*, and not an *explanation*.

But when, after much groping, we succeed in formulating with the aid of this vibration a body of fundamental hypotheses, when we see in the plan drawn by these hypotheses a vast domain of optics, hitherto encumbered by so many details in so confused a way, become ordered and organized, it is impossible for us to believe that this order and this organization are not the reflected image of a real order and organization; that the phenomena which are brought together by the theory, e.g., interference bands and colorations of thin layers, are not in truth slightly different manifestations of the same property of light; and that phenomena separated by the theory, e.g., the spectra of diffraction and of dispersion, do not have good reasons for being in fact essentially different.

Thus, physical theory never gives us the explanation of experimental laws; it never reveals realities hiding under the sensible appearances; but the more complete it becomes, the more we apprehend that the logical order in which theory orders experimental laws is the reflection of an ontological order, the more we suspect that the relations it establishes among the data of observation correspond to real relations among things,* and the more we feel that theory tends to be a natural classification.

The physicist cannot take account of this conviction. The method at his disposal is limited to the data of observation. It therefore cannot prove that the order established among experimental laws reflects an order transcending experience; which is all the more reason why his method cannot suspect the nature of the real relations corresponding to the relations established by theory.

But while the physicist is powerless to justify this conviction, he is nonetheless powerless to rid his reason of it. In vain is he filled with the idea that his theories have no power to grasp reality, and that they serve only to give experimental laws a summary and classificatory representation. He cannot compel himself to believe that a system capable of ordering so simply and so easily a vast number of laws, so disparate at first encounter, should be a purely artificial system. Yielding to an intuition which Pascal would have recognized as one of those reasons of the heart

* Cf. H. Poincaré, *La Science et l'Hypothèse* (Paris, 1903), p. 190. (Translator's note: Translated by Bruce Halsted, "Science and Hypothesis" in *Foundations of Science* [Lancaster, Pa.: Science Press, 1905].)

"that reason does not know," he asserts his faith in a real order reflected in his theories more clearly and more faithfully as time goes on.

Thus the analysis of the methods by which physical theories are constructed proves to us with complete evidence that these theories cannot be offered as explanations of experimental laws; and, on the other hand, an act of faith, as incapable of being justified by this analysis as of being frustrated by it, assures us that these theories are not a purely artificial system, but a natural classification. And so, we may here apply that profound thought of Pascal: "We have an impotence to prove, which cannot be conquered by any dogmatism; we have an idea of truth which cannot be conquered by any Pyrrhonian skepticism."

THEORY ANTICIPATING EXPERIMENT

There is one circumstance which shows with particular clarity our belief in the natural character of a theoretical classification; this circumstance is present when we ask of a theory that it tell us the results of an experiment before it has occurred, when we give it the bold injunction: "Be a prophet for us."

A considerable group of experimental laws had been established by investigators; the theorist has proposed to condense the laws into a very small number of hypotheses, and has succeeded in doing so; each one of the experimental laws is correctly represented by a consequence of these hypotheses.

But the consequences that can be drawn from these hypotheses are unlimited in number; we can, then, draw some consequences which do not correspond to any of the experimental laws previously known, and which simply represent possible experimental laws.

Among these consequences, some refer to circumstances realizable in practice, and these are particularly interesting, for they can be submitted to test by facts. If they represent exactly the experimental laws governing these facts, the value of the theory will be augmented, and the domain governed by the theory will annex new laws. If, on the contrary, there is among these consequences one which is sharply in disagreement with the facts whose law was to be represented by the theory, the latter will have to be more or less modified, or perhaps completely rejected.

Now, on the occasion when we confront the predictions of the theory with reality, suppose we have to bet for or against the theory; on which side shall we lay our wager?

If the theory is a purely artificial system, if we see in the hypotheses on which it rests statements skillfully worked out so that they represent the experimental laws already known, but if the theory fails to hint at any reflection of the real relations among the invisible realities, we shall think that such a theory will fail to confirm a new law. That, in the space left free among the drawers adjusted for other laws, the hitherto unknown law should find a drawer already made into which it may be fitted exactly would be a marvelous feat of chance. It would be folly for us to risk a bet on this sort of expectation.

If, on the contrary, we recognize in the theory a natural classification, if we feel that its principles express profound and real relations among things, we shall not be surprised to see its consequences anticipating experience and stimulating the discovery of new laws; we shall bet fearlessly in its favor.

The highest test, therefore, of our holding a classification as a natural one is to ask it to indicate in advance things which the future alone will reveal. And when the experiment is made and confirms the predictions obtained from our theory, we feel strengthened in our conviction that the relations established by our reason among abstract notions truly correspond to relations among things.

Thus, modern chemical symbolism, by making use of developed formulas, establishes a classification in which diverse compounds are ordered. The wonderful order this classification brings about in the tremendous arsenal of chemistry already assures us that the classification is not a purely artificial system. The relations of analogy and derivation by substitution it establishes among diverse compounds have meaning only in our mind; yet, we are convinced that they correspond to kindred relations among substances themselves, whose nature remains deeply hidden but whose reality does not seem doubtful. Nevertheless, for this conviction to change into overwhelming certainty, we must see the theory write in advance the formulas of a multitude of bodies and, yielding to these indications, synthesis must bring to light a large number of substances whose composition and several properties we should know even before they exist.

Just as the syntheses announced in advance sanction chemical notation as a natural classification, so physical theory will prove that it is the reflection of a real order by anticipating observation.

Now the history of physics provides us with many examples of this clairvoyant guesswork; many a time has a theory forecast laws not yet observed, even laws which appear improbable, stimulating the experimenter to discover them and guiding him toward that discovery.

The Académie des Sciences had set, as the subject for the physics prize that was to be awarded in the public meeting of March 1819, the general examination of the phenomena of the diffraction of light. Two memoirs were presented, and one by Fresnel was awarded the prize, the commission of judges consisting of Biot, Arago, Laplace, Gay-Lussac, and Poisson.

From the principles put forward by Fresnel, Poisson deduced through an elegant analysis the following strange consequence: If a small, opaque, and circular screen intercepts the rays emitted by a point source of light, there should exist behind the screen, on the very axis of this screen, points which are not only bright, but which shine exactly as though the screen were not interposed between them and the source of light.

Such a corollary, so contrary, it seems, to the most obvious experimental certainties, appeared to be a very good ground for rejecting the theory of diffraction proposed by Fresnel. Arago had confidence in the natural character arising from the clairvoyance of this theory. He tested it, and observation gave results which agreed absolutely with the improbable predictions from calculation.*

Thus physical theory, as we have defined it, gives to a vast group of experimental laws a condensed representation, favorable to intellectual economy.

It classifies these laws and, by classifying, renders them more easily and safely utilizable. At the same time, putting order into the whole, it adds to their beauty.

It assumes, while being completed, the characteristics of a natural classification. The groups it establishes permit hints as to the real affinities of things.

This characteristic of natural classification is marked, above all, by the fruitfulness of the theory which anticipates experimental laws not yet observed, and promotes their discovery.

That sufficiently justifies the search for physical theories, which cannot be called a vain and idle task even though it does not pursue the explanation of phenomena.

THE FUNCTION OF GENERAL LAWS IN HISTORY

C. G. HEMPEL

1. It is a rather widely held opinion that history, in contradistinction to the so-called physical sciences, is concerned with the description of particular events of the past rather than with the search for general laws which might govern those events. As a characterization of the type of problem in which some historians are mainly interested, this view probably can not be denied; as a statement of the theoretical function of general laws in scientific historical research, it is certainly unacceptable. The following considerations are an attempt to substantiate this point by showing in some detail that general laws have quite analogous functions in history and in the natural sciences, that they form an indispensable instrument of historical research, and that they even constitute the common basis of various procedures which are often considered as characteristic of the social in contradistinction to the natural sciences.

* *Oeuvres complètes d'Augustin Fresnel*, 3 vols. (Paris, 1866–1870), 1, 236, 365, 368.

Reprinted from *The Journal of Philosophy* (vol. XXXIX, No. 2, 1942, pp. 35–48) by permission of the author and editors.

By a general law, we shall here understand a statement of universal conditional form which is capable of being confirmed or disconfirmed by suitable empirical findings. The term "law" suggests the idea that the statement in question is actually well confirmed by the relevant evidence available; as this qualification is, in many cases, irrelevant for our purpose, we shall frequently use the term "hypothesis of universal form" or briefly "universal hypothesis" instead of "general law," and state the condition of satisfactory confirmation separately, if necessary. In the context of this paper, a universal hypothesis may be assumed to assert a regularity of the following type: In every case where an event of a specified kind C occurs at a certain place and time, an event of a specified kind E will occur at a place and time which is related in a specified manner to the place and time of the occurrence of the first event. (The symbols "C" and "E" have been chosen to suggest the terms "cause" and "effect," which are often, though by no means always, applied to events related by a law of the above kind.)

2.1 The main function of general laws in the natural sciences is to connect events in patterns which are usually referred to as *explanation* and *prediction*.

The explanation of the occurrence of an event of some specific kind E at a certain place and time consists, as it is usually expressed, in indicating the causes or determining factors of E. Now the assertion that a set of events—say, of the kinds C_1, C_2, . . . C_n—have caused the event to be explained, amounts to the statement that, according to certain general laws, a set of events of the kinds mentioned is regularly accompanied by an event of kind E. Thus, the scientific explanation of the event in question consists of

(1) a set of statements asserting the occurrence of certain events C_1, . . . C_n at certain times and places,
(2) a set of universal hypotheses, such that
(*a*) the statements of both groups are reasonably well confirmed by empirical evidence,
(*b*) from the two groups of statements the sentence asserting the occurrence of event E can be logically deduced.

In a physical explanation, group (1) would describe the initial and boundary conditions for the occurrence of the final event; generally, we shall say that group (1) states the *determining conditions* for the event to be explained, while group (2) contains the general laws on which the explanation is based; they imply the statement that whenever events of the kind described in the first group occur, an event of the kind to be explained will take place.

Illustration: Let the event to be explained consist in the cracking of an automobile radiator during a cold night. The sentences of group (1) may state the following initial and boundary conditions: The car was left in the street all night. Its radiator, which consists of iron, was completely filled with water, and the lid was screwed on tightly. The temperature during the night dropped from 39° F. in the evening to 25° F. in the morning; the air pressure was normal. The bursting pressure of the radiator material is so and so much.—Group (2) would contain empirical laws such as the following: Below 32° F., under normal atmospheric pressure, water freezes. Below 39.2° F., the pressure of a mass of water increases with decreasing temperature, if the volume remains constant or decreases; when the water freezes, the pressure again increases. Finally, this group would have to include a quantitative law concerning the change of pressure of water as a function of its temperature and volume.

From statements of these two kinds, the conclusion that the radiator cracked during the night can be deduced by logical reasoning; an explanation of the considered event has been established.

2.2 It is important to bear in mind that the symbols "E," "C," "C_1," "C_2," etc., which were used above, stand for kinds or properties of events, not for what is sometimes called individual events. For the object of description and explanation in every branch of empirical science is always the occurrence of an event of a certain *kind* (such as a drop in temperature by 14° F., an eclipse of the moon, a cell-division, an earthquake, an increase in employment, a political assassination) at a given place and time, or in a given empirical object (such as the radiator of a certain car, the planetary system, a specified historical personality, etc.) at a certain time.

What is sometimes called the complete description of an individual event (such as the earthquake of San Francisco in 1906 or the assassination of Julius Caesar) would require a statement of all the properties exhibited by the spatial region or the individual object involved, for the period of time occupied by the event in question. Such a task can never be completely accomplished.

A fortiori, it is impossible to explain an individual event in the sense of accounting for *all* its characteristics by means of universal hypotheses, although the explanation of what happened at a specified place and time may gradually be made more and more specific and comprehensive.

But there is no difference, in this respect, between history and the natural sciences: both can give an account of their subject-matter only in terms of general concepts, and history can "grasp the unique individuality" of its objects of study no more and no less than can physics or chemistry.

3. The following points result more or less directly from the above study of scientific explanation and are of special importance for the questions here to be discussed.

3.1 A set of events can be said to have caused the event to be explained only if general laws can be indicated which connect "causes" and "effect" in the manner characterized above.

3.2 No matter whether the cause-effect terminology is used or not, a scientific explanation has been achieved only if empirical laws of the kind mentioned under (2) in 2.1 have been applied.*

* Maurice Mandelbaum, in his generally very clarifying analysis of relevance and causation in history (*The Problem of Historical Knowledge*, New York, 1938, Chs. 7, 8) seems to hold that there is a difference between the "causal analysis" or "causal explanation" of an event and the establishment of scientific laws governing it in the

3.3 The use of universal empirical hypotheses as explanatory principles distinguishes genuine from pseudo-explanation, such as, say, the attempt to account for certain features of organic behavior by reference to an entelechy, for whose functioning no laws are offered, or the explanation of the achievements of a given person in terms of his "mission in history," his "predestined fate," or similar notions. Accounts of this type are based on metaphors rather than laws; they convey pictorial and emotional appeals instead of insight into factual connections; they substitute vague analogies and intuitive "plausibility" for deduction from testable statements and are therefore unacceptable as scientific explanations.

Any explanation of scientific character is amenable to objective checks; these include

(*a*) an empirical test of the sentences which state the determining conditions;
(*b*) an empirical test of the universal hypotheses on which the explanation rests;
(*c*) an investigation of whether the explanation is logically conclusive in the sense that the sentence describing the event to be explained follows from the statements of groups (1) and (2).

4. The function of general laws in *scientific prediction* can now be stated very briefly. Quite generally, prediction in empirical science consists in deriving a statement about a certain future event (for example, the relative position of the planets to the sun, at a future date) from (1) statements describing certain known (past or present) conditions (for example, the positions and momenta of the planets at a past or present moment, and (2) suitable general laws (for example, the laws of celestial mechanics). Thus, the logical structure of a scientific prediction is the same as that of a scientific explanation, which has been described in 2.1. In particular, prediction no less than explanation throughout empirical science involves reference to universal empirical hypotheses.

The customary distinction between explanation and prediction rests mainly on a pragmatical difference between the two: While in the case of an explanation, the final event is known to have happened, and its determining conditions have to be sought, the situation is reversed in the case of a prediction: here, the initial conditions are given, and their "effect"–which, in the typical case, has not yet taken place–is to be determined.

In view of the structural equality of explanation and prediction, it may be said that an explanation as characterized in 2.1 is not complete unless it might as well have functioned as a prediction: If the final event can be

---

sense stated above. He argues that "scientific laws can only be formulated on the basis of causal analysis," but that "they are not substitutes for full causal explanations" (*l.c.*, p. 238). For the reasons outlined above, this distinction does not appear to be justified: every "causal explanation" is an "explanation by scientific laws"; for in no other way than by reference to empirical laws can the assertion of a causal connection between certain events be scientifically substantiated.

derived from the initial conditions and universal hypotheses stated in the explanation, then it might as well have been predicted, before it actually happened, on the basis of a knowledge of the initial conditions and the general laws. Thus, e.g., those initial conditions and general laws which the astronomer would adduce in explanation of a certain eclipse of the sun are such that they might also have served as a sufficient basis for a forecast of the eclipse before it took place.

However, only rarely, if ever, are explanations stated so completely as to exhibit this predictive character (which the test referred to under (*c*) in 3.3 would serve to reveal). Quite commonly, the explanation offered for the occurrence of an event is incomplete. Thus, we may hear the explanation that a barn burnt down "because" a burning cigarette was dropped in the hay, or that a certain political movement has spectacular success "because" it takes advantage of widespread racial prejudices. Similarly, in the case of the broken radiator, the customary way of formulating an explanation would be restricted to pointing out that the car was left in the cold, and the radiator was filled with water.–In explanatory statements like these, the general laws which confer upon the stated conditions the character of "causes" or "determining factors" are completely omitted (sometimes, perhaps, as a "matter of course"), and, furthermore, the enumeration of the determining conditions of group (1) is incomplete; this is illustrated by the preceding examples, but even by the earlier analysis of the broken-radiator case: as a closer examination would reveal, even that much more detailed statement of determining conditions and universal hypotheses would require amplification in order to serve as a sufficient basis for the deduction of the conclusion that the radiator broke during the night.

In some instances, the incompleteness of a given explanation may be considered as inessential. Thus, e.g., we may feel that the explanation referred to in the last example could be made complete if we so desired; for we have reasons to assume that we know the kind of determining conditions and of general laws which are relevant in this context.

Very frequently, however, we encounter "explanations" whose incompleteness can not simply be dismissed as inessential. The methodological consequences of this situation will be discussed later (especially in 5.3 and 5.4).

5.1 The preceding considerations apply to *explanation in history* as well as in any other branch of empirical science. Historical explanation, too, aims at showing that the event in question was not "a matter of chance," but was to be expected in view of certain antecedent or simultaneous conditions. The expectation referred to is not prophecy or divination, but rational scientific anticipation which rests on the assumption of general laws.

If this view is correct, it would seem strange that while most historians do suggest explanations of historical events, many of them deny the possibility of resorting to any general laws in history. It is, however, possible to account for this situation by a closer study of explanation in history, as may become clear in the course of the following analysis.

5.2 In some cases, the universal hypotheses underlying a historical explanation are rather explicitly stated, as is illustrated by the italicized passages in the following attempt to explain the tendency of government agencies to perpetuate themselves and to expand (italics the author's):

As the activities of the government are enlarged, more people develop a vested interest in the continuation and expansion of governmental functions. *People who have jobs do not like to lose them; those who are habituated to certain skills do not welcome change; those who have become accustomed to the exercise of a certain kind of power do not like to relinquish their control*—if anything, *they want to develop greater power and correspondingly greater prestige.* . . .

Thus, government offices and bureaus, once created, in turn institute drives, not only to fortify themselves against assault, but to enlarge the scope of their operations.*

Most explanations offered in history or sociology, however, fail to include an explicit statement of the general regularities they presuppose; and there seem to be at least two reasons which account for this:

First, the universal hypotheses in question frequently relate to individual or social psychology, which somehow is supposed to be familiar to everybody through his everyday experience; thus, they are tacitly taken for granted. This is a situation quite similar to that characterized in 4.

Second, it would often be very difficult to formulate the underlying assumptions explicitly with sufficient precision and at the same time in such a way that they are in agreement with all the relevant empirical evidence available. It is highly instructive, in examining the adequacy of a suggested explanation, to attempt a reconstruction of the universal hypotheses on which it rests. Particularly, such terms as "hence," "therefore," "consequently," "because," "naturally," "obviously," etc., are often indicative of the tacit presupposition of some general law: they are used to tie up the initial conditions with the event to be explained; but that the latter was "naturally" to be expected as "a consequence" of the stated conditions follows only if suitable general laws are presupposed. Consider, for example, the statement that the Dust Bowl farmers migrate to California "because" continual drought and sandstorms render their existence increasingly precarious, and because California seems to them to offer so much better living conditions. This explanation rests on some such universal hypothesis as that populations will tend to migrate to regions which offer better living conditions. But it would obviously be difficult accurately to state this hypothesis in the form of a general law which is reasonably well confirmed by all the relevant evidence available. Similarly, if a particular revolution is explained by reference to the growing discontent, on the part of a large part of the population, with certain prevailing conditions, it is clear that a general regularity is assumed in this explanation, but we are hardly in a position to state just what extent and what specific form the discontent has to assume, and what the environmental conditions have to be, to bring about a revolution. Analogous remarks apply to all historical explanations in terms of

* Donald W. McConnell, *Economic Behavior;* New York, 1939; pp. 894–895.

class struggle, economic or geographic conditions, vested interests of certain groups, tendency to conspicuous consumption, etc.: All of them rest on the assumption of universal hypotheses* which connect certain characteristics of individual or group life with others; but in many cases, the content of the hypotheses which are tacitly assumed in a given explanation can be reconstructed only quite approximately.

5.3 It might be argued that the phenomena covered by the type of explanation just mentioned are of a statistical character, and that therefore only probability hypotheses need to be assumed in their explanation, so that the question as to the "underlying general laws" would be based on a false premise. And indeed, it seems possible and justifiable to construe certain explanations offered in history as based on the assumption of probability hypotheses rather than of general "deterministic" laws, i.e., laws in the form of universal conditionals. This claim may be extended to many of the explanations offered in other fields of empirical science as well. Thus, e.g., if Tommy comes down with the measles two weeks after his brother, and if he has not been in the company of other persons having the measles, we accept the explanation that he caught the disease from his brother. Now, there is a general hypothesis underlying this explanation; but it can hardly be said to be a general law to the effect that any person who has not had the measles before will get them without fail if he stays in the company of somebody else who has the measles; that a contagion will occur can be asserted only with a high probability.

Many an explanation offered in history seems to admit of an analysis of this kind: if fully and explicitly formulated, it would state certain initial conditions, and certain probability hypotheses,** such that the occurrence of the event to be explained is made highly probable by the initial conditions in view of the probability hypotheses. But no matter whether explanations in history be construed as "causal" or as "probabilistic" in character, it remains true that in general the initial conditions and especially the universal hypotheses involved are not clearly indicated, and can not unambiguously be supplemented. (In the case of probability hypotheses, for example, the probability values involved will at best be known quite roughly.)

5.4 What the explanatory analyses of historical events offer is, then, in most cases not an explanation in one of the meanings developed above, but something that might be called an *explanation sketch*. Such a sketch

* What is sometimes, misleadingly, called an explanation by means of a certain *concept* is, in empirical science, actually an explanation in terms of *universal hypotheses* containing that concept. "Explanations" involving concepts which do not function in empirically testable hypotheses—such as "entelechy" in biology, "historic destination of a race" or "self-unfolding of absolute reason" in history—are mere metaphors without cognitive content.

** E. Zilsel, in a very stimulating paper on "Physics and the Problem of Historico-Sociological Laws" (*Philosophy of Science*, Vol. 8, 1941, pp. 567–579), suggests that all specifically historical laws are of a statistical character similar to that of the "macro-laws" in physics. The above remarks, however, are not restricted to specifically historical laws since explanation in history rests to a large extent on non-historical laws (cf. section 8 of this paper).

consists of a more or less vague indication of the laws and initial conditions considered as relevant, and it needs "filling out" in order to turn into a full-fledged explanation. This filling-out requires further empirical research, for which the sketch suggests the direction. (Explanation sketches are common also outside of history; many explanations in psychoanalysis, for instance, illustrate this point.)

Obviously, an explanation sketch does not admit of an empirical test to the same extent as does a complete explanation; and yet, there is a difference between a scientifically acceptable explanation sketch and a pseudo-explanation (or a pseudo-explanation sketch). A scientifically acceptable explanation sketch needs to be filled out by more specific statements; but it points into the direction where these statements are to be found; and concrete research may tend to confirm or to infirm those indications; i.e., it may show that the kind of initial conditions suggested are actually relevant; or it may reveal that factors of a quite different nature have to be taken into account in order to arrive at a satisfactory explanation.—The filling-out process required by an explanation sketch will, in general, assume the form of a gradually increasing precision of the formulations involved; but at any stage of this process, those formulations will have some empirical import: it will be possible to indicate, at least roughly, what kind of evidence would be relevant in testing them, and what findings would tend to confirm them. In the case of non-empirical explanations or explanation sketches, on the other hand—say, by reference to the historical destination of a certain race, or to a principle of historical justice—the use of empirically meaningless terms makes it impossible even roughly to indicate the type of investigation that would have a bearing upon those formulations, and that might lead to evidence either confirming or infirming the suggested explanation.

5.5 In trying to appraise the soundness of a given explanation, one will first have to attempt to reconstruct as completely as possible the argument constituting the explanation or the explanation sketch. In particular, it is important to realize what the underlying explaining hypotheses are, and to judge of their scope and empirical foundation. A resuscitation of the assumptions buried under the gravestones "hence," "therefore," "because," and the like will often reveal that the explanation offered is poorly founded or downright unacceptable. In many cases, this procedure will bring to light the fallacy of claiming that a large number of details of an event have been explained when, even on a very liberal interpretation, only some broad characteristics of it have been accounted for. Thus, for example, the geographic or economic conditions under which a group lives may account for certain general features of, say, its art or its moral codes; but to grant this does not mean that the artistic achievements of the group or its system of morals has thus been explained in detail; for this would imply that from a description of the prevalent geographic or economic conditions alone, a detailed account of certain aspects of the cultural life of the group can be deduced by means of specifiable general laws.

A related error consists in singling out one of several important groups of factors which would have to be stated in the initial conditions, and then claiming that the phenomenon in question is "determined" by and thus can be explained in terms of that one group of factors.

Occasionally, the adherents of some particular school of explanation or interpretation in history will adduce, as evidence in favor of their approach, a successful historical prediction which was made by a representative of their school. But though the predictive success of a theory is certainly relevant evidence of its soundness, it is important to make sure that the successful prediction is in fact obtainable by means of the theory in question. It happens sometimes that the prediction is actually an ingenious guess which may have been influenced by the theoretical outlook of its author, but which can not be arrived at by means of his theory alone. Thus, an adherent of a quite metaphysical "theory" of history may have a sound feeling for historical developments and may be able to make correct predictions, which he will even couch in the terminology of his theory, though they could not have been attained by means of it. To guard against such pseudo-confirming cases would be one of the functions of test (*c*) in 3.3.

6. We have tried to show that in history no less than in any other branch of empirical inquiry, scientific explanation can be achieved only by means of suitable general hypotheses, or by theories, which are bodies of systematically related hypotheses. This thesis is clearly in contrast with the familiar view that genuine explanation in history is obtained by a method which characteristically distinguishes the social from the natural sciences, namely, *the method of empathetic understanding:* The historian, we are told, imagines himself in the place of the persons involved in the events which he wants to explain; he tries to realize as completely as possible the circumstances under which they acted, and the motives which influenced their actions; and by this imaginary self-identification with his heroes, he arrives at an understanding and thus at an adequate explanation of the events with which he is concerned.

This method of empathy is, no doubt, frequently applied by laymen and by experts in history. But it does not in itself constitute an explanation; it rather is essentially a heuristic device; its function is to suggest certain psychological hypotheses which might serve as explanatory principles in the case under consideration. Stated in crude terms, the idea underlying this function is the following: The historian tries to realize how he himself would act under the given conditions, and under the particular motivations of his heroes; he tentatively generalizes his findings into a general rule and uses the latter as an explanatory principle in accounting for the actions of the persons involved. Now, this procedure may sometimes prove heuristically helpful; but its use does not guarantee the soundness of the historical explanation to which it leads. The latter rather depends upon the factual correctness of the empirical generalizations which the method of understanding may have suggested.

Nor is the use of this method indispensable for historical explanation. A historian may, for example, be incapable of feeling himself into the rôle of a paranoiac historic personality, and yet he may well be able to explain certain of his actions; notably by reference to the principles of abnormal psychology. Thus, whether the historian is or is not in a position to identify himself with his historical hero, is irrelevant for the correctness of his explanation; what counts, is the soundness of the general hypotheses involved, no matter whether they were suggested by empathy or by a strictly behavioristic procedure. Much of the appeal of the "method of understanding" seems to be due to the fact that it tends to present the phenomena in question as somehow "plausible" or "natural" to us;* this is often done by means of attractively worded metaphors. But the kind of "understanding" thus conveyed must clearly be separated from scientific understanding. In history as anywhere else in empirical science, the explanation of a phenomenon consists in subsuming it under general empirical laws; and the criterion of its soundness is not whether it appeals to our imagination, whether it is presented in suggestive analogies, or is otherwise made to appear plausible—all this may occur in pseudo-explanations as well—but exclusively whether it rests on empirically well confirmed assumptions concerning initial conditions and general laws.

7.1 So far, we have discussed the importance of general laws for explanation and prediction, and for so-called understanding in history. Let us now survey more briefly some other procedures of historical research which involve the assumption of universal hypotheses.

Closely related to explanation and understanding is the so-called *interpretation of historical phenomena* in terms of some particular approach or theory. The interpretations which are actually offered in history consist either in subsuming the phenomena in question under a scientific explanation or explanation sketch; or in an attempt to subsume them under some general idea which is not amenable to any empirical test. In the former case, interpretation clearly is explanation by means of universal hypotheses; in the latter, it amounts to a pseudo-explanation which may have emotive appeal and evoke vivid pictorial associations, but which does not further our theoretical understanding of the phenomena under consideration.

7.2 Analogous remarks apply to the procedure of ascertaining the "*meaning*" of given historical events; its scientific import consists in determining what other events are relevantly connected with the event in question, be it as "causes," or as "effects"; and the statement of the relevant connections assumes, again, the form of explanations or explanation sketches which involve universal hypotheses; this will be seen more clearly in the subsequent section.

7.3 In the historical explanation of some social institutions great emphasis is laid upon an analysis of the *development* of the institution up to the stage under consideration. Critics of this approach have objected that

* For a criticism of this kind of plausibility, cf. Zilsel, *l.c.*, pp. 577–578, and sections 7 and 8 in the same author's "Problems of Empiricism," in *International Encyclopedia of Unified Science*, Vol. II, 8.

a mere description of this kind is not a genuine explanation. This argument may be given a slightly different aspect in terms of the preceding reflections: A description of the development of an institution is obviously not simply a statement of *all* the events which temporally preceded it; only those events are meant to be included which are "*relevant*" to the formation of that institution. And whether an event is relevant to that development is not a question of the value attitude of the historian, but an objective question depending upon what is sometimes called a causal analysis of the rise of that institution.* Now, the causal analysis of an event consists in establishing an explanation for it, and since this requires reference to general hypotheses, so do assumptions about relevance, and, consequently, so does the adequate analysis of the historical development of an institution.

7.4 Similarly, the use of the notions of *determination* and of *dependence* in the empirical sciences, including history, involves reference to general laws.** Thus, e.g., we may say that the pressure of a gas depends upon its temperature and volume, or that temperature and volume determine the pressure, in virtue of Boyle's law. But unless the underlying laws are stated explicitly, the assertion of a relation of dependence or of determination between certain magnitudes or characteristics amounts at best to claiming that they are connected by some unspecified empirical law; and that is a very meager assertion indeed: If, for example, we know only that there is some empirical law connecting two metrical magnitudes (such as length and temperature of a metal bar), we can not even be sure that a change of one of the two will be accompanied by a change of the other (for the law may connect the same value of the "dependent" or "determined" magnitude with different values of the other), but only that with any specific value of one of the variables, there will always be associated one and the same value of the other; and this is obviously much less than most authors mean to assert when they speak of determination or dependence in historical analysis.

Therefore, the sweeping assertion that economic (or geographic, or any other kind of) conditions "determine" the development and change of all other aspects of human society, has explanatory value only in so far as it can be substantiated by explicit laws which state just what kind of

* See the detailed and clear exposition of this point in M. Mandelbaum's book; *l.c.*, Chs. 6–8.

** According to Mandelbaum, history, in contradistinction to the physical sciences, consists "not in the formulation of laws of which the particular case is an instance, but in the description of the events in their actual determining relationships to each other; in seeing events as the products and producers of change" (*l.c.*, pp. 13–14). This is essentially a view whose untenability has been pointed out already by Hume; it is the belief that a careful examination of two specific events alone, without any reference to similar cases and to general regularities, can reveal that one of the events produces or determines the other. This thesis does not only run counter to the scientific meaning of the concept of determination which clearly rests on that of general law, but it even fails to provide any objective criteria which would be indicative of the intended relationship of determination or production. Thus, to speak of empirical determination independently of any reference to general laws means to use a metaphor without cognitive content.

change in human culture will regularly follow upon specific changes in the economic (geographic, etc.) conditions. Only the establishment of concrete laws can fill the general thesis with scientific content, make it amenable to empirical tests, and confer upon it an explanatory function. The elaboration of such laws with as much precision as possible seems clearly to be the direction in which progress in scientific explanation and understanding has to be sought.

8. The considerations developed in this paper are entirely neutral with respect to the problem of "*specifically historical laws*": neither do they presuppose a particular way of distinguishing historical from sociological and other laws, nor do they imply or deny the assumption that empirical laws can be found which are historical in some specific sense, and which are well confirmed by empirical evidence.

But it may be worth mentioning here that those universal hypotheses to which historians explicitly or tacitly refer in offering explanations, predictions, interpretations, judgments of relevance, etc., are taken from *various* fields of scientific research, in so far as they are not pre-scientific generalizations of everyday experiences. Many of the universal hypotheses underlying historical explanation, for instance, would commonly be classified as psychological, economical, sociological, and partly perhaps as historical laws; in addition, historical research has frequently to resort to general laws established in physics, chemistry, and biology. Thus, e.g., the explanation of the defeat of an army by reference to lack of food, adverse weather conditions, disease, and the like, is based on a—usually tacit—assumption of such laws. The use of tree rings in dating events in history rests on the application of certain biological regularities. Various methods of testing the authenticity of documents, paintings, coins, etc., make use of physical and chemical theories.

The last two examples illustrate another point which is relevant in this context: Even if a historian should propose to restrict his research to a "*pure description*" of the past, without any attempt at offering explanations, statements about relevance and determination, etc., he would continually have to make use of general laws. For the object of his studies would be the past—forever inaccessible to his direct examination. He would have to establish his knowledge by indirect methods: by the use of universal hypotheses which connect his present data with those past events. This fact has been obscured partly because some of the regularities involved are so familiar that they are not considered worth mentioning at all; and partly because of the habit of relegating the various hypotheses and theories which are used to ascertain knowledge about past events, to the "auxiliary sciences" of history. Quite probably, some of the historians who tend to minimize, if not to deny, the importance of general laws for history, are actuated by the feeling that only "genuinely historical laws" would be of interest for history. But once it is realized that the discovery of historical laws (in some specified sense of this very vague notion) would not make history methodologically autonomous and independent of the other branches of scientific research, it would seem that the problem of the existence of historical laws ought to lose some of its weight.

The remarks made in this section are but special illustrations of two broader principles of the theory of science: first, the separation of "pure description" and "hypothetical generalization and theory-construction" in empirical science is unwarranted; in the building of scientific knowledge the two are inseparably linked. And, second, it is similarly unwarranted and futile to attempt the demarcation of sharp boundary lines between the different fields of scientific research, and an autonomous development of each of the fields. The necessity, in historical inquiry, to make extensive use of universal hypotheses of which at least the overwhelming majority come from fields of research traditionally distinguished from history is just one of the aspects of what may be called the methodological unity of empirical science.

EXPLAINING AND JUSTIFYING ACTIONS

WILLIAM DRAY

1. *HISTORICAL UNDERSTANDING AS 'EMPATHETIC'*

. . . What I now wish to say may be regarded as an attempt to rehabilitate to some extent a second traditional doctrine of idealist philosophers of history: the view that the objects of historical study are fundamentally different from those, for example, of the natural sciences, because they are the actions of beings like ourselves; and that even if (for the sake of argument) we allow that natural events may be explained by subsuming them under empirical laws, it would still be true that this procedure is inappropriate in history. Sometimes such a view will be supported by the belief that human actions—at any rate the ones we call 'free'—do not fall under law at all. Sometimes it will be alleged only that even if they do fall under law, discovery of the law would still not enable us to understand them in the sense proper to this special subject-matter. It is the second of these claims which I especially want to consider here.

The doctrine is commonly expressed with the aid of a characteristic set of terms. To understand a human action, it will be said, it is necessary for the inquirer somehow to discover its 'thought-side'; it is not sufficient merely to know the pattern of overt behaviour. The historian must *penetrate* behind appearances, achieve *insight* into the situation, *identify*

Reprinted, with slight omissions, from *Laws and Explanation in History*, Chapter 5, Clarendon Press, Oxford, 1960, by permission of the publishers and William Dray.

himself sympathetically with the protagonist, *project* himself imaginatively into his situation. He must *revive, re-enact, re-think, re-experience* the hopes, fears, plans, desires, views, intentions, &c., of those he seeks to understand. To explain action in terms of covering law would be to achieve, at most, an external kind of understanding. The historian, by the very nature of his self-imposed task, seeks to do more than this.

It is worth noticing that historians themselves, and not just professional philosophers of history, often describe their task in these terms. Professor Butterfield is representative of a large group of his professional colleagues when he insists that "the only understanding we ever reach in history is but a refinement, more or less subtle and sensitive, of the difficult—and sometimes deceptive—process of imagining oneself in another person's place". And elsewhere in *History and Human Relations*, he writes:

> Our traditional historical writing . . . has refused to be satisfied with any merely causal or stand-offish attitude towards the personalities of the past. It does not treat them as mere things, or just measure such features of them as the scientist might measure; and it does not content itself with merely reporting about them in the way an external observer would do. It insists that the story cannot be told correctly unless we see the personalities from the inside, feeling with them as an actor might feel the part he is playing—thinking their thoughts over again and sitting in the position not of the observer but of the doer of action. If it is argued that this is imposible—as indeed it is—not merely does it still remain the thing to aspire to, but in any case the historian must put himself in the place of the historical personage, must feel his predicament, must think as though he were that man. Without this art not only is it impossible to tell the story correctly but it is impossible to interpret the very documents on which the reconstruction depends. Traditional historical writing emphasizes the importance of sympathetic imagination for the purpose of getting inside human beings. We may even say that this is part of the science of history for it produces communicable results—the insight of one historian may be ratified by scholars in general, who then give currency to the interpretation that is produced. . . .*

Among covering law logicians there is an 'official' answer to philosophers or historians who talk in this way about the peculiarities of 'historical understanding'. The answer is that although there is something right about it, the element of truth in such an account is not a point of logic; it is a mixture of psychological description and methodological precept. As a psychological description of the historian's state of mind when he succeeds in explaining the action of one of his characters, the notion of 'empathy' or 'imaginative understanding', as it is often called, will be allowed some merit—although it will be represented as involving us all too easily in the philosophical error of thinking that merely having certain experiences, or thinking certain thoughts similar to those of the historical agents, itself constitutes understanding or explaining. Similarly, as a suggestion as to how to go about discovering what the agent's motives were, the 'empathy' theory will be admitted to have a certain methodological point—although the reservation will be made that the

* pp. 145–6. See also pp. 116–17.

principle involved often leads the investigator astray. Professor Hempel puts the position succinctly in the following passage:

The historian, we are told, imagines himself in the place of the persons involved in the events which he wants to explain; he tries to realize as completely as possible the circumstances under which they acted, and the motives which influenced their actions; and by this imaginary self-identification with his heroes, he arrives at an understanding and thus at an adequate explanation of the events with which he is concerned.

This method of empathy is, no doubt, frequently applied by laymen and by experts in history. But it does not in itself constitute an explanation; it rather is essentially a heuristic device; its function is to suggest certain psychological hypotheses which might serve as explanatory principles in the case under consideration. Stated in crude terms, the idea underlying this function is the following: the historian tries to realize how he himself would act under the given conditions, and under the particular motivations of his heroes; he tentatively generalizes his findings into a general rule and uses the latter as an explanatory principle in accounting for the actions of the persons involved. Now, this procedure may sometimes prove heuristically helpful; but its use does not guarantee the soundness of the historical explanation to which it leads. The latter rather depends upon the factual correctness of the empirical generalizations which the method of understanding may have suggested.

Nor is the use of this method indispensable for historical explanation. A historian may, for example, be incapable of feeling himself into the role of a paranoiac historic personality, and yet be able to explain certain of his actions; notably by reference to the principles of abnormal psychology. Thus whether the historian is or is not in a position to identify himself with his historical hero, is irrelevant for the correctness of his explanation; what counts, is the soundness of the general hypotheses involved, no matter whether they were suggested by empathy, or by a strictly behaviouristic procedure.*

Now I do not wish to deny that there is any value at all in this sort of objection. But I think it important to show that the argument does not cut as deeply as covering law theorists commonly assume. For in recognizing the mixture of psychological and methodological elements in many statements of the idealist position, and in denying that these amount to an analysis of logical structure, these theorists fail to notice what it is about explanations of human actions in history which make the idealists want to say what they do—albeit in a quasi-psychological and quasi-methodological way. And what is left out, I wish to maintain, should properly be taken into account in a *logical* analysis of explanation as it is given in history. I shall argue that idealist theory partially, and perhaps defectively, formulates a certain pragmatic criterion operating in explanations of action given by historians, and that when this is ignored, we are quite properly puzzled as to why certain alleged explanations, which meet the covering law requirements, would be dismissed by historians as unsatisfactory—perhaps even as 'no explanation at all'.

* Carl G. Hempel, 'The Function of General Laws in History', *Readings in Philosophical Analysis*, ed. H. Feil and W. Sellars, New York, 1949, p. 467 [and reprinted in this section]. A similar argument is used by R. M. Crawford, 'History as Science', *Historical Studies, Australia and New Zealand*, 1947, p. 157; R. S. Peters, 'Motives and Cause', *Proceedings of the Aristotelian Society*, Supp. Vol., 1952, p. 143; P. L. Gardiner, *The Nature of Historical Explanation*, Oxford, 1952, p. 129; A. Danto, in 'Mere Chronicle and History Proper', *Journal of Philosophy*, 1953, p. 176.

The discussion to follow may be regarded in part as an attempt to 'make sense' of what Collingwood, in particular, has to say about historical understanding—and I make no apology for this. But although some reference will be made to dicta of his, I shall not offer any close textual discussion of his account. I shall try, rather, to bring out independently, by reference to examples, features which covering law theory seems to me to miss, going on thereafter to discuss likely misunderstandings of, and objections to, the logical point which appears to emerge out of such an examination.

2. *EXPLAINING AND JUSTIFYING ACTIONS*

The following extract from G. M. Trevelyan's *The English Revolution* is typical of a wide range of explanations of individual actions to be found in ordinary historical writing. In the course of an account of the invasion of England by William of Orange, Trevelyan asks: "Why did Louis make the greatest mistake of his life in withdrawing military pressure from Holland in the summer of 1688?" His answer is:

> He was vexed with James, who unwisely chose this moment of all, to refuse the help and advice of his French patron, upon whose friendship he had based his whole policy. But Louis was not entirely passion's slave. No doubt he felt irritation with James, but he also calculated that, even if William landed in England, there would be civil war and long troubles, as always in that factious island. Meanwhile, he could conquer Europe at leisure. "For twenty years," says Lord Acton, "it had been his desire to neutralize England by internal broils, and he was glad to have the Dutch out of the way (in England) while he dealt a blow at the Emperor Leopold (in Germany)." He thought "it was impossible that the conflict between James and William should not yield him an opportunity." This calculation was not as absurd as it looks after the event. It was only defeated by the unexpected solidity of a new type of Revolution.*

What Trevelyan here makes quite explicit is that, when we ask for the explanation of an action, what we very often want is a reconstruction of the agent's *calculation* of means to be adopted toward his chosen end in the light of the circumstances in which he found himself. To explain the action we need to know what considerations convinced him that he should act as he did.

But the notion of discovering the agent's calculation, it must be admitted, takes us no more than one preliminary step towards a satisfactory analysis of such explanations; and it may in itself be misleading. It must not be assumed, for instance, that the agent "calculated" in the sense of deriving by strict deductive reasoning the practical conclusion he drew—i.e. that the various considerations are elements in a calculus. Indeed, Trevelyan's explanation provides an obvious example to the contrary. Nor should we assume that the explanatory calculation must have been recited in propositional form, either aloud or silently—a notion which

* pp. 105–6.

one might be forgiven for extracting out of Collingwood's discussion of the way thought must be re-enacted by historians in order to understand intelligent, purposive actions. Not all high-grade actions are performed deliberately in the sense that they are undertaken with a plan consciously preformulated.

Indeed, it is tempting to say that in such cases there is *no* calculation to be *re*constructed by the historian. But such an admission need not affect the main point; for in so far as we say an action is purposive at all, no matter at what level of conscious deliberation, there is a calculation which could be constructed for it: the one the agent would have gone through if he had had time, if he had not seen what to do in a flash, if he had been called upon to account for what he did after the event, &c. And it is by eliciting some such calculation that we explain the action. It might be added that if the agent is to understand his *own* actions, i.e. after the event, he may have to do so by constructing a calculation in exactly the same way, although at the time he recited no propositions to himself. No doubt there are special dangers involved in such construction after the fact. But although we may have to examine very critically any particular example, the point is that when we do consider ourselves justified in accepting an explanation of an individual action, it will most often assume the general *form* of an agent's calculation.

Since the calculation gives what we should normally call the agent's *reasons* for acting as he did, I shall refer hereafter to this broad class of explanations as 'rational'. It should be clear that this use of the expression 'rational explanation' is a narrower one than is often found in philosophical and semi-philosophical literature. It is sometimes said, for instance, that all science, all systematic inquiry, seeks a rational explanation for what is observed, where all that is meant is an explanation which takes account of all the facts considered puzzling, and which does not violate, say, the canons of coherence and induction. I intend something much more restricted than this: an explanation which displays the *rationale* of what was done.

The goal of such explanation is to show that what was done was the thing to have done for the reasons given, rather than merely the thing that is done on such occasions, perhaps in accordance with certain laws (loose or otherwise). The phrase 'thing to have done' betrays a crucially important feature of explanations in terms of agent calculations—a feature quite different from any we have noticed so far. For the infinitive 'to do' here functions as a value term. I wish to claim therefore that there is an element of *appraisal* of what was done in such explanations; that what we want to know when we ask to have the action explained is in what way it was *appropriate*. In the ordinary course of affairs, a demand for explanation is often recognized to be at the same time a challenge to the agent to produce either justification or excuse for what was done. In history, too, I want to argue, it will often be found impossible to bring out the point of what is offered as explanation unless the overlapping of these notions, when it is human actions we are interested in, is explicitly recognized.

Once again, however, I must be on guard against overstating the point; for I do not wish to imply that anything that is explained on the rational model is thereby certified *without qualification* as the right, or proper, or intelligent thing to have done. In saying that the explanation must exhibit what was done as appropriate or justified it is always necessary to add the philosopher's proviso: 'in a sense.'

The sense in question may be clarified if we note a scale along which rational explanations can be ranged. The scale falls away from the simple case in which we can say: 'I find his action perfectly intelligible; he did exactly as I should have done'. It is a small step from such a case to one where we can understand an action when we see that it is what we should agree was the thing to do in view of the agent's peculiar circumstances. In such a case the explanation would consist of an account of these circumstances; they are the missing data which permit the construction of a calculation certifying the action as appropriate. Sometimes, of course, the agent is found to have been mistaken about the facts–including (as Trevelyan's example of Louis XIV shows) his views about what the results of certain lines of action will be. The agent is thus mistaken about the nature of his circumstances; yet his action can still be explained in the rational way so long as by bringing his erroneous beliefs to bear, the calculation can be satisfactorily constructed. It may also be necessary, at times, to take note explicitly of the agent's purposes, which may be quite different from the ones which the investigator would have had in the same circumstances, or even in the circumstances the agent envisaged. And the calculation may also have to take into account certain peculiar principles of the agent; for the action is rationally explained if it is in accordance with the agent's principles–no matter what we think of these.

There are thus gradations of rational explanation, depending on the amount of 'foreign' data which the investigator must bring in to complete the calculation: beliefs, purposes, principles, &c., of the agent which are different from those we might have assumed in absence of evidence to the contrary. Rational explanation may be regarded as an attempt to reach a kind of logical equilibrium at which point an action is *matched* with a calculation. A demand for explanation arises when the equilibrium is upset–when from the 'considerations' obvious to the investigator it is impossible to see the point of what was done. The function of the historian's explanatory story will in many cases be to sketch in the corrections to these 'obvious' considerations which require to be made if the reader is to be able to say: 'Now I understand what he was about.'*

* A certain apparent difficulty about our use of the words 'understand' and 'explain' disappears in the light of such a 'scale' of rational explanation. Ordinarily, I think, we tend to assume that these two notions are correlative: when I know the explanation of something then I understand it; and when I understand it, I am in a position to give the explanation. But the relation between the two is more complicated than that, for in many cases we should hesitate to claim understanding of what was done even though we know the explanation. This would probably not often be so in cases where, in order to give a rational explanation, all we have to do is supply the agent's beliefs, whether correct or not. But if references has to be made to quite peculiar purposes and principles in the calculation we shall probably be less comfort-

In the light of this account, it should be clear how restricted is the sense in which a rational explanation, as I use the term here, must show that what was done was the appropriate or right thing to have done. It is not necessary for the historian to show that the agent had reason for what he did; it is sufficient for explanation to show that he had reasons. But the element of appraisal remains in that what the historian declares to have been the agent's reasons must really *be* reasons (from the agent's point of view). To record what the agent *said* his reasons were would not be enough to provide a rational explanation unless the cogency of such reported reasons could be appreciated by the historian, when any peculiar beliefs, purposes, or principles of the agent were taken into account. Reported reasons, if they are to be explanatory in the rational way, must be *good* reasons at least in the sense that *if* the situation had been as the agent envisaged it (whether or not we, from our point of vantage, concur in his view of it), then what was done would have been the thing to have done. The historian must be able to 'work' the agent's calculation.

3. *THE POINT OF THE 'IDENTIFICATION' METAPHOR*

If my account of rational explanation is correct, what should we say about the view that historical understanding is 'empathetic'? It seems to me that our being able to range rational explanations along a scale in the way described above gives a real point to the 'projection' metaphors used by empathy theorists. Perhaps it is because the scale has been either ignored or misunderstood that what such theorists have said has been so easily written off as obvious but uninteresting, or as interesting but dangerous.

Covering law logicians commonly speak of empathy as a 'methodological dodge'. And it might, I suppose, be claimed that if an old, practised historian were to say to a novice: 'You will never understand the way medieval knights behaved unless you drop your 20th century prejudices and try to see things from their point of view', he *may* be telling the novice how to get on with his job, and thus be making a point which might be called 'methodological'. But I cannot believe that what the old hand offers his young colleague is (in Hempel's words) "a heuristic device" whose function is "to suggest certain psychological hypotheses which might serve as explanatory principles in the case under consideration". As Hempel goes on to explain, by this he means that the historian,

---

able—and show it by hedging a little about the propriety of saying we 'understand' the action thus explained. In a sense we understand a certain action so long as, not our principles, but the agent's, enjoin it. But if we find his principles uncommonly wrong-headed, or perhaps in moral cases even revolting, we may want to say: 'Although I see how he figured it out. I find it quite impossible to understand his acting that way.' That is, we allow our notions of 'explanation' and 'understanding' to get out of step in order to register our awareness of just how far we are having to descend the scale in order to achieve what I have called an explanatory equilibrium.

since he lacks empirically tested psychological laws which fit, say, the behaviour of medieval knights, must do something about repairing the deficiency if he is ever to give an explanation of knightly activities; for according to the covering law theory there is no explanation without empirical laws. Clearly the historian, especially the novice, is in no position to work over the whole field himself in search of the required laws. So, according to Hempel, he takes a short cut; he imagines himself in the knight's position, asks himself what *he* would have done, generalizes the answer as an empirical law covering knights (i.e. from a single imaginary case), and in this way satisfies the logical requirements of the model.

Hempel warns us, of course, that the use of the 'device' does not "guarantee the soundness of the historical explanation to which it leads", which depends rather "upon the factual correctness of the empirical generalizations which the method of understanding may have suggested". That is, we may presume, further empirical confirmation of the generalization must come in before we can regard the explanation as anything more than an inspired guess. In Hempel's terminology, the generalization is only a "hypothesis" until it has received the sort of empirical confirmation and testing that any respectable scientific law must undergo, losing in the process the marks of its Athena-like origin.

In the light of what was said in the previous section, it should be clear how misleading this is as an account of 'empathetic understanding'. No doubt there *is* a methodological side to the doctrine; and it might be formulated in some such way as: 'Only by putting yourself in the agent's position can you *find out* why he did what he did'. Here the suggestion is admittedly that by an imaginative technique we shall discover some *new information*—the agent's motives or reasons for acting. When Collingwood says that historical understanding consists of penetrating to the thought-side of actions—discovering the thought and nothing further—the temptation to interpret this in the methodological way is understandably strong. But there is another way in which the doctrine can be formulated: 'Only by putting yourself in the agent's position can you *understand* why he did what he did'. The point of the 'projection' metaphor is, in this case, more plausibly interpreted as a logical one. Its function is not to remind us of *how we come to know* certain facts, but to formulate, however tentatively, certain *conditions which must be satisfied* before a historian is prepared to say: 'Now I have the explanation'.

To dismiss 'empathy' as a mere 'methodological dodge' is to assume, falsely, that all there is to notice when rational explanations are given is a second-rate method of obtaining the same sort of result as can be obtained more reliably by direct attempts to subsume what is to be explained under an empirical covering law. But, as I have tried to show, at least part of what is meant by talking about the 'need to project', &c., is not achievable at all by the method recommended by covering law theorists. To accept Hempel's argument against 'empathy' is to obliterate a distinction between explanation types: a distinction between representing something as the thing generally done, and representing it as the appropriate thing to have done. Thus, when Hempel, after the passage quoted, goes on to say: "The kind of understanding thus conveyed must be clearly separated from scientific understanding", I have no objection to make, provided that by 'scientific understanding' is meant 'knowing to fall under an empirical law'. But Hempel's account of the alternative is quite unsatisfactory. For 'empathetic understanding', interpreted as 'rational explanation', is *not* a matter of "presenting the phenomena in question as somehow 'plausible' or 'natural' to us . . . by means of attractively worded metaphors".

No doubt the widespread resistance to admitting the need to cite anything more than antecedent conditions and a general law in explaining actions owes something to the air of mystery surrounding the language in which 'empathy' theory is often framed: 'projection', 'identification', 'imagination', 'insight', 'intuition', &c. Such words arouse the suspicion that, if the conditions of the covering law theory are not met, it will be necessary to claim that the historian's explanation somehow goes beyond the limits of empirical inquiry into the realm of the unverifiable. As Gardiner puts it, historians often seem to be credited with "an additional power of knowing which allows them to 'penetrate into' the minds of the subjects of their study and take, as it were, psychological X-ray photographs".* And in the bulletin of the American Social Science Research Council already referred to, historians are warned against a view of 'historical understanding' supposed to be "achieved not by introducing general laws or relevant antecedent events, but by an act of 'intuition', 'imaginative identification', 'empathy' or 'valuation' which makes the historical occurrence plausible or intelligible", and whose adequacy is determined by "a self-certifying insight".** To allow the legitimacy of empathy appears to many of its opponents as the granting of a licence to eke out scanty evidence with imaginative filler.

It is therefore worth my denying explicitly that what I have called rational explanation is in any damaging sense beyond empirical inquiry. As I have pointed out already, it has an inductive, empirical side, for we build up to explanatory equilibrium *from the evidence*. To get inside Disraeli's shoes the historian does not simply ask himself: 'What would I have done?'; he reads Disraeli's dispatches, his letters, his speeches, &c.—and not with the purpose of discovering antecedent conditions falling under some empirically validated law, but rather in the hope of appreciating the problem as Disraeli saw it. The attempt to provide rational explanation is thus—if you like the term—'scientific' explanation in a broad sense; there is no question of the investigator letting his imagination run riot. Indeed, many 'empathy' theorists have expressly guarded against such a misinterpretation of their views. To Butterfield, for instance, historical understanding is not a deliberate commission of the sin

* Op. cit., p. 128.
** *Bulletin No. 54*, p. 128.

of anachronism; it is a "process of emptying oneself in order to catch the outlook and feelings of men not like-minded with oneself".*

It is true, of course, that the *direction* of inquiry in the explanation of actions is generally from what the inquirer presumes the relevant agent calculation to be—using his own, or his society's conception of rational purposes and principles—to what he discovers to be the peculiar data of the historical agent: a direction suggested by the scale already indicated. In view of this, Butterfield's admonition to 'empty ourselves' is a little sweeping. In achieving rational explanation of an action we do project—but we project from our own point of view. In each case, the inclusion of 'foreign' data in the calculation requires positive evidence that the agent was *not* like-minded with us. The historian does not build up to explanatory equilibrium from scratch. But this is far from admitting the covering law objection that the whole direction of the inquiry amounts to a vicious methodology. The procedure is self-corrective.

There is thus no reason to think that what I am calling 'rational' explanations are put forward as self-evidently true, as some philosophers who talk of 'insight' may seem to imply. Collingwood has sometimes been thought to provide justification for those who attack empathy theory on this account—e.g. when he represents the understanding of an action as an immediate leap to the discovery of its 'inside', without the aid of any general laws, and (it may appear) without the use of any inductive reasoning at all.** But it is always possible that a mistake has been made in the inductive reasoning which provided the factual information for the calculation. It is always possible that further data may come in which will upset the logical equilibrium—perhaps evidence that the agent did not know something which it was at first thought he did. The ability of the historian to go through what he takes to be a relevant calculation does not guarantee the correctness of the explanation given; correct *form* is never a guarantee of correct *content*. But this is nothing more than the normal hazard of any empirical inquiry.

4. *GENERALIZATIONS AND PRINCIPLES OF ACTION*

Some exponents of the covering law model, while accepting the thesis of the two preceding sections, may object that this only amounts to recognizing an additional condition of a pragmatic sort which explanations must often satisfy in ordinary historical writing. It may be held, therefore, that what I say about rational explanation affects the claims of covering law theory only on its sufficient condition side. It seems to me, however, that in cases where we want to elicit the rationale of what was done, there are special reasons for regarding the model as false or mislead-

* Op. cit., p. 146.

** e.g. "When [the historian] knows what happened, he already knows why it happened" (*The Idea of History*, p. 214).

ing on its necessary condition side as well. For in an important sense, rational explanation falls short of, as well as goes beyond, subsuming a case under a general empirical law.

Any argument to the effect that a satisfactory or complete rational explanation must subsume what is explained under an empirically ascertainable 'regularity' depends on treating the data of the agent's calculation as 'antecedent conditions' (no doubt a very complicated set). It will be said that no matter what *else* is said about these conditions, they must be data from which what was done could have been predicted; and that the only difficulties we should encounter in trying to formulate the implicit covering law linking these to actions of the kind performed would be the ones discussed in Chapter II above (which I propose to ignore here). If we say: 'Disraeli attacked Peel because Peel was ruining the landed class', we mean *inter alia* that anyone like Disraeli in certain respects would have done the same thing in a situation similar in certain respects—the respects in question being discovered by pressing for amplification of the single reason given.

Now this objection is an important one, because its plausibility arises out of a genuine characteristic of rational explanation which ought to be made clear. For it is quite true that 'reasons for acting' as well as 'conditions for predicting' have a kind of generality or universality. If y is a good reason for A to do x, then y would be a good reason for anyone sufficiently like A to do x under sufficiently similar circumstances. But this universality of reasons is unlike the generality of an empirically validated law in a way which makes it especially hazardous to say that by giving a rational explanation, an historian commits himself to the truth of a corresponding law. For if a negative instance is found for a general empirical law, the law itself must be modified or rejected, since it states that people *do* behave in a certain way under certain circumstances. But if a negative instance is found for the sort of general statement which might be extracted out of a rational explanation, the latter would not necessarily be falsified. For that statement would express a judgement of the form: 'When in a situation of type $C_1 \ldots C_n$ the thing to do is x'. The 'implicit law' in such explanation is better called a *principle of action* than a generalization (or even a principle of inference).

It is true that finding a large number of negative instances—finding that people often do not act in accordance with it—would create a presumption against the claim of a given principle to universal validity. But it would not *compel* its withdrawal; and if it was not withdrawn, the explanatory value of the principle for those actions which *were* in accordance with it would remain. It is true, too, that if a particular person often acted at variance with a principle which he was said to hold, the statement that he held that principle would come into question. But that statement would not *necessarily* be falsified; and if it were retained, we could still explain in the rational way those of his actions which *were* in accordance with it. The connexion between a principle of action and the 'cases' falling under it is thus intentionally and peculiarly loose.

I do not deny, of course, that we often *can* predict successfully a person's response to a situation if we know, among other things, what his principles are (in so far as they are peculiar). In representing the action as the thing to have done, even in the extended sense required for rational explanation, we to some extent license the conclusion that it was the thing to have expected. Having said '*A* did *x* because of *y*', where *y* is *A*'s reason for doing *x*, we could also say that a bystander who knew the fact *y*, and also knew what *A*'s purposes and principles were, should not be surprised at *A*'s doing *x*. It is thus easy enough, under the guidance of a general theory of explanation which requires it, to slip into believing that the real force of the original explanation resides in alleviating such surprise; that its point is to show that this is the kind of thing we can expect to be done by such a person in such circumstances, and that the justification for the expectation must be found in experience of similar cases.

The widespread failure to distinguish between explanations which 'apply' empirical laws and those which 'apply' principles of action may owe something to the fact that the word 'because' is systematically ambiguous in this connexion. Taken in isolation, it is very seldom beyond all doubt whether a given explanatory statement of the form 'He did *x* because of *y*' is to be taken in the rational sense or not, i.e. whether the 'because' derives its explanatory force from an empirical law or a principle. The particular 'because' does not carry its language level on its face; this has to be determined by other means. It is thus often possible to interpret an explanation at the wrong level for a long time without committing any obvious logical errors. And this leaves plenty of room for manœuvring by philosophers who have a thesis to maintain which requires that only one level be recognized.

Whether an explanation of a piece of behaviour is to be interpreted rationally or not will often depend on the context of utterance; we may have to ask how the explanation would be argued for, what else would be said if it were expanded, &c. Take the following example from Trevelyan's discussion of the problem of the early eighteenth-century smog in London:

> On days when the north-east wind carried the smoke-cloud, even Chelsea became dangerous to the asthmatic, as the mild philosopher Earl of Shaftesbury had reason to complain. There is no wonder that King William with his weak lungs had lived at Hampton Court when he could, and at Kensington when he must.*

The explanation offered can easily be reduced to a 'because' statement. But what exactly does the historian mean to imply: does he mean that any person *would* have done so, circumstances being what they were? Or does he mean that any *sensible* person would have done so? The explanation could surely be pushed either way, depending on how we cared to read it. And the explanation may be satisfactory (in the sense of 'adequate for its type') no matter which way it is read. Butterfield would no doubt elect to defend it in the second, or rational, way, while Gardiner, in the

* *English Social History*, London, 1946, p. 337.

interests of his thesis, could choose the regularity way without obvious logical error. We cannot settle the issue between them until the writer gives us a more definite indication of what he intends. It is worth noticing, in this connexion, that many of the examples used by Gardiner to support the covering law model could be plausibly re-analysed in the rational way. The force of the explanation of Louis XIV's unpopularity in terms of his policies being detrimental to French interests is very likely to be found in the detailed description of the aspirations, beliefs, and problems of Louis's subjects. Given these men and their situation, Louis and his policies, their dislike of the king was an *appropriate* response.

Nor is the ambiguity confined to the word 'because'; it can be traced through a wide variety of terms used to describe and explain actions. It can be found, for instance, in the terms 'natural' and 'humanly possible', which Mr. W. H. Walsh employs in *An Introduction to Philosophy of History*, when arguing that explanations of action in history are accomplished by means of basic non-technical generalizations.* "We are agreed", Walsh declares, "that to understand an historical situation we must bring some kind of general knowledge to bear on it, and the first question to ask here is clearly in what this general knowledge consists." Against the positivists he maintains that the most important generalizations used in an historian's explanations do not come from any of the sciences; they are fundamental judgements about human nature—"judgments about the characteristic responses human beings made to the various challenges set them in the course of their lives, whether by the natural conditions in which they live, or by their fellow beings". These constitute a 'science of human nature' distinguishable from scientific psychology; they provide the historian with a criterion of what is 'humanly possible', when he seeks to understand the past.

But the 'science of human nature' here described does not differ logically from scientific psychology; it is really just the common-sense psychology of the plain man. If left at that, Walsh's argument would make no other point against the positivists than Hempel's own admission that, because of the unfortunate backwardness of the science of psychology, historians must formulate many of the 'laws of human nature' required on the basis of their own experience. But the facts of historical writing which stimulate Walsh's sympathy with the idealists seem to me to require our drawing, not a distinction merely between different *sources* of empirical laws used, but between different *types* of explanation. For we sometimes want to explain actions not by representing them as instances of laws, but as the reasonable thing to have done; and when we do, if we appeal to 'general knowledge' at all, it is to principles of behaviour rather than empirical generalizations; to knowledge of what to do rather than of what is usually or always done.

Walsh does not put it this way, yet there are suggestions of the point in some of his remarks. For instance, in pointing out that the basic general knowledge which historians bring to their work differs from one his-

* Chap. III, sections 4, 5.

torian to another, he includes both knowledge of how men *do* and (he adds 'perhaps') *should* behave.* And again, in a footnote, he considers favourably Ryle's term 'knowledge how' (i.e. practical knowledge of some kind) as a characterization of what is to be included in the envisaged 'science of human nature'** There is a hint of the same view in his acceptance of the suggestion that the 'science' in question is continuous with common sense—which, it may be remarked, is generally taken to cover our knowledge of what to do, as well as of what is generally done.† And the use of 'challenge-response' terminology in describing the nature of the fundamental judgements concerned points roughly in the same direction.‡

Walsh's terms 'humanly possible' and 'human nature' are located at the centre of the difficulty; they straddle the distinction between explanation types, or between the levels of language at which we talk about actions. Consider the following explanatory remark of Ramsey Muir about a political decision of George III. "The king", he writes, ". . . naturally chose Shelburne rather than the hated Whigs".§ In a way, this word does, as Walsh might say, represent the action as a characteristic response, in that anyone with George III's political memories would have tried to keep the Whigs out. But there is a very strong suggestion, too, that this response was *appropriate* in a rational sense; to say the choice naturally went to Shelburne is to imply that this was obviously the right thing for the king to do—from his point of view. Similarly, saying that an historian has a keen appreciation of what is 'humanly possible' *may* refer to the sort of law-governed phenomenon Walsh cites, e.g. "that men who undergo great physical privations are for the most part lacking in mental energy". But I think it may just as well refer to the fundamental principles on which any man may be expected to order his activities.

* p. 69.
** p. 67.
† p. 66.
‡ p. 65.
§ *A Short History of the British Commonwealth*, vol. ii, p. 105.

Further Readings

CAUSALITY

Braithwaite, R. B., *Scientific Explanation*, Cambridge University Press, Fair Lawn, N.J., 1953, chaps. 9 and 10.

Broad, C. D., *The Mind and Its Place in Nature*, Routledge & Kegan Paul, London, 1951, chaps. 3 and 10.

Ducasse, C. J., *Nature, Mind, and Death*, Open Court, La Salle, Ill., 1951, Part II.

Ewing, A. C., *The Fundamental Questions of Philosophy*, Routledge & Kegan Paul, London, 1951, chap. 8.

Ewing, A. C., *Idealism*, Methuen, London, 1934, chap. 4.

Hume, David, *A Treatise of Human Nature*, Doubleday, Garden City, N.Y., first published 1739–1740, Book I.

Margenau, Henry, *The Nature of Physical Reality*, McGraw-Hill, New York, 1950, chap. 19.

Nagel, Ernest, *The Structure of Science*, Harcourt, Brace & World, New York, 1961, chaps. 4 and 10.

Pap, Arthur, *An Introduction to the Philosophy of Science*, Free Press, New York, 1962, Part IV.

Pap, Arthur, "Philosophical Analysis, Translation Schemas, and the Regularity Theory of Causation," *Journal of Philosophy, 43* (1952).

Russell, Bertrand, "On the Notion of Cause," in *Mysticism and Logic*, Allen & Unwin, London, 1917.

Schlick, Moritz, "Causality in Everyday Life and in Recent Science," in Herbert Feigl and Wilfred Sellars (eds.), *Readings in Philosophical Analysis*, Appleton-Century-Crofts, New York, 1949.

INDUCTION

Black, Max, *Language and Philosophy*, Cornell University Press, Ithaca, N.Y., 1949, chap. 3.

Black, Max, *Problems of Analysis*, Cornell University Press, Ithaca, N.Y., 1954, chaps. 10–12.

Edwards, Paul, "Bertrand Russell's Doubts About Induction," *Mind, 58* (1949).

Feigl, Herbert, "The Logical Character of the Principle of Induction," *Philosophy of Science, 1* (1934).

Kneale, William, *Probability and Induction*, Oxford University Press, Fair Lawn, N.J., 1949.

Reichenbach, Hans, *Experience and Prediction*, University of Chicago Press, Chicago, 1938, chap. 5.

Salmon, Wesley, "Inductive Inference," in Bernard Baumrin (ed.), *Delaware Seminar in the Philosophy of Science*. Wiley, New York, 1963.

Salmon, Wesley, "Should We Attempt to Justify Induction?" *Philosophical Studies, 8* (1957).

Strawson, P. F., *Introduction to Logical Theory*, Wiley, New York, 1952, chap. 9.

Wright, G. H. von., *The Logical Problem of Induction*, Macmillan, New York, 1957.

SCIENTIFIC REALISM

Boltzmann, Ludwig, *Die Grundprinzipien und Grundgleichungen der Mechanik* in *Populäre Schriften*, Barth, Munich, 1905, vol. I.

Craig, William, "Replacement of Auxiliary Expressions," *Philosophical Review, 65* (1956).

Feigl, Herbert, "Existential Hypotheses," *Philosophy of Science, 17* (1950).

Feyerabend, P. K., "An Attempt at a Realistic Interpretation of Experience," *Proceedings of the Aristotelian Society, 58* (1958).

Hempel, Carl G., "The Theoretician's Dilemma," in Herbert Feigl, Michael Scriven, and Grover Maxwell (eds.), *Minnesota Studies in Philosophy of Science*, University of Minnesota Press, Minneapolis, 1958, vol. II.

Mach, Ernst, *The Science of Mechanics*, trans. Thomas J. McCormack, ed. Charles S. Peirce, Open Court, La Salle, Ill., 1902.

Margenau, Henry, *The Nature of Physical Reality*, McGraw-Hill, New York, 1950, chaps. 2, 4, 5, 8, 15, and 21.

Maxwell, Grover, "The Ontological Status of Theoretical Entities," in Herbert Feigl and Grover Maxwell (eds.), *Minnesota Studies in Philosophy of Science*, University of Minnesota Press, Minneapolis, 1962, vol. III.

Nagel, Ernest, *The Structure of Science*, Harcourt, Brace & World, New York, 1961, chap. 6.

Rozeboom, William W., "The Factual Content of Theoretical Concepts," in Herbert Feigl and Grover Maxwell (eds.), *Minnesota Studies in Philosophy of Science*, University of Minnesota Press, Minneapolis, 1962, vol. III.

Ryle, Gilbert, *The Concept of Mind*, Barnes & Noble, New York, 1949, chap. 5.

Smart, J. J. C., "The Reality of Theoretical Entities," *Australasian Journal of Philosophy, 34* (1956).

Toulmin, Stephen, *The Philosophy of Science*, Harper & Row, New York, 1953, chaps. 3 and 4.

Watson, W. H., *On Understanding Physics*, Cambridge University Press, New York, 1938, chap. 3.

EXPLANATION (GENERAL)

Braithwaite, R. B., *Scientific Explanation*, Cambridge University Press, New York, 1953.

Brodbeck, May, "Explanation, Prediction, and 'Imperfect Knowledge,'" in Herbert Feigl and Grover Maxwell (eds.), *Minnesota Studies in Philosophy of Science*, University of Minnesota Press, Minneapolis, 1962, vol. III.

Campbell, N. R., *What Is Science?* Dover, New York, 1952.

Feigl, Herbert, "Some Remarks on the Meaning of Scientific Explanation," *Psychological Review, 52* (1948).

Feyerabend, P. K., "Explanation, Reduction, and Empiricism," in Herbert Feigl and Grover Maxwell (eds.), *Minnesota Studies in Philosophy of Science*, University of Minnesota Press, Minneapolis, 1962, vol. III.

Hempel, Carl G., "Deductive-Nomological vs. Statistical Explanation," in Herbert Feigl and Grover Maxwell (eds.), *Minnesota Studies in Philosophy of Science*, University of Minnesota Press, Minneapolis, 1962, vol. III.

Hempel, Carl G., "Explanation and Prediction," in Bernard Baumrin (ed.), *Delaware Seminar on the Philosophy of Science*, Wiley, New York, 1963.

Hempel, Carl G., *Philosophy of Natural Science*. Prentice-Hall, Englewood Cliffs, N.J., 1965.

Hempel, Carl G., and Paul Oppenheim, "Studies in the Logic of Explanation," *Philosophy of Science, 15* (1948).

Hospers, John, "On Explanation," *Journal of Philosophy, 43* (1946).

Nagel, Ernest, *The Structure of Science*, Harcourt, Brace & World, New York, 1961, chaps. 2, 3, 7, and 12.

Pap, Arthur, *An Introduction to the Philosophy of Science*, Free Press, Glencoe, N.Y., 1962, chaps. 18 and 19.

Scriven, Michael, "Explanations, Predictions, and Laws," in Herbert Feigl and Grover Maxwell (eds.), *Minnesota Studies in Philosophy of Science*, University of Minnesota Press, Minneapolis, 1962, vol. III.

Scriven, Michael, "The Limits of Physical Explanation," in *Delaware Seminar in the Philosophy of Science*, Wiley, New York, 1963.

Toulmin, Stephen, *The Philosophy of Science*, Harper & Row, New York, 1953, chaps. 3 and 4.

EXPLANATION OF HUMAN BEHAVIOR

Collingwood, R. G., *The Idea of History*, Oxford University Press, Fair Lawn, N.J., 1946.

Danto, Arthur, *Analytical Philosophy of History*, Cambridge University Press, New York, 1965.

Danto, Arthur, "On Explanations in History," *Philosophy of Science, 23* (1956).

Dray, William, *Philosophy of History*, Prentice-Hall, Englewood Cliffs, N.J., 1964.

Dray, William (ed.), *Philosophical Analysis and History*, Harper & Row, New York, 1966.

Gallie, W. B., *Philosophy and the Historical Understanding*, Schocken, New York, 1964.

Gardiner, Patrick, *The Nature of Historical Explanation*, Oxford University Press, Fair Lawn, N.J., 1952.

Gardiner, Patrick (ed.), *Theories of History*, Free Press, New York, 1959.

Hempel, Carl G., "Explanation in Science and in History," in Robert G. Colodny (ed.), *Frontiers of Science and Philosophy*, University of Pittsburgh Press, Pittsburgh, Pa., 1962.

Hook, Sidney (ed.), *Philosophy and History*, New York University Press, New York, 1963.

Mandelbaum, Maurice, "Historical Explanation: The Problem of 'Covering Laws,'" *History and Theory, 1* (1960–1961).

Natanson, Maurice, (ed.), *Philosophy of the Social Sciences*, Random House, New York, 1963.

Passmore, John, "Explanation in Everyday Life, in Science, and in History," *History and Theory, 2* (1962–1963).

Peters, R. S., *The Concept of Motivation*, Routledge & Kegan Paul, London, 1958.

Schutz, Alfred, "The Social World and the Theory of Social Action," *Social Research, 27* (1960).

Taylor, Charles, *The Explanation of Behavior*, Humanities Press, New York, 1964.

Walsh, W. H., *Introduction to Philosophy of History*, Hutchinson, London, 1951.

White, M. G., *Foundations of Historical Knowledge*, Harper & Row, New York, 1965.

Winch, Peter, *The Idea of a Social Science*, Routledge & Kegan Paul, London, 1958.

V

MORAL EVALUATION AND JUSTIFICATION

ALMOST EVERYONE has opinions about what things are good or bad, what actions are right or wrong, which people to praise and which to blame. Reflective men will attempt to justify these opinions, that is, to give reasons for making the moral judgments and the moral choices that they in fact make. Indeed, some will try to base their judgments and their actions on moral principles, principles which will give them a way of dealing with different and various moral questions. Particular moral decisions will be justified by the principles that dictated them. The task then will be to justify the principles themselves.

Many, however, feel no real need to reflect until a moral conflict arises. One may be in a situation in which he must do one of two things, each of which he thinks is wrong. Suppose, for example, one believes that it is wrong to break a promise and that it is wrong to cause needless harm to another. Suppose further that by keeping a promise he has made, he will cause great harm to an innocent bystander. He is then confronted with a moral problem which his moral opinions are, by themselves, inadequate to solve. They would require him to both keep and not keep the promise. He must, therefore, reflect in order to work out a way to balance the conflicting moral claims upon him.

Again, one might find that his inclination conflicts with what he believes it is his duty to do. Should he help someone who is being attacked on the street or should he leave well enough alone and avoid possible injury? Should he return the wallet full of money he has just found? The question most apt to arise in situations like this is: *Why* should I do what I think is right? One must reflect in order to satisfy the need he feels to give reasons for doing what he takes to be his duty.

A dilemma may be created when a moral principle seems to conflict with general human happiness or with personal happiness and well-being. For example, one might feel that birth control is morally wrong and yet realize that the practice of it in overpopulated countries would greatly increase the well-being of the peoples in those countries. We might ask, then, what role the happiness or well-being of men plays in a moral situation. Can a person have an obligation to do something which he knows will produce consequences less conducive to human happiness than those of some alternative action?

Should a person come in contact with people whose moral beliefs conflict with his, he will probably be led to re-examine his own beliefs. If, for example, he found that a different society held apparently different views about the value of the freedom of the individual or the value of a human life, he may well be led to ask himself what reason he has for holding the views that he does. Might there be no justification? Or if there is a justification, of what sort is it?

I

When the philosopher turns to moral questions, he may be concerned with either or both of *two* kinds of questions: normative ones and meta-ethical ones.

Normative ethical questions are those of the form: What things are good or bad, what actions right or wrong? What ought I to do? What ought I to believe? Answers to these questions would include the reasons one has for believing that certain things are good or bad, etc. These are questions *within* ethics.

Meta-ethics is concerned with questions *about* ethics. They are not, however, questions that an anthropologist would ask about the values of a particular tribe or that a psychologist would ask about the psychological mechanism which accounts for one's doing his duty. The philosopher's meta-ethical inquiry is best described as a conceptual, not a scientific, inquiry. Questions which are examined in this realm include the following: What is the meaning of "good," "right," "ought," etc? Do ethical terms refer to anything? Can moral judgments be true or false? Do they report states of affairs or do they have other functions? What is a moral principle, e.g., how does it differ from a legal principle? How do we justify moral judgments? Can we give reasons for saying that certain things are good or bad, certain actions right or wrong? Is there a logic peculiar to ethical reasoning as opposed to mathematical or scientific reasoning? What is the relation between facts and values? (This question is more often asked in the form: How can we derive a statement with an "ought" in it from ones which contain only "is"?) Are moral statements necessarily true?

There is another sort of meta-ethical question, concerned not with problems of meaning and justification, but rather with the relation between moral judgments and action. Here the moral philosopher would consider whether men's actions are free or determined, and if they are determined whether or not it is appropriate to blame or praise certain actions. Can we hold a person responsible for something if he had no choice as to whether or not to do it?

Another important problem is how is it that moral judgments determine our actions. The moral philosopher might produce a theory of motivation designed to answer this question: he might say that men always act self-interestedly or, again, that they are capable of acting altruistically. Perhaps this will take him into the realm of psychology, insofar as he would want evidence for a theory of what moves men to act.

Presumably, a reflective person who is examining his own set of values will touch on some of these meta-ethical questions. For example, before one can give a completely adequate answer to the question whether there are any absolute moral principles and, if so, what they are, he must find out what he believes a moral principle is, e.g., how it differs from or is similar to legal or scientific principles. Also, if one is concerned to find out what obligations he has, he should ask what he means by "obligation."

In general, however, it is the philosopher who will study meta-ethical questions in detail. Some twentieth century philosophers have gone so far as to say that normative ethics is not the special province of the philosopher; his concern, as a philosopher, should be solely with meta-ethical questions.

While normative ethics and meta-ethics are, in some ways, independent, they are not unrelated to each other. Not only will a consideration of the meaning of ethical terms and judgments help to clarify normative questions, but also the results of answers to meta-ethical questions will influence normative ethics in its content. If, for example, one decides that moral judgments are merely expressions of attitudes or emotions, then reasons given for normative judgments would be attempts to persuade, attempts to create similar attitudes or emotions in the listener, rather than reasons to justify an objective truth. Again, if "right" means "in accord with the judgments of one's society," then in justifying the claim that x is right, one will try to show it is approved of by one's society.

While it is difficult to classify the views of moral philosophers, because of the complexity of the subject matter, among other things, it is possible to indicate the main kinds of views which have been held with relation to normative questions and meta-ethical questions.

II

In general, philosophers who are concerned with normative questions have given two kinds of answers. One is that the value of an action is determined by the consequences of the action. This is called a *teleological* theory. For example, some philosophers say that an act is right if and only if it would produce the greatest balance of pleasure over pain or displeasure. If one is in a situation where he can perform no action that will produce more pleasure than pain, then the right action is that which will produce the least pain.

Philosophers justify this claim that an action is right if and only if it brings about the greatest possible balance of pleasure over pain in different ways. One way is to say that "right" with respect to actions just *means* "conducive to the greatest balance of pleasure over pain"; another is that since men desire pleasure, it is right that they attain it where possible. Still another is that "right" means "willed by God" and God has arranged the pleasures and pains following from actions so that just those actions willed by God have the consequence of producing the greatest balance of pleasure.

Others have said that not only pleasure, but knowledge, or beauty, or self-realization are values the production of which determines the rightness of an action. What is essential to a teleological theory is that the moral value of an action is determined by its consequences. (See Aristotle, "The Good as the End of Action," in this section.)

The other kind of answer given to normative questions is embodied in what are called *formalist* theories. Some philosophers say that the value of an action lies within the action itself. For example, certain actions like breaking promises or killing are wrong in themselves, independent of such consequences as might follow from them. The justification that might be given is that one intuits the truth of rules like "Killing is wrong" in much the way that we intuit the truth of "Two and two are four." One who offered this justification would say that moral rules expressed necessary truths. Another variation of the formalist theory is that the value of an action is determined by the principle in accord with which the action was performed. One holding such a view would have to specify a way to pick out acceptable from nonacceptable principles. (See Kant, "The Metaphysics of Morals," in this section. Also see Rawls, "Two Concepts of Rules," for an interesting discussion involving both teleological and formalist elements.)

III

It is most difficult to classify meta-ethical views because the number of questions which can be called meta-ethical is so great.

However, with respect to the meta-ethical questions concerning the meaning and nature of ethical terms and judgments, there are three kinds of views.

Naturalism maintains that ethical judgments are like judgments about the empirical world. More specifically, the view is that moral concepts can be analyzed in terms of concepts exemplified in sense-experience. For example, some hold that "good" means "conducive to happiness," where happiness is explained in terms of pleasure, self-realization, etc., all of which can be defined empirically. On this view, we can see whether or not an action is good by looking in the world to see if it produces pleasure, for example, and this procedure is similar to the one we use to find out what color crows are, or how many people are in the next room.

Since moral judgments can be restated as empirical judgments, they are, like empirical judgments, either true or false. Therefore, were one man to say killing was wrong, and another it was not wrong, one of them must be wrong. That is, it is, on this view, possible to disagree about ethical matters. (See Mill, "Utilitarianism," in this section, for a discussion related to naturalism.)

A more sophisticated form of naturalism is that the term "good" cannot be analyzed by itself; but the contexts ("good table," "good show," "good thing to do," "good man,") in which it appears can be analyzed in terms of empirical notions. For example, "good table" might be analyzed as "a table which is sturdy or which has a smooth surface." One can determine empirically whether a given table has some or all of these properties. The task of the meta-ethical philosopher, then, is to analyze notions like "morally good man" in a similar fashion.

The view called *intuitionism* agrees with naturalism that moral judgments are either true or false. It disagrees, however, as to whether moral judgments are about the empirical world, that is, whether moral concepts can be analyzed in terms of empirical concepts. The intuitionist says that moral judgments are not about matters of empirical fact, but that since they are either true or false, they must be about something. What they are about, then, is values, things different from the constituents of the sensible world. One comes to know the truth of a statement about values by *seeing* that the statement is true.

Intuitionists are most often formalists with respect to normative questions. That is, they feel that the statements whose truth we intuit are statements about actions considered in themselves, not about their consequences. However, an intuitionist may hold a teleological theory and claim that the rightness of an act is determined by examining its consequences. He would deny that "right" *means* "having as a consequence the production of the greatest amount of pleasure," for he denies that moral terms can be analyzed in terms of empirical ones (though he might say that one moral term can be analyzed in terms of another moral term: "right" means "productive of the greatest good").

The intuitionist who is a teleologist might say that one can intuit that all actions which have the property of being right also have the property of producing the greatest pleasure. He might claim that the statement "All and only right acts are those which produce greatest amounts of pleasure" is synthetic and known *a priori*, in other words, it is necessarily true, but it is not seen to be true merely by analyzing the meanings of its terms. (See Moore, "The Subject Matter of Ethics," in this section.)

Finally, the third major meta-ethical theory is called *noncognitivism*. A noncognitivist agrees with the intuitionist that ethical concepts are neither empirical nor analyzable in terms of empirical concepts, but he disagrees with the intuitionists as to whether moral judgments can be true or false. He says that moral judgments are not statements, or are not primarily or solely used to state facts, but are more like expressions of emotions or attitudes, or like commands or orders. A noncognitivist is concerned to point out the expressive and persuasive elements in our use of ethical terms, and that, therefore, one who makes a moral judgment is expressing his attitudes toward the object of the judgment or recommending that we choose it. (See Stevenson, "The Emotive Meaning of Ethical Terms," in this section.)

The noncognitivist, then, is concerned with the relation between a moral judgment and human choice and actions. He wants to emphasize the fact that a man's moral beliefs and opinions influence the way he acts. Cognitivists, on the other hand, emphasize the relation between the moral judgment and the empirical or nonempirical facts in terms of which moral judgments can be analyzed. Any adequate moral theory should address itself both to the connection between moral judgments and considerations of fact, experience, and reason, and to the connection between moral judgments and human actions.

The resultant tension might be characterized as follows: The naturalist reduces moral terms to empirical terms and thereby shows what kinds of actions are right. The intuitionist claims to intuit the truth of certain moral rules, such as, murder is wrong, and thereby to discover what actions are right. These views, however, must be supplemented by an account of why one should do the things which are shown to be right. The noncognitivist, on the other hand, says that to make a moral judgment is already to be inclined to act in a certain way. The connection with action, with doing what is right, is manifest. They claim further that moral judgments are not about anything, either empirical or nonempirical; that is, there is no direct connection between them and fact, experience, or reason. Noncognitivists are, however, left with the conclusion that moral judgments are neither true nor false and that, therefore, there can be no real moral disagreement, only disagreement in attitudes. I might say murder is wrong, and you might say it is not wrong, but since we are only expressing our respective attitudes toward murder, we cannot say that either of us is right or wrong. The notions of right and wrong do not seem to apply. Noncognitivists then must give some account of why it appears that moral disagreement is possible; they must discuss the relation between moral judgments and fact, experience, or reason.

One other question, mentioned above briefly, which is treated in this section is that raised by Plato: "Why should I be moral?" The selection from Baier, "Why I Should Be Moral," attempts to answer this question in a way which relates to a number of the views expressed by philosophers included in this section. The question is basically concerned with the relation of duty and self-interest.

The following selections exemplify a number of the positions which have been indicated above. They give a sense of the variety of views held by philosophers as they address themselves to problems of normative and meta-ethics. They give an indication of what serious ethical inquiry can produce.

WHY SHOULD I BE MORAL?

PLATO

I thought that, with these words, I was quit of the discussion; but it seems this was only a prelude. Glaucon, undaunted as ever, was not content to let Thrasymachus abandon the field.

Socrates, he broke out, you have made a show of proving that justice is better than injustice in every way. Is that enough, or do you want us to be really convinced?

Certainly I do, if it rests with me.

Then you are not going the right way about it. I want to know how you classify the things we call good. Are there not some which we should wish to have, not for their consequences, but just for their own sake, such as harmless pleasures and enjoyments that have no further result beyond the satisfaction of the moment?

Yes, I think there are good things of that description.

And also some that we value both for their own sake and for their consequences—things like knowledge and health and the use of our eyes?

Yes.

And a third class which would include physical training, medical treatment, earning one's bread as a doctor or otherwise—useful, but burdensome things, which we want only for the sake of the profit or other benefit they bring.

Yes, there is that third class. What then?

In what class do you place justice?

I should say, in the highest, as a thing which anyone who is to gain happiness must value both for itself and for its results.

Well, that is not the common opinion. Most people would say it was one of those things, tiresome and disagreeable in themselves, which we cannot avoid practising for the sake of reward or a good reputation.

I know, said I; that is why Thrasymachus has been finding fault with it all this time and praising injustice. But I seem to be slow in seeing his point.

Listen to me, then, and see if you agree with mine. There was no need, I think, for Thrasymachus to yield so readily, like a snake you had charmed into submission; and nothing so far said about justice and injustice has been established to my satisfaction. I want to be told what each of them really is, and what effect each has, in itself, on the soul that harbours it, when all rewards and consequences are left out of account.

This selection is reprinted from the *The Republic of Plato*, translated by F. M. Cornford. Oxford University Press, 1945. Reprinted by permission.

So here is my plan, if you approve. I shall revive Thrasymachus' theory. First, I will state what is commonly held about the nature of justice and its origin; secondly, I shall maintain that it is always practised with reluctance, not as good in itself, but as a thing one cannot do without; and thirdly, that this reluctance is reasonable, because the life of injustice is much the better life of the two—so people say. That is not what I think myself, Socrates; only I am bewildered by all that Thrasymachus and ever so many others have dinned into my ears; and I have never yet heard the case for justice stated as I wish to hear it. You, I believe, if anyone, can tell me what is to be said in praise of justice in and for itself; that is what I want. Accordingly, I shall set you an example by glorifying the life of injustice with all the energy that I hope you will show later in denouncing it and exalting justice in its stead. Will that plan suit you?

Nothing could be better, I replied. Of all subjects this is one on which a sensible man must always be glad to exchange ideas.

Good, said Glaucon. Listen then, and I will begin with my first point: the nature and origin of justice.

What people say is that to do wrong is, in itself, a desirable thing; on the other hand, it is not at all desirable to suffer wrong, and the harm to the sufferer outweighs the advantage to the doer. Consequently, when men have had a taste of both, those who have not the power to seize the advantage and escape the harm decide that they would be better off if they made a compact neither to do wrong nor to suffer it. Hence they began to make laws and covenants with one another; and whatever the law prescribed they called lawful and right. That is what right or justice is and how it came into existence; it stands half-way between the best thing of all—to do wrong with impunity—and the worst, which is to suffer wrong without the power to retaliate. So justice is accepted as a compromise, and valued, not as good in itself, but for lack of power to do wrong; no man worthy of the name, who had that power, would ever enter into such a compact with anyone; he would be mad if he did. That, Socrates, is the nature of justice according to this account, and such the circumstances in which it arose.

The next point is that men practise it against the grain, for lack of power to do wrong. How true that is, we shall best see if we imagine two men, one just, the other unjust, given full licence to do whatever they like, and then follow them to observe where each will be led by his desires. We shall catch the just man taking the same road as the unjust; he will be moved by self-interest, the end which it is natural to every creature to pursue as good, until forcibly turned aside by law and custom to respect the principle of equality.

Now, the easiest way to give them that complete liberty of action would be to imagine them possessed of the talisman found by Gyges, the ancestor of the famous Lydian. The story tells how he was a shepherd in the King's service. One day there was a great storm, and the ground where his flock was feeding was rent by an earthquake. Astonished at the sight, he went down into the chasm and saw, among other wonders of which the story tells, a brazen horse, hollow, with windows in its sides. Peering in, he saw a dead body, which seemed to be of more than human size. It was naked save for a gold ring, which he took from the finger and made his way out. When the shepherds met, as they did every month, to send an account to the King of the state of his flocks, Gyges came wearing the ring. As he was sitting with the others, he happened to turn the bezel of the ring inside his hand. At once he became invisible, and his companions, to his surprise, began to speak of him as if he had left them. Then, as he was fingering the ring, he turned the bezel outwards and became visible again. With that, he set about testing the ring to see if it really had this power, and always with the same result: according as he turned the bezel inside or out he vanished and reappeared. After this discovery he contrived to be one of the messengers sent to the court. There he seduced the Queen, and with her help murdered the King and seized the throne.

Now suppose there were two such magic rings, and one were given to the just man, the other to the unjust. No one, it is commonly believed, would have such iron strength of mind as to stand fast in doing right or keep his hands off other men's goods, when he could go to the market-place and fearlessly help himself to anything he wanted, enter houses and sleep with any woman he chose, set prisoners free and kill men at his pleasure, and in a word go about among men with the powers of a god. He would behave no better than the other; both would take the same course. Surely this would be strong proof that men do right only under compulsion; no individual thinks of it as good for him personally, since he does wrong whenever he finds he has the power. Every man believes that wrongdoing pays him personally much better, and, according to this theory, that is the truth. Granted full licence to do as he liked, people would think him a miserable fool if they found him refusing to wrong his neighbours or to touch their belongings, though in public they would keep up a pretence of praising his conduct, for fear of being wronged themselves. So much for that.

Finally, if we are really to judge between the two lives, the only way is to contrast the extremes of justice and injustice. We can best do that by imagining our two men to be perfect types, and crediting both to the full with the qualities they need for their respective ways of life. To begin with the unjust man: he must be like any consummate master of a craft, a physician or a captain, who, knowing just what his art can do, never tries to do more, and can always retrieve a false step. The unjust man, if he is to reach perfection, must be equally discreet in his criminal attempts, and he must not be found out, or we shall think him a bungler; for the highest pitch of injustice is to seem just when you are not. So we must endow our man with the full complement of injustice; we must allow him to have secured a spotless reputation for virtue while committing the blackest crimes; he must be able to retrieve any mistake, to defend himself with convincing eloquence if his misdeeds are denounced, and, when force is required, to bear down all opposition by his courage and strength and by his command of friends and money.

Now set beside this paragon the just man in his simplicity and nobleness, one who, in Aeschylus' words, 'would be, not seem, the best.' There must, indeed, be no such seeming; for if his character were apparent, his reputation would bring him honours and rewards, and then we should not know whether it was for their sake that he was just or for justice's sake alone. He must be stripped of everything but justice, and denied every advantage the other enjoyed. Doing no wrong, he must have the worst reputation for wrong-doing, to test whether his virtue is proof against all that comes of having a bad name; and under this lifelong imputation of wickedness, let him hold on his course of justice unwavering to the point of death. And so, when the two men have carried their justice and injustice to the last extreme, we may judge which is the happier.

THE GOOD AS THE END OF ACTION

ARISTOTLE

Every art and every investigation, and likewise every practical pursuit or undertaking, seems to aim at some good: hence it has been well said that the Good is that at which all things aim. (It is true that a certain variety is to be observed among the ends at which the arts and sciences aim: in some cases the activity of practising the art is itself the end, whereas in others the end is some product over and above the mere exercise of the art; and in the arts whose ends are certain things beside the practice of the arts themselves, these products are essentially superior in value to the activities.) But as there are numerous pursuits and arts and sciences, it follows that their ends are correspondingly numerous: for instance, the end of the science of medicine is health, that of the art of shipbuilding a vessel, that of strategy victory, that of domestic economy wealth. Now in cases where several such pursuits are subordinate to some single faculty—as bridle-making and the other trades concerned with horses' harness are subordinate to horsemanship, and this and every other military pursuit to the science of strategy, and similarly other arts to different arts again—in all these cases, I say, the ends of the master arts are things more to be desired than the ends of the arts subordinate to them; since the latter ends are only pursued for the sake of the former. (And it makes no difference whether the ends of the pursuits are the activities themselves or some other thing beside these, as in the case of the sciences mentioned.)

If therefore among the ends at which our actions aim there be one which we will for its own sake, while we will the others only for the sake

This selection is reprinted from *Nicomachean Ethics*, Book I, translated by H. Rackham, 1926, by permission of Harvard University Press, Cambridge, Mass., and the Loeb Classical Library.

of this, and if we do not choose everything for the sake of something else (which would obviously result in a process *ad infinitum*, so that all desire would be futile and vain), it is clear that this one ultimate End must be the Good, and indeed the Supreme Good. Will not then a knowledge of this Supreme Good be also of great practical importance for the conduct of life? Will it not better enable us to attain our proper object, like archers having a target to aim at? If this be so, we ought to make an attempt to comprehend at all events in outline what exactly this Supreme Good is, and of which of the sciences or faculties it is the object.

Now it would seem that this supreme End must be the object of the most authoritative of the sciences—some science which is pre-eminently a master-craft. But such is manifestly the science of Politics; for it is this that ordains which of the sciences are to exist in states, and what branches of knowledge the different classes of the citizens are to learn, and up to what point; and we observe that even the most highly esteemed of the faculties, such as strategy, domestic economy, oratory, are subordinate to the political science. Inasmuch then as the rest of the sciences are employed by this one, and as it moreover lays down laws as to what people shall do and what things they shall refrain from doing, the end of this science must include the ends of all the others. Therefore, the Good of man must be the end of the science of Politics. For even though it be the case that the Good is the same for the individual and for the state, nevertheless, the good of the state is manifestly a greater and more perfect good, both to attain and to preserve. To secure the good of one person only is better than nothing; but to secure the good of a nation or a state is a nobler and more divine achievement.

This then being its aim, our investigation is in a sense the study of Politics.

Now our treatment of this science will be adequate, if it achieves that amount of precision which belongs to its subject matter. The same exactness must not be expected in all departments of philosophy alike, any more than in all the products of the arts and crafts. The subjects studied by political science are Moral Nobility and Justice; but these conceptions involve much difference of opinion and uncertainty, so that they are sometimes believed to be mere conventions and to have no real existence in the nature of things. And a similar uncertainty surrounds the conception of the Good, because it frequently occurs that good things have harmful consequences: people have before now been ruined by wealth, and in other cases courage has cost men their lives. We must therefore be content if, in dealing with subjects and starting from premises thus uncertain, we succeed in presenting a rough outline of the truth: when our subjects and our premises are merely generalities, it is enough if we arrive at generally valid conclusions. Accordingly we may ask the student also to accept the various views we put forward in the same spirit; for it is the mark of an educated mind to expect that amount of exactness in each kind which the nature of the particular subject admits. It is equally unreasonable to accept merely probable conclusions from a mathematician, and to demand strict demonstration from an orator.

Again, each man judges correctly those matters with which he is acquainted; it is of these that he is a competent critic. To criticize a particular subject, therefore, a man must have been trained in that subject: to be a good critic generally, he must have had an all-round education. Hence the young are not fit to be students of Political Science. For they have no experience of life and conduct, and it is these that supply the premises and subject matter of this branch of philosophy. And moreover they are led by their feelings; so that they will study the subject to no purpose or advantage, since the end of this science is not knowledge but action. And it makes no difference whether they are young in years or immature in character: the defect is not a question of time, it is because their life and its various aims are guided by feeling; for to such persons their knowledge is of no use, any more than it is to persons of defective self-restraint. But Moral Science may be of great value to those who guide their desires and actions by principle.

Let so much suffice by way of introduction as to the student of the subject, the spirit in which our conclusions are to be received, and the object that we set before us.

To resume, inasmuch as all studies and undertakings are directed to the attainment of some good, let us discuss what it is that we pronounce to be the aim of Politics, that is, what is the highest of all the goods that action can achieve. As far as the name goes, we may almost say that the great majority of mankind are agreed about this; for both the multitude and persons of refinement speak of it as Happiness, and conceive 'the good life' or 'doing well' to be the same thing as 'being happy.' But what constitutes happiness is a matter of dispute; and the popular account of it is not the same as that given by the philosophers. Ordinary people identify it with some obvious and visible good, such as pleasure or wealth or honour—some say one thing and some another, indeed very often the same man says different things at different times: when he falls sick he thinks health is happiness, when he is poor, wealth. At other times, feeling conscious of their own ignorance, men admire those who propound something grand and above their heads; and it has been held by some thinkers that beside the many good things we have mentioned, there exists another Good, that is good in itself, and stands to all those goods as the cause of their being good.

Now perhaps it would be a somewhat fruitless task to review all the different opinions that are held. It will suffice to examine those which are most widely accepted, or which seem to be supported by some measure of reason.

And we must not overlook the distinction between arguments that start from first principles and those that lead to first principles. This is a matter that was rightly raised by Plato, who used to enquire whether the true procedure is to start from or to lead up to one's first principles, as in a race-course one may run from the judges to the far end of the track or the reverse. Now no doubt it is proper to start from the known. But 'the known' has two meanings—'what is familiar to us,' which is one thing, and 'what is intelligible in itself,' which is another. Perhaps then for us at all events it is proper to start from what is known to us. This is why in order to be a competent student of the Right and Just, and in short of the topics of Politics in general, the pupil is bound to have had a right moral upbringing. For the starting-point or first principle is the fact that a thing is so; if this be satisfactorily ascertained, there will be no need also to know the reason why it is so. And the man of good moral training knows first principles already, or can easily acquire them. As for the person who neither knows nor can learn, let him hear the words of Hesiod:

> Best is the man who can himself advise;
> He too is good who hearkens to the wise;
> But who, himself being witless, will not heed
> Another's wisdom, is a fool indeed.

But let us continue from the point where we digressed. To judge from the recognized types of Lives, the more or less reasoned conceptions of the Good or Happiness that prevail are the following. On the one hand the generality of men and the most vulgar identify the Good with pleasure, and accordingly look no higher than the Life of Enjoyment—for there are three specially prominent Lives, the one just mentioned, the Life of Politics, and thirdly, the Life of Contemplation. The generality of mankind then show themselves to be utterly slavish, by preferring what is only a life for cattle; but they get a hearing for their view as reasonable because many persons of high position share the feelings of Sardanapallus.

Men of refinement, on the other hand, and men of action think that the Good is honour—for this may be said to be the end of the Life of Politics. But honour after all seems too superficial to be the Good for which we are seeking; since it appears to depend on those who confer it more than on him upon whom it is conferred, whereas we instinctively feel that the Good must be something proper to its possessor and not easy to be taken away from him. Moreover men's motive in pursuing honour seems to be to assure themselves of their own merit; at least they seek to be honoured by men of judgement and by people who know them, that is, they desire to be honoured on the ground of virtue. It is clear therefore that in the opinion at all events of men of action, virtue is a greater good than honour; and one might perhaps accordingly suppose that virtue rather than honour is the end of the Political Life. But even virtue proves on examination to be too incomplete to be the End; since it appears possible to possess it while you are asleep, or without putting it into practice throughout the whole of your life; and also for the virtuous man to suffer the greatest misery and misfortune—though no one would pronounce a man living a life of misery to be happy, unless for the sake of maintaining a paradox. But we need not pursue this subject, since it has been sufficiently treated in the ordinary discussions.

The third type of life is the Life of Contemplation, which we shall consider in the sequel.

The Life of Money-making is a hard kind of life; and clearly wealth is not the Good we are in search of, for it is only good as being useful, a means to something else. On this score indeed one might conceive the ends before mentioned to have a better claim, for they are approved for their own sakes. But even they do not really seem to be the Supreme Good; however, many arguments against them have been disseminated, so we may dismiss them.

But perhaps it is desirable that we should examine the notion of a Universal Good, and review the difficulties that it involves, although such an enquiry goes against the grain because of our friendship for the authors of the Theory of Ideas. Still perhaps it would appear desirable, and indeed it would seem to be obligatory, especially for a philosopher, to sacrifice even one's closest personal ties in defence of the truth. Both are dear to us, but it is a sacred duty to put truth first.

The originators of this theory, then, used not to postulate Ideas of groups of things in which they posited an order of priority and posteriority (for which reason they did not construct an Idea of numbers in general). But Good is predicated alike in the Categories of Substance, of Quality, and of Relation; yet the Absolute, or Substance, is prior in nature to the Relative, which seems to be a sort of offshoot or 'accident' of Substance; so that there cannot be a common Idea corresponding to the absolutely good and the relatively good.

Again, the word 'good' is used in as many senses as the word 'is'; for we may predicate good in the Category of Substance, for instance of God, or intelligence; in that of Quality, of the virtues; in that of Quantity, of the due amount; in that of Relation, of the useful; in that of Time, of a favourable opportunity; in that of Place, of a suitable 'habitat'; and so on. So clearly good cannot be a single and universal general notion; if it were, it would not be predicable in all the Categories, but only in one.

Again, things that come under a single Idea must be objects of a single science; hence there ought to be a single science dealing with all good things. But as a matter of fact there are a number of sciences even for the goods in one Category, for example, opportunity: for opportunity in war comes under the science of strategy, in disease under that of medicine; and the due amount in diet comes under medicine, in bodily exercise under gymnastics.

One might also raise the question what precisely they mean by their expression 'the Ideal so-and-so,' seeing that one and the same definition of man applies both to 'the Ideal man' and to 'man,' for in so far as both are man, there will be no difference between them; and if so, no more will there be any difference between 'the Ideal Good' and 'Good' in so far as both are good. Nor yet will the Ideal Good be any more good because it is eternal, seeing that a white thing that lasts a long time is no whiter than one that lasts only a day.

The Pythagoreans seem to give a more probable doctrine on the subject of the Good when they place Unity in their column of goods; and indeed Speusippus appears to have followed them. But this subject must be left for another discussion.

We can descry an objection that may be raised against our arguments on the ground that the theory in question was not intended to apply to every sort of good, and that only things pursued and accepted for their own sake are pronounced good as belonging to a single species, while things productive or preservative of these in any way, or preventive of their opposites, are said to be good as a means to these, and in a different sense. Clearly then the term 'goods' would have two meanings, (1) things good in themselves and (2) things good as a means to these; let us then separate things good in themselves from things useful as means, and consider whether the former are called good because they fall under a single Idea. But what sort of things is one to class as good in themselves? Are they not those things which are sought after even without any accessory advantage, such as wisdom, sight, and certain pleasures and honours? for even if we also pursue these things as means to something else, still one would class them among things good in themselves. Or is there nothing else good in itself except the Idea? If so, the species will be of no use. If on the contrary the class of things good in themselves includes these objects, the same notion of good ought to be manifested in all of them, just as the same notion of white is manifested in snow and in white paint. But as a matter of fact the notions of honour and wisdom and pleasure, as being good, are different and distinct. Therefore, good is not a general term corresponding to a single Idea.

But in what sense then are different things called good? For they do not seem to be a case of things that bear the same name merely by chance. Possibly things are called good in virtue of being derived from one good; or because they all contribute to one good. Or perhaps it is rather by way of a proportion: that is, as sight is good in the body, so intelligence is good in the soul, and similarly another thing in something else.

Perhaps however this question must be dismissed for the present, since a detailed investigation of it belongs more properly to another branch of philosophy. And likewise with the Idea of the Good; for if the goodness predicated of various things in common actually is a unity or something existing separately and absolute, it clearly will not be practicable or attainable by man; but the Good which we are now seeking is a good within human reach.

But possibly someone may think that to know the Ideal Good may be desirable as an aid to achieving those goods which are practicable and attainable: having the Ideal Good as a pattern we shall more easily know what things are good for us, and knowing them, obtain them. Now it is true that this argument has a certain plausibility; but it does not seem to square with the actual procedure of the sciences. For these all aim at some good, and seek to make up their deficiencies, but they do not trouble about a knowledge of the Ideal Good. Yet if it were so potent an aid, it is improbable that all the professors of the arts and sciences should not know it, nor even seek to discover it. Moreover, it is not easy to see *how* a knowledge of the Ideal Good will help a weaver or carpenter in the practice of his own craft, or how anybody will be a better physician or general for having contemplated the absolute Idea. In fact it does not appear that the physician studies even health in the abstract; he studies the health of the human being—or rather of some particular human being, for it is individuals that he has to cure.

Let us here conclude our discussion of this subject.

We may now return to the Good which is the object of our search, and try to find out what exactly it can be. For good appears to be one thing in one pursuit or art and another in another: it is different in medicine from what it is in strategy, and so on with the rest of the arts. What definition of the Good then will hold true in all the arts? Perhaps we may define it as that for the sake of which everything else is done. This applies to something different in each different art—to health in the case of medicine, to victory in that of strategy, to a house in architecture, and to something else in each of the other arts; but in every pursuit or undertaking it describes the end of that pursuit or undertaking, since in all of them it is for the sake of the end that everything else is done. Hence if there be something which is the end of all the things done by human action, this will be the practicable Good—or if there be several such ends, the sum of these will be the Good. Thus by changing its ground the argument has reached the same result as before. We must attempt however to render this still more precise.

Now there do appear to be several ends at which our actions aim; but as we choose some of them—for instance wealth, or flutes, and instruments generally—as a means to something else, it is clear that not all of them are final ends; whereas the Supreme Good seems to be something final or perfect. Consequently if there be some one thing which alone is a final end, this thing—or if there be several final ends, the one among them which is the most final—will be the Good which we are seeking. In speaking of degrees of finality, we mean that a thing pursued as an end in itself is more final than one pursued as a means to something else, and that a thing never chosen as a means to anything else is more final than things chosen both as ends in themselves and as means to that thing; and accordingly a thing chosen always as an end and never as a means we call absolutely final. Now happiness above all else appears to be absolutely final in this sense, since we always choose it for its own sake and never as a means to something else; whereas honour, pleasure, intelligence, and excellence in its various forms, we choose indeed for their own sakes (since we should be glad to have each of them although no extraneous advantage resulted from it), but we also choose them for the sake of happiness, in the belief that they will be a means to our securing it. But no one chooses happiness for the sake of honour, pleasure, etc., nor as a means to anything whatever other than itself.

The same conclusion also appears to follow from a consideration of the self-sufficiency of happiness—for it is felt that the final good must be a thing sufficient in itself. The term self-sufficient, however, we employ with reference not to oneself alone, living a life of isolation, but also to one's parents and children and wife, and one's friends and fellow citizens in general, since man is by nature a social being. On the other hand a limit has to be assumed in these relationships; for if the list be extended to one's ancestors and descendants and to the friends of one's friends, it will go on *ad infinitum.* But this is a point that must be considered later on; we take a self-sufficient thing to mean a thing which merely standing by itself alone renders life desirable and lacking in nothing, and such a thing we deem happiness to be. Moreover, we think happiness the most desirable of all good things without being itself reckoned as one among the rest; for if it were so reckoned, it is clear that we should consider it more desirable when even the smallest of other good things were combined with it, since this addition would result in a larger total of good, and of two goods the greater is always the more desirable.

Happiness, therefore, being found to be something final and self-sufficient, is the End at which all actions aim.

To say however that the Supreme Good is happiness will probably appear a truism; we still require a more explicit account of what constitutes happiness. Perhaps then we may arrive at this by ascertaining what is man's function. For the goodness or efficiency of a flute-player or sculptor or craftsman of any sort, and in general of anybody who has some function or business to perform, is thought to reside in that function; and similarly it may be held that the good of man resides in the function of man, if he has a function.

Are we then to suppose that, while the carpenter and the shoemaker have definite functions or businesses belonging to them, man as such has none, and is not designed by nature to fulfil any function? Must we not rather assume that, just as the eye, the hand, the foot and each of the various members of the body manifestly has a certain function of its own, so a human being also has a certain function over and above all the functions of his particular members? What then precisely can this function be? The mere act of living appears to be shared even by plants, whereas we are looking for the function peculiar to man; we must therefore set aside the vital activity of nutrition and growth. Next in the scale will come some form of sentient life; but this too appears to be shared by horses, oxen, and animals generally. There remains therefore what may be called the practical life of the rational part of man. (This part has two divisions, one rational as obedient to principle, the other as possessing principle and exercising intelligence.) Rational life again has two meanings; let us assume that we are here concerned with the active exercise of the rational faculty, since this seems to be the more proper sense of the term. If then the function of man is the active exercise of the soul's faculties in conformity with rational principle, or at all events not in dissociation from rational principle, and if we acknowledge the function of an individual and of a good individual of the same class (for instance, a harper and a good harper, and so generally with all classes) to be generically the same, the qualification of the latter's superiority in excellence being added to the function in his case (I mean that if the function of a harper is to play the harp, that of a good harper is to play the harp well): if this is so, and if we declare that the function of man is a certain form of life, and define that form of life as the exercise of the soul's faculties and activities in association with rational principle, and say that the function of a good man is to perform these activities well and rightly, and if a function is well performed when it is performed in accordance with its own proper excellence—if then all this be so, the Good of man proves to be the active exercise of his soul's faculties in conformity with excellence or virtue, or if there be several human excellences or virtues, in conformity with the best and most perfect among them.

Moreover, to be happy takes a complete lifetime. For one swallow does not make summer, nor does one fine day; and similarly one day or a brief period of happiness does not make a man supremely blessed and happy.

THE METAPHYSIC OF MORALS

IMMANUEL KANT

Nothing can possibly be conceived in the world, or even out of it, which can be called good without qualification, except a *good will.* Intelligence, wit, judgment, and the other *talents* of the mind, however they may be named, or courage, resolution, perseverance, as qualities of temperament, are undoubtedly good and desirable in many respects; but these gifts of nature may also become extremely bad and mischievous if the will which is to make use of them, and which, therefore, constitutes what is called *character*, is not good. It is the same with the *gifts of fortune*. Power, riches, honor, even health, and the general well-being and contentment with one's condition which is called *happiness*, inspire pride, and often presumption, if there is not a good will to correct the influence of these on the mind, and with this also to rectify the whole principle of acting, and adapt it to its end. The sight of a being who is not adorned with a single feature of a pure and good will, enjoying unbroken prosperity, can never give pleasure to an impartial rational spectator. Thus a good will appears to constitute the indispensable condition even of being worthy of happiness.

There are even some qualities which are of service to this good will

Reprinted from *Fundamental Principles of the Metaphysic of Morals,* translated by Thomas K. Abbott, from *Kant's Critique of Practical Reason and Other Works on the Theory of Ethics* (1898), First and Second Sections, with omissions.

itself, and may facilitate its action, yet which have no intrinsic unconditional value, but always presuppose a good will, and this qualifies the esteem that we justly have for them, and does not permit us to regard them as absolutely good. Moderation in the affections and passions, self-control, and calm deliberation are not only good in many respects, but even seem to constitute part of the intrinsic worth of the person; but they are far from deserving to be called good without qualification, although they have been so unconditionally praised by the ancients. For without the principles of a good will, they may become extremely bad; and the coolness of a villain not only makes him far more dangerous, but also directly makes him more abominable in our eyes than he would have been without it.

A good will is good not because of what it performs or effects, not by its aptness for the attainment of some proposed end, but simply by virtue of the volition—that is, it is good in itself, and considered by itself is to be esteemed much higher than all that can be brought about by it in favor of any inclination, nay, even of the sum-total of all inclinations. Even if it should happen that, owing to special disfavor of fortune, or the niggardly provision of a step-motherly nature, this will should wholly lack power to accomplish its purpose, if with its greatest efforts it should yet achieve nothing, and there should remain only the good will (not, to be sure, a mere wish, but the summoning of all means in our power), then, like a jewel, it would still shine by its own light, as a thing which has its whole value in itself. Its usefulness or fruitlessness can neither add to nor take away anything from this value. It would be, as it were, only the setting to enable us to handle it the more conveniently in common commerce, or to attract to it the attention of those who are not yet connoisseurs, but not to recommend it to true connoisseurs, or to determine its value.

There is, however, something so strange in this idea of the absolute value of the mere will, in which no account is taken of its utility, that notwithstanding the thorough assent of even common reason to the idea, yet a suspicion must arise that it may perhaps really be the product of mere high-flown fancy, and that we may have misunderstood the purpose of nature in assigning reason as the governor of our will. Therefore we will examine this idea from this point of view.

In the physical constitution of an organized being, that is, a being adapted suitably to the purposes of life, we assume it as a fundamental principle that no organ for any purpose will be found but what is also the fittest and best adapted for that purpose. Now in a being which has reason and a will, if the proper object of nature were its *conservation*, its *welfare*, in a word, its *happiness*, then nature would have hit upon a very bad arrangement in selecting the reason of the creature to carry out this purpose. For all the actions which the creature has to perform with a view to this purpose, and the whole rule of its conduct, would be far more surely prescribed to it by instinct, and that end would have been attained thereby much more certainly than it ever can be by reason. Should reason have been communicated to this favored creature over and above, it must only have served it to contemplate the happy constitution of its nature, to admire it, to congratulate itself thereon, and to feel thankful for it to the beneficent cause, but not that it should subject its desires to that weak and delusive guidance, and meddle bunglingly with the purpose of nature. In a word, nature would have taken care that reason should not break forth into *practical exercise*, nor have the presumption, with its weak insight, to think out for itself the plan of happiness and of the means of attaining it. Nature would not only have taken on herself the choice of the ends but also of the means, and with wise foresight would have entrusted both to instinct.

And, in fact, we find that the more a cultivated reason applies itself with deliberate purpose to the enjoyment of life and happiness, so much the more does the man fail of true satisfaction. And from this circumstance there arises in many, if they are candid enough to confess it, a certain degree of *misology*, that is, hatred of reason, especially in the case of those who are most experienced in the use of it, because after calculating all the advantages they derive—I do not say from the invention of all the arts of common luxury, but even from the sciences (which seem to them to be after all only a luxury of the understanding)—they find that they have, in fact, only brought more trouble on their shoulders rather than gained in happiness; and they end by envying rather than despising the more common stamp of men who keep closer to the guidance of mere instinct, and do not allow their reason much influence on their conduct. And this we must admit, that the judgment of those who would very much lower the lofty eulogies of the advantages which reason gives us in regard to the happiness and satisfaction of life, or who would even reduce them below zero, is by no means morose or ungrateful to the goodness with which the world is governed, but that there lies at the root of these judgments the idea that our existence has a different and far nobler end, for which, and not for happiness, reason is properly intended, and which must, therefore, be regarded as the supreme condition to which the private ends of man must, for the most part, be postponed.

For as reason is not competent to guide the will with certainty in regard to its objects and the satisfaction of all our wants (which it to some extent even multiplies), this being an end to which an implanted instinct would have led with much greater certainty; and since, nevertheless, reason is imparted to us as a practical faculty, that is, as one which is to have influence on the *will*, therefore, admitting that nature generally in the distribution of her capacities has adapted the means to the end, its true destination must be to produce a *will*, not merely good as a *means* to something else, but *good in itself*, for which reason was absolutely necessary. This will then, though not indeed the sole and complete good, must be the supreme good and the condition of every other, even of the desire of happiness. Under these circumstances, there is nothing inconsistent with the wisdom of nature in the fact that the cultivation of the reason, which is requisite for the first and unconditional purpose, does in many ways interfere, at least in this life, with the attainment of the second, which is always conditional—namely, happiness. Nay, it may even reduce it to nothing, without nature thereby failing of her purpose. For reason recognizes the establishment of a good will as its highest practical destination, and in attaining this purpose is capable only of a satisfaction of its own proper kind, namely, that from the attainment of an end, which end again is determined by reason only, notwithstanding that this may involve many a disappointment to the ends of inclination.

We have then to develop the notion of a will which deserves to be highly esteemed for itself, and is good without a view to anything further, a notion which exists already in the sound natural understanding, requiring rather to be cleared up than to be taught, and which in estimating the value of our actions always takes the first place and constitutes the condition of all the rest. In order to do this, we will take the notion of duty, which includes that of a good will, although implying certain subjective restrictions and hindrances. These, however, far from concealing it or rendering it unrecognizable, rather bring it out by contrast and make it shine forth so much the brighter.

I omit here all actions which are already recognized as inconsistent with duty, although they may be useful for this or that purpose, for with these the question whether they are done *from duty* cannot arise at all, since they even conflict with it. I also set aside those actions which really conform to duty, but to which men have *no* direct *inclination*, performing them because they are impelled thereto by some other inclination. For in this case we can readily distinguish whether the action which agrees with duty is done *from duty* or from a selfish view. It is much harder to make this distinction when the action accords with duty, and the subject has besides a *direct* inclination to it. For example, it is always a matter of duty that a dealer should not overcharge an inexperienced purchaser; and wherever there is much commerce the prudent tradesman does not overcharge, but keeps a fixed price for everyone, so that a child buys of him as well as any other. Men are thus *honestly* served; but this is not enough to make us believe that the tradesman has so acted from duty and from principles of honesty; his own advantage required it; it is out of the question in this case to suppose that he might besides have a direct inclination in favor of the buyers, so that, as it were, from love he should give no advantage to one over another. Accordingly the action was done neither from duty nor from direct inclination, but merely with a selfish view.

On the other hand, it is a duty to maintain one's life; and, in addition, everyone has also a direct inclination to do so. But on this account the often anxious care which most men take for it has no intrinsic worth, and their maxim has no moral import. They preserve their life *as duty requires*, no doubt, but not *because duty requires*. On the other hand, if adversity and hopeless sorrow have completely taken away the relish for life, if the unfortunate one, strong in mind, indignant at his fate rather than desponding or dejected, wishes for death, and yet preserves his life without loving it—not from inclination or fear, but from duty—then his maxim has a moral worth.

To be beneficent when we can is a duty; and besides this, there are many minds so sympathetically constituted that, without any other motive of vanity or self-interest, they find a pleasure in spreading joy around them, and can take delight in the satisfaction of others so far as it is their own work. But I maintain that in such a case an action of this kind, however proper, however amiable it may be, has nevertheless no true moral worth, but is on a level with other inclinations, for example, the inclination to honor, which, if it is happily directed to that which is in fact of public utility and accordant with duty, and consequently honorable, deserves praise and encouragement, but not esteem. For the maxim lacks the moral import, namely, that such actions be done *from duty*, not from inclination. Put the case that the mind of that philanthropist was clouded by sorrow of his own, extinguishing all sympathy with the lot of others, and that while he still has the power to benefit others in distress, he is not touched by their trouble because he is absorbed with his own; and now suppose that he tears himself out of this dead insensibility and performs the action without any inclination to it, but simply from duty, then first has his action its genuine moral worth. Further still, if nature has put little sympathy in the heart of this or that man, if he, supposed to be an upright man, is by temperament cold and indifferent to the sufferings of others, perhaps because in respect of his own he is provided with the special gift of patience and fortitude, and supposes, or even requires, that others should have the same—and such a man would certainly not be the meanest product of nature—but if nature had not specially framed him for a philanthropist, would he not still find in himself a source from whence to give himself a far higher worth than that of a good-natured temperament could be? Unquestionably. It is just in this that the moral worth of the character is brought out which is incomparably the highest of all, namely, that he is beneficent, not from inclination, but from duty.

To secure one's own happiness is a duty, at least indirectly; for discontent with one's condition, under a pressure of many anxieties and amidst unsatisfied wants, might easily become a great *temptation to transgression of duty*. But here again, without looking to duty, all men have already the strongest and most intimate inclination to happiness, because it is just in this idea that all inclinations are combined in one total. But the precept of happiness is often of such a sort that it greatly interferes with some inclinations, and yet a man cannot form any definite and certain conception of the sum of satisfaction of all of them which is called happiness. It is not then to be wondered at that a single inclination, definite both as to what it promises and as to the time within which it can be gratified, is often able to overcome such a fluctuating idea, and that a gouty patient, for instance, can choose to enjoy what he likes, and to suffer what he may, since, according to his calculation, on this occasion at least, he has [only] not sacrificed the enjoyment of the present moment to a possibly mistaken expectation of a happiness which is supposed to be found in health. But even in this case, if the general desire for happiness did not influence his will, and supposing that in his particular case health was not a necessary element in this calculation, there yet remains in this, as in all other cases, this law—namely, that he should promote his happiness not from inclination but from duty, and by this would his conduct first acquire true moral worth.

It is in this manner, undoubtedly, that we are to understand those passages of Scripture also in which we are commanded to love our neighbor, even our enemy. For love, as an affection, cannot be commanded, but beneficence for duty's sake may, even though we are not impelled to it by any inclination—nay, are even repelled by a natural and unconquerable aversion. This is *practical* love, and not *pathological*—a love which is seated in the will, and not in the propensions of sense—in principles of action and not of tender sympathy; and it is this love alone which can be commanded.

The second proposition is: That an action done from duty derives its moral worth, *not from the purpose* which is to be attained by it, but from the maxim by which it is determined, and therefore does not depend on the realization of the object of the action, but merely on the *principle of volition* by which the action has taken place, without regard to any object of desire. It is clear from what precedes that the purposes which we may have in view in our actions, or their effects regarded as ends and springs of the will, cannot give to actions any unconditional or moral worth. In what, then, can their worth lie if it is not to consist in the will and in reference to its expected effect? It cannot lie anywhere but in the *principle of the will* without regard to the ends which can be attained by the action. For the will stands between its *a priori* principle, which is formal, and its *a posteriori* spring, which is material, as between two roads, and as it must be determined by something, it follows that it must be determined by the formal principle of volition when an action is done from duty, in which case every material principle has been withdrawn from it.

The third proposition, which is a consequence of the two preceding, I would express thus: *Duty is the necessity of acting from respect for the law.* I may have *inclination* for an object as the effect of my proposed action, but I cannot have *respect* for it just for this reason that it is an effect and not an energy of will. Similarly, I cannot have respect for inclination, whether my own or another's; I can at most, if my own, approve it; if another's, sometimes even love it, that is, look on it as favorable to my own interest. It is only what is connected with my will as a principle, by no means as an effect—what does not subserve my inclination, but overpowers it, or at least in case of choice excludes it from its calculation—in other words, simply the law of itself, which can be an object of respect, and hence a command. Now an action done from duty must wholly exclude the influence of inclination, and with it every object of the will, so that nothing remains which can determine the will except objectively the *law*, and subjectively *pure respect* for this practical law, and consequently the maxim* that I should follow this law even to the thwarting of all my inclinations.

Thus the moral worth of an action does not lie in the effect expected from it, nor in any principle of action which requires to borrow its motive from this expected effect. For all these effects—agreeableness of one's condition, and even the promotion of the happiness of others—could have been also brought about by other causes, so that for this there would have been no need of the will of a rational being; whereas it is in this alone that the supreme and unconditional good can be found. The pre-eminent good which we call moral can therefore consist in nothing else than *the conception of law* in itself, *which certainly is only possible in a rational being*, in so far as this conception, and not the expected effect, determines the will. This is a good which is already present in the person who acts accordingly, and we have not to wait for it to appear first in the result.**

But what sort of law can that be the conception of which must determine the will, even without paying any regard to the effect expected from it, in order that this will may be called good absolutely and without qualification? As I have deprived the will of every impulse which could arise to it from obedience to any law, there remains nothing but the universal conformity of its actions to law in general, which alone is to serve the will as a principle, that is, I am never to act otherwise than so *that I could also will that my maxim should become a universal law.* Here, now, it is the simple conformity to law in general, without assuming any particular law applicable to certain actions, that serves the will as its principle, and must so serve it if duty is not to be a vain delusion and a chimerical

* A *maxim* is the subjective principle of volition. The objective principle (*i.e.*, that which would also serve subjectively as a practical principle to all rational beings if reason had full power over the faculty of desire) is the practical *law.*

** It might be here objected to me that I take refuge behind the word *respect* in an obscure feeling, instead of giving a distinct solution of the question by a concept of the reason. But although respect is a feeling, it is not a feeling *received* through influence, but is *self-wrought* by a rational concept, and, therefore, is specifically distinct from all feelings of the former kind, which may be referred either to inclination or fear. What I recognize immediately as a law for me, I recognize with respect. This merely signifies the consciousness that my will is *subordinate* to a law, without the intervention of other influences on my sense. The immediate determination of the will by the law, and the consciousness of this, is called *respect*, so that this is regarded as an *effect* of the law on the subject, and not as the *cause* of it. Respect is properly the conception of a worth which thwarts my self-love. Accordingly it is something which is considered neither as an object of inclination nor of fear, although it has something analogous to both. The *object* of respect is the *law* only, that is, the law which we impose on *ourselves*, and yet recognize as necessary in itself. As a law, we are subjected to it without consulting self-love; as imposed by us on ourselves, it is a result of our will. In the former aspect it has an analogy to fear, in the latter to inclination. Respect for a person is properly only respect for the law (of honesty, etc.) of which he gives us an example. Since we also look on the improvement of our talents as a duty, we consider that we see in a person of talents, as it were, the *example of a law* (viz. to become like him in this by exercise), and this constitutes our respect. All so-called moral *interest* consists simply in *respect* for the law.

notion. The common reason of men in its practical judgments perfectly coincides with this, and always has in view the principle here suggested. Let the question be, for example: May I when in distress make a promise with the intention not to keep it? I readily distinguish here between the two significations which the question may have: whether it is prudent or whether it is right to make a false promise? The former may undoubtedly often be the case. I see clearly indeed that it is not enough to extricate myself from a present difficulty by means of this subterfuge, but it must be well considered whether there may not hereafter spring from this lie much greater inconvenience than that from which I now free myself, and as, with all my supposed *cunning*, the consequences cannot be so easily foreseen but that credit once lost may be much more injurious to me than any mischief which I seek to avoid at present, it should be considered whether it would not be more *prudent* to act herein according to a universal maxim, and to make it a habit to promise nothing except with the intention of keeping it. But it is soon clear to me that such a maxim will still only be based on the fear of consequences. Now it is a wholly different thing to be truthful from duty, and to be so from apprehension of injurious consequences. In the first case, the very notion of the action already implies a law for me; in the second case, I must first look about elsewhere to see what results may be combined with it which would affect myself. For to deviate from the principle of duty is beyond all doubt wicked; but to be unfaithful to my maxim of prudence may often be very advantageous to me, although to abide by it is certainly safer. The shortest way, however, and an unerring one, to discover the answer to this question whether a lying promise is consistent with duty, is to ask myself, Should I be content that my maxim (to extricate myself from difficulty by a false promise) should hold good as a universal law, for myself as well as for others; and should I be able to say to myself, "Every one may make a deceitful promise when he finds himself in a difficulty from which he cannot otherwise extricate himself"? Then I presently become aware that, while I can will the lie, I can by no means will that lying should be a universal law. For with such a law there would be no promises at all, since it would be in vain to allege my intention in regard to my future actions to those who would not believe this allegation, or if they over-hastily did so, would pay me back in my own coin. Hence my maxim, as soon as it should be made a universal law, would necessarily destroy itself.

I do not, therefore, need any far-reaching penetration to discern what I have to do in order that my will may be morally good. Inexperienced in the course of the world, incapable of being prepared for all its contingencies, I only ask myself: Canst thou also will that thy maxim should be a universal law? If not, then it must be rejected, and that not because of a disadvantage accruing from it to myself or even to others, but because it cannot enter as a principle into a possible universal legislation, and reason extorts from me immediate respect for such legislation. I do not indeed as yet *discern* on what this respect is based (this the philosopher may inquire), but at least I understand this—that it is an estimation of the worth which far outweighs all worth of what is recommended by inclination, and that the necessity of acting from *pure* respect for the practical law is what constitutes duty, to which every other motive must give place because it is the condition of a will being good *in itself*, and the worth of such a will is above everything.

Thus, then, without quitting the moral knowledge of common human reason, we have arrived at its principle. And although, no doubt, common men do not conceive it in such an abstract and universal form, yet they always have it really before their eyes and use it as the standard of their decision. Here it would be easy to show how, with this compass in hand, men are well able to distinguish, in every case that occurs, what is good, what bad, conformably to duty or inconsistent with it, if, without in the least teaching them anything new, we only, like Socrates, direct their attention to the principle they themselves employ; and that, therefore, we do not need science and philosophy to know what we should do to be honest and good, yea, even wise and virtuous. Indeed we might well have conjectured beforehand that the knowledge of what every man is bound to do, and therefore also to know, would be within the reach of every man, even the commonest. Here we cannot forbear admiration when we see how great an advantage the practical judgment has over the theoretical in the common understanding of men. In the latter, if common reason ventures to depart from the laws of experience and from the perceptions of the senses, it falls into mere inconceivabilities and self-contradictions, at least into a chaos of uncertainty, obscurity, and instability. But in the practical sphere it is just when the common understanding excludes all sensible springs from practical laws that its power of judgment begins to show itself to advantage. It then becomes even subtle, whether it be that it chicanes with its own conscience or with other claims respecting what is to be called right, or whether it desires for its own instruction to determine honestly the worth of actions; and, in the latter case, it may even have as good a hope of hitting the mark as any philosopher whatever can promise himself. Nay, it is almost more sure of doing so, because the philosopher cannot have any other principle, while he may easily perplex his judgment by a multitude of considerations foreign to the matter, and so turn aside from the right way. Would it not therefore be wiser in moral concerns to acquiesce in the judgment of common reason, or at most only to call in philosophy for the purpose of rendering the system of morals more complete and intelligible, and its rules more convenient for use (especially for disputation), but not so as to draw off the common understanding from its happy simplicity, or to bring it by means of philosophy into a new path of inquiry and instruction?

Innocence is indeed a glorious thing; only, on the other hand, it is very sad that it cannot well maintain itself, and is easily seduced. On this account even wisdom—which otherwise consists more in conduct than in knowledge—yet has need of science, not in order to learn from it, but to secure for its precepts admission and permanence. Against all the commands of duty which reason represents to man as so deserving of respect, he feels in himself a powerful counterpoise in his wants and inclinations, the entire satisfaction of which he sums up under the name of happiness. Now reason issues its commands unyieldingly, without promising anything to the inclinations, and, as it were, with disregard and contempt for these claims, which are so impetuous and at the same time so plausible, and which will not allow themselves to be suppressed by any command. Hence there arises a natural *dialectic*, that is, a disposition to argue against these strict laws of duty and to question their validity, or at least their purity and strictness; and, if possible, to make them more accordant with our wishes and inclinations, that is to say, to corrupt them at their very source and entirely to destroy their worth—a thing which even common practical reason cannot ultimately call good.

. . .

Everything in nature works according to laws. Rational beings alone have the faculty of acting according *to the conception* of laws—that is, according to principles, that is, have a *will*. Since the deduction of actions from principles requires *reason*, the will is nothing but practical reason. If reason infallibly determines the will, then the actions of such a being which are recognized as objectively necessary are subjectively necessary also, that is, the will is a faculty to choose *that only* which reason independent on inclination recognizes as practically necessary, that is, as good. But if reason of itself does not sufficiently determine the will, if the latter is subject also to subjective conditions (particular impulses) which do not always coincide with the objective conditions, in a word, if the will does not *in itself* completely accord with reason (which is actually the case with men), then the actions which objectively are recognized as necessary are subjectively contingent, and the determination of such a will according to objective laws is *obligation*, that is to say, the relation of the objective laws to a will that is not thoroughly good is conceived as the determination of the will of a rational being by principles of reason, but which the will from its nature does not of necessity follow.

The conception of an objective principle, in so far as it is obligatory for a will, is called a command (of reason), and the formula of the command is called an Imperative.

All imperatives are expressed by the word *ought* [or *shall*], and thereby indicate the relation of an objective law of reason to a will which from its subjective constitution is not necessarily determined by it (an obligation). They say that something would be good to do or to forbear, but they say it to a will which does not always do a thing because it is conceived to be good to do it. That is practically *good*, however, which determines the will by means of the conceptions of reason, and consequently not from subjective causes, but objectively, that is, on principles which are valid for every rational being as such. It is distinguished from the *pleasant* as that which influences the will only by means of sensation from merely subjective causes, valid only for the sense of this or that one, and not as a principle of reason which holds for every one.*

A perfectly good will would therefore be equally subject to objective laws (viz., laws of good), but could not be conceived as *obliged* thereby to act lawfully, because of itself from its subjective constitution it can only be determined by the conception of good. Therefore no imperatives hold for the Divine will, or in general for a *holy* will; *ought* is here out of place because the volition is already of itself necessarily in unison with the law. Therefore imperatives are only formulae to express the relation of objective laws of all volition to the subjective imperfection of the will of this or that rational being, for example, the human will.

Now all *imperatives* command either *hypothetically* or *categorically*. The former represent the practical necessity of a possible action as means to something else that is willed (or at least which one might possibly will). The categorical imperative would be that which represented an action as necessary of itself without reference to another end, that is, as objectively necessary.

Since every practical law represents a possible action as good, and on this account, for a subject who is practically determinable by reason as necessary, all imperatives are formulae determining an action which is necessary according to the principle of a will good in some respects. If now the action is good only as a means *to something else*, then the imperative is *hypothetical;* if it is conceived of as good *in itself* and consequently as being necessarily the principle of a will which of itself conforms to reason, then it is *categorical.*

Thus the imperative declares what action possible by me would be good, and presents the practical rule in relation to a will which does not forthwith perform an action simply because it is good, whether because the subject does not always know that it is good, or because, even if it know this, yet its maxims might be opposed to the objective principles of practical reason.

Accordingly the hypothetical imperative only says that the action is good for some purpose, *possible* or *actual.* In the first case it is a *problematical*, in the second an *assertorial* practical principle. The cate-

* The dependence of the desires on sensations is called inclination, and this accordingly always indicates a *want.* The dependence of a contingently determinable will on principles of reason is called an *interest.* This, therefore, is found only in the case of a dependent will which does not always of itself conform to reason; in the Divine will we cannot conceive any interest. But the human will can also *take an interest* in a thing without therefore acting *from interest.* The former signifies the *practical* interest in the action, the latter the *pathological* in the object of the action. The former indicates only dependence of the will on principles of reason in themselves; the second, dependence on principles of reason for the sake of inclination, reason supplying only the practical rules how the requirement of the inclination may be satisfied. In the first case the action interests me; in the second the object of the action (because it is pleasant to me). We have seen in the first section that in an action done from duty we must look not to the interest in the object, but only to that in the action itself, and in its rational principle (viz., the law).

gorical imperative which declares an action to be objectively necessary in itself without reference to any purpose, that is, without any other end, is valid as an *apodictic* (practical) principle.

Whatever is possible only by the power of some rational being may also be conceived as a possible purpose of some will; and therefore the principles of action as regards the means necessary to attain some possible purpose are in fact infinitely numerous. All sciences have a practical part consisting of problems expressing that some end is possible for us, and of imperatives directing how it may be attained. These may, therefore, be called in general imperatives of *skill.* Here there is no question whether the end is rational and good, but only what one must do in order to attain it. The precepts for the physician to make his patient thoroughly healthy, and for a poisoner to ensure certain death, are of equal value in this respect, that each serves to effect its purpose perfectly. Since in early youth it cannot be known what ends are likely to occur to us in the course of life, parents seek to have their children taught a *great many things,* and provide for their *skill* in the use of means for all sorts of arbitrary ends, of none of which can they determine whether it may not perhaps hereafter be an object to their pupil, but which it is at all events *possible* that he might aim at; and this anxiety is so great that they commonly neglect to form and correct their judgment on the value of the things which may be chosen as ends.

There is *one* end, however, which may be assumed to be actually such to all rational beings (so far as imperatives apply to them, viz., as dependent beings), and, therefore, one purpose which they not merely *may* have, but which we may with certainty assume that they all actually *have* by a natural necessity, and this is *happiness.* The hypothetical imperative which expresses the practical necessity of an action as means to the advancement of happiness is *assertorial.* We are not to present it as necessary for an uncertain and merely possible purpose, but for a purpose which we may presuppose with certainty and *a priori* in every man, because it belongs to his being. Now skill in the choice of means to his own greatest well-being may be called *prudence,** in the narrowest sense. And thus the imperative which refers to the choice of means to one's own happiness, that is, the precept of prudence, is still always *hypothetical;* the action is not commanded absolutely, but only as means to another purpose.

Finally, there is an imperative which commands a certain conduct immediately, without having as its condition any other purpose to be attained by it. This imperative is *categorical.* It concerns not the matter of the action, or its intended result, but its form and the principle of which

* The word *prudence* is taken in two senses: in the one it may bear the name of knowledge of the world, in the other that of private prudence. The former is a man's ability to influence others so as to use them for his own purposes. The latter is the sagacity to combine all these purposes for his own lasting benefit. This latter is properly that to which the value even of the former is reduced, and when a man is prudent in the former sense, but not in the latter, we might better say of him that he is clever and cunning, but, on the whole, imprudent.

it is itself a result; and what is essentially good in it consists in the mental disposition, let the consequence be what it may. This imperative may be called that of *morality*.

There is a marked distinction also between the volitions on these three sorts of principles in the *dissimilarity* of the obligation of the will. In order to mark this difference more clearly, I think they would be most suitably named in their order if we said they are either *rules* of skill, or *counsels* of prudence, or *commands* (*laws*) of morality. For it is *law* only that involves the conception of an *unconditional* and objective necessity, which is consequently universally valid; and commands are laws which must be obeyed, that is, must be followed, even in opposition to inclination. *Counsels*, indeed, involve necessity, but one which can only hold under a contingent subjective condition, viz., they depend on whether this or that man reckons this or that as part of his happiness; the categorical imperative, on the contrary, is not limited by any condition, and as being absolutely, although practically, necessary may be quite properly called a command. We might also call the first kind of imperatives *technical* (belonging to art), the second *pragmatic** (belonging to welfare), the third *moral* (belonging to free conduct generally, that is, to morals).

. . .

When I conceive a hypothetical imperative, in general I do not know beforehand what it will contain until I am given the condition. But when I conceive a categorical imperative, I know at once what it contains. For as the imperative contains besides the law only the necessity that the maxims** shall conform to this law, while the law contains no conditions restricting it, there remains nothing but the general statement that the maxim of the action should conform to a universal law, and it is this conformity alone that the imperative properly represents as necessary.

There is therefore but one categorical imperative, namely, this: *Act only on that maxim whereby thou canst at the same time will that it should become a universal law.*

Now if all imperatives of duty can be deduced from this one imperative as from their principle, then, although it should remain undecided whether what is called duty is not merely a vain notion, yet at least we

* It seems to me that the proper signification of the word *pragmatic* may be most accurately defined in this way. For *sanctions* are called pragmatic which flow properly, not from the law of the states as necessary enactments, but from *precaution* for the general welfare. A history is composed pragmatically when it teaches *prudence*, that is, instructs the world how it can provide for its interests better, or at least as well as the men of former time.

** A "maxim" is a subjective principle of action, and must be distinguished from the *objective principle*, namely, practical law. The former contains the practical rule set by reason according to the conditions of the subject (often its ignorance or its inclinations), so that it is the principle on which the subject *acts;* but the law is the objective principle valid for every rational being, and is the principle on which it *ought to act*—that is an imperative.

shall be able to show what we understand by it and what this notion means.

Since the universality of the law according to which effects are produced constitutes what is properly called *nature* in the most general sense (as to form)—that is, the existence of things so far as it is determined by general laws—the imperative of duty may be expressed thus: *Act as if the maxim of thy action were to become by thy will a universal law of nature.*

We will now enumerate a few duties, adopting the usual division of them into duties to ourselves and to others, and into perfect and imperfect duties.*

1. A man reduced to despair by a series of misfortunes feels wearied of life, but is still so far in possession of his reason that he can ask himself whether it would not be contrary to his duty to himself to take his own life. Now he inquires whether the maxim of his action could become a universal law of nature. His maxim is: From self-love I adopt it as a principle to shorten my life when its longer duration is likely to bring more evil than satisfaction. It is asked then simply whether this principle founded on self-love can become a universal law of nature. Now we see at once that a system of nature of which it should be a law to destroy life by means of the very feeling whose special nature it is to impel to the improvement of life would contradict itself, and therefore could not exist as a system of nature; hence that maxim cannot possibly exist as a universal law of nature, and consequently would be wholly inconsistent with the supreme principle of all duty.

2. Another finds himself forced by necessity to borrow money. He knows that he will not be able to repay it, but sees also that nothing will be lent to him unless he promises stoutly to repay it in a definite time. He desires to make this promise, but he has still so much conscience as to ask himself: Is it not unlawful and inconsistent with duty to get out of a difficulty in this way? Suppose, however, that he resolves to do so, then the maxim of his action would be expressed thus: When I think myself in want of money, I will borrow money and promise to repay it, although I know that I never can do so. Now this principle of self-love or of one's own advantage may perhaps be consistent with my whole future welfare; but the question now is, Is it right? I change then the suggestion of self-love into a universal law, and state the question thus: How would it be if my maxim were a universal law? Then I see at once that it could never hold as a universal law of nature, but would necessarily contradict itself. For supposing it to be a universal law that everyone when he thinks

* It must be noted here that I reserve the division of duties for a future *metaphysic of morals;* so that I give it here only as an arbitrary one (in order to arrange my examples). For the rest, I understand by a perfect duty one that admits no exception in favor of inclination, and then I have not merely external but also internal perfect duties. This is contrary to the use of the word adopted in the schools; but I do not intend to justify it here, as it is all one for my purpose whether it is admitted or not. [*Perfect* duties are usually understood to be those which can be enforced by external law; *imperfect,* those which cannot be enforced. They are also called respectively *determinate* and *indeterminate, officia juris* and *officia virtutis.*]

himself in a difficulty should be able to promise whatever he pleases, with the purpose of not keeping his promise, the promise itself would become impossible, as well as the end that one might have in view in it, since no one would consider that anything was promised to him, but would ridicule all such statements as vain pretenses.

3. A third finds in himself a talent which with the help of some culture might make him a useful man in many respects. But he finds himself in comfortable circumstances and prefers to indulge in pleasure rather than to take pains in enlarging and improving his happy natural capacities. He asks, however, whether his maxim of neglect of his natural gifts, besides agreeing with his inclination to indulgence, agrees also with what is called duty. He sees then that a system of nature could indeed subsist with such a universal law, although men (like the South Sea islanders) should let their talents rest and resolve to devote their lives merely to idleness, amusement, and propagation of their species—in a word, to enjoyment; but he cannot possibly *will* that this should be a universal law of nature, or be implanted in us as such by a natural instinct. For, as a rational being, he necessarily wills that his faculties be developed, since they serve him, and have been given him, for all sorts of possible purposes.

4. A fourth, who is in prosperity, while he sees that others have to contend with great wretchedness and that he could help them, thinks: What concern is it of mine? Let everyone be as happy as Heaven pleases, or as he can make himself; I will take nothing from him nor even envy him, only I do not wish to contribute anything to his welfare or to his assistance in distress! Now no doubt, if such a mode of thinking were a universal law, the human race might very well subsist, and doubtless even better than in a state in which everyone talks of sympathy and good-will, or even takes care occasionally to put it into practice, but, on the other side, also cheats when he can, betrays the rights of men, or otherwise violates them. But although it is possible that a universal law of nature might exist in accordance with that maxim, it is impossible to *will* that such a principle should have the universal validity of a law of nature. For a will which resolved this would contradict itself, inasmuch as many cases might occur in which one would have need of the love and sympathy of others, and in which, by such a law of nature, sprung from his own will, he would deprive himself of all hope of the aid he desires.

These are a few of the many actual duties, or at least what we regard as such, which obviously fall into two classes on the one principle that we have laid down. We must be *able to will* that a maxim of our action should be a universal law. This is the canon of the moral appreciation of the action generally. Some actions are of such a character that their maxim cannot without contradiction be even *conceived* as a universal law of nature, far from it being possible that we should *will* that it *should* be so. In others, this intrinsic impossibility is not found, but still it is impossible to *will* that their maxim should be raised to the universality of a law of nature, since such a will would contradict itself. It is easily seen that the former violate strict or rigorous (inflexible) duty; the latter only laxer (meritorious) duty. Thus it has been completely shown by these examples how all duties depend as regards the nature of the obligation (not the object of the action) on the same principle.

If now we attend to ourselves on occasion of any transgression of duty, we shall find that we in fact do not will that our maxim should be a universal law, for that is impossible for us; on the contrary, we will that the opposite should remain a universal law, only we assume the liberty of making an *exception* in our own favor or (just for this time only) in favor of our inclination. Consequently, if we considered all cases from one and the same point of view, namely, that of reason, we should find a contradiction in our own will, namely, that a certain principle should be objectively necessary as a universal law, and yet subjectively should not be universal, but admit of exceptions. As, however, we at one moment regard our action from the point of view of a will wholly conformed to reason, and then again look at the same action from the point of view of a will affected by inclination, there is not really any contradiction, but an antagonism of inclination to the precept of reason, whereby the universality of the principle is changed into a mere generality, so that the practical principle of reason shall meet the maxim half way. Now, although this cannot be justified in our own impartial judgment, yet it proves that we do really recognize the validity of the categorical imperative and (with all respect for it) only allow ourselves a few exceptions which we think unimportant and forced from us.

UTILITARIANISM

JOHN STUART MILL

There are few circumstances among those which make up the present condition of human knowledge more unlike what might have been expected, or more significant of the backward state in which speculation on the most important subjects still lingers, than the little progress which has been made in the decision of the controversy respecting the criterion of right and wrong. From the dawn of philosophy, the question concerning the *summum bonum*, or, what is the same thing, concerning the foundation of morality, has been accounted the main problem in speculative thought, has occupied the most gifted intellects and divided them into sects and schools carrying on a vigorous warfare against one another. And after more than two thousand years the same discussions continue, philosophers are still ranged under the same contending banners, and neither thinkers nor mankind at large seem nearer to being

From *Utilitarianism* (1863), Chapters I, II, and IV.

unanimous on the subject than when the youth Socrates listened to the old Protagoras and asserted (if Plato's dialogue be grounded on a real conversation) the theory of utilitarianism against the popular morality of the so-called sophist.

It is true that similar confusion and uncertainty and, in some cases, similar discordance exist respecting the first principles of all the sciences, not excepting that which is deemed the most certain of them—mathematics, without much impairing, generally indeed without impairing at all, the trustworthiness of the conclusions of those sciences. An apparent anomaly, the explanation of which is that the detailed doctrines of a science are not usually deduced from, nor depend for their evidence upon, what are called its first principles. Were it not so, there would be no science more precarious, or whose conclusions were more insufficiently made out, than algebra, which derives none of its certainty from what are commonly taught to learners as its elements, since these, as laid down by some of its most eminent teachers, are as full of fictions as English law, and of mysteries as theology. The truths which are ultimately accepted as the first principles of a science are really the last results of metaphysical analysis practiced on the elementary notions with which the science is conversant; and their relation to the science is not that of foundations to an edifice, but of roots to a tree, which may perform their office equally well though they be never dug down to and exposed to light. But though in science the particular truths precede the general theory, the contrary might be expected to be the case with a practical art, such as morals or legislation. All action is for the sake of some end, and rules of action, it seems natural to suppose, must take their whole character and color from the end to which they are subservient. When we engage in a pursuit, a clear and precise conception of what we are pursuing would seem to be the first thing we need, instead of the last we are to look forward to. A test of right and wrong must be the means, one would think, of ascertaining what is right or wrong, and not a consequence of having already ascertained it.

The difficulty is not avoided by having recourse to the popular theory of a natural faculty, a sense or instinct, informing us of right and wrong. For—besides that the existence of such a moral instinct is itself one of the matters in dispute—those believers in it who have any pretensions to philosophy have been obliged to abandon the idea that it discerns what is right or wrong in the particular case in hand, as our other senses discern the sight or sound actually present. Our moral faculty, according to all those of its interpreters who are entitled to the name of thinkers, supplies us only with the general principles of moral judgments; it is a branch of our reason, not of our sensitive faculty; and must be looked to for the abstract doctrines of morality, not for perception of it in the concrete. The intuitive, no less than what may be termed the inductive, school of ethics insists on the necessity of general laws. They both agree that the morality of an individual action is not a question of direct perception, but of the application of a law to an individual case. They recognize also, to a great extent, the same moral laws, but differ as to their evidence and the source from which they derive their authority. According to the one opinion, the principles of morals are evident *a priori*, requiring nothing to command assent except that the meaning of the terms be understood. According to the other doctrine, right and wrong, as well as truth and falsehood, are questions of observation and experience. But both hold equally that morality must be deduced from principles; and the intuitive school affirm as strongly as the inductive that there is a science of morals. Yet they seldom attempt to make out a list of the *a priori* principles which are to serve as the premises of the science; still more rarely do they make any effort to reduce those various principles to one first principle or common ground of obligation. They either assume the ordinary precepts of morals as of *a priori* authority, or they lay down as the common groundwork of those maxims some generality much less obviously authoritative than the maxims themselves, and which has never succeeded in gaining popular acceptance. Yet to support their pretensions there ought either to be some one fundamental principle or law at the root of all morality, or, if there be several, there should be a determinate order of precedence among them; and the one principle, or the rule for deciding between the various principles when they conflict, ought to be self-evident.

To inquire how far the bad effects of this deficiency have been mitigated in practice, or to what extent the moral beliefs of mankind have been vitiated or made uncertain by the absence of any distinct recognition of an ultimate standard, would imply a complete survey and criticism of past and present ethical doctrine. It would, however, be easy to show that whatever steadiness or consistency these moral beliefs have attained has been mainly due to the tacit influence of a standard not recognized. Although the nonexistence of an acknowledged first principle has made ethics not so much a guide as a consecration of men's actual sentiments, still, as men's sentiments, both of favor and of aversion, are greatly influenced by what they suppose to be the effects of things upon their happiness, the principle of utility, or, as Bentham latterly called it, the greatest happiness principle, has had a large share in forming the moral doctrines even of those who most scornfully reject its authority. Nor is there any school of thought which refuses to admit that the influence of actions on happiness is a most material and even predominant consideration in many of the details of morals, however unwilling to acknowledge it as the fundamental principle of morality and the source of moral obligation. I might go much further and say that to all those *a priori* moralists who deem it necessary to argue at all, utilitarian arguments are indispensable. It is not my present purpose to criticize these thinkers; but I cannot help referring, for illustration, to a systematic treatise by one of the most illustrious of them, the *Metaphysics of Ethics* by Kant. This remarkable man, whose system of thought will long remain one of the landmarks in the history of philosophical speculation, does, in the treatise in question, lay down a universal first principle as the origin and ground of moral obligation; it is this: "So act that the rule on which thou actest would admit of being adopted as a law by all rational beings." But when he begins to deduce from this precept any of the actual duties of morality, he fails, almost grotesquely, to show that there would be any contradiction, any logical (not to say physical) impossibility, in the adoption by all rational beings of the most outrageously immoral rules of conduct. All he shows is that the *consequences* of their universal adoption would be such as no one would choose to incur.

On the present occasion, I shall, without further discussion of the other theories, attempt to contribute something towards the understanding and appreciation of the "utilitarian" or "happiness" theory, and towards such proof as it is susceptible of. It is evident that this cannot be proof in the ordinary and popular meaning of the term. Questions of ultimate ends are not amenable to direct proof. Whatever can be proved to be good must be so by being shown to be a means to something admitted to be good without proof. The medical art is proved to be good by its conducing to health; but how is it possible to prove that health is good? The art of music is good, for the reason, among others, that it produces pleasure; but what proof is it possible to give that pleasure is good? If, then, it is asserted that there is a comprehensive formula, including all things which are in themselves good, and that whatever else is good is not so as an end but as a means, the formula may be accepted or rejected, but is not a subject of what is commonly understood by proof. We are not, however, to infer that its acceptance or rejection must depend on blind impulse, or arbitrary choice. There is a larger meaning of the word "proof," in which this question is as amenable to it as any other of the disputed questions of philosophy. The subject is within the cognizance of the rational faculty; and neither does that faculty deal with it solely in the way of intuition. Considerations may be presented capable of determining the intellect either to give or withhold its assent to the doctrine; and this is equivalent to proof.

. . .

The creed which accepts as the foundation of morals "utility" or the "greatest happiness principle" holds that actions are right in proportion as they tend to promote happiness; wrong as they tend to produce the reverse of happiness. By happiness is intended pleasure and the absence of pain; by unhappiness, pain and the privation of pleasure. To give a clear view of the moral standard set up by the theory, much more requires to be said; in particular, what things it includes in the ideas of pain and pleasure, and to what extent this is left an open question. But these supplementary explanations do not affect the theory of life on which this theory of morality is grounded—namely, that pleasure and freedom from pain are the only things desirable as ends; and that all desirable things (which are as numerous in the utilitarian as in any other scheme) are desirable either for the pleasure inherent in themselves or as means to the promotion of pleasure and the prevention of pain.

Now such a theory of life excites in many minds, and among them in some of the most estimable in feeling and purpose, inveterate dislike. To suppose that life has (as they express it) no higher end than pleasure—no better and nobler object of desire and pursuit—they designate as utterly mean and groveling, as a doctrine worthy only of swine, to whom the followers of Epicurus were, at a very early period, contemptuously likened; and modern holders of the doctrine are occasionally made the subject of equally polite comparisons by its German, French, and English assailants.

When thus attacked, the Epicureans have always answered that it is not they, but their accusers, who represent human nature in a degrading light, since the accusation supposes human beings to be capable of no pleasures except those of which swine are capable. If this supposition were true, the charge could not be gainsaid, but would then be no longer an imputation; for if the sources of pleasure were precisely the same to human beings and to swine, the rule of life which is good enough for the one would be good enough for the other. The comparison of the Epicurean life to that of beasts is felt as degrading, precisely because a beast's pleasures do not satisfy a human being's conceptions of happiness. Human beings have faculties more elevated than the animal appetites and, when once made conscious of them, do not regard anything as happiness which does not include their gratification. I do not, indeed, consider the Epicureans to have been by any means faultless in drawing out their scheme of consequences from the utilitarian principle. To do this in any sufficient manner, many Stoic, as well as Christian, elements require to be included. But there is no known Epicurean theory of life which does not assign to the pleasures of the intellect, of the feelings and imagination, and of the moral sentiments a much higher value as pleasures than to those of mere sensation. It must be admitted, however, that utilitarian writers in general have placed the superiority of mental over bodily pleasures chiefly in the greater permanency, safety, uncostliness, etc., of the former—that is, in their circumstantial advantages rather than in their intrinsic nature. And on all these points utilitarians have fully proved their case; but they might have taken the other and, as it may be called, higher ground with entire consistency. It is quite compatible with the principle of utility to recognize the fact that some kinds of pleasure are more desirable and more valuable than others. It would be absurd that, while in estimating all other things, quality is considered as well as quantity, the estimation of pleasures should be supposed to depend on quantity alone.

If I am asked what I mean by difference of quality in pleasures, or what makes one pleasure more valuable than another merely, as a pleasure, except its being greater in amount, there is but one possible answer. Of two pleasures, if there be one to which all or almost all who have experience of both give a decided preference, irrespective of any feeling of moral obligation to prefer it, that is the more desirable pleasure. If one of the two is, by those who are competently acquainted with both, placed so far above the other that they prefer it, even though knowing it to be attended with a greater amount of discontent, and would not resign it for any quantity of the other pleasure which their nature is capable of, we are justified in ascribing to the preferred enjoyment a superiority in quality so far outweighing quantity as to render it, in comparison, of small account.

Now it is an unquestionable fact that those who are equally acquainted with and equally capable of appreciating and enjoying both do give a most marked preference to the manner of existence which employs their higher faculties. Few human creatures would consent to be changed into any of the lower animals for a promise of the fullest allowance of a beast's pleasures; no intelligent human being would consent to be a fool, no instructed person would be an ignoramus, no person of feeling and conscience would be selfish and base, even though they should be persuaded that the fool, the dunce, or the rascal is better satisfied with his lot than they are with theirs. They would not resign what they possess more than he for the most complete satisfaction of all the desires which they have in common with him. If they ever fancy they would, it is only in cases of unhappiness so extreme that to escape from it they would exchange their lot for almost any other, however undesirable in their own eyes. A being of higher faculties requires more to make him happy, is capable probably of more acute suffering, and certainly accessible to it at more points, than one of an inferior type; but in spite of these liabilities, he can never really wish to sink into what he feels to be a lower grade of existence. We may give what explanation we please of this unwillingness; we may attribute it to pride, a name which is given indiscriminately to some of the most and to some of the least estimable feelings of which mankind are capable; we may refer it to the love of liberty and personal independence, and appeal to which was with the Stoics one of the most effective means for the inculcation of it; to the love of power or to the love of excitement, both of which do really enter into and contribute to it; but its most appropriate appellation is a sense of dignity, which all human beings possess in one form or other, and in some, though by no means in exact, proportion to their higher faculties, and which is so essential a part of the happiness of those in whom it is strong that nothing which conflicts with it could be otherwise than momentarily an object of desire to them. Whoever supposes that this preference takes place at a sacrifice of happiness—that the superior being, in anything like equal circumstances, is not happier than the inferior—confounds the two very different ideas of happiness and content. It is indisputable that the being whose capacities of enjoyment are low has the greatest chance of having them fully satisfied; and a highly endowed being will always feel that any happiness which he can look for, as the world is constituted, is imperfect. But he can learn to bear its imperfections, if they are at all bearable; and they will not make him envy the being who is indeed unconscious of the imperfections, but only because he feels not at all the good which those imperfections qualify. It is better to be a human being dissatisfied than a pig satisfied; better to be Socrates dissatisfied than a fool satisfied. And if the fool, or the pig, are of a different opinion, it is because they only know their own side of the question. The other party to the comparison knows both sides.

. . .

According to the greatest happiness principle, as above explained, the ultimate end, with reference to and for the sake of which all other things are desirable—whether we are considering our own good or that of other people—is an existence exempt as far as possible from pain, and as rich as possible in enjoyments, both in point of quantity and quality; the test of quality and the rule for measuring it against quantity being the preference felt by those who, in their opportunities of experience, to which must be added their habits of self-consciousness and self-observation, are best furnished with the means of comparison. This, being according to the utilitarian opinion the end of human action, is necessarily also the standard of morality, which may accordingly be defined "the rules and precepts for human conduct," by the observance of which an existence such as has been described might be, to the greatest extent possible, secured to all mankind; and not to them only, but, so far as the nature of things admits, to the whole sentient creation.

Against this doctrine, however, arises another class of objectors who say that happiness, in any form, cannot be the rational purpose of human life and action; because, in the first place, it is unattainable; and they contemptuously ask, What right hast thou to be happy?—a question which Mr. Carlyle clinches by the addition, What right, a short time ago, hadst thou even *to be?* Next they say that men can do *without* happiness; that all noble human beings have felt this, and could not have become noble but by learning the lesson of *Entsagen*, or renunciation; which lesson, thoroughly learnt and submitted to, they affirm to be the beginning and necessary condition of all virtue.

The first of these objections would go to the root of the matter were it well founded; for if no happiness is to be had at all by human beings, the attainment of it cannot be the end of morality or of any rational conduct. Though, even in that case, something might still be said for the utilitarian theory, since utility includes not solely the pursuit of happiness, but the prevention or mitigation of unhappiness; and if the former aim be chimerical, there will be all the greater scope and more imperative need for the latter, so long at least as mankind think fit to live and do not take refuge in the simultaneous act of suicide recommended under certain conditions by Novalis. When, however, it is thus positively asserted to be impossible that human life should be happy, the assertion, if not something like a verbal quibble, is at least an exaggeration. If by happiness be meant a continuity of highly pleasurable excitement, it is evident enough that this is impossible. A state of exalted pleasure lasts only moments or in some cases, and with some intermissions, hours or days, and is the occasional brilliant flash of enjoyment, not its permanent and steady flame. Of this the philosophers who have taught that happiness is the end of life were as fully aware as those who taunt them. The happiness which they meant was not a life of rapture, but moments of such, in an existence made up of few and transitory pains, many and various pleasures, with a decided predominance of the active over the passive, and having as the foundation of the whole not to expect more from life than it is capable of bestowing. A life thus composed, to those who have been fortunate enough to obtain it, has always appeared worthy of the name of happiness. And such an existence is even now the lot of many during some considerable portion of their lives. The present wretched education and wretched social arrangements are the only real hindrance to its being attainable by almost all.

The objectors perhaps may doubt whether human beings, if taught to consider happiness as the end of life, would be satisfied with such a moderate share of it. But great numbers of mankind have been satisfied with much less. The main constituents of a satisfied life appear to be two, either of which by itself is often found sufficient for the purpose: tranquillity and excitement. With much tranquillity, many find that they can be content with very little pleasure; with much excitement, many can reconcile themselves to a considerable quantity of pain. There is assuredly no inherent impossibility of enabling even the mass of mankind to unite both, since the two are so far from being incompatible that they are in natural alliance, the prolongation of either being a preparation for, and exciting a wish for, the other. It is only those in whom indolence amounts to a vice that do not desire excitement after an interval of repose; it is only those in whom the need of excitement is a disease that feel the tranquillity which follows excitement dull and insipid, instead of pleasurable in direct proportion to the excitement which preceded it. When people who are tolerably fortunate in their outward lot do not find in life sufficient enjoyment to make it valuable to them, the cause generally is caring for nobody but themselves. To those who have neither public nor private affections, the excitements of life are much curtailed, and in any case dwindle in value as the time approaches when all selfish interests must be terminated by death; while those who leave after them objects of personal affection, and especially those who have also cultivated a fellow feeling with the collective interests of mankind, retain as lively an interest in life on the eve of death as in the vigor of youth and health. Next to selfishness, the principal cause which makes life unsatisfactory is want of mental cultivation. A cultivated mind—I do not mean that of a philosopher, but any mind to which the fountains of knowledge have been opened, and which has been taught, in any tolerable degree, to exercise its faculties—finds sources of inexhaustible interest in all that surrounds it: in the objects of nature, the achievements of art, the imaginations of poetry, the incidents of history, the ways of mankind, past and present, and their prospects in the future. It is possible, indeed, to become indifferent to all this, and that too without having exhausted a thousandth part of it, but only when one has had from the beginning no moral or human interest in these things, and has sought in them only the gratification of curiosity.

Now there is absolutely no reason in the nature of things why an amount of mental culture sufficient to give an intelligent interest in these objects of contemplation should not be the inheritance of everyone born in a civilized country. As little is there an inherent necessity that any human being should be a selfish egotist, devoid of every feeling or care but those which center in his own miserable individuality. Something far superior to this is sufficiently common even now, to give ample earnest of what the human species may be made. Genuine private affections and a sincere interest in the public good are possible, though in unequal degrees, to every rightly brought up human being. In a world in which there is so much to interest, so much to enjoy, and so much also to correct and improve, everyone who has this moderate amount of moral and intellectual requisites is capable of an existence which may be called enviable; and unless such a person, through bad laws or subjection to the will of others, is denied the liberty to use the sources of happiness within his reach, he will not fail to find this enviable existence, if he escape the positive evils of life, the great sources of physical and mental suffering—such as indigence, disease, and the unkindness, worthlessness, or premature loss of objects of affection. The main stress of the problem lies, therefore, in the contest with these calamities from which it is a rare good fortune entirely to escape; which, as things now are, cannot be obviated, and often cannot be in any material degree mitigated. Yet no one whose opinion deserves a moment's consideration can doubt that most of the great positive evils of the world are in themselves removable, and will, if human affairs continue to improve, be in the end reduced within narrow limits. Poverty, in any sense implying suffering, may be completely extinguished by the wisdom of society combined with the good sense and providence of individuals. Even that most intractable of enemies, disease, may be indefinitely reduced in dimensions by good physical and moral education and proper control of noxious influences, while the progress of science holds out a promise for the future of still more direct conquests over this detestable foe. And every advance in that direction relieves us from some, not only of the chances which cut short our own lives, but, what concerns us still more, which deprive us of those in whom our happiness is wrapt up. As for vicissitudes of fortune and other disappointments connected with worldly circumstances, these are principally the effect, either of gross imprudence, of ill-regulated desires, or of bad or imperfect social institutions. All the grand sources, in short, of human suffering are in a great degree, many of them almost entirely, conquerable by human care and effort; and though their removal is grievously slow—though a long succession of generations will perish in the breach before the conquest is completed, and this world becomes all that, if will and knowledge were not wanting, it might easily be made—yet every mind sufficiently intelligent and generous to bear a part, however small and inconspicuous, in the endeavor will draw a noble enjoyment from the contest itself, which he would not for any bribe in the form of selfish indulgence consent to be without.

And this leads to the true estimation of what is said by the objectors concerning the possibility and the obligation of learning to do without happiness. Unquestionably it is possible to do without happiness; it is done involuntarily by nineteen-twentieths of mankind, even in those parts of our present world which are least deep in barbarism; and it often has to be done voluntarily by the hero or the martyr, for the sake of something which he prizes more than his individual happiness. But this something, what is it, unless the happiness of others or some of the requisites of happiness? It is noble to be capable of resigning entirely one's own portion of happiness, or chances of it; but, after all, this self-sacrifice must be for some end; it is not its own end; and if we are told that its end is not happiness but virtue, which is better than happiness, I ask, would the sacrifice be made if the hero or martyr did not believe that it would earn for others immunity from similar sacrifices? Would it be made if he thought that his renunciation of happiness for himself would produce no fruit for any of his fellow creatures, but to make their lot like his, and place them also in the condition of persons who have renounced happiness? All honor to those who can abnegate for themselves the personal enjoyment of life when by such renunciation they contribute worthily to increase the amount of happiness in the world; but he who does it or professes to do it for any other purpose is no more deserving of admiration than the ascetic mounted on his pillar. He may be an inspiriting proof of what men *can* do, but assuredly not an example of what they *should*.

Though it is only in a very imperfect state of the world's arrangements that anyone can best serve the happiness of others by the absolute sacrifice of his own, yet, so long as the world is in that imperfect state, I fully acknowledge that the readiness to make such a sacrifice is the highest virtue which can be found in man. I will add that in this condition of the world, paradoxical as the assertion may be, the conscious ability to do without happiness gives the best prospect of realizing such happiness as is attainable. For nothing except that consciousness can raise a person above the chances of life, by making him feel that, let fate and fortune do their worst, they have not power to subdue him; which, once felt, frees him from excess of anxiety concerning the evils of life, and enables him, like many a Stoic in the worst times of the Roman Empire, to cultivate in tranquillity the sources of satisfaction accessible to him, without concerning himself about the uncertainty of their duration any more than about their inevitable end.

Meanwhile, let utilitarians never cease to claim the morality of self-devotion as a possession which belongs by as good a right to them as either to the Stoic or to the Transcendentalist. The utilitarian morality does recognize in human beings the power of sacrificing their own greatest good for the good of others. It only refuses to admit that the sacrifice is itself a good. A sacrifice which does not increase or tend to increase the sum total of happiness, it considers as wasted. The only self-renunciation which it applauds is devotion to the happiness, or to some of the means of happiness, of others, either of mankind collectively or of individuals within the limits imposed by the collective interests of mankind.

I must again repeat what the assailants of utilitarianism seldom have the justice to acknowledge, that the happiness which forms the utilitarian standard of what is right in conduct is not the agent's own happiness but that of all concerned. As between his own happiness and that of others, utilitarianism requires him to be as strictly impartial as a disinterested and benevolent spectator. In the golden rule of Jesus of Nazareth, we read the complete spirit of the ethics of utility. "To do as you would be done by," and "to love your neighbor as yourself," constitute the ideal perfection of utilitarian morality. As the means of making the nearest approach to this ideal, utility would enjoin, first, that laws and social arrangements should place the happiness or (as, speaking practically, it may be called) the interest of every individual as nearly as possible in harmony with the interest of the whole; and, secondly, that education and opinion, which have so vast a power over human character, should so use that power as to establish in the mind of every individual an indissoluble association between his own happiness and the good of the whole, especially between his own happiness and the practice of such modes of conduct, negative and positive, as regard for the universal happiness prescribes; so that not only he may be unable to conceive the possibility of happiness to himself, consistently with conduct opposed to the general good, but also that a direct impulse to promote the general good may be in every individual one of the habitual motives of action, and the sentiments connected therewith may fill a large and prominent place in every human being's sentient existence. If the impugners of the utilitarian morality represented it to their own minds in this its true character, I know not what recommendation possessed by any other morality they could possibly affirm to be wanting to it; what more beautiful or more exalted developments of human nature any other ethical system can be supposed to foster, or what springs of action, not accessible to the utilitarian, such systems rely on for giving effect to their mandates.

. . .

It has already been remarked that questions of ultimate ends do not admit of proof, in the ordinary acceptation of the term. To be incapable of proof by reasoning is common to all first principles, to the first premises of our knowledge, as well as to those of our conduct. . . .

Questions about ends are, in other words, questions about what things are desirable. The utilitarian doctrine is that happiness is desirable, and the only thing desirable as an end; all other things being only desirable as means to that end. What ought to be required of this doctrine, what conditions is it requisite that the doctrine should fulfill—to make good its claim to be believed?

The only proof capable of being given that an object is visible is that people actually see it. The only proof that a sound is audible is that people hear it; and so of the other sources of our experience. In like manner, I apprehend, the sole evidence it is possible to produce that anything is desirable is that people do actually desire it. If the end which the utilitarian doctrine proposes to itself were not, in theory and in practice, acknowledged to be an end, nothing could ever convince any person that it was so. No reason can be given why the general happiness is desirable, except that each person, so far as he believes it to be attainable, desires his own happiness. This, however, being a fact, we have not only all the proof which the case admits of, but all which it is possible to require, that happiness is a good, that each person's happiness is a good to that person, and the general happiness, therefore, a good to the aggregate of all persons. Happiness has made out its title as *one* of the ends of conduct and, consequently, one of the criteria of morality.

THE SUBJECT-MATTER OF ETHICS

G. E. MOORE

1. It is very easy to point out some among our every-day judgments, with the truth of which Ethics is undoubtedly concerned. Whenever we say, 'So and so is a good man,' or 'That fellow is a villain'; whenever we ask, 'What ought I to do?' or 'Is it wrong for me to do like this?'; whenever we hazard such remarks as 'Temperance is a virtue and drunkenness a vice'—it is undoubtedly the business of Ethics to discuss such questions and such statements; to argue what is the true answer when we ask what it is right to do, and to give reasons for thinking that our statements about the character of persons or the morality of actions are true or false. In the vast majority of cases, where we make statements involving any of the terms 'virtue,' 'vice,' 'duty,' 'right,' 'ought,' 'good,' 'bad,' we are making ethical judgments; and if we wish to discuss their truth, we shall be discussing a point of Ethics.

So much as this is not disputed; but it falls very far short of defining the province of Ethics. That province may indeed be defined as the whole truth about that which is at the same time common to all such judgments and peculiar to them. But we have still to ask the question: What is it that is thus common and peculiar? And this is a question to which very

This selection is reprinted from *Principia Ethica*, 1903, Chapter 1, by permission of Cambridge University Press, New York.

different answers have been given by ethical philosophers of acknowledged reputation, and none of them, perhaps, completely satisfactory.

2. If we take such examples as those given above, we shall not be far wrong in saying that they are all of them concerned with the question of 'conduct'—with the question, what, in the conduct of us, human beings, is good, and what is bad, what is right, and what is wrong. For when we say that a man is good, we commonly mean that he acts rightly; when we say that drunkenness is a vice, we commonly mean that to get drunk is a wrong or wicked action. And this discussion of human conduct is, in fact, that with which the name 'Ethics' is most intimately associated. It is so associated by derivation; and conduct is undoubtedly by far the commonest and most generally interesting object of ethical judgments.

Accordingly, we find that many ethical philosophers are disposed to accept as an adequate definition of 'Ethics' the statement that it deals with the question what is good or bad in human conduct. They hold that its enquiries are properly confined to 'conduct' or to 'practice'; they hold that the name 'practical philosophy' covers all the matter with which it has to do. Now, without discussing the proper meaning of the word (for verbal questions are properly left to the writers of dictionaries and other persons interested in literature; philosophy, as we shall see, has no concern with them), I may say that I intend to use 'Ethics' to cover more than this—a usage, for which there is, I think, quite sufficient authority. I am using it to cover an enquiry for which, at all events, there is no other word: the general enquiry into what is good.

Ethics is undoubtedly concerned with the question what good conduct is; but, being concerned with this, it obviously does not start at the beginning, unless it is prepared to tell us what is good as well as what is conduct. For 'good conduct' is a complex notion: all conduct is not good; for some is certainly bad and some may be indifferent. And on the other hand, other things, beside conduct, may be good; and if they are so, then, 'good' denotes some property, that is common to them and conduct; and if we examine good conduct alone of all good things, then we shall be in danger of mistaking for this property, some property which is not shared by those other things: and thus we shall have made a mistake about Ethics even in this limited sense; for we shall not know what good conduct really is. This is a mistake which many writers have actually made, from limiting their enquiry to conduct. And hence I shall try to avoid it by considering first what is good in general; hoping, that if we can arrive at any certainty about this, it will be much easier to settle the question of good conduct: for we all know pretty well what 'conduct' is. This, then, is our first question: What is good? and What is bad? and to the discussion of this question (or these questions) I give the name of Ethics, since that science must, at all events, include it.

3. But this is a question which may have many meanings. If, for example, each of us were to say 'I am doing good now' or 'I had a good dinner yesterday,' these statements would each of them be some sort of answer to our question, although perhaps a false one. So, too, when A

asks B what school he ought to send his son to, B's answer will certainly be an ethical judgment. And similarly all distribution of praise or blame to any personage or thing that has existed, now exists, or will exist, does give some answer to the question 'What is good?' In all such cases some particular thing is judged to be good or bad: the question 'What?' is answered by 'This.' But this is not the sense in which a scientific Ethics asks the question. Not one, of all the many million answers of this kind, which must be true, can form a part of an ethical system; although that science must contain reasons and principles sufficient for deciding on the truth of all of them. There are far too many persons, things and events in the world, past, present, or to come, for a discussion of their individual merits to be embraced in any science. Ethics, therefore, does not deal at all with facts of this nature, facts that are unique, individual, absolutely particular; facts with which such studies as history, geography, astronomy, are compelled, in part at least, to deal. And, for this reason, it is not the business of the ethical philosopher to give personal advice or exhortation.

4. But there is another meaning which may be given to the question 'What is good?' 'Books are good' would be an answer to it, though an answer obviously false; for some books are very bad indeed. And ethical judgments of this kind do indeed belong to Ethics; though I shall not deal with many of them. Such is the judgment 'Pleasure is good'—a judgment, of which Ethics should discuss the truth, although it is not nearly as important as that other judgment, with which we shall be much occupied presently—'Pleasure *alone* is good.' It is judgments of this sort, which are made in such books on Ethics as contain a list of 'virtues'—in Aristotle's 'Ethics' for example. But it is judgments of precisely the same kind, which form the substance of what is commonly supposed to be a study different from Ethics, and one much less respectable—the study of Casuistry. We may be told that Casuistry differs from Ethics, in that it is much more detailed and particular, Ethics much more general. But it is most important to notice that Casuistry does not deal with anything that is absolutely particular—particular in the only sense in which a perfectly precise line can be drawn between it and what is general. It is not particular in the sense just noticed, the sense in which this book is a particular book, and A's friend's advice particular advice. Casuistry may indeed be *more* particular and Ethics *more* general; but that means that they differ only in degree and not in kind. And this is universally true of 'particular' and 'general,' when used in this common, but inaccurate, sense. So far as Ethics allows itself to give lists of virtues or even to name constituents of the Ideal, it is indistinguishable from Casuistry. Both alike deal with what is general, in the sense in which physics and chemistry deal with what is general. Just as chemistry aims at discovering what are the properties of oxygen, *wherever it occurs*, and not only of this or that particular specimen of oxygen; so Casuistry aims at discovering what actions are good, *whenever they occur*. In this respect Ethics and Casuistry alike are to be classed with such sciences as physics, chemistry and

physiology, in their absolute distinction from those of which history and geography are instances. And it is to be noted that, owing to their detailed nature, casuistical investigations are actually nearer to physics and to chemistry than are the investigations usually assigned to Ethics. For just as physics cannot rest content with the discovery that light is propagated by waves of ether, but must go on to discover the particular nature of the ether-waves corresponding to each several colour; so Casuistry, not content with the general law that charity is a virtue, must attempt to discover the relative merits of every different form of charity. Casuistry forms, therefore, part of the ideal of ethical science: Ethics cannot be complete without it. The defects of Casuistry are not defects of principle; no objection can be taken to its aim and object. It has failed only because it is far too difficult a subject to be treated adequately in our present state of knowledge. The casuist has been unable to distinguish, in the cases which he treats, those elements upon which their value depends. Hence he often thinks two cases to be alike in respect of value, when in reality they are alike only in some other respect. It is to mistakes of this kind that the pernicious influence of such investigations has been due. For Casuistry is the goal of ethical investigation. It cannot be safely attempted at the beginning of our studies, but only at the end.

5. But our question 'What is good?' may have still another meaning. We may, in the third place, mean to ask, not what thing or things are good, but how 'good' is to be defined. This is an enquiry which belongs only to Ethics, not to Casuistry; and this is the enquiry which will occupy us first.

It is an enquiry to which most special attention should be directed; since this question, how 'good' is to be defined, is the most fundamental question in all Ethics. That which is meant by 'good' is, in fact, except its converse 'bad,' the *only* simple object of thought which is peculiar to Ethics. Its definition is, therefore, the most essential point in the definition of Ethics; and moreover a mistake with regard to it entails a far larger number of erroneous ethical judgments than any other. Unless this first question be fully understood, and its true answer clearly recognised, the rest of Ethics is as good as useless from the point of view of systematic knowledge. True ethical judgments, of the two kinds last dealt with, may indeed be made by those who do not know the answer to this question as well as by those who do; and it goes without saying that the two classes of people may lead equally good lives. But it is extremely unlikely that the *most general* ethical judgments will be equally valid, in the absence of a true answer to this question: I shall presently try to shew that the gravest errors have been largely due to beliefs in a false answer. And, in any case, it is impossible that, till the answer to this question be known, any one should know *what is the evidence* for any ethical judgment whatsoever. But the main object of Ethics, as a systematic science, is to give correct *reasons* for thinking that this or that is good; and, unless this question be answered, such reasons cannot be given. Even, therefore, apart from the fact that a false answer leads to false conclusions, the present enquiry is a most necessary and important part of the science of Ethics.

6. What, then, is good? How is good to be defined? Now, it may be thought that this is a verbal question. A definition does indeed often mean the expressing of one word's meaning in other words. But this is not the sort of definition I am asking for. Such a definition can never be of ultimate importance in any study except lexicography. If I wanted that kind of definition I should have to consider in the first place how people generally used the word 'good'; but my business is not with its proper usage, as established by custom. I should, indeed, be foolish, if I tried to use it for something which it did not usually denote: if, for instance, I were to announce that, whenever I used the word 'good,' I must be understood to be thinking of that object which is usually denoted by the word 'table.' I shall, therefore, use the word in the sense in which I think it is ordinarily used; but at the same time I am not anxious to discuss whether I am right in thinking that it is so used. My business is solely with that object or idea, which I hold, rightly or wrongly, that the word is generally used to stand for. What I want to discover is the nature of that object or idea, and about this I am extremely anxious to arrive at an agreement.

But, if we understand the question in this sense, my answer to it may seem a very disappointing one. If I am asked 'What is good?' my answer is that good is good, and that is the end of the matter. Or if I am asked 'How is good to be defined?' my answer is that it cannot be defined, and that is all I have to say about it. But disappointing as these answers may appear, they are of the very last importance. To readers who are familiar with philosophic terminology, I can express their importance by saying that they amount to this: That propositions about the good are all of them synthetic and never analytic; and that is plainly no trivial matter. And the same thing may be expressed more popularly, by saying that, if I am right, then nobody can foist upon us such an axiom as that 'Pleasure is the only good' or that 'The good is the desired' on the pretence that this is 'the very meaning of the word.'

7. Let us, then, consider this position. My point is that 'good' is a simple notion, just as 'yellow' is a simple notion; that, just as you cannot, by any manner of means, explain to any one who does not already know it, what yellow is, so you cannot explain what good is. Definitions of the kind that I was asking for, definitions which describe the real nature of the object or notion denoted by a word, and which do not merely tell us what the word is used to mean, are only possible when the object or notion in question is something complex. You can give a definition of a horse, because a horse has many different properties and qualities, all of which you can enumerate. But when you have enumerated them all, when you have reduced a horse to his simplest terms, then you can no longer define those terms. They are simply something which you think of or perceive, and to any one who cannot think of or perceive them, you can never, by any definition, make their nature known. It may perhaps be

objected to this that we are able to describe to others, objects which they have never seen or thought of. We can, for instance, make a man understand what a chimaera is, although he has never heard of one or seen one. You can tell him that it is an animal with a lioness's head and body, with a goat's head growing from the middle of its back, and with a snake in place of a tail. But here the object which you are describing is a complex object; it is entirely composed of parts, with which we are all perfectly familiar—a snake, a goat, a lioness; and we know, too, the manner in which those parts are to be put together, because we know what is meant by the middle of a lioness's back, and where her tail is wont to grow. And so it is with all objects, not previously known, which we are able to define: they are all complex; all composed of parts, which may themselves, in the first instance, be capable of similar definition, but which must in the end be reducible to simplest parts, which can no longer be defined. But yellow and good, we say, are not complex: they are notions of that simple kind, out of which definitions are composed and with which the power of further defining ceases.

8. When we say, as Webster says, 'The definition of horse is "A hoofed quadruped of the genus Equus,"' we may, in fact, mean three different things. (1) We may mean merely: 'When I say "horse," you are to understand that I am talking about a hoofed quadruped of the genus Equus.' This might be called the arbitrary verbal definition: and I do not mean that good is indefinable in that sense. (2) We may mean, as Webster ought to mean: 'When most English people say "horse," they mean a hoofed quadruped of the genus Equus.' This may be called the verbal definition proper, and I do not say that good is indefinable in this sense either; for it is certainly possible to discover how people use a word: otherwise, we could never have known that 'good' may be translated by 'gut' in German and by 'bon' in French. But (3) we may, when we define horse, mean something much more important. We may mean that a certain object, which we all of us know, is composed in a certain manner: that it has four legs, a head, a heart, a liver, etc., etc., all of them arranged in definite relations to one another. It is in this sense that I deny good to be definable. I say that it is not composed of any parts, which we can substitute for it in our minds when we are thinking of it. We might think just as clearly and correctly about a horse, if we thought of all its parts and their arrangement instead of thinking of the whole: we could, I say, think how a horse differed from a donkey just as well, just as truly, in this way, as now we do, only not so easily; but there is nothing whatsoever which we could so substitute for good; and that is what I mean, when I say that good is indefinable.

9. But I am afraid I have still not removed the chief difficulty which may prevent acceptance of the proposition that good is indefinable. I do not mean to say that *the* good, that which is good, is thus indefinable; if I did think so, I should not be writing on Ethics, for my main object is to help towards discovering that definition. It is just because I think there will be less risk of error in our search for a definition of 'the good,' that

I am now insisting that *good* is indefinable. I must try to explain the difference between these two. I suppose it may be granted that 'good' is an adjective. Well 'the good,' 'that which is good,' must therefore be the substantive to which the adjective 'good' will apply: it must be the whole of that to which the adjective will apply, and the adjective must *always* truly apply to it. But if it is that to which the adjective will apply, it must be something different from that adjective itself; and the whole of that something different, whatever it is, will be our definition of *the* good. Now it may be that this something will have other adjectives, beside 'good,' that will apply to it. It may be full of pleasure, for example; it may be intelligent: and if these two adjectives are really part of its definition, then it will certainly be true, that pleasure and intelligence are good. And many people appear to think that, if we say 'Pleasure and intelligence are good,' or if we say 'Only pleasure and intelligence are good,' we are defining 'good.' Well, I cannot deny that propositions of this nature may sometimes be called definitions; I do not know well enough how the word is generally used to decide upon this point. I only wish it to be understood that that is not what I mean when I say there is no possible definition of good, and that I shall not mean this if I use the word again. I do most fully believe that some true proposition of the form 'Intelligence is good and intelligence alone is good' can be found; if none could be found, our definition of *the* good would be impossible. As it is, I believe *the* good to be definable; and yet I still say that good itself is indefinable.

10. 'Good,' then, if we mean by it that quality which we assert to belong to a thing, when we say that the thing is good, is incapable of any definition, in the most important sense of that word. The most important sense of 'definition' is that in which a definition states what are the parts which invariably compose a certain whole; and in this sense 'good' has no definition because it is simple and has no parts. It is one of those innumerable objects of thought which are themselves incapable of definition, because they are the ultimate terms by reference to which whatever *is* capable of definition must be defined. That there must be an indefinite number of such terms is obvious, on reflection; since we cannot define anything except by an analysis, which, when carried as far as it will go, refers us to something, which is simply different from anything else, and which by that ultimate difference explains the peculiarity of the whole which we are defining: for every whole contains some parts which are common to other wholes also. There is, therefore, no intrinsic difficulty in the contention that 'good' denotes a simple and indefinable quality. There are many other instances of such qualities.

Consider yellow, for example. We may try to define it, by describing its physical equivalent; we may state what kind of light-vibrations must stimulate the normal eye, in order that we may perceive it. But a moment's reflection is sufficient to shew that those light-vibrations are not themselves what we mean by yellow. *They* are not what we perceive. Indeed we should never have been able to discover their existence, unless we had first been struck by the patent difference of quality between the different colours. The most we can be entitled to say of those vibrations is that they are what corresponds in space to the yellow which we actually perceive.

Yet a mistake of this simple kind has commonly been made about 'good.' It may be true that all things which are good are *also* something else, just as it is true that all things which are yellow produce a certain kind of vibration in the light. And it is a fact, that Ethics aims at discovering what are those other properties belonging to all things which are good. But far too many philosophers have thought that when they named those other properties they were actually defining good; that these properties, in fact, were simply not 'other,' but absolutely and entirely the same with goodness. This view I propose to call the 'naturalistic fallacy' and of it I shall now endeavour to dispose.

11. Let us consider what it is such philosophers say. And first it is to be noticed that they do not agree among themselves. They not only say that they are right as to what good is, but they endeavour to prove that other people who say that it is something else, are wrong. One, for instance, will affirm that good is pleasure, another, perhaps, that good is that which is desired; and each of these will argue eagerly to prove that the other is wrong. But how is that possible? One of them says that good is nothing but the object of desire, and at the same time tries to prove that it is not pleasure. But from his first assertion, that good just means the object of desire, one of two things must follow as regards his proof:

(1) He may be trying to prove that the object of desire is not pleasure. But, if this be all, where is his Ethics? The position he is maintaining is merely a psychological one. Desire is something which occurs in our minds, and pleasure is something else which so occurs; and our would-be ethical philosopher is merely holding that the latter is not the object of the former. But what has that to do with the question in dispute? His opponent held the ethical proposition that pleasure was the good, and although he should prove a million times over the psychological proposition that pleasure is not the object of desire, he is no nearer proving his opponent to be wrong. The position is like this. One man says a triangle is a circle: another replies 'A triangle is a straight line, and I will prove to you that I am right: *for*' (this is the only argument) 'a straight line is not a circle.' 'That is quite true,' the other may reply; 'but nevertheless a triangle is a circle, and you have said nothing whatever to prove the contrary. What is proved is that one of us is wrong, for we agree that a triangle cannot be both a straight line and a circle: but which is wrong, there can be no earthly means of proving, since you define triangle as straight line and I define it as circle.'—Well, that is one alternative which any naturalistic Ethics has to face; if good is *defined* as something else, it is then impossible either to prove that any other definition is wrong or even to deny such definition.

(2) The other alternative will scarcely be more welcome. It is that the discussion is after all a verbal one. When A says 'Good means pleasant'

and B says 'Good means desired,' they may merely wish to assert that most people have used the word for what is pleasant and for what is desired respectively. And this is quite an interesting subject for discussion: only it is not a whit more an ethical discussion than the last was. Nor do I think that any exponent of naturalistic Ethics would be willing to allow that this was all he meant. They are all so anxious to persuade us that what they call the good is what we really ought to do. 'Do, pray, act so, because the word "good" is generally used to denote actions of this nature': such, on this view, would be the substance of their teaching. And in so far as they tell us how we ought to act, their teaching is truly ethical, as they mean it to be. But how perfectly absurd is the reason they would give for it! 'You are to do this, because most people use a certain word to denote conduct such as this.' 'You are to say the thing which is not, because most people call it lying.' That is an argument just as good!—My dear sirs, what we want to know from you as ethical teachers, is not how people use a word; it is not even, what kind of actions they approve, which the use of this word 'good' may certainly imply: what we want to know is simply what *is* good. We may indeed agree that what most people do think good, is actually so; we shall at all events be glad to know their opinions: but when we say their opinions about what *is* good, we do mean what we say; we do not care whether they call that thing which they mean 'horse' or 'table' or 'chair,' 'gut' or 'bon' or 'ἀγαθός'; we want to know what it is that they so call. When they say 'Pleasure is good,' we cannot believe that they merely mean 'Pleasure is pleasure' and nothing more than that.

12. Suppose a man says 'I am pleased'; and suppose that is not a lie or a mistake but the truth. Well, if it is true, what does that mean? It means that his mind, a certain definite mind, distinguished by certain definite marks from all others, has at this moment a certain definite feeling called pleasure. 'Pleased' *means* nothing but having pleasure, and though we may be more pleased or less pleased, and even, we may admit for the present, have one or another kind of pleasure; yet in so far as it is pleasure we have, whether there be more or less of it, and whether it be of one kind or another, what we have is one definite thing, absolutely indefinable, some one thing that is the same in all the various degrees and in all the various kinds of it that there may be. We may be able to say how it is related to other things: that, for example, it is in the mind, that it causes desire, that we are conscious of it, etc., etc. We can, I say, describe its relations to other things, but define it we can *not*. And if anybody tried to define pleasure for us as being any other natural object; if anybody were to say, for instance, that pleasure *means* the sensation of red, and were to proceed to deduce from that that pleasure is a colour, we should be entitled to laugh at him and to distrust his future statements about pleasure. Well, that would be the same fallacy which I have called the naturalistic fallacy. That 'pleased' does not mean 'having the sensation of red,' or anything else whatever, does not prevent us from understanding what it does mean. It is enough for us to know that 'pleased' does mean

'having the sensation of pleasure,' and though pleasure is absolutely indefinable, though pleasure is pleasure and nothing else whatever, yet we feel no difficulty in saying that we are pleased. The reason is, of course, that when I say 'I am pleased,' I do *not* mean that 'I' am the same thing as 'having pleasure.' And similarly no difficulty need be found in my saying that 'pleasure is good' and yet not meaning that 'pleasure' is the same thing as 'good,' that pleasure *means* good, and that good *means* pleasure. If I were to imagine that when I said 'I am pleased,' I meant that I was exactly the same thing as 'pleased,' I should not indeed call that a naturalistic fallacy, although it would be the same fallacy as I have called naturalistic with reference to Ethics. The reason of this is obvious enough. When a man confuses two natural objects with one another, defining the one by the other, if for instance, he confuses himself, who is one natural object, with 'pleased' or with 'pleasure' which are others, then there is no reason to call the fallacy naturalistic. But if he confuses 'good,' which is not in the same sense a natural object, with any natural object whatever, then there is a reason for calling that a naturalistic fallacy; its being made with regard to 'good' marks it as something quite specific, and this specific mistake deserves a name because it is so common. As for the reasons why good is not to be considered a natural object, they may be reserved for discussion in another place. But, for the present, it is sufficient to notice this: Even if it were a natural object, that would not alter the nature of the fallacy nor diminish its importance one whit. All that I have said about it would remain quite equally true: only the name which I have called it would not be so appropriate as I think it is. And I do not care about the name: what I do care about is the fallacy. It does not matter what we call it, provided we recognise it when we meet with it. It is to be met with in almost every book on Ethics; and yet it is not recognised: and that is why it is necessary to multiply illustrations of it, and convenient to give it a name. It is a very simple fallacy indeed. When we say that an orange is yellow, we do not think our statement binds us to hold that 'orange' means nothing else than 'yellow,' or that nothing can be yellow but an orange. Supposing the orange is also sweet! Does that bind us to say that 'sweet' is exactly the same thing as 'yellow,' that 'sweet' must be defined as 'yellow'? And supposing it be recognised that 'yellow' just means 'yellow' and nothing else whatever, does that make it any more difficult to hold that oranges are yellow? Most certainly it does not: on the contrary, it would be absolutely meaningless to say that oranges were yellow, unless yellow did in the end mean just 'yellow' and nothing else whatever—unless it was absolutely indefinable. We should not get any very clear notion about things, which are yellow—we should not get very far with our science, if we were bound to hold that everything which was yellow, *meant* exactly the same thing as yellow. We should find we had to hold that an orange was exactly the same thing as a stool, a piece of paper, a lemon, anything you like. We could prove any number of absurdities; but should we be the nearer to the truth? Why, then, should it be different with 'good'? Why, if good is good and indefinable, should I be held to deny that pleasure is good? Is there any difficulty in holding both to be true at once? On the contrary, there is no meaning in saying that pleasure is good, unless good is something different from pleasure. It is absolutely useless, so far as Ethics is concerned, to prove, as Mr. Spencer tries to do, that increase of pleasure coincides with increase of life, unless good *means* something different from either life or pleasure. He might just as well try to prove that an orange is yellow by shewing that it always is wrapped up in paper.

13. In fact, if it is not the case that 'good' denotes something simple and indefinable, only two alternatives are possible: either it is a complex, a given whole, about the correct analysis of which there may be disagreement; or else it means nothing at all, and there is no such subject as Ethics. In general, however, ethical philosophers have attempted to define good, without recognising what such an attempt must mean. They actually use arguments which involve one or both of the absurdities considered in § 11. We are, therefore, justified in concluding that the attempt to define good is chiefly due to want of clearness as to the possible nature of definition. There are, in fact, only two serious alternatives to be considered, in order to establish the conclusion that 'good' does denote a simple and indefinable notion. It might possibly denote a complex, as 'horse' does; or it might have no meaning at all. Neither of these possibilities has, however, been clearly conceived and seriously maintained, as such, by those who presume to define good; and both may be dismissed by a simple appeal to facts.

(1) The hypothesis that disagreement about the meaning of good is disagreement with regard to the correct analysis of a given whole, may be most plainly seen to be incorrect by consideration of the fact that, whatever definition be offered, it may be always asked, with significance, of the complex so defined, whether it is itself good. To take, for instance, one of the more plausible, because one of the more complicated, of such proposed definitions, it may easily be thought, at first sight, that to be good may mean to be that which we desire to desire. Thus if we apply this definition to a particular instance and say 'When we think that A is good, we are thinking that A is one of the things which we desire to desire,' our proposition may seem quite plausible. But, if we carry the investigation further, and ask ourselves 'Is it good to desire to desire A?' it is apparent, on a little reflection, that this question is itself as intelligible, as the original question 'Is A good?'—that we are, in fact, now asking for exactly the same information about the desire to desire A, for which we formerly asked with regard to A itself. But it is also apparent that the meaning of this second question cannot be correctly analysed into 'Is the desire to desire A one of the things which we desire to desire?': we have not before our minds anything so complicated as the question 'Do we desire to desire to desire to desire A?' Moreover any one can easily convince himself by inspection that the predicate of this proposition—'good'—is positively different from the notion of 'desiring to desire' which enters into its subject: 'That we should desire to desire A is good'

is *not* merely equivalent to 'That A should be good is good.' It may indeed be true that what we desire to desire is always also good; perhaps, even the converse may be true: but it is very doubtful whether this is the case, and the mere fact that we understand very well what is meant by doubting it, shews clearly that we have two different notions before our minds.

(2) And the same consideration is sufficient to dismiss the hypothesis that 'good' has no meaning whatsoever. It is very natural to make the mistake of supposing that what is universally true is of such a nature that its negation would be self-contradictory: the importance which has been assigned to analytic propositions in the history of philosophy shews how easy such a mistake is. And thus it is very easy to conclude that what seems to be a universal ethical principle is in fact an identical proposition; that, if, for example, whatever is called 'good' seems to be pleasant, the proposition 'Pleasure is the good' does not assert a connection between two different notions, but involves only one, that of pleasure, which is easily recognised as a distinct entity. But whoever will attentively consider with himself what is actually before his mind when he asks the question 'Is pleasure (or whatever it may be) after all good?' can easily satisfy himself that he is not merely wondering whether pleasure is pleasant. And if he will try this experiment with each suggested definition in succession, he may become expert enough to recognise that in every case he has before his mind a unique object, with regard to the connection of which with any other object, a distinct question may be asked. Every one does in fact understand the question 'Is this good?' When he thinks of it, his state of mind is different from what it would be, were he asked 'Is this pleasant, or desired, or approved?' It has a distinct meaning for him, even though he may not recognise in what respect it is distinct. Whenever he thinks of 'intrinsic value,' or 'intrinsic worth,' or says that a thing 'ought to exist,' he has before his mind the unique object—the unique property of things—which I mean by 'good.' Everybody is constantly aware of this notion, although he may never become aware at all that it is different from other notions of which he is also aware. But, for correct ethical reasoning, it is extremely important that he should become aware of this fact; and, as soon as the nature of the problem is clearly understood, there should be little difficulty in advancing so far in analysis.

THE EMOTIVE MEANING OF ETHICAL TERMS

C. L. STEVENSON

I

Ethical questions first arise in the form "Is so and so good?", or "Is this alternative better than that?" These questions are difficult partly because we don't quite know what we are seeking. We are asking, "Is there a needle in that haystack?" without even knowing just what a needle is. So the first thing to do is to examine the questions themselves. We must try to make them clearer, either by defining the terms in which they are expressed, or by any other method that is available.

The present paper is concerned wholly with this preliminary step of making ethical questions clear. In order to help answer the question "Is X good?" we must *substitute* for it a question which is free from ambiguity and confusion.

It is obvious that in substituting a clearer question we must not introduce some utterly different kind of question. It won't do (to take an extreme instance of a prevalent fallacy) to substitute for "Is X good?" the question "Is X pink with yellow trimmings?" and then point out how easy the question really is. This would beg the original question, not help answer it. On the other hand, we must not expect the substituted question to be strictly "identical" with the original one. The original question may embody hypostatization, anthropomorphism, vagueness, and all the other ills to which our ordinary discourse is subject. If our substituted question is to be clearer, it must remove these ills. The questions will be identical only in the sense that a child is identical with the man he later becomes. Hence we must not demand that the substitution strike us, on immediate introspection, as making no change in meaning.

Just how, then, must the substituted question be related to the original? Let us assume (inaccurately) that it must result from replacing "good" by some set of terms which define it. The question then resolves itself to this: How must the defined meaning of "good" be related to its original meaning?

I answer that it must be *relevant*. A defined meaning will be called "relevant" to the original meaning under these circumstances: Those who have understood the definition must be able to say all that they then want

Reprinted from *Mind*, Vol. 46 (1937) by permission of the author and the editor; also reprinted, with changes, in C. L. Stevenson, *Facts and Values: Studies in Ethical Analysis*, Yale University Press, New Haven, 1963.

to say by using the term in the defined way. They must never have occasion to use the term in the old, unclear sense. (If a person did have to go on using the word in the old sense, then to this extent his meaning would not be clarified, and the philosophical task would not be completed.) It frequently happens that a word is used so confusedly and ambiguously that we must give it *several* defined meanings, rather than one. In this case only the whole set of defined meanings will be called "relevant," and any one of them will be called "partially relevant." This is not a rigorous treatment of *relevance*, by any means; but it will serve for the present purposes.

Let us now turn to our particular task—that of giving a relevant definition of "good." Let us first examine some of the ways in which others have attempted to do this.

The word "good" has often been defined in terms of *approval*, or similar psychological attitudes. We may take as typical examples: "good" means *desired by me* (Hobbes); and "good" means *approved by most people* (Hume, in effect). It will be convenient to refer to definitions of this sort as "interest theories," following Mr. R. B. Perry, although neither "interest" nor "theory" is used in the most usual way.

Are definitions of this sort relevant?

It is idle to deny their *partial* relevance. The most superficial inquiry will reveal that "good" is exceedingly ambiguous. To maintain that "good" is *never* used in Hobbes's sense, and never in Hume's, is only to manifest an insensitivity to the complexities of language. We must recognize, perhaps, not only these senses, but a variety of similar ones, differing both with regard to the kind of interest in question, and with regard to the people who are said to have the interest.

But this is a minor matter. The essential question is not whether interest theories are *partially* relevant, but whether they are *wholly* relevant. This is the only point for intelligent dispute. Briefly: Granted that some senses of "good" may relevantly be defined in terms of interest, is there some *other* sense which is *not* relevantly so defined? We must give this question careful attention. For it is quite possible that when philosophers (and many others) have found the question "Is X good?" so difficult, they have been grasping for this *other* sense of "good", and not any sense relevantly defined in terms of interest. If we insist on defining "good" in terms of interest, and answer the question when thus interpreted, we may be begging *their* question entirely. Of course this *other* sense of "good" may not exist, or it may be a complete confusion; but that is what we must discover.

Now many have maintained that interest theories are *far* from being completely relevant. They have argued that such theories neglect the very sense of "good" which is most vital. And certainly, their arguments are not without plausibility.

Only . . . what *is* this "vital" sense of "good"? The answers have been so vague, and so beset with difficulties, that one can scarcely determine.

There are certain requirements, however, with which this "vital" sense has been expected to comply—requirements which appeal strongly to our common sense. It will be helpful to summarize these, showing how they exclude the interest theories:

In the first place, we must be able sensibly to *disagree* about whether something is "good". This condition rules out Hobbes's definition. For consider the following argument: "This is good." "That isn't so; it's not good." As translated by Hobbes, this becomes: "I desire this." "That isn't so, for *I* don't." The speakers are not contradicting one another, and think they are, only because of an elementary confusion in the use of pronouns. The definition, "good" means *desired by my community*, is also excluded, for how could people from different communities disagree?*

In the second place, "goodness" must have, so to speak, a magnetism. A person who recognizes X to be "good" must *ipso facto* acquire a stronger tendency to act in its favour than he otherwise would have had. This rules out the Humian type of definition. For according to Hume, to recognize that something is "good" is simply to recognize that the majority approve of it. Clearly, a man may see that the majority approve of X without having, himself, a stronger tendency to favour it. This requirement excludes any attempt to define "good" in terms of the interest of people *other* than the speaker.**

In the third place, the "goodness" of anything must not be verifiable solely by use of the scientific method. "Ethics must not be psychology." This restriction rules out all of the traditional interest theories, without exception. It is so sweeping a restriction that we must examine its plausibility. What are the methodological implications of interest theories which are here rejected?

According to Hobbes's definition, a person can prove his ethical judgments, with finality, by showing that he is not making an introspective error about his desires. According to Hume's definition, one may prove ethical judgments (roughly speaking) by taking a vote. *This* use of the empirical method, at any rate, seems highly remote from what we usually accept as proof, and reflects on the complete relevance of the definitions which imply it.

But aren't there more complicated interest theories which are immune from such methodological implications? No, for the same factors appear; they are only put off for a while. Consider, for example, the definition: "X is good" means *most people would approve of X if they knew its nature and consequences*. How, according to this definition, could we prove that a certain X was good? We should first have to find out, empirically, just what X was like, and what its consequences would be. To this extent the empirical method, as required by the definition, seems beyond intelligent objection. But what remains? We should next have to discover whether most people would approve of the sort of thing we had discovered X to be. This couldn't be determined by popular vote—but only because it would be too difficult to explain to the voters, beforehand,

* See G. E. Moore's *Philosophical Studies*, pp. 332–334.
** See G. C. Field's *Moral Theory*, pp. 52, 56–57.

what the nature and consequences of X really were. Apart from this, voting would be a pertinent method. We are again reduced to counting noses, as a *perfectly final* appeal.

Now we need not scorn voting entirely. A man who rejected interest theories as irrelevant might readily make the following statement: "If I believed that X would be approved by the majority, when they knew all about it, I should be strongly *led* to say that X was good." But he would continue: "*Need* I say that X was good, under the circumstances? Wouldn't my acceptance of the alleged 'final proof' result simply from my being democratic? What about the more aristocratic people? They would simply say that the approval of most people, even when they knew all about the object of their approval, simply had nothing to do with the goodness of anything, and they would probably add a few remarks about the low state of people's interests." It would indeed seem, from these considerations, that the definition we have been considering has presupposed democratic ideals from the start; it has dressed up democratic propaganda in the guise of a definition.

The omnipotence of the empirical method, as implied by interest theories and others, may be shown unacceptable in a somewhat different way. Mr. G. E. Moore's familiar objection about the open question is chiefly pertinent in this regard. No matter what set of scientifically knowable properties a thing may have (says Moore, in effect), you will find, on careful introspection, that it is an open question to ask whether anything having these properties is *good*. It is difficult to believe that this recurrent question is a totally confused one, or that it seems open only because of the ambiguity of "good". Rather, we must be using some sense of "good" which is not definable, relevantly, in terms of anything scientifically knowable. That is, the scientific method is not sufficient for ethics.*

These, then, are the requirements with which the "vital" sense of "good" is expected to comply: (1) goodness must be a topic for intelligent disagreement; (2) it must be "magnetic"; and (3) it must not be discoverable solely through the scientific method.

II

Let us now turn to my own analysis of ethical judgments. First let me present my position dogmatically, showing to what extent I vary from tradition.

I believe that the three requirements, given above, are perfectly sensible; that there is some *one* sense of "good" which satisfies all three requirements; and that no traditional interest theory satisfies them all. But this does not imply that "good" must be explained in terms of a Platonic

* See G. E. Moore's *Principia Ethica*, chap. i. I am simply trying to preserve the spirit of Moore's objection, and not the exact form of it.

Idea, or of a Categorical Imperative, or of an unique, unanalyzable property. On the contrary, the three requirements can be met by a *kind* of interest theory. *But we must give up a presupposition which all the traditional interest theories have made.*

Traditional interest theories hold that ethical statements are *descriptive* of the existing state of interests—that they simply *give information* about interests. (More accurately, ethical judgments are said to describe what the state of interests is, was, or will be, or to indicate what the state of interests *would* be under specified circumstances.) It is this emphasis on description, on information, which leads to their incomplete relevance. Doubtless there is always *some* element of description in ethical judgments, but this is by no means all. Their major use is not to indicate facts, but to *create an influence*. Instead of merely describing people's interests, they *change* or *intensify* them. They *recommend* an interest in an object, rather than state that the interest already exists.

For instance: When you tell a man that he oughtn't to steal, your object isn't merely to let him know that people disapprove of stealing. You are attempting, rather, to get *him* to disapprove of it. Your ethical judgment has a quasi-imperative force which, operating through suggestion, and intensified by your tone of voice, readily permits you to begin to *influence*, to *modify*, his interests. If in the end you do not succeed in getting *him* to disapprove of stealing, you will feel that you've failed to convince him that stealing is wrong. You will continue to feel this, even though he fully acknowledges that you disapprove of it, and that almost everyone else does. When you point out to him the consequences of his actions—consequences which you suspect he already disapproves of—these *reasons* which support your ethical judgment are simply a means of facilitating your influence. If you think you can change his interests by making vivid to him how others will disapprove of him, you will do so; otherwise not. So the consideration about other people's interest is just an additional means you may employ, in order to move him, and is not a part of the ethical judgment itself. Your ethical judgment doesn't merely describe interests to him, it directs his very interests. The difference between the traditional interest theories and my view is like the difference between describing a desert and irrigating it.

Another example: A munition maker declares that war is a good thing. If he merely meant that he approved of it, he would not have to insist so strongly, nor grow so excited in his argument. People would be quite easily convinced that he approved of it. If he merely meant that most people approved of war, or that most people would approve of it if they knew the consequences, he would have to yield his point if it were proved that this wasn't so. But he wouldn't do this, nor does consistency require it. He is not *describing* the state of people's approval; he is trying to *change* it by his influence. If he found that few people approved of war, he might insist all the more strongly that it was good, for there would be more changing to be done.

This example illustrates how "good" may be used for what most of us would call bad purposes. Such cases are as pertinent as any others. I am not indicating the *good* way of using "good". I am not influencing people, but am describing the way this influence sometimes goes on. If the reader wishes to say that the munition maker's influence is bad—that is, if the reader wishes to awaken people's disapproval of the man, and to make him disapprove of his own actions—I should at another time be willing to join in this undertaking. But this is not the present concern. I am not using ethical terms, but am indicating how they *are* used. The munition maker, in his use of "good", illustrates the persuasive character of the word just as well as does the unselfish man who, eager to encourage in each of us a desire for the happiness of all, contends that the supreme good is peace.

Thus ethical terms are *instruments* used in the complicated interplay and readjustment of human interests. This can be seen plainly from more general observations. People from widely separated communities have different moral attitudes. Why? To a great extent because they have been subject to different social influences. Now clearly this influence doesn't operate through sticks and stones alone; words play a great part. People praise one another, to encourage certain inclinations, and blame one another, to discourage others. Those of forceful personalities issue commands which weaker people, for complicated instinctive reasons, find it difficult to disobey, quite apart from fears of consequences. Further influence is brought to bear by writers and orators. Thus social influence is exerted, to an enormous extent, by means that have nothing to do with physical force or material reward. The ethical terms facilitate such influence. Being suited for use in *suggestion*, they are a means by which men's attitudes may be led this way or that. The reason, then, that we find a greater similarity in the moral attitudes of one community than in those of different communities is largely this: ethical judgments propagate themselves. One man says "This is good"; this may influence the approval of another person, who then makes the same ethical judgment, which in turn influences another person, and so on. In the end, by a process of mutual influence, people take up more or less the same attitudes. Between people of widely separated communities, of course, the influence is less strong; hence different communities have different attitudes.

These remarks will serve to give a general idea of my point of view. We must now go into more detail. There are several questions which must be answered: How does an ethical sentence acquire its power of influencing people—why is it suited to suggestion? Again, what has this influence to do with the *meaning* of ethical terms? And finally, do these considerations really lead us to a sense of "good" which meets the requirements mentioned in the preceding section?

Let us deal first with the question about *meaning*. This is far from an easy question, so we must enter into a preliminary inquiry about meaning in general. Although a seeming digression, this will prove indispensable.

III

Broadly speaking, there are two different *purposes* which lead us to use language. On the one hand we use words (as in science) to record, clarify, and communicate *beliefs*. On the other hand we use words to give vent to our feelings (interjections), or to create moods (poetry), or to incite people to actions or attitudes (oratory).

The first use of words I shall call "descriptive"; the second, "dynamic". Note that the distinction depends solely upon the *purpose* of the *speaker*.

When a person says "Hydrogen is the lightest known gas", his purpose *may* be simply to lead the hearer to believe this, or to believe that the speaker believes it. In that case the words are used descriptively. When a person cuts himself and says "Damn", his purpose is not ordinarily to record, clarify, or communicate any belief. The word is used dynamically. The two ways of using words, however, are by no means mutually exclusive. This is obvious from the fact that our purposes are often complex. Thus when one says "I want you to close the door", part of his purpose, ordinarily, is to lead the hearer to believe that he has this want. To that extent the words are used descriptively. But the major part of one's purpose is to lead the hearer to *satisfy* the want. To that extent the words are used dynamically.

It very frequently happens that the same sentence may have a dynamic use on one occasion, and may not have a dynamic use on another; and that it may have different dynamic uses on different occasions. For instance: A man says to a visiting neighbour, "I am loaded down with work". His purpose may be to let the neighbour know how life is going with him. This would *not* be a dynamic use of words. He may make the remark, however, in order to drop a hint. This *would* be dynamic usage (as well as descriptive). Again, he may make the remark to arouse the neighbour's sympathy. This would be a *different* dynamic usage from that of hinting.

Or again, when we say to a man, "Of course you won't make those mistakes any more", we *may* simply be making a prediction. But we are more likely to be using "suggestion", in order to encourage him and hence *keep* him from making mistakes. The first use would be descriptive; the second, mainly dynamic.

From these examples it will be clear that we can't determine whether words are used dynamically or not, merely by reading the dictionary—even assuming that everyone is faithful to dictionary meanings. Indeed, to know whether a person is using a word dynamically, we must note his tone of voice, his gestures, the general circumstances under which he is speaking, and so on.

We must now proceed to an important question: What has the dynamic use of words to do with their *meaning?* One thing is clear—we must not define "meaning" in a way that would make meaning vary with dynamic usage. If we did, we should have no use for the term. All that we could say about such "meaning" would be that it is very complicated, and subject to constant change. So we must certainly distinguish between the dynamic use of words and their meaning.

It doesn't follow, however, that we must define "meaning" in some non-psychological fashion. We must simply restrict the psychological field. Instead of identifying meaning with *all* the psychological causes and effects that attend a word's utterance, we must identify it with those that it has a *tendency* (causal property, dispositional property) to be connected with. The tendency must be of a particular kind, moreover. It must exist for all who speak the language; it must be persistent; and must be realizable more or less independently of determinate circumstances attending the word's utterance. There will be further restrictions dealing with the interrelation of words in different contexts. Moreover, we must include, under the psychological responses which the words tend to produce, not only immediately introspectable experiences, but *dispositions* to react in a given way with appropriate stimuli. I hope to go into these matters in a subsequent paper. Suffice it now to say that I think "meaning" may be thus defined in a way to include "propositional" meaning as an important kind. Now a word may *tend* to have causal relations which in fact it sometimes doesn't; and it may sometimes have causal relations which it *doesn't tend* to have. And since the tendency of words which constitutes their meaning must be of a particular kind, and may include, as responses, dispositions to reactions, of which any of *several* immediate experiences may be a sign, then there is nothing surprising in the fact that words have a permanent meaning, in spite of the fact that the immediately introspectable experiences which attend their usage are so highly varied.

When "meaning" is defined in this way, meaning will not include dynamic use. For although words are sometimes accompanied by dynamic purposes, they do not *tend* to be accompanied by them in the way above mentioned. *E.g.*, there is no tendency realizable independently of the determinate circumstances under which the words are uttered.

There will be a kind of meaning, however, in the sense above defined, which has an intimate relation to dynamic usage. I refer to "emotive" meaning (in a sense roughly like that employed by Ogden and Richards).* The emotive meaning of a word is a tendency of a word, arising through the history of its usage, to produce (result from) *affective* responses in people. It is the immediate aura of feeling which hovers about a word. Such tendencies to produce affective responses cling to words very tenaciously. It would be difficult, for instance, to express merriment by using the interjection "alas". Because of the persistence of such affective tendencies (among other reasons) it becomes feasible to classify them as "meanings".

* See *The Meaning of Meaning*, by C. K. Ogden and I. A. Richards. On p. 125, second edition, there is a passage on ethics which was the source of the ideas embodied in this paper.

Just *what* is the relation between emotive meaning and the dynamic use of words? Let us take an example. Suppose that a man is talking with a group of people which includes Miss Jones, aged 59. He refers to her, without thinking, as an "old maid". Now even if his purposes are perfectly innocent—even if he is using the words purely descriptively—Miss Jones won't think so. She will think he is encouraging the others to have contempt for her, and will draw in her skirts, defensively. The man might have done better if instead of saying "old maid" he had said "elderly spinster". The latter words could have been put to the same descriptive use, and would not so readily have caused suspicions about the dynamic use.

"Old maid" and "elderly spinster" differ, to be sure, only in emotive meaning. From the example it will be clear that certain words, because of their emotive meaning, are suited to a certain kind of dynamic use—so well suited, in fact, that the hearer is likely to be misled when we use them in any other way. The more pronounced a word's emotive meaning is, the less likely people are to use it purely descriptively. Some words are suited to encourage people, some to discourage them, some to quiet them, and so on.

Even in these cases, of course, the dynamic purposes are not to be identified with any sort of meaning; for the emotive meaning accompanies a word much more persistently than do the dynamic purposes. But there is an important contingent relation between emotive meaning and dynamic purpose: the former assists the latter. Hence if we define emotively laden terms in a way that neglects their emotive meaning, we are likely to be confusing. *We lead people to think that the terms defined are used dynamically less often than they are.*

IV

Let us now apply these remarks in defining "good". This word may be used morally or non-morally. I shall deal with the non-moral usage almost entirely, but only because it is simpler. The main points of the analysis will apply equally well to either usage.

As a preliminary definition, let us take an inaccurate approximation. It may be more misleading than helpful, but will do to begin with. Roughly, then, the sentence "X is good" means *We like* X. ("We" includes the hearer or hearers.)

At first glance this definition sounds absurd. If used, we should expect to find the following sort of conversation: A. "This is good." B. "But I *don't* like it. What led you to believe that I did?" The unnaturalness of B's reply, judged by ordinary word-usage, would seem to cast doubt on the relevance of my definition.

B's unnaturalness, however, lies simply in this: he is assuming that "We like it" (as would occur implicitly in the use of "good") is being used descriptively. This won't do. When "We like it" is to take the place of

"This is good", the former sentence must be used not purely descriptively, but dynamically. More specifically, it must be used to promote a very subtle (and for the non-moral sense in question, a very easily resisted) kind of *suggestion.* To the extent that "we" refers to the hearer, it must have the dynamic use, essential to suggestion, of leading the hearer to *make* true what is said, rather than merely to believe it. And to the extent that "we" refers to the speaker, the sentence must have not only the descriptive use of indicating belief about the speaker's interest, but the quasi-interjectory, dynamic function of giving direct expression to the interest. (This immediate expression of feelings assists in the process of suggestion. It is difficult to disapprove in the face of another's enthusiasm.)

For an example of a case where "We like this" is used in the dynamic way that "This is good" is used, consider the case of a mother who says to her several children, "One thing is certain, *we all like to be neat*". If she really believed this, she wouldn't bother to say so. But she is not using the words descriptively. She is *encouraging* the children to like neatness. By telling them that they like neatness, she will lead them to *make* her statement true, so to speak. If, instead of saying "We all like to be neat" in this way, she had said "It's a good thing to be neat", the effect would have been approximately the same.

But these remarks are still misleading. Even when "We like it" is used for suggestion, it isn't quite like "This is good". The latter is more subtle. With such a sentence as "This is a good book", for example, it would be practically impossible to use instead "We like this book". When the latter is used, it must be accompanied by so exaggerated an intonation, to prevent its becoming confused with a descriptive statement, that the force of suggestion becomes stronger, and ludicrously more overt, than when "good" is used.

The definition is inadequate, further, in that the definiens has been restricted to dynamic usage. Having said that dynamic usage was different from meaning, I should not have to mention it in giving the *meaning* of "good".

It is in connection with this last point that we must return to emotive meaning. The word "good" has a pleasing emotive meaning which fits it especially for the dynamic use of suggesting favourable interest. But the sentence "We like it" has no such emotive meaning. Hence my definition has neglected emotive meaning entirely. Now to neglect emotive meaning is likely to lead to endless confusions, as we shall presently see; so I have sought to make up for the inadequacy of the definition by letting the restriction about dynamic usage take the place of emotive meaning. What I should do, of course, is to find a definiens whose emotive meaning, like that of "good", simply does *lead* to dynamic usage.

Why didn't I do this? I answer that it isn't possible, if the definition is to afford us increased clarity. No two words, in the first place, have quite the same emotive meaning. The most we can hope for is a rough approximation. But if we seek for such an approximation for "good", we shall find nothing more than synonyms, such as "desirable" or "valuable"; and these are profitless because they do not clear up the connection between "good" and favourable interest. If we reject such synonyms, in favour of non-ethical terms, we shall be highly misleading. For instance: "This is good" has something like the meaning of "I *do* like this; do so as well". But this is certainly not accurate. For the imperative makes an appeal to the conscious efforts of the hearer. Of course he can't like something just by trying. He must be led to like it through suggestion. Hence an ethical sentence differs from an imperative in that it enables one to make changes in a much more subtle, less fully conscious way. Note that the ethical sentence centres the hearer's attention not on his interests, but on the object of interest, and thereby facilitates suggestion. Because of its subtlety, moreover, an ethical sentence readily permits counter-suggestion, and leads to the give and take situation which is so characteristic of arguments about values.

Strictly speaking, then, it is impossible to define "good" in terms of favourable interest if emotive meaning is not to be distorted. Yet it is possible to say that "This is good" is *about* the favourable interest of the speaker and the hearer or hearers, and that it has a pleasing emotive meaning which fits the words for use in suggestion. This is a rough description of meaning, not a definition. But it serves the same clarifying function that a definition ordinarily does; and that, after all, is enough.

A word must be added about the moral use of "good". This differs from the above in that it is about a different kind of interest. Instead of being about what the hearer and speaker *like*, it is about a stronger sort of approval. When a person *likes* something, he is pleased when it prospers, and disappointed when it doesn't. When a person *morally approves* of something, he experiences a rich feeling of security when it prospers, and is indignant, or "shocked" when it doesn't. These are rough and inaccurate examples of the many factors which one would have to mention in distinguishing the two kinds of interest. In the moral usage, as well as in the non-moral, "good" has an emotive meaning which adapts it to suggestion.

And now, are these considerations of any importance? Why do I stress emotive meanings in this fashion? Does the omission of them really lead people into errors? I think, indeed, that the errors resulting from such omissions are enormous. In order to see this, however, we must return to the restrictions, mentioned in section I, with which the "vital" sense of "good" has been expected to comply.

V

The first restriction, it will be remembered, had to do with disagreement. Now there is clearly some sense in which people disagree on ethical points; but we must not rashly assume that all disagreement is modelled after the sort that occurs in the natural sciences. We must distinguish between "disagreement in belief" (typical of the sciences) and "disagreement in interest". Disagreement in belief occurs when A believes *p* and B disbelieves it. Disagreement in interest occurs when A has a favourable interest in X, when B has an unfavourable one in it, and when neither is content to let the other's interest remain unchanged.

Let me give an example of disagreement in interest. A. "Let's go to a cinema to-night." B. "I don't want to do that. Let's go to the symphony." A continues to insist on the cinema, B on the symphony. This is disagreement in a perfectly conventional sense. They can't agree on where they want to go, and each is trying to redirect the other's interest. (Note that imperatives are used in the example.)

It is disagreement in *interest* which takes place in ethics. When C says "This is good", and D says "No, it's bad", we have a case of suggestion and counter-suggestion. Each man is trying to redirect the other's interest. There obviously need be no domineering, since each may be willing to give ear to the other's influence; but each is trying to move the other none the less. It is in this sense that they disagree. Those who argue that certain interest theories make no provision for disagreement have been misled, I believe, simply because the traditional theories, in leaving out emotive meaning, give the impression that ethical judgments are used descriptively only; and of course when judgments are used purely descriptively, the only disagreement that can arise is disagreement *in belief*. Such disagreement may be disagreement in belief *about* interests; but this is not the same as disagreement *in* interest. My definition doesn't provide for disagreement in belief about interests, any more than does Hobbes's; but that is no matter, for there is no reason to believe, at least on common-sense grounds, that this kind of disagreement exists. There is only disagreement *in* interest. (We shall see in a moment that disagreement in interest does not remove ethics from sober argument—that this kind of disagreement may often be resolved through empirical means.)

The second restriction, about "magnetism", or the connection between goodness and actions, requires only a word. This rules out *only* those interest theories which do *not* include the interest of the speaker, in defining "good". My account does include the speaker's interest; hence is immune.

The third restriction, about the empirical method, may be met in a way that springs naturally from the above account of disagreement. Let us put the question in this way: When two people disagree over an ethical matter, can they completely resolve the disagreement through empirical considerations, assuming that each applies the empirical method exhaustively, consistently, and without error?

I answer that sometimes they can, and sometimes they cannot; and that at any rate, even when they can, the relation between empirical knowledge and ethical judgments is quite different from the one which traditional interest theories seem to imply.

This can best be seen from an analogy. Let's return to the example where A and B couldn't agree on a cinema or a symphony. The example differed from an ethical argument in that imperatives were used, rather than ethical judgments; but was analogous to the extent that each person was endeavouring to modify the other's interest. Now how would these peopl argue the case, assuming that they were too intelligent just to shout at one another?

Clearly, they would give "reasons" to support their imperatives. A might say, "But you know, Garbo is at the Bijou". His hope is that B, who admires Garbo, will acquire a desire to go to the cinema when he knows what play will be there. B may counter, "But Toscanini is guest conductor to-night, in an all-Beethoven programme". And so on. Each supports his imperative ("*Let's* do so and so") by reasons which may be empirically established.

To generalize from this: disagreement in interest may be rooted in disagreement in belief. That is to say, people who disagree in interest would often cease to do so if they knew the precise nature and consequences of the object of their interest. To this extent disagreement in interest may be resolved by securing agreement in belief, which in turn may be secured empirically.

This generalization holds for ethics. If A and B, instead of using imperatives, had said, respectively, "It would be *better* to go to the cinema", and "It would be better to go to the symphony", the reasons which they would advance would be roughly the same. They would each give a more thorough account of the object of interest, with the purpose of completing the redirection of interest which was begun by the suggestive force of the ethical sentence. On the whole, of course, the suggestive force of the ethical statement merely exerts enough pressure to start such trains of reasons, since the reasons are much more essential in resolving disagreement in interest than the persuasive effect of the ethical judgment itself.

Thus the empirical method is relevant to ethics simply because our knowledge of the world is a determining factor to our interests. But note that empirical facts are not inductive grounds from which the ethical judgment problematically follows. (This is what traditional interest theories imply.) If someone said "Close the door", and added the reason "We'll catch cold", the latter would scarcely be called an inductive ground of the former. Now imperatives are related to the reasons which support them in the same way that ethical judgments are related to reasons.

Is the empirical method *sufficient* for attaining ethical agreement? Clearly not. For empirical knowledge resolves disagreement in interest only to the extent that such disagreement is rooted in disagreement in belief. Not all disagreement in interest is of this sort. For instance: A is of a sympathetic nature, and B isn't. They are arguing about whether a public dole would be good. Suppose that they discovered all the consequences of the dole. Isn't it possible, even so, that A will say that it's good, and B that it's bad? The disagreement in interest may arise not from limited factual knowledge, but simply from A's sympathy and B's coldness. Or again, suppose, in the above argument, that A was poor and unemployed, and that B was rich. Here again the disagreement might not be due to different factual knowledge. It would be due to the different social positions of the men, together with their predominant self-interest.

When ethical disagreement is not rooted in disagreement in belief, is there *any* method by which it may be settled? If one means by "method" a *rational* method, then there is no method. But in any case there is a "way". Let's consider the above example, again, where disagreement was due to A's sympathy and B's coldness. Must they end by saying, "Well, it's just a matter of our having different temperaments"? Not necessarily. A, for instance, may try to *change* the temperament of his opponent. He may pour out his enthusiasms in such a moving way—present the sufferings of the poor with such appeal—that he will lead his opponent to see life through different eyes. He may build up, by the contagion of his feelings, an influence which will modify B's temperament, and create in him a sympathy for the poor which didn't previously exist. This is often the only way to obtain ethical agreement, if there is any way at all. It is persuasive, not empirical or rational; but that is no reason for neglecting it. There is no reason to scorn it, either, for it is only by such means that our personalities are able to grow, through our contact with others.

The point I wish to stress, however, is simply that the empirical method is instrumental to ethical agreement only to the extent that disagreement in interest is rooted in disagreement in belief. There is little reason to believe that all disagreement is of this sort. Hence the empirical method is not sufficient for ethics. In any case, ethics is not psychology, since psychology doesn't endeavour to *direct* our interests; it discovers facts about the ways in which interests are or can be directed, but that's quite another matter.

To summarize this section: my analysis of ethical judgments meets the three requirements for the "vital" sense of "good" that were mentioned in section I. The traditional interest theories fail to meet these requirements simply because they neglect emotive meaning. This neglect leads them to neglect dynamic usage, and the sort of disagreement that results from such usage, together with the method of resolving the disagreement. I may add that my analysis answers Moore's objection about the open question. Whatever scientifically knowable properties a thing may have, it *is* always open to question whether a thing having these (enumerated) qualities is good. For to ask whether it is good is to ask for *influence*. And whatever I may know about an object, I can still ask, quite pertinently, to be influenced with regard to my interest in it.

VI

And now, have I really pointed out the "vital" sense of "good"?

I suppose that many will still say "No", claiming that I have simply failed to set down *enough* requirements which this sense must meet, and that my analysis, like all others given in terms of interest, is a way of begging the issue. They will say: "When we ask 'Is X good?' we don't want mere influence, mere advice. We decidedly don't want to be influenced through persuasion, nor are we fully content when the influence is supported by a wide scientific knowledge of X. The answer to our question will, of course, modify our interests. But this is only because an unique sort of *truth* will be revealed to us—a truth which must be apprehended *a priori*. We want our interests to be guided by this truth, and by nothing else. To substitute for such a truth mere emotive meaning and suggestion is to conceal from us the very object of our search."

I can only answer that I do not understand. What is this truth to be *about?* For I recollect no Platonic Idea, nor do I know what to *try* to recollect. I find no indefinable property, nor do I know what to look for. And the "self-evident" deliverances of reason, which so many philosophers have claimed, seem, on examination, to be deliverances of their respective reasons only (if of anyone's) and not of mine.

I strongly suspect, indeed, that any sense of "good" which is expected both to unite itself in synthetic *a priori* fashion with other concepts, and to influence interests as well, is really a great confusion. I extract from this meaning the power of influence alone, which I find the only intelligible part. If the rest is confusion, however, then it certainly deserves more than the shrug of one's shoulders. What I should like to do is to *account* for the confusion—to examine the psychological needs which have given rise to it, and to show how these needs may be satisfied in another way. This is *the* problem, if confusion is to be stopped at its source. But it is an enormous problem, and my reflections on it, which are at present worked out only roughly, must be reserved until some later time.

I may add that if "X is good" is essentially a vehicle for suggestion, it is scarcely a statement which philosophers, any more than many other men, are called upon to make. To the extent that ethics predicates the ethical terms of anything, rather than explains their meaning, it ceases to be a reflective study. Ethical statements are social instruments. They are used in a cooperative enterprise that leads to a mutual readjustment of human interests. Philosophers have a part in this; but so too do all men.

TWO CONCEPTS OF RULES

JOHN RAWLS

In this paper I want to show the importance of the distinction between justifying a practice* and justifying a particular action falling under it, and I want to explain the logical basis of this distinction and how it is possible to miss its significance. While the distinction has frequently been made, and is now becoming commonplace, there remains the task of explaining the tendency either to overlook it altogether, or to fail to appreciate its importance.

To show the importance of the distinction I am going to defend utilitarianism against those objections which have traditionally been made against it in connection with punishment and the obligation to keep promises. I hope to show that if one uses the distinction in question then one can state utilitarianism in a way which makes it a much better explication of our considered moral judgments than these traditional objections would seem to admit. Thus the importance of the distinction is shown by the way it strengthens the utilitarian view regardless of whether that view is completely defensible or not.

To explain how the significance of the distinction may be overlooked, I am going to discuss two conceptions of rules. One of these conceptions conceals the importance of distinguishing between the justification of a rule or practice and the justification of a particular action falling under it. The other conception makes it clear why this distinction must be made and what is its logical basis.

. . .

II

I shall now consider the question of promises. The objection to utilitarianism in connection with promises seems to be this: it is believed that on the utilitarian view when a person makes a promise the only ground upon which he should keep it, if he should keep it, is that by keeping it he will realize the most good on the whole. So that if one asks the question

A selection from "Two Concepts of Rules" from *The Philosophical Review,* Vol. 64, 1955. Reprinted by permission of the editors and the author.

* I use the word "practice" throughout as a sort of technical term meaning any form of activity specified by a system of rules which defines offices, roles, moves, penalties, defenses, and so on, and which gives the activity its structure. As examples one may think of games and rituals, trials and parliaments.

"Why should I keep *my* promise?" the utilitarian answer is understood to be that doing so in *this* case will have the best consequences. And this answer is said, quite rightly, to conflict with the way in which the obligation to keep promises is regarded.

Now of course critics of utilitarianism are not unaware that one defense sometimes attributed to utilitarians is the consideration involving the practice of promise-keeping.* In this connection they are supposed to argue something like this: it must be admitted that we feel strictly about keeping promises, more strictly than it might seem our view can account for. But when we consider the matter carefully it is always necessary to take into account the effect which our action will have on the practice of making promises. The promisor must weigh, not only the effects of breaking his promise on the particular case, but also the effect which his breaking his promise will have on the practice itself. Since the practice is of great utilitarian value, and since breaking one's promise always seriously damages it, one will seldom be justified in breaking one's promise. If we view our individual promises in the wider context of the practice of promising itself we can account for the strictness of the obligation to keep promises. There is always one very strong utilitarian consideration in favor of keeping them, and this will insure that when the question arises as to whether or not to keep a promise it will usually turn out that one should, even where the facts of the particular case taken by itself would seem to justify one's breaking it. In this way the strictness with which we view the obligation to keep promises is accounted for.

Ross has criticized this defense as follows: however great the value of the practice of promising, on utilitarian grounds, there must be some value which is greater, and one can imagine it to be obtainable by breaking a promise. Therefore there might be a case where the promisor could argue that breaking his promise was justified as leading to a better state of affairs on the whole. And the promisor could argue in this way no matter how slight the advantage won by breaking the promise. If one were to challenge the promisor his defense would be that what he did was best on the whole in view of all the utilitarian considerations, which in this case *include* the importance of the practice. Ross feels that such a defense would be unacceptable. I think he is right insofar as he is protesting against the appeal to consequences in general and without further explanation. Yet it is extremely difficult to weigh the force of Ross's argument. The kind of case imagined seems unrealistic and one feels that it needs to be described. One is inclined to think that it would either turn out that such a case came under an exception defined by the practice itself, in which case there would not be an appeal to consequences in general on the particular case, or it would happen that the

* Ross, *The Right and the Good*, pp. 37–39, and *Foundations of Ethics* (Oxford, 1939), pp. 92–94. I know of no utilitarian who has used this argument except W. A. Pickard-Cambridge in "Two Problems about Duty," *Mind*, n.s., XLI (April, 1932), 153–157, although the argument goes with G. E. Moore's version of utilitarianism in *Principia Ethica* (Cambridge, 1903). To my knowledge it does not appear in the classical utilitarians; and if one interprets their view correctly this is no accident.

circumstances were so peculiar that the conditions which the practice presupposes no longer obtained. But certainly Ross is right in thinking that it strikes us as wrong for a person to defend breaking a promise by a general appeal to consequences. For a general utilitarian defense is not open to the promisor: it is not one of the defenses allowed by the practice of making promises.

Ross gives two further counterarguments: First, he holds that it overestimates the damage done to the practice of promising by a failure to keep a promise. One who breaks a promise harms his own name certainly, but it isn't clear that a broken promise always damages the practice itself sufficiently to account for the strictness of the obligation. Second, and more important, I think, he raises the question of what one is to say of a promise which isn't known to have been made except to the promisor and the promisee, as in the case of a promise a son makes to his dying father concerning the handling of the estate. In this sort of case the consideration relating to the practice doesn't weigh on the promisor at all, and yet one feels that this sort of promise is as binding as other promises. The question of the effect which breaking it has on the practice seems irrelevant. The only consequence seems to be that one can break the promise without running any risk of being censured; but the obligation itself seems not the least weakened. Hence it is doubtful whether the effect on the practice ever weighs in the particular case; certainly it cannot account for the strictness of the obligation where it fails to obtain. It seems to follow that a utilitarian account of the obligation to keep promises cannot be successfully carried out.

From what I have said in connection with punishment, one can foresee what I am going to say about these arguments and counterarguments. They fail to make the distinction between the justification of a practice and the justification of a particular action falling under it, and therefore they fall into the mistake of taking it for granted that the promisor, like Carritt's official,* is entitled without restriction to bring utilitarian considerations to bear in deciding whether to keep *his* promise. But if one considers what the practice of promising is one will see, I think, that it is such as not to allow this sort of general discretion to the promisor. Indeed, the point of the practice is to abdicate one's title to act in accordance with utilitarian and prudential considerations in order that the future may be tied down and plans coordinated in advance. There are obvious utilitarian advantages in having a practice which denies to the promisor, as a defense, any general appeal to the utilitarian principle in accordance with which the practice itself may be justified. There is nothing contradictory, or surprising, in this: utilitarian (or aesthetic) reasons might properly be given in arguing that the game of chess, or baseball, is satisfactory just as it is, or in arguing that it should be changed in various respects, but a player in a game cannot properly appeal to such considerations as reasons for his making one move rather than another. It is a mistake to think that if the practice is justified on utilitarian grounds

* See E. F. Carritt, *Ethical and Political Thinking* (Oxford, 1947), p. 65.

then the promisor must have complete liberty to use utilitarian arguments to decide whether or not to keep his promise. The practice forbids this general defense; and it is a purpose of the practice to do this. Therefore what the above arguments presuppose—the idea that if the utilitarian view is accepted then the promisor is bound if, and only if, the application of the utilitarian principle to his own case shows that keeping it is best on the whole—is false. The promisor is bound because he promised: weighing the case on its merits is not open to him.

Is this to say that in particular cases one cannot deliberate whether or not to keep one's promise? Of course not. But to do so is to deliberate whether the various excuses, exceptions and defenses, which are understood by, and which constitute an important part of, the practice, apply to one's own case. Various defenses for not keeping one's promise are allowed, but among them there isn't the one that, on general utilitarian grounds, the promisor (truly) thought his action best on the whole, even though there may be the defense that the consequences of keeping one's promise would have been *extremely* severe. While there are too many complexities here to consider all the necessary details, one can see that the general defense isn't allowed if one asks the following question: what would one say of someone who, when asked why he broke his promise, replied simply that breaking it was best on the whole? Assuming that his reply is sincere and that his belief was reasonable (i.e., one need not consider the possibility that he was mistaken), I think that one would question whether or not he knows what it means to say "I promise" (in the appropriate circumstances). It would be said of someone who used this excuse without further explanation that he didn't understand what defenses the practice, which defines a promise, allows to him. If a child were to use this excuse one would correct him; for it is part of the way one is taught the concept of a promise to be corrected if one uses this excuse. The point of having the practice would be lost if the practice did allow this excuse.

It is no doubt part of the utilitarian view that every practice should admit the defense that the consequences of abiding by it would have been extremely severe; and utilitarians would be inclined to hold that some reliance on people's good sense and some concession to hard cases is necessary. They would hold that a practice is justified by serving the interests of those who take part in it; and as with any set of rules there is understood a background of circumstances under which it is expected to be applied and which need not—indeed which cannot—be fully stated. Should these circumstances change, then even if there is no rule which provides for the case, it may still be in accordance with the practice that one be released from one's obligation. But this sort of defense allowed by a practice must not be confused with the general option to weigh each particular case on utilitarian grounds which critics of utilitarianism have thought it necessarily to involve.

The concern which utilitarianism raises by its justification of punishment is that it may justify too much. The question in connection with promises is different: it is how utilitarianism can account for the obligation to keep promises at all. One feels that the recognized obligation to keep one's promise and utilitarianism are incompatible. And to be sure, they are incompatible if one interprets the utilitarian view as necessarily holding that each person has complete liberty to weigh every particular action on general utilitarian grounds. But must one interpret utilitarianism in this way? I hope to show that, in the sorts of cases I have discussed, one cannot interpret it in this way.

III

So far I have tried to show the importance of the distinction between the justification of a practice and the justification of a particular action falling under it by indicating how this distinction might be used to defend utilitarianism against two long-standing objections. One might be tempted to close the discussion at this point by saying that utilitarian considerations should be understood as applying to practices in the first instance and not to particular actions falling under them except insofar as the practices admit of it. One might say that in this modified form it is a better account of our considered moral opinions and let it go at that. But to stop here would be to neglect the interesting question as to how one can fail to appreciate the significance of this rather obvious distinction and can take it for granted that utilitarianism has the consequence that particular cases may always be decided on general utilitarian grounds. I want to argue that this mistake may be connected with misconceiving the logical status of the rules of practices; and to show this I am going to examine two conceptions of rules, two ways of placing them within the utilitarian theory.

The conception which conceals from us the significance of the distinction I am going to call the summary view. It regards rules in the following way: one supposes that each person decides what he shall do in particular cases by applying the utilitarian principle; one supposes further that different people will decide the same particular case in the same way and that there will be recurrences of cases similar to those previously decided. Thus it will happen that in cases of certain kinds the same decision will be made either by the same person at different times or by different persons at the same time. If a case occurs frequently enough one supposes that a rule is formulated to cover that sort of case. I have called this conception the summary view because rules are pictured as summaries of past decisions arrived at by the *direct* application of the utilitarian principle to particular cases. Rules are regarded as reports that cases of a certain sort have been found on *other* grounds to be properly decided in a certain way (although, of course, they do not *say* this).

There are several things to notice about this way of placing rules within the utilitarian theory.

1. The point of having rules derives from the fact that similar cases

tend to recur and that one can decide cases more quickly if one records past decisions in the form of rules. If similar cases didn't recur, one would be required to apply the utilitarian principle directly, case by case, and rules reporting past decisions would be of no use.

2. The decisions made on particular cases are logically prior to rules. Since rules gain their point from the need to apply the utilitarian principle to many similar cases, it follows that a particular case (or several cases similar to it) may exist whether or not there is a rule covering that case. We are pictured as recognizing particular cases prior to there being a rule which covers them, for it is only if we meet with a number of cases of a certain sort that we formulate a rule. Thus we are able to describe a particular case as a particular case of the requisite sort whether there is a rule regarding *that* sort of case or not. Put another way: what the *A*'s and the *B*'s refer to in rules of the form 'Whenever *A* do *B*' may be described as *A*'s and *B*'s whether or not there is the rule 'Whenever *A* do *B*', or whether or not there is any body of rules which make up a practice of which that rule is a part.

To illustrate this consider a rule, or maxim, which could arise in this way: suppose that a person is trying to decide whether to tell someone who is fatally ill what his illness is when he has been asked to do so. Suppose the person to reflect and then decide, on utilitarian grounds, that he should not answer truthfully; and suppose that on the basis of this and other like occasions he formulates a rule to the effect that when asked by someone fatally ill what his illness is, one should not tell him. The point to notice is that someone's being fatally ill and asking what his illness is, and someone's telling him, are things that can be described as such whether or not there is this rule. The performance of the action to which the rule refers doesn't require the stage-setting of a practice of which this rule is a part. This is what is meant by saying that on the summary view particular cases are logically prior to rules.

3. Each person is in principle always entitled to reconsider the correctness of a rule and to question whether or not it is proper to follow it in a particular case. As rules are guides and aids, one may ask whether in past decisions there might not have been a mistake in applying the utilitarian principle to get the rule in question, and wonder whether or not it is best in this case. The reason for rules is that people are not able to apply the utilitarian principle effortlessly and flawlessly; there is need to save time and to post a guide. On this view a society of rational utilitarians would be a society without rules in which each person applied the utilitarian principle directly and smoothly, and without error, case by case. On the other hand, ours is a society in which rules are formulated to serve as aids in reaching these ideally rational decisions on particular cases, guides which have been built up and tested by the experience of generations. If one applies this view to rules, one is interpreting them as maxims, as "rules of thumb"; and it is doubtful that anything to which the summary conception did apply would be called a *rule*. Arguing as if one regarded rules in this way is a mistake one makes while doing philosophy.

4. The concept of a *general* rule takes the following form. One is

pictured as estimating on what percentage of the cases likely to arise a given rule may be relied upon to express the correct decision, that is, the decision that would be arrived at if one were to correctly apply the utilitarian principle case by case. If one estimates that by and large the rule will give the correct decision, or if one estimates that the likelihood of making a mistake by applying the utilitarian principle directly on one's own is greater than the likelihood of making a mistake by following the rule, and if these considerations held of persons generally, then one would be justified in urging its adoption as a general rule. In this way *general* rules might be accounted for on the summary view. It will still make sense, however, to speak of applying the utilitarian principle case by case, for it was by trying to foresee the results of doing this that one got the initial estimates upon which acceptance of the rule depends. That one is taking a rule in accordance with the summary conception will show itself in the naturalness with which one speaks of the rule as a guide, or as a maxim, or as a generalization from experience, and as something to be laid aside in extraordinary cases where there is no assurance that the generalization will hold and the case must therefore be treated on its merits. Thus there goes with this conception the notion of a particular exception which renders a rule suspect on a particular occasion.

The other conception of rules I will call the practice conception. On this view rules are pictured as defining a practice. Practices are set up for various reasons, but one of them is that in many areas of conduct each person's deciding what to do on utilitarian grounds case by case leads to confusion, and that the attempt to coordinate behavior by trying to foresee how others will act is bound to fail. As an alternative one realizes that what is required is the establishment of a practice, the specification of a new form of activity; and from this one sees that a practice necessarily involves the abdication of full liberty to act on utilitarian and prudential grounds. It is the mark of a practice that being taught how to engage in it involves being instructed in the rules which define it, and that appeal is made to those rules to correct the behavior of those engaged in it. Those engaged in a practice recognize the rules as defining it. The rules cannot be taken as simply describing how those engaged in the practice in fact behave: it is not simply that they act as if they were obeying the rules. Thus it is essential to the notion of a practice that the rules are publicly known and understood as definitive; and it is essential also that the rules of a practice can be taught and can be acted upon to yield a coherent practice. On this conception, then, rules are not generalizations from the decisions of individuals applying the utilitarian principle directly and independently to recurrent particular cases. On the contrary, rules define a practice and are themselves the subject of the utilitarian principle.

• • •

If one compares the two conceptions of rules I have discussed, one can see how the summary conception misses the significance of the distinction between justifying a practice and justifying actions falling under it. On this view rules are regarded as guides whose purpose it is to indicate the ideally rational decision on the given particular case which the flawless application of the utilitarian principle would yield. One has, in principle, full option to use the guides or to discard them as the situation warrants without one's moral office being altered in any way: whether one discards the rules or not, one always holds the office of a rational person seeking case by case to realize the best on the whole. But on the practice conception, if one holds an office defined by a practice then questions regarding one's actions in this office are settled by reference to the rules which define the practice. If one seeks to question these rules, then one's office undergoes a fundamental change: one then assumes the office of one empowered to change and criticize the rules, or the office of a reformer, and so on. The summary conception does away with the distinction of offices and the various forms of argument appropriate to each. On that conception there is one office and so no offices at all. It therefore obscures the fact that the utilitarian principle must, in the case of actions and offices defined by a practice, apply to the practice, so that general utilitarian arguments are not available to those who act in offices so defined.*

. . .

I have tried to show that when we fit the utilitarian view together with the practice conception of rules, where this conception is appropriate, we can formulate it in a way which saves it from several traditional objections. I have further tried to show how the logical force of the distinction between justifying a practice and justifying an action falling under it is connected with the practice conception of rules and cannot be understood as long as one regards the rules of practices in accordance with the summary view. Why, when doing philosophy, one may be inclined to so regard them, I have not discussed. The reasons for this are evidently very deep and would require another paper.

* How do these remarks apply to the case of the promise known only to father and son? Well, at first sight the son certainly holds the office of promisor, and so he isn't allowed by the practice to weigh the particular case on general utilitarian grounds. Suppose instead that he wishes to consider himself in the office of one empowered to criticize and change the practice, leaving aside the question as to his right to move from his previously assumed office to another. Then he may consider utilitarian arguments as applied to the practice; but once he does this he will see that there are such arguments for not allowing a general utilitarian defense in the practice for this sort of case. For to do so would make it impossible to ask for and to give a kind of promise which one often wants to be able to ask for and to give. Therefore he will not want to change the practice, and so as a promisor he has no option but to keep his promise.

WHY I SHOULD BE MORAL

KURT BAIER

THE SUPREMACY OF MORAL REASONS

Are moral reasons really superior to reasons of self-interest as we all believe? Do we really have reason on our side when we follow moral reasons against self-interest? What reasons could there be for being moral? Can we really give an answer to 'Why should we be moral?' It is obvious that all these questions come to the same thing. When we ask, 'Should we be moral?' or 'Why should we be moral?' or 'Are moral reasons superior to all others?' we ask to be shown the reason for being moral. What is this reason?

Let us begin with a state of affairs in which reasons of self-interest are supreme. In such a state everyone keeps his impulses and inclinations in check when and only when they would lead him into behavior detrimental to his own interest. Everyone who follows reason will discipline himself to rise early, to do his exercises, to refrain from excessive drinking and smoking, to keep good company, to marry the right sort of girl, to work and study hard in order to get on, and so on. However, it will often happen that people's interests conflict. In such a case, they will have to resort to ruses or force to get their own way. As this becomes known, men will become suspicious, for they will regard one another as scheming competitors for the good things in life. The universal supremacy of the rules of self-interest must lead to what Hobbes called the state of nature. At the same time, it will be clear to everyone that universal obedience to certain rules overriding self-interest would produce a state of affairs which serves everyone's interest much better than his unaided pursuit of it in a state where everyone does the same. Moral rules are universal rules designed to override those of self-interest when following the latter is harmful to others. 'Thou shalt not kill,' 'Thou shalt not lie,' 'Thou shalt not steal' are rules which forbid the inflicting of harm on someone else even when this might be in one's interest.

The very *raison d'être* of a morality is to yield reasons which overrule the reasons of self-interest in those cases when everyone's following self-interest would be harmful to everyone. Hence moral reasons are superior to all others.

"But what does this mean?" it might be objected. "If it merely means that we do so regard them, then you are of course right, but your conten-

Reprinted from Kurt Baier, *The Moral Point by View*, © 1958, by permission of the author and Cornell University Press, Ithaca, N.Y.

tion is useless, a mere point of usage. And how could it mean any more? If it means that we not only do so regard them, but *ought* so to regard them, then there must be *reasons* for saying this. But there could not be any reasons for it. If you offer reasons of self-interest, you are arguing in a circle. Moreover, it cannot be true that it is always in my interest to treat moral reasons as superior to reasons of self-interest. If it were, self-interest and morality could never conflict, but they notoriously do. It is equally circular to argue that there are moral reasons for saying that one ought to treat moral reasons as superior to reasons of self-interest. And what other reasons are there?"

The answer is that we are now looking at the world from the point of view of *anyone*. We are not examining particular alternative courses of action before this or that person; we are examining two alternative worlds, one in which moral reasons are always treated by everyone as superior to reasons of self-interest and one in which the reverse is the practice. And we can see that the first world is the better world, because we can see that the second world would be the sort which Hobbes describes as the state of nature.

This shows that I ought to be moral, for when I ask the question 'What ought I to do?' I am asking, 'Which is the course of action supported by the best reasons?' But since it has just been shown that moral reasons are superior to reasons of self-interest, I have been given a reason for being moral, for following moral reasons rather than any other, namely, they are better reasons than any other.

But is this always so? Do we have a reason for being moral whatever the conditions we find ourselves in? Could there not be situations in which it is not true that we have reasons for being moral, that, on the contrary, we have reasons for ignoring the demands of morality? Is not Hobbes right in saying that in a state of nature the laws of nature, that is, the rules of morality, bind only *in foro interno?*

Hobbes argues as follows.

(i) To live in a state of nature is to live outside society. It is to live in conditions in which there are no common ways of life and, therefore, no reliable expectations about other people's behavior other than that they will follow their inclination or their interest.

(ii) In such a state reason will be the enemy of co-operation and mutual trust. For it is too risky to hope that other people will refrain from protecting their own interests by the preventive elimination of probable or even possible dangers to them. Hence reason will counsel everyone to avoid these risks by preventive action. But this leads to war.

(iii) It is obvious that everyone's following self-interest leads to a state of affairs which is desirable from no one's point of view. It is, on the contrary, desirable that everybody should follow rules overriding self-interest whenever that is to the detriment of others. In other words, it is desirable to bring about a state of affairs in which all obey the rules of morality.

(iv) However, Hobbes claims that in the state of nature it helps nobody if a single person or a small group of persons begins to follow the rules of morality, for this could only lead to the extinction of such individuals or groups. In such a state, it is therefore contrary to reason to be moral.

(v) The situation can change, reason can support morality, only when the presumption about other people's behavior is reversed. Hobbes thought that this could be achieved only by the creation of an absolute ruler with absolute power to enforce his laws. We have already seen that this is not true and that it is quite different if people live in a society, that is, if they have common ways of life, which are taught to all members and somehow enforced by the group. Its members have reason to expect their fellows generally to obey its rules, that is, its religion, morality, customs, and law, even when doing so is not, on certain occasions, in their interest. Hence they too have reason to follow these rules.

Is this argument sound? One might, of course, object to step (i) on the grounds that this is an empirical proposition for which there is little or no evidence. For how can we know whether it is true that people in a state of nature would follow only their inclinations or, at best, reasons of self-interest, when nobody now lives in that state or has ever lived in it?

However, there is some empirical evidence to support this claim. For in the family of nations, individual states are placed very much like individual persons in a state of nature. The doctrine of the sovereignty of nations and the absence of an effective international law and police force are a guarantee that nations live in a state of nature, without commonly accepted rules that are somehow enforced. Hence it must be granted that living in a state of nature leads to living in a state in which individuals act either on impulse or as they think their interest dictates. For states pay only lip service to morality. They attack their hated neighbors when the opportunity arises. They start preventive wars in order to destroy the enemy before he can deliver his knockout blow. Where interests conflict, the stronger party usually has his way, whether his claims are justified or not. And where the relative strength of the parties is not obvious, they usually resort to arms in order to determine "whose side God is on." Treaties are frequently concluded but, morally speaking, they are not worth the paper they are written on. Nor do the partners regard them as contracts binding in the ordinary way, but rather as public expressions of the belief of the governments concerned that for the time being their alliance is in the interest of the allies. It is well understood that such treaties may be canceled before they reach their predetermined end or simply broken when it suits one partner. In international affairs, there are very few examples of *Nibelungentreue*, although statesmen whose countries have profited from keeping their treaties usually make such high moral claims.

It is, moreover, difficult to justify morality in international affairs. For suppose a highly moral statesman were to demand that his country adhere to a treaty obligation even though this meant its ruin or possibly its extinction. Suppose he were to say that treaty obligations are sacred and must be kept whatever the consequences. How could he defend such a policy? Perhaps one might argue that someone has to make a start in order to create mutual confidence in international affairs. Or one might say that setting a good example is the best way of inducing others to follow suit. But such a defense would hardly be sound. The less skeptical one is about the genuineness of the cases in which nations have adhered to their treaties from a sense of moral obligation, the more skeptical one must be about the effectiveness of such examples of virtue in effecting a change of international practice. Power politics still govern in international affairs.

We must, therefore, grant Hobbes the first step in his argument and admit that in a state of nature people, as a matter of psychological fact, would not follow the dictates of morality. But we might object to the next step that knowing this psychological fact about other people's behavior constitutes a reason for behaving in the same way. Would it not still be immoral for anyone to ignore the demands of morality even though he knows that others are likely or certain to do so, too? Can we offer as a justification for morality the fact that no one is entitled to do wrong just because someone else is doing wrong? This argument begs the question whether it *is* wrong for anyone in this state to disregard the demands of morality. It cannot be wrong to break a treaty or make preventive war if we have no reason to obey the moral rules. For to say that it is wrong to do so is to say that we ought not to do so. But if we have no reason for obeying the moral rule, then we have no reason overruling self-interest, hence no reason for keeping the treaty when keeping it is not in our interest, hence it is not true that we have a reason for keeping it, hence not true that we ought to keep it, hence not true that it is wrong not to keep it.

I conclude that Hobbes's argument is sound. Moralities are systems of principles whose acceptance by everyone as overruling the dictates of self-interest is in the interest of everyone alike, though following the rules of a morality is not of course identical with following self-interest. If it were, there could be no conflict between a morality and self-interest and no point in having moral rules overriding self-interest. Hobbes is also right in saying that the application of this system of rules is in accordance with reason only in social conditions, that is, when there are well-established ways of behavior.

The answer to our question 'Why should we be moral?' is therefore as follows. We should be moral because being moral is following rules designed to overrule self-interest whenever it is in the interest of everyone alike that everyone should set aside his interest. It is not self-contradictory to say this, because it may be in one's interest *not* to follow one's interest at times. We have already seen that enlightened self-interest acknowledges this point. But while enlightened self-interest does not require any genuine sacrifice from anyone, morality does. In the interest of the possibility of the good life for everyone, voluntary sacrifices are sometimes required from everybody. Thus, a person might do better for himself by following enlightened self-interest rather than morality. It is not possible, however, that *everyone* should do better for himself by following enlightened self-interest rather than morality. The best possible life *for everyone* is possible only by everyone's following the rules of morality, that is, rules which quite frequently may require individuals to make genuine sacrifices.

It must be added to this, however, that such a system of rules has the support of reason only where people live in societies, that is, in conditions in which there are established common ways of behavior. Outside society, people have no reason for following such rules, that is, for being moral. In other words, outside society, the very distinction between right and wrong vanishes.

WHY SHOULD WE FOLLOW REASON?

But someone might now ask whether and why he should follow reason itself. He may admit that moral reasons are superior to all others, but doubt whether he ought to follow reason. He may claim that this will have to be proved first, for if it is not true that he ought to follow reason, then it is not true that he ought to follow the strongest reason either.

What is it to follow reason? As we have explained, it involves two tasks, the theoretical, finding out what it would be in accordance with reason to do in a certain situation, what contrary to reason, and the practical task, to act accordingly. It was shown in Chapter Three how this is done. We must also remind ourselves that there are many different ways in which what we do or believe or feel can be contrary to reason. It may be *irrational*, as when, for no reason at all, we set our hand on fire or cut off our toes one by one, or when, in the face of conclusive evidence to the contrary, someone *believes* that her son killed in the war is still alive, or when someone is *seized by fear* as a gun is pointed at him although he knows for certain that it is not loaded. What we do, believe, or feel is called irrational if it is the case not only that there are conclusive or overwhelming reasons against doing, believing, or feeling these things, but also that we must know there are such reasons and we still persist in our action, belief, or feeling.

Or it may be *unreasonable*, as when we make demands which are excessive or refuse without reason to comply with requests which are reasonable. We say of demands or requests that they are excessive if, though we are entitled to make them, the party against whom we make them has good reasons for not complying, as when the landlord demands the immediate vacation of the premises in the face of well-supported pleas of hardship by the tenant.

Being unreasonable is a much weaker form of going counter to reason than being irrational. The former applies in cases where there is a conflict of reasons and where one party does not acknowledge the obvious force of the case of the other or, while acknowledging it, will not modify his behavior accordingly. A person is irrational only if he flies in the face of reason, if, that is, all reasons are on one side and he acts contrary to it when he either acknowledges that this is so or, while refusing to acknowledge it, has no excuse for failing to do so.

Again, someone may be *inconsistent*, as when he refuses a Jew admission to a club although he has always professed strong positive views on racial equality. Behavior or remarks are inconsistent if the agent or author professes principles adherence to which would require him to say or do the opposite of what he says or does.

Or a person may be *illogical*, as when he does something which, as anyone can see, cannot or is not at all likely to lead to success. Thus when I cannot find my glasses or my fountain pen, the logical thing to do is to look for them where I can remember I had them last or where I usually have them. It would be illogical of me to look under the bed or in the oven unless I have special reason to think they might be there. To say of a person that he is a logical type is to say that he always does what, on reflection, anyone would agree is most likely to lead to success. Scatterbrains, people who act rashly, without thinking, are the opposite of logical.

When we speak of following reason, we usually mean 'doing what is supported by the best reasons because it is so supported' or perhaps 'doing what we think (rightly or wrongly) is supported by the best reasons because we think it is so supported.' It might, then, occur to someone to ask, 'Why should I follow reason?' During the last hundred years or so, reason has had a very bad press. Many thinkers have sneered at it and have recommended other guides, such as the instincts, the unconscious, the voice of the blood, inspiration, charisma, and the like. They have advocated that one should not follow reason but be guided by these other forces.

However, in the most obvious sense of the question 'Should I follow reason?' this is a tautological question like 'Is a circle a circle?'; hence the advice 'You should not follow reason' is as nonsensical as the claim 'A circle is not a circle.' Hence the question 'Why should I follow reason?' is as silly as 'Why is a circle a circle?' We need not, therefore, take much notice of the advocates of unreason. They show by their advocacy that they are not too clear on what they are talking about.

How is it that 'Should I follow reason?' is a tautological question like 'Is a circle a circle?' Questions of the form 'Shall I do this?' or 'Should I do this?' or 'Ought I to do this?' are, as was shown (in Chapter Three), requests to someone (possibly oneself) to deliberate on one's behalf. That is to say, they are requests to survey the facts and weigh the reasons for and against this course of action. These questions could therefore be paraphrased as follows. 'I wish to do what is supported by the best reasons. Tell me whether this is so supported.' As already mentioned, 'following reason' means 'doing what is supported by the best reasons.' Hence the question 'Shall (should, ought) I follow reason?' must be paraphrased as 'I wish to do what is supported by the best reasons. Tell me whether doing what is supported by the best reasons is doing what is supported by the best reasons.' It is, therefore, not worth asking.

The question '*Why* should I follow reason?' simply does not make sense. Asking it shows complete lack of understanding of the meaning of 'why questions.' 'Why should I do this?' is a request to be given the reason for saying that I should do this. It is normally asked when someone has already said, 'You should do this' and answered by giving the reason. But since 'Should I follow reason?' means 'Tell me whether doing what is supported by the best reasons is doing what is supported by the best reasons,' there is simply no possibility of adding 'Why?' For the question now comes to this, 'Tell me the reason why doing what is supported by the best reasons is doing what is supported by the best reasons.' It is exactly like asking, 'Why is a circle a circle?'

However, it must be admitted that there is another possible interpretation to our question according to which it makes sense and can even be answered. 'Why should I follow reason?' may not be a request for a reason in support of a tautological remark, but a request for a reason why one should enter on the theoretical task of deliberation. As already explained, following reason involves the completion of two tasks, the theoretical and the practical. The point of the theoretical is to give guidance in the practical task. We perform the theoretical only because we wish to complete the practical task in accordance with the outcome of the theoretical. On our first interpretation, 'Should I follow reason?' means 'Is the practical task completed when it is completed in accordance with the outcome of the theoretical task?' And the answer to this is obviously 'Yes,' for that is what we mean by 'completion of the practical task.' On our second interpretation, 'Should I follow reason?' is not a question about the practical but about the theoretical task. It is not a question about whether, given that one is prepared to perform both these tasks, they are properly completed in the way indicated. It is a question about whether one should enter on the whole performance at all, whether the "game" is worth playing. And this is a meaningful question. It might be better to "follow inspiration" than to "follow reason," in this sense: better to close one's eyes and wait for an answer to flash across the mind.

But while, so interpreted, 'Should I follow reason?' makes sense, it seems to me obvious that the answer to it is 'Yes, because it pays.' Deliberation is the only reliable method. Even if there were other reliable methods, we could only tell whether they were reliable by checking them against this method. Suppose some charismatic leader counsels, 'Don't follow reason, follow me. My leadership is better than that of reason'; we would still have to check his claim against the ordinary methods of reason. We would have to ascertain whether in following his advice we were doing the best thing. And this we can do only by examining whether he has advised us to do what is supported by the best reasons.

His claim to be better than reason can in turn only be supported by the fact that he tells us precisely the same as reason does.

Is there any sense, then, in his claim that his guidance is preferable to that of reason? There may be, for working out what is supported by the best reasons takes a long time. Frequently, the best thing to do is to do something quickly now rather than the most appropriate thing later. A leader may have the ability to "see," to "intuit," what is the best thing to do more quickly than it is possible to work this out by the laborious methods of deliberation. In evaluating the qualities of leadership of such a person, we are evaluating *his ability to perform correctly the practical task of following reason* without having to go through the lengthy operations of the theoretical. Reason is required to tell us whether anyone has qualities of leadership better than ordinary, in the same way that pencil and paper multiplications are required to tell us whether a mathematical prodigy is genuine or a fraud.

Lastly, it must be said that sometimes it may be better even for an ordinary person without charisma not to follow reason but to do something at once, for quick action may be needed.

Further Readings

Austin, J. L., "A Plea for Excuses," *Philosophical Papers*, Oxford University Press, London, 1963.

Ayer, A. J., *Language, Truth and Logic*, Dover, New York, 1950.

Baier, Kurt, *The Moral Point of View*, Cornell University Press, Ithaca, 1958.

Bentham, Jeremy, *An Introduction to the Principles of Morals and Legislation*, ed. Laurence J. Lafleur, Hafner, New York, 1948 (first published 1789).

Bradley, F. H., *Ethical Studies*, Liberal Arts, New York, 1951.

Brandt, Richard B., "Blameworthiness and Obligation," in Melden.

Brandt, Richard B., *Ethical Theory*, Prentice-Hall, Englewood Cliffs, N.J., 1959.

Brandt, Richard B., (ed.), *Value and Obligation*, Harcourt, Brace & World, New York, 1961.

Broad, C. D., *Five Types of Ethical Theory*, Harcourt, Brace & World, New York, 1934.

Butler, J., *Fifteen Sermons Upon Human Nature*, 1726, *Works*, J. Bernard (ed.), Macmillan, London, 1900.

Camus, Albert, *The Myth of Sisyphus*, Knopf, New York, 1955.

Dewey, John, "The Construction of the Good," in Sellars and Hospers.

Dewey, John, *Theory of Moral Life*, ed. Arnold Isenberg, Holt, Rinehart and Winston, New York, 1960.

Ewing, A. C., *The Definition of Good*, Macmillan, New York, 1947.

Foot, Philippa, "Moral Arguments," *Mind*, *67* (1958).

Foot, Philippa, "Moral Beliefs," *Proceedings of the Aristotelian Society*, 1958–1959.

Firth, Roderick, "Ethical Absolutism and the Ideal Observer Theory," *Philosophy and Phenomenological Research*, *12* (1952).

Frankena, William, *Ethics*, (Foundations of Philosophy Series), Prentice-Hall, Englewood Cliffs, N.J., 1963.

Frankena, William, "The Naturalistic Fallacy," *Mind*, *48* (1939), also in Sellars and Hospers.

Frankena, William, "Obligation and Ability," in Black, Max (eds.), *Philosophical Analysis*, Cornell University Press, Ithaca, N.Y., 1950.

Hare, R. M., *Freedom and Reason*, Clarendon Press, Oxford, 1963.

Hospers, John, *Human Conduct*, Harcourt, Brace & World, New York, 1961.

Hume, David, *Enquiry Concerning the Principles of Morals*, Open Court, La Salle, Ill., 1912.

Hume, David, *Treatise Concerning Human Nature*, ed. L. A. Selby-Bigge, Oxford University Press, New York, 1941, Book III.

Katz, Jerrold, "Semantic Theory and the Meaning of 'Good,'" *Journal of Philosophy*, *61*, 23 (1964).

Locke, John, *Essays on the Law of Nature*, trans. W. von Leyden, Oxford University Press, Oxford, 1954.

Melden, A. I., *Essays in Moral Philosophy*, University of Washington Press, Seattle, 1958.

Mill, John Stuart, *Utilitarianism*, Longmans, London, 1907, Chapter III.

Moore, G. E., *Ethics*, Oxford University Press, Oxford, 1912.

Nietzsche, Friedrich, *The Genealogy of Morals*, trans. Francis Golffing, Doubleday, Garden City, N.Y., 1956.

Nowell-Smith, P. H., *Ethics*, Penguin, Baltimore, 1954.

Plantinga, Alvin, "An Existentialists Ethics," *Review of Metaphysics*, *12* (1958).

Plato, *Euthyphro*, *Republic*, *Protagoras*, *Philebus*, *Gorgias*.

Prichard, H. A., *Moral Obligation*. Clarendon Press, Oxford, 1949, especially Chapter I.

Rawls, John, "Outline of a Decision Procedure for Ethics," *Philosophical Review*, *60* (1951).

Rawls, John, "The Sense of Justice," *Philosophical Review*, *72* (1963).

Ross, Sir David, *The Right and the Good*, Oxford University Press, Oxford, 1930.

Sartre, Jean-Paul, *Existentialism and Human Emotions*, Philosophical Library, New York, 1957.

Selby-Bigge, L. A. (ed.), *British Moralists*, Bobbs-Merrill, Indianapolis, 1964 (first issued 1897).

Sellars, W., and J. Hospers, (eds.), *Readings in Ethical Theory*, Appleton-Century-Crofts, New York, 1952.

Sidgwick, Henry, *The Methods of Ethics*, 7th ed., Macmillan, New York, 1874.

Sidgwick, Henry, *Outlines of the History of Ethics*, Beacon Press, Boston, 1960 (first issued 1886).

Singer, Marcus, *Generalization in Ethics*, Knopf, New York, 1961.

Smart, J. J. C., *An Outline of a System of Utilitarian Ethics*, Melbourne University Press, Melbourne, 1961.

Spinoza, Baruch, *Ethics*, 1677, in *Spinoza Selections*, Scribner, New York, 1930.

Stevenson, C. L., *Ethics and Language*, Yale University Press, New Haven, 1943.

Stevenson, C. L., "The Nature of Ethical Disagreement," in Brandt (ed.), *Value and Obligation*.

Strawson, P. F., "Ethical Intuitionism," *Philosophy*, *24*, *88* (1949), also in Brandt (ed.), *Value and Obligation*, and Sellars and Hospers.

Toulmin, S. E., *The Place of Reason in Ethics*, Cambridge University Press, Cambridge, 1950.

Urmson, J. O., "On Grading," *Mind*, *59* (1950), also in A. Flew (ed.), *Logic and Language, Second Series*, Blackwell, Oxford, 1959.

Vendler, Zeno, "The Grammar of Goodness," *Philosophical Review*, *60* (1964).

von Wright, G. H., *The Varieties of Goodness*, Routledge & Kegan Paul, London, 1963.

Warnock, Mary, *Ethics Since 1900*, Oxford University Press, London, 1960.

VI

POLITICAL PHILOSOPHY

Almost everyone is affected by politics. Each of us is a citizen of a country, an inhabitant of a state, a city, and perhaps a township. We belong to clubs, other organizations, and possibly a political party. In each of these politics plays a significant role.

As a participant in each of these associations, a person stands in various political relations to the other members of the association. In different cases he may have different roles in the association. A man may be an official of his union or professional group, and he may hold office in local government. Yet, he may be only a voter on the national level. Each political association has a set of roles or offices as part of its organization. There are, in most cases, specified procedures for filling the offices, and specified rights and duties accruing to the officeholder. Some (or all) of those who reside within the territory under the jurisdiction of governments play one or more roles in the various political groups to which they belong. Some, like convicts, are deprived not only of the right to hold office, but also of the right to vote. So with respect to political organizations extending outside the prison, they play only the role of persons obligated to obey laws (if, indeed, that is a role at all). Within the prison, however, they may hold political office, such as captain of a prison athletic team.

Central to a political system is some system of relationships involving power and authority. The power and authority is vested in the holders of the offices within the system. The government in a political system might then be said to be the class of the office holders in that system. This, of course, is a rather vague definition. What the government of a political system is depends upon how broadly the notion of an office is taken. In a democracy, for example, one might say that each voter has an office—that of elector—in which case the government would probably encompass most of the population. On the other hand, it could be said that the voters elect the real office-holders, in which case the government would consist of elected officials plus their appointees. This would probably be a small minority of the entire population. It is important to keep one's concepts clear in any discussion of politics in general, and political philosophy in particular.

Since politics, like language, is so close and so important to so many people, philosophers have taken a great interest in a number of questions involving political systems, government, and authority.

Although some of what philosophers say about these matters would apply to any political system (including fraternities and football teams), by and large, the interest of philosophers is in a political system called a state or a nation. It is difficult to make clear exactly what this is. Some philosophers say that a state is a combination of the residents of an area with a government which has supreme authority over them. Others suggest that the government is what controls the legitimate application of physical force within the area. Still others use the term "state" to refer only to the government (in one of the senses just mentioned).

The questions that political philosophers have been concerned with cover a wide area. They range from normative questions, such as, What is the best form of government? and What political obligations does a citizen of a state have? to conceptual questions like, What is justice? What is political obligation? Is it a property or a relation or neither? In between these are questions such as, What makes a government legitimate? When does a government have what is called "authority"? What political powers should a government have and what should it not have? What should be the relation between the individual and the government?

The selections included below focus on one or more of these questions and attempt to answer them or at least comment on them. In these selections a number of important notions are examined and reexamined. We will mention two important ones:

Self-Preservation and Self-Protection

Some philosophers argue that men by nature are brutish and prone to harm others in order to further their own interests. Left to themselves, that is, without any government, they would be constantly at war with one another. This would mean that men lived short, miserable lives.

To remedy this, men unite to form a government and give to the government all political power. This, it is argued, is necessary for the state to continue in existence, since a weakened government would not be able to keep the state going. Without a government of some sort, men would revert to the state of war. On this view, then, self-preservation is what is central to the formation of a government, and, in a sense, is a key factor in determining what powers the government may legitimately have. (See Hobbes, "The Origin and Nature of the State," in this section. See also Baier, "Why I Should Be Moral," in Section V for a discussion of Hobbes' argument.)

Another view uses the notion of self-protection to draw a line between the power a government may legitimately use and the power it may not legitimately use. The claim here is that the only time a government (or any group of people) has the right to interfere with the liberty of a citizen is when that citizen's action will harm another person. As long as his actions do not harm another, then he should be left to himself. (See Mill, "On Liberty," in this section.)

Yet another view is that a government has no right to take the life of its citizens, for every man, no matter what he has done, has the right to have a chance to make amends. (See Camus, "Reflections on the Guillotine," in this section.)

Finally, it may be claimed that the desire of men to preserve themselves is presupposed in any discussion of political systems, for presumably one purpose of a political system is, in some way, to facilitate men's lives together, and this presupposes that men want, at least, to keep themselves alive. (See Hart, "Morality and the Law," in this section.)

It is clear from this that any adequate political philosophy, and any adequate system of political beliefs held by anyone, will have to pay special attention to the place of self-preservation and self-protection in human activity. The desire for self-preservation found in human beings may serve as a necessary precondition for there being political systems. It may also give purpose to any political system. Finally, it may play a role in determining the legitimate exercise of a government's political power.

The Minority

A number of philosophers have discussed democratic political systems in particular. They have taken a special interest in the question of the minority. (This is related to more general questions about the relation between an individual citizen and the government, and between a citizen and other citizens in a state.) This is clearly a problem for anyone who claims, as many have, that democracy is in some way the best political system.

The problem arises because a person who is in the minority is sometimes forced to do certain things which he does not choose to do. For example, the majority may attempt to force its will on the minority and, in a sense, give the minority no more liberty than it gives to a group of slaves. Engels argues that, as a matter of fact, modern society has to face the enslavement on the majority by the bourgeois minority. (See Engels, "The Materialist Conception of History," in this section.)

Hart points out that while a political system may have to offer protections and benefits to some of its members in order to continue in existence, it is clear that it need not offer them to all. (The fact that there are slaves in some societies bears witness to this.) One problem concerning minorities, then, is that they may be treated as slaves in a presumably free society.

An attempt to solve this problem is suggested by Mill, as we mentioned above. The legitimate use of the power of the government or the majority is to be limited to the prevention of one citizen harming another. (Of course, it is difficult to find a clear notion of *harm*. A member of an intolerant majority might say that he was psychologically harmed by the presence in his country of an individual of a certain ethnic group.)

Wolff suggests that there may be an even more fundamental problem, i.e., to become a citizen in any state where one may have to obey laws he would not otherwise choose to obey is to surrender one's moral autonomy. Certainly this possibility exists in any state with a single man as a ruler. But it also exists in a majority-rule democracy, since it is possible that a citizen will be in the minority on some issue and find himself obligated to obey a law he would not have chosen. If, then, democracy is to make good its claim to be a privileged form of political system, it must, according to this view, provide some way for a person to be a citizen without thereby surrendering his autonomy. (See Wolff, "Democracy and the Minority," in this section.)

It is obvious, then, that a political philosopher will probably have to say something about the place of the minority. At least he will have to deal with the broader questions concerning the rights of the individual citizen in a state with respect to his government.

Of course, careful studies in political philosophy deal with far more than these issues. The selection from Engels, for example, deals with political relationships as connected to economic relationships, and concentrates on the latter as being of the utmost importance in understanding the place of man in society. Other selections treat such topics as the relation between morality and law, and the question of whether or not a man's political obligations are self-imposed. Yet the two issues chosen as a sample provide a good example of the concepts and problems with which a political philosopher must deal.

THE ORIGIN AND NATURE OF THE STATE

THOMAS HOBBES

The principal parts of philosophy are two. For two chief kinds of bodies, and very different from one another, offer themselves to such as search after their generation and properties; one whereof being the work of nature, is called a *natural body*, the other is called a *commonwealth*, and is made by the wills and agreement of men. And from these spring the two parts of philosophy, called *natural* and *civil*. But seeing that, for the knowledge of the properties of a commonwealth, it is necessary first

From *Elements of Philosophy*, Chap. 1 (1655), and *The Leviathan*, Chaps. 13, 17, 21, 26 (1651).

to know the dispositions, affections, and manners of men, civil philosophy is again commonly divided into two parts, whereof one, which treats of men's dispositions and manners, is called *ethics;* and the other, which takes cognizance of their civil duties, is called *politics*, or simply *civil philosophy*. In the first place, therefore (after I have set down such premises as appertain to the nature of philosophy in general), I will discourse of *bodies natural;* in the second, of the *dispositions and manners of men;* and in the third, *of the civil duties of subjects*.

. . .

So that in the nature of men, we find three principal causes of quarrel. First, competition; second, diffidence; thirdly, glory.

The first, maketh men invade for gain; the second, for safety; and the third, for reputation. The first use violence to make themselves masters of other men's persons, wives, children, and cattle; the second, to defend them; the third, for trifles, as a word, a smile, a different opinion, and any other sign of undervalue, either direct in their persons, or by reflection in their kindred, their friends, their nation, their profession, or their name.

Hereby it is manifest, that during the time men live without a common power to keep them all in awe, they are in that condition which is called war; and such a war, as is of every man, against every man. For WAR, consisteth not in battle only, or the act of fighting; but in a tract of time, wherein the will to contend by battle is sufficiently known; and therefore the notion of *time* is to be considered in the nature of war, as it is in the nature of weather. For as the nature of foul weather lieth not in a shower or two of rain, but in an inclination thereto of many days together; so the nature of war consisteth not in actual fighting, but in the known disposition thereto, during all the time there is no assurance to the contrary. All other time is PEACE.

Whatsoever therefore is consequent to a time of war, where every man is enemy to every man, the same is consequent to the time, wherein men live without other security than what their own strength and their own invention shall furnish them withal. In such condition, there is no place for industry, because the fruit thereof is uncertain: and consequently no culture of the earth; no navigation, nor use of the commodities that may be imported by sea; no commodious building; no instruments of moving, and removing, such things as require much force; no knowledge of the face of the earth; no account of time; no arts; no letters; no society; and which is worst of all, continual fear, and danger of violent death; and the life of man, solitary, poor, nasty, brutish, and short.

It may seem strange to some man that has not well weighed these things, that nature should thus dissociate, and render men apt to invade and destroy one another; and he may, therefore, not trusting to this inference, made from the passions, desire perhaps to have the same confirmed by experience. Let him therefore consider with himself, when taking a journey, he arms himself, and seeks to go well accompanied;

when going to sleep, he locks his doors; when even in his house he locks his chests; and this when he knows there be laws, and public officers, armed, to revenge all injuries shall be done him; what opinion he has of his fellow subjects, when he rides armed; of his fellow citizens, when he locks his doors; and of his children, and servants, when he locks his chests. Does he not there as much accuse mankind by his actions, as I do by my words? But neither of us accuse man's nature in it. The desires and other passions of man are in themselves no sin. No more are the actions that proceed from those passions, till they know a law that forbids them: which till laws be made they cannot know: nor can any law be made, till they have agreed upon the person that shall make it.

It may peradventure be thought there was never such a time nor condition of war as this; and I believe it was never generally so, over all the world: but there are many places where they live so now. For the savage people in many places of America, except the government of small families, the concord whereof dependeth on natural lust, have no government at all; and live at this day in that brutish manner as I said before. Howsoever, it may be perceived what manner of life there would be, where there were no common power to fear, by the manner of life, which men that have formerly lived under a peaceful government, use to degenerate into, in a civil war.

But though there had never been any time, wherein particular men were in a condition of war one against another; yet in all times, kings and persons of sovereign authority, because of their independency, are in continual jealousies, and in the state and posture of gladiators; having their weapons pointing, and their eyes fixed on one another; that is, their forts, garrisons, and guns upon the frontiers of their kingdoms; and continual spies upon their neighbors; which is a posture of war. But because they uphold thereby the industry of their subjects, there does not follow from it, that misery, which accompanies the liberty of particular men.

To this war of every man against every man, this also is consequent; that nothing can be unjust. The notions of right and wrong, justice and injustice have there no place. Where there is no common power, there is no law: where no law, no injustice. Force, and fraud, are in war the two cardinal virtues. Justice, and injustice are none of the faculties neither of the body, nor mind. If they were, they might be in a man that were alone in the world, as well as his senses, and passions. They are qualities that relate to men in society, not in solitude. It is consequent also to the same condition, that there be no propriety, no dominion no *mine* and *thine* distinct; but only that to be every man's that he can get, and for so long as he can keep it. And thus much for the ill condition, which man by mere nature is actually placed in; though with a possibility to come out of it, consisting partly in the passions, partly in his reason.

The passions that incline men to peace are fear of death, desire of such things as are necessary to commodious living, and a hope by their industry to obtain them. And reason suggesteth convenient articles of peace, upon which men may be drawn to agreement.

. . .

The final cause, end, or design of men, who naturally love liberty, and dominion over others, in the introduction of that restraint upon themselves, in which we see them live in commonwealths, is the foresight of their own preservation, and of a more contented life thereby; that is to say, of getting themselves out from that miserable condition of war, which is necessarily consequent . . . to the natural passions of men, when there is no visible power to keep them in awe, and tie them by fear of punishment to the performance of their covenants, and observation of those laws of nature set down.

. . .

It is true, that certain living creatures, as bees, and ants, live sociably one with another, which are therefore by Aristotle numbered amongst political creatures; and yet have no other direction, than their particular judgments and appetites; nor speech, whereby one of them can signify to another what he thinks expedient for the common benefit; and, therefore, some man may perhaps desire to know why mankind cannot do the same. To which I answer:

First, that men are continually in competition for honor and dignity, which these creatures are not; and consequently amongst men there ariseth on that ground envy and hatred, and finally war; but amongst these not so.

Secondly, that amongst these creatures, the common good differeth not from the private; and being by nature inclined to their private, they procure thereby the common benefit. But man, whose joy consisteth in comparing himself with other men, can relish nothing but what is eminent.

Thirdly, that these creatures, having not, as man, the use of reason, do not see, nor think they see any fault in the administration of their common business; whereas amongst men, there are very many that think themselves wiser, and able to govern the public better than the rest; and these strive to reform and innovate, one this way, another that way; and thereby bring it into distraction and civil war.

Fourthly, that these creatures, though they have some use of voice in making known to one another their desires, and other affections; yet they want that art of words, by which some men can represent to others that which is good, in the likeness of evil; and evil, in the likeness of good; and augment, or diminish the apparent greatness of good and evil; discontenting men, and troubling their peace at their pleasure.

Fifthly, irrational creatures cannot distinguish between *injury* and *damage;* and, therefore, as long as they be at ease, they are not offended with their fellows, whereas man is then most troublesome, when he is most at ease: for then it is that he loves to show his wisdom, and control the actions of them that govern the commonwealth.

Lastly, the agreement of these creatures is natural; that of men is by covenant only, which is artificial: and, therefore, it is no wonder if there be somewhat else required, besides covenant, to make their agreement constant and lasting; which is a common power, to keep them in awe and to direct their actions to the common benefit.

The only way to erect such a common power, as may be able to defend them from the invasion of foreigners, and the injuries of one another, and thereby to secure them in such sort, as that by their own industry, and by the fruits of the earth, they may nourish themselves and live contentedly is to confer all their power and strength upon one man, or upon one assembly of men, that may reduce all their wills, by plurality of voices, unto one will: which is as much as to say, to appoint one man, or assembly of men, to bear their person; and every one to own, and acknowledge himself to be author of whatsoever he that so beareth their person, shall act, or cause to be acted, in those things which concern the common peace and safety; and therein to submit their wills, every one to his will, and their judgments, to his judgment. This is more than consent, or concord; it is a real unity of them all, in one and the same person, made by covenant of every man with every man, in such manner, as if every man should say to every man, *I authorize and give up my right of governing myself, to this man, or to this assembly of men, on this condition, that thou give up thy right to him, and authorize all his actions in like manner.* This done, the multitude so united in one person, is called a COMMONWEALTH, in Latin CIVITAS. This is the generation of that great LEVIATHAN, or rather, to speak more reverently, of that *mortal god*, to which we owe under the *immortal God*, our peace and defense. For by this authority, given him by every particular man in the commonwealth, he hath the use of so much power and strength conferred on him, that by terror thereof, he is enabled to perform the wills of them all, to peace at home, and mutual aid against their enemies abroad. And in him consisteth the essence of the commonwealth; which, to define it, is *one person, of whose acts as a great multitude, by mutual covenants one with another, have made themselves every one the author, to the end he may use the strength and means of them all, as he shall think expedient, for their peace and common defense.*

And he that carrieth this person, is called SOVEREIGN, and said to have *sovereign power;* and every one besides, his SUBJECT.

The attaining to this sovereign power is by two ways. One, by natural force; as when a man maketh his children, to submit themselves, and their children, to his government, as being able to destroy them if they refuse; or by war subdueth his enemies to his will, giving them their lives on that condition. The other, is when men agree amongst themselves to submit to some men, or assembly of men, voluntarily, on confidence to be protected by him against all others. This latter may be called a political commonwealth, or commonwealth by *institution;* and the former, a commonwealth by *acquisition.*

. . .

But as men, for the attaining of peace, and conservation of themselves thereby, have made an artificial man, which we call a commonwealth; so also have they made artificial chains, called *civil laws,* which they themselves, by mutual covenants, have fastened at one end, to the lips of that man, or assembly, to whom they have given the sovereign power; and at the other end to their own ears. These bonds in their own nature but weak, may nevertheless be made to hold, by the danger, though not by the difficulty of breaking them.

In relation to these bonds only it is, that I am to speak now, of the *liberty* of *subjects.* For seeing there is no commonwealth in the *world,* wherein there be rules enough set down, for the regulating of all the actions and words of men; as being a thing impossible: it followeth necessarily, that in all kinds of actions by the laws praetermitted, men have the liberty of doing what their own reasons shall suggest, for the most profitable to themselves. For if we take liberty in the proper sense, for corporal liberty; that is to say, freedom from chains and prison, it were very absurd for men to clamor as they do for the liberty they so manifestly enjoy. Again, if we take liberty for an exemption from laws, it is no less absurd for men to demand as they do, that liberty by which all other men may be masters of their lives. And yet, as absurd as it is, this is it they demand; not knowing that the laws are of no power to protect them, without a sword in the hands of a man, or men, to cause those laws to be put in execution. The liberty of a subject lieth therefore only in those things, which in regulating their actions, the sovereign hath praetermitted: such as is the liberty to buy, and sell, and otherwise contract with one another; to choose their own abode, their own diet, their own trade of life, and institute their children as they themselves think fit; and the like.

Nevertheless we are not to understand that by such liberty the sovereign power of life and death is either abolished, or limited. For it has been already shown that nothing the sovereign representative can do to a subject, on what pretense soever, can properly be called injustice, or injury; because every subject is author of every act the sovereign doth; so that he never wanteth right to anything, otherwise, than as he himself is the subject of God, and bound thereby to observe the laws of nature. And therefore it may, and doth often happen in commonwealths, that a subject may be put to death by the command of the sovereign power; and yet neither do the other wrong; as when Jephtha caused his daughter to be sacrificed: in which, and the like cases, he that so dieth, had liberty to do the action, for which he is nevertheless, without injury put to death. And the same holdeth also in a sovereign prince, that putteth to death an innocent subject. For though the action be against the law of nature, as being contrary to equity, as was the killing of Uriah, by David; yet it was not an injury to Uriah, but to God. Not to Uriah, because the right to do what he pleased was given him by Uriah himself: and yet to God, because David was God's subject, and prohibited all iniquity by the law of nature: which distinction, David himself, when he repented the fact, evidently confirmed, saying, *To thee only have I sinned.* In the same manner, the people of Athens, when they banished the most potent of their commonwealth for ten years, thought they committed no injustice; and yet they never questioned what crime he had done; but what hurt he would do: nay they commanded the banishment of they knew not whom; and every citizen bringing his oystershell into the market place, written with the name of him he desired should be banished, without actually accusing him, sometimes banished an Aristides, for his reputation of justice; and sometimes a scurrilous jester, as Hyperbolus, to make a jest of it. And yet a man cannot say the sovereign people of Athens wanted right to banish them; or an Athenian the liberty to jest, or to be just.

The liberty, whereof there is so frequent and honorable mention, in the histories, and philosophy of the ancient Greeks, and Romans, and in the writings, and discourse of those that from them have received all their learning in the politics, is not the liberty of particular men; but the liberty of the commonwealth: which is the same with that which every man then should have, if there were no civil laws, nor commonwealth at all. And the effects of it also be the same. For as amongst masterless men, there is perpetual war, of every man against his neighbor; no inheritance, to transmit to the son, nor to expect from the father; no propriety of goods, or lands; no security; but a full and absolute liberty in every particular man; so in states and commonwealths not dependent on one another, every commonwealth, not every man, has an absolute liberty to do what it shall judge, that is to say, what that man, or assembly that representeth it, shall judge most conducing to their benefit. But withal, they live in the condition of a perpetual war, and upon the confines of battle, with their frontiers armed, and cannons planted against their neighbors round about. The Athenians, and Romans were free; that is, free commonwealths: not that any particular men had the liberty to resist their own representative; but that their representative had the liberty to resist or invade other people. There is written on the turrets of the city of Lucca in great characters at this day the word LIBERTAS; yet no man can thence infer that a particular man has more liberty, or immunity from the service of the commonwealth there, than in Constantinople. Whether a commonwealth be monarchical, or popular, the freedom is still the same.

But it is an easy thing for men to be deceived, by the specious name of liberty; and for want of judgment to distinguish, mistake that for their private inheritance, and birthright, which is the right of the public only. And when the same error is confirmed by the authority of men in reputation for their writings on this subject, it is no wonder if it produce sedition, and change of government. In these western parts of the world, we are made to receive our opinions concerning the institution, and rights of commonwealths, from Aristotle, Cicero, and other men, Greeks and Romans, that living under popular states, derived those rights, not from the principles of nature, but transcribed them into their books, out of the practice of their own commonwealths, which were popular; as the grammarians describe the rules of language, out of the practice of the time; or the rules of poetry, out of the poems of Homer and Virgil. And because the Athenians were taught to keep them from desire of changing their government, that they were freemen, and all that lived under monarchy were slaves; therefore Aristotle puts it down in his *Politics*, (*lib. 6 cap. 2.*) *In democracy,* LIBERTY *is to be supposed: for it is commonly held that no man is* FREE *in any other government.* And as Aristotle, so Cicero and other writers have grounded their civil doctrine on the opinions of the Romans, who were taught to hate monarchy, at first, by them that having deposed their sovereign, shared amongst them the sovereignty of Rome; and afterwards by their successors. And by reading of these Greek and Latin authors, men from their childhood have gotten a habit, under a false show of liberty, of favoring tumults, and of licentious controlling the actions of their sovereigns, and again of controlling those controllers; with the effusion of so much blood, as I think I may truly say, there was never anything so dearly bought, as these western parts have bought the learning of the Greek and Latin tongues.

To come now to the particulars of the true liberty of a subject; that is to say, what are the things, which though commanded by the sovereign, he may nevertheless, without injustice, refuse to do; we are to consider, what rights we pass away, when we make a commonwealth; or, which is all one, what liberty we deny ourselves, by owning all the actions, without exception, of the man, or assembly, we make our sovereign. For in the act of our *submission* consisteth both our *obligation* and our *liberty;* which must therefore be inferred by arguments taken from thence; there being no obligation on any man, which ariseth not from some act of his own; for all men equally, are by nature free. And because such arguments, must either be drawn from the express words, *I authorize all his actions*, or from the intention of him that submitteth himself to his power, which intention is to be understood by the end for which he so submitteth; the obligation, and liberty of the subject, is to be derived, either from those words, or others equivalent; or else from the end of the institution of sovereignty, namely, the peace of the subjects within themselves, and their defense against a common enemy.

First, therefore, seeing sovereignty by institution is by covenant of every one to every one; and sovereignty by acquisition, by covenants of the vanquished to the victor, or child to the parent; it is manifest, that every subject has liberty in all those things, the right whereof cannot by covenant be transferred. . . . Covenants, not to defend a man's own body, are void. Therefore:

If the sovereign command a man, though justly condemned, to kill, wound, or maim himself; or not to resist those that assault him; or to abstain from the use of food, air, medicine, or any other thing, without which he cannot live; yet hath that man the liberty to disobey.

If a man be interrogated by the sovereign, or his authority, concerning a crime done by himself, he is not bound, without assurance of pardon, to confess it; because no man . . . can be obliged by covenant to accuse himself.

Again, the consent of a subject to sovereign power is contained in these words, *I authorize, or take upon me, all his actions;* in which there is no restriction at all of his own former natural liberty: for by allowing him to *kill me,* I am not bound to kill myself when he commands me. It is one thing to say, *kill me, or my fellow, if you please;* another thing to say, *I will kill myself, or my fellow.* It followeth therefore, that

No man is bound by the words themselves, either to kill himself, or any other man; and consequently, that the obligation a man may sometimes have, upon the command of the sovereign to execute any dangerous, or dishonorable office, dependeth not on the words of our submission; but on the intention, which is to be understood by the end thereof. When therefore our refusal to obey frustrates the end for which the sovereignty was ordained, then there is no liberty to refuse: otherwise there is.

Upon this ground, a man that is commanded as a soldier to fight against the enemy, though his sovereign have right enough to punish his refusal with death, may nevertheless in many cases refuse, without injustice; as when he substituteth a sufficient soldier in his place: for in this case he deserteth not the service of the commonwealth. And there is allowance to be made for natural timorousness; not only to women, of whom no such dangerous duty is expected, but also to men of feminine courage. When armies fight, there is on one side, or both, a running away; yet when they do it not out of treachery, but fear, they are not esteemed to do it unjustly, but dishonorably. For the same reason, to avoid battle is not injustice, but cowardice. But he that inrolleth himself a soldier, or taketh impress money, taketh away the excuse of a timorous nature; and is obliged, not only to go to the battle, but also not to run from it, without his captain's leave. And when the defense of the commonwealth requireth at once the help of all that are able to bear arms, everyone is obliged; because otherwise the institution of the commonwealth, which they have not the purpose, or courage to preserve, was in vain.

To resist the sword of the commonwealth, in defense of another man, guilty or innocent, no man hath liberty; because such liberty takes away from the sovereign the means of protecting us and is therefore destructive of the very essence of government. But in case a great many men together have already resisted the sovereign power unjustly, or committed some capital crime, for which every one of them expecteth death, whether have they not the liberty then to join together, and assist, and defend one another? Certainly they have: for they but defend their lives, which the guilty man may as well do as the innocent. There was indeed injustice in the first breach of their duty; their bearing of arms subsequent to it, though it be to maintain what they have done, is no new unjust act. And if it be only to defend their persons, it is not unjust at all. But the offer of pardon taketh from them, to whom it is offered, the plea of self-defense, and maketh their perseverance in assisting, or defending, the rest, unlawful.

As for other liberties, they depend on the silence of the law. In cases where the sovereign has prescribed no rule, there the subject hath the liberty to do, or forbear, according to his own discretion. And therefore such liberty is in some places more, and in some less; and in some times more, in other times less, according as they that have the sovereignty shall think most convenient. As for example, there was a time, when in England a man might enter into his own land, and dispossess such as wrongfully possessed it, by force. But in after times, that liberty of forcible entry was taken away by a statute made, by the king, in parliament. And in some places of the world, men have the liberty of many wives; in other places, such liberty is not allowed.

If a subject have a controversy with his sovereign of debt, or of right of possession of lands or goods, or concerning any service required at his hands, or concerning any penalty, corporal, or pecuniary, grounded on a precedent law; he hath the same liberty to sue for his right, as if it were against a subject; and before such judges, as are appointed by the sovereign. For seeing the sovereign demandeth by force of a former law, and not by virtue of his power, he declareth thereby, that he requireth no more than shall appear to be due by that law. The suit therefore is not contrary to the will of the sovereign; and consequently the subject hath the liberty to demand the hearing of his cause; and sentence, according to that law. But if he demand, or take anything by pretense of his power; there lieth, in that case, no action of law; for all that is done by him in virtue of his power, is done by the authority of every subject, and consequently he that brings an action against the sovereign, brings it against himself.

If a monarch, or sovereign assembly, grant a liberty to all, or any of his subjects, which grant standing, he is disabled to provide for their safety, the grant is void; unless he directly renounce, or transfer the sovereignty to another. For in that he might openly, if it had been his will, and in plain terms, have renounced, or transferred it, and did not; it is to be understood it was not his will, but that the grant proceeded from ignorance of the repugnancy between such a liberty and the sovereign power; and therefore the sovereignty is still retained; and consequently all those powers, which are necessary to the exercising thereof; such as are the power of war and peace, of judicature, of appointing officers and councillors, of levying money, and the rest. . . .

The obligation of subjects to the sovereign is understood to last as long, and no longer, than the power lasteth, by which he is able to protect them. For the right men have by nature to protect themselves, when none else can protect them, can by no covenant be relinquished. The sovereignty is the soul of the commonwealth; which once departed from the body, the members do no more receive their motion from it. The end of obedience is protection; which, wheresoever a man seeth it, either in his own, or in another's sword, nature applieth his obedience to it, and his endeavor to maintain it. And though sovereignty, in the intention of them that make it, be immortal; yet it is in its own nature, not only subject to violent death, by foreign war; but also through the ignorance and passions of men, it hath in it, from the very institution, many seeds of a natural mortality, by intestine discord.

. . .

The law of nature, and the civil law, contain each other, and are of equal extent. For the laws of nature, which consist in equity, justice, gratitude, and other moral virtues on these depending, in the condition of mere nature . . . are not properly laws, but qualities that dispose men to peace, and to obedience. When a commonwealth is once settled, then are they actually laws, and not before; as being then the commands of the commonweath; and therefore also civil laws: for it is the sovereign power that obliges men to obey them. For in the differences of private men, to declare what is equity, what is justice, and what is moral virtue, and to make them binding, there is need of the ordinances of sovereign power, and punishments to be ordained for such as shall break them; which ordinances are therefore part of the civil law. The law of nature, therefore, is a part of the civil law in all commonwealths of the world. Reciprocally also, the civil law is a part of the dictates of nature. For justice, that is to say, performance of covenant, and giving to every man his own, is a dictate of the law of nature. But every subject in a commonwealth hath covenanted to obey the civil law, (either one with another, as when they assemble to make a common representative, or with the representative itself one by one, when subdued by the sword they promise obedience, that they may receive life). And therefore obedience to the civil law is part also of the law of nature. Civil and natural law are not different kinds, but different parts of law; whereof one part being written, is called civil, the other unwritten, natural. But the right of nature, that is, the natural liberty of man, may by the civil law be abridged, and restrained: nay, the end of making laws, is no other, but such restraint; without the which there cannot possibly be any peace. And law was brought into the world for nothing else, but to limit the natural liberty of particular men, in such manner, as they might not hurt, but assist one another, and join together against a common enemy.

ON LIBERTY

JOHN STUART MILL

The subject of this Essay is not the so-called Liberty of the Will, so unfortunately opposed to the misnamed doctrine of Philosophical Necessity; but Civil, or Social Liberty: the nature and limits of the power which can be legitimately exercised by society over the individual. A question seldom stated, and hardly ever discussed, in general terms, but which profoundly influences the practical controversies of the age by its latent presence, and is likely soon to make itself recognised as the vital question of the future. It is so far from being new, that, in a certain sense, it has divided mankind, almost from the remotest ages; but in the stage of progress into which the more civilised portions of the species have now entered, it presents itself under new conditions, and requires a different and more fundamental treatment.

The struggle between Liberty and Authority is the most conspicuous feature in the portions of history with which we are earliest familiar, particularly in that of Greece, Rome, and England. But in old times this contest was between subjects, or some classes of subjects, and the Government. By liberty, was meant protection against the tyranny of the political rulers. The rulers were conceived (except in some of the popular governments of Greece) as in a necessarily antagonistic position to the people whom they ruled. They consisted of a governing One, or a governing tribe or caste, who derived their authority from inheritance or conquest, who, at all events, did not hold it at the pleasure of the governed, and whose supremacy men did not venture, perhaps did not desire, to contest, whatever precautions might be taken against its oppressive exercise. Their power was regarded as necessary, but also as highly dangerous; as a weapon which they would attempt to use against their subjects, no less than against external enemies. To prevent the weaker members of the community from being preyed upon by innumerable vultures, it was needful that there should be an animal of prey stronger than the rest, commissioned to keep them down. But as the king of the vultures would be no less bent upon preying on the flock than any of the minor harpies, it was indispensable to be in a perpetual attitude of defence against his beak and claws. The aim, therefore, of patriots was to set limits to the power which the ruler should be suffered to exercise over the community; and this limitation was what they meant by liberty. It was attempted in two ways. First, by obtaining a recognition of certain

From Chapters One and Two of *On Liberty*, first published in 1859.

immunities, called political liberties or rights, which it was to be regarded as a breach of duty in the ruler to infringe, and which if he did infringe, specific resistance, or general rebellion, was held to be justifiable. A second, and generally a later expedient, was the establishment of constitutional checks, by which the consent of the community, or of a body of some sort, supposed to represent its interests, was made a necessary condition to some of the more important acts of the governing power. To the first of these modes of limitation, the ruling power, in most European countries, was compelled, more or less, to submit. It was not so with the second; and, to attain this, or when already in some degree possessed, to attain it more completely, became everywhere the principal object of the lovers of liberty. And so long as mankind were content to combat one enemy by another, and to be ruled by a master, on condition of being guaranteed more or less efficaciously against his tyranny, they did not carry their aspirations beyond this point.

A time, however, came, in the progress of human affairs, when men ceased to think it a necessity of nature that their governors should be an independent power, opposed in interest to themselves. It appeared to them much better that the various magistrates of the State should be their tenants or delegates, revocable at their pleasure. In that way alone, it seemed, could they have complete security that the powers of government would never be abused to their disadvantage. By degrees this new demand for elective and temporary rulers became the prominent object of the exertions of the popular party, wherever any such party existed; and superseded, to a considerable extent, the previous efforts to limit the power of rulers. As the struggle proceeded for making the ruling power emanate from the periodical choice of the ruled, some persons began to think that too much importance had been attached to the limitation of the power itself. *That* (it might seem) was a resource against rulers whose interests were habitually opposed to those of the people. What was now wanted was, that the rulers should be identified with the people; that their interest and will should be the interest and will of the nation. The nation did not need to be protected against its own will. There was no fear of its tyrannising over itself. Let the rulers be effectually responsible to it, promptly removable by it, and it could afford to trust them with power of which it could itself dictate the use to be made. Their power was but the nation's own power, concentrated, and in a form convenient for exercise. This mode of thought, or rather perhaps of feeling, was common among the last generation of European liberalism, in the Continental section of which it still apparently predominates. Those who admit any limit to what a government may do, except in the case of such governments as they think ought not to exist, stand out as brilliant exceptions among the political thinkers of the Continent. A similar tone of sentiment might by this time have been prevalent in our own country, if the circumstances which for a time encouraged it, had continued unaltered.

But, in political and philosophical theories, as well as in persons, success discloses faults and infirmities which failure might have concealed from observation. The notion, that the people have no need to limit their power over themselves, might seem axiomatic, when popular government was a thing only dreamed about, or read of as having existed at some distant period of the past. Neither was that notion necessarily disturbed by such temporary aberrations as those of the French Revolution, the worst of which were the work of a usurping few, and which, in any case, belonged, not to the permanent working of popular institutions, but to a sudden and convulsive outbreak against monarchical and aristocratic despotism. In time, however, a democratic republic came to occupy a large portion of the earth's surface, and made itself felt as one of the most powerful members of the community of nations; and elective and responsible government became subject to the observations and criticisms which wait upon a great existing fact. It was now perceived that such phrases as 'self-government,' and 'the power of the people over themselves,' do not express the true state of the case. The 'people' who exercise the power are not always the same people with those over whom it is exercised; and the 'self-government' spoken of is not the government of each by himself, but of each by all the rest. The will of the people, moreover, practically means the will of the most numerous or the most active *part* of the people; the majority, or those who succeed in making themselves accepted as the majority; the people, consequently *may* desire to oppress a part of their number; and precautions are as much needed against this as against any other abuse of power. The limitation, therefore, of the power of government over individuals loses none of its importance when the holders of power are regularly accountable to the community, that is, to the strongest party therein. This view of things, recommending itself equally to the intelligence of thinkers and to the inclination of those important classes in European society to whose real or supposed interests democracy is adverse, has had no difficulty in establishing itself; and in political speculations "the tyranny of the majority" is now generally included among the evils against which society requires to be on its guard.

Like other tyrannies, the tyranny of the majority was at first, and is still vulgarly, held in dread, chiefly as operating through the acts of the public authorities. But reflecting persons perceived that when society is itself the tyrant—society collectively over the separate individuals who compose it—its means of tyrannising are not restricted to the acts which it may do by the hands of its political functionaries. Society can and does execute its own mandates: and if it issues wrong mandates instead of right, or any mandates at all in things with which it ought not to meddle, it practises a social tyranny more formidable than many kinds of political oppression, since, though not usually upheld by such extreme penalties, it leaves fewer means of escape, penetrating much more deeply into the details of life, and enslaving the soul itself. Protection, therefore, against the tyranny of the magistrate is not enough: there needs protection also against the tyranny of the prevailing opinion and feeling; against the tendency of society to impose, by other means than civil penalties, its own ideas and practices as rules of conduct on those who dissent from them; to fetter the development, and, if possible, prevent the formation, of any individuality not in harmony with its ways, and compels all characters to fashion themselves upon the model of its own. There is a limit to the legitimate interference of collective opinion with individual independence: and to find that limit, and maintain it against encroachment, is as indispensable to a good condition of human affairs, as protection against political despotism.

But though this proposition is not likely to be contested in general terms, the practical question, where to place the limit—how to make the fitting adjustment between individual independence and social control—is a subject on which nearly everything remains to be done. All that makes existence valuable to any one, depends on the enforcement of restraints upon the actions of other people. Some rules of conduct, therefore, must be imposed, by law in the first place, and by opinion on many things which are not fit subjects for the operation of law. What these rules should be is the principal question in human affairs; but if we except a few of the most obvious cases, it is one of those which least progress has been made in resolving. No two ages, and scarcely any two countries, have decided it alike; and the decision of one age or country is a wonder to another. Yet the people of any given age and country no more suspect any difficulty in it, than if it were a subject on which mankind had always been agreed. The rules which obtain among themselves appear to them self-evident and self-justifying. This all but universal illusion is one of the examples of the magical influence of custom, which is not only, as the proverb says, a second nature, but is continually mistaken for the first. The effect of custom, in preventing any misgiving respecting the rules of conduct which mankind impose on one another, is all the more complete because the subject is one on which it is not generally considered necessary that reasons should be given, either by one person to others or by each to himself. People are accustomed to believe, and have been encouraged in the belief by some who aspire to the character of philosophers, that their feelings, on subjects of this nature, are better than reasons, and render reasons unnecessary. The practical principle which guides them to their opinions on the regulation of human conduct, is the feeling in each person's mind that everybody should be required to act as he, and those with whom he sympathises, would like them to act. No one, indeed, acknowledges to himself that his standard of judgment is his own liking; but an opinion on a point of conduct, not supported by reasons, can only count as one person's preference; and if the reasons, when given, are a mere appeal to a similar preference felt by other people, it is still only many people's liking instead of one. To an ordinary man, however, his own preference, thus supported, is not only a perfectly satisfactory reason, but the only one he generally has for any of his notions of morality, taste, or propriety, which are not expressly written in his religious creed; and his chief guide in the interpretation even of that. Men's opinions, accordingly, on what is laudable or blamable, are affected by all the multifarious causes which influence their wishes in regard to the conduct of others, and which are as numerous as those which determine their wishes on any other subject. Sometimes their reason—at other times their prejudices or superstitions: often their social affections, not seldom their anti-social ones, their envy or jealousy, their arrogance or contemptuousness: but most commonly their desires or fears for themselves—their legitimate or illegitimate self-interest. Wherever there is an ascendant class, a large portion of the morality of the country emanates from its class interests, and its feelings of class superiority. The morality between Spartans and Helots, between planters and negroes, between princes and subjects, between nobles and roturiers, between men and women, has been for the most part the creation of these class interests and feelings: and the sentiments thus generated react in turn upon the moral feelings of the members of the ascendant class, in their relations among themselves. Where, on the other hand, a class, formerly ascendant, has lost its ascendancy, or where its ascendancy is unpopular, the prevailing moral sentiments frequently bear the impress of an impatient dislike of superiority. Another grand determining principle of the rules of conduct, both in act and forbearance, which have been enforced by law or opinion, has been the servility of mankind towards the supposed preferences or aversions of their temporal masters or of their gods. This servility, though essentially selfish, is not hypocrisy; it gives rise to perfectly genuine sentiments of abhorrence; it made men burn magicians and heretics. Among so many baser influences, the general and obvious interests of society have of course had a share, and a large one, in the direction of the moral sentiments: less, however, as a matter of reason, and on their own account, than as a consequence of the sympathies and antipathies which grew out of them: and sympathies and antipathies which had little or nothing to do with the interests of society, have made themselves felt in the establishment of moralities with quite as great force.

The likings and dislikings of society, or of some powerful portion of it, are thus the main thing which has practically determined the rules laid down for general observance, under the penalties of law or opinion. And in general, those who have been in advance of society in thought and feeling, have left this condition of things unassailed in principle, however they may have come into conflict with it in some of its details. They have occupied themselves rather in inquiring what things society ought to like or dislike, than in questioning whether its likings or dislikings should be a law to individuals. They preferred endeavouring to alter the feelings of mankind on the particular points on which they were themselves heretical, rather than make common cause in defence of freedom, with heretics generally. The only case in which the higher ground has been taken on principle and maintained with consistency, by any but an individual here and there, is that of religious belief: a case instructive in many ways, and not least so as forming a most striking instance of the fallibility of what is called the moral sense: for the *odium theologicum*, in a sincere bigot, is one of the most unequivocal cases of moral feeling. Those who first broke the yoke of what called itself the Universal Church, were in general as little willing to permit difference of religious opinion as that church itself. But when the heat of the conflict was over, without giving a complete victory to any party, and each church or sect was reduced to limit its hopes to retaining possession of the ground it already occupied; minorities, seeing that they had no chance of becoming majorities, were under the necessity of pleading to those whom they could not convert, for permission to differ. It is accordingly on this battle field, almost solely, that the rights of the individual against society have been asserted on broad grounds of principle, and the claim of society to exercise authority over dissentients openly controverted. The great writers to whom the world owes what religious liberty it possesses, have mostly asserted freedom of conscience as an indefeasible right, and denied absolutely that a human being is accountable to others for his religious belief. Yet so natural to mankind is intolerance in whatever they really care about, that religious freedom has hardly anywhere been practically realised, except where religious indifference, which dislikes to have its peace disturbed by theological quarrels, has added its weight to the scale. In the minds of almost all religious persons, even in the most tolerant countries, the duty of toleration is admitted with tacit reserves. One person will bear with dissent in matters of church government, but not of dogma; another can tolerate everybody short of a Papist or a Unitarian; another every one who believes in revealed religion; a few extend their charity a little further, but stop at the belief in a God and in a future state. Wherever the sentiment of the majority is still genuine and intense, it is found to have abated little of its claim to be obeyed.

. . .

The object of this Essay is to assert one very simple principle, as entitled to govern absolutely the dealings of society with the individual in the way of compulsion and control, whether the means used be physical force in the form of legal penalties, or the moral coercion of public opinion. That principle is, that the sole end for which mankind are warranted, individually or collectively, in interfering with the liberty of action of any of their number, is self-protection. That the only purpose for which power can be rightfully exercised over any member of a civilised community, against his will, is to prevent harm to others. His own good, either physical or moral is not a sufficient warrant. He cannot rightfully be compelled to do or forbear because it will be better for him to do so, because it will make him happier, because, in the opinions of others, to do so would be wise, or even right. These are good reasons for remonstrating with him, or reasoning with him, or persuading him, or entreating him, but not for compelling him, or visiting him with any evil in case he do otherwise. To justify that, the conduct from which it is desired to deter him must be calculated to produce evil to some one else. The only part of the conduct of any one, for which he is amenable to society, is that which concerns others. In the part which merely concerns himself, his independence is, of right, absolute. Over himself, over his own body and mind, the individual is sovereign.

It is, perhaps, hardly necessary to say that this doctrine is meant to apply only to human beings in the maturity of their faculties. We are not speaking of children, or of young persons below the age which the law may fix as that of manhood or womanhood. Those who are still in a state to require being taken care of by others, must be protected against their own actions as well as against external injury. For the same reason, we may leave out of consideration those backward states of society in which the race itself may be considered as in its nonage. The early difficulties in the way of spontaneous progress are so great, that there is seldom any choice of means for overcoming them; and a ruler full of the spirit of improvement is warranted in the use of any expedients that will attain an end, perhaps otherwise unattainable. Despotism is a legitimate mode of government in dealing with barbarians, provided the end be their improvement, and the means justified by actually effecting that end. Liberty, as a principle, has no application to any state of things anterior to the time when mankind have become capable of being improved by free and equal discussion. Until then, there is nothing for them but implicit obedience to an Akbar or a Charlemagne, if they are so fortunate as to find one. But as soon as mankind have attained the capacity of being guided to their own improvement by conviction or persuasion (a period long since reached in all nations with whom we need here concern ourselves), compulsion, either in the direct form or in that of pains and penalties for non-compliance, is no longer admissible as a means to their own good, and justifiable only for the security of others.

It is proper to state that I forego any advantage which could be derived to my argument from the idea of abstract right, as a thing independent of utility. I regard utility as the ultimate appeal on all ethical questions; but it must be utility in the largest sense, grounded on the permanent interests of a man as a progressive being. Those interests, I contend, authorise the subjection of individual spontaneity to external control, only in respect to those actions of each, which concern the interest of other people. If any one does an act hurtful to others, there is a *prima facie* case for punishing him, by law, or, where legal penalties are not safely applicable, by general disapprobation. There are also many positive acts for the benefit of others, which he may rightfully be compelled to perform; such as to give evidence in a court of justice; to bear his fair share in the common defence, or in any other joint work necessary to the interest of the society of which he enjoys the protection; and to perform certain acts of individual beneficence, such as saving a fellow-creature's life, or interposing to protect the defenceless against ill-usage, things which whenever it is obviously a man's duty to do, he may rightfully be made responsible to society for not doing. A person may cause evil to others not only by his actions but by his inaction, and in either case he is justly accountable to them for the injury. The latter case, it is true, requires a much more cautious exercise of compulsion than the former. To make any one answerable for doing evil to others is the rule; to make him answerable for not preventing evil is, comparatively speaking, the exception. Yet there are many cases clear enough and grave enough to justify that exception. In all things which regard the external relations of the individual, he is *de jure* amenable to those whose interests are concerned, and, if need be, to society as their protector. There are often good reasons for not holding him to the responsibility; but these reasons must arise from the special expediences of the case: either because it is a kind of case in which he is on the whole likely to act better, when left to his own discretion, than when controlled in any way in which society have it in their power to control him; or because the attempt to exercise control would produce other evils, greater than those which it would prevent. When such reasons as these preclude the enforcement of responsibility, the conscience of the agent himself should step into the vacant judgment seat, and protect those interests of others which have no external protection; judging himself all the more rigidly, because the case does not admit of his being made accountable to the judgment of his fellow-creatures.

But there is a sphere of action in which society, as distinguished from the individual, has, if any, only an indirect interest; comprehending all that portion of a person's life and conduct which affects only himself, or if it also affects others, only with their free, voluntary, and undeceived consent and participation. When I say only himself, I mean directly, and in the first instance; for whatever affects himself, may affect others through himself; and the objection which may be grounded on this contingency, will receive consideration in the sequel. This, then, is the appropriate region of human liberty. It comprises, first, the inward domain of consciousness; demanding liberty of conscience in the most comprehensive sense; liberty of thought and feeling; absolute freedom of opinion and sentiment on all subjects, practical or speculative, scientific, moral, or theological. The liberty of expressing and publishing opinions may seem to fall under a different principle, since it belongs to that part of the conduct of an individual which concerns other people; but, being almost of as much importance as the liberty of thought itself, and resting in great part on the same reasons, is practically inseparable from it. Secondly, the principle requires liberty of tastes and pursuits; of framing the plan of our life to suit our own character; of doing as we like, subject to such consequences as may follow: without impediment from our fellow-creatures, so long as what we do does not harm them, even though they should think our conduct foolish, perverse, or wrong. Thirdly, from this liberty of each individual, follows the liberty, within the same limits, of combination among individuals; freedom to unite, for any purpose not involving harm to others: the persons combining being supposed to be of full age, and not forced or deceived.

No society in which these liberties are not, on the whole, respected, is free, whatever may be its form of government; and none is completely free in which they do not exist absolute and unqualified. The only freedom which deserves the name, is that of pursuing our own good in our own way, so long as we do not attempt to deprive others of theirs, or impede their efforts to obtain it. Each is the proper guardian of his own health, whether bodily, *or* mental and spiritual. Mankind are greater gainers by suffering each other to live as seems good to themselves, than by compelling each to live as seems good to the rest.

Though this doctrine is anything but new, and, to some persons, may have the air of a truism, there is no doctrine which stands more directly opposed to the general tendency of existing opinion and practice. Society has expanded fully as much effort in the attempt (according to its lights) to compel people to conform to its notions of personal as of social excellence. The ancient commonwealths thought themselves entitled to practise, and the ancient philosophers countenanced, the regulation of every part of private conduct by public authority, on the ground that the State had a deep interest in the whole bodily and mental discipline of every one of its citizens; a mode of thinking which may have been admissible in small republics surrounded by powerful enemies, in constant peril of being subverted by foreign attack or internal commotion, and to which even a short interval of relaxed energy and self-command might so easily be fatal that they could not afford to wait for the salutary permanent effects of freedom. In the modern world, the greater size of political communities, and, above all, the separation between spiritual and temporal authority (which placed the direction of men's consciences in other hands than those which controlled their worldly affairs), prevented so great an interference by law in the details of private life; but the engines of moral repression have been wielded more strenuously against divergence from the reigning opinion in self-regarding, than even in social matters; religion, the most powerful of the elements which have entered into the formation of moral feeling, having almost always been governed either by the ambition of a hierarchy, seeking control over every department of human conduct, or by the spirit of Puritanism. . . .

Apart from the peculiar tenets of individual thinkers, there is also in the world at large an increasing inclination to stretch unduly the powers of society over the individual, both by the force of opinion and even by that of legislation; and as the tendency of all the changes taking place in the world is to strengthen society, and diminish the power of the individual, this encroachment is not one of the evils which tend spontaneously to disappear, but, on the contrary, to grow more and more formidable. The disposition of mankind, whether as rulers or as fellow-citizens, to impose their own opinions and inclinations as a rule of conduct on others, is so energetically supported by some of the best and by some of the worst feelings incident to human nature, that it is hardly ever kept under restraint by anything but want of power; and as the power is not declining, but growing, unless a strong barrier of moral conviction can be raised against the mischief, we must expect, in the present circumstances of the world, to see it increase. . . .

We have now recognized the necessity to the mental well-being of mankind (on which all their other well-being depends) of freedom of opinion, and freedom of the expression of opinion, on four distinct grounds; which we will now briefly recapitulate.

First, if any opinion is compelled to silence, that opinion may, for aught we can certainly know, be true. To deny this is to assume our own infallibility.

Secondly, though the silenced opinion be an error, it may, and very commonly does, contain a portion of truth; and since the general or prevailing opinion on any subject is rarely or never the whole truth, it is only by the collision of adverse opinions that the remainder of the truth has any chance of being supplied.

Thirdly, even if the received opinion be not only true, but the whole truth; unless it is suffered to be, and actually is, vigorously and earnestly contested, it will, by most of those who receive it, be held in the manner of a prejudice, with little comprehension or feeling of its rational grounds. And not only this, but, fourthly, the meaning of the doctrine itself will be in danger of being lost, or enfeebled, and deprived of its vital effect on the character and conduct: the dogma becoming a mere formal profession, inefficacious for good, but cumbering the ground, and preventing the growth of any real and heartfelt conviction, from reason or personal experience.

DEMOCRACY AND THE MINORITY

ROBERT PAUL WOLFF

I. THE CONFLICT BETWEEN AUTHORITY AND AUTONOMY

SECTION 1. THE CONCEPT OF AUTHORITY

Politics is the exercise of the power of the state, or the attempt to influence that exercise. Political philosophy is therefore, strictly speaking, the philosophy of the state. If we are to determine the content of political philosophy, and whether indeed it exists, we must begin with the concept of the state.

The state is a group of persons who have and exercise supreme authority within a given territory. Strictly, we should say that a state is a group of persons who have supreme authority within a given territory *or over a certain population.* A nomadic tribe may exhibit the authority structure of a state, so long as its subjects do not fall under the superior authority of a territorial state. The state may include all the persons who fall under its authority, as does the democratic state according to its theorists; it may also consist of a single individual to whom all the rest are subject. We may doubt whether the one-person state has ever actually existed, although Louis XIV evidently thought so when he announced, "L'état, c'est moi." The distinctive characteristic of the state is supreme authority, or what political philosophers used to call "sovereignty." Thus one speaks of "popular sovereignty," which is the doctrine that the people are the state, and of course the use of "sovereign" to mean "king" reflects the supposed concentration of supreme authority in a monarchy.

Authority is the right to command, and correlatively, the right to be obeyed. It must be distinguished from power, which is the ability to compel compliance, either through the use or the threat of force. When I turn over my wallet to a thief who is holding me at gunpoint, I do so because the fate with which he threatens me is worse than the loss of money which I am made to suffer. I grant that he has power over me, but I would hardly suppose that he has *authority*, that is, that he has a right to demand my money and that I have an obligation to give it to him. When the government presents me with a bill for taxes, on the other hand, I pay it (normally) even though I do not wish to, and even if I think I can get away with not paying. It is, after all, the duly constituted government, and hence it has a *right* to tax me. It has *authority* over me. Sometimes, of course, I cheat the government, but even so, I acknowledge its authority, for who would speak of "cheating" a thief?

To *claim* authority is to claim the right to be obeyed. To *have* authority is then—what? It may mean to have that right, or it may mean to have one's claim acknowledged and accepted by those at whom it is directed. The term "authority" is ambiguous, having both a descriptive and a normative sense. Even the descriptive sense refers to norms or obligations, of course, but it does so by *describing* what men believe they ought to do, rather than by *asserting* that they ought to do it.

Corresponding to the two senses of authority, there are two concepts of the state. Descriptively, the state may be defined as a group of persons who are *acknowledged* to have supreme authority within a territory—acknowledged, that is, by those over whom the authority is asserted. The study of the forms, characteristics, institutions, and functioning of *de facto* states, as we may call them, is the province of political science. If we take the term in its prescriptive signification, the state is a group of persons who have the *right* to exercise supreme authority within a territory. The discovery, analysis, and demonstration of the forms and principles of legitimate authority—of the right to rule—is called political philosophy.

What is meant by *supreme* authority? Some political philosophers, speaking of authority in the normative sense, have held that the true state has ultimate authority over all matters whatsoever that occur within its venue. Jean-Jacques Rousseau, for example, asserted that the social contract by which a just political community is formed "gives to the body politic absolute command over the members of which it is formed; and it is this power, when directed by the general will, that bears . . . the name of 'sovereignty'." John Locke, on the other hand, held that the supreme authority of the just state extends only to those matters which it is proper for a state to control. The state is, to be sure, the highest authority, but its right to command is less than absolute. One of the questions which political philosophy must answer is whether there is any limit to the range of affairs over which a just state has authority.

An authoritative command must also be distinguished from a persuasive argument. When I am commanded to do something, I may choose to comply even though I am not being threatened, because I am brought to believe that it is something which I ought to do. If that is the case, then I am not, strictly speaking, obeying a command, but rather acknowledging the force of an argument or the rightness of a prescription. The person who issues the "command" functions merely as the *occasion* for my becoming aware of my duty, and his role might in other instances be filled by an admonishing friend, or even by my own conscience. I might, by an extension of the term, say that the prescription has authority over me, meaning simply that I ought to act in accordance with it. But the person himself has no authority—or, to be more precise, my complying with his command does not constitute an acknowledgment on my part of any such authority. Thus authority resides in persons; they possess it—if indeed they do at all—by virtue of who they are and not by virtue of what they command. My duty to obey is a duty owed to them, not to the moral law or to the beneficiaries of the actions I may be commanded to perform.

That men accede to claims of supreme authority is plain. Hence, political science has an appropriate field of objects, and there can be no doubt about its existence as a branch of social science. That men *ought* to accede to claims of supreme authority is not so obvious, and it therefore remains an open question whether the discipline of political philosophy has any subject matter at all. Our first question must therefore be, Under what conditions and for what reasons does one man have supreme authority over another? The same question can be restated, Under what conditions can a state (understood normatively) exist?

Kant has given us a convenient title for this sort of investigation. He called it a "deduction," meaning by the term not a proof of one proposition from another, but a demonstration of the legitimacy of a concept. When a concept is empirical, its deduction is accomplished merely by pointing to instances of its objects. But when the concept in question is non-empirical, its deduction must proceed in a different manner. All normative concepts are non-empirical, for they refer to what ought to be rather than to what is. Hence, we cannot justify the use of the concept of (normative) supreme authority by presenting instances. We must demonstrate by an *a priori* argument that there can be forms of human community in which some men have a moral right to rule. In short, the fundamental task of political philosophy is to provide a *deduction of the concept of the state.*

To complete this deduction, it is not enough to show that there are circumstances in which men have an obligation to do what the *de facto* authorities command. Even under the most unjust of governments there are frequently good reasons for obedience rather than defiance. It may be that the government has commanded its subjects to do what in fact they already have an independent obligation to do; or it may be that the evil consequences of defiance far outweigh the indignity of submission. A government's commands may promise beneficent effects, either intentionally or not. For these reasons, and for reasons of prudence as well, a man may be right to comply with the commands of the government under whose *de facto* authority he finds himself. But none of this settles the question of legitimate authority. That is a matter of the *right* to command, and of the correlative obligation *to obey the person who issues the command.*

The point of the last paragraph cannot be too strongly stressed. Obedience is not a matter of doing what someone tells you to do. It is a matter of doing what he tells you to do *because he tells you to do it.* Legitimate, or *de jure*, authority thus concerns the grounds and sources of moral obligation.

Since it is indisputable that there are men who believe that others have authority over them, it might be thought that we could use that fact to prove that somewhere, at some time or other, there must have been men who really did possess legitimate authority. We might think, that is to say, that although some claims to authority are wrong, it could not be that *all* such claims are wrong, since then we never would have had the concept of legitimate authority at all. By a similar argument, some philosophers have tried to show that not all our experiences are dreams, or more generally that in experience not everything is mere appearance rather than reality. The point is that terms like "dream" and "appearance" are defined by contrast with "waking experience" or "reality." Hence we could only have developed a use for them by being presented with situations in which some experiences were dreams and others not, or some things mere appearance and others reality.

Whatever the force of that argument in general, it cannot be applied to the case of *de facto* versus *de jure* authority, for the key component of both concepts, namely "right," is imported into the discussion from the realm of moral philosophy generally. Insofar as we concern ourselves with the possibility of a just state, we assume that moral discourse is meaningful and that adequate deductions have been given of concepts like "right," "duty," and "obligation." Thus, political philosophy is a dependent or derivative discipline, just as the philosophy of science is dependent upon the general theory of knowledge and on the branches of metaphysics which concern themselves with the reality and nature of the physical world.

What can be inferred from the existence of *de facto* states is that men *believe* in the existence of legitimate authority, for of course a *de facto* state is simply a state whose subjects believe it to be legitimate (i.e., really to have the authority which it claims for itself). They may be wrong.

Indeed, *all* beliefs in authority may be wrong—there may be not a single state in the history of mankind which has now or ever has had a right to be obeyed. It might even be impossible for such a state to exist; that is the question we must try to settle. But so long as men believe in the authority of states, we can conclude that they possess the concept of *de jure* authority.

The normative concept of the state, as the human community which possesses rightful authority within a territory, thus defines the subject matter of political philosophy proper. However, even if it should prove impossible to present a deduction of the concept—if, that is, there can be no *de jure* state—still a large number of moral questions can be raised concerning the individual's relationship with *de facto* states. We may ask, for example, whether there are any moral principles which ought to guide the state in its law-making, such as the principle of utilitarianism, and under what conditions it is right for the individual to obey the laws. We may explore the social ideals of equality and achievement, or the principles of punishment, or the justifications for war. All such investigations are essentially applications of general moral principles to the particular phenomena of (*de facto*) politics. Hence, it would be appropriate to reclaim a word which has fallen on bad days, and call that branch of the study of politics *casuistical politics*. Since there are men who acknowledge claims to authority, there are *de facto* states. Assuming that moral discourse in general is legitimate, there must be moral questions which arise in regard to such states. Hence, casuistical politics as a branch of ethics does exist. It remains to be decided whether political philosophy proper exists.

SECTION 2. THE CONCEPT OF AUTONOMY

The fundamental assumption of moral philosophy is that men are responsible for their actions. From this assumption it follows necessarily, as Kant pointed out, that men are metaphysically free, which is to say that in some sense they are capable of choosing how they shall act. Being able to choose how he acts makes a man responsible, but merely choosing is not in itself enough to constitute *taking* responsibility for one's actions. Taking responsibility involves attempting to determine what one ought to do, and that, as philosophers since Aristotle have recognized, lays upon one the additional burdens of gaining knowledge, reflecting on motives, predicting outcomes, criticizing principles, and so forth.

Every man who possesses both free will and reason has an obligation to take responsibility for his actions, even though he may not be actively engaged in a continuing process of reflection, investigation, and deliberation about how he ought to act. A man will sometimes announce his willingness to take responsibility for the consequences of his actions, even though he has not deliberated about them, or does not intend to do so in the future. Such a declaration is, of course, an advance over the refusal to take responsibility; it at least acknowledges the existence of the obligation. But it does not relieve the man of the duty to engage in the reflective process which he has thus far shunned. It goes without saying that a man may take responsibility for his actions and yet act wrongly. When we describe someone as a responsible individual, we do not imply that he always *does* what is right, but only that he does not neglect the duty of attempting to ascertain what is right.

The responsible man is not capricious or anarchic, for he acknowledges himself bound by certain moral constraints. Nevertheless, he is himself the judge of those constraints. He may listen to the advice of others, but he makes it his own by determining for himself whether it is good advice. He may learn from others about his moral obligations, but only in the sense that a mathematician learns from other mathematicians—namely, by hearing from them arguments whose validity he recognizes even though he did not think of them himself. He does not learn in the sense that one learns from an explorer, by accepting as true his accounts of things one cannot see for oneself.

Since the responsible man arrives at moral decisions which he expresses to himself in the form of imperatives, we may say that he gives laws to himself, or is self-legislating. In short, he is *autonomous*. As Kant argued, moral autonomy is a combination of freedom and responsibility; it is a submission to laws which one has made for oneself. The autonomous man, insofar as he is autonomous, is not subject to the will of another. He may do what another tells him, but not *because* he has been told to do it. He is therefore, in the political sense of the word, *free*. We see that while freedom of the will is the necessary condition of *morality*, freedom from subjection, or "liberty," is the necessary condition of moral autonomy.

Since man's responsibility for his actions is a consequence of his capacity for choice, he cannot give it up or put it aside. He can refuse to acknowledge it, however, either deliberately or by simply failing to recognize his moral condition. All men refuse to take responsibility for their actions at some time or other during their lives, and some men so consistently shirk their duty that they present more the appearance of overgrown children than of adults. Inasmuch as moral autonomy is simply the condition of taking full responsibility for one's actions, it follows that men can forfeit their autonomy at will. That is to say, a man can decide to obey the commands of another without making any attempt to determine for himself whether what is commanded is good or wise. (This is an important point, and it should not be confused with the false assertion that a man can give up his responsibility for his actions. Even after he has subjected himself to the will of another, an individual remains responsible for what he does. But by refusing to engage in moral deliberation, by accepting as final the commands of the others, he forfeits his autonomy. Rousseau is therefore right when he says that a man cannot become a slave even through his own choice, if he means that even slaves are morally responsible for their acts. But he is wrong if he means that men cannot place themselves voluntarily in a position of servitude and mindless obedience.)

There are many forms and degrees of forfeiture of autonomy. A man can give up his independence of judgment with regard to a single question, or in respect of a single type of question. For example, when I place myself in the hands of my doctor, I commit myself to whatever course of treatment he prescribes, but only in regard to my health. I do not make him my legal counselor as well. A man may forfeit autonomy on some or all questions for a specific period of time, or during his entire life. He may submit himself to all commands, whatever they may be, save for some specified acts (such as killing) which he refuses to perform. All these and many more are the forms and degrees of giving up autonomy. From the example of the doctor, it is obvious that there are at least some situations in which it is reasonable to give up one's autonomy. Indeed, we may wonder whether, in a complex world of technical expertise, it is ever reasonable *not* to do so!

Since the concept of taking and forfeiting responsibility is central to the discussion which follows, it is worth devoting a bit more space to clarifying it. Taking responsibility for one's actions means making the final decisions about what one should do. For the autonomous man, there is no such thing, strictly speaking, as a *command*. If someone in my environment is issuing what are intended as commands, and if he or others expect those commands to be obeyed, that fact will be taken account of in my deliberations. I may decide that I ought to do what that person is commanding me to do, and it may even be that his issuing the command is the factor in the situation which makes it desirable for me to do so. For example, if I am on a sinking ship, and the captain is giving orders for manning the life boats, and if everyone else is obeying the captain *because he is the captain*, I may decide that under the circumstances I had better do what he says, since the confusion caused by disobeying him would be generally harmful. But insofar as I make such a decision, I am not *obeying his command;* that is, I am not acknowledging him as having authority over me. I would make the same decision, for exactly the same reasons, if one of the passengers had started to issue "orders" and had, in the confusion, come to be obeyed.

In politics, as in life generally, men frequently forfeit their autonomy. There are a number of causes for this fact, and also a number of arguments which have been offered to justify it. Most men feel so strongly the force of tradition or bureaucracy that they accept unthinkingly the claims to authority which are made by their nominal rulers. It is the rare individual in the history of the race who rises even to the level of questioning the right of his masters to command and the duty of himself and his fellows to obey. Once the dangerous question has been started, however, a variety of arguments can be brought forward to demonstrate the authority of the rulers. Among the most ancient is Plato's assertion that men should submit to the authority of those with superior knowledge, wisdom, or insight. A sophisticated modern version has it that the educated portion of a democratic population is more likely to be politically active, and that it is just as well for the ill-informed segment of the electorate to remain passive since its entrance into the political arena only supports the efforts of demagogues and extremists. As a number of American political scientists have put it, the apathy of the American masses is a cause of stability and hence a good thing.

The moral condition demands that we acknowledge responsibility and achieve autonomy wherever and whenever possible. Sometimes this involves moral deliberation and reflection, at other times, the gathering of special, even technical, information. The contemporary American citizen, for example, has an obligation to master enough modern science to enable him to follow debates about nuclear policy and come to an independent conclusion. There are great, perhaps insurmountable, obstacles to the achievement of a complete and rational autonomy in the modern world. Nevertheless, so long as we recognize our responsibility for our actions, and acknowledge the power of reason within us, we must acknowledge as well the continuing obligation to make ourselves the authors of such commands as we may obey. The paradox of man's condition in the modern world is that the more fully he recognizes his right and duty to be his own master, the more completely he becomes the passive object of a technology and bureaucracy whose complexities he cannot hope to understand. It is only several hundred years since a reasonably well-educated man could claim to understand the major issues of government as well as his king or parliament. Ironically, the high school graduate of today, who cannot master the issues of foreign and domestic policy on which he is asked to vote, could quite easily have grasped the problems of 18th century statecraft.

SECTION 3. THE CONFLICT BETWEEN AUTHORITY AND AUTONOMY

The defining mark of the state is authority, the right to rule. The primary obligation of man is autonomy, the refusal to be ruled. It would seem, then, that there can be no resolution of the conflict between the autonomy of the individual and the putative authority of the state. Insofar as a man fulfills his obligation to make himself the author of his decisions, he will resist the state's claim to have authority over him. That is to say, he will deny that he has a duty to obey the laws of the state *simply because they are the laws.* In that sense, it would seem that anarchism is the only political doctrine consistent with the virtue of autonomy.

Now, of course, an anarchist may grant the necessity of complying with the law under certain circumstances or for the time being. He may even doubt that there is any real prospect of eliminating the state as a human institution. But he will never view the commands of the state as *legitimate,* as having a binding moral force. In a sense, we might characterize the anarchist as a man without a country, for despite the ties which bind him to the land of his childhood, he stands in precisely the same moral relationship to "his" government as he does to the government of any other country in which he might happen to be staying for a time. When I take a vacation in Great Britain, I obey its laws, both because of prudential self-interest and because of the obvious moral considerations concerning the value of order, the general good consequences of preserving a system of property, and so forth. On my return to the United States, I have a sense of re-entering *my* country, and if I think about the matter at all, I imagine myself to stand in a different and more intimate relation to American laws. They have been promulgated by *my* government, and I therefore have a special obligation to obey them. But the anarchist tells me that my feeling is purely sentimental, and has no objective moral basis. All authority is equally illegitimate, although of course not therefore equally worthy or unworthy of support, and my obedience to American laws, if I am to be morally autonomous, must proceed from the same considerations which determine me abroad.

Earlier, we concluded that the fundamental task of political philosophy was to provide a deduction of the concept of the *de jure* state. It is now clear that the principal obstacle to such a deduction is the apparent conflict between the conditions of legitimate authority and the duty of moral autonomy.

II. THE SOLUTION OF CLASSICAL DEMOCRACY

SECTION 1. DEMOCRACY IS THE ONLY FEASIBLE SOLUTION

There is only one form of political community which offers any hope of resolving the conflict between authority and autonomy, and that is democracy.

The argument runs thus: men cannot be free so long as they are subject to the will of others, whether one man (a monarch) or several (aristocrats). But if men rule themselves, if they are both law-givers and law-obeyers, then they can combine the benefits of government with the blessing of freedom. Rule *for* the people is merely benevolent slavery, but rule by the people is true freedom. Insofar as a man participates in the affairs of state, he is ruler as well as ruled. His obligation to submit to the laws stems not from the divine right of the monarch, nor from the hereditary authority of a noble class, but from the fact that he himself is the source of the laws which govern him. Therein lies the peculiar merit and moral claim of a democratic state.

Democracy attempts a natural extension of the duty of autonomy to the realm of collective action. Just as the truly responsible man gives laws to himself, and thereby binds himself to what he conceives to be right, so a society of responsible men can collectively bind themselves to laws collectively made, and thereby bind themselves to what they have together judged to be right. The government of a democratic state is then, strictly speaking, no more than a servant of the people as a whole, charged with the execution of laws which have been commonly agreed upon.

SECTION 2. UNANIMOUS DIRECT DEMOCRACY

There is, in theory, a solution to the problem which has been posed, and this fact is in itself quite important. However, the solution requires the imposition of impossibly restrictive conditions which make it applicable only to a rather bizarre variety of actual situations. The solution is a direct democracy—that is, a political community in which every person votes on every issue—governed by a rule of unanimity. Under unanimous direct democracy, every member of the society wills freely every law which is actually passed. Hence, he is only confronted as a citizen with laws to which he has consented. Since a man who is constrained only by the dictates of his own will is autonomous, it follows that under the conditions of unanimous direct democracy, men can harmonize the duty of autonomy with the commands of authority.

It might be argued that even this limiting case is not genuine, since each man is obeying himself, and hence is not submitting to a legitimate authority. However, the case is really different from the pre-political (or extra-political) case of self-determination, for the authority to which each citizen submits is not that of himself simply, but that of the entire community taken collectively. The laws are issued in the name of the sovereign, which is to say the total population of the community. The power which enforces the law (should there be any citizen who, having voted for a law, now resists its application to himself) is the power of all, gathered together into the police power of the state. By this means, the moral conflict between duty and interest which arises from time to time within each man is externalized, and the voice of duty now speaks with the authority of law. Each man, in a manner of speaking, encounters his better self in the form of the state, for its dictates are simply the laws which he has, after due deliberation, willed to be enacted.

Unanimous direct democracy is feasible only so long as there is substantial agreement among *all* the members of a community on the matters of major importance. Since by the rule of unanimity a single negative vote defeats any motion, the slightest disagreement over significant questions will bring the operations of the society to a halt. It will cease to function as a political community and fall into a condition of anarchy (or at least into a condition of non-legitimacy; a *de facto* government may of course emerge and take control). However, it should not be thought that unanimous direct democracy requires for its existence a perfect harmony of the interests or desires of the citizens. It is perfectly consistent with such a system that there be sharp, even violent, oppositions within the community, perhaps of an economic kind. The only necessity is that when the citizens come together to deliberate on the means for resolving such conflicts, they agree unanimously on the laws to be adopted.

Since unanimous democracy can exist only under limited conditions, it might be thought that there is very little point in discussing it at all. For two reasons, however, unanimous direct democracy has great theoretical importance. First, it *is* a genuine solution to the problem of autonomy and authority, and as we shall see, this makes it rather unusual. More important still, unanimous direct democracy is the (frequently unexpressed) ideal which underlies a great deal of classical democratic theory. The devices of majoritary rule and representation are introduced in order to overcome obstacles which stand in the way of unanimity and direct democracy. Unanimity is clearly thought to be the method of making decisions which is most obviously legitimate; other forms are presented as compromises with this ideal, and the arguments in favor of them seek to show that the authority of a unanimous democracy is not fatally weakened by the necessity of using representation or majority rule. One evidence of the theoretical primacy of unanimous direct democracy is the fact that in all social contract theories, the original collective adoption of the social contract is always a unanimous decision made by everyone who can later be held accountable to the new state. Then the various compromise devices are introduced as practical measures, and their legitimacy is derived from the legitimacy of the original contract. The assumption that unanimity creates a *de jure* state is usually not even argued for with any vigor; it seems to most democratic theorists perfectly obvious.

SECTION 3. MAJORITARIAN DEMOCRACY

The principal theoretical weakness of unanimous direct democracy is its requirement that decisions be taken unanimously in order for them to acquire the authority of law. As a practical matter, of course, this requirement severely limits the actual situations in which a state can flourish, but it is perhaps an even more serious failing of unanimous democracy that it offers no way at all for men of good will to resolve their differences. Presumably, in order for the concept of a just state to have more than idle interest, it must at least in theory be possible for conflicts to be resolved without a loss of autonomy on the part of the citizens or of authority on the part of the state. The conflicts need not be motivated by divisive self-interest; they may simply be disagreements over the best way to pursue the common good.

The solution which immediately springs to the fore is, of course, majority rule. Where the electorate are divided, take a vote; give to each man one vote, and let the group as a whole be committed by the preponderance of voices. So widespread is the belief in majority rule that there is not a single variant of democratic theory which does not call upon it as the means for composing differences and arriving at decisions. Our task is to discover an argument which demonstrates the legitimacy of that authority which guides itself by the rule of the majority. In other words, we must inquire whether the members of a democratic polity are morally bound to obey the decisions of the majority, and if so, why.

The problem, of course, concerns those who find themselves in the minority on any question. The members of the majority bear the same relation to the law they have passed as do all the citizens in a unanimous democracy. Since the majority have willed the law, they are bound by it, and remain autonomous in submitting to its authority. A member of the minority, however, has voted against the law, and he appears to be in the position of a man who, deliberating on a moral question, rejects an alternative only to find it forced upon him by a superior power. His readiness to deliberate, and to be committed by his decision, manifests his desire to be autonomous, but insofar as he must submit to the will of the majority it seems that his desire is frustrated.

One common justification of majority rule is that, on prudential or general moral grounds, it works better than any other system which has been devised.

But any defence which might be based on considerations of interest or good consequences, is strictly irrelevant to our inquiry. As a justification for an individual's decision to obey the state, it may be perfectly adequate; but as a demonstration of the *authority* of the state—as a proof, that is, of the right of the state to command the individual and of his obligation to obey, *whatever may be commanded*—it fails completely. If the individual retains his autonomy by reserving to himself in each instance the final decision whether to obey, he thereby denies the authority of the state; if, on the other hand, he submits to the state and accepts its claim to authority, then so far as any of the above arguments indicate, he loses his autonomy.

Indeed, the prudential and casuistical defences of democracy do not succeed in distinguishing it morally from any other form of political community. A man might find that his affairs flourished in a dictatorship or monarchy, and even that the welfare of the people as a whole was effectively advanced by the policies of such a state. Democracy, then, could claim to be no more than one type of *de facto* government among many, and its virtues, if any, would be purely relative. Perhaps, as Winston Churchill once remarked, democracy is the worst form of government except for all the others, but if so, then the "citizens" of America are as much subjects of an alien power as the Spaniards under Franco or the Russians under Stalin. They are merely more fortunate in their rulers.

A more serious case for majority rule can be founded on the terms of the contract by which the political order is constituted. According to many theorists of democracy, the transition from unanimous rule, as exemplified by the adoption of the social contract, to majority rule, on which the subsequent functionings of the society depend, is provided for by a clause in the original agreement. Everyone pledges himself henceforth to abide by the rule of the majority, and whenever a citizen objects to being required to obey laws for which he has not voted, he can be recalled to his promise. On that pact, it is asserted, rests the moral authority of a majoritarian state.

But this argument is no better than the previous one. A promise to abide by the will of the majority creates an obligation, *but it does so precisely by giving up one's autonomy*. It is perfectly possible to forfeit autonomy, as we have already seen. Whether it is wise, or good, or right to do so is, of course, open to question, but *that* one can do so is obvious. Hence, if citizens contract to govern themselves by majority rule, they thereby obligate themselves in just the manner that they would be obligated by any promise. The state then has a right to command them, assuming that it is guided only by the majority. But the citizens have created a legitimate state at the price of their own autonomy! They have bound themselves to obey laws which they do not will, and indeed even laws which they vigorously reject. Insofar as democracy originates in such a promise, it is no more than voluntary slavery, and the characterization which Rousseau gives of the English form of representation can as well be applied here.

If the only argument for majority rule is its legitimation by unanimous vote at the founding convention, then presumably *any* method of decision-making at all which was given that sanction would be equally legitimate. If we hold that majority rule has some special validity, then it must be because of the character of majority rule itself, and not because of a promise which we may be thought to have made to abide by it. What is required, therefore, is a direct justification of majority rule itself, that is, a demonstration that under majority rule the minority do not forfeit their autonomy in submitting to the decisions of the collectivity.

. . .

We appear to be left with no plausible reason for believing that a direct democracy governed by majority rule preserves the moral autonomy of the individual while conferring legitimate authority on the sovereign. The problem remains, that those who submit to laws against which they have voted are no longer autonomous, even though they may have submitted voluntarily. The strongest argument for the moral authority of a majoritarian government is that it is founded upon the unanimous promise of obedience of its subjects. If such a promise may be supposed to exist, then the government does indeed have a moral right to command. But we have discovered no moral reason why men should by their promise bring a democratic state into being rather than a state of any other sort. The implicit claim of all democratic theory, I repeat, is that it offers a solution to the problem of combining political liberty (autonomy) with political authority. This claim is justified for the special case of unanimous direct democracy. But none of the arguments which we have considered thus far succeed in demonstrating that this claim is also valid for majoritarian democracy.

This is not to deny that there are many other reasons for favoring democracy of one sort or another under the conditions which prevail today in advanced industrial societies. For example, one might reply impatiently to all the foregoing argumentation that majority rule seems to work well enough, and that minorities do not show signs of feeling trampled upon, for all that they may be frustrated or disappointed. To which one need only reply that the psychology of politics is not at issue here. Men's feelings of loss of autonomy, like their feelings of loyalty, are determined by such factors as the relative degree of satisfaction and frustration of deeply-held desires which they experience. Modern interest-group democracy is, under some circumstances, an effective means of reducing frustrations, or at least of reducing the connection between frustration and political disaffection. But many other forms of political organization might accomplish this result, such as benevolent autocracy or charismatic dictatorship. If democracy is to make good its title as the only morally legitimate form of politics, then it must solve the problem of the heteronymous minority.

THE MATERIALIST CONCEPTION OF HISTORY

FRIEDRICH ENGELS

The materialist conception of history starts from the principle that production, and next to production the exchange of its products, is the basis of every social system; that in every society arising in history the allotment of products, and with it the division of society into classes or ranks, depends upon what is produced, how it is produced, and how when produced it is exchanged. Accordingly the ultimate causes of all social changes and political revolutions are not to be looked for in the heads of men, in their growing insight into eternal truth and justice, but in changes of the methods of production and exchange; they are to be looked for not in the *philosophy*, but in the *economy* of the epoch in question. The awakening perception that existing social arrangements are unreasonable and unjust, that reason has become nonsense and goodness a scourge, is only a symptom of the fact that in the methods of production and forms of exchange alterations have silently gone on, to which the social system fitted for earlier economic conditions no longer corresponds. That amounts to saying that the means for removing the evils revealed must itself, more or less developed, be present in the altered conditions of production. This means is not something to be invented out of the head, but something to be discovered by means of the head in the material facts of production lying before us.

Reprinted from *Anti-Dührung: Herr Eugen Dührung's Revolution in Science*, translated by R. C. K. Ensor, 1878.

How does modern Socialism accord with this conception?

The present social system has been, as is now pretty generally conceded, created by the now dominant class, the bourgeoisie. The method of production proper to the bourgeoisie, designated, since Marx, as the capitalistic method of production, was incompatible with the local and fixed privileges and the reciprocal personal ties of the feudal system; the bourgeoisie shattered the feudal system and erected on its ruins the bourgeois conception of society, the empire of free competition, of free locomotion, of equal rights for the possessors of commodities, and of all the other bourgeois fine things. The capitalistic method of production could now unfold itself freely. The productive forces elaborated under the direction of the bourgeoisie developed, after steam and the new machinery had transformed the old manufacture into the great industry, with hitherto unheard-of rapidity on a hitherto unheard-of scale. But as in its time manufacture and the handicraft developed under its influence came into conflict with the feudal fetters of the guilds, so the great industry in its fuller development comes into conflict with the limitations in which the capitalistic method of production has confined it. The new productive forces have already quite outgrown the bourgeois form of their utilization; and this conflict between productive forces and methods of production is not a conflict which has originated in the heads of men, like the conflict between human original sin and divine righteousness, but it exists in facts, is objective, outside of us, independent of the will or the course even of those human beings who have brought it about. Modern Socialism is nothing more than the mirroring in thought of this conflict in fact, its ideal reflection in the heads of the class, primarily, which directly suffers by it, the working-class.

In what does this conflict consist?

Before capitalistic production—that is, in the Middle Ages—there everywhere existed petty industry, on the basis of the workers owning privately their means of production: the agriculture of the small free or subject peasants, the handicraft of the towns. The means of work—land, agricultural implements, workshop, manual tools—were means of work for the individual, only calculated for individual use, so necessarily upon a small, pigmy, restricted scale. But for that very reason they belonged as a rule to the producer himself. To concentrate these fragmentary, cramped means of production, to expand them, to transform them into the powerfully operative lever of the production of to-day, was just the *rôle* in history of the capitalistic method of production and its agent, the bourgeoisie. How it carried this out historically after the fifteenth century in the three stages of simple co-operation, manufacture, and the great industry, Marx has depicted expressly in the fourth section of *Capital*. But the bourgeoisie, as is there proved, could not change those limited means of production into mighty productive forces, without changing them from means of production of the individual into *social* means of production only to be utilized by a *collectivity* of men. In place of the spinning-wheel, the hand-loom, and the smith's hammer, came the spinning-mule, the power-loom, and the steam-hammer; in place of the individual workshop, the factory enabling hundreds and thousands to work together. And along with the means of production, production itself changed from a series of individual performances into a series of social acts, and the products from products of individuals into social products. The yarn, the cloth, the hardware, which now came from the factory, were the common product of many workers, through whose hands they had to go in order before they were ready. No individual can say of them: "I made that; that is *my* product."

Where, however, the natural division of labour within society is the basic form of production, it stamps on the products the form of *commodities*, whose reciprocal exchange, purchase and sale, puts the individual producers in a position to satisfy their manifold needs. And in the Middle Ages this was the case. The peasant, *e.g.*, sold farm-produce to the handicraftsman, and bought from him in return the products of handicraft. Upon this society of individual producers, producers of commodities, intruded the new method of production. In the midst of the natural undesigned division of labour prevailing all through society, it set up the designed division of labour as organized in the individual factory; by the side of individual production appeared social production. The products of both were sold on the same market, therefore at prices at least approximately equal. But the designed organization was more powerful than the natural division of labour; the factories with their social labour got out their products more cheaply than the small individual producers. Individual production failed in one sphere after another; social production revolutionized the entire former method of production. But this its revolutionary character was so little recognized, that on the contrary it was introduced as a means for augmenting and advancing the production of commodities. It arose in immediate connection with definite machinery, already discovered for the production and exchange of commodities: merchant's capital, handicraft, wage-labour. While it appeared itself as a new form of the production of commodities, the forms of appropriation in force for the production of commodities remained also in full force for it.

In the production of commodities, as developed in the Middle Ages, there could arise no question as to whose should be the product of labour. As a rule, the individual producer had made it out of raw material belonging to him, and often produced by him, with his own instruments of work, and his own manual labour or that of his family. There was absolutely no need for him first to appropriate it; it belonged to him entirely of itself. A man's ownership of the product rested, therefore, on his own work. Even where outside assistance was used, this as a rule remained secondary, and commonly involved some other benefit beside wages; the guild apprentice and companion worked less for the money and the wage than for their own training to be masters. Then came the concentration of the means of production in great workshops and factories, and its alteration into a really social means of production. But the social means of production and products were treated as though they were still, as they had been, the means of production, and products, of individuals. As the possessor of the means of production had hitherto appropriated the product, because it as a rule was his own product and the labour of outside assistants was the exception, so now the possessor of the means of production continued to appropriate the product, although it was no longer his product, but exclusively the product of outside labour. Thus the products now made socially were not appropriated by those who had really set the means of production in motion and really made the products, but by the *capitalists*. Production, and the means of it, have really become social. But they are subject to a form of appropriation, which presupposes the private production of individuals, in which every-one possesses and brings to market his own product. The method of production is subject to this form of appropriation, although it does away with what this form presupposes.* In this contradiction, which lends to the new method of production its capitalistic character, the whole discord of the present lies already in germ. The more the new method of production came to dominate all important fields of production and all important countries, the more glaringly came perforce to light *the incompatibility of social production and capitalistic appropriation.*

The first capitalists found, as we said, the form of wage-labour already to hand. But wage-labour as an exception, a side occupation, a supplement, a transitional stage. The country labourer, who from time to time went to earn day-wages, had his few acres of his own land, from which alone he could if necessary live. The guild ordinances provided that the companion of to-day should pass on to be the master of to-morrow. But as soon as the means of production were changed and became social, and were concentrated into the hands of capitalists, this was altered. The means of production, as well as the product, of the small individual producer became more and more valueless; nothing was left for him but to go to the capitalist for wages. Wage-labour, previously an exception and a supplement, became the rule and the fundamental form of all production; formerly a side occupation, it became now the exclusive activity of the worker. The temporary wage-worker turned into the lifelong wage-worker. The multitude of lifelong wage-workers was, besides, colossally increased through the simultaneous collapse of the feudal system, dissolution of the retinues of the feudal lords, dismissal of peasants from their court posts, etc. The cleavage was complete between the means of production concentrated in the hands of the capitalists on the one side, and the producers reduced to possessing nothing but their

* It need not here be explained, that although the *form* of appropriation remains the same, its *character* is no less revolutionized by the process described above than is production. If I appropriate my own product, or if I appropriate some one else's, those are naturally two very different sorts of appropriation. Note too, that wage-labour, in which the whole capitalistic method of production is contained in germ, is very old; in an individualized and scattered form it subsisted for centuries beside slavery. But the germ could not develop into the capitalistic method of production, until the historical conditions for it had come about.

labour power on the other. The contradiction between social production and capitalistic appropriation appeared as *an opposition between proletariate and bourgeoisie.*

We saw that the capitalistic method of production intruded itself upon a society of individual producers producing commodities, the means of whose social connection was the exchange of their products. But every society resting on production of commodities has the peculiarity, that in it the producers have lost the control over their own social relations. Every one produces for himself with his means of production, whatever it may be, and for his individual exchange requirements. No one knows how much of his article comes to the market, or how much of it is needed; no one knows whether his individual product meets a real need, whether he will be able to balance his expenses, or to sell it at all. There is a prevailing anarchy of social production. But production of commodities, like every other form of production, has its peculiar, inherent laws, inseparable from it; and these laws are fixed, in spite of the anarchy, in it and through it. They appear in the single persistent form of social connection, in exchange, and they assert themselves against the individual producers as the coercive laws of competition. They are therefore at the outset unknown to these producers themselves, and have first to be gradually discovered by them through long experience. They are fixed not by the producers nor in the producers' interest, but as the blindly-operative natural laws of their form of production. The product governs the producer.

In mediæval society, that is, in the first centuries, production was essentially directed to producers' uses. It in the main satisfied only the needs of the producer and his family. Where, as in the country, there existed relations of personal dependence, it contributed also to satisfy the needs of the feudal lord. In this case no exchange took place, and the products did not acquire the character of commodities from it either. The peasant's family produced nearly everything that it needed, furniture and clothing no less than food. Only when it went so far as to produce a surplus over and above its own requirements and the tribute in kind due to the feudal lord, did it also produce commodities; this surplus, thrown into the social exchange, exposed for sale, became a commodity. The town handicraftsmen had of course from the beginning to produce for exchange. But they, too, worked principally to satisfy their own requirements; they had gardens and small fields; they sent their cattle into the common forest, which at the same time supplied them with timber and firewood; the women spun flax, wool, etc. Production for the purpose of exchange, production of commodities, was only beginning. Hence a restricted exchange, a restricted market, a stable method of production, local exclusiveness against outsiders, local unity within: the manor in the country, the guild in the town.

But with the extension of production, and in particular with the rise of the capitalistic method of production, the hitherto dormant laws of the production of commodities became more openly and powerfully realized.

The old associations were relaxed, the old exclusive limits broken through, the producers converted more and more into independent, isolated producers of commodities. The anarchy of social production became apparent, and was more and more accentuated. But the main instrument, by which the capitalists' method of production enhanced this anarchy in social production, was the exact opposite of anarchy: the increasing organization of production on social lines in every separate producing establishment. With this instrument it put an end to the old peaceful stability. Where it was introduced into a branch of industry, it suffered no older industrial methods to remain beside it. Where it took hold of handicraft, it annihilated the old handicraft. The field of labour became a battle-field. The great geographical discoveries, and the colonizations which followed them, multiplied many times over the area of the market, and emphasized the change from handicraft to manufacture. Not only did the struggle break out between the separate local producers; the local struggles grew on their side to national ones, the commercial wars of the seventeenth and eighteenth centuries. Finally, the great industry and the establishment of the world-market made the struggle universal and at the same time gave it an unheard-of severity. Between single capitalists as between whole industries, and whole countries, the favour of natural or artificial conditions of production decided the question of existence. The weaker was mercilessly eliminated. It is Darwin's struggle for individual existence, transferred with heightened ferocity from nature to society. The natural standpoint of the beast appears as the summit of human development. The contradiction between social production and capitalistic appropriation, reproduces itself as an opposition between the organization of production in the individual factory and the anarchy of production in the entire society.

In these two manifestations of the contradiction imminent in it by reason of its origin, the capitalistic method of production moves, describing without any way out that vicious circle, which already Fourier discovered it in. What Fourier, of course, could not see in his time, is that this circle gradually contracts, that the movement rather describes a spiral, and must reach its end, like the movement of the planets, by a collision with the centre. It is the driving force of the social anarchy of production, which converts the great majority of human beings more and more into proletarians, and again it is the masses of proletarians which finally will put a stop to the anarchy of production. It is the driving force of the social anarchy of production, which converts the infinite perfectibility of the machines of the great industry into an imperative command that every individual industrial capitalist shall perfect his machinery more and more, on pain of ruin. But to perfect machinery means to render superfluous human labour. If the introduction and increase of machinery means the crushing out of millions of manual workers by a few machine-workers, the improvement of machinery means the crushing out of more and more of the machine-workers themselves; and, in the last instance, the production of a number of available wage-workers exceeding the average demand of capital for employees,—a regular reserve-army of industry, as I called it as far back as 1845,—available for the times when industry is working at high pressure, thrown on the pavement by the collapse which necessarily follows, at all times a lead weight tied round the feet of the working-class in its struggle for existence against capital, a regulator for depressing the wage of labour to the low level set by the capitalist demand. So it comes about that machinery, as Marx puts it, is the most powerful weapon of capital against the working-class, that the means of work is continually dashing the means of subsistence out of the worker's hand, that the worker's own product turns into a tool for the worker's enslavement. Thus it happens that the economising of the means of work leads to most reckless squandering of labour-force and robbery of what the labour-function should normally start from; that machinery, the strongest instrument for shortening work-time, is transformed into the surest instrument for converting the whole lifetime of the worker and his family into available work-time for capital to profit by; that the overemployment of one man comes to imply the unemployment of another, and that the great industry, which hunts the whole world over for fresh consumers, limits the consumption of the masses at home to a starvation minimum, and undermines thereby its own domestic market. "The law which keeps the relative surplus population or reserve army of industry, continually balancing the extent and energy of the accumulation of capital, rivets the worker more firmly to capital than Hephaestus' wedges riveted Prometheus to the rocks. It causes an accumulation of misery corresponding to the accumulation of capital. The accumulation of wealth at the one pole is therefore at the same time an accumulation of misery, hard work, slavery, ignorance, brutalization, and moral degradation at the opposite pole, *i.e.* on the side of the class, which produces its own product in the form of capital."* And to expect any other division of the products from the capitalistic method of production, is like wanting the electrodes of a battery, while remaining connected with it, to leave water undecomposed, instead of developing oxygen at the positive pole and hydrogen at the negative.

We saw that the maximised capacity for improvement of modern machinery turns, through the anarchy of production in society, into an imperative command that the individual industrial capitalist shall continually improve his machinery, continually raise its productive power. Into a similar imperative command turns the mere *de facto* possibility of his extending his sphere of production. The enormous power of expansion of the great industry, compared to which that of gases is simply child's play, now manifests itself to us as a qualitative and quantitative *demand for expansion*, which laughs at every opposing check. Such a check is formed by the consumption, the outlet, the markets, for the products of the great industry. But the capacity of expansion of markets, extensive and intensive alike, is governed immediately by quite other laws, with a far less energetic operation. The expansion of markets cannot keep pace with the

* Marx, *Capital.*

expansion of production. The clash becomes inevitable, and as it can give rise to no solution as long as it does not explode the capitalistic method of production itself, it becomes periodic. Capitalistic production gives rise to a new "vicious circle."

In fact, since 1825, when the first general crisis broke out, the whole industrial and commercial world, the production and exchange of all the civilized nations and their more or less barbarous dependencies, gets out of joint just about once every ten years. Transport comes to a standstill, the markets are glutted, products lie unremoved, as abundant as they are impossible to get rid of, ready money goes out of sight, credit disappears, factories are idle, the working masses lack the means of subsistence because they have produced too much of it, bankruptcy follows bankruptcy, and bankrupt after bankrupt is sold up. The standstill lasts for years, productive forces as well as products are squandered and destroyed wholesale, till the accumulated masses of commodities are finally disposed of more or less below value, and production and exchange gradually resume their course. After a while the pace becomes marked; it falls into a trot; the trot of industry passes into a gallop, and this again increases to the unbridled career of a complete industrial, commercial, banking, and speculative steeplechase, so at last to attain once more the breakneck leap into the grave of the crisis. And so all over again and again. Since 1825 we have now experienced this five times, and at the present moment (1877) are experiencing it for the sixth. And the character of these crises is so sharply marked out that Fourier named them all when he named the first one: "*crise pléthorique*"—crisis from over-supply.*

In the crises the contradiction between social production and capitalistic appropriation breaks out violently. The circulation of commodities is for the moment annihilated; the medium of circulation, money, becomes a hindrance to circulation; all the laws of the production and circulation of commodities are turned upside down. The economic clashing has reached its maximum; the method of production is in revolt against the method of exchange, the productive forces are in revolt against the method of production, out of which they have grown.

The fact that the social organization of production inside the factory has developed itself to the point at which it is incompatible with the anarchy of production existing beside and beyond it in society; this fact is made obvious to the capitalists themselves, by the powerful concentration of capitals, which, during crises, is achieved by means of the ruin of many great, and still more small, capitalists. The whole mechanism of the capitalistic method of production gives out under the pressure of the productive forces which it has itself created. It can no longer convert all these masses of the means of production into capital; they lie fallow, and for that very reason, the reserve army of industry must lie fallow also. Means

* This theory, and its premiss that the workers only get a small fraction of the value of their work, was advanced also by the theoretic Socialist Rodbertus. Unchecked capitalism, in this view, minimizes the purchasing-power of the majority, while maximizing their producing-power; hence the crises.

of production, means of subsistence, available workers, all elements of production and of the general wealth, are present in superfluity. But "superfluity is the source of want and need" (Fourier), because it is just it which impedes the conversion of the means of production and subsistence into capital. For in capitalist society the means of production cannot come into action, unless they have previously been converted into capital, into means for the exploitation of human labour-force. Between them and the workers stands, like a spectre, the necessity for them and the means of subsistence to take the character of capital. It alone prevents the harmonious working of the material and personal factors in production; it alone forbids the means of production to function, and the workers to work and live. On the one hand, therefore, the capitalistic method of production becomes convinced of its own incapacity to control further these productive forces. On the other, these productive forces themselves bring increasing pressure to bear for the removal of the contradiction, for their release from their character as capital, for actual recognition of their character as social productive forces.

It is this opposition of the powerfully growing productive forces to their character as capital, this increasing pressure for the recognition of their social character, which compels the capitalist class itself more and more, so far as this is at all possible inside the capitalistic conditions, to treat them as social productive forces. Both the high-pressure periods of industry, with their limitless inflation of credit, and the crisis itself by the collapse of great capitalist firms, lead to that form of the socialization of larger quantities of the means of production, which confronts us in the different sorts of joint-stock companies. Many of these means of production and traffic are from the first so colossal, that, like the railways, they exclude every other form of capitalist exploitation. At a certain stage of development, this form also ceases to suffice; the official representative of capitalist society, the State, must take over their management. This need for conversion into State property appears first in the case of the great traffic concerns: the post, telegraphs, and railways.

If the crises revealed the inability of the bourgeoisie to control further the modern productive forces, the conversion of the great producing and traffic concerns into joint-stock companies and State property shows that the bourgeoisie can be dispensed with for that purpose. Every social function of capitalists is now discharged by salaried servants. The capitalist has no social activity left, except to pocket incomes, to cut off coupons, and to gamble on the Stock Exchange, where the different capitalists relieve each other of their capital. If the capitalistic method of production at first crushed out the workers, so now it crushes out the capitalists, and rejects them, just like the workers, into the surplus population, though not immediately into the reserve-army of industry.

But neither the conversion into joint-stock companies, nor that into State property, takes away the character of capital from the productive forces. In the case of joint-stock companies this is palpable. And the modern State, again, is only the organization, which bourgeois society gives itself in order to uphold the universal outward conditions of the capitalistic method of production against the encroachments, not only of the workers, but of individual capitalists. The modern State, as indeed its form shows, is an essentially capitalist machine, a State of the capitalists, the ideal of capitalist aggregate. The more productive forces it takes over into its ownership, the more does it become a real capitalist aggregate, the more does it exploit its citizens. The workers remain wage-workers, proletarians. The relationship of capital is not removed; rather it culminates. But at the culmination comes transformation. State-ownership of productive forces is not the solution of the conflict; but it contains in itself the formal means of the solution, the handle to it.

This solution can only be found in the actual recognition of the social nature of the modern productive forces, so that the methods of production, appropriation, and exchange shall be harmonized with the social character of the means of production. This can only take place, if society, openly and without beating round the bush, seizes hold of the productive forces, which have outgrown every management but its own. Thereby the social character of the means of production and products,—which to-day turns against the producers themselves, breaks down periodically the methods of production and exchange, and only accomplishes itself in violence and destruction, as a blindly working natural law,—will be brought to its full effect by the producers acting with their eyes open, and will transform itself from a cause of disturbance and periodical collapse into the most powerful lever of production itself.

The forces operative in society operate just like natural forces—blindly, violently, destructively, so long as we do not recognize them and reckon with them. But when once we have recognized them and grasped their activity, their direction, and their workings, it only depends upon ourselves to subject them more and more to our will and to attain our objects by their means. And this holds particularly true of the powerful productive forces of to-day. So long as we obstinately refuse to understand their nature and their character—and to thwart this understanding the whole capitalistic method of production and its defenders strive,—so long do these forces work themselves out in spite of us, against us, so long do they dominate us, as we have in detail described. But once they are apprehended in their nature, they can, in the hands of the associated producers, be converted from demonic masters into willing servants. It is the difference between the destructive force of electricity in the lightning of the storm, and the fettered electricity of the telegraph and the arc-light; the difference between a fiery conflagration, and fire working in the service of man. With this treatment of the modern productive forces in accordance with their ultimately recognized nature, the social anarchy of production is replaced by a socially designed regulation of production according to the acquirements of the collectivity and of every individual; the capitalistic method of appropriation, in which the product enslaves first the producer and afterwards the appropriator too, is replaced by that method of appropriating the products which is founded in the very nature of the modern means of production: on the one hand, direct social appropriation as a means for the maintenance and extension of production; on the other hand, direct individual appropriation as a means of subsistence and enjoyment.

While the capitalistic method of production more and more converts the great majority of the population into proletarians, it is creating the power which is compelled, on pain of perishing, to achieve this revolution. While it more and more forces the great socialized means of production to be converted into State property, it is itself pointing the path for this revolution's achievement. *The proletariate seizes the power of the State, and converts the means of production into State property at once.* But it thereby abolishes itself as a proletariate, abolishes all class distinctions and class antagonisms, and abolishes the State as State. Society, hitherto, stirred by class antagonisms, needed the State, *i.e.* an organization of the exploiting class in each period to maintain their external conditions of production, and especially, therefore, to hold down by force the exploited classes in the conditions of oppression afforded by the existing methods of production (slavery, serfdom or bondage, and wage-labour). The State was the official representative of the whole of society, its embodiment in a visible corporation; but it was this only in so far as it was the State of that class which itself for its period represented the whole of society—in antiquity the State of the slave-holding burgesses, in the Middle Ages that of the feudal nobility, in our time that of the bourgeoisie. When at last it really becomes representative of the whole of society, it renders itself superfluous. As soon as there is no longer a class in society to be held in subjection, as soon as, along with the class-domination and the struggle for individual existence based on the anarchy of production hitherto, the resultant clashings and excesses disappear—there is no longer anything to be repressed, which might necessitate a special repressive force, a State. The first act in which the State really appears as representative of the whole of society—the appropriation of the means of production in the name of society—is at the same time its last independent act as a State. The interference of a State authority in social relations grows superfluous in one sphere after another, and then of its own accord becomes dormant. For government of persons is substituted control of things and management of the processes of production. The State is not "abolished," it dies out. In this context should be considered the phrase "free popular State," both in its temporary rightness for purposes of agitation, and in its ultimate scientific inadequacy; so, too, should the demand of the so-called Anarchists, that the State should be abolished in twenty-four hours.

The appropriation of all the means of production by society has, ever since the appearance in history of the capitalistic method of production, hovered often more or less hazily as the future ideal before the eyes of individuals and of whole sects. But it could not become possible, could not be historically necessary, until the material conditions were present for it to be carried out. Neither it nor any other social advance becomes realizable through the acquired perception that the existence of classes is contrary to justice, equality, etc.; nor through mere willingness to abolish these classes, but through certain new economic conditions. The splitting of society into an exploiting and an exploited, a ruling and a subject class, was the necessary result of the former slight development of production. As long as the aggregate labour of society gives a yield only slightly in excess of what was needed for the bare existence of everybody, as long, therefore, as labour claims all, or nearly all, the time of the great majority of the members of society, so long does society necessarily divide itself into classes. Beside this great majority, which drudges exclusively at labour, is formed a class freed from directly productive work, which looks after the common concerns of society—management of labour, State affairs, justice, science, the arts, etc. The law of the division of labour, therefore, is what lies at the base of the division of classes. But that does not prevent this division of classes from having been established through violence and robbery, guile and fraud, nor the ruling class from having, when once in the saddle, secured their domination at the expense of the working class, and transformed the management of society into an exploitation of the masses.

But if on this view the division into classes has a certain historical justification, it has it only for a given period of time, for given social conditions. It was based on the insufficiency of production; it will be swept away by the full unfolding of the modern productive forces. And, in fact, the abolition of classes in society presupposes a degree of historical development, at which the existence, not merely of this or that particular ruling class, but of a ruling class at all, and therefore of the class-distinction itself, has become an obsolete anachronism. It presupposes, therefore, a high degree of the development of production, at which for a special class in society to appropriate the means of production and products, and with them political supremacy and the monopoly of education and intellectual management, is not only superfluous, but economically, politically, and intellectually a hindrance to development. This point is now reached. While the bourgeoisie itself is hardly unaware any longer of its political and intellectual bankruptcy, its economic bankruptcy is repeated regularly every ten years. In every crisis society is suffocated under the weight of its own productive forces and products, which it cannot utilize; and stands helpless before the absurd contradiction, that the producers have nothing to consume because there is a dearth of consumers. The expansive power of the means of production is bursting the bonds which the capitalistic method of production puts upon it. Its emancipation from these bonds is the sole condition to be fulfilled for an uninterrupted, ever rapidly advancing development of productive forces, and with it a practically unlimited increase of production itself. Nor is that all. Social appropriation of the means of production removes not only the present artificial check on production, but also the positive squandering and spoiling of productive forces and products, which at present is the inevitable accompaniment of production and culminates in the crises. Moreover, it sets free for the community a mass of the means of production and products, by doing away with the imbecile expenditure upon luxuries which the now ruling classes and their political representatives practise. The possibility of securing for all members of society, by means of social production, an existence, which not only is in a material sense perfectly adequate and daily growing wealthier, but also guarantees to them the perfectly free training and exercise of their physical and mental faculties—this possibility was never ours until now, but ours it now is.

When society takes possession of the means of production, there is no more production of commodities, and therefore no more subjection of the producer to the product. The anarchy inside social production is replaced by systematic conscious organization. The struggle for individual existence ceases. In a certain sense this marks the final separation of man from the animal kingdom, and his passage from animal conditions of existence to really human ones. The circle of conditions of life environing men, which hitherto dominated them, now passes under their domination and control; they now for the first time become real, conscious masters of nature, because, and in that, they are masters of their own association. The laws of their own social action, which previously withstood them as external overmastering laws of nature, are now applied, and so mastered, by men, with full practical knowledge. The peculiar association of men, which hitherto confronted them as something doled out by nature and history, now becomes their own free act. The objective eternal powers, which controlled history, come under the control of men themselves. Henceforth for the first time men will make their own history quite consciously; henceforth the social causes which they set in motion will predominantly and in a steadily increasing measure have the results which they wish them to have. Mankind leap from the realm of necessity into the realm of freedom.

To perform this act of world-emancipation is the mission in history of the modern proletariate. To investigate its historical conditions, and so its very nature, and to make the class which is called upon to act—the oppressed class of to-day—aware of the conditions and the nature of its own action, is the object of the theoretic expression of the proletarian movement—scientific Socialism.

MORALITY AND THE LAW

H. L. A. HART

. . . The doctrine of Natural Law is part of an older conception of nature in which the observable world is not merely a scene of such regularities, and knowledge of nature is not merely a knowledge of them. Instead, on this older outlook every nameable kind of existing thing, human, animate, and inanimate, is conceived not only as tending to maintain itself in existence but as proceeding towards a definite optimum state which is the specific good—or the *end* (τέλος, *finis*) appropriate for it.

This is the teleological conception of nature as containing in itself levels of excellence which things realize. The stages by which a thing of any kind progresses to its specific or proper end are regular, and may be formulated in generalizations describing the thing's characteristic mode of change, or action, or development; to that extent the teleological view of nature overlaps with modern thought. The difference is that on the teleological view, the events regularly befalling things are not thought of *merely* as occurring regularly, and the questions whether they *do* occur regularly and whether they *should* occur or whether it is *good* that they occur are not regarded as separate questions. On the contrary (except for some rare monstrosities ascribed to 'chance') what generally occurs can both be explained and evaluated as good or what ought to occur, by exhibiting it as a step towards the proper end or goal of the thing concerned. The laws of a thing's development therefore should show both how it should and how it does regularly behave or change.

This mode of thinking about nature seems strange when stated abstractly. It may appear less fantastic if we recall some of the ways in which even now we refer at least to living things, for a teleological view is still reflected in common ways of describing their development. Thus in the case of an acorn, growth into an oak is something which is not only regularly achieved by acorns, but is distinguished unlike its decay (which is also regular) as an optimum state of maturity in the light of which the intermediate stages are both explained and judged as good or bad, and the 'function' of its various parts and structural changes identified. The normal growth of leaves is required if it is to obtain the moisture necessary for 'full' or 'proper' development, and it is the 'function' of leaves to supply this. Hence we think and speak of this growth as what 'ought naturally to occur'. In the case of the action or movements of

Reprinted from Chapter IX of H. L. A. Hart's *The Concept of Law*, 1961, by permission of the Clarendon Press, Oxford.

inanimate things, such ways of talking seem much less plausible unless they are artefacts designed by human beings for a purpose. The notion that a stone on falling to the ground is realizing some appropriate 'end' or returning to its 'proper place', like a horse galloping home to a stable, is now somewhat comic.

Indeed, one of the difficulties in understanding a teleological view of nature is that just as it minimized the differences between statements of what regularly happens and statements of what ought to happen, so too it minimizes the difference, so important in modern thought, between human beings *with* a purpose of their own which they consciously strive to realize and other living or inanimate things. For in the teleological view of the world, man, like other things, is thought of as tending towards a specific optimum state or end which is set for him and the fact, that he, unlike other things, may do this consciously, is not conceived as a radical difference between him and the rest of nature. This specific human end or good is in part, like that of other living things, a condition of biological maturity and developed physical powers; but it also includes, as its distinctively human element, a development and excellence of mind and character manifested in thought and conduct. Unlike other things, man is able by reasoning and reflection to discover what the attainment of this excellence of mind and character involves and to desire it. Yet even so, on this teleological view, this optimum state is not man's good or end because he desires it; rather he desires it because it is already his natural end.

Again, much of this teleological point of view survives in some of the ways in which we think and speak of human beings. It is latent in our identification of certain things as human *needs* which it is *good* to satisfy and of certain things done to or suffered *by* human beings as *harm* or *injury*. Thus, though it is true that some men may refuse to eat or rest because they wish to die, we think of eating and resting as something more than things which men regularly do or just happen to desire. Food and rest are human needs, even if some refuse them when they are needed. Hence we say not only that it is natural for all men to eat and sleep, but that all men ought to eat and rest sometimes, or that it is naturally good to do these things. The force of the word 'naturally', in such judgments of human conduct, is to differentiate them both from judgments which reflect mere conventions or human prescriptions ('You ought to take off your hat'), the content of which cannot be discovered by thought or reflection, and also from judgments which merely indicate what is required for achieving some particular objective, which at a given time one man may happen to have and another may not. The same outlook is present in our conception of the *functions* of bodily organs and the line we draw between these and mere causal properties. We say it is the function of the heart to circulate the blood, but not that it is the function of a cancerous growth to cause death.

These crude examples designed to illustrate teleological elements still alive in ordinary thought about human action, are drawn from the lowly sphere of biological fact which man shares with other animals. It will be rightly observed that what makes sense of this mode of thought and expression is something entirely obvious: it is the tacit assumption that the proper end of human activity is survival, and this rests on the simple contingent fact that most men most of the time wish to continue in existence. The actions which we speak of as those which are naturally good to do, are those which are required for survival; the notions of a human need, of harm, and of the *function* of bodily organs or changes rests on the same simple fact. Certainly if we stop here, we shall have only a very attenuated version of Natural Law: for the classical exponents of this outlook conceived of survival (*perseverare in esse suo*) as merely the lowest stratum in a much more complex and far more debatable concept of the human end or good for man. Aristotle included in it the disinterested cultivation of the human intellect, and Aquinas the knowledge of God, and both these represent values which may be and have been challenged. Yet other thinkers, Hobbes and Hume among them, have been willing to lower their sights: they have seen in the modest aim of survival the central indisputable element which gives empirical good sense to the terminology of Natural Law. 'Human nature cannot by any means subsist without the association of individuals: and that association never could have place were no regard paid to the laws of equity and justice.'*

This simple thought has in fact very much to do with the characteristics of both law and morals, and it can be disentangled from more disputable parts of the general teleological outlook in which the end or good for man appears as a specific way of life about which, in fact, men may profoundly disagree. Moreover, we can, in referring to survival, discard, as too metaphysical for modern minds, the notion that this is something antecedently fixed which men necessarily desire because it is their proper goal or end. Instead we may hold it to be a mere contingent fact which could be otherwise, that in general men do desire to live, and that we may mean nothing more by calling survival a human goal or end than that men do desire it. Yet even if we think of it in this commonsense way, survival has still a special status in relation to human conduct and in our thought about it, which parallels the prominence and the necessity ascribed to it in the orthodox formulations of Natural Law. For it is not merely that an overwhelming majority of men do wish to live, even at the cost of hideous misery, but that this is reflected in whole structures of our thought and language, in terms of which we describe the world and each other. We could not subtract the general wish to live and leave intact concepts like danger and safety, harm and benefit, need and function, disease and cure; for these are ways of simultaneously describing and appraising things by reference to the contribution they make to survival which is accepted as an aim.

There are, however, simpler, less philosophical, considerations than these which show acceptance of survival as an aim to be necessary, in a

* Hume, *Treatise of Human Nature,* III. ii, 'Of Justice and Injustice'.

sense more directly relevant to the discussion of human law and morals. We are committed to it as something presupposed by the terms of the discussion; for our concern is with social arrangements for continued existence, not with those of a suicide club. We wish to know whether, among these social arrangements, there are some which may illuminatingly be ranked as natural laws discoverable by reason, and what their relation is to human law and morality. To raise this or any other question concerning *how* men should live together, we must assume that their aim, generally speaking, is to live. From this point the argument is a simple one. Reflection on some very obvious generalizations—indeed truisms—concerning human nature and the world in which men live, show that as long as these hold good, there are certain rules of conduct which any social organization must contain if it is to be viable. Such rules do in fact constitute a common element in the law and conventional morality of all societies which have progressed to the point where these are distinguished as different forms of social control. With them are found, both in law and morals, much that is peculiar to a particular society and much that may seem arbitrary or a mere matter of choice. Such universally recognized principles of conduct which have a basis in elementary truths concerning human beings, their natural environment, and aims, may be considered the *minimum content* of Natural Law, in contrast with the more grandiose and more challengeable constructions which have often been proffered under that name. In the next section we shall consider, in the form of five truisms, the salient characteristics of human nature upon which this modest but important minimum rests.

2. *THE MINIMUM CONTENT OF NATURAL LAW*

In considering the simple truisms which we set forth here, and their connexion with law and morals, it is important to observe that in each case the facts mentioned afford a *reason* why, given survival as an aim, law and morals should include a specific content. The general form of the argument is simply that without such a content laws and morals could not forward the minimum purpose of survival which men have in associating with each other. In the absence of this content men, as they are, would have no reason for obeying voluntarily any rules; and without a minimum of co-operation given voluntarily by those who find that it is in their interest to submit to and maintain the rules, coercion of others who would not voluntarily conform would be impossible. It is important to stress the distinctively rational connexion between natural facts and the content of legal and moral rules in this approach, because it is both possible and important to inquire into quite different forms of connexion between natural facts and legal or moral rules. Thus, the still young sciences of psychology and sociology may discover or may even have discovered that, unless certain physical, psychological, or economic conditions are satisfied, e.g. unless young children are fed and nurtured in certain ways within the family, no system of laws or code of morals can be established, or that only those laws can function successfully which conform to a certain type. Connexions of this sort between natural conditions and systems of rules are not mediated by *reasons*; for they do not relate the existence of certain rules to the conscious aims or purpose of those whose rules they are. Being fed in infancy in a certain way may well be shown to be a necessary condition or even a *cause* of a population developing or maintaining a moral or legal code, but it is not a *reason* for their doing so. Such causal connexions do not of course conflict with the connexions which rest on purposes or conscious aims; they may indeed be considered more important or fundamental than the latter, since they may actually explain why human beings have those conscious aims or purposes which Natural Law takes as its starting-points. Causal explanations of this type do not rest on truisms nor are they mediated by conscious aims or purposes: they are for sociology or psychology like other sciences to establish by the methods of generalization and theory, resting on observation and, where possible, on experiment. Such connexions therefore are of a different kind from those which relate the content of certain legal and moral rules to the facts stated in the following truisms.

(i) HUMAN VULNERABILITY

The common requirements of law and morality consist for the most part not of active services to be rendered but of forbearances, which are usually formulated in negative form as prohibitions. Of these the most important for social life are those that restrict the use of violence in killing or inflicting bodily harm. The basic character of such rules may be brought out in a question: If there were not these rules what point could there be for beings such as ourselves in having rules of *any* other kind? The force of this rhetorical question rests on the fact that men are both occasionally prone to, and normally vulnerable to, bodily attack. Yet though this is a truism it is not a necessary truth; for things might have been, and might one day be, otherwise. There are species of animals whose physical structure (including exoskeletons or a carapace) renders them virtually immune from attack by other members of their species and animals who have no organs enabling them to attack. If men were to lose their vulnerability to each other there would vanish one obvious reason for the most characteristic provision of law and morals: *Thou shalt not kill.*

(ii) APPROXIMATE EQUALITY

Men differ from each other in physical strength, agility, and even more in intellectual capacity. Nonetheless it is a fact of quite major importance for the understanding of different forms of law and morality, that no individual is so much more powerful than others, that he is able, without co-operation, to dominate or subdue them for more than a short period. Even the strongest must sleep at times and, when asleep, loses temporarily his superiority. This fact of approximate equality, more than any other, makes obvious the necessity for a system of mutual forbearance and compromise which is the base of both legal and moral obligation. Social life with its rules requiring such forbearances is irksome at times; but it is at any rate less nasty, less brutish, and less short than unrestrained aggression for beings thus approximately equal. It is, of course, entirely consistent with this and an equal truism that when such a system of forbearance is established there will always be some who will wish to exploit it, by simultaneously living within its shelter and breaking its restrictions. This, indeed is, as we later show, one of the natural facts which makes the step from merely moral to organized, legal forms of control a necessary one. Again, things might have been otherwise. Instead of being approximately equal there might have been some men immensely stronger than others and better able to dispense with rest, either because some were in these ways far above the present average, or because most were far below it. Such exceptional men might have much to gain by aggression and little to gain from mutual forbearance or compromise with others. But we need not have recourse to the fantasy of giants among pygmies to see the cardinal importance of the fact of approximate equality: for it is illustrated better by the facts of international life, where there are (or were) vast disparities in strength and vulnerability between the states. This inequality, as we shall later see, between the units of international law is one of the things that has imparted to it a character so different from municipal law and limited the extent to which it is capable of operating as an organized coercive system.

(iii) LIMITED ALTRUISM

Men are not devils dominated by a wish to exterminate each other, and the demonstration that, given only the modest aim of survival, the basic rules of law and morals are necessities, must not be identified with the false view that men are predominantly selfish and have no disinterested interest in the survival and welfare of their fellows. But if men are not devils, neither are they angels; and the fact that they are a mean between these two extremes is something which makes a system of mutual forbearances both necessary and possible. With angels, never tempted to harm others, rules requiring forbearances would not be necessary. With devils prepared to destroy, reckless of the cost to themselves, they would be impossible. As things are, human altruism is limited in range and intermittent, and the tendencies to aggression are frequent enough to be fatal to social life if not controlled.

(iv) LIMITED RESOURCES

It is a merely contingent fact that human beings need food, clothes, and shelter; that these do not exist at hand in limitless abundance; but are scarce, have to be grown or won from nature, or have to be constructed by human toil. These facts alone make indispensable some minimal form of the institution of property (though not necessarily individual property), and the distinctive kind of rule which requires respect for it. The simplest forms of property are to be seen in rules excluding persons generally other than the 'owner' from entry on, or the use of land, or from taking or using material things. If crops are to grow, land must be secure from indiscriminate entry, and food must, in the intervals between its growth or capture and consumption, be secure from being taken by others. At all times and places life itself depends on these minimal forbearances. Again, in this respect, things might have been otherwise than they are. The human organism might have been constructed like plants, capable of extracting food from air, or what it needs might have grown without cultivation in limitless abundance.

The rules which we have so far discussed are *static* rules, in the sense that the obligations they impose and the incidence of these obligations are not variable by individuals. But the division of labour, which all but the smallest groups must develop to obtain adequate supplies, brings with it the need for rules which are *dynamic* in the sense that they enable individuals to create obligations and to vary their incidence. Among these are rules enabling men to transfer, exchange, or sell their products; for these transactions involve the capacity to alter the incidence of those initial rights and obligations which define the simplest form of property. The same inescapable division of labour, and perennial need for co-operation, are also factors which make other forms of dynamic or obligation-creating rule necessary in social life. These secure the recognition of promises as a source of obligation. By this device individuals are enabled by words, spoken or written, to make themselves liable to blame or punishment for failure to act in certain stipulated ways. Where altruism is not unlimited, a standing procedure providing for such self-binding operations is required in order to create a minimum form of confidence in the future behaviour of others, and to ensure the predictability necessary for co-operation. This is most obviously needed where what is to be exchanged or jointly planned are mutual services, or wherever goods which are to be exchanged or sold are not simultaneously or immediately available.

(v) LIMITED UNDERSTANDING AND STRENGTH OF WILL

The facts that make rules respecting persons, property, and promises necessary in social life are simple and their mutual benefits are obvious. Most men are capable of seeing them and of sacrificing the immediate short-term interests which conformity to such rules demands. They may indeed obey, from a variety of motives: some from prudential calculation that the sacrifices are worth the gains, some from a disinterested interest in the welfare of others, and some because they look upon the rules as worthy of respect in themselves and find their ideals in devotion to them.

On the other hand, neither understanding of long-term interest, nor the strength or goodness of will, upon which the efficacy of these different motives towards obedience depends, are shared by all men alike. All are tempted at times to prefer their own immediate interests and, in the absence of a special organization for their detection and punishment, many would succumb to the temptation. No doubt the advantages of mutual forbearance are so palpable that the number and strength of those who would co-operate voluntarily in a coercive system will normally be greater than any likely combination of malefactors. Yet, except in very small closely-knit societies, submission to the system of restraints would be folly if there were no organization for the coercion of those who would then try to obtain the advantages of the system without submitting to its obligations. 'Sanctions' are therefore required not as the normal motive for obedience, but as a *guarantee* that those who would voluntarily obey shall not be sacrificed to those who would not. To obey, without this, would be to risk going to the wall. Given this standing danger, what reason demands is *voluntary* co-operation in a *coercive* system.

It is to be observed that the same natural fact of approximate equality between men is of crucial importance in the efficacy of organized sanctions. If some men were vastly more powerful than others, and so not dependent on their forbearance, the strength of the malefactors might exceed that of the supporters of law and order. Given such inequalities, the use of sanctions could not be successful and would involve dangers at least as great as those which they were designed to suppress. In these circumstances instead of social life being based on a system of mutual forbearances, with force used only intermittently against a minority of malefactors, the only viable system would be one in which the weak submitted to the strong on the best terms they could make and lived under their 'protection'. This, because of the scarcity of resources, would lead to a number of conflicting power centres, each grouped round its 'strong man': these might intermittently war with each other, though the natural sanction, never negligible, of the risk of defeat might ensure an uneasy peace. Rules of a sort might then be accepted for the regulation of issues over which the 'powers' were unwilling to fight. Again we need not think in fanciful terms of pygmies and giants in order to understand the simple logistics of approximate equality and its importance for law. The international scene, where the units concerned have differed vastly in strength, affords illustration enough. For centuries the disparities between states have resulted in a system where organized sanctions have been impossible, and law has been confined to matters which did not affect 'vital' issues. How far atomic weapons, when available to all, will redress the balance of unequal power, and bring forms of control more closely resembling municipal criminal law, remains to be seen.

The simple truisms we have discussed not only disclose the core of good sense in the doctrine of Natural Law. They are of vital importance for the understanding of law and morals, and they explain why the definition of the basic forms of these in purely formal terms, without reference to any specific content or social needs, has proved so inadequate. Perhaps the major benefit to jurisprudence from this outlook is the escape it affords from certain misleading dichotomies which often obscure the discussion of the characteristics of law. Thus, for example, the traditional question whether every legal system *must* provide for sanctions can be presented in a fresh and clearer light, when we command the view of things presented by this simple version of Natural Law. We shall no longer have to choose between two unsuitable alternatives which are often taken as exhaustive: on the one hand that of saying that this is required by 'the' meaning of the words 'law' or 'legal system', and on the other that of saying that it is 'just a fact' that most legal systems do provide for sanctions. Neither of these alternatives is satisfactory. There are no settled principles forbidding the use of the word 'law' of systems where there are no centrally organized sanctions, and there is good reason (though no compulsion) for using the expression 'international law' of a system, which has none. On the other hand we do need to distinguish the place that sanctions must have within a municipal system, if it is to serve the minimum purposes of beings constituted as men are. We can say, given the setting of natural facts and aims, which make sanctions both possible and necessary in a municipal system, that this is a *natural necessity;* and some such phrase is needed also to convey the status of the minimum forms of protection for persons, property, and promises which are similarly indispensable features of municipal law. It is in this form that we should reply to the positivist thesis that 'law may have any content'. For it is a truth of some importance that for the adequate description not only of law but of many other social institutions, a place must be reserved, besides definitions and ordinary statements of fact, for a third category of statements: those the truth of which is contingent on human beings and the world they live in retaining the salient characteristics which they have.

3. *LEGAL VALIDITY AND MORAL VALUE*

The protections and benefits provided by the system of mutual forbearances which underlies both law and morals may, in different societies, be extended to very different ranges of persons. It is true that the denial of these elementary protections to any class of human beings, willing to accept the corresponding restrictions, would offend the principles of morality and justice to which all modern states pay, at any rate, lip service. Their professed moral outlook is, in general, permeated by the conception that in these fundamentals at least, human beings are entitled to be treated alike and that differences of treatment require more to justify them than just an appeal to the interests of others.

Yet it is plain that neither the law nor the accepted morality of societies need extend their minimal protections and benefits to all within their scope, and often they have not done so. In slave-owning societies the sense that the slaves are human beings, not mere objects to be used, may be lost by the dominant group, who may yet remain morally most sensitive to each other's claims and interests. Huckleberry Finn, when asked if the explosion of a steamboat boiler had hurt anyone, replied, 'No'm: killed a nigger.' Aunt Sally's comment 'Well it's lucky because sometimes people do get hurt' sums up a whole morality which has often prevailed among men. Where it does prevail, as Huck found to his cost, to extend to slaves the concern for others which is natural between members of the dominant group may well be looked on as a grave moral offence, bringing with it all the sequelae of moral guilt. Nazi Germany and South Africa offer parallels unpleasantly near to us in time.

Though the law of some societies has occasionally been in advance of the accepted morality, normally law follows morality and even the homicide of a slave may be regarded only as a waste of public resources or as an offence against the master whose property he is. Even where slavery is not officially recognized, discriminations on grounds of race, colour, or creed may produce a legal system and a social morality which does not recognize that all men are entitled to a minimum of protection from others.

These painful facts of human history are enough to show that, though a society to be viable must offer *some* of its members a system of mutual forbearances, it need not, unfortunately, offer them to all. It is true, as we have already emphasized in discussing the need for and the possibility of sanctions, that if a system of rules is to be imposed by force on any, there must be a sufficient number who accept it voluntarily. Without their voluntary co-operation, thus creating *authority*, the coercive power of law and government cannot be established. But coercive power, thus established on its basis of authority, may be used in two principal ways. It may be exerted only against malefactors who, though they are afforded the protection of the rules, yet selfishly break them. On the other hand, it may be used to subdue and maintain, in a position of permanent inferiority, a subject group whose size, relatively to the master group, may be large or small, depending on the means of coercion, solidarity, and discipline available to the latter, and the helplessness or inability to organize of the former. For those thus oppressed there may be nothing in the system to command their loyalty but only things to fear. They are its victims, not its beneficiaries.

In the earlier chapters of this book we stressed the fact that the existence of a legal system is a social phenomenon which always presents two aspects, to both of which we must attend if our view of it is to be realistic. It involves the attitudes and behaviour involved in the voluntary acceptance of rules and also the simpler attitudes and behaviour involved in mere obedience or acquiescence.

Hence a society with law contains those who look upon its rules from the internal point of view as accepted standards of behaviour, and not merely as reliable predictions of what will befall them, at the hands of officials, if they disobey. But it also comprises those upon whom, either because they are malefactors or mere helpless victims of the system, these legal standards have to be imposed by force or threat of force; they are concerned with the rules merely as a source of possible punishment. The balance between these two components will be determined by many different factors. If the system is fair and caters genuinely for the vital interests of all those from whom it demands obedience, it may gain and retain the allegiance of most for most of the time, and will accordingly be stable. On the other hand it may be a narrow and exclusive system run in the interests of the dominant group, and it may be made continually more repressive and unstable with the latent threat of upheaval. Between these two extremes various combinations of these attitudes to law are to be found, often in the same individual.

Reflection on this aspect of things reveals a sobering truth: the step from the simple form of society, where primary rules of obligation are the only means of social control, into the legal world with its centrally organized legislature, courts, officials, and sanctions brings its solid gains at a certain cost. The gains are those of adaptability to change, certainty, and efficiency, and these are immense; the cost is the risk that the centrally organized power may well be used for the oppression of numbers with whose support it can dispense, in a way that the simpler régime of primary rules could not.

. . .

REFLECTIONS ON THE GUILLOTINE

ALBERT CAMUS

To simplify matters, let us say that our civilization has lost the only values that, in a certain way, can justify that penalty and, on the other hand, suffers from evils that necessitate its suppression. In other words, the abolition of the death penalty ought to be asked for by all thinking members of our society, for reasons both of logic and of realism.

Of logic, to begin with. Deciding that a man must have the definitive punishment imposed on him is tantamount to deciding that that man has no chance of making amends. This is the point, to repeat ourselves, where the arguments clash blindly and crystallize in a sterile opposition. But it so

Reprinted from Albert Camus' "Reflections on the Guillotine" in *Resistance, Rebellion and Death*, pp. 220–230, 1961, by permission of Alfred A. Knopf, Inc.

happens that none among us can settle the question, for we are all both judges and interested parties. Whence our uncertainty as to our right to kill and our inability to convince each other. Without absolute innocence, there is no supreme judge. Now, we have all done wrong in our lives even if that wrong, without falling within the jurisdiction of the laws, went as far as the unknown crime. There are no just people—merely hearts more or less lacking in justice. Living at least allows us to discover this and to add to the sum of our actions a little of the good that will make up in part for the evil we have added to the world. Such a right to live, which allows a chance to make amends, is the natural right of every man, even the worst man. The lowest of criminals and the most upright of judges meet side by side, equally wretched in their solidarity. Without that right, moral life is utterly impossible. None among us is authorized to despair of a single man, except after his death, which transforms his life into destiny and then permits a definitive judgment. But pronouncing the definitive judgment before his death, decreeing the closing of accounts when the creditor is still alive, is no man's right. On this limit, at least, whoever judges absolutely condemns himself absolutely.

Bernard Fallot of the Masuy gang, working for the Gestapo, was condemned to death after admitting the many terrible crimes of which he was guilty, and declared himself that he could not be pardoned. "My hands are too red with blood," he told a prison mate.* Public opinion and the opinion of his judges certainly classed him among the irremediable, and I should have been tempted to agree if I had not read a surprising testimony. This is what Fallot said to the same companion after declaring that he wanted to die courageously: "Shall I tell you my greatest regret? Well, it is not having known the Bible I now have here. I assure you that I wouldn't be where I now am." There is no question of giving in to some conventional set of sentimental pictures and calling to mind Victor Hugo's good convicts. The age of enlightenment, as people say, wanted to suppress the death penalty on the pretext that man was naturally good. Of course he is not (he is worse or better). After twenty years of our magnificent history we are well aware of this. But precisely because he is not absolutely good, no one among us can pose as an absolute judge and pronounce the definitive elimination of the worst among the guilty, because no one of us can lay claim to absolute innocence. Capital judgment upsets the only indisputable human solidarity—our solidarity against death—and it can be legitimized only by a truth or a principle that is superior to man.

In fact, the supreme punishment has always been, throughout the ages, a religious penalty. Inflicted in the name of the king, God's representative on earth, or by priests or in the name of society considered as a sacred body, it denies, not human solidarity, but the guilty man's membership in the divine community, the only thing that can give him life. Life on earth is taken from him, to be sure, but his chance of making amends is left

* Jean Bocognano: *Quartier des fauves, prison de Fresnes* (Editions du Fuseau).

him. The real judgment is not pronounced; it will be in the other world. Only religious values, and especially belief in eternal life, can therefore serve as a basis for the supreme punishment because, according to their own logic, they keep it from being definitive and irreparable. Consequently, it is justified only insofar as it is not supreme.

The Catholic Church, for example, has always accepted the necessity of the death penalty. It inflicted that penalty itself, and without stint, in other periods. Even today it justifies it and grants the State the right to apply it. The Church's position, however subtle, contains a very deep feeling that was expressed directly in 1937 by a Swiss National Councillor from Fribourg during a discussion in the National Council. According to M. Grand, the lowest of criminals when faced with execution withdraws into himself. "He repents and his preparation for death is thereby facilitated. The Church has saved one of its members and fulfilled its divine mission. This is why it has always accepted the death penalty, not only as a means of self-defense, but *as a powerful means of salvation.** . . . Without trying to make of it a thing of the Church, the death penalty can point proudly to its almost divine efficacy, like war."

By virtue of the same reasoning, probably, there could be read on the sword of the Fribourg executioner the words: "Lord Jesus, thou art the judge." Hence the executioner is invested with a sacred function. He is the man who destroys the body in order to deliver the soul to the divine sentence, which no one can judge beforehand. Some may think that such words imply rather scandalous confusions. And, to be sure, whoever clings to the teaching of Jesus will look upon that handsome sword as one more outrage to the person of Christ. In the light of this, it is possible to understand the dreadful remark of the Russian condemned man about to be hanged by the Tsar's executioners in 1905 who said firmly to the priest who had come to console him with the image of Christ: "Go away and commit no sacrilege." The unbeliever cannot keep from thinking that men who have set at the center of their faith the staggering victim of a judicial error ought at least to hesitate before committing legal murder. Believers might also be reminded that Emperor Julian, before his conversion, did not want to give official offices to Christians because they systematically refused to pronounce death sentences or to have anything to do with them. For five centuries Christians therefore believed that the strict moral teaching of their master forbade killing. But Catholic faith is not nourished solely by the personal teaching of Christ. It also feeds on the Old Testament, on St. Paul, and on the Church Fathers. In particular, the immortality of the soul and the universal resurrection of bodies are articles of dogma. As a result, capital punishment is for the believer a temporary penalty that leaves the final sentence in suspense, an arrangement necessary only for terrestrial order, an administrative measure which, far from signifying the end for the guilty man, may instead favor his redemption. I am not saying that all believers agree with this, and I

* My italics.

can readily imagine that some Catholics may stand closer to Christ than to Moses or St. Paul. I am simply saying that faith in the immortality of the soul allowed Catholicism to see the problem of capital punishment in very different terms and to justify it.

But what is the value of such a justification in the society we live in, which in its institutions and its customs has lost all contact with the sacred? When an atheistic or skeptical or agnostic judge inflicts the death penalty on an unbelieving criminal, he is pronouncing a definitive punishment that cannot be reconsidered. He takes his place on the throne of God,* without having the same powers and even without believing in God. He kills, in short, because his ancestors believed in eternal life. But the society that he claims to represent is in reality pronouncing a simple measure of elimination, doing violence to the human community united against death, and taking a stand as an absolute value because society is laying claim to absolute power. To be sure, it delegates a priest to the condemned man, through tradition. The priest may legitimately hope that fear of punishment will help the guilty man's conversion. Who can accept, however, that such a calculation should justify a penalty most often inflicted and received in a quite different spirit? It is one thing to believe before being afraid and another to find faith after fear. Conversion through fire or the guillotine will always be suspect, and it may seem surprising that the Church has not given up conquering infidels through terror. In any case, society that has lost all contact with the sacred can find no advantage in a conversion in which it professes to have no interest. Society decrees a sacred punishment and at the same time divests it both of excuse and of usefulness. Society proceeds sovereignly to eliminate the evil ones from her midst as if she were virtue itself. Like an honorable man killing his wayward son and remarking: "Really, I didn't know what to do with him." She assumes the right to select as if she were nature herself and to add great sufferings to the elimination as if she were a redeeming god.

To assert, in any case, that a man must be absolutely cut off from society because he is absolutely evil amounts to saying that society is absolutely good, and no one in his right mind will believe this today. Instead of believing this, people will more readily think the reverse. Our society has become so bad and so criminal only because she has respected nothing but her own preservation or a good reputation in history. Society has indeed lost all contact with the sacred. But society began in the nineteenth century to find a substitute for religion by proposing herself as an object of adoration. The doctrines of evolution and the notions of selection that accompany them have made of the future of society a final end. The political utopias that were grafted onto those doctrines placed at the end of time a golden age that justified in advance any enterprises whatever. Society became accustomed to legitimizing what might serve her future and, consequently, to making use of the supreme punishment

* As everyone knows, the jury's decision is preceded by the words: "Before God and my conscience. . . ."

in an absolute way. From then on, society considered as a crime and a sacrilege anything that stood in the way of her plan and her temporal dogmas. In other words, after being a priest, the executioner became a government official. The result is here all around us. The situation is such that this mid-century society which has lost the right, in all logic, to decree capital punishment ought now to suppress it for reasons of realism.

In relation to crime, how can our civilization be defined? The reply is easy: for thirty years now, State crimes have been far more numerous than individual crimes. I am not even speaking of wars, general or localized, although bloodshed too is an alcohol that eventually intoxicates like the headiest of wines. But the number of individuals killed directly by the State has assumed astronomical proportions and infinitely outnumbers private murders. There are fewer and fewer condemned by common law and more and more condemned for political reasons. The proof is that each of us, however honorable he may be, can foresee the possibility of being someday condemned to death, whereas that eventuality would have seemed ridiculous at the beginning of the century. Alphonse Karr's witty remark: "Let the noble assassins begin" has no meaning now. Those who cause the most blood to flow are the same ones who believe they have right, logic, and history on their side.

Hence our society must now defend herself not so much against the individual as against the State. It may be that the proportions will be reversed in another thirty years. But, for the moment, our self-defense must be aimed at the State first and foremost. Justice and expediency command the law to protect the individual against a State given over to the follies of sectarianism or of pride. "Let the State begin and abolish the death penalty" ought to be our rallying cry today.

Bloodthirsty laws, it has been said, make bloodthirsty customs. But any society eventually reaches a state of ignominy in which, despite every disorder, the customs never manage to be as bloodthirsty as the laws. Half of Europe knows that condition. We French knew it in the past and may again know it. Those executed during the Occupation led to those executed at the time of the Liberation, whose friends now dream of revenge. Elsewhere States laden with too many crimes are getting ready to drown their guilt in even greater massacres. One kills for a nation or a class that has been granted divine status. One kills for a future society that has likewise been given divine status. Whoever thinks he has omniscience imagines he has omnipotence. Temporal idols demanding an absolute faith tirelessly decree absolute punishments. And religions devoid of transcendence kill great numbers of condemned men devoid of hope.

How can European society of the mid-century survive unless it decides to defend individuals by every means against the State's oppression? Forbidding a man's execution would amount to proclaiming publicly that society and the State are not absolute values, that nothing authorizes them to legislate definitively or to bring about the irreparable. Without the death penalty, Gabriel Péri and Brasillach would perhaps be among us. We could then judge them according to our opinion and proudly proclaim our judgment, whereas now they judge us and we keep silent. Without the death penalty Rajk's corpse would not poison Hungary; Germany, with less guilt on her conscience, would be more favorably looked upon by Europe; the Russian Revolution would not be agonizing in shame; and Algerian blood would weigh less heavily on our consciences. Without the death penalty, Europe would not be infected by the corpses accumulated for the last twenty years in its tired soil. On our continent, all values are upset by fear and hatred between individuals and between nations. In the conflict of ideas the weapons are the cord and the guillotine. A natural and human society exercising her right of repression has given way to a dominant ideology that requires human sacrifices. "The example of the gallows," it has been written,* "is that a man's life ceases to be sacred when it is thought useful to kill him." Apparently it is becoming ever more useful; the example is being copied; the contagion is spreading everywhere. And together with it, the disorder of nihilism. Hence we must call a spectacular halt and proclaim, in our principles and institutions, that the individual is above the State. And any measure that decreases the pressure of social forces upon the individual will help to relieve the congestion of a Europe suffering from a rush of blood, allowing us to think more clearly and to start on the way toward health. Europe's malady consists in believing nothing and claiming to know everything. But Europe is far from knowing everything, and, judging from the revolt and hope we feel, she believes in something: she believes that the extreme of man's wretchedness, on some mysterious limit, borders on the extreme of his greatness. For the majority of Europeans, faith is lost. And with it, the justifications faith provided in the domain of punishment. But the majority of Europeans also reject the State idolatry that aimed to take the place of faith. Henceforth in mid-course, both certain and uncertain, having made up our minds never to submit and never to oppress, we should admit at one and the same time our hope and our ignorance, we should refuse absolute law and the irreparable judgment. We know enough to say that this or that major criminal deserves hard labor for life. But we don't know enough to decree that he be shorn of his future—in other words, of the chance we all have of making amends. Because of what I have just said, in the unified Europe of the future the solemn abolition of the death penalty ought to be the first article of the European Code we all hope for.

* By Francart.

Further Readings

Aquinas, Thomas, "Treatise on Law" in *Summa Theologica,* Benziger, New York, 1947, II, I, questions 90–97.

Aristotle, *Politics,* Harvard University Press, Cambridge, Mass., 1932.

Barry, Brian, *Political Argument,* Humanities Press, New York, 1965.

Benn, S. I., and R. S. Peters, *Social Principles and the Democratic State,* Allen & Unwin, London, 1959.

Bentham, Jeremy, *An Introduction to the Principles of Morals and Legislation,* ed. Laurence J. Lafleur, Hafner, New York, 1948, first published 1789.

Berlin, I., *Two Concepts of Liberty,* Oxford University Press, Fair Lawn, N.J., 1958.

Brown, Stuart M., Jr., "Inalienable Rights," *Philosophical Review, 64* (1955).

Carritt, E. F., *Ethical and Political Thinking,* Clarendon Press, Oxford, 1947.

Cohen, M. R., *Law and the Social Order,* Harcourt, New York, 1933.

Engels, F., *Anti-Dührung: Herr Eugen Duhring's Revolution in Science,* Foreign Languages Publishing House, Moscow, 1962.

Frankena, William, "Natural and Inalienable Rights," *Philosophical Review, 64* (1955).

Hart, H. L. A., "Are There Any Natural Rights?" *Philosophical Review, 64* (1955).

Hart, H. L. A., "The Ascription of Responsibility and Rights," *Proceedings of the Aristotelian Society,* 1948–1949, also in A. Flew (ed.), *Logic and Language, First Series,* Blackwell, Oxford, 1951.

Hart, H. L. A., *Law, Liberty, and Morality,* Random House, New York, 1963.

Hobbes, Thomas, *De Cive,* ed. Sterling P. Lamprecht, Appleton-Century-Crofts, New York, 1949, first published 1642.

Hook, S., *From Hegel to Marx,* University of Michigan Press, Ann Arbor, 1962.

Hume, David, *Treatise of Human Nature,* ed. L. A. Selby-Bigge, Oxford University Press, New York, 1941, Book III, Parts 1 and 2.

Kant, Immanuel, *Philosophy of Law,* translated by W. Hastie, T. and T. Clark, Edinburgh, 1887.

Laslett, P., (ed.), *Philosophy, Politics and Society,* First Series, Macmillan, New York, 1956.

Laslett, P. and W. G. Runciman, (eds.), *Philosophy, Politics and Society,* Second Series, Blackwell, Oxford, 1964.

Locke, John, *The Second Treatise of Government in Two Treatises on Government,* edited by T. Cook, Heffner, New York, 1956.

Mabbott, J. D., *The State and the Citizen,* Hutchinson, London, 1948.

Macdonald, Margaret, "Natural Rights," *Proceedings of the Aristotelian Society,* 1947–1948.

Machiavelli, Niccolo, *The Prince* (1513), Random House, New York, 1939.

Olafson, F. A. (ed.), *Justice and Social Policy,* Prentice-Hall, Englewood Cliffs, N.J., 1961.

Plato, *Crito, Republic, Laws,* in The Collected Dialogues of Plato, Edith Hamilton and Huntington Cairns, (eds.) Pantheon, New York, 1961.

Rawls, John, "Justice as Fairness," *Philosophical Review,* 67 (1958), also in Laslett and Runciman.

Rousseau, Jean-Jacques, *Social Contract.* Everyman's Library, New York, 1947.

Sartre, Jean-Paul, *Critique de la raison dialectique,* Gallimard, Paris, 1960.

Sartre, Jean-Paul, "Marxism and Revolution," in *Literary and Philosophical Essays,* Rider, London, 1955.

Strauss, Leo, *Natural Right and History,* The University of Chicago Press, Chicago, 1953.

Venable, Vernon, *Human Nature: The Marxist View,* Knopf, New York, 1946.

Weldon, T. D., *The Vocabulary of Politics,* Penguin, Baltimore, 1953.

Weldon, T. D., *The Vocabulary of Politics,* Penguin, Baltimore, 1953.

VII

KNOWLEDGE, PERCEPTION, AND NECESSARY TRUTH

I

N OBVIOUS THING to do when we want to know something is to use our senses. If we want to know how many people are in the next room, we go to look. If we want to know what color crows are, we look at crows. If we want to find out the results of the latest tennis match, we listen to the radio. Indeed, a great deal of what we know is based on sensory experience.

Because of this, philosophers have been concerned with sense perception, which is commonly held to be the basis of empirical knowledge. They have raised a number of questions, some of which are "What, if anything, can I know on the basis of sense perception?" and "What are the objects of perception?"

The philosopher's interest in perception is not the same as that of the scientist, who talks about light waves, sound waves, nerves; nor is it the same as that of the psychologist who talks about the threshold of perception or the ability of a person to discriminate colors. Even so, any adequate account of perception should at least be compatible with the physiologist's or the psychologist's account.

One of the philosopher's main concerns is with the objects of perception, with what it is that we perceive. A number of different theories have been developed in an attempt to explain what are taken to be the facts of the case.

Most people, were they to think at all about the objects of perception, would say that they perceive a world of objects which is external to them and which exists independently of their perception of it. This view is called *realism.*

They would also say that objects have certain properties that we can learn about by, for example, looking at them or touching them. Among these properties are size, shape, color, motion, temperature, odor, and taste. Not all objects have all of these properties, but many of them do. We can learn through perception that an object has a given one of them and, roughly, at least, which one it has. This aspect of the commonsense view, according to which objects have the properties that perception tells us they have, has been called *naive*. Therefore, the ordinary man's theory of perception can be called *naive realism*.

Philosophers have subjected this theory to close scrutiny and a number of them have concluded that it is inadequate. A typical argument which is designed to show that the view called naive realism is incorrect is this:

First of all, we have to acknowledge that we do not always perceive things as they really are. A straight stick put into water looks bent, a coin from most angles looks elliptical, and men are sometimes subject to illusions, delusions, hallucinations. In particular, look at a round coin from an angle. What you see is elliptical. Since nothing can be both round and elliptical at the same time, it follows that what you perceive is something other than the round coin. There are not, however, two coins on the table, one round and the other elliptical. Therefore, what you really see, the "elliptical coin", is an "object" that is private or subjective. It is something in you, so to speak, rather than in the physical world. These private objects are often called *sense-data*.

A person might grant this much, but argue that it is *only* in a case like the above that he perceives a sense-datum rather than a physical object. That is, when his sense-perception is of a round coin (as it is when he looks straight down at the coin), then he is actually perceiving the coin and not a sense-datum. However, a philosopher who holds a sense-data theory would ask, "Is the experience of the one so different from the experience of the other that we have reason to believe that in each case we are perceiving a totally different kind of object, a sense-datum in the one case and a material object in the other?" There is nothing qualitatively different between the experience of the elliptical coin and the round one. Since the experience of the elliptical coin is really an experience of a sense-datum, it is clear, this philosopher would say, that the experience of the round coin is too. He concludes, then, that our perceptions are always of sense-data and never of physical objects.

One view put forward (by Locke) is that while it is true that all we immediately perceive are sense-data, or *ideas*, these ideas are caused to appear in our minds by physical objects. This view, which is like that proposed by physiologists, is called the *causal theory of perception*. It is aimed at preserving realism, while doing justice to the fact that the objects of our perceptions are mental entities. Locke's version of the causal theory is coupled with the view that several of the ideas we get in perception have no counterparts in physical objects. In particular, objects have, strictly speaking, no color or smell or taste. Rather, they emit light waves or sound waves, which cause in us the experience of seeing colors or hearing sounds. One who holds this view questions the "naive" aspect of naive realism and is said to hold a view called *critical realism.* It is easy to see how the critical realist can use the causal theory of perception to explain how it is that we have ideas of color or sound. (See Locke, "Perception and the External World," in this section.)

Philosophers have been quick to point out difficulties with this position. In particular, it was noted (by Berkeley) that the causal theory opened the door to scepticism. If we perceive only ideas, what reason have we to believe that there are any physical objects causing them, that is, that there are any physical objects in the causal theorist's sense? We cannot get outside of our ideas to find out if there are any such things. (See Berkeley, "To Be Is to Be Perceived," in this section.)

Some philosophers have accepted the sceptical conclusion that we can never know whether there are physical objects, and others have tried to justify the causal theorist's inference from our ideas to physical objects on the grounds that the "hypothesis" that there are physical objects is the best way to explain the fact that we have sense experience. There is a third position that has been developed called *idealism.* According to this view objects are just collections of ideas. There are no physical things existing without the mind. Therefore, we do immediately perceive physical objects, and since objects are collections of ideas, the objects we perceive are in the mind. This view attempts to avoid the scepticism which arises if physical objects are thought to lie hidden behind ideas, and yet to grant that we perceive ideas.

Idealism has been attacked on a number of grounds. Perhaps the most straightforward objection (given by Moore) is that it is simply false to say that objects are in the mind. He argued as follows: hold up your two hands, clearly they exist, therefore, objects external to the mind exist. (See Moore, "Proof of an External World," in this section.)

One other influential view about perception is that the distinction between sense-data and physical objects is not a distinction between two types of entities, the one private and the other public. Physical objects are neither identical with collections of sense-data nor entities hidden from us by the veil of sense data. Rather, the relation between the two may be conceived as the relation between two languages: a sense-datum language and a physical object language. Philosophers who hold this view argue that we have the concept of a physical object because our perceptual experiences manifest a great deal of order and regularity, that is, the concept of a physical object provides a convenient way of grouping our experiences. For example, we have the concept of an apple because whenever we have the experience of a certain kind of red, round sense datum, we get certain taste sensations whenever we perform certain actions. Since these sense-data of sight, touch, and taste, normally go together, we can, given some of them, reliably predict the occurrence of the others. Therefore, any statement about a physical object can be translated, without loss of meaning, into statements about the occurrence of present or future sense experiences, i.e., sense-data. Any statement about the apple can be translated into statements about the kinds of sense experiences one would have if he were to do such and such (look at it, lift it up, bite it).

The apple is not identical with my present sense-data because the concept of apple includes reference to other future and possible sense data, nor is it an entity that lies behind and produces sense-data because it is itself defined in terms of sense-data. This view is known as *phenomenalism.* (See Ayer, "Sense Data and Physical Objects," in this section.)

All of these views have been put forward in an attempt to give an account of perception and of the objects of perception. They indicate how difficult it is to give a coherent account of such matters. Recent work in perception has reviewed the various arguments given in behalf of sense-data and questioned whether sense data (if indeed there are any such entities) play the important epistemological role many have supposed them to play. (See Quinton, "The Problem of Perception," in this section.)

The following selections will illustrate many of the views discussed above.

II

While a great deal of our knowledge comes through our senses, many philosophers have felt that such knowledge is not of the highest kind. One reason for this is that judgments made on the basis of sensory experience are fallible, that is, our senses can deceive us. In fact, some have claimed that the senses are unreliable as sources of knowledge.

Another reason for being dissatisfied with the senses is that they are limited in that they can tell us, at best, about only this crow or that one. They cannot tell us anything about all crows. We cannot examine each crow that was, is, or will be, to see whether it is black. In other words, sensory knowledge is not truly general.

For many, however, the most important limitation of the senses is that they can tell us only what *is* the case and not what *must be* the case. That is, even if we could examine every bachelor, the most we could conclude on the basis of our experience is that all bachelors happen to be unmarried. We could not conclude that all bachelors have to be unmarried. These philosophers would say that the highest truths are those that are *necessarily* true, and such truths can never be justified solely on the basis of sensory experience. A necessary truth, then, is one which states what must be the case. A nonnecessary truth states what happens to be the case. These truths are called *contingent.*

Some have said that the senses teach us only what *is* the case, but they cannot teach us what *ought to be* the case. In other words, moral truths can never be derived from any statements concerned solely with sense-experience.

The question arises, then, as to what are the necessary truths that man can know. Some, like Mill, have felt that there are very few kinds of truths that are necessarily true. In particular, Mill believed that mathematical truths were only well-confirmed empirical generalizations. (See Mill, "Empirical Theory of Mathematical Truths," in this section.) Others have felt that it was possible to apprehend necessary truths about the nature of the universe, about moral values, and about theology. The apprehension of such truths is independent of the senses. This is not to say that a man could know these truths without having had any experience at all, but rather that no sensory experience would be needed to justify them. To take a simple example, we may need some sort of experience to learn what the words "bachelor" and "unmarried" mean, but once we know what they mean, we can come to see the truth of "All bachelors are unmarried" without having to examine any bachelors. On the other hand, even if a person knows what "crow" and "black" mean, he still must consult experience before he can know the truth of "All crows are black." Philosophers have marked this distinction by saying that if we know something independently of the evidence of the senses, our knowledge of it is *a priori;* if we require sensory evidence, our knowledge is *a posteriori.*

Philosophers are in general agreement that what we can know *a priori* are necessary truths. In fact, we can know them *a priori* precisely because they are necessary truths. Since it is a necessary truth that all bachelors are unmarried, that is, since one must be unmarried in order to be a bachelor, we need not consult the senses to see whether all bachelors are in fact unmarried. Hence, our knowledge that they are unmarried is *a priori.*

Many philosophers claim that all and only necessary truths are those knowable *a priori*, and all and only contingent truths are knowable *a posteriori.* Beyond this point, however, philosophers disagree radically. The heart of the issue is this: Can we know *a priori* anything which is *about the world?* Many have believed that it is possible to know certain things about the world without consulting the senses for evidence. They believed that man can come to know necessary truths about reality, morality, and God, without having to gather evidence through experience. Thus, we can know *a priori* necessary truths about the most important things.

On the other hand, many philosophers have said that this is impossible. The only way to learn about the world is to consult the world through our senses. In no case are there necessary truths about the world. Some might agree that if we could know things *a priori* about the world "it would be grand," but we cannot.

The disagreement can be made clearer by introducing another distinction which philosophers have drawn—the distinction between *analytic truths* and *synthetic truths.* While there is some variation in the formulations of what an analytic truth is, most philosophers would agree that an analytic truth is one whose negation is self-contradictory. For example, if one said that not all bachelors are unmarried he would be contradicting himself, and therefore "All bachelors are unmarried" is analytic. Most would agree that analytic truths are not informative, that is, they give no information about the world (although they may be quite interesting in other ways). They are true solely in virtue of the meanings of the terms contained in them, and therefore, according to many philosophers, they can give information only about the meanings of terms. A synthetic statement, on the other hand, is one that is not analytic. (See Section VIII, "Language and Meaning," for a discussion of the meanings of terms.)

It is generally agreed by all who accept the distinction between analytic and synthetic truths that all analytic truths are known *a priori.* Since we know that all bachelors are unmarried, or that all cats are animals, merely by examining the meanings of the terms "bachelor," "unmarried," "cat," and "animal," we know the truth of these without having to make use of sensory evidence.

Similarly, it is agreed that all truths known *a posteriori* are synthetic. That is, if experience is needed to supply evidence for our knowing something, e.g., that all crows are black, then it is obviously not the case that we could have known this merely by contemplating the meanings of "crow" and "black."

Here the agreement ends. Those philosophers who claim that we can know things about the world independently of the evidence of the senses say that there is a category of synthetic truths which are known *a priori.* In other words, they claim that certain truths which do not *merely* express relations among the meanings of terms can be known without relying upon sensory evidence. (See Kant, "On Our Knowledge of Synthetic A Priori Judgments," in this section.)

This is denied vehemently by others. They claim that the only things we can know *a priori* are truths like "All cats are animals," which are necessary truths, but are true merely because of the meanings of the terms, i.e., are analytic. No information about the world can be gotten *a priori,* independently of experience. According to these philosophers, every synthetic proposition which is true can be known to be true only if we consult experience. That is, synthetic propositions can be known only *a posteriori.* (See Lewis, "A Pragmatic Conception of the *A Priori,*" in this section.)

It is important to keep in mind that the dispute as to whether or not there are synthetic propositions which can be known *a priori* is not merely a technical philosophic problem (even though a number of the issues involved within it are extremely technical).

If we can know truths about the world which are necessary and universal, then we can transcend sense-experience and, hopefully, gain fundamental metaphysical, moral, and theological knowledge. If, on the other hand, such knowledge is a fiction, then it is only through sense-experience that man can know the world.

If we can come to know for certain that God exists or that certain actions are right or wrong, it is important that we realize this and appreciate the consequent gains for religion and morality. If, however, knowledge of necessary truths is no more than understanding the meanings of terms, then it is equally important that we realize this so as not to be led into accepting some set of theological, moral, or metaphysical doctrines without demanding evidence for them.

So far certain *traditional* distinctions have been noted and views involving them have been sketched. One important criticism of traditional distinctions should be considered. Terms like "analytic" and "necessary truth" have been used by many philosophers. Others, however, have become suspicious of these terms and have begun to question whether they have been clearly enough explicated to play so important a role as they customarily do in philosophic discussions. As traditionally conceived, the central problem for the philosopher interested in necessary truth is whether or not there are synthetic propositions which can be known to be true *a priori*. This is the philosophers' formulation of the question whether or not it is possible to have knowledge of necessary truths which are about the world. If one is to couch the problem in terms like "analytic" and "synthetic," then one must, it is felt, be prepared to give some clear and careful characterization of these terms. Some philosophers have denied that this can be done and suggest, therefore, that the traditional formulations of the problem of knowledge are in error. It is sometimes argued that there *is* no sharp distinction between analytic and synthetic truths, a distinction which is, of course, assumed by those who argue about whether there can be synthetic truths known *a priori*. In light of this criticism, new ways of looking at human knowledge have been suggested. (See Quine, "One Dogma of Empiricism," in this section.)

In the following selections are included a number of important discussions of the questions outlined above. Many of them are concerned with the various distinctions we have noted:

(1) Necessary vs. contingent
(2) *A priori* vs. *a posteriori*
(3) Analytic vs. synthetic
(4) About the world vs. not about the world.

They discuss the classifications of various propositions in light of these distinctions and present arguments to show that certain combinations of these can or cannot be realized. In particular, the question of synthetic truths which can be known *a priori* is examined. Some, on the other hand, criticize the very distinctions which many philosophers presuppose, specifically the analytic-synthetic distinction.

While the issues involved are interesting and fascinating in themselves, they derive their ultimate importance from their bearing on the nature of human knowledge and its possibilities. The selections illustrate how philosophers, in an attempt to answer a question of great importance, reformulate the question and isolate certain issues so as to bring the problems into sharper focus. They also indicate how philosophers are critical of their own distinctions and seek continually to reformulate problems in the interests of greater understanding. They express the belief that the possibility and likelihood of finding a solution to a given problem is in large part a function of the way in which the problem is stated.

PERCEPTION AND THE EXTERNAL WORLD

JOHN LOCKE

THE CAUSAL THEORY OF PERCEPTION

1. Concerning the simple ideas of Sensation, it is to be considered,—that whatsoever is so constituted in nature as to be able, by affecting our senses, to cause any perception in the mind, doth thereby produce in the understanding a simple idea; which, whatever be the external cause of it, when it comes to be taken notice of by our discerning faculty, it is by the mind looked on and considered there to be a real positive idea in the understanding, as much as any other whatsoever; though, perhaps, the cause of it be but a privation of the subject.

2. Thus the ideas of heat and cold, light and darkness, white and black, motion and rest, are equally clear and positive ideas in the mind; though, perhaps, some of the causes which produce them are barely privations, in those subjects from whence our senses derive those ideas. These the understanding, in its view of them, considers all as distinct positive ideas, without taking notice of the causes that produce them: which is an inquiry not belonging to the idea, as it is in the understanding, but to the nature of the things existing without us. These are two very different things, and carefully to be distinguished; it being one thing to perceive and know the idea of white or black, and quite another to examine what kind of particles they must be, and how ranged in the superficies, to make any object appear white or black.

. . .

7. To discover the nature of our *ideas* the better, and to discourse of them intelligibly, it will be convenient to distinguish them *as they are ideas or perceptions in our minds;* and *as they are modifications of matter in the bodies that cause such perceptions in us:* that so we may not think (as perhaps usually is done) that they are exactly the images and resemblances of something inherent in the subject; most of those of

Reprinted from *An Essay Concerning Human Understanding* Book II, Chapter VIII; Book IV, Chapter XI, first published 1690.

sensation being in the mind no more the likeness of something existing without us, than the names that stand for them are the likeness of our ideas, which yet upon hearing they are apt to excite in us.

8. Whatsoever the mind perceives *in itself*, or is the immediate object of perception, thought, or understanding, that I call *idea*; and the power to produce any idea in our mind, I call *quality* of the subject wherein that power is. Thus a snowball having the power to produce in us the ideas of white, cold, and round,—the power to produce those ideas in us, as they are in the snowball, I call qualities; and as they are sensations or perceptions in our understandings, I call them ideas; which *ideas*, if I speak of sometimes as in the things themselves, I would be understood to mean those qualities in the objects which produce them in us.

9. [Qualities thus considered in bodies are,

First, such as are utterly inseparable from the body, in what state soever it be;] and such as in all the alterations and changes it suffers, all the force can be used upon it, it constantly keeps; and such as sense constantly finds in every particle of matter which has bulk enough to be perceived; and the mind finds inseparable from every particle of matter, though less than to make itself singly be perceived by our senses: v.g. Take a grain of wheat, divide it into two parts; each part has still solidity, extension, figure, and mobility: divide it again, and it retains still the same qualities; and so divide it on, till the parts become insensible; they must retain still each of them all those qualities. For division (which is all that a mill, or pestle, or any other body, does upon another, in reducing it to insensible parts) can never take away either solidity, extension, figure, or mobility from any body, but only makes two or more distinct separate masses of matter, of that which was but one before; all which distinct masses, reckoned as so many distinct bodies, after division, make a certain number. [These I call *original* or *primary qualities* of body, which I think we may observe to produce simple ideas in us, viz. solidity, extension, figure, motion or rest, and number.

10. *Secondly*, such qualities which in truth are nothing in the objects themselves but powers to produce various sensations in us by their primary qualities, i.e. by the bulk, figure, texture, and motion of their insensible parts, as colours, sounds, tastes, &c. These I call *secondary qualities*. To these might be added a *third* sort, which are allowed to be barely powers; though they are as much real qualities in the subject as those which I, to comply with the common way of speaking, call qualities, but for distinction, secondary qualities. For the power in fire to produce a new colour, or consistency, in *wax* or *clay*,—by its primary qualities, is as much a quality in fire, as the power it has to produce in *me* a new idea or sensation of warmth or burning, which I felt not before,—by the same primary qualities, viz. the bulk, texture, and motion of its insensible parts.]

11. [The next thing to be considered is, how bodies produce ideas in us; and that is manifestly by impulse, the only way which we can conceive bodies to operate in.]

12. If then external objects be not united to our minds when they produce ideas therein; and yet we perceive these *original* qualities in such of them as singly fall under our senses, it is evident that some motion must be thence continued by our nerves, or animal spirits, by some parts of our bodies, to the brains or the seat of sensation, there to produce in our minds the particular ideas we have of them. And since the extension, figure, number, and motion of bodies of an observable bigness, may be perceived at a distance by the sight, it is evident some singly imperceptible bodies must come from them to the eyes, and thereby convey to the brain some motion; which produces these ideas which we have of them in us.

13. After the same manner that the ideas of these original qualities are produced in us, we may conceive that the ideas of *secondary* qualities are also produced, viz. by the operation of insensible particles on our senses. For, it being manifest that there are bodies and good store of bodies, each whereof are so small, that we cannot by any of our senses discover either their bulk, figure, or motion,—as is evident in the particles of the air and water, and others extremely smaller than those; perhaps as much smaller than the particles of air and water, as the particles of air and water are smaller than peas or hail-stones;—let us suppose at present that the different motions and figures, bulk and number, of such particles, affecting the several organs of our senses, produce in us those different sensations which we have from the colours and smells of bodies; v.g. that a violet, by the impulse of such insensible particles of matter, of peculiar figures and bulks, and in different degrees and modifications of their motions, causes the ideas of the blue colour, and sweet scent of that flower to be produced in our minds. It being no more impossible to conceive that God should annex such ideas to such motions, with which they have no similitude, than that he should annex the idea of pain to the motion of a piece of steel dividing our flesh, with which that idea hath no resemblance.

14. What I have said concerning colours and smells may be understood also of tastes and sounds, and other the like sensible qualities; which, whatever reality we by mistake attribute to them, are in truth nothing in the objects themselves, but powers to produce various sensations in us; and depend on those primary qualities, viz. bulk, figure, texture, and motion of parts [as I have said].

15. From whence I think it easy to draw this observation,—that the ideas of primary qualities of bodies are resemblances of them, and their patterns do really exist in the bodies themselves, but the ideas produced in us by these secondary qualities have no resemblance of them at all. There is nothing like our ideas, existing in the bodies themselves. They are, in the bodies we denominate from them, only a power to produce those sensations in us: and what is sweet, blue, or warm in idea, is but the certain bulk, figure, and motion of the insensible parts, in the bodies themselves, which we call so.

16. Flame is denominated hot and light; snow, white and cold; and

manna, white and sweet, from the ideas they produce in us. Which qualities are commonly thought to be the same in those bodies that those ideas are in us, the one the perfect resemblance of the other, as they are in a mirror, and it would by most men be judged very extravagant if one should say otherwise. And yet he that will consider that the same fire that, at one distance produces in us the sensation of warmth, does, at a nearer approach, produce in us the far different sensation of pain, ought to bethink himself what reason he has to say—that this idea of warmth, which was produced in him by the fire, is *actually in the fire*; and his idea of pain, which the same fire produced in him the same way, is *not* in the fire. Why are whiteness and coldness in snow, and pain not, when it produces the one and the other idea in us; and can do neither, but by the bulk, figure, number, and motion of its solid parts?

17. The particular bulk, number, figure, and motion of the parts of fire or snow are really in them,—whether any one's senses perceive them or no: and therefore they may be called *real* qualities, because they really exist in those bodies. But light, heat, whiteness, or coldness, are no more really in them than sickness or pain is in manna. Take away the sensation of them; let not the eyes see light or colours, nor the ears hear sounds; let the palate not taste, nor the nose smell, and all colours, tastes, odours, and sounds, *as they are such particular ideas*, vanish and cease, and are reduced to their causes, i.e. bulk, figure, and motion of parts.

18. A piece of manna of a sensible bulk is able to produce in us the idea of a round or square figure; and by being removed from one place to another, the idea of motion. This idea of motion represents it as it really is in manna moving: a circle or square are the same, whether in idea or existence, in the mind or in the manna. And this, both motion and figure, are really in the manna, whether we take notice of them or no: this everybody is ready to agree to. Besides, manna, by the bulk, figure, texture, and motion of its parts, has a power to produce the sensations of sickness, and sometimes of acute pains or gripings in us. That these ideas of sickness and pain are *not* in the manna, but effects of its operations on us, and are nowhere when we feel them not; this also every one readily agrees to. And yet men are hardly to be brought to think that sweetness and whiteness are not really in manna; which are but the effects of the operations of manna, by the motion, size, and figure of its particles, on the eyes and palate: as the pain and sickness caused by manna are confessedly nothing but the effects of its operations on the stomach and guts, by the size, motion, and figure of its insensible parts, (for by nothing else can a body operate, as has been proved): as if it could not operate on the eyes and palate, and thereby produce in the mind particular distinct ideas, which in itself it has not, as well as we allow it can operate on the guts and stomach, and thereby produce distinct ideas, which in itself it has not. These ideas, being all effects of the operations of manna on several parts of our bodies, by the size, figure, number, and motion of its parts;—why those produced by the eyes and palate should rather be thought to be really in the manna, than those produced by the stomach and guts; or

why the pain and sickness, ideas that are the effect of manna, should be thought to be nowhere when they are not felt; and yet the sweetness and whiteness, effects of the same manna on other parts of the body, by ways equally as unknown, should be thought to exist in the manna, when they are not seen or tasted, would need some reason to explain.

19. Let us consider the red and white colours in porphyry. Hinder light from striking on it, and its colours vanish; it no longer produces any such ideas in us: upon the return of light it produces these appearances on us again. Can any one think any real alterations are made in the porphyry by the presence or absence of light; and that those ideas of whiteness and redness are really in porphyry in the light, when it is plain *it has no colour in the dark?* It has, indeed, such a configuration of particles, both night and day, as are apt, by the rays of light rebounding from some parts of that hard stone, to produce in us the idea of redness, and from others the idea of whiteness; but whiteness or redness are not in it at any time, but such a texture that hath the power to produce such a sensation in us.

20. Pound an almond, and the clear white colour will be altered into a dirty one, and the sweet taste into an oily one. What real alteration can the beating of the pestle make in any body, but an alteration of the texture of it?

21. Ideas being thus distinguished and understood, we may be able to give an account how the same water, at the same time, may produce the idea of cold by one hand and of heat by the other: whereas it is impossible that the same water, if those ideas were really in it, should at the same time be both hot and cold. For, if we imagine *warmth*, as it is in our hands, to be nothing but a certain sort and degree of motion in the minute particles of our nerves or animal spirits, we may understand how it is possible that the same water may, at the same time, produce the sensations of heat in one hand and cold in the other; which yet *figure* never does, that never producing the idea of a square by one hand which has produced the idea of a globe by another. But if the sensation of heat and cold be nothing but the increase or diminution of the motion of the minute parts of our bodies, caused by the corpuscles of any other body, it is easy to be understood, that if that motion be greater in one hand than in the other; if a body be applied to the two hands, which has in its minute particles a greater motion than in those of one of the hands, and a less than in those of the other, it will increase the motion of the one hand and lessen it in the other; and so cause the different sensations of heat and cold that depend thereon.

22. I have in what just goes before been engaged in physical inquiries a little further than perhaps I intended. But, it being necessary to make the nature of sensation a little understood; and to make the difference between the *qualities* in bodies, and the *ideas* produced by them in the mind, to be distinctly conceived, without which it were impossible to discourse intelligibly of them;—I hope I shall be pardoned this little excursion into natural philosophy; it being necessary in our present

inquiry to distinguish the *primary* and *real* qualities of bodies, which are always in them (viz. solidity, extension, figure, number, and motion, or rest, and are sometimes perceived by us, viz. when the bodies they are in are big enough singly to be discerned), from those *secondary* and *imputed* qualities, which are but the powers of several combinations of those primary ones, when they operate without being distinctly discerned;—whereby we may also come to know what ideas are, and what are not, resemblances of something really existing in the bodies we denominate from them.

23. The qualities, then, that are in bodies, rightly considered, are of three sorts:—

First, The bulk, figure, number, situation, and motion or rest of their solid parts. Those are in them, whether we perceive them or not; and when they are of that size that we can discover them, we have by these an idea of the thing as it is in itself; as is plain in artificial things. These I call *primary qualities.*

Secondly, The power that is in any body, by reason of its insensible primary qualities, to operate after a peculiar manner on any of our senses, and thereby produce in *us* the different ideas of several colours, sounds, smells, tastes, &c. These are usually called *sensible qualities.*

Thirdly, The power that is in any body, by reason of the particular constitution of its primary qualities, to make such a change in the bulk, figure, texture, and motion of *another body*, as to make it operate on our senses differently from what it did before. Thus the sun has a power to make wax white, and fire to make lead fluid. [These are usually called *powers.*]

The first of these, as has been said, I think may be properly called real, original, or primary qualities; because they are in the things themselves, whether they are perceived or not: and upon their different modifications it is that the secondary qualities depend.

The other two are only powers to act differently upon other things: which powers result from the different modifications of those primary qualities.

24. But, though the two latter sorts of qualities are powers barely, and nothing but powers, relating to several other bodies, and resulting from the different modifications of the original qualities, yet they are generally otherwise thought of. For the *second* sort, viz. the powers to produce several ideas in us, by our senses, are looked upon as real qualities in the things thus affecting us: but the *third* sort are called and esteemed barely powers. v.g. The idea of heat or light, which we receive by our eyes, or touch, from the sun, are commonly thought real qualities existing in the sun, and something more than mere powers in it. But when we consider the sun in reference to wax, which it melts or blanches, we look on the whiteness and softness produced in the wax, not as qualities in the sun, but effects produced by powers in it. Whereas, if rightly considered, these qualities of light and warmth, which are perceptions in me when I am warmed or enlightened by the sun, are no otherwise in the sun, than

the changes made in the wax, when it is blanched or melted, are in the sun. They are all of them equally *powers in the sun, depending on its primary qualities*; whereby it is able, in the one case, so to alter the bulk, figure, texture, or motion of some of the insensible parts of my eyes or hands, as thereby to produce in me the idea of light or heat; and in the other, it is able so to alter the bulk, figure, texture, or motion of the insensible parts of the wax, as to make them fit to produce in me the distinct ideas of white and fluid.

25. The reason why the one are ordinarily taken for real qualities, and the other only for bare powers, seems to be, because the ideas we have of distinct colours, sounds, &c., containing nothing at all in them of bulk, figure, or motion, we are not apt to think them the effects of these primary qualities; which appear not, to our senses, to operate in their production, and with which they have not any apparent congruity or conceivable connexion. Hence it is that we are so forward to imagine, that those ideas are the resemblances of something really existing in the objects themselves: since sensation discovers nothing of bulk, figure, or motion of parts in their production; nor can reason show how bodies, *by their bulk, figure, and motion*, should produce in the mind the ideas of blue or yellow, &c. But, in the other case, in the operations of bodies changing the qualities one of another, we plainly discover that the quality produced hath commonly no resemblance with anything in the thing producing it; wherefore we look on it as a bare effect of power. For, through receiving the idea of heat or light from the sun, we are apt to think *it* is a perception and resemblance of such a quality in the sun; yet when we see wax, or a fair face, receive change of colour from the sun, we cannot imagine *that* to be the reception or resemblance of anything in the sun, because we find not those different colours in the sun itself. For, our senses being able to observe a likeness or unlikeness of sensible qualities in two different external objects, we forwardly enough conclude the production of any sensible quality in any subject to be an effect of bare power, and not the communication of any quality which was really in the efficient, when we find no such sensible quality in the thing that produced it. But our senses, not being able to discover any unlikeness between the idea produced in us, and the quality of the object producing it, we are apt to imagine that our ideas are resemblances of something in the objects, and not the effects of certain powers placed in the modification of their primary qualities, with which primary qualities the ideas produced in us have no resemblance.

26. To conclude. Beside those before-mentioned primary qualities in bodies, viz. bulk, figure, extension, number, and motion of their solid parts; all the rest, whereby we take notice of bodies, and distinguish them one from another, are nothing else but several powers in them, depending on those primary qualities; whereby they are fitted, either by immediately operating on our bodies to produce several different ideas in us; or else, by operating on other bodies, so to change their primary qualities as to render them capable of producing ideas in us different from what

before they did. The former of these, I think, may be called secondary qualities *immediately perceivable*: the latter, secondary qualities, *mediately perceivable.*

OF OUR KNOWLEDGE OF THE EXISTENCE OF OTHER THINGS

1. The knowledge of our own being we have by intuition. The existence of a God, reason clearly makes known to us, as has been shown.

The knowledge of the existence of *any other thing* we can have only by *sensation*: for there being no necessary connexion of real existence with any *idea* a man hath in his memory; nor of any other existence but that of God with the existence of any particular man: no particular man can know the existence of any other being, but only when, by actual operating upon him, it makes itself perceived by him. For, the having the idea of anything in our mind, no more proves the existence of that thing, than the picture of a man evidences his being in the world, or the visions of a dream make thereby a true history.

2. It is therefore the *actual receiving* of ideas from without that gives us notice of the existence of other things, and makes us know, that something doth exist at that time without us, which causes that idea in us; though perhaps we neither know nor consider how it does it. For it takes not from the certainty of our senses, and the ideas we receive by them, that we know not the manner wherein they are produced: v.g. whilst I write this, I have, by the paper affecting my eyes, that idea produced in my mind, which, whatever object causes, I call *white*; by which I know that that quality or accident (i.e. whose appearance before my eyes always causes that idea) doth really exist, and hath a being without me. And of this, the greatest assurance I can possibly have, and to which my faculties can attain, is the testimony of my eyes, which are the proper and sole judges of this thing; whose testimony I have reason to rely on as so certain, that I can no more doubt, whilst I write this, that I see white and black, and that something really exists that causes that sensation in me, than that I write or move my hand; which is a certainty as great as human nature is capable of, concerning the existence of anything, but a man's self alone, and of God.

3. The notice we have by our senses of the existing of things without us, though it be not altogether so certain as our intuitive knowledge, or the deductions of our reason employed about the clear abstract ideas of our own minds; yet it is an assurance that deserves the name of *knowledge*. If we persuade ourselves that our faculties act and inform us right concerning the existence of those objects that affect them, it cannot pass for an ill-grounded confidence: for I think nobody can, in earnest, be so sceptical as to be uncertain of the existence of those things which he sees and feels. At least, he that can doubt so far, (whatever he may have with

his own thoughts,) will never have any controversy with me; since he can never be sure I say anything contrary to his own opinion. As to myself, I think God has given me assurance enough of the existence of things without me: since, by their different application, I can produce in myself both pleasure and pain, which is one great concernment of my present state. This is certain: the confidence that our faculties do not herein deceive us, is the greatest assurance we are capable of concerning the existence of material beings. For we cannot act anything but by our faculties; nor talk of knowledge itself, but by the help of those faculties which are fitted to apprehend even what knowledge is.

But besides the assurance we have from our senses themselves, that they do not err in the information they give us of the existence of things without us, when they are affected by them, we are further confirmed in this assurance by other concurrent reasons:—

4. I. It is plain those perceptions are produced in us by exterior causes affecting our senses: because those that want the *organs* of any sense, never can have the ideas belonging to that sense produced in their minds. This is too evident to be doubted: and therefore we cannot but be assured that they come in by the organs of that sense, and no other way. The organs themselves, it is plain, do not produce them: for then the eyes of a man in the dark would produce colours, and his nose smell roses in the winter: but we see nobody gets the relish of a pineapple, till he goes to the Indies, where it is, and tastes it.

5. II. Because sometimes I find that *I cannot avoid the having those ideas produced in my mind*. For though, when my eyes are shut, or windows fast, I can at pleasure recall to my mind the ideas of light, or the sun, which former sensations had lodged in my memory; so I can at pleasure lay by *that* idea, and take into my view that of the smell of a rose, or taste of sugar. But, if I turn my eyes at noon towards the sun, I cannot avoid the ideas which the light or sun then produces in me. So that there is a manifest difference between the ideas laid up in my memory, (over which, if they were there only, I should have constantly the same power to dispose of them, and lay them by at pleasure,) and those which force themselves upon me, and I cannot avoid having. And therefore it must needs be some exterior cause, and the brisk acting of some objects without me, whose efficacy I cannot resist, that produces those ideas in my mind, whether I will or no. Besides, there is nobody who doth not perceive the difference in himself between contemplating the sun, as he hath the idea of it in his memory, and actually looking upon it: of which two, his perception is so distinct, that few of his ideas are more distinguishable one from another. And therefore he hath certain knowledge that they are not *both* memory, or the actions of his mind, and fancies only within him; but that actual seeing hath a cause without.

6. III. Add to this, that many of those ideas are *produced in us with pain*, which afterwards we remember without the least offence. Thus, the pain of heat or cold, when the idea of it is revived in our minds, gives us no disturbance; which, when felt, was very troublesome; and is again,

when actually repeated: which is occasioned by the disorder the external object causes in our bodies when applied to them: and we remember the pains of hunger, thirst, or the headache, without any pain at all; which would either never disturb us, or else constantly do it, as often as we thought of it, were there nothing more but ideas floating in our minds, and appearances entertaining our fancies, without the real existence of things affecting us from abroad. The same may be said of *pleasure*, accompanying several actual sensations. And though mathematical demonstration depends not upon sense, yet the examining them by diagrams gives great credit to the evidence of our sight, and seems to give it a certainty approaching to that of demonstration itself. For, it would be very strange, that a man should allow it for an undeniable truth, that two angles of a figure, which he measures by lines and angles of a diagram, should be bigger one than the other, and yet doubt of the existence of those lines and angles, which by looking on he makes use of to measure that by.

7. IV. Our *senses* in many cases *bear witness to the truth of each other's report*, concerning the existence of sensible things without us. He that *sees* a fire, may, if he doubt whether it be anything more than a bare fancy, *feel* it too; and be convinced, by putting his hand in it. Which certainly could never be put into such exquisite pain by a bare idea or phantom, unless that the pain be a fancy too: which yet he cannot, when the burn is well, by raising the idea of it, bring upon himself again.

Thus I see, whilst I write this, I can change the appearance of the paper; and by designing the letters, tell *beforehand* what new idea it shall exhibit the very next moment, by barely drawing my pen over it: which will neither appear (let me fancy as much as I will) if my hands stand still; or though I move my pen, if my eyes be shut: nor, when those characters are once made on the paper, can I choose afterwards but see them as they are; that is, have the ideas of such letters as I have made. Whence it is manifest, that they are not barely the sport and play of my own imagination, when I find that the characters that were made at the pleasure of my own thoughts, do not obey them; nor yet cease to be, whenever I shall fancy it, but continue to affect my senses constantly and regularly, according to the figures I made them. To which if we will add, that the sight of those shall, from another man, draw such sounds as I beforehand design they shall stand for, there will be little reason left to doubt that those words I write do really exist without me, when they cause a long series of regular sounds to affect my ears, which could not be the effect of my imagination, nor could my memory retain them in that order.

8. But yet, if after all this any one will be so sceptical as to distrust his senses, and to affirm that all we see and hear, feel and taste, think and do, during our whole being, is but the series and deluding appearances of a long dream, whereof there is no reality; and therefore will question the existence of all things, or our knowledge of anything: I must desire him to consider, that, if all be a dream, then he doth but dream that he makes

the question, and so it is not much matter that a waking man should answer him. But yet, if he pleases, he may dream that I make him this answer, That the certainty of things existing in *rerum natura* when we have the testimony of our senses for it is not only as great as our frame can attain to, but as our condition needs. For, our faculties being suited not to the full extent of being, nor to a perfect, clear, comprehensive knowledge of things free from all doubt and scruple; but to the preservation of us, in whom they are; and accommodated to the use of life: they serve to our purpose well enough, if they will but give us certain notice of those things, which are convenient or inconvenient to us. For he that sees a candle burning, and hath experimented the force of its flame by putting his finger in it, will little doubt that this is something existing without him, which does him harm, and puts him to great pain: which is assurance enough, when no man requires greater certainty to govern his actions by than what is as certain as his actions themselves. And if our dreamer pleases to try whether the glowing heat of a glass furnace be barely a wandering imagination in a drowsy man's fancy, by putting his hand into it, he may perhaps be wakened into a certainty greater than he could wish, that it is something more than bare imagination. So that this evidence is as great as we can desire, being as certain to us as our pleasure or pain, i.e. happiness or misery; beyond which we have no concernment, either of knowing or being. Such an assurance of the existence of things without us is sufficient to direct us in the attaining the good and avoiding the evil which is caused by them, which is the important concernment we have of being made acquainted with them.

9. In fine, then, when our senses do actually convey into our understandings any idea, we cannot but be satisfied that there doth something *at that time* really exist without us, which doth affect our senses, and by them give notice of itself to our apprehensive faculties, and actually produce that idea which we then perceive: and we cannot so far distrust their testimony, as to doubt that such *collections* of simple ideas as we have observed by our senses to be united together, do really exist together. But this knowledge extends as far as the present testimony of our senses, employed about particular objects that do then affect them, and no further. For if I saw such a collection of simple ideas as is wont to be called *man*, existing together one minute since, and am now alone, I cannot be certain that the same man exists now, since there is no *necessary connexion* of his existence a minute since with his existence now: by a thousand ways he may cease to be, since I had the testimony of my senses for his existence. And if I cannot be certain that the man I saw last to-day is now in being, I can less be certain that he is so who hath been longer removed from my senses, and I have not seen since yesterday, or since the last year: and much less can I be certain of the existence of men that I never saw. And, therefore, though it be highly probable that millions of men do now exist, yet, whilst I am alone, writing this, I have not that certainty of it which we strictly call knowledge; though the great likelihood of it puts me past doubt, and it be reasonable for me to

do several things upon the confidence that there are men (and men also of my acquaintance, with whom I have to do) now in the world: but this is but probability, not knowledge.

10. Whereby yet we may observe how foolish and vain a thing it is for a man of a narrow knowledge, who having reason given him to judge of the different evidence and probability of things, and to be swayed accordingly; how vain, I say, it is to expect demonstration and certainty in things not capable of it; and refuse assent to very rational propositions, and act contrary to very plain and clear truths, because they cannot be made out so evident, as to surmount every the least (I will not say reason, but) pretence of doubting. He that, in the ordinary affairs of life, would admit of nothing but direct plain demonstration, would be sure of nothing in this world, but of perishing quickly. The wholesomeness of his meat or drink would not give him reason to venture on it: and I would fain know what it is he could do upon such grounds as are capable of no doubt, no objection.

TO BE IS TO BE PERCEIVED

GEORGE BERKELEY

1. It is evident to anyone who takes a survey of the objects of human knowledge, that they are either ideas (1) actually imprinted on the senses, or else such as are (2) perceived by attending to the passions and operations of the mind, or lastly (3) ideas formed by help of memory and imagination, either compounding, dividing, or barely representing those originally perceived in the aforesaid ways. By sight I have the ideas of lights and colors, with their several degrees and variations. By touch I perceive hard and soft, heat and cold, motion and resistance, and of all these more and less either as to quantity or degree. Smelling furnishes me with odors, the palate with tastes, and hearing conveys sounds to the mind in all their variety of tone and composition. And as several of these are observed to accompany each other, they come to be marked by one name, and so to be reputed as one thing. Thus, for example, a certain color, taste, smell, figure, and consistence, having been observed to go together, are accounted one distinct thing, signified by the name "apple." Other collections of ideas constitute a stone, a tree, a book, and the like sensible things; which, as they are pleasing or disagreeable, excite the passions of love, hatred, joy, grief, and so forth.

2. But besides all that endless variety of ideas or objects of knowledge, there is likewise something which knows or perceives them, and exercises

Reprinted from *Of the Principles of Human Knowledge,* first published 1710.

divers operations, as willing, imagining, remembering, about them. This perceiving, active being is what I call *mind*, *spirit*, *soul*, or *myself*. By which words I do not denote any one of my ideas, but a thing entirely distinct from them wherein they exist, or, which is the same thing, whereby they are perceived; for the existence of an idea consists in being perceived.

3. That neither our thoughts, nor passions, nor ideas formed by the imagination, exist without the mind, is what everybody will allow. And it seems no less evident that the various sensations or ideas imprinted on the sense, however blended or combined together (that is, whatever objects they compose), cannot exist otherwise than in a mind perceiving them. I think an intuitive knowledge may be obtained of this by anyone that shall attend to what is meant by the term "exist" when applied to sensible things. The table I write on I say exists—that is, I see and feel it; and if I were out of my study I should say it existed—meaning thereby that if I was in my study I might perceive it, or that some other spirit actually does perceive it. There was an odor, that is, it was smelt; there was a sound, that is, it was heard; a color or figure, and it was perceived by sight or touch. This is all that I can understand by these and the like expressions. For as to what is said of the absolute existence of unthinking things without any relation to their being perceived, that seems perfectly unintelligible. Their *esse* is *percipi*, nor is it possible they should have any existence out of the minds or thinking things which perceive them.

4. It is indeed an opinion strangely prevailing amongst men, that houses, mountains, rivers, and in a word all sensible objects, have an existence, natural or real, distinct from their being perceived by the understanding. But with how great an assurance and acquiescence soever this principle may be entertained in the world, yet whoever shall find in his heart to call it in question may, if I mistake not, perceive it to involve a manifest contradiction. For what are the forementioned objects but the things we perceive by sense? and what do we perceive *besides our own ideas or sensations?* and is it not plainly repugnant that any one of these, or any combination of them, should exist unperceived?

5. If we thoroughly examine this tenet it will perhaps be found at bottom to depend on the doctrine of *abstract ideas*. For can there be a nicer strain of abstraction than to distinguish the existence of sensible objects from their being perceived, so as to conceive them existing unperceived? Light and colors, heat and cold, extension and figures—in a word the things we see and feel—what are they but so many sensations, notions, ideas, or impressions on the sense? And is it possible to separate, even in thought, any of these from perception? For my part, I might as easily divide a thing from itself. I may, indeed, divide in my thoughts, or conceive apart from each other, those things which perhaps I never perceived by sense so divided. Thus I imagine the trunk of a human body without the limbs, or conceive the smell of a rose without thinking on the rose itself. So far, I will not deny, I can abstract, if that may properly be called abstraction which extends only to the conceiving separately such

objects as it is possible may really exist or be actually perceived asunder. But my conceiving or imagining power does not extend beyond the possibility of real existence or perception. Hence, as it is impossible for me to see or feel anything without an actual sensation of that thing, so it is impossible for me to conceive in my thoughts any sensible thing or object distinct from the sensation or perception of it.

6. Some truths there are so near and obvious to the mind that a man need only open his eyes to see them. Such I take this important one to be, to wit, that all the choir of heaven and furniture of the earth, in a word all those bodies which compose the mighty frame of the world, have not any subsistence without a mind, that their *being* is to be perceived or known; that consequently so long as they are not actually perceived by me, or do not exist in my mind or that of any other created spirit, they must either have no existence at all, or else subsist in the mind of some Eternal Spirit; it being perfectly unintelligible, and involving all the absurdity of abstraction, to attribute to any single part of them an existence independent of a spirit. To be convinced of which, the reader need only reflect and try to separate in his own thoughts the *being* of a sensible thing from its *being perceived.*

7. From what has been said it follows there is not any other substance than *spirit*, or that which perceives. But for the fuller proof of this point, let it be considered the sensible qualities are color, figure, motion, smell, taste, etc.—that is, the ideas perceived by sense. Now, for an idea to exist in an unperceiving thing is a manifest contradiction, for to have an idea is all one as to perceive; that therefore wherein color, figure, and the like qualities exist must perceive them; hence it is clear there can be no unthinking substance or *substratum* of those ideas.

8. But, say you, though the ideas themselves do not exist without the mind, yet there may be things *like* them, whereof they are copies or resemblances, which things exist without the mind in an unthinking substance. I answer, an idea can be like nothing but an idea; a color or figure can be like nothing but another color or figure. If we look but never so little into our thoughts, we shall find it impossible for us to conceive a likeness except only between our ideas. Again, I ask whether those supposed originals or external things, of which our ideas are the pictures or representations, be themselves perceivable or no? If they are, then they are ideas and we have gained our point; but if you say they are not, I appeal to anyone whether it be sense to assert a color is like something which is invisible; hard or soft, like something which is intangible; and so of the rest.

9. Some there are who make a distinction betwixt *primary* and *secondary* qualities. By the former they mean extension, figure, motion, rest, solidity or impenetrability, and number; by the latter they denote all other sensible qualities, as colors, sounds, tastes, and so forth. The ideas we have of these they acknowledge not to be the resemblances of anything existing without the mind, or unperceived, but they will have our ideas of the primary qualities to be patterns or images of things which

exist without the mind, in an unthinking substance which they call *matter*. By *matter*, therefore, we are to understand an inert, senseless substance, in which extension, figure, and motion do actually subsist. But it is evident from what we have already shown, that extension, figure, and motion are only ideas existing in the mind, and that an idea can be like nothing but another idea, and that consequently neither they nor their archetypes can exist in an unperceiving substance. Hence, it is plain that the very notion of what is called *matter*, or *corporeal substance*, involves a contradiction in it.

10. They who assert that figure, motion, and the rest of the primary or original qualities do exist without the mind in unthinking substances, do at the same time acknowledge that color, sounds, heat, cold, and suchlike secondary qualities, do not; which they tell us are sensations existing in the mind alone, that depend on and are occasioned by the different size, texture, and motion of the minute particles of matter. This they take for an undoubted truth, which they can demonstrate beyond all exception. Now, if it be certain that those original qualities are inseparably united with the other sensible qualities, and not, even in thought, capable of being abstracted from them, it plainly follows that they exist only in the mind. But I desire anyone to reflect and try whether he can, by any abstraction of thought, conceive the extension and motion of a body without all other sensible qualities. For my own part, I see evidently that it is not in my power to frame an idea of a body extended and moving, but I must withal give it some color or other sensible quality which is acknowledged to exist only in the mind. In short, extension, figure, and motion, abstracted from all other qualities, are inconceivable. Where therefore the other sensible qualities are, there must these be also, to wit, in the mind and nowhere else.

. . .

14. I shall farther add that, after the same manner as modern philosophers prove certain sensible qualities to have no existence in matter, or without the mind, the same thing may be likewise proved of all other sensible qualities whatsoever. Thus, for instance, it is said that heat and cold are affections only of the mind, and not at all patterns of real beings, existing in the corporeal substances which excite them, for that the same body which appears cold to one hand seems warm to another. Now, why may we not as well argue that figure and extension are not patterns or resemblances of qualities existing in matter, because to the same eye at different stations, or eyes of a different texture at the same station, they appear various, and cannot therefore be the images of anything settled and determinate without the mind? Again, it is proved that sweetness is not really in the sapid thing, because the thing remaining unaltered the sweetness is changed into bitter, as in case of a fever or otherwise vitiated palate. Is it not as reasonable to say that motion is not without the mind, since if the succession of ideas in the mind become swifter, the motion, it

is acknowledged, shall appear slower without any alteration in any external object?

15. In short, let anyone consider those arguments which are thought manifestly to prove that colors and tastes exist only in the mind, and he shall find they may with equal force be brought to prove the same thing of extension, figure, and motion—though it must be confessed this method of arguing does not so much prove that there is no extension or color in an outward object, as that we do not know by sense which is the true extension or color of the object. But the arguments foregoing plainly show it to be impossible that any color or extension at all, or other sensible quality whatsoever, should exist in an unthinking subject without the mind, or in truth, that there should be any such thing as an outward object.

16. But let us examine a little the received opinion. It is said extension is a mode or accident of matter, and that matter is the *substratum* that supports it. Now I desire that you would explain to me what is meant by matter's *supporting* extension. Say you, I have no idea of matter and therefore cannot explain it. I answer, though you have no positive, yet, if you have any meaning at all, you must at least have a relative idea of matter; though you know not what it is, yet you must be supposed to know what relation it bears to accidents, and what is meant by its supporting them. It is evident "support" cannot here be taken in its usual or literal sense—as when we say that pillars support a building; in what sense therefore must it be taken?

17. If we inquire into what the most accurate philosophers declare themselves to mean by *material substance*, we shall find them acknowledge they have no other meaning annexed to those sounds but the idea of *Being in general*, together with the relative notion of its supporting accidents. The general idea of Being appeareth to me the most abstract and incomprehensible of all other; and as for its supporting accidents, this, as we have just now observed, cannot be understood in the common sense of those words; it must therefore be taken in some other sense, but what that is they do not explain. So that when I consider the two parts or branches which make the signification of the words *material substance*, I am convinced there is no distinct meaning annexed to them. But why should we trouble ourselves any farther, in discussing this material *substratum* or support of figure and motion, and other sensible qualities? Does it not suppose they have an existence without the mind? And is not this a direct repugnancy, and altogether inconceivable?

18. But though it were possible that solid, figured, movable substances may exist without the mind, corresponding to the ideas we have of bodies, yet how is it possible for us to know this? Either we must know it by sense or by reason. As for our senses, by them we have the knowledge only of our sensations, ideas, or those things that are immediately perceived by sense, call them what you will; but they do not inform us that things exist without the mind, or unperceived, like to those which are perceived. This the materialists themselves acknowledge. It remains

therefore that if we have any knowledge at all of external things, it must be by reason, inferring their existence from what is immediately perceived by sense. But what reason can induce us to believe the existence of bodies without the mind, from what we perceive, since the very patrons of matter themselves do not pretend there is any necessary connection betwixt them and our ideas? I say it is granted on all hands (and what happens in dreams, frenzies, and the like, puts it beyond dispute) that *it is possible we might be affected with all the ideas we have now, though there were no bodies existing without, resembling them.* Hence, it is evident the supposition of external bodies is not necessary for the producing our ideas; since it is granted they are produced sometimes, and might possibly be produced always in the same order we see them in at present, without their concurrence.

19. But, though we might possibly have all our sensations without them, yet perhaps it may be thought easier to conceive and explain the manner of their production by supposing external bodies in their likeness rather than otherwise; and so it might be at least probable there are such things as bodies that excite their ideas in our minds. But neither can this be said; for though we give the materialists their external bodies, they by their own confession are never the nearer knowing how our ideas are produced, since they own themselves unable to comprehend in what manner body can act upon spirit, or how it is possible it should imprint any idea in the mind. Hence it is evident the production of ideas or sensations in our minds can be no reason why we should suppose matter or corporeal substances, since that is acknowledged to remain equally inexplicable with or without this supposition. If therefore it were possible for bodies to exist without the mind, yet to hold they do so, must needs be a very precarious opinion; since it is to suppose, without any reason at all, that God has created innumerable beings that are entirely useless, and serve to no manner of purpose.

20. In short, if there were external bodies, it is impossible we should ever come to know it; and if there were not, we might have the very same reasons to think there were that we have now. Suppose (what no one can deny possible) an intelligence without the help of external bodies, to be affected with the same train of sensations or ideas that you are, imprinted in the same order and with like vividness in his mind. I ask whether that intelligence hath not all the reason to believe the existence of corporeal substances, represented by his ideas, and exciting them in his mind, that you can possibly have for believing the same thing? Of this there can be no question; which one consideration were enough to make any reasonable person suspect the strength of whatever arguments he may think himself to have for the existence of bodies without the mind.

. . .

22. I am afraid I have given cause to think I am needlessly prolix in handling this subject. For, to what purpose is it to dilate on that which

may be demonstrated with the utmost evidence in a line or two, to anyone that is capable of the least reflection? It is but looking into your own thoughts, and so trying whether you can conceive it possible for a sound, or figure, or motion, or color to exist without the mind or unperceived. This easy trial may perhaps make you see that what you contend for is a downright contradiction. Insomuch that I am content to put the whole upon this issue: if you can but conceive it possible for one extended movable substance, or, in general, for any one idea, or anything like an idea, to exist otherwise than in a mind perceiving it, I shall readily give up the cause; and, as for all that compages of external bodies you contend for, I shall grant you its existence, though you cannot either give me any reason why you believe it exists, or assign any use to it when it is supposed to exist. I say, the bare possibility of your opinion's being true shall pass for an argument that it is so.

23. But, say you, surely there is nothing easier than for me to imagine trees, for instance, in a park, or books existing in a closet, and nobody by to perceive them. I answer, you may so, there is no difficulty in it; but what is all this, I beseech you, more than framing in your mind certain ideas which you call books and trees, and the same time omitting to frame the idea of anyone that may perceive them? But do not you yourself perceive or think of them all the while? This therefore is nothing to the purpose; it only shews you have the power of imagining or forming ideas in your mind: but it doth not shew that you can conceive it possible the objects of your thought may exist without the mind. To make out this, it is necessary that you conceive them existing unconceived or unthought of, which is a manifest repugnancy. When we do our utmost to conceive the existence of external bodies, we are all the while only contemplating our own ideas. But the mind taking no notice of itself, is deluded to think it can and doth conceive bodies existing unthought of or without the mind, though at the same time they are apprehended by or exist in itself. A little attention will discover to anyone the truth and evidence of what is here said, and make it unnecessary to insist on any other proofs against the existence of *material substance.*

. . .

33. The ideas imprinted on the senses by the Author of nature are called *real things;* and those excited in the imagination, being less regular, vivid, and constant, are more properly termed *ideas,* or *images* of *things,* which they copy and represent. But then our sensations, be they never so vivid and distinct, are nevertheless ideas, that is, they exist in the mind, or are perceived by it, as truly as the ideas of its own framing. The ideas of sense are allowed to have more reality in them, that is, to be more strong, orderly, and coherent than the creatures of the mind; but this is no argument that they exist without the mind. They are also less dependent on the spirit, or thinking substance which perceives them, in that they are

excited by the will of another and more powerful spirit; yet still they are *ideas*, and certainly no idea, whether faint or strong, can exist otherwise than in a mind perceiving it.

34. Before we proceed any farther it is necessary we spend some time in answering objections which may probably be made against the principles we have hitherto laid down. In doing of which, if I seem too prolix to those of quick apprehensions, I hope it may be pardoned, since all men do not equally apprehend things of this nature, and I am willing to be understood by everyone.

First, then, it will be objected that by the foregoing principles all that is real and substantial in nature is banished out of the world, and instead thereof a chimerical scheme of *ideas* takes place. All things that exist, exist only in the mind, that is, they are purely notional. What therefore becomes of the sun, moon, and stars? What must we think of houses, rivers, mountains, trees, stones; nay, even of our own bodies? Are all these but so many chimeras and illusions on the fancy? To all which, and whatever else of the same sort may be objected, I answer that by the principles premised we are not deprived of any one thing in nature. Whatever we see, feel, hear, or anywise conceive or understand remains as secure as ever, and is as real as ever. There is a *rerum natura*, and the distinction between realities and chimeras retains its full force. This is evident from Sec. 29, 30, and 33, where we have shewn what is meant by *real things* in opposition to *chimeras* or ideas of our own framing; but then they both equally exist in the mind, and in that sense they are alike *ideas*.

35. I do not argue against the existence of any one thing that we can apprehend either by sense or reflection. That the things I see with my eyes and touch with my hands do exist, really exist, I make not the least question. The only thing whose existence we deny is that which *philosophers* call matter or corporeal substance. And in doing of this there is no damage done to the rest of mankind, who, I dare say, will never miss it. The atheist indeed will want the color of an empty name to support his impiety; and the philosophers may possibly find they have lost a great handle for trifling and disputation.

36. If any man thinks this detracts from the existence or reality of things, he is very far from understanding what hath been premised in the plainest terms I could think of. Take here an abstract of what has been said. There are spiritual substances, minds, or human souls, which will or excite ideas in themselves at pleasure; but these are faint, weak, and unsteady in respect of others they perceive by sense—which, being impressed upon them according to certain rules or laws of nature, speak themselves the effects of a mind more powerful and wise than human spirits. These latter are said to have more *reality* in them than the former; by which is meant that they are more affecting, orderly, and distinct, and that they are not fictions of the mind perceiving them. And in this sense the sun that I see by day is the real sun, and that which I imagine by night is the idea of the former. In the sense here given of "reality" it is evident that every vegetable, star, mineral, and in general each part of the

mundane system, is as much as a real being by our principles as by any other. Whether others mean anything by the term "reality" different from what I do, I entreat them to look into their own thoughts and see.

37. It will be urged that thus much at least is true, to wit, that we take away all corporeal substances. To this my answer is that if the word "substance" be taken in the vulgar sense—for a combination of sensible qualities, such as extension, solidity, weight, and the like—this we cannot be accused of taking away. But if it be taken in a philosophic sense—for the support of accidents or qualities without the mind—then indeed I acknowledge that we take it away, if one may be said to take away that which never had any existence, not even in the imagination.

38. But after all, say you, it sounds very harsh to say we eat and drink ideas, and are clothed with ideas. I acknowledge it does so; the word "idea" not being used in common discourse to signify the several combinations of sensible qualities which are called "things"; and it is certain that any expression which varies from the familiar use of language will seem harsh and ridiculous. But this doth not concern the truth of the proposition, which in other words is no more than to say, we are fed and clothed with those things which we perceive immediately by our senses. The hardness or softness, the color, taste, warmth, figure, or suchlike qualities, which combined together constitute the several sorts of victuals and apparel, have been shewn to exist only in the mind that perceives them; and this is all that is meant by calling them "ideas"; which word if it was as ordinarily used as "things," would sound no harsher nor more ridiculous than it. I am not for disputing about the propriety, but the truth of the expression. If therefore you agree with me that we eat and drink and are clad with the immediate objects of sense, which cannot exist unperceived or without the mind, I shall readily grant it is more proper or conformable to custom that they should be called things rather than ideas.

39. If it be demanded why I make use of the word "idea," and do not rather in compliance with custom call them "thing"; I answer, I do it for two reasons:—first, because the term "thing" in contradistinction to "idea," is generally supposed to denote somewhat existing without the mind; secondly, because "thing" hath a more comprehensive signification than "idea," including spirit or thinking things as well as ideas. Since therefore the objects of sense exist only in the mind, and are withal thoughtless and inactive, I chose to mark them by the word "idea," which implies those properties.

40. But, say what we can, someone perhaps may be apt to reply, he will still believe his senses, and never suffer any arguments, how plausible soever, to prevail over the certainty of them. Be it so; assert the evidence of sense as high as you please, we are willing to do the same. That what I see, hear, and feel doth exist, that is to say, is perceived by me, I no more doubt than I do of my own being. But I do not see how the testimony of sense can be alleged as a proof for the existence of anything which is not perceived by sense. We are not for having any man turn sceptic and disbelieve his senses; on the contrary, we give them all the stress and

assurance imaginable; nor are there any principles more opposite to scepticism than those we have laid down. . .

41. *Secondly*, it will be objected that there is a great difference betwixt real fire for instance, and the idea of fire, betwixt dreaming or imagining oneself burnt, and actually being so: if you suspect it to be only the idea of fire which you see, do but put your hand into it and you will be convinced with a witness. This and the like may be urged in opposition to our tenets. To all which the answer is evident from what hath been already said; and I shall only add in this place, that if real fire be very different from the idea of fire, so also is the real pain that it occasions very different from the idea of the same pain, and yet nobody will pretend that real pain either is, or can possibly be, in an unperceiving thing, or without the mind, any more than its idea.

PROOF OF AN EXTERNAL WORLD

G. E. MOORE

. . . It should, I think, be noted, first of all, that the use of the word 'mind', which is being adopted when it is said that any bodily pains which I feel are 'in my mind', is one which is not quite in accordance with any usage common in ordinary speech, although we are very familiar with it in philosophy. Nobody, I think, would say that bodily pains which I feel are 'in my mind', unless he was also prepared to say that it is *with* my mind that I feel bodily pains; and to say this latter is, I think, not quite in accordance with common non-philosophic usage. It is natural enough to say that it is with my mind that I remember, and think, and imagine, and feel *mental* pains—e.g. disappointment, but not, I think, quite so natural to say that it is with my mind that I feel *bodily* pains, e.g. a severe headache; and perhaps even less natural to say that it is with my mind that I see and hear and smell and taste. There is, however, a well-established philosophical usage according to which seeing, hearing, smelling, tasting, and having a bodily pain are just as much *mental* occurrences or processes as are remembering, or thinking, or imagining. This usage was, I think, adopted by philosophers, because they saw a real resemblance between such statements as 'I saw a cat', 'I heard a clap of thunder', 'I smelt a strong smell of onions', 'My finger smarted horribly', on the one hand, and such statements as 'I remembered having seen him', 'I was thinking out a plan of action', 'I pictured the scene to myself', 'I felt bitterly

Reprinted from *The Proceedings of the British Academy*, 1939, by permission of the editor.

disappointed', on the other—a resemblance which puts all these statements in one class together, as contrasted with other statements in which 'I' or 'my' is used, such as, e.g., 'I was less than four feet high', 'I was lying on my back', 'My hair was very long'. What is the resemblance in question? It is a resemblance which might be expressed by saying that all the first eight statements are the sort of statements which furnish data for psychology, while the three latter are not. It is also a resemblance which may be expressed, in a way now common among philosophers, by saying that in the case of all the first eight statements, if we make the statement more specific by adding a date, we get a statement such that, if it is true, then it *follows* that I was 'having an experience' at the date in question, whereas this does not hold for the three last statements. For instance, if it is true that I saw a cat between 12 noon and 5 minutes past, to-day, it *follows* that I was 'having some experience' between 12 noon and 5 minutes past, to-day; whereas from the proposition that I was less than four feet high in December 1877, it does not *follow* that I had any experiences in December 1877. . . . I think that what has been meant by saying that any pain which I feel or any after-image which I see with my eyes closed is '*in* my mind', can be explained by saying that what is meant is neither more nor less than that there would be a contradiction in supposing *that very same pain* or *that very same after-image* to have existed at a time at which I was having no experience; or, in other words, that from the proposition, with regard to any time, that *that* pain or *that* after-image existed at that time, it *follows* that I was having some experience at the time in question. And if so, then we can say that the felt difference between bodily pains which I feel and after-images which I see, on the one hand, and my body on the other, which has led philosophers to say that any such pain or after-image is '*in* my mind', whereas my body *never* is but is always 'outside of' or 'external to' my mind, is just this, that whereas there is a contradiction in supposing a pain which I feel or an after-image which I see to exist at a time when I am having no experience, there is no contradiction in supposing my body to exist at a time when I am having no experience; and we can even say, I think, that just this and nothing more is what they have meant by these puzzling and misleading phrases 'in my mind' and 'external to my mind'.

But now, if to say of anything, e.g. my body, that it is external to *my* mind, means merely that from a proposition to the effect that it existed at a specified time, there in no case follows the further proposition that *I* was having an experience at the time in question, then to say of anything that it is external to *our* minds, will mean similarly that from a proposition to the effect that it existed at a specified time, it in no case follows that any of *us* were having experiences at the time in question. And if by *our* minds be meant, as is, I think, usually meant, the minds of human beings living on the earth, then it will follow that any pains which animals may feel, any after-images they may see, any experiences they may have, though not external to *their* minds, yet are external to *ours*. And this at once makes plain how different is the conception 'external to our minds' from the conception 'to be met with in space'; for, of course, pains which animals feel or after-images which they see are no more to be met with in space than are pains which *we* feel are after-images which *we* see. From the proposition that there are external objects–objects that are not in any of *our* minds, it does *not* follow that there are things to be met with in space; and hence 'external to our minds' is not a mere synonym for 'to be met with in space': that is to say, 'external to our minds' and 'to be met with in space' are two different conceptions. And the true relation between these conceptions seems to me to be this. We have already seen that there are ever so many kinds of 'things', such that, in the case of each of these kinds, from the proposition that there is at least one thing of that kind there *follows* the proposition that there is at least one thing to be met with in space: e.g. this follows from 'There is at least one star', from 'There is at least one human body', from 'There is at least one shadow', &c. And I think we can say that of every kind of thing of which this is true, it is also true that from the proposition that there is at least one 'thing' of that kind there *follows* the proposition that there is at least one thing external to our minds: e.g. for 'There is at least one star' there follows not only 'There is at least one thing to be met with in space' but also 'There is at least one external thing', and similarly in all other cases. My reason for saying this is as follows. Consider any kind of thing, such that anything of that kind, if there is anything of it, must be 'to be met with in space': e.g. consider the kind 'soap-bubble'. If I say of anything which I am perceiving, 'That is a soap-bubble', I am, it seems to me, certainly implying that there would be no contradiction in asserting that it existed before I perceived it and that it will continue to exist, even if I cease to perceive it. This seems to me to be part of what is meant by saying that it is a real soap-bubble, as distinguished, for instance, from an hallucination of a soap-bubble. Of course, it by no means follows, that if it really is a soap-bubble, it did in fact exist before I perceived it or will continue to exist after I cease to perceive it: soap-bubbles are an example of a kind of 'physical object' and 'thing to be met with in space', in the case of which it is notorious that particular specimens of the kind often do exist only so long as they are perceived by a particular person. But a thing which I perceive would not be a soap-bubble unless its existence at any given time were *logically independent* of my perception of it at that time; unless that is to say, from the proposition, with regard to a particular time, that it existed at that time, it *never* follows that I perceived it at that time. But, if it is true that it would not be a soap-bubble, unless it *could* have existed at any given time without being perceived by me at that time, it is certainly also true that it would not be a soap-bubble, unless it *could* have existed at any given time, without its being true that I was having any experience of any kind at the time in question: it would not be a soap-bubble, unless, whatever time you take, from the proposition that it existed at that time it does *not* follow that I was having any experience at that time. That is to say, from the proposition with regard to anything which I am perceiving that it is a soap-bubble, there *follows* the proposition that it is external to *my* mind. But if, when I say that anything which I perceive is a soap-bubble, I am implying that it is external to *my* mind, I am, I think, certainly also implying that it is also external to all other minds: I am implying that it is not a thing of a sort such that things of that sort *can* only exist at a time when somebody is having an experience. I think, therefore, that from any proposition of the form 'There's a soap-bubble!' there does really *follow* the proposition 'There's an external object!' 'There's an object external to *all* our minds!' And, if this is true of the kind 'soap-bubble', it is certainly also true of any other kind (including the kind 'unicorn') which is such that, if there are any things of that kind, it follows that there are *some* things to be met with in space.

I think, therefore, that in the case of all kinds of 'things', which are such that if there is a pair of things, both of which are of one of these kinds, or a pair of things one of which is of one of them and one of them of another, then it will follow at once that there are some things to be met with in space, it is true also that if I can prove that there are a pair of things, one of which is of one of these kinds and another of another, or a pair both of which are of one of them, then I shall have proved *ipso facto* that there are at least two 'things outside of us'. That is to say, if I can prove that there exist now both a sheet of paper and a human hand, I shall have proved that there are now 'things outside of us'; if I can prove that there exist now both a shoe and sock, I shall have proved that there are now 'things outside of us'; &c.; and similarly I shall have proved it, if I can prove that there exist now two sheets of paper, or two human hands, or two shoes, or two socks, &c. Obviously, then, there are thousands of different things such that, if, at any time, I can prove any one of them, I shall have proved the existence of things outside of us. Cannot I prove any of these things?

It seems to me that, so far from its being true, as Kant declares to be his opinion, that there is only one possible proof of the existence of things outside of us, namely the one which he has given, I can now give a large number of different proofs, each of which is a perfectly rigorous proof; and that at many other times I have been in a position to give many others. I can prove now, for instance, that two human hands exist. How? By holding up my two hands, and saying, as I make a certain gesture with the right hand, 'Here is one hand', and adding, as I make a certain gesture with the left, 'and here is another'. And if, by doing this, I have proved *ipso facto* the existence of external things, you will all see that I can also do it now in numbers of other ways: there is no need to multiply examples.

But did I prove just now that two human hands were then in existence? I do want to insist that I did; that the proof which I gave was a perfectly rigorous one; and that it is perhaps impossible to give a better or more rigorous proof of anything whatever. Of course, it would not have been a proof unless three conditions were satisfied; namely (1) unless the premiss which I adduced as proof of the conclusion was different from the conclusion I adduced it to prove; (2) unless the premiss which I adduced was something which I *knew* to be the case, and not merely something which I believed but which was by no means certain, or something which, though in fact true, I did not know to be so; and (3) unless the conclusion did really follow from the premiss. But all these three conditions were in fact satisfied by my proof. (1) The premiss which I adduced in proof was quite certainly different from the conclusion, for the conclusion was merely 'Two human hands exist at this moment'; but the premiss was something far more specific than this—something which I expressed by showing you my hands, making certain gestures, and saying the words 'Here is one hand, and here is another'. It is quite obvious that the two were different, because it is quite obvious that the conclusion might have been true, even if the premiss had been false. In asserting the premiss I was asserting much more than I was asserting in asserting the conclusion. (2) I certainly did at the moment *know* that which I expressed by the combination of certain gestures with saying the words 'There is one hand and here is another'. I *knew* that there was one hand in the place indicated by combining a certain gesture with my first utterance of 'here' and that there was another in the different place indicated by combining a certain gesture with my second utterance of 'here'. How absurd it would be to suggest that I did not know it, but only believed it, and that perhaps it was not the case! You might as well suggest that I do not know that I am now standing up and talking—that perhaps after all I'm not, and that it's not quite certain that I am! And finally (3) it is quite certain that the conclusion did follow from the premiss. This is as certain, as it is that if there is one hand here and another here *now*, then it follows that there are two hands in existence *now*.

My proof, then, of the existence of things outside of us did satisfy three of the conditions necessary for a rigorous proof. Are there any other conditions necessary for a rigorous proof, such that perhaps it did not satisfy one of them? Perhaps there may be; I do not know; but I do want to emphasize that, so far as I can see, we all of us do constantly take proofs of this sort as absolutely conclusive proofs of certain conclusions—as finally settling certain questions, as to which we were previously in doubt. Suppose, for instance, it were a question whether there were as many as three misprints on a certain page in a certain book. A says there are, B is inclined to doubt it. How could A prove that he is right? Surely he *could* prove it by taking the book, turning to the page, and pointing to three separate places on it, saying 'There's one misprint here, another here, and another here': surely that is a method by which it *might* be proved! Of course, A would not have proved, by doing this, that there were at least three misprints on the page in question, unless it was certain that there was a misprint in each of the places to which he pointed. But to say that he *might* prove it in this way, is to say that it *might* be certain that there was. And if such a thing as that could ever be certain, then assuredly it was certain just now that there was one hand in one of the two places I indicated and another in the other.

. . .

But now I am perfectly well aware that, in spite of all that I have said, many philosophers will still feel that I have not given any satisfactory proof of the point in question. And I want briefly, in conclusion, to say something as to why this dissatisfaction with my proofs should be felt.

One reason why, is, I think, this. Some people understand 'proof of an external world' as including a proof of things which I haven't attempted to prove and haven't proved. It is not quite easy to say *what* it is that they want proved—*what* it is that is such that unless they got a proof of it, they would not say that they had a proof of the existence of external things; but I can make an approach to explaining what they want by saying that if I had proved the propositions which I used as *premisses* in my two proofs, then they would perhaps admit that I had proved the existence of external things, but, in the absence of such a proof (which, of course, I have neither given, nor attempted to give), they will say that I have not given what they mean by a proof of the existence of external things. In other words they want a proof of what I assert *now* when I hold up my hands and say 'Here's one hand and here's another'; and, in the other case, they want a proof of what I assert *now* when I say 'I did hold up two hands above this desk just now'. Of course, what they really want is not merely a proof of these two propositions, but something like a general statement as to how *any* propositions of this sort may be proved. This, of course, I haven't given; and I do not believe it can be given: if this is what is meant by proof of the existence of external things, I do not believe that any proof of the existence of external things is possible. Of course, in some cases what might be called a proof of propositions which seem like these can be got. If one of you suspected that one of my hands was artificial he might be said to get a proof of my proposition 'Here's one hand, and here's another', by coming up and examining the suspected hand close up, perhaps touching and pressing it, and so establishing that it really was a human hand. But I do not believe that any proof is possible in nearly all cases. How am I to prove now that 'Here's one hand, and here's another'? I do not believe I can do it. In order to do it, I should need to prove for one thing, as Descartes pointed out, that I am not now dreaming. But how can I prove that I am not? I have, no doubt, conclusive reasons for asserting that I am not now dreaming; I have conclusive evidence that I am awake: but that is a very different thing from being able to prove it. I could not tell you what all my evidence is; and I should require to do this at least, in order to give you a proof.

But another reason, why some people would feel dissatisfied with my proofs is, I think, not merely that they want a proof of something which I haven't proved, but that they think that, if I cannot give such extra proofs, then the proofs that I have given are not conclusive proofs at all. And this, I think, is a definite mistake. They would say: 'If you cannot prove your premiss that here is one hand and here is another, then you do not know it. But you yourself have admitted that, if you did not know it, then your proof was not conclusive. Therefore your proof was not, as you say it was, a conclusive proof.' This view that, if I cannot prove such things as these, I do not know them, is, I think, the view that Kant was expressing in the sentence which I quoted at the beginning of this lecture, when he implies that so long as we have no proof of the existence of external things, their existence must be accepted merely on *faith*. He means to say, I think, that if I cannot prove that there is a hand here, I must accept it merely as a matter of faith—I cannot know it. Such a view, though it has been very common among philosophers, can, I think, be shown to be wrong—though shown only by the use of premisses which are not known to be true, unless we do know of the existence of external things. I can know things, which I cannot prove; and among things which I certainly did know, even if (as I think) I could not prove them, were the premisses of my two proofs. I should say, therefore, that those, if any, who are dissatisfied with these proofs merely on the ground that I did not know their premisses, have no good reason for their dissatisfaction.

SENSE-DATA AND PHYSICAL OBJECTS

A. J. AYER

The problem of specifying the relationship of material things to sense-data, to which the causal theory of perception has been shown to provide so unsatisfactory an answer, is apt to be obscured by being represented as a problem about the inter-relationship of two different classes of objects. There is, indeed, a sense in which it is correct to say that both sense-data and material things exist, inasmuch as sentences that are used to describe sense-data and sentences that are used to describe material things both very frequently express true propositions. But it would not be correct to infer from this that there really were both material things and sense-data, in the sense in which it can truly be said that there really are chairs as well as tables, or that there are tastes as well as sounds. For whereas, in these cases, the existential propositions refer to different empirical "facts", this does not hold good in the case of sense-data and material things. All the same, the term "material thing" is not synonymous with any term or set of terms that stand for species of sense-data. It is indeed

Reprinted from A. J. Ayer, *The Foundations of Empirical Knowledge*, Part V, Chap. 22, 1940, by permission of the author and Macmillan & Co., Ltd., London, and St. Martin's Press, Inc., New York.

logically necessary that any situation that in any degree establishes the existence of a material thing should also establish the existence of a sense-datum; for we have constructed the sense-datum language in such a way that whenever it is true that a material thing is perceived, it must also be true that a sense-datum is sensed; and this applies also to the cases where the existence of the material thing is inferred from observations of its "physical effects". But it is not wholly a matter of convention that a situation which establishes the existence of a sense-datum should also be evidence in some degree for the existence of a material thing. For this depends, as I shall show, upon certain special features of our sensory experience, which it might conceivably not have possessed. Moreover, while a situation which directly establishes the existence of a sense-datum does so conclusively, no such situations can conclusively establish the existence of a material thing. The degree to which the existence of the material thing is established will depend upon the character of the sense-data in question, and especially upon the nature of the contexts in which they occur; but whatever the strength of this evidence may be, it will always be logically compatible with the hypothesis that this material thing is not in all respects what it appears to be, or even that it does not exist at all. Additional evidence may weaken this hypothesis to an extent that makes it very foolish still to entertain it; but it may also substantiate it, as the fact that there are illusions shows. At the same time, it is to be remarked that this additional evidence, whether favourable or not, will always consist in the occurrence of further sense-data. Indeed there is nothing else in which one can legitimately suppose it to consist, once one has accepted the rule that the word "sense-datum" is to be used to stand for whatever is, in fact, observed. And since it is impossible, by any valid process of inference, to make a transition from what is observed to anything that is conceived as being, in principle, unobservable, all that the evidence in question will be evidence for or against is the possible occurrence of further sense-data still. And from this it seems to follow that, even though the term "material thing" is not synonymous with any set of terms that stand for species of sense-data, any proposition that refers to a material thing must somehow be expressible in terms of sense-data, if it is to be empirically significant.

A common way of expressing this conclusion is to say that material things are nothing but collections of actual and possible sense-data. But this is a misleading formula and one that provokes objections which a more accurate way of speaking might avoid. Thus, it is sometimes argued, by those who reject this "phenomenalistic" analysis of the nature of material things, that to conceive of such things as houses or trees or stones as mere collections of actual and possible sense-data is to ignore their "unity" and "substantiality", and that, in any case, it is hard to see how anything can be composed of so shadowy a being as a possible sense-datum. But these objections are founded upon the mistaken assumption that a material thing is supposed to consist of sense-data, as a patchwork quilt consists of different coloured pieces of silk. To remove this misconception, it must be made clear that what the statement that material things consist of sense-data must be understood to designate is not a factual but a linguistic relationship. What is being claimed is simply that the propositions which are ordinarily expressed by sentences which refer to material things could also be expressed by sentences which referred exclusively to sense-data; and the inclusion of possible as well as actual sense-data among the elements of the material things must be taken only to imply a recognition that some of these statements about sense-data will have to be hypothetical. As for the belief in the "unity" and "substantiality" of material things, I shall show that it may be correctly represented as involving no more than the attribution to visual and tactual sense-data of certain relations which do, in fact, obtain in our experience. And I shall show that it is only the contingent fact that there are these relations between sense-data that makes it profitable to describe the course of our experience in terms of the existence and behaviour of material things.

It may seem that an attempt to carry out this plan of "reducing" material things to sense-data would be at variance with my previous attempt to draw a sharp distinction between them. But the purpose of making this distinction was simply to increase the utility and clarity of the sense-datum language by ensuring that its sentences should not be of the same logical form as those that refer to material things. And here it may be explained that two sentences may be said to have the same logical form if they can be correlated in such a way that to each expression that occurs in either one of them there corresponds in the other an expression of the same logical type; and that two expressions may be said to be of the same logical type if any sentence that significantly contains either one of them remains significant when the other is put in its place. It follows that if sentences referring to sense-data are of a different logical form from sentences referring to material things, it must not be assumed that precisely the same things can be said about them. To say, for example, that this was being written with a "pennish" group of sense-data, instead of saying that it was being written with a pen, would be neither true nor false but nonsensical. But this does not rule out the possibility that a proposition which is expressed by a sentence referring to a material thing can equally well be expressed by an entirely different set of sentences, which refer to sense-data; and this is what those who assert that material things are "logical constructions" out of sense-data must be understood to claim. Their view is sometimes put in the form of an assertion that "to say anything about a material thing is to say something, but not the same thing about classes of sense-data";* but if this is taken to imply that any significant statement about a material thing can actually be translated, without alteration of meaning, into a definite set of statements about sense-data, it is not strictly accurate, for a reason I shall presently give.

An objection which is often brought against phenomenalists is that

* *Vide* A. E. Duncan-Jones, "Does Philosophy Analyse Common Sense?" *Aristotelian Society Supplementary Proceedings,* 1937, pp. 140–41.

they begin with a false conception of the nature of "perceptual situations". Thus, it is held by some philosophers that what is directly observed is usually not a sense-datum at all, but a material thing; so that the view that material things must be reducible to sense-data, on the ground that these alone are observable, is fundamentally erroneous. But this, as I have shown,* is not the expression of a disagreement about any matter of fact, but only of a preference for a different form of language. It is indeed legitimate to use the phrase "direct observation" in such a way that things like houses and trees and stones can properly be said to be directly observable; and this usage can perfectly well be made to cover the case of delusive as well as veridical perceptions, provided that it is allowed that what is "directly observed" may not in fact exist, and that it may not really have the properties that it appears to have. But I have shown that it is also legitimate to use the phrase "direct observation" in such a way that it is only what is designated by the term "sense-datum", or some equivalent term, that can be said to be directly observable; and that it is this usage that, for my present purpose, is to be preferred. And one reason why it is to be preferred is to be found in the fact, which I have already mentioned, that whereas the proposition that a sense-datum is veridically sensed does not entail that any material thing is veridically perceived, the proposition that a material thing is veridically perceived can always be represented as entailing that some sense-datum or other is veridically sensed. Indeed, it is inconceivable that any sense-datum should not be sensed veridically, since it has been made self-contradictory to say of an experienced sense-datum that it does not exist or that it does not really have the properties that it appears to have. And because there is this logical relationship between "perceiving a material thing" and "sensing a sense-datum", it follows that, while a reference to a material thing will not elucidate the meaning of a sentence which is used to describe a sense-datum, except in so far as the poverty of our language may make it convenient to identify this sense-datum as one of a type that is ordinarily associated with a special sort of material thing, a reference to sense-data will provide a general elucidation of the meaning of statements about material things by showing what is the kind of evidence by which they may be verified. And this may be regarded as the purpose of the phenomenalist analysis.

Besides the philosophers who maintain that material things are themselves "directly observed", there are others who object to phenomenalism on the ground that even if the occurrence of illusions shows that what is directly observed is not a material thing, it is still not just a sense-datum. Thus Professor Stout, for one, has argued that "the evidence of sense-perception flatly contradicts phenomenalism", on the ground that to regard what is immediately experienced as being just a sensible appearance is to ignore an essential factor which he calls "perceptual seeming".**

* In Part I.
** "Phenomenalism", *Proceedings of the Aristotelian Society*, 1938–9, pp. 1–18.

According to him, it is because of "perceptual seeming" that one is able to "perceive one thing as behind another, although it is so hidden that there is no sensible appearance of it", or that one can "perceive things as having insides, when they are not transparent".* But while this line of argument may have some force against those who employ a physiological criterion for determining the character of sense-data, it does not affect us at all, inasmuch as our use of the word sense-datum is not bound up with any special empirical theory about the nature of what is given. If one accepts the view of certain psychologists that there are experiences that may properly be described as experiences of "seeing the inside of a solid object" or "seeing an object when it is screened by another", then the inference one must draw is not that what is observed on such occasions is "more than a mere sense-datum", but that the character of people's visual sense-fields is empirically different from what a misplaced attention to the laws of physiology might lead one to suppose. It is true that the terms in which the psychologists describe such experiences are not purely sensory; but the reason for this is that it is only by referring to material things that they can actually expect to make their meaning understood. We must not, therefore, be misled into supposing that what they are intending to describe is anything more than a sensory phenomenon. The statement that someone is having the experience of "seeing the inside of a solid object" must not, in this context, be taken to exclude the possibility that no such physical object is actually there.

It may, however, be admitted that not only in cases of this sort, but in the vast majority of cases in which one senses a visual or tactual sense-datum, one tends to take it for granted that there is a physical object "there"; and it may be that this is what Professor Stout is referring to when he talks of "perceptual seeming". But this is a fact that I do not think any phenomenalist would wish to deny. The view that material things are, in the sense I have just explained, logical constructions out of sense-data does not imply that "perceiving a material thing" need involve any conscious process of inference from the occurrence of one sense-datum to the possible occurrence of another. The phenomenalist is perfectly free to admit that the sensing of a visual or tactual sense-datum is, in most cases, accompanied by an unreflecting assumption of the existence of some material thing. But the question in which he is interested is, What exactly is it that is here unreflectingly assumed? And his answer, which certainly cannot be refuted by any such appeal to psychology as Professor Stout relies on, is that it is the possibility of obtaining further sense-data.

It would seem that the best way to justify the claim that "to say anything about a material thing is always to say something, though not the same thing, about certain sense-data", would be to provide a number of specimen translations. But this is what no one has ever yet been able to do. It may be suggested that the reason why it has never been done is that

* *Loc. cit.* pp. 10–11.

no one has yet devised a sufficiently elaborate vocabulary. With our current resources of language we are able to classify visual sense-data only in a very general way, tactual data even less specifically, and kinaesthetic data hardly at all: and the result is that when we wish to distinguish the sense-data that belong to one sort of material thing from those that belong to another we are unable to achieve it except by referring to the material things in question. But suppose that someone took the trouble to name all the different varieties of sensible characteristics with which he was acquainted. Even so, he would still not be able to translate any statement about a material thing into a finite set of statements about sense-data. It is not inconceivable that someone should construct and make use of such a sensory language, though in practice he would find it very difficult to make himself understood; but what he succeeded in expressing by these means would never be precisely equivalent even to the singular statements that we make about material things. For when statements are equivalent to one another, they can always be represented as standing in a relationship of mutual entailment. And, in the case I am now considering, this condition cannot be fulfilled.

I have indeed already admitted that no finite set of singular statements about sense-data can ever formally entail a statement about a material thing, inasmuch as I have recognized that statements about material things are not conclusively verifiable. For when we try to reproduce the content of a statement about a material thing by specifying the empirical situations that would furnish us with direct tests of its validity, we find that the number of these possible tests is infinite. Admittedly, when someone makes a statement of this kind he does not actually envisage an infinite series of possible verifications. He may very well be satisfied, in familiar circumstances, with the single sense-experience on which his statement is based; and if he does think it necessary to test it further, the subsequent occurrence, in the appropriate conditions, of only a limited number of "favourable" sense-data will be sufficient, in the absence of contrary evidence, to convince him that it is true. And this is an entirely reasonable procedure, as I have shown.* But the fact remains that however many favourable tests he may make he can never reach a stage at which it ceases to be conceivable that further sense-experience will reverse the verdict of the previous evidence. He will never be in a position to demonstrate that he will not subsequently have experiences that will entitle him to conclude that his original statement was false after all. And this implies that the content of a statement about a material thing cannot be exhaustively specified by any finite number of references to sense-data. This difficulty could indeed be met by introducing into the sense-datum language a suitable set of expressions which would be understood to refer to infinite series of sense-data. But I am afraid that most philosophers would not admit that this gave them the sort of translation that they wanted. For all that would seem to be achieved by the introduction of these new expressions would be a mere renaming of material things.

* Part I, section 4.

But not only is the occurrence of any one particular, finite series of sense-data never formally sufficient to establish the truth of a statement about a material thing; it is never even necessary. There is, indeed, a sense in which it can be said that every statement about a material thing entails some set of statements or other about sense-data, inasmuch as it is only by the occurrence of some sense-datum that any statement about a material thing is ever in any degree verified. But there is no set of statements about the occurrence of particular sense-data of which it can truly be said that precisely this is entailed by a given statement about a material thing. And the reason for this is that what is required to verify a statement about a material thing is never just the occurrence of a sense-datum of an absolutely specific kind, but only the occurrence of one or other of the sense-data that fall within a fairly indefinite range. In other words, not only can we go on testing a statement about a material thing as long as we like without being able to arrive at a formal demonstration of its truth; but for any test that we actually do carry out there are always an indefinite number of other tests, differing to some extent either in respect of their conditions or their results, which would have done just as well. And this means that if we try to describe what at any given moment would afford us direct evidence for the truth of a statement about a material thing by putting forward a disjunction of statements about sense-data, we shall find once again that this disjunction will have to be infinite.*

But if one infers from this that sentences referring to material things cannot be translated, without alteration of meaning, into sentences referring to sense-data, one must not then conclude that to speak about a material thing is to speak about something altogether different from sense-data, or that it is to speak about sense-data but about something else besides. For that would be a mistake analogous to that of supposing that because sentences referring indefinitely to what is red cannot be translated into a finite number of sentences referring to particular red things, therefore "redness" is the name of an object with a distinct existence of its own, or that because sentences referring to "someone" cannot be translated into a finite disjunction of sentences referring to particular persons, therefore "someone" is the name of a peculiar being, a "subsistent entity" perhaps, who is distinct from any person that one can actually meet. If we cannot produce the required translations of sentences referring to material things into sentences referring to sense-data, the reason is not that it is untrue that "to say anything about a material thing is always to say something about sense-data", but only that one's references to material things are vague in their application to phenomena and that the series of sense-data that they may be understood to specify are composed of infinite sets of terms.

This does not mean, however, that nothing can be done in the way of "analysing material things in terms of sense-data". It would not, indeed, be profitable to seek in any such analysis a means of distinguishing one

* Cf. John Wisdom, "Metaphysics and Verification", *Mind,* October 1938, pp. 478–81.

material thing from another. It is not by a verbal analysis in terms of sense-data that one can hope to make clear what is meant, for example, by "a pen" as opposed to "a pencil", or by "a steamship" as opposed to "a canoe". One can give a verbal, as well as an ostensive, indication of the meaning of such words; but it will not exclude the use of other expressions that belong to a physical rather than to a purely sensory terminology. At the same time, there are certain general features about the way in which any expression referring to a material thing applies to phenomena that one can profitably undertake to analyse. That is to say, one may be able to explain what are the relations between sense-data that make it possible for us successfully to employ the physical terminology that we do. If I may now use the metaphor of construction without being misunderstood, I can describe the task I am about to undertake as that of showing what are the general principles on which, from our resources of sense-data, we "construct" the world of material things.

THE PROBLEM OF PERCEPTION

A. M. QUINTON

I

The problem of perception is to give an account of the relationship of sense-experience to material objects. This relationship has traditionally been seen as logical, a matter of showing how beliefs about objects can be established or supported by what we know in immediate experience. For, it is held, only our knowledge of experience is direct, immediate, by acquaintance; what we know or claim to know about objects is indirect, derivative, by inference from what we know directly. Consequently if our beliefs about objects are to have any secure foundation, it must consist in what we know directly, by acquaintance, about sense-data. From this starting-point philosophers have gone on to present varying accounts of the type of inference involved. An extreme view is Hume's, that the passage from experiences to objects rests on 'a kind of fallacy or illusion'. Lockean causal theories assert that the connexion between experiences and objects is contingent and that knowledge of experience is good inductive evidence for beliefs, logically distinct from it about objects. The species of inference involved is transcendental hypothesis of the type to be found in scientific arguments for the existence of such unobservables as electrons or chromosomes. For phenomenalism the

Reprinted from *Mind*, n.s. Vol. LXIV (1955), pp. 28–51, by permission of the author and editor.

connexion between experiences and objects is necessary, to speak of objects is to speak in an abbreviated way about certain pervasive kinds of regularity in experience. The species of inference involved is simple inductive extrapolation. There are not two worlds, an inner and an outer, but two terminologies. The terminology of objects is used to refer to what is invariant as between the private worlds of experience.

Each view derives strength from the weaknesses of its opponent. The most emphasised weakness of phenomenalism is that, if it were true, unobserved objects would be mere possibilities and actual effects would have to arise from merely potential causes. Mill's view that objects are permanent possibilities of sensation is confronted by a fundamental and unargued incredulity. A more serious difficulty arises about the antecedents of the hypothetical statements which describe the permanent possibilities in question. For these antecedents mention objects. To assume, as phenomenalists often cheerfully do, that these references can be replaced by references to 'orienting experiences' is to beg the very question at issue. One cannot *assume* that statements about experiences are equivalent in meaning to statements about objects in order to *show* that they are. Against the causal theory it is argued that, given the sense-datum theory, it would be impossible ever to know that the logically distinct, unobservable, transcendental causes existed. For a causal inference is only legitimate if it is at least possible to obtain evidence for the existence of the cause which is independent of the events it is held to explain.

In the face of this impasse sense-datum theorists have tended to adopt a middle position of compromise. Causal theorists liken their procedure to the 'model-building' of natural scientists. The external world is a theoretical construction, fruitful and various in its predictive and explanatory consequences. Phenomenalists modify their thesis of the strict logical equivalence of statements about experiences and about objects, in view of the difficulties, in principle and practice, of translating one into the other. Both extremes are abandoned in favour of the view that it is a simple, convenient and fruitful theoretical construction. But this is rather a method of refusing to face the difficulties than of overcoming them. For what sort of theoretical construction is involved, a substantial model of the not-yet-observed like a theory of atomic structure or a mere *façon de parler* like theories of magnetic and gravitational fields?

My purpose in this paper is to overcome these difficulties by a more radical procedure, that of refuting the premise from which both problematic doctrines derive, that we are never directly aware of or acquainted with objects.

My principal target will be the conception of direct awareness or acquaintance itself. The sense-datum theory holds that corresponding to the two kinds of objects of knowledge are two kinds of knowledge—direct and indirect. Thus while no knowledge of material objects is direct, all or only knowledge of experience is direct. In more linguistic terms, while no statements about objects are basic, all or only statements about experience are basic. A piece of knowledge, then, is direct if, and only if, it can be expressed by a basic statement. But this translation is of little help since neither of the crucial terms, 'direct' and 'basic', is clearly intelligible, let alone more intelligible than the other.

Two main kinds of definition are commonly offered of these expressions, one in terms of certainty, the other in terms of inference. By the former I directly know that *p* (or '*p*' is a basic statement) if I know for certain that *p*. It is held that beliefs about objects are never certain, beliefs about experience are always certain and that for any uncertain belief to be even probable something else must be certain. Consequently all beliefs about objects that are to any extent probable must be logically derived from beliefs about experience. I shall hold that all three of the premises for this conclusion are false. The incorrigibility of statements about experience has been defended, notably by Ayer, on the ground that the only mistakes to which we are liable in making such statements are 'verbal'. I shall attempt to show that this too is false. Sometimes a definition in terms of inference is preferred. I directly know that *p* (or '*p*' is a basic statement) if I know that *p* without inference. It is not, of course, maintained that in coming to form a belief about an object I undertake any conscious process of reasoning. What is involved is 'implicit' inference. Nevertheless, it is held, reasons exist for beliefs about objects which it is the philosopher's business to render explicit and without reference to which no justification of these beliefs can be provided. I shall argue that there is no relevant sense of 'reason' in which a reason for them always exists.

Why should this have been thought to be so? The sense-datum theory, seemingly a variant of the empiricist principle that all our knowledge of matters of fact is based on sense-experience, tends to assume that principle's authority. But this, like other oracles, owes much of its reputation to ambiguity. It can be taken to assert three different things, two of which are uncontentious while the third deserves close inspection. First, it is an unexciting truth of physiology that sensations, physical stimulations of the sense-organs, are causally necessary conditions of our knowledge of matters of fact. Second, the establishment of any truth about objects logically requires that someone shall have seen, touched or otherwise perceived something. The chains of inference and testimony cannot hang unsupported but must terminate in observation. In this use 'sense-experience' does not mean anything so definite as 'sense-datum', it has no phenomenological flavour. Seeing a tomato is just as much an observation as seeing a round, red, shiny patch. Finally, 'based on sense-experience' can be taken to mean 'logically derived from sense-experience'. The logical derivation in question here is of statements about objects from statements about experiences. It is this third interpretation of the principle that constitutes the sense-datum theory and which I shall attempt to refute.

These definitions of 'direct' and 'basic' in terms of certainty and inference are not, however, the starting-points of sense-datum theories of perception. They are rather conclusions to the argument from illusion in terms of which the expressions 'direct' and 'basic' are normally introduced. This argument holds that objects are not always what they appear to be and that there need be no discoverable difference between two situations in one of which an object is and in the other is not what it appears to be. In consequence, all that we really know is what appears to be the case, since, even when what appears to be the case *is* the case, we cannot there and then tell whether it is or not. Since we know only what appears to be the case, the only things we really perceive are appearances. Some philosophers have protested weakly against the later stages of this argument. I hope to substantiate and fortify their protest.

The mistake lies in the identification of what appears to be the case with our sense-experience. We always know what appears to be the case. So it is appearances, not objects, that we really perceive. But what else are these appearances but our current sense-fields, our sense-experience? The three forms of words; 'this appears to be ϕ', 'there is a ϕ appearance', 'there is a ϕ sense-datum', are held to be equivalent in meaning. I shall argue that a statement of what appears to be the case is rarely a description of our sense-experience and is normally a modified, guarded claim about what *is* the case, expressing an inclination to believe something about objects. The ostensible firmness and incorrigibility of these assertions is a consequence, not of their referring to a class of private, given entities, but rather of the modesty of the claim they make. So what the argument from illusion establishes is not that we always infallibly know what our sense-experience is like, but only that, whether or not we *know* what is the case, we can always say, without much fear of contradiction, what we are inclined to *believe* is the case. These statements do not, then, express a special kind of direct knowledge by acquaintance nor are they premises from which statements about objects could be inferred. For they are not claims to knowledge at all, but more or less tentative expressions of belief, and what is tentatively affirmed is precisely the same as, and thus cannot be a premise for, what, in the conclusion of the supposed inference, we claim to know without hesitation. I shall argue, however, that we can, and rather infrequently do, describe our experience and that we can do this in statements containing such expressions as 'look', 'appear' and 'seem'.

The consequences of this distinction of 'appearances' from sense-data are that knowledge about experience is much less common than is widely supposed and that the greater part of our 'knowledge of appearances' is not capable of figuring as premises in inferences to beliefs about objects.

Before embarking on this another familiar argument for the sense-datum theory must be considered: what may be called the argument from scientific knowledge. There is conclusive evidence for the fact that many of our sense-experiences occur appreciably later than the events of which they give us knowledge, in particular the experiences caused by what is astronomically visible or less remotely audible. More generally, every sense-experience is at the end of a temporally extended causal chain whose first member is the supposedly perceived occurrence. Consequently, what we directly perceive, the object of acquaintance, cannot be the same as that about which we claim knowledge. But this involves no new issue of principle. It shows objects and experiences to be temporally distinct where the argument from illusion shows them to be much more generally different in character. It only shows that we do not directly perceive objects if the supposed consequence of the argument from illusion—that we perceive only our sense-experience directly—is already accepted.

The view common to all versions of the sense-datum theory that the perception of objects is really a kind of inference seems to arise from a belief that, while perception proper must be infallible, inference need not be, and thus that all mistakes are fallacies. But both perception and inference are learnt, intelligent activities which we can presumably perform with varying degrees of efficiency and success. That perception is an acquired skill has perhaps been an inducement to regard it as inference to those who suppose all intelligence activities to be species of reasoning.

Ultimately the problem of perception is that of the relation of thought or language to the world. There is a distressing correspondence with primitive cosmology. Some statements are supported by others, but what supports these others, what is tortoise to their elephant? For the whole system of knowledge cannot support itself in mid-air; it is not self-contained. There is a dilemma here. Either the ultimate support is logically related to the body of knowledge and is thus automatically brought inside the body of knowledge, since only statements can stand in logical relations, and, if so, the question of dependence on the extralinguistic world breaks out again. Or it is not and there is no answer in terms of correct inference to the request for a justification of reliance on this ultimate support.

Philosophers have sought to evade this dilemma by recourse to the Janus-faced notion of experience. The fact that we cannot, it seems, have an experience without somehow being conscious or aware of it has seemed to provide foundation-stones for the edifice of knowledge which are at once statements, capable of standing in logical relations to the rest of the structure, and parts, perhaps the sole constituents, of the extralinguistic world, self-describing entities. I shall contend that there are no such things and opt for the second horn of the dilemma which, as I hope to show, is a less painful resting-place than it might seem.

II

Our first problem is to evaluate the argument from illusion. From the unexceptionable premises that things are not always what they appear to be and that we cannot always tell, there and then, whether they are or not, it is concluded that we have direct knowledge only of appearances, never of objects. For there need be no immediately discoverable difference between two appearances of which one is in fact 'veridical' and the other 'delusive'. So what we really perceive are appearances, whether they are veridical or not depends on something that lies outside the perceptual situation. But what are these appearances that we perceive? They are, it is said, sense-data, the given, immediate experience, they are the current states of our sense-fields.

Of some uses of 'appear', 'seem', etc. it is clearly untrue to say that they figure in descriptions of experience. 'They appear to be away', said when the twice-rung doorbell of a house with drawn curtains remains unanswered, means much the same as 'they must be away' or 'they are probably away'. We are not here describing, but drawing conclusions from, what we observe. The word 'appear' serves to indicate that these conclusions are drawn with less than full confidence. There is nothing 'basic' about them.

But there is another use of 'appear' in which no reason can be given for statements containing it and which do report observations. 'It appears to be green' we might say of a distant house. If challenged we can only repeat, or perhaps correct, ourselves or protest, 'well, that is how it appears to me'. But such a statement would normally be made in answer to such questions as 'what colour is that house' and could be replaced by 'it's green, I think' or 'it's green, isn't it?' They report observations in a tentative way where we know, believe or suspect that the circumstances are unfavorable to an accurate report, that there is something wrong with or abnormal about the conditions of observation. They resemble ordinary categorical descriptions, 'that house is green', in subject-matter, but differ from them in expressing inclinations to believe rather than full beliefs.

There is a third use of 'appear', which resembles the one last mentioned, in that no reasons or evidence can be given for statements containing it, but differs from it in that certain conventional conditions of observation are supposed to obtain, whether they do or not. 'It looks to me (here, now) elliptical' we say of a plate we know to be tilted and round, supposing it to be at right angles to our line of vision. This statement answers the question 'how does it strike you, look to you, what exactly do you see?' It is replaceable by 'there is an elliptical patch in the centre of my visual field'. It is in this type of case only that the description of appearances and experience coincide.

Consider that old friend the stick half in, half out, of water. One might say of it (*a*) 'it is straight', (*b*) 'it looks bent but is really straight', (*c*) 'it looks bent', (*d*) 'it is bent'. Statement (*a*) is true, (*b*) describes the stick correctly and points out how one might be led to make a mistake about it if unaware of an abnormality (a refracting medium) in the conditions of observation, (*c*) gives tentative expression to the inclination mistakenly to believe (*d*) which is straightforwardly false. 'It looks bent' is the puzzling case. For it may be a guarded way of saying 'it is bent' (denied by 'it isn't bent') or a way of saying 'most people would be inclined to say it was bent' (denied by 'it doesn't') or a way of saying 'it looks bent to me, here, now' (which can only be denied by 'oh surely not').

So, even when not used to give tentative conclusions from evidence, the verb 'appear' and its cognates are seldom used to describe experience, but primarily to give tentative descriptions of objects. In other words, the 'appearances' that survive the argument from illusion as the proper objects of acquaintance are not ordinarily sense-experiences. These seemingly rock-bottom matters of fact are, in a way, incorrigible and, *ex hypothesi*, uninferred. But their incorrigibility is imperfect and spurious. Imperfect because both 'this is ϕ, I think' and 'this is ϕ, most people would say' can be contradicted (by 'it isn't' and 'they wouldn't') and revised accordingly. Spurious because it arises, not from their making a definite claim about something private, but from their making a weak, indefinite claim about something public. And, though uninferred, they cannot play the part of premises in inferences to categorical descriptions of objects. 'This appears to be ϕ' is no more evidence of a reason for 'this is ϕ' than are 'this may be ϕ' or 'this is probably ϕ.' All three are simply modified ways of saying 'this is ϕ', appropriate for one who is inclined, but not inclined quite confidently enough, to make the categorical statement itself.

This is not to deny that we can and do describe our experience. All I have tried to show is that we describe it very much less often than is usually supposed. Being unsure about the circumstances is a common enough occurrence. But the description of experience proper is a sophisticated procedure and one seldom called for. It is an essential accomplishment for painters, broadcasting engineers, doctors of the eye and ear, cooks and experimental psychologists. But unless we fall into their hands there is little need for us to become proficient in it. The sophistication arises with the deliberate supposition that conditions obtain which we have no reason to suppose do so in fact and perhaps every reason to suppose do not. The fact that we have laboriously to learn perspective drawing is an indication of this, as is the notorious unreliability of eyewitnesses.

That we seldom do describe our experience and then usually with difficulty does not entail that we could not set up and become proficient in the use of a private language. But it would involve a remarkable change in our attitude to the world. Normally we observe in a context of beliefs about where we are and what we are doing that the sophisticated naiveté of phenomenology would exclude. To attend to one's experience involves a radical shift in attitude, a determined effort to resist the solicitations of that submerged constellation of beliefs within which our perceptual discoveries are made.

To this extent, then, I am in sympathy with those who have argued that if the stick half in water looks bent then something really *is* bent. When I say the stick looks bent, I should discover, if I were to direct my attention to it, that my visual field contained a bent brown line. Whether it follows from this that I am in some way aware of this feature of my visual field is a question that will be answered later. But there is something to be said against this line of argument which is commonly ignored. No doubt when the stick looks bent, something else is bent. But consider these cases. I see a small glassy object in a radio shop and say 'that looks like a valve'. But in fact it is a wineglass. For this error there is no sensory cue; it is the outcome of my general beliefs about the contents of radio shops. Again, I see what is in fact half a pair of spectacles beside a box which I mistakenly suppose to be obscuring the rest. Even when I know better, it still looks just like a pair to me but it is unlikely that my visual field contains anything corresponding to the second lens.

I have been at pains to emphasise the uncommon and sophisticated nature of the description of experience because of the supposed consequence of the argument from illusion, that in every perceptual situation, even if no object is in fact perceived or if objects are misperceived, still something is perceived, our sense-experience. It would seem *prima facie* that one cannot be said to perceive something unless one is in a position to describe it. But I am not in a position to describe my experience unless I am in the appropriate, sophisticated, phenomenological frame of mind.

Normally if someone says mistakenly that he sees something we are not inclined to say that he really saw something else. We should say of Macbeth that he thought he saw the dagger, imagined he could see it, was under the impression he could see it, but that he did not actually see it at all. In cases of illusion, as against hallucination, there will be something that really is perceived, but it will be a perfectly ordinary public object, not a private experience. If I take a piece of mud on the doormat to be a letter, it will be said that what I actually saw was a piece of mud.

In general, it is not the case, when I am mistaken about what I claim to perceive, either that I am in a position to describe my experience or that I would be said really to have perceived my experience. There are reasons, nevertheless, which have led philosophers to believe that I am aware of my experience, acquainted with it, in such circumstances.

It is not only when in the hands of those professionally concerned with it that we attend to and describe our experience. We are sometimes forced to do so by total ignorance of the conditions of observation. Waking up in unfamiliar circumstances we may, if no other assumption seems inviting, suppose that the conventional phenomenological conditions obtain. In exceptional circumstances of this kind, as we come round from an anaesthetic for example, a description of our visual experience is a possible answer to the question 'can you see anything?' But it is worth noticing that in such cases we can also say, with even better warrant perhaps, 'no, just a lot of yellow streaks' instead of 'yes, a lot of yellow streaks'. Only in a very marginal sense is a description of one's visual experience to be called 'seeing' at all.

In a way, then, we can be said sometimes to 'see' our visual experience: when we are trying to describe it or when we are not in a position to describe anything else. But what of the case of a man lying in the sun on his back with his eyes open and his mind far away? Does he see the blue expanse with shifting white patches on it that he could describe if he were to turn his attention to his visual field? And what of the man who is carefully watching a hen to discover where the gap in the hen-run is? Does he see the green expanse of the downs beyond, that he would in fact find occupying the greater part of his visual field if he were to attend to it? Compare these cases with a less problematic kind of seeing. Suppose you show me round your garden and afterwards ask me 'did you see the tulip tree?' If I say 'no', you may say 'you must have done, it's right beside the summer-house I showed you'. If I still deny seeing it, even after another look to refresh my memory, then I cannot have seen it. Yet one might be inclined here to think that I must have seen it all the same. There it was, ten yards away, in broad daylight, right in the middle of my field of vision. But perhaps I was concentrating on the summer-house or thinking of something else altogether. One's visual field is in much the same case as the tulip tree in this example. However far one's attention may have strayed, it seems, nevertheless, that one is inescapably *confronted* by it. So philosophers have said that whenever we think we see anything we really do see the contents of our visual fields. But this is an extremely hypothetical kind of seeing. All we can say is that if I had been in a different frame of mind I should have noticed the tree; I should have been able to describe the contents of my visual field.

In every perceptual situation, then, we know what appears to be the case, but this is not usually to be in a position to describe our experience. It may be true that we can be said to have sense-experiences in every perceptual situation (they are, no doubt, the *causes* of our inclinations to believe) but this is quite another matter from being aware of them, noticing them, being in a position to describe them, and nothing less than this can be involved in the claim of the sense-datum theory that it is our experience which we really perceive.

But can having experiences and being aware of them be clearly distinguished in this way? For having an experience is a mental event of the kind, it would be argued, the only direct evidence for whose existence is its presence in consciousness. One might distinguish two senses of 'awareness'. In the wider sense I am aware of any mental event that I am in any way conscious of. In the narrower sense I am only aware of what I notice or attend to, of what I am in a position to describe, of what, in fact, I have some statable knowledge of. Now it might be argued that one was aware of all experience in the wider sense and that this was sufficient reason for saying that all experience was really perceived. I do not think that this distinction can be maintained. It is not that we are really aware of a great many things which we do not notice or attend to but rather that we suppose ourselves to have a great deal of experience for whose existence we have little or no direct evidence. For ordinarily 'be aware of' and 'notice' are largely interchangeable. Both imply claims to knowledge. There are differences of nuance: to become aware of a smell of decay is to have it borne in upon one, to notice a smell of decay is to have discovered it. In implying claims to knowledge both words resemble the perceptual verbs 'see', 'hear', etc. One cannot be aware *of* something without knowing something about it, being aware *that* something is the case.

Now we are, perhaps, usually vaguely aware of the character of our experience, but far too indefinitely for the knowledge involved to support the complicated structure of beliefs that the sense-datum theory would erect on it. The faint and undetailed nature of this underlying awareness of experience is attested to by the fact that when asked to recall our experience we have more or less to reconstruct it from the objects perceived. We attend to experience often enough to know the sort of experiences normally associated with various kinds of object in various conditions. When we transfer our attention from objects to experience an enormously richer awareness of the latter is obtained. We then suppose that we were in fact having experiences of as complex and detailed a kind while attending to the objects, although we were unaware of the complexity and detail. This move is not inference supported by recollection, but a convention. It is assumed that, given unchanged objects, medium, and sense-organs, a change of attention brings about no change in the associated experiences. The idealist's problem 'does attention alter its object'? is thus a matter of convention not of fact. The convention described here lays down that it does not. By this a distinction is introduced between experiences which we have and which we are aware of. It gives a sense to the expression 'unnoticed experience'. One could equally well, if not better, opt for the other alternative and speak, not of 'unnoticed', but of 'possible' experiences, that is the experiences one would be aware of were one to adopt the phenomenological frame of mind. There is a close analogy with the problem of unsensed sense-data. Should we speak with Russell of 'sensibilia' or with Ayer of 'possible sense-data'? In each case considerations of continuity urge one convention, conceptual economy and epistemological rigour the other. In our problem continuity makes a stronger claim. For while there is a clear distinction between sensed and unsensed sense-data, there would seem to be an unbroken continuum of grades of awareness. At any rate to have an experience of which one is not aware is not so much an event as the possibility of an event, it is to be able, by appropriately directing one's attention, to become aware of an experience. The nature of these possibilities is discovered inductively. I conclude that, whether we decide to say we have experiences of which we are not aware or merely that we could have them, anything we can say about them or their possibility depends on the limited number we are aware of. It is only these, meagre or absent in most perceptual situations, which we can be said to perceive.

III

I have argued that experience cannot be the sole object of acquaintance since it is not the case that in every perceptual situation we are aware of it. If this argument is accepted it can be reinforced—if not replaced—by considering what is *meant* by saying that experience alone is the object of acquaintance. I shall first consider the view that this is so because only of experience can we have certain knowledge.

That statements about objects can never be certain (an elliptical way of saying that we can never know for certain that they are true) is sometimes affirmed on the ground that they are empirical. For it is an essential feature of empirical statements that they can be shown to be false and, it is argued, if a statement can be false there can be reasonable doubt of its truth. But if there can be reasonable doubt of its truth it cannot be certain. This argument has the notorious consequence that only necessary truths can be certain. This is not, as some have argued, merely inconvenient in assimilating one useful distinction to another, it is the outcome of a definite mistake. For it is not correct to say that a statement is certain only if there *can* be no reasonable doubt of its truth; a statement is certain, rather, if there *is* no reasonable doubt of its truth.

This familiar argument, in trying to prove that no empirical statement is certain, tries to prove too much. For, if it were correct, the supposed difference in epistemological status between objects and experiences could not consist in a difference in respect of certainty between the statements describing them. I shall consider two arguments designed to show that, in fact, there is always reasonable doubt about descriptions of objects. Both assert that descriptions of objects have implications which inevitably 'go beyond' or 'lie outside' the current observation.

The first holds that there is no limit to the set of other statements which follow from a given statement about objects. For at any time, however remote from the time to which the original statement refers, evidence will exist and could be obtained for or against it. If at any time there is no evidence, however tenuous, for or against it, it is then untestable and, therefore, without meaning. At any rate the possibility of evidence arising for any statement, however remote its reference, cannot be ruled out. So, it is argued, however much favourable evidence for the truth of a statement may have accumulated, it is always possible that all the evidence to come may point to and, in the end, enforce the opposite conclusion.

If, as I shall argue later, it is also the case that descriptions of experience can be revised, that there can be evidence for and against them distinct from the occurrence of the experience itself, then precisely the same argument can be applied to them and so no difference in epistemological status is established. In effect this argument comes to the same as the previous one; revision in the face of unfavourable evidence is as much a universal feature of empirical statements as falsifiability.

But, waiving this point for the moment, the argument is fallacious in concluding that statements with 'open consequences' are never certain. For if the statement of unfavourable evidence q is remote, in the way described, from the original statement p, then q alone will not entail the falsity of p but only in conjunction with some generalization or law of nature *r*. So *q* will only falsify or disconfirm *p* to the extent that *r* is accepted as true and applicable. It is not *p* and *q* simply that are incompatible but *p, q and r*. If *q* turns out to be true we are not therefore compelled to abandon *p*. The more remote *q* is from *p*, the more tenuous the connexion, the more we shall be inclined to abandon *r*. This critical point between abandoning *p* and abandoning *r* in face of *q* may be hard to locate, but for every statement it will exist and for every statement circumstances can be indicated in which its 'logical neighbourhood' is so densely populated with favourable evidence that no remote unfavourable evidence whatever would be taken as refuting it. So it does not follow from the fact that the set of a statement's consequences is open that there is always reasonable doubt of its truth.

The second argument about implications asserts that statements about objects are always and necessarily predictive, that they always logically imply something which the current observation is not sufficient to establish. A statement about objects always forms part of a system of beliefs of varying size, at least including assumptions about the normality—or controllable abnormality—of the conditions of observation. But this has no disastrous consequences. In the first place, no infinite regress is generated. The entailed consequences (or assumptions about the conditions of observation) are themselves statements about objects, but *their* entailed consequences (or conditions) will not all be distinct from the original statement. The implications do not fray off endlessly into the unknown, they are, rather, elements in finite, and indeed decently small, systems of mutual support. And in the second place, arising out of this, it is wrong to regard statements about objects as necessarily predictive under all circumstances. For it is perfectly possible to establish all the members of such a set of mutually supporting statements. Knowledge of the conditions of observation constitutes just such a framework which a statement about objects completes, supports and is supported by. I am not here going back on my earlier criticism of the coherence theory. These coherent sets of statements are not self-sufficient. For their members are conventionally correlated with observed situations. Loose talk about semantic or ostensive rules has ignored the indeterminacy of this correlation, the existence of slack in the application of statements about objects which the systems in which they figure take up.

In the normal course of events it is not that the entailed consequences or conditions are yet to be discovered but that they are known already. This 'systematic' character of our knowledge of objects does indeed distinguish it from our knowledge of experience, consistently with what has gone before since it is the logical correlate of the perceptual as against the phenomenological frame of mind. In the extreme, limiting case (waking up, etc.), where we have no knowledge of the conditions, all descriptions of objects are likely to be less than certain. But we are not usually in this unfortunate position and single observations can give us certain knowledge about objects.

Even if statements about objects were never certain this would not prove them to be derived from statements about experience, if being less than certain were not identified with being probable and if it were not held that nothing can be probable unless something else is certain.

The crucial error in these interconnected doctrines is the supposition that certainty and probability are exhaustive as well as mutually exclusive. Any assertion made with full confidence may be called certain but only one kind of assertion made with less than full confidence is called probable. 'It appears to be cloudy over there' is perfectly good, if weak, evidence for 'it will probably rain'. Yet the whole point of saying that it appears to be, rather than that it is, cloudy over there is to indicate lack of confidence, uncertainty. That is, a less than certain conclusion can be based on less than certain premises which are not themselves the result of inference. The word 'probably' qualifies assertions which are both tentatively advanced, held to be less than certain, and are the conclusions of inferences. This latter characteristic allows us always to challenge, to ask for the reasons for, a statement that something is probably the case and warrants the view that probability is always relative to evidence. But this evidence may itself be tentative and less than certain. To express just this 'uninferred' hesitancy is, as was shown earlier, the principal office of the words 'look', 'appear' and 'seem'. But can we describe experience in this way? The sole use we have for forms of words where these verbs are reiterated (it seems to look ϕ) is where neither verb is used to describe experience (I am inclined to think that most people would say it was ϕ). But this does not entail that phenomenological uses of these verbs cannot be tentative, that 'this looks to me, here, now, ϕ' must be certain. To modify these we use adverbial devices like 'roughly', 'more or less', 'sort of' or add the rider 'I think'. We avoid 'appear' and its kin because they suggest assignable reservations, that we realise or suspect something to be amiss with the conditions of observation or, in non-perceptual uses ('he appears to have died about 300 B.C.'), that we realise that better evidence could, in principle, be obtained. But there are no better conditions in which to describe our experiences than those in which they occur, no better evidence than that they occur. The corrigibility of a statement, in other words, does not entail that 'appear' and the rest apply to it; they apply only where assignable reservations are indicated.

Less than certain statements are not all probable; they are so only if they are the conclusions of inferences, and the premises of these inferences may be less than certain without themselves being inferred. They will be what appears to be the case if I can assign the reservations from which my tentativeness arises or what is, I think, roughly the case, if I cannot.

Finally we must consider a familiar argument against the view that all descriptions of experience are certain. A statement of fact must be expressed by a sentence containing a predicate, a general or descriptive word, and must, therefore, involve the classification of what it refers to, the discrimination of this from other things to which the predicate does not apply. Things, including experiences, do not confront us already sorted out, classified, discriminated. And like any other learnt, regular procedure classification can be carried out wrongly. The use of predicates in classifying and discriminating is essentially a matter of relating what we are describing to the things which are the standard for the application of the predicate, with which it is conventionally correlated, by which it is 'ostensively defined'.

For we can and do revise our descriptions of experience, however convinced we were of their correctness at the time we made them. Such revision could only be excluded by the presumption that recollected experiences, formerly described as ϕ, and now recalled as noticeably different from something else we want to call ϕ, must always be misrecollected. But our recollections have a credibility of their own which does not depend on what is recollected matching something which we now describe with the same predicate we applied to it. Not only can we revise past descriptions of experience, we can also be hesitant about present descriptions. Sometimes we can find no precedent for a perfectly distinct and definite but unique impression; sometimes, while inclined to give a certain description, there is some peculiarity in the situation which we cannot precisely identify and which makes us hesitate. There is a range of cases between these extremes of inadequate vocabulary and indistinct experience.

Against this view it is argued that the errors corrected by such a revision are merely *verbal*. 'All that one can properly mean . . . by saying that one doubts whether this (sense-datum) is green is that one is doubting whether "green" is the correct word to use.' (Ayer). But what else is one doubting when one doubts whether this *object* is green? There is a difference, of course, in that one can have another, better, look at the object but not at the sense-datum. But it does not follow from this that all mistakes that do not depend on unfavourable conditions of observation are not really mistakes at all. What, after all, is a 'merely verbal' error? Properly speaking, only mistaken expressions of belief due to slips of the tongue or pen or laziness and inattention. Linguistic incapacity, the source of mistaken descriptions of experience, is quite another matter. Professor Ayer has recently argued that experience is described 'not by relating it to anything else but by indicating that a certain word applies to it in virtue of a meaning-rule of the language'. The suggestion is that the application of meaning-rules is such a simple matter that it is impossible to perform it wrongly except by a slip. But meaning-rules do not have the bemusing simplicity of their 'semantic' formulation (the word 'red' applies to red things). The class of things to which a predicate applies is indeterminately bounded. Some blue things are more obviously blue than others. Again we are not equally and perfectly accomplished in the application of all predicates. We can manage 'red' and 'round' fairly well, but are less efficient with 'mauve' and 'rhomboidal'. Even if we were trained up to the highest pitch of descriptive efficiency with the predicates we do understand, it is wrong to imagine that that notoriously blunt instrument, our descriptive vocabulary, would provide a precisely appropriate caption for every situation, that it could deal exhaustively with the fecundity of experience. Behind this theory of semantic rules lurks a pair of metaphysical assumptions: that universals, in one-one correlation with predicates, are wide open to some kind of direct apprehension and that there is a decent limit to their variety. The implied analogy with the rules by means of which the truths of mathematics and logic are established is misleading. These rules are precise, definite and can be clearly stated and communicated; careful tests can be made of whether they have been employed correctly. No such laborious check of the correct employment of 'meaning-rules' is possible with the private, fluid and unstable constituents of our sense-experience.

Lack of clarity about the relation between the mere occurrence of an experience and its description has contributed to the view that we cannot, without lying or slips, misdescribe experience. Experience just happens. But being what it is we cannot help being aware of it. Yet it occurs in every perceptual situation. This confusion of the phenomenologically scrutinised with the more or less hypothetical unnoticed experience is responsible for the view that simply to have an experience is to know it for what it is. Those who have, consistently enough, denied that experience as such is properly speaking either a kind of knowledge or true or false at all, have avoided the confusion at the cost of abolishing their problem. For from mere events nothing can be logically derived; only from statements, from what can be known to be true, can other statements be inferred.

I conclude that statements about objects and about experience are sometimes certain, sometimes not. In this respect there is no sharp distinction between the two. Whether a description of objects is certain will depend largely on the circumstances in which it is given and what is known about them. Its familiarity and stability will no doubt determine whether a description of experience is certain. We can err about both from linguistic incapacity and the loose correlation of language and the world, about objects on account of unfavourable conditions of observation and about experiences (and occasionally objects) on account of their evanescence. Such difference as there is between the respective sources of error is not sufficient to substantiate a theory of acquaintance or to show one category to be logically prior to the other.

IV

Some philosophers, realising that certainty as a criterion of acquaintance or basic statements is not sufficient to distinguish objects and experience in the way the sense-datum theory requires, have proposed a different definition in terms of inference. On this view we know directly, by acquaintance, what we know without inference; basic statements are primitive, uninferred; and, while no descriptions of experience are inferred, all descriptions of objects are. The task of theory of knowledge, it is held, is to make a rational reconstruction of our knowledge of matters of fact in which the uninferred premises from which alone this knowledge can be validly derived are explicitly set out. It is agreed that we are rarely, if ever, conscious of carrying out these inferences. It is thought, nevertheless, that experiential premises must somehow 'underlie' what we believe about objects.

If this account is correct two conditions must be satisfied. Statements about experiences must count as reasons or evidence for statements about objects and they must in some, no doubt rather obscure, sense be accepted by those who make statements about objects. This second, seemingly platitudinous, requirement deserves emphasis. A fact cannot be a man's reason or evidence for an assertion unless, however implicitly, he is aware of it. Someone's implicit or unconscious awareness of facts about objects can be established by observation of his behaviour. But there is no such criterion available for detecting his awareness of his experience. The view, mistaken as I have argued, that we cannot help being aware of our experience no doubt explains why it has not been thought necessary to provide any criterion for the occurrence of this supposed awareness. If my argument against the view that in every perceptual situation we are aware of our own experience is accepted, it follows that the second condition of the inference theory is unsatisfied and that the theory is mistaken. For our experiences could only be our reasons or evidence for our beliefs about objects if we were to become aware of them through adopting a completely different, phenomenological, frame of mind in our traffic with the external world. Like any other facts, facts about experience must be discovered before they can be appealed to. But even if my argument on this is not accepted, the inference theory is mistaken since the first condition mentioned is not satisfied either.

The best proof that statements about experience were reasons or evidence for statements about objects would be that we did in fact commonly infer from the one to the other. This, however, is admittedly not the case. But, as it stands, this is of little importance. In the first place, the psychological criterion involved is exceedingly vague, seeming to do no more than mark off as cases of inference those in which a thoughtful pause supervenes between observation and announcement. Furthermore, there are many cases, unquestionably of knowledge by inference, where it is not in the least likely that any conscious process of reasoning has taken place. A girl, sitting in the drawing-room, hears the front door slam and says 'Father's home'. I hear a pattering on the roof and say 'it's raining'. I see a small pool on the kitchen floor and say 'the dog has misbehaved'. We only infer consciously in situations that are unfamiliar or complex, in the predicament of the weekend guest or the new boy on the first day of term. The detective, the busybody, the scientist are more or less professionally concerned to make the most of a small stock of data. Conscious, deliberate thinking is both exhausting and infrequent, a last resort to be appealed to only when all habitual capacities have failed. But most of our perceptual knowledge is of familiar states of affairs and acquired in familiar conditions.

That a statement is employed as a premise in a conscious process of reasoning is not the only feature of our use of that statement which shows it to count as a reason or evidence for the conclusion. More fundamental surely, is that we *give* it as our reason when challenged on the other.

Consider these five cases. I can at once reproduce the course of reasoning that led me to say that it is Mother's hat on top of the garage. This is conscious inference, where the reason given is a premise already consciously affirmed. Secondly, I can, without hesitation, answer 'by the way he sways about' when asked how I can tell someone is drunk, although I recollect no process of inferring. Thirdly, I may take some time over or require assistance in accounting for my claim that Towzer is ill by the glazed look in his eye. Fourthly, I may be unable to give any reason of my own and unwilling to accept any reason offered by another for my assertion that X dislikes Y. Yet commonly in this type of case I may be sure a reason does exist for my belief, may be extremely confident of the truth of my belief and turn out, in the end, to be quite right. Finally, consider standing in broad daylight three feet away from a large and perfectly normal chestnut cart-horse and saying 'that is a horse' or, more adventurously, 'that horse is brown'. This resembles the previous case in that one would be quite unable to give or accept any reason whatever for one's assertion. It differs from it in that one would not be in the very least abashed or apologetic about this. For, in these conditions, the challenge 'how can you tell?' is simply devoid of sense.

Still, if it were made, one might perhaps answer 'well, because it looks like a horse'. If this were intended as a description of one's experience, as interchangeable with 'there is now a shiny brown patch of a characteristic shape in the centre of my visual field', it would not be to answer the question but rather to change the subject, perhaps to offer a causal explanation of one's belief. But this interpretation proposed by the sense-datum theory, a wildly unnatural interpretation of what is, in the circumstances, a wildly unnatural remark, is surely mistaken. The statement would more naturally be intended and understood as a modification of, an infusion of tentativeness into, the original claim, expressing a lack of confidence inspired by the nagging question. As such it is not a reason. To repeat oneself in a more cautious way is not to substantiate but merely to attenuate one's original assertion. 'It looks like a horse' resembles 'it is probably a horse' or 'I think it's a horse' and not 'it has thick legs and no horns' which might be advanced to support the claim that some comparatively distant animal was a horse. For there are, of course, plenty of situations in which reasons do exist for statements about objects.

A statement cannot be inferred, then, if no reason or evidence for it exists, or, more exactly, if it does not make sense to ask for or give a reason for it. Whether or not it does make sense to ask for a reason depends on the circumstances in which the statement is made. The sentence, the form of words, 'that is a horse', may be used in an enormous variety of circumstances. In some of these it will make sense to ask 'how can you tell', in others not. The latter may be called the standard conditions of its use. It will be in such circumstances that the use of the sentence will normally be learnt. This accomplished, it will be possible to use it in an increasingly adventurous way in increasingly non-standard conditions. Connexions are established between assertions and their reasons through the discovery of a vast array of factual concomitances. That standard conditions are those in which we learn how to use a sentence helps to explain why the statements they are used to make are basic and uninferred. For in these conditions they are directly correlated with an observable situation, they are not introduced by means of other statements. (This explains 'implicit inference'. I implicitly infer, acknowledge a reason for, a statement if I was introduced to it by means of other statements but can now make it without conscious consideration of them.) For some sentences there are no standard conditions (generalizations or such implicitly general sentences as 'she is naturally shy'). With others the nature of their standard conditions may vary from person to person. A wife will be able to tell at once that her husband is depressed where others have no inkling of the fact. (A difference in capacity that leads us to speak of intuition.) Again prolonged success in a certain nonstandard use of a sentence may lead us to incorporate the conditions of this use into the standard. I say 'it is raining' when I cannot actually see the rain falling but only drops of water bouncing off the wet street. The addition of unwillingness to inability to answer the question 'how can you tell?' shows that these conditions have become standard. Standard conditions are those in which we have a right to feel certain of the truth of an assertion. The suggestion of uncertainty conveyed by the protest 'that's only an inference' would be made more obviously by the equivalent protest 'you are in no position to be sure' (*i.e.* 'these are not standard conditions'.) The lawyer, who asks for a description of what one *actually* saw, devoid of inference and conjecture, is asking for a standard description, that is, a description for which the conditions one was then in were standard.

The notions of acquaintance and of the basic statements which it warrants have, therefore, a foundation in our ordinary way of thinking and speaking. The failure to locate them in their right place is due in part to the failure to distinguish between sentences and statements. For because of multiplicity of uses there are no 'basic sentences'. What we know for certain and without inference in any situation is what the circumstances we are in are the standard conditions for. This will normally be a statement about objects. But there are circumstances in which, knowing nothing about the conditions or that they are highly abnormal, we can take no description of objects as standard. In such a situation we can do no more than tentatively say what appears to be the case. If we are not prepared to do this we can, by an appropriate shift of attention, describe our experience. This last-ditch feature of statements about experience is another encouragement to the sense-datum theorist.

More important is the fact that standard conditions are not a perfect guarantee of the truth of a statement made in them. For standard conditions do not involve that all of a statement's entailed consequences have been established. The horse in the example may just possibly be a brilliantly contrived deception, a flat painted board. We could make our standard stringent enough to cater for this, by insisting on the establishment of entailed consequences, without abandoning statements about objects as basic. But it would be laborious and inconvenient to do so. The programme of convenience embodied in our actual standards is abetted by the order of nature which is uniform enough to make the risks of standard description negligible. Our standards depend on contingencies but some contingencies are highly reliable and regular. Error, as Descartes pointed out, is a product of the will rather than the understanding and arises almost entirely with nonstandard descriptions.

This minute residual imperfection is the ultimate source of the sense-datum theory. The metaphysical demand behind the theory is for an infallible basis for knowledge. So a new standard is proposed which is thought to be perfect. The justification of the new standard is that the knowledge of conditions required is always available, conditions are always standard for the description of experience. I have argued that we are not, in fact, always in standard conditions for the description of experience but rather that it is always in our power, by an appropriate shift of attention, to produce such conditions. If this is so, the sense-datum theory can be no more than the proposal of a new and exceedingly cumbrous way of thinking and speaking to be adopted from fear of a very minor risk. But whether it is true or not, whether the sense-datum theory is a proposal or, what it claims to be, an account of what actually occurs, the supposed improvement is illusory. For, in taking steps to set one exaggerated doubt at rest, it provides the opportunity for another to arise. Admittedly descriptions of experience, for which conditions are always standard, do not depend on a knowledge of conditions which may not be forthcoming. But they have weaknesses of their own. The objects we describe are largely stable and persistent; if we are unsure about them we can always look again. But experience is fleeting and momentary; to attend to it again is to make the insecure hypothesis that it has not changed. The systematic, mutually corroborative character of our beliefs about objects is not a weakness but a strength. Similarly the atomic, disconnected character of experiences, which has encouraged the view that they are self-describing entities, is a weakness. I conclude, then, that experiences are not only not in fact the basis of our empirical knowledge but that they would be inferior to the basis we have, since we are just as much open to error about them, though not entirely the same way; and we should have to revise our way of thinking and speaking completely to use them as a basis.

The relation between experiences and objects, then, neither is nor should be logical. On the contrary it is causal, a matter of psychological fact. Our beliefs about objects are based on experience in a way that requires not justification but explanation. Experiences are not *my* reasons for my beliefs about objects—to have an experience is not to know or believe anything which could be a reason in this sense—though they may be *the* reasons for my believing what I do from the point of view of the psychologist. They may, that is, be the causes of my beliefs and explain them. But they could only be my reasons for my beliefs about objects if I already knew something independently about the relations between experiences and objects.

We learn, it is said, to interpret our experiences, to give rein to Hume's principle of the imagination, to apply Kant's schematized category of substance. These forms of words at least point out that perception is an intelligent activity (not an infallible reflex), but they point it out so uncompromisingly that it is overintellectualised. Interpreting experiences suggests literary scholarship or detective work. But not all intellectual processes are types of reasoning. These phrases refer to the psychological preconditions of recognizing objects for what they are. They point out that we must learn to use the language we do use, that this is an exercise of skill not an automatism and, further, that the situations in which any one sentence may be correctly uttered are extremely various. But they do not demand and could not evoke any logical justification of our practice of thinking and speaking of a common world of objects. We cannot set out the logical relation of an assertion about objects with the experiences that occasion it, because there is no such relation. This is not to sever language from the world altogether, the sin of the coherence theory. It is simply to say that the relations that obtain within the body of our knowledge do not also connect it with what is outside.

I have considered the three principal methods of establishing the sense-datum theory: the arguments from illusion, certainty and inference. Those who hold statements about experience to be basic have misconstrued all three. Statements about experience are not known in every perceptual situation, for we cannot know what we are not aware of, they are no more certain than statements about objects and they do not differ from all statements about objects in being uninferred. Doctrines about acquaintance and basic statements are the outcome of a search for perfect standard conditions. But no standard conditions are perfect and there is no reason to say that descriptions of experience are or ought to be our standard. Our empirical knowledge already has a basis and as good a one as we can obtain. It is to be found, as we should expect, in those situations in which the use of our language is taught and learnt.

ON OUR KNOWLEDGE OF SYNTHETIC *A PRIORI* JUDGMENTS

IMMANUEL KANT

I. THE DISTINCTION BETWEEN PURE AND EMPIRICAL KNOWLEDGE

There can be no doubt that all our knowledge begins with experience. For how should our faculty of knowledge be awakened into action did not objects affecting our senses partly of themselves produce representations, partly arouse the activity of our understanding to compare these representations, and, by combining or separating them, work up the raw material of the sensible impressions into that knowledge of objects which is entitled experience? In the order of time, therefore, we have no knowledge antecedent to experience, and with experience all our knowledge begins.

But though all our knowledge begins with experience, it does not follow that it all arises out of experience. For it may well be that even our empirical knowledge is made up of what we receive through impressions and of what our own faculty of knowledge (sensible impressions serving merely as the occasion) supplies from itself. If our faculty of knowledge makes any such addition, it may be that we are not in a position to distinguish it from the raw material, until with long practice of attention we have become skilled in separating it.

This, then, is a question which at least calls for closer examination, and does not allow of any off-hand answer:—whether there is any knowledge that is thus independent of experience and even of all impressions of the senses. Such knowledge is entitled *a priori*, and distinguished from the *empirical*, which has its sources *a posteriori*, that is, in experience.

The expression '*a priori*' does not, however, indicate with sufficient precision the full meaning of our question. For it has been customary to say, even of much knowledge that is derived from empirical sources, that we have it or are capable of having it *a priori*, meaning thereby that we do not derive it immediately from experience, but from a universal rule—a rule which is itself, however, borrowed by us from experience. Thus we would say of a man who undermined the foundations of his house,

This selection consists of the first six sections of the introduction to the second edition of Kant's *Critique of Pure Reason*, first published in 1781, translated by Norman Kemp Smith. It is used by permission of Macmillan & Co., Ltd., London, and St. Martin's Press, New York.

that he might have known *a priori* that it would fall, that is, that he need not have waited for the experience of its actual falling. But still he could not know this completely *a priori*. For he had first to learn through experience that bodies are heavy, and therefore fall when their supports are withdrawn.

In what follows, therefore, we shall understand by *a priori* knowledge, not knowledge independent of this or that experience, but knowledge absolutely independent of all experience. Opposed to it is empirical knowledge, which is knowledge possible only *a posteriori*, that is, through experience. *A priori* modes of knowledge are entitled pure when there is no admixture of anything empirical. Thus, for instance, the proposition, 'every alteration has its cause', while an *a priori* proposition, is not a pure proposition, because alteration is a concept which can be derived only from experience.

II. We are in Possession of Certain Modes of a priori *Knowledge, and Even the Common Understanding is Never Without Them*

What we here require is a criterion by which to distinguish with certainty between pure and empirical knowledge. Experience teaches us that a thing is so and so, but not that it cannot be otherwise. First, then, if we have a proposition which in being thought is thought as *necessary*, it is an *a priori* judgment; and if, besides, it is not derived from any proposition except one which also has the validity of a necessary judgment, it is an absolutely *a priori* judgment. Secondly, experience never confers on its judgments true or strict, but only assumed and comparative *universality*, through induction. We can properly only say, therefore, that, so far as we have hitherto observed, there is no exception to this or that rule. If, then, a judgment is thought with strict universality, that is, in such manner that no exception is allowed as possible, it is not derived from experience, but is valid absolutely *a priori*. Empirical universality is only an arbitrary extension of a validity holding in most cases to one which holds in all, for instance, in the proposition, 'all bodies are heavy'. When, on the other hand, strict universality is essential to a judgment, this indicates a special source of knowledge, namely, a faculty of *a priori* knowledge. Necessity and strict universality are thus sure criteria of *a priori* knowledge, and are inseparable from one another. But since in the employment of these criteria the contingency of judgments is sometimes more easily shown than their empirical limitation, or, as sometimes also happens, their unlimited universality can be more convincingly proved than their necessity, it is advisable to use the two criteria separately, each by itself being infallible.

Now it is easy to show that there actually are in human knowledge judgments which are necessary and in the strictest sense universal, and which are therefore pure *a priori* judgments. If an example from the sciences be desired, we have only to look to any of the propositions of mathematics; if we seek an example from the understanding in its quite ordinary employment, the proposition, 'every alteration must have a cause', will serve our purpose. In the latter case, indeed, the very concept of a cause so manifestly contains the concept of a necessity of connection with an effect and of the strict universality of the rule, that the concept would be altogether lost if we attempted to derive it, as Hume has done, from a repeated association of that which happens with that which precedes, and from a custom of connecting representations, a custom originating in this repeated association, and constituting therefore a merely subjective necessity. Even without appealing to such examples, it is possible to show that pure *a priori* principles are indispensable for the possibility of experience, and so to prove their existence *a priori*. For whence could experience derive its certainty, if all the rules, according to which it proceeds, were always themselves empirical, and therefore contingent? Such rules could hardly be regarded as first principles. At present, however, we may be content to have established the fact that our faculty of knowledge does have a pure employment, and to have shown what are the criteria of such an employment.

Such *a priori* origin is manifest in certain concepts, no less than in judgments. If we remove from our empirical concept of a body, one by one, every feature in it which is [merely] empirical, the colour, the hardness or softness, the weight, even the impenetrability, there still remains the space which the body (now entirely vanished) occupied, and this cannot be removed. Again, if we remove from our empirical concept of any object, corporeal or incorporeal, all properties which experience has taught us, we yet cannot take away that property through which the object is thought as substance or as inhering in a substance (although this concept of substance is more determinate than that of an object in general). Owing, therefore, to the necessity with which this concept of substance forces itself upon us, we have no option save to admit that it has its seat in our faculty of *a priori* knowledge.

III. PHILOSOPHY STANDS IN NEED OF A SCIENCE WHICH SHALL DETERMINE THE POSSIBILITY, THE PRINCIPLES, AND THE EXTENT OF ALL A PRIORI *KNOWLEDGE*

But what is still more extraordinary than all the preceding is this, that certain modes of knowledge leave the field of all possible experiences and have the appearance of extending the scope of our judgments beyond all limits of experience, and this by means of concepts to which no corresponding object can ever be given in experience.

It is precisely by means of the latter modes of knowledge, in a realm beyond the world of the senses, where experience can yield neither guidance nor correction, that our reason carries on those enquiries which owing to their importance we consider to be far more excellent, and in their purpose far more lofty, than all that the understanding can learn in the field of appearances. Indeed we prefer to run every risk of error rather than desist from such urgent enquiries, on the ground of their dubious character, or from disdain and indifference. These unavoidable problems set by pure reason itself are *God*, *freedom*, and *immortality*. The science which, with all its preparations, is in its final intention directed solely to their solution is metaphysics; and its procedure is at first dogmatic, that is, it confidently sets itself to this task without any previous examination of the capacity or incapacity of reason for so great an undertaking.

Now it does indeed seem natural that, as soon as we have left the ground of experience, we should, through careful enquiries, assure ourselves as to the foundations of any building that we propose to erect, not making use of any knowledge that we possess without first determining whence it has come, and not trusting to principles without knowing their origin. It is natural, that is to say, that the question should first be considered, how the understanding can arrive at all this knowledge *a priori*, and what extent, validity, and worth it may have. Nothing, indeed, could be more natural, if by the term 'natural' we signify what fittingly and reasonably ought to happen. But if we mean by 'natural' what ordinarily happens, then on the contrary nothing is more natural and more intelligible than the fact that this enquiry has been so long neglected. For one part of this knowledge, the mathematical, has long been of established reliability, and so gives rise to a favourable presumption as regards the other part, which may yet be of quite different nature. Besides, once we are outside the circle of experience, we can be sure of not being *contradicted* by experience. The charm of extending our knowledge is so great that nothing short of encountering a direct contradiction can suffice to arrest us in our course; and this can be avoided, if we are careful in our fabrications—which none the less will still remain fabrications. Mathematics gives us a shining example of how far, independently of experience, we can progress in *a priori* knowledge. It does, indeed, occupy itself with objects and with knowledge solely in so far as they allow of being exhibited in intuition. But this circumstance is easily overlooked, since this intuition can itself be given *a priori*, and is therefore hardly to be distinguished from a bare and pure concept. Misled by such a proof of the power of reason, the demand for the extension of knowledge recognises no limits. The light dove, cleaving the air in her free flight, and feeling its resistance, might imagine that its flight would be still easier in empty space. It was thus that Plato left the world of the senses, as setting too narrow limits to the understanding, and ventured out beyond it on the wings of the ideas, in the empty space of the pure understanding. He did not observe that with all his efforts he made no advance—meeting no resistance that might, as it were, serve as a support upon which he could take a stand, to which he could apply his powers, and so set his understanding in motion. It is, indeed, the common fate of human reason to complete its speculative structures as speedily as may be, and only afterwards to enquire whether the foundations are reliable. All sorts of excuses will then be appealed to, in order to reassure us of their solidity, or rather indeed to enable us to dispense altogether with so late and so dangerous an enquiry. But what keeps us, during the actual building, free from all apprehension and suspicion, and flatters us with a seeming thoroughness, is this other circumstance, namely, that a great, perhaps the greatest, part of the business of our reason consists in analysis of the concepts which we already have of objects. This analysis supplies us with a considerable body of knowledge, which, while nothing but explanation or elucidation of what has already been thought in our concepts, though in a confused manner, is yet prized as being, at least as regards its form, new insight. But so far as the matter or content is concerned, there has been no extension of our previously possessed concepts, but only an analysis of them. Since this procedure yields real knowledge *a priori*, which progresses in an assured and useful fashion, reason is so far misled as surreptitiously to introduce, without itself being aware of so doing, assertions of an entirely different order, in which it attaches to given concepts others completely foreign to them, and moreover attaches them *a priori*. And yet is is not known how reason can be in position to do this. Such a question is never so much as thought of. I shall therefore at once proceed to deal with the difference between these two kinds of knowledge.

IV. THE DISTINCTION BETWEEN ANALYTIC AND SYNTHETIC JUDGMENTS

In all judgments in which the relation of a subject to the predicate is thought (I take into consideration affirmative judgments only, the subsequent application to negative judgments being easily made), this relation is possible in two different ways. Either the predicate B belongs to the subject A, as something which is (covertly) contained in this concept A; or B lies outside the concept A, although it does indeed stand in connection with it. In the one case I entitle the judgment analytic, in the other synthetic. Analytic judgments (affirmative) are therefore those in which the connection of the predicate with the subject is thought through identity; those in which this connection is thought without identity should be entitled synthetic. The former, as adding nothing through the predicate to the concept of the subject, but merely breaking it up into those constituent concepts that have all along been thought in it, although confusedly, can also be entitled explicative. The latter, on the other hand, add to the concept of the subject a predicate which has not been in any wise thought in it, and which no analysis could possibly extract from it; and they may therefore be entitled ampliative. If I say, for instance, 'All bodies are extended', this is an analytic judgment. For I do not require to go beyond the concept which I connect with 'body' in order to find extension as bound up with it. To meet with this predicate, I have merely to analyse the concept, that is, to become conscious to myself of the manifold which I always think in that concept. The judgment is therefore analytic. But when I say, 'All bodies are heavy', the predicate is something quite different from anything that I think in the mere concept of body in general; and the addition of such a predicate therefore yields a synthetic judgment.

Judgments of experience, as such, are one and all synthetic. For it would be absurd to found an analytic judgment on experience. Since, in framing the judgment, I must not go outside my concept, there is no need to appeal to the testimony of experience in its support. That a body is extended is a proposition that holds *a priori* and is not empirical. For, before appealing to experience, I have already in the concept of body all the conditions required for my judgment. I have only to extract from it, in accordance with the principle of contradiction, the required predicate, and in so doing can at the same time become conscious of the necessity of the judgment—and that is what experience could never have taught me. On the other hand, though I do not include in the concept of a body in general the predicate 'weight', none the less this concept indicates an object of experience through one of its parts, and I can add to that part other parts of this same experience, as in this way belonging together with the concept. From the start I can apprehend the concept of body analytically through the characters of extension, impenetrability, figure, etc., all of which are thought in the concept. Now, however, looking back on the experience from which I have derived this concept of body, and finding weight to be invariably connected with the above characters, I attach it as a predicate to the concept; and in doing so I attach it synthetically, and am therefore extending my knowledge. The possibility of the synthesis of the predicate 'weight' with the concept of 'body' thus rests upon experience. While the one concept is not contained in the other, they yet belong to one another, though only contingently, as parts of a whole, namely, of an experience which is itself a synthetic combination of intuitions.

But in *a priori* synthetic judgments this help is entirely lacking. [I do not here have the advantage of looking around in the field of experience.] Upon what, then, am I to rely, when I seek to go beyond the concept A, and to know that another concept B is connected with it? Through what is the synthesis made possible? Let us take the proposition, 'Everything which happens has its cause'. In the concept of 'something which happens', I do indeed think an existence which is preceded by a time, etc., and from this concept analytic judgments may be obtained. But the concept of a 'cause' lies entirely outside the other concept, and signifies something different from 'that which happens', and is not therefore in any way contained in this latter representation. How come I then to predicate of that which happens something quite different, and to apprehend that the concept of cause, though not contained in it, yet belongs, and indeed necessarily belongs, to it? What is here the unknown = X which gives support to the understanding when it believes that it can discover outside the concept A a predicate B foreign to this concept, which it yet at the same time considers to be connected with it? It cannot be experience, because the suggested principle has connected the second representation with the first, not only with greater universality, but also with the character of necessity, and therefore completely *a priori* and on the basis of mere concepts. Upon such synthetic, that is, ampliative principles, all our *a priori* speculative knowledge must ultimately rest; analytic judgments are very important, and indeed necessary, but only for obtaining that clearness in the concepts which is requisite for such a sure and wide synthesis as will lead to a genuinely new addition to all previous knowledge.

V. IN ALL THEORETICAL SCIENCES OF REASON SYNTHETIC A PRIORI *JUDGMENTS ARE CONTAINED AS PRINCIPLES*

1. *All mathematical judgments, without exception, are synthetic.* This fact, though incontestably certain and in its consequences very important, has hitherto escaped the notice of those who are engaged in the analysis of human reason, and is, indeed, directly opposed to all their conjectures. For as it was found that all mathematical inferences proceed in accordance with the principle of contradiction (which the nature of all apodeictic certainty requires), it was supposed that the fundamental propositions of the science can themselves be known to be true through that principle. This is an erroneous view. For though a synthetic proposition can indeed be discerned in accordance with the principle of contradiction, this can only be if another synthetic proposition is presupposed, and if it can then be apprehended as following from this other proposition; it can never be so discerned in and by itself.

First of all, it has to be noted that mathematical propositions, strictly so called, are always judgments *a priori*, not empirical; because they carry with them necessity, which cannot be derived from experience. If this be demurred to, I am willing to limit my statement to *pure* mathematics, the very concept of which implies that it does not contain empirical, but only pure *a priori* knowledge.

We might, indeed, at first suppose that the proposition $7 + 5 = 12$ is a merely analytic proposition, and follows by the principle of contradiction from the concept of a sum of 7 and 5. But if we look more closely we find that the concept of the sum of 7 and 5 contains nothing save the union of the two numbers into one, and in this no thought is being taken as to what that single number may be which combines both. The concept of 12 is by no means already thought in merely thinking this union of 7 and 5; and I may analyse my concept of such a possible sum as long as I please, still I shall never find the 12 in it. We have to go outside these concepts, and call in the aid of the intuition which corresponds to one of them, our five fingers, for instance, or, as Segner does in his *Arithmetic*, five points, adding to the concept of 7, unit by unit, the five given in intuition. For starting with the number 7, and for the concept of 5 calling in the aid of the fingers of my hand as intuition, I now add one by one to the number 7 the units which I previously took together to form the number 5, and with the aid of that figure [the hand] see the number 12 come into being. That 5 should be added to 7, I have indeed already thought in the concept of a sum = 7 + 5, but not that this sum is equivalent to the number 12. Arithmetical propositions are therefore always synthetic. This is still more evident if we take larger numbers. For it is then obvious that, however we might turn and twist our concepts, we could never, by the mere analysis of them, and without the aid of intuition discover what [the number is that] is the sum.

Just as little is any fundamental proposition of pure geometry analytic. That the straight line between two points is the shortest, is a synthetic proposition. For my concept of *straight* contains nothing of quantity, but only of quality. The concept of the shortest is wholly an addition, and cannot be derived, through any process of analysis, from the concept of the straight line. Intuition, therefore, must here be called in; only by its aid is the synthesis possible. What here causes us commonly to believe that the predicate of such apodeictic judgments is already contained in our concept, and that the judgment is therefore analytic, is merely the ambiguous character of the terms used. We are required to join in thought a certain predicate to a given concept, and this necessity is inherent in the concepts themselves. But the question is not what we *ought* to join in thought to the given concept, but what we *actually* think in it, even if only obscurely; and it is then manifest that, while the predicate is indeed attached necessarily to the concept, it is so in virtue of an intuition which must be added to the concept, not as thought in the concept itself.

Some few fundamental propositions, presupposed by the geometrician, are, indeed, really analytic, and rest on the principle of contradiction. But, as identical propositions, they serve only as links in the chain of method and not as principles; for instance, $a = a$; the whole is equal to itself; or $(a + b) > a$, that is, the whole is greater than its part. And even these propositions, though they are valid according to pure concepts, are only admitted in mathematics because they can be exhibited in intuition.

2. *Natural science (physics) contains* a priori *synthetic judgments as principles*. I need cite only two such judgments: that in all changes of the material world the quantity of matter remains unchanged; and that in all communication of motion, action and reaction must always be equal. Both propositions, it is evident, are not only necessary, and therefore in their origin *a priori*, but also synthetic. For in the concept of matter I do

not think its permanence, but only its presence in the space which it occupies. I go outside and beyond the concept of matter, joining to it *a priori* in thought something which I have not thought *in* it. The proposition is not, therefore, analytic, but synthetic, and yet is thought *a priori*; and so likewise are the other propositions of the pure part of natural science.

3. *Metaphysics*, even if we look upon it as having hitherto failed in all its endeavours, is yet, owing to the nature of human reason, a quite indispensable science, and *ought to contain* a priori *synthetic knowledge*. For its business is not merely to analyse concepts which we make for ourselves *a priori* of things, and thereby to clarify them analytically, but to extend our *a priori* knowledge. And for this purpose we must employ principles which add to the given concept something that was not contained in it, and through *a priori* synthetic judgments venture out so far that experience is quite unable to follow us, as, for instance, in the proposition, that the world must have a first beginning, and such like. Thus metaphysics consists, at least *in intention*, entirely of *a priori* synthetic propositions.

VI. THE GENERAL PROBLEM OF PURE REASON

Much is already gained if we can bring a number of investigations under the formula of a single problem. For we not only lighten our own task, by defining it accurately, but make it easier for others, who would test our results, to judge whether or not we have succeeded in what we set out to do. Now the proper problem of pure reason is contained in the question: How are *a priori* synthetic judgments possible?

That metaphysics has hitherto remained in so vacillating a state of uncertainty and contradiction, is entirely due to the fact that this problem, and perhaps even the distinction between analytic and synthetic judgments, has never previously been considered. Upon the solution of this problem, or upon a sufficient proof that the possibility which it desires to have explained does in fact not exist at all, depends the success or failure of metaphysics. Among philosophers, David Hume came nearest to envisaging this problem, but still was very far from conceiving it with sufficient definiteness and universality. He occupied himself exclusively with the synthetic proposition regarding the connection of an effect with its cause (*principium causalitatis*), and he believed himself to have shown that such an *a priori* proposition is entirely impossible. If we accept his conclusions, then all that we call metaphysics is a mere delusion whereby we fancy ourselves to have rational insight into what, in actual fact, is borrowed solely from experience, and under the influence of custom has taken the illusory semblance of necessity. If he had envisaged our problem in all its universality, he would never have been guilty of this statement, so destructive of all pure philosophy. For he would then have recognised that, according to his own argument, pure mathematics, as certainly containing *a priori* synthetic propositions, would also not be possible; and from such an assertion his good sense would have saved him.

In the solution of the above problem, we are at the same time deciding as to the possibility of the employment of pure reason in establishing and developing all those sciences which contain a theoretical *a priori* knowledge of objects, and have therefore to answer the questions:

How is pure mathematics possible?
How is pure science of nature possible?

Since these sciences actually exist, it is quite proper to ask *how* they are possible; for that they must be possible is proved by the fact that they exist.* But the poor progress which has hitherto been made in metaphysics, and the fact that no system yet propounded can, in view of the essential purpose of metaphysics, be said really to exist, leaves everyone sufficient ground for doubting as to its possibility.

Yet, in a certain sense, this *kind of knowledge* is to be looked upon as given; that is to say, metaphysics actually exists, if not as a science, yet still as natural disposition (*metaphysica naturalis*). For human reason, without being moved merely by the idle desire for extent and variety of knowledge, proceeds impetuously, driven on by an inward need, to questions such as cannot be answered by any empirical employment of reason, or by principles thence derived. Thus in all men, as soon as their reason has become ripe for speculation, there has always existed and will always continue to exist some kind of metaphysics. And so we have the question:

How is metaphysics, as natural disposition, possible?

that is, how from the nature of universal human reason do those questions arise which pure reason propounds to itself, and which it is impelled by its own need to answer as best it can?

But since all attempts which have hitherto been made to answer these natural questions—for instance, whether the world has a beginning or is from eternity—have always met with unavoidable contradictions, we cannot rest satisfied with the mere natural disposition to metaphysics, that is, with the pure faculty of reason itself, from which, indeed, some sort of metaphysics (be it what it may) always arises. It must be possible for reason to attain to certainty whether we know or do not know the objects of metaphysics, that is, to come to a decision either in regard to the objects of its enquiries or in regard to the capacity or incapacity of

* Many may still have doubts as regards pure natural science. We have only, however, to consider the various propositions that are to be found at the beginning of (empirical) physics, properly so-called, those, for instance, relating to the permanence in the quantity of matter, to inertia, to the equality of action and reaction, etc., in order to be soon convinced that they constitute a *physica pura*, or *rationalis*, which well deserves, as an independent science, to be separately dealt with in its whole extent, be that narrow or wide.

reason to pass any judgment upon them, so that we may either with confidence extend our pure reason or set to it sure and determinate limits. This last question, which arises out of the previous general problem, may, rightly stated, take the form:

How is metaphysics, as science, possible?

Thus the critique of reason, in the end, necessarily leads to scientific knowledge; while its dogmatic employment, on the other hand, lands us in dogmatic assertions to which other assertions, equally specious, can always be opposed—that is, in *scepticism.*

This science cannot be of any very formidable prolixity, since it has to deal not with the objects of reason, the variety of which is inexhaustible, but only with itself and the problems which arise entirely from within itself, and which are imposed upon it by its own nature, not by the nature of things which are distinct from it. When once reason has learnt completely to understand its own power in respect of objects which can be presented to it in experience, it should easily be able to determine, with completeness and certainty, the extent and the limits of its attempted employment beyond the bounds of all experience.

We may, then, and indeed we must, regard as abortive all attempts, hitherto made, to establish a metaphysic *dogmatically*. For the analytic part in any such attempted system, namely, the mere analysis of the concepts that inhere in our reason *a priori,* is by no means the aim of, but only a preparation for, metaphysics proper, that is, the extension of its *a priori* synthetic knowledge. For such a purpose, the analysis of concepts is useless, since it merely shows what is contained in these concepts, not how we arrive at them *a priori.* A solution of this latter problem is required, that we may be able to determine the valid employment of such concepts in regard to the objects of all knowledge in general. Nor is much self-denial needed to give up these claims, seeing that the undeniable, and in the dogmatic procedure of reason also unavoidable, contradictions of reason with itself have long since undermined the authority of every metaphysical system yet propounded. Greater firmness will be required if we are not to be deterred by inward difficulties and outward opposition from endeavouring, through application of a method entirely different from any hitherto employed, at last to bring to a prosperous and fruitful growth a science indispensable to human reason—a science whose every branch may be cut away but whose root cannot be destroyed.

AN EMPIRICAL THEORY OF MATHEMATICAL TRUTHS

JOHN STUART MILL

If, as laid down in the two preceding chapters, the foundation of all sciences, even deductive or demonstrative sciences, is induction, if every step in the ratiocinations even of geometry is an act of induction, and if a train of reasoning is but bringing many inductions to bear upon the same subject of inquiry and drawing a case within one induction by means of another, wherein lies the peculiar certainty always ascribed to the sciences which are entirely, or almost entirely, deductive? Why are they called the exact sciences? Why are mathematical certainty and the evidence of demonstration common phrases to express the very highest degree of assurance attainable by reason? Why are mathematics by almost all philosophers, and (by some) even those branches of natural philosophy which, through the medium of mathematics, have been converted into deductive sciences, considered to be independent of the evidence of experience and observation and characterized as systems of necessary truth?

The answer I conceive to be that this character of necessity ascribed to the truths of mathematics and even (with some reservations to be hereafter made) the peculiar certainty attributed to them is an illusion, in order to sustain which, it is necessary to suppose that those truths relate to, and express the properties of, purely imaginary objects. It is acknowledged that the conclusions of geometry are deduced, partly at least, from the so-called definitions, and that those definitions are assumed to be correct representations, as far as they go, of the objects with which geometry is conversant. Now we have pointed out that from a definition as such no proposition, unless it be one concerning the meaning of a word, can ever follow, and that what apparently follows from a definition follows in reality from an implied assumption that there exists a real thing comformable thereto. This assumption, in the case of the definitions of geometry, is not strictly true; there exist no real things exactly conformable to the definitions. There exist no points without magnitude; no lines without breadth, nor perfectly straight; no circles with all their radii exactly equal, nor squares with all their angles perfectly right. It will perhaps be said that the assumption does not extend to the actual, but only

From John Stuart Mill, *System of Logic*, 10th ed., Book II, Longmans, Green & Co., 1879.

to the possible, existence of such things. I answer that, according to any test we have of possibility, they are not even possible. Their existence, so far as we can form any judgment, would seem to be inconsistent with the physical constitution of our planet at least, if not of the universe. To get rid of this difficulty and at the same time to save the credit of the supposed system of necessary truth, it is customary to say that the points, lines, circles, and squares which are the subject of geometry exist in our conceptions merely and are part of our minds, which minds, by working on their own materials, construct an *a priori* science, the evidence of which is purely mental and has nothing whatever to do with outward experience. By howsoever high authorities this doctrine may have been sanctioned, it appears to me psychologically incorrect. The points, lines, circles, and squares which anyone has in his mind are (I apprehend) simply copies of the points, lines, circles, and squares which he has known in his experience. Our idea of a point I apprehend to be simply our idea of the *minimum visibile*, the smallest portion of surface which we can see. A line, as defined by geometers, is wholly inconceivable. We can reason about a line as if it had no breadth, because we have a power, which is the foundation of all the control we can exercise over the operations of our minds, the power, when a perception is present to our senses or a conception to our intellects, of *attending* to a part only of that perception or conception instead of the whole. But we cannot *conceive* a line without breadth; we can form no mental picture of such a line; all the lines which we have in our minds are lines possessing breadth. If anyone doubts this, we may refer him to his own experience. I much question if anyone who fancies that he can conceive what is called a mathematical line thinks so from the evidence of his consciousness; I suspect it is rather because he supposes that, unless such a conception were possible, mathematics could not exist as a science, a supposition which there will be no difficulty in showing to be entirely groundless.

Since, then, neither in nature nor in the human mind do there exist any objects exactly corresponding to the definitions of geometry, while yet that science cannot be supposed to be conversant about nonentities, nothing remains but to consider geometry as conversant with such lines, angles, and figures as really exist, and the definitions, as they are called, must be regarded as some of our first and most obvious generalizations concerning those natural objects. The correctness of those generalizations, *as* generalizations, is without a flaw; the equality of all the radii of a circle is true of all circles, so far as it is true of any one, but it is not exactly true of any circle; it is only nearly true, so nearly that no error of any importance in practice will be incurred by feigning it to be exactly true. When we have occasion to extend these inductions or their consequences to cases in which the error would be appreciable—to lines of perceptible breadth or thickness, parallels which deviate sensibly from equidistance, and the like—we correct our conclusions by combining with them a fresh set of propositions relating to the aberration, just as we also take in propositions relating to the physical or chemical properties of the material if those properties happen to introduce any modification into the result, which they easily may, even with respect to figure and magnitude, as in the case, for instance, of expansion by heat. So long, however, as there exists no practical necessity for attending to any of the properties of the object except its geometrical properties or to any of the natural irregularities in those, it is convenient to neglect the consideration of the other properties and of the irregularities and to reason as if these did not exist; accordingly, we formally announce in the definitions that we intend to proceed on this plan. But it is an error to suppose, because we resolve to confine our attention to a certain number of the properties of an object, that we therefore conceive, or have an idea of, the object denuded of its other properties. We are thinking, all the time, of precisely such objects as we have seen and touched and with all the properties which naturally belong to them, but, for scientific convenience, we feign them to be divested of all properties except those which are material to our purpose and in regard to which we design to consider them.

The peculiar accuracy supposed to be characteristic of the first principles of geometry thus appears to be fictitious. The assertions on which the reasonings of the science are founded do not, any more than in other sciences, exactly correspond with the fact, but we suppose that they do so, for the sake of tracing the consequences which follow from the supposition. The opinion of Dugald Stewart respecting the foundations of geometry is, I conceive, substantially correct: that it is built on hypotheses; that it owes to this alone the peculiar certainty supposed to distinguish it; and that in any science whatever, by reasoning from a set of hypotheses, we may obtain a body of conclusions as certain as those of geometry, that is, as strictly in accordance with the hypotheses and as irresistibly compelling assent, *on condition* that those hypotheses are true.*

When, therefore, it is affirmed that the conclusions of geometry are necessary truths, the necessity consists in reality only in this, that they correctly follow from the suppositions from which they are deduced. Those suppositions are so far from being necessary that they are not even true; they purposely depart, more or less widely, from the truth. The only sense in which necessity can be ascribed to the conclusions of any

* It is justly remarked by Professor Bain (*Logic*, II, 134) that the word Hypothesis is used here in a somewhat peculiar sense. An hypothesis, in science, usually means a supposition not proved to be true, but surmised to be so, because if true it would account for certain known facts, and the final result of the speculation may be to prove its truth. The hypotheses spoken of in the text are of a different character; they are known not to be literally true, while as much of them as is true is not hypothetical, but certain. The two cases, however, resemble in the circumstance that in both we reason, not from a truth, but from an assumption, and the truth, therefore, of the conclusions is conditional, not categorical. This suffices to justify, in point of logical propriety, Stewart's use of the term. It is, of course, needful to bear in mind that the hypothetical element in the definitions of geometry is the assumption that what is very nearly true is exactly so. This unreal exactitude might be called a fiction as properly as an hypothesis, but that appellation, still more than the other, would fail to point out the close relation which exists between the fictitious point or line and the points and lines of which we have experience.

scientific investigation is that of legitimately following from some assumption which, by the conditions of the inquiry, is not to be questioned. In this relation, of course, the derivative truths of every deductive science must stand to the inductions or assumptions on which the science is founded, and which, whether true or untrue, certain or doubtful in themselves, are always supposed certain for the purposes of the particular science.

. . .

It remains to inquire what is the ground of our belief in axioms—what is the evidence on which they rest? I answer, they are experimental truths, generalizations from observation. The proposition, Two straight lines cannot enclose a space—or, in other words, two straight lines which have once met, do not meet again, but continue to diverge—is an induction from the evidence of our senses.

. . .

It is not necessary to show that the truths which we call axioms are originally *suggested* by observation and that we should never have known that two straight lines cannot enclose a space if we had never seen a straight line, thus much being admitted by Dr. Whewell and by all, in recent times, who have taken his view of the subject. But they contend that it is not experience which *proves* the axiom, but that its truth is perceived *a priori*, by the constitution of the mind itself, from the first moment when the meaning of the proposition is apprehended, and without any necessity for verifying it by repeated trials, as is requisite in the case of truths really ascertained by observation.

They cannot, however, but allow that the truth of the axiom, Two straight lines cannot enclose a space, even if evident independently of experience, is also evident from experience. Whether the axiom needs confirmation or not, it receives confirmation in almost every instant of our lives, since we cannot look at any two straight lines which intersect one another without seeing that from that point they continue to diverge more and more. Experimental proof crowds in upon us in such endless profusion, and without one instance in which there can be even a suspicion of an exception to the rule, that we should soon have stronger ground for believing the axiom, even as an experimental truth, than we have for almost any of the general truths which we confessedly learn from the evidence of our senses. Independently of *a priori* evidence, we should certainly believe it with an intensity of conviction far greater than we accord to any ordinary physical truth, and this, too, at a time of life much earlier than that from which we date almost any part of our acquired knowledge, and much too early to admit of our retaining any recollection of the history of our intellectual operations at that period. Where, then, is the necessity for assuming that our recognition of these truths has a different origin from the rest of our knowledge when its existence is perfectly accounted for by supposing its origin to be the same? when the causes which produce belief in all other instances exist in this instance, and in a degree of strength as much superior to what exists in other cases as the intensity of the belief itself is superior? The burden of proof lies on the advocates of the contrary opinion; it is for them to point out some fact inconsistent with the supposition that this part of our knowledge of nature is derived from the same sources as every other part.*

. . .

What we have now asserted, however, cannot be received as universally true of deductive or demonstrative sciences until verified by being applied to the most remarkable of all those sciences, that of Numbers; the theory of the Calculus, Arithmetic and Algebra. It is harder to believe of the doctrines of this science than of any other, either that they are not truths *a priori* but experimental truths, or that their peculiar certainty is owing to their being not absolute but only conditional truths. This, therefore, is a case which merits examination apart, and the more so because on this subject we have a double set of doctrines to contend with: that of the *a priori* philosophers on one side; and, on the other, a theory the most opposite to theirs which was at one time very generally received and is still far from being altogether exploded among metaphysicians.

This theory attempts to solve the difficulty apparently inherent in the case by representing the propositions of the science of numbers as merely verbal and its processes as simple transformations of language, substitu-

* Some persons find themselves prevented from believing that the axiom, Two straight lines cannot enclose a space, could ever became known to us through experience, by a difficulty which may be stated as follows: If the straight lines spoken of are those contemplated in the definition—lines absolutely without breadth and absolutely straight—that such are incapable of enclosing a space is not proved by experience, for lines such as these do not present themselves in our experience. If, on the other hand, the lines meant are such straight lines as we do meet with in experience, lines straight enough for practical purposes, but in reality slightly zigzag, and with some, however trifling, breadth; as applied to these lines the axiom is not true, for two of them may, and sometimes do, enclose a small portion of space. In neither case, therefore, does experience prove the axiom.

Those who employ this argument to show that geometrical axioms cannot be proved by induction show themselves unfamiliar with a common and perfectly valid mode of inductive proof: proof by approximation. Though experience furnishes us with no lines so unimpeachably straight that two of them are incapable of enclosing the smallest space, it presents us with gradations of lines possessing less and less either of breadth or of flexure, of which series the straight line of the definition is the ideal limit. And observation shows that just as much and as nearly as the straight lines of experience approximate to having no breadth or flexure, so much and so nearly does the space-enclosing power of any two of them approach to zero. The inference that if they had no breadth or flexure at all they would enclose no space at all, is a correct inductive inference from these facts, conformable to one of the four Inductive Methods hereinafter characterized—the Method of Concomitant Variations, of which the Mathematical Doctrine of Limits presents the extreme case.

tions of one expression for another. The proposition, Two and one is equal to three, according to these writers, is not a truth, is not the assertion of a really existing fact, but a definition of the word three, a statement that mankind have agreed to use the name three as a sign exactly equivalent to two and one, to call by the former name whatever is called by the other more clumsy phrase. According to this doctrine, the longest process in algebra is but a succession of changes in terminology by which equivalent expressions are substituted one for another, a series of translations of the same fact from one into another language; though how, after such a series of translations, the fact itself comes out changed (as when we demonstrate a new geometrical theorem by algebra) they have not explained, and it is a difficulty which is fatal to their theory.

It must be acknowledged that there are peculiarities in the processes of arithmetic and algebra which render the theory in question very plausible, and have not unnaturally made those sciences the stronghold of Nominalism. The doctrine that we can discover facts, detect the hidden processes of nature, by an artful manipulation of language is so contrary to common sense that a person must have made some advances in philosophy to believe it: men fly to so paradoxical a belief to avoid, as they think, some even greater difficulty which the vulgar do not see. What has led many to believe that reasoning is a mere verbal process is that no other theory seemed reconcilable with the nature of the science of numbers. For we do not carry any ideas along with us when we use the symbols of arithmetic or of algebra. In a geometrical demonstration we have a mental diagram, if not one on paper; AB, AC, are present to our imagination as lines, intersecting other lines, forming an angle with one another, and the like; but not so *a* and *b*. These may represent lines or any other magnitudes, but those magnitudes are never thought of; nothing is realised in our imagination but *a* and *b*. The ideas which, on the particular occasion, they happen to represent are banished from the mind during every intermediate part of the process between the beginning, when the premises are translated from things into signs, and the end, when the conclusion is translated back from signs into things. Nothing, then, being in the reasoner's mind but the symbols, what can seem more inadmissible than to contend that the reasoning process has to do with anything more? We seem to have come to one of Bacon's prerogative instances, an *experimentum crucis* on the nature of reasoning itself.

Nevertheless, it will appear on consideration that this apparently so decisive instance is no instance at all; that there is in every step of an arithmetical or algebraical calculation a real induction, a real inference of facts from facts; and that what disguises the induction is simply its comprehensive nature and the consequent extreme generality of the language. All numbers must be numbers of something; there are no such things as numbers in the abstract. *Ten* must mean ten bodies, or ten sounds, or ten beatings of the pulse. But though numbers must be numbers of something, they may be numbers of anything. Propositions, therefore, concerning numbers have the remarkable peculiarity that they are propositions concerning all things whatever, all objects, all existences of every kind known to our experience. All things possess quantity, consist of parts which can be numbered, and in that character possess all the properties which are called properties of numbers. That half of four is two must be true whatever the word four represents, whether four hours, four miles, or four pounds weight. We need only conceive a thing divided into four equal parts (and all things may be conceived as so divided) to be able to predicate of it every property of the number four, that is, every arithmetical proposition in which the number four stands on one side of the equation. Algebra extends the generalisation still farther; every number represents that particular number of all things without distinction, but every algebraical symbol does more; it represents all numbers without distinction. . . .

There is another circumstance which, still more than that which we have now mentioned, gives plausibility to the notion that the propositions of arithmetic and algebra are merely verbal. That is that when considered as propositions respecting things, they all have the appearance of being identical propositions. The assertion, Two and one is equal to three, considered as an assertion respecting objects, as for instance Two pebbles and one pebble are equal to three pebbles, does not affirm equality between two collections of pebbles, but absolute identity. It affirms that if we put one pebble to two pebbles, those very pebbles are three. The objects, therefore, being the very same, and the mere assertion that "objects are themselves" being insignificant, it seems but natural to consider the proposition Two and one is equal to three, as asserting mere identity of signification between the two names.

This, however, though it looks so plausible, will not bear examination. The expression "two pebbles and one pebble" and the expression "three pebbles" stand, indeed, for the same aggregation of objects, but they by no means stand for the same physical fact. They are names of the same objects, but of those objects in two different states; though they *de*note the same things, their *con*notation is different. Three pebbles in two separate parcels, and three pebbles in one parcel, do not make the same impression on our senses; and the assertion that the very same pebbles may by an alteration of place and arrangement be made to produce either the one set of sensations or the other, though a very familiar proposition, is not an identical one. It is a truth known to us by early and constant experience, an inductive truth, and such truths are the foundation of the science of numbers. The fundamental truths of that science all rest on the evidence of sense; they are proved by showing to our eyes and our fingers that any given number of objects—ten balls, for example—may by separation and rearrangement exhibit to our senses all the different sets of numbers the sum of which is equal to ten. All the improved methods of teaching arithmetic to children proceed on a knowledge of this fact. All who wish to carry the child's *mind* along with them in learning arithmetic, all who wish to teach numbers, and not mere ciphers—now teach it through the evidence of the senses, in the manner we have described.

We may, if we please, call the proposition, "Three is two and one," a definition of the number three and assert that arithmetic, as it has been asserted that geometry, is a science founded on definitions. But they are definitions in the geometrical sense, not the logical; asserting not the meaning of a term only, but along with it an observed matter of fact. The proposition, "A circle is a figure bounded by a line which has all its points equally distant from a point within it," is called the definition of a circle; but the proposition from which so many consequences follow and which is really a first principle in geometry is that figures answering to this description exist. And thus we may call "Three is two and one" a definition of three; but the calculations which depend on that proposition do not follow from the definition itself, but from an arithmetical theorem presupposed in it, namely, that collections of objects exist which, while they impress the senses thus, ○○○, may be separated into two parts, thus, ○○ ○. This proposition being granted, we term all such parcels Threes, after which the enunciation of the above-mentioned physical fact will serve also for a definition of the word Three.

The science of number is thus no exception to the conclusion we previously arrived at that the processes even of deductive sciences are altogether inductive and that their first principles are generalisations from experience.

A PRAGMATIC CONCEPTION OF THE *A PRIORI*

C. I. LEWIS

The conception of the *a priori* points two problems which are perennial in philosophy; the part played in knowledge by the mind itself, and the possibility of "necessary truth" or of knowledge "independent of experience." But traditional conceptions of the *a priori* have proved untenable. That the mind approaches the flux of immediacy with some godlike foreknowledge of principles which are legislative for experience, that there is any natural light or any innate ideas, it is no longer possible to believe.

Nor shall we find the clue to the *a priori* in any compulsion of the mind to incontrovertible truth or any peculiar kind of demonstration which establishes first principles. All truth lays upon the rational mind the same compulsion to belief; as Mr. Bosanquet has pointed out, this character belongs to all propositions or judgments once their truth is established.

Reprinted from the *Journal of Philosophy*. Vol, 20, 1923, by permission of the editors.

The difficulties of the conception are due, I believe, to two mistakes: whatever is *a priori* is necessary, but we have misconstrued the relation of necessary truth to mind. And the *a priori* is independent of experience, but in so taking it, we have misunderstood its relation to empirical fact. What is *a priori* is necessary truth not because it compels the mind's acceptance, but precisely because it does not. It is given experience, brute fact, the *a posteriori* element in knowledge which the mind must accept willy-nilly. The *a priori* represents an attitude in some sense freely taken, a stipulation of the mind itself, and a stipulation which might be made in some other way if it suited our bent or need. Such truth is necessary as opposed to contingent, not as opposed to voluntary. And the *a priori* is independent of experience not because it prescribes a form which the data of sense must fit, or anticipates some preëstablished harmony of experience with the mind, but precisely because it prescribes nothing to experience. That is a *a priori* which is true, *no matter what.* What it anticipates is not the given, but our attitude toward it: it concerns the uncompelled initiative of mind or, as Josiah Royce would say, our categorical ways of acting.

The traditional example of the *a priori par excellence* is the laws of logic. These can not be derived from experience since they must first be taken for granted in order to prove them. They make explicit our general modes of classification. And they impose upon experience no real limitation. Sometimes we are asked to tremble before the spectre of the "alogical," in order that we may thereafter rejoice that we are saved from this by the dependence of reality upon mind. But the "alogical" is pure bogey, a word without a meaning. What kind of experience could defy the principle that everything must either be or not be, that nothing can both be and not be, or that if x is y and y is z, then x is z? If anything imaginable or unimaginable could violate such laws, then the ever-present fact of change would do it every day. The laws of logic are purely formal; they forbid nothing but what concerns the use of terms and the corresponding modes of classification and analysis. The law of contradiction tells us that nothing can be both white and not-white, but it does not and can not tell us whether black is not-white, or soft or square is not-white. To discover *what contradicts what* we must always consult the character of experience. Similarly the law of the excluded middle formulates our decision that whatever is not designated by a certain term shall be designated by its negative. It declares our purpose to make, for every term, a complete dichotomy of experience, instead—as we might choose—of classifying on the basis of a tripartite division into opposities (as black and white) and the middle ground between the two. Our rejection of such tripartite division represents only our penchant for simplicity.

Further laws of logic are of similar significance. They are principles of procedure, the parliamentary rules of intelligent thought and speech. Such laws are independent of experience because they impose no limitations wherever upon it. They are legislative because they are addressed to ourselves—because definition, classification, and inference represent no operations of the objective world, but only our own categorical attitudes of mind.

And further, the ultimate criteria of the laws of logic are pragmatic. Those who suppose that there is, for example, *a* logic which everyone would agree to if he understood it and understood himself, are more optimistic than those versed in the history of logical discussion have a right to be. The fact is that there are several logics, markedly different, each self-consistent in its own terms and such that whoever, using it, avoids false premises, will never reach a false conclusion. Mr. Russell, for example, bases *his* logic on an implication relation such that if twenty sentences be cut from a newspaper and put in a hat, and then two of these be drawn at random, one of them will certainly imply the other, and it is an even bet that the implication will be mutual. Yet upon a foundation so remote from ordinary modes of inference the whole structure of *Principia Mathematica* is built. This logic—and there are others even more strange—is utterly consistent and the results of it entirely valid. Over and above all questons of consistency, there are issues of logic which can not be determined—nay, can not even be argued—except on pragmatic grounds of conformity to human bent and intellectual convenience. That we have been blind to this fact, itself reflects traditional errors in the conception of the *a priori.*

We may note in passing one less important illustration of the *a priori*—the propositon "true by definition." Definitions and their immediate consequences, analytic propositions generally, are necessarily true, true under all possible circumstances. Definition is legislative because it is in some sense arbitrary. Not only is the meaning assigned to words more or less a matter of choice—that consideration is relatively trivial—but the manner in which the precise classifications which definition embodies shall be effected, is something not dictated by experience. If experience were other than it is, the definition and its corresponding classification might be inconvenient, fantastic, or useless, but it could not be false. Mind makes classifications and determines meanings; in so doing it creates the *a priori* truth of analytic judgments. But that the manner of this creation responds to pragmatic considerations, is so obvious that it hardly needs pointing out.

If the illustrations so far given seem trivial or verbal, that impression may be corrected by turning to the place which the *a priori* has in mathematics and in natural science. Arithmetic, for example, depends *en toto* upon the operation of counting or correlating, a procedure which can be carried out at will in any world containing identifiable things—even identifiable ideas—regardless of the further characters of experience. Mill challenged this *a priori* character of arithmetic. He asked us to suppose a demon sufficiently powerful and maleficent so that every time two things were brought together with two other things, this demon should always introduce a fifth. The implication which he supposed to follow is that under such circumstances $2 + 2 = 5$ would be a universal law of arithmetic. But Mill was quite mistaken. In such a world we should be obliged to become a little clearer than is usual about the distinction between arithmetic and physics, that is all. If two black marbles were put in the same urn with two white ones, the demon could take his choice of colors, but it would be evident that there were more black marbles or more white ones than were put in. The same would be true of all objects in any wise identifiable. We should simply find ourselves in the presence of an extraordinary physical law, which we should recognize as universal in our world, that whenever two things were brought into proximity with two others, an additional and similar thing was always created by the process. Mill's world would be physically most extraordinary. The world's work would be enormously facilitated if hats or locomotives or tons of coal could be thus multiplied by anyone possessed originally of two pairs. But the laws of mathematics would remain unaltered. It is because this is true that arithmetic is *a priori*. Its laws prevent *nothing;* they are compatible with anything which happens or could conceivably happen in nature. They would be true in any possible world. Mathematical addition is not a physical transformation. Physical changes which result in an increase or decrease of the countable things involved are matters of everyday occurrence. Such physical processes present us with phenomena in which the purely mathematical has to be separated out by abstraction. Those laws and those laws only have necessary truth which we are prepared to maintain, no matter what. It is because we shall always separate out that part of the phenomenon not in conformity with arithmetic and designate it by some other category—physical change, chemical reaction, optical illusion—that arithmetic is *a priori*.

The *a priori* element in science and in natural law is greater than might be supposed. In the first place, all science is based upon definitive concepts. The formulation of these concepts is, indeed, a matter determined by the commerce between our intellectual or our pragmatic interests and the nature of experience. Definition is classification. The scientific search is for such classification as will make it possible to correlate appearance and behavior, to discover law, to penetrate to the "essential nature" of things in order that behavior may become predictable. In other words, if definition is unsuccessful, as early scientific definitions mostly have been, it is because the classification thus set up corresponds with no natural cleavage and does not correlate with any important uniformity of behavior. A name itself must represent *some* uniformity in experience or it names nothing. What does not repeat itself or recur in intelligible fashion is not a thing. Where the definitive uniformity is a clue to other uniformities, we have successful scientific definition. Other definitions can not be said to be false; they are merely useless. In scientific classification the search is, thus, for *things worth naming*. But the naming, classifying, defining activity is essentially prior to investigation. We can not interrogate experience in general. Until our meaning is definite and our classification correspondingly exact, experience can not conceivably answer our questions.

In the second place, the fundamental laws of any science—or those treated as fundamental—are *a priori* because they formulate just such definitive concepts or categorical tests by which alone investigation becomes possible. If the lightning strikes the railroad track at two places, *A* and *B*, how shall we tell whether these events are simultaneous? "We . . . require a definition of simultaneity such that this definition supplies us with the method by means of which . . . we can decide whether or not both the lightning strokes occurred simultaneously. As long as this requirement is not satisfied, I allow myself to be deceived as a physicist (and of course the same applies if I am not a physicist), when I imagine that I am able to attach a meaning to the statement of simultaneity. . . .

"After thinking the matter over for some time you then offer the following suggestion with which to test simultaneity. By measuring along the rails, the connecting line *AB* should be measured up and an observer placed at the mid-point *M* of the distance *AB*. This observer should be supplied with an arrangement (*e.g.*, two mirrors inclined at 90°) which allows him visually to observe both places *A* and *B* at the same time. If the observer perceives the two flashes at the same time, then they are simultaneous.

"I am very pleased with this suggestion, but for all that I can not regard the matter as quite settled, because I feel constrained to raise the following objection: 'Your definition would certainly be right, if I only knew that the light by means of which the observer at *M* perceives the lightning flashes travels along the length *A—M* with the same velocity as along the length *B—M*. But an examination of this supposition would only be possible if we already had at our disposal the means of measuring time. It would thus appear as though we were moving here in a logical circle.'

"After further consideration you cast a somewhat disdainful glance at me—and rightly so—and you declare: 'I maintain my previous definition nevertheless, because in reality it assumes absolutely nothing about light. There is only *one* demand to be made of the definition of simultaneity, namely, that in every real case it must supply us with an empirical decision as to whether or not the conception which has to be defined is fulfilled. That light requires the same time to traverse the path *A—M* as for the path *B—M* is in reality *neither a supposition nor a hypothesis* about the physical nature of light, but a *stipulation* which I can make of my own freewill in order to arrive at a definition of simultaneity.' . . . We are thus led also to a definition of 'time' in physics."*

As this example from the theory of relativity well illustrates, we can not even ask the questions which discovered law would answer until we have first by *a priori* stipulation formulated definitive criteria. Such concepts are not verbal definitions, nor classifications merely; they are themselves laws which prescribe a certain uniformity of behavior to whatever is thus named. Such definitive laws are *a priori;* only so can we

* Einstein, *Relativity*, pp. 26–28: italics are the author's.

enter upon the investigation by which further laws are sought. Yet it should also be pointed out that such *a priori* laws are subject to abandonment if the structure which is built upon them does not succeed in simplifying our interpretation of phenomena. If, in the illustration given, the relation "simultaneous with," as defined, should not prove transitive—if event *A* should prove simultaneous with *B*, and *B* with *C*, but not *A* with *C*—this definition would certainly be rejected.

And thirdly, there is that *a priori* element in science—as in other human affairs—which constitutes the criteria of the real as opposed to the unreal in experience. An object itself is a uniformity. Failure to behave in certain categorical ways marks it as unreal. Uniformities of the type called "natural law" are the clues to reality and unreality. A mouse which disappears where no hole is, is no real mouse; a landscape which recedes as we approach is but illusion. As the queen remarked in the episode of the wishing-carpet; "If this were real, then it would be a miracle. But miracles do not happen. Therefore I shall wake presently." That the uniformities of natural law are the only reliable criteria of the real, is inescapable. But such a criterion is *ipso facto a priori.* No conceivable experience could dictate the alteration of a law so long as failure to obey that law marked the content of experience as unreal.

This is one of the puzzles of empiricism. We deal with experience: what any reality may be which underlies experience, we have to learn. What we desire to discover is natural law, the formulation of those uniformities which obtain amongst the real. But experience as it comes to us contains not only the real but all the content of illusion, dream, hallucination, and mistake. The *given* contains both real and unreal, confusingly intermingled. If we ask for uniformities of this unsorted experience, we shall not find them. Laws which characterize all experience, of real and unreal both, are non-existent and would in any case be worthless. What we seek are the uniformities of the *real;* but *until we have such laws, we can not sift experience and segregate the real.*

The obvious solution is that the enrichment of experience, the separation of the real from the illusory or meaningless, and the formulation of natural law, all grow up together. If the criteria of the real are *a priori,* that is not to say that no conceivable character of experience would lead to alteration of them. For example, spirits can not be photographed. But if photographs of spiritistic phenomena, taken under properly guarded conditions, should become sufficiently frequent, this *a priori* dictum would be called in question. What we should do would be to redefine our terms. Whether "spook" was spirit or matter, whether the definition of "spirit" or of "matter" should be changed; all this would constitute one interrelated problem. We should reopen together the question of definition or classification, of criteria for this sort of real, and of natural law. And the solution of one of these would mean the solution of all. Nothing could *force* a redefinition of spirit or of matter. A sufficiently fundamental relation to human bent, to human interests, would guarantee continuance unaltered even in the face of unintelligible and baffling experiences. In such problems, the mind finds itself uncompelled save by its own purposes and needs. I *may* categorize experience as I will; but *what* categorical distinctions will best serve my interests and objectify my own intelligence? What the mixed and troubled experience shall be—that is beyond me. But what I shall do with it—that is my own question, when the character of experience is sufficiently before me. I am coerced only by my own need to understand.

It would indeed be inappropriate to characterize as *a priori* a law which we are wholly prepared to alter in the light of further experience, even though in an isolated case we should discard as illusory any experience which failed to conform. But the crux of the situation lies in this; beyond such principles as those of logic, which we seem fully prepared to maintain no matter what, there must be further and more particular criteria of the real prior to any investigation of nature whatever. We can not even interrogate experience without a network of categories and definitive concepts. And we must further be prepared to say what experimental findings will answer what questions, and how. Without tests which represent anterior principle, there is no question which experience could answer at all. Thus the most fundamental laws in any category—or those which we regard as most fundamental—are *a priori*, even though continued failure to render experience intelligible in such terms might result eventually in the abandonment of that category altogether. Matters so comparatively small as the behavior of Mercury and of starlight passing the sun's limb may, if there be persistent failure to bring them within the field of previously accepted modes of explanation, result in the abandonment of the independent categories of space and time. But without the definitions, fundamental principles, and tests, of the type which constitute such categories, no experience whatever could prove or disprove anything. And to that mind which should find independent space and time absolutely necessary conceptions, no possible experiment could prove the principles of relativity. "There must be some error in the experimental findings, or some law not yet discovered," represents an attitude which can never be rendered impossible. And the only sense in which it could be proved unreasonable would be the pragmatic one of comparison with another method of categorical analysis which more successfully reduced all such experience to order and law.

At the bottom of all science and all knowledge are categories and definitive concepts which represent fundamental habits of thought and deep-lying attitudes which the human mind has taken in the light of its total experience. But a new and wider experience may bring about some alteration of these attitudes, even though by themselves they dictate nothing as to the content of experience, and no experience can conceivably prove them invalid.

Perhaps some will object to this conception on the ground that only such principles should be designated *a priori* as the human mind *must* maintain, no matter what; that if, for example, it is shown possible to arrive at a consistent doctrine of physics in terms of relativity, even by the most arduous reconstruction of our fundamental notions, then the present conceptions are by that fact shown not to be *a priori*. Such objection is especially likely from those who would conceive the *a priori* in terms of an absolute mind or an absolutely universal human nature. We should readily agree that a decision by popular approval or a congress of scientists or anything short of such a test as would bring to bear the full weight of human capacity and interest, would be ill-considered as having to do with the *a priori*. But we wish to emphasize two facts: first, that in the field of those conceptions and principles which have altered in human history, there are those which could neither be proved nor disproved by any experience, but represent the uncompelled initiative of human thought—that without this uncompelled initiative no growth of science, nor any science at all, would be conceivable. And second, that the difference between such conceptions as are, for example, concerned in the decision of relativity versus absolute space and time, and those more permanent attitudes such as are vested in the laws of logic, there is only a difference of degree. The dividing line between the *a priori* and the *a posteriori* is that between principles and definitive concepts which *can* be maintained in the face of all experience and those genuinely empirical generalizations which *might* be proven flatly false. The thought which both rationalism and empiricism have missed is that there are principles, representing the initiative of mind, which impose upon experience no limitations whatever, but that such conceptions are still subject to alteration on pragmatic grounds when the expanding boundaries of experience reveal their infelicity as intellectual instruments.

Neither human experience nor the human mind has a character which is universal, fixed, and absolute. "The human mind" does not exist at all save in the sense that all humans are very much alike in fundamental respects, and that the language habit and the enormously important exchange of ideas has greatly increased our likeness in those respects which are here in question. Our categories and definitions are peculiarly social products, reached in the light of experiences which have much in common, and beaten out, like other pathways, by the coincidence of human purposes and the exigencies of human coöperation. Concerning the *a priori* there need be neither universal agreement nor complete historical continuity. Conceptions, such as those of logic, which are least likely to be affected by the opening of new ranges of experience, represent the most stable of our categories; but none of them is beyond the possibility of alteration.

Mind contributes to experience the element of order, of classification, categories, and definition. Without such, experience would be unintelligible. Our knowledge of the validity of these is simply consciousness of our own fundamental ways of acting and our own intellectual intent. Without this element, knowledge is impossible, and it is here that whatever truths are necessary and independent of experience must be found. But the commerce between our categorical ways of acting, our pragmatic interests, and the particular character of experience, is closer than we have realized. No explanation of any one of these can be complete without consideration of the other two.

Pragmatism has sometimes been charged with oscillating between two contrary notions; the one, that experience is "through and through malleable to our purpose," the other, that facts are "hard" and uncreated by the mind. We here offer a mediating conception: through all our knowledge runs the element of the *a priori*, which is indeed malleable to our purpose and responsive to our need. But throughout, there is also that other element of experience which is "hard," "independent," and unalterable to our will.

ONE DOGMA OF EMPIRICISM

W. V. O. QUINE

Modern empiricism has been conditioned in large part by two dogmas. One is a belief in some fundamental cleavage between truths which are *analytic*, or grounded in meanings independently of matters of fact, and truths which are *synthetic*, or grounded in fact. The other dogma is *reductionism:* the belief that each meaningful statement is equivalent to some logical construct upon terms which refer to immediate experience. Both dogmas, I shall argue, are ill founded. One effect of abandoning them is, as we shall see, a blurring of the supposed boundary between speculative metaphysics and natural science. Another effect is a shift toward pragmatism.

I. BACKGROUND FOR ANALYTICITY

Kant's cleavage between analytic and synthetic truths was foreshadowed in Hume's distinction between relations of ideas and matters of fact, and in Leibniz's distinction between truths of reason and truths of fact. Leibniz spoke of the truths of reason as true in all possible worlds. Pictur-

Reprinted from *The Philosophical Review*, Vol. 60, 1951, by permission of the author and the editors.

Much of this paper is devoted to a critique of analyticity which I have been urging orally and in correspondence for years past. My debt to the other participants in those discussions, notably Carnap, Church, Goodman, Tarski, and White, is large and indeterminate. White's excellent essay "The Analytic and the Synthetic: An Untenable Dualism," in *John Dewey: Philosopher of Science and Freedom* (New York, 1950), says much of what needed to be said on the topic; but in the present paper I touch on some further aspects of the problem. I am grateful to Dr. Donald L. Davidson for valuable criticism of the first draft.

esqueness aside, this is to say that the truths of reason are those which could not possibly be false. In the same vein we hear analytic statements defined as statements whose denials are self-contradictory. But this definition has small explanatory value; for the notion of self-contradictoriness, in the quite broad sense needed for this definition of analyticity, stands in exactly the same need of clarification as does the notion of analyticity itself.* The two notions are the two sides of a single dubious coin.

Kant conceived of an analytic statement as one that attributes to its subject no more than is already conceptually contained in the subject. This formulation has two shortcomings: it limits itself to statements of subject-predicate form, and it appeals to a notion of containment which is left at a metaphorical level. But Kant's intent, evident more from the use he makes of the notion of analyticity than from his definition of it, can be restated thus: a statement is analytic when it is true by virtue of meanings and independently of fact. Pursuing this line, let us examine the concept of *meaning* which is presupposed.

We must observe to begin with that meaning is not to be identified with naming, or reference. Consider Frege's example of 'Evening Star' and 'Morning Star'. Understood not merely as a recurrent evening apparition but as a body, the Evening Star is the planet Venus, and the Morning Star is the same. The two singular terms *name* the same thing. But the meanings must be treated as distinct, since the identity 'Evening Star = Morning Star' is a statement of fact established by astronomical observation. If 'Evening Star' and 'Morning Star' were alike in meaning, the identity 'Evening Star = Morning Star' would be analytic.

Again there is Russell's example of 'Scott' and 'the author of *Waverley*'. Analysis of the meanings of words was by no means sufficient to reveal to George IV that the person named by these two singular terms was one and the same.

The distinction between meaning and naming is no less important at the level of abstract terms. The terms '9' and 'the number of planets' name one and the same abstract entity but presumably must be regarded as unlike in meaning; for astronomical observation was needed, and not mere reflection on meanings, to determine the sameness of the entity in question.

Thus far we have been considering singular terms. With general terms, or predicates, the situation is somewhat different but parallel. Whereas a singular term purports to name an entity, abstract or concrete, a general term does not; but a general term is *true of* an entity, or of each of many, or of none. The class of all entities of which a general term is true is called the *extension* of the term. Now paralleling the contrast between the meaning of a singular term and the entity named, we must distinguish equally between the meaning of a general term and its extension. The general terms 'creature with a heart' and 'creature with a kidney', e.g., are perhaps alike in extension but unlike in meaning.

* See White, *op. cit.*, p. 324.

Confusion of meaning with extension, in the case of general terms, is less common than confusion of meaning with naming in the case of singular terms. It is indeed a commonplace in philosophy to oppose intension (or meaning) to extension, or, in a variant vocabulary, connotation to denotation.

The Aristotelian notion of essence was the forerunner, no doubt, of the modern notion of intension or meaning. For Aristotle it was essential in men to be rational, accidental to be two-legged. But there is an important difference between this attitude and the doctrine of meaning. From the latter point of view it may indeed be conceded (if only for the sake of argument) that rationality is involved in the meaning of the word 'man' while two-leggedness is not; but two-leggedness may at the same time be viewed as involved in the meaning of 'biped' while rationality is not. Thus from the point of view of the doctrine of meaning it makes no sense to say of the actual individual, who is at once a man and a biped, that his rationality is essential and his two-leggedness accidental or vice versa. Things had essences, for Aristotle, but only linguistic forms have meanings. Meaning is what essence becomes when it is divorced from the object of reference and wedded to the word.

For the theory of meaning the most conspicuous question is as to the nature of its objects: what sort of things are meanings? They are evidently intended to be ideas, somehow—mental ideas for some semanticists, Platonic ideas for others. Objects of either sort are so elusive, not to say debatable, that there seems little hope of erecting a fruitful science about them. It is not even clear, granted meanings, when we have two and when we have one; it is not clear when linguistic forms should be regarded as *synonymous*, or alike in meaning, and when they should not. If a standard of synonymy should be arrived at, we may reasonably expect that the appeal to meanings as entities will not have played a very useful part in the enterprise.

A felt need for meant entities may derive from an earlier failure to appreciate that meaning and reference are distinct. Once the theory of meaning is sharply separated from the theory of reference, it is a short step to recognizing as the business of the theory of meaning simply the synonymy of linguistic forms and the analyticity of statements; meanings themselves, as obscure intermediary entities, may well be abandoned.

The description of analyticity as truth by virtue of meanings started us off in pursuit of a concept of meaning. But now we have abandoned the thought of any special realm of entities called meanings. So the problem of analyticity confronts us anew.

Statements which are analytic by general philosophical acclaim are not, indeed, far to seek. They fall into two classes. Those of the first class, which may be called *logically true*, are typified by:

(1) No unmarried man is married.

The relevant feature of this example is that it is not merely true as it stands, but remains true under any and all reinterpretations of 'man' and 'married'. If we suppose a prior inventory of *logical* particles, comprising 'no', 'un-', 'not', 'if', 'then', 'and', etc., then in general a logical truth is a statement which is true and remains true under all reinterpretations of its components other than the logical particles.

But there is also a second class of analytic statements, typified by:

(2) No bachelor is married.

The characteristic of such a statement is that it can be turned into a logical truth by putting synonyms for synonyms; thus (2) can be turned into (1) by putting 'unmarried man' for its synonym 'bachelor'. We still lack a proper characterization of this second class of analytic statements, and therewith of analyticity generally, inasmuch as we have had in the above description to lean on a notion of 'synonymy' which is no less in need of clarification than analyticity itself.

. . .

II. DEFINITION

There are those who find it soothing to say that the analytic statements of the second class reduce to those of the first class, the logical truths, by *definition;* 'bachelor', e.g., is *defined* as 'unmarried man'. But how do we find that 'bachelor' is defined as 'unmarried man'? Who defined it thus, and when? Are we to appeal to the nearest dictionary, and accept the lexicographer's formulation as law? Clearly this would be to put the cart before the horse. The lexicographer is an empirical scientist, whose business is the recording of antecedent facts; and if he glosses 'bachelor' as 'unmarried man' it is because of his belief that there is a relation of synonymy between these forms, implicit in general or preferred usage prior to his own work. The notion of synonymy presupposed here has still to be clarified, presumably in terms relating to linguistic behavior. Certainly the "definition" which is the lexicographer's report of an observed synonymy cannot be taken as the ground of the synonymy.

Definition is not, indeed, an activity exclusively of philologists. Philosophers and scientists frequently have occasion to "define" a recondite term by paraphrasing it into terms of a more familiar vocabulary. But ordinarily such a definition, like the philologist's, is pure lexicography, affirming a relationship of synonymy antecedent to the exposition in hand.

Just what it means to affirm synonymy, just what the interconnections may be which are necessary and sufficient in order that two linguistic forms be properly describable as synonymous, is far from clear; but, whatever these interconnections may be, ordinarily they are grounded in usage. Definitions reporting selected instances of synonymy come then as reports upon usage.

There is also, however, a variant type of definitional activity which does not limit itself to the reporting of pre-existing synonymies. I have in mind what Carnap calls *explication*—an activity to which philosophers are given, and scientists also in their more philosophical moments. In explication the purpose is not merely to paraphrase the definiendum into an outright synonym, but actually to improve upon the definiendum by refining or supplementing its meaning. But even explication, though not merely reporting a pre-existing synonymy between definiendum and definiens, does rest nevertheless on *other* pre-existing synonymies. The matter may be viewed as follows. Any word worth explicating has some contexts which, as wholes, are clear and precise enough to be useful; and the purpose of explication is to preserve the usage of these favored contexts while sharpening the usage of other contexts. In order that a given definition be suitable for purposes of explication, therefore, what is required is not that the definiendum in its antecedent usage be synonymous with the definiens, but just that each of these favored contexts of the definiendum, taken as a whole in its antecedent usage, be synonymous with the corresponding context of the definiens.

Two alternative definientia may be equally appropriate for the purposes of a given task of explication and yet not be synonymous with each other; for they may serve interchangeably within the favored contexts but diverge elsewhere. By cleaving to one of these definientia rather than the other, a definition of explicative kind generates, by fiat, a relationship of synonymy between definiendum and definiens which did not hold before. But such a definition still owes its explicative function, as seen, to pre-existing synonymies.

There does, however, remain still an extreme sort of definition which does not hark back to prior synonymies at all; viz., the explicitly conventional introduction of novel notations for purposes of sheer abbreviation. Here the definiendum becomes synonymous with the definiens simply because it has been created expressly for the purpose of being synonymous with the definiens. Here we have a really transparent case of synonymy created by definition; would that all species of synonymy were as intelligible. For the rest, definition rests on synonymy rather than explaining it.

. . .

III. INTERCHANGEABILITY

A natural suggestion, deserving close examination, is that the synonymy of two linguistic forms consists simply in their interchangeability in all contexts without change of truth value; interchangeability, in Leibniz's phrase, *salva veritate*. Note that synonyms so conceived need not even be free from vagueness, as long as the vaguenesses match.

But it is not quite true that the synonyms 'bachelor' and 'unmarried man' are everywhere interchangeable *salva veritate*. Truths which become false under substitution of 'unmarried man' for 'bachelor' are easily constructed with help of 'bachelor of arts' or 'bachelor's buttons'. Also with help of quotation, thus:

'Bachelor' has less than ten letters.

Such counterinstances can, however, perhaps be set aside by treating the phrases 'bachelor of arts' and 'bachelor's buttons' and the quotation ' 'bachelor' ' each as a single indivisible word and then stipulating that the interchangeability *salva veritate* which is to be the touchstone of synonymy is not supposed to apply to fragmentary occcurrences inside of a word. This account of synonymy, supposing it acceptable on other counts, has indeed the drawback of appealing to a prior conception of "word" which can be counted on to present difficulties of formulation in its turn. Nevertheless some progress might be claimed in having reduced the problem of synonymy to a problem of wordhood. Let us pursue this line a bit, taking "word" for granted.

The question remains whether interchangeability *salva veritate* (apart from occurrences within words) is a strong enough condition for synonymy, or whether, on the contrary, some nonsynonymous expressions might be thus interchangeable. Now let us be clear that we are not concerned here with synonymy in the sense of complete identity in psychological associations or poetic quality; indeed no two expressions are synonymous in such a sense. We are concerned only with what may be called *cognitive synonymy*. Just what this is cannot be said without successfully finishing the present study; but we know something about it from the need which arose for it in connection with analyticity in Section I. The sort of synonymy needed there was merely such that any analytic statement could be turned into a logical truth by putting synonyms for synonyms. Turning the tables and assuming analyticity, indeed, we could explain cognitive synonymy of terms as follows (keeping to the familiar example): to say that 'bachelor' and 'unmarried man' are cognitively synonymous is to say no more nor less than that the statement:

(3) All and only bachelors are unmarried men.

is analytic.*

What we need is an account of cognitive synonymy not presupposing analyticity—if we are to explain analyticity conversely with help of cognitive synonymy as undertaken in Section I. And indeed such an

* This is cognitive synonymy in a primary, broad sense. Carnap (*Meaning and Necessity*, pp. 56 ff.) and Lewis (*Analysis of Knowledge and Valuation* [La Salle, Ill., 1946], pp. 83 ff.) have suggested how, once this notion is at hand, a narrower sense of cognitive synonymy which is preferable for some purposes can in turn be derived. But this special ramification of concept-building lies aside from the present purposes and must not be confused with the broad sort of cognitive synonymy here concerned.

independent account of cognitive synonymy is at present up for consideration, viz., interchangeability *salva veritate* everywhere except within words. The question before us, to resume the thread at last, is whether such interchangeability is a sufficient condition for cognitive synonymy. We can quickly assure ourselves that it is, by examples of the following sort. The statement:

(4) Necessarily all and only bachelors are bachelors.

is evidently true, even supposing 'necessarily' so narrowly construed as to be truly applicable only to analytic statements. Then, *if* 'bachelor' and 'unmarried man' are interchangeable *salva veritate*, the result:

(5) Necessarily, all and only bachelors are unmarried men.

of putting 'unmarried man' for an occurrence of 'bachelor' in (4) must, like (4), be true. But to say that (5) is true is to say that (3) is analytic, and hence that 'bachelor' and 'unmarried man' are cognitively synonymous.

Let us see what there is about the above argument that gives it its air of hocus-pocus. The condition of interchangeability *salva veritate* varies in its force with variations in the richness of the language at hand. The above argument supposes we are working with a language rich enough to contain the adverb 'necessarily', this adverb being so construed as to yield truth when and only when applied to an analytic statement. But can we condone a language which contains such an adverb? Does the adverb really make sense? To suppose that it does is to suppose that we have already made satisfactory sense of 'analytic'. Then what are we so hard at work on right now?

Our argument is not flatly circular, but something like it. It has the form, figuratively speaking, of a closed curve in space.

Interchangeability *salva veritate* is meaningless until relativized to a language whose extent is specified in relevant respects. Suppose now we consider a language containing just the following materials. There is an indefinitely large stock of one- and many-place predicates, mostly having to do with extralogical subject matter. The rest of the language is logical. The atomic sentences consist each of a predicate followed by one or more variables; and the complex sentences are built up of atomic ones by truth functions and quantification. In effect such a language enjoys the benefits also of descriptions and class names and indeed singular terms generally, these being contextually definable in known ways.* Such a language can be adequate to classical mathematics and indeed to scientific discourse generally, except in so far as the latter involves debatable devices such as modal adverbs and contrary-to-fact conditionals. Now a language of this type is *extensional*, in this sense: any two predicates which *agree extensionally* (i.e., are true of the same objects) are interchangeable *salva veritate*.

* See, e.g., my *Mathematical Logic* (New York, 1940; Cambridge, Mass., 1947), sec. 24, 26, 27; or *Methods of Logic* (New York, 1950), sec. 37 ff.

In an extensional language, therefore, interchangeability *salva veritate* is no assurance of cognitive synonymy of the desired type. That 'bachelor' and 'unmarried man' are interchangeable *salva veritate* in an extensional language assures us of no more than that (3) is true. There is no assurance here that the extensional agreement of 'bachelor' and 'unmarried man' rests on meaning rather than merely on accidental matters of fact, as does extensional agreement of 'creature with a heart' and 'creature with a kidney'.

For most purposes extensional agreement is the nearest approximation to synonymy we need care about. But the fact remains that extensional agreement falls far short of cognitive synonymy of the type required for explaining analyticity in the manner of Section I. The type of cognitive synonymy required there is such as to equate the synonymy of 'bachelor' and 'unmarried man' with the analyticity of (3), not merely with the truth of (3).

So we must recognize that interchangeability *salva veritate*, if construed in relation to an extensional language, is not a sufficient condition of cognitive synonymy in the sense needed for deriving analyticity in the manner of Section I. If a language contains an intensional adverb 'necessarily' in the sense lately noted, or other particles to the same effect, then interchangeability *salva veritate* in such a language does afford a sufficient condition of cognitive synonymy; but such a language is intelligible only if the notion of analyticity is already clearly understood in advance.

The effort to explain cognitive synonymy first, for the sake of deriving analyticity from it afterward as in Section I, is perhaps the wrong approach. Instead we might try explaining analyticity somehow without appeal to cognitive synonymy. Afterward we could doubtless derive cognitive synonymy from analyticity satisfactorily enough if desired. We have seen that cognitive synonymy of 'bachelor' and 'unmarried man' can be explained as analyticity of (3). The same explanation works for any pair of one-place predicates, of course, and it can be extended in obvious fashion to many-place predicates. Other syntactical categories can also be accommodated in fairly parallel fashion. Singular terms may be said to be cognitively synonymous when the statement of identity formed by putting '=' between them is analytic. Statements may be said simply to be cognitively synonymous when their biconditional (the result of joining them by 'if and only if') is analytic.* If we care to lump all categories into a single formulation, at the expense of assuming again the notion of "word" which was appealed to early in this section, we can describe any two linguistic forms as cognitively synonymous when the two forms are interchangeable (apart from occurrences within "words") *salva* (no longer *veritate* but) *analyticitate*. Certain technical questions arise, indeed, over cases of ambiguity or homonymy; let us not pause for them, however, for we are already digressing. Let us rather turn our

* The 'if and only if' itself is intended in the truth functional sense. See Carnap, *Meaning and Necessity*, p. 14.

backs on the problem of synonymy and address ourselves anew to that of analyticity.

IV. SEMANTICAL RULES

Analyticity at first seemed most naturally definable by appeal to a realm of meanings. On refinement, the appeal to meanings gave way to an appeal to synonymy or definition. But definition turned out to be a will-o'-the-wisp, and synonymy turned out to be best understood only by dint of a prior appeal to analyticity itself. So we are back at the problem of analyticity.

I do not know whether the statement 'Everything green is extended' is analytic. Now does my indecision over this example really betray an incomplete understanding, an incomplete grasp of the "meanings", of 'green' and 'extended'? I think not. The trouble is not with 'green' or 'extended', but with 'analytic'.

It is often hinted that the difficulty in separating analytic statements from synthetic ones in ordinary language is due to the vagueness of ordinary language and that the distinction is clear when we have a precise artificial language with explicit "semantical rules." This, however, as I shall now attempt to show, is a confusion.

The notion of analyticity about which we are worrying is a purported relation between statements and languages: a statement *S* is said to be *analytic for* a language *L*, and the problem is to make sense of this relation generally, i.e., for variable '*S*' *and* '*L*'. The point that I want to make is that the gravity of this problem is not perceptibly less for artificial languages than for natural ones. The problem of making sense of the idiom '*S* is analytic for *L*', with variable '*S*' and '*L*', retains its stubbornness even if we limit the range of the variable '*L*' to artificial languages. Let me now try to make this point evident.

For artificial languages and semantical rules we look naturally to the writings of Carnap. His semantical rules take various forms, and to make my point I shall have to distinguish certain of the forms. Let us suppose, to begin with, an artificial language L_0 whose semantical rules have the form explicitly of a specification, by recursion or otherwise, of all the analytic statements of L_0. The rules tell us that such and such statements, and only those, are the analytic statements of L_0. Now here the difficulty is simply that the rules contain the word 'analytic', which we do not understand! We understand what expressions the rules attribute analyticity to, but we do not understand what the rules attribute to those expressions. In short, before we can understand a rule which begins "A statement *S* is analytic for language L_0 if and only if . . . ," we must understand the general relative term 'analytic for'; we must understand '*S* is analytic for *L*' where '*S*' and '*L*' are variables.

Alternatively we may, indeed, view the so-called rule as a conventional definition of a new simple symbol 'analytic-for-L_0', which might better be written untendentiously as '*K*' so as not to seem to throw light on the interesting word 'analytic'. Obviously any number of classes *K*, *M*, *N*, etc. of statements of L_0 can be specified for various purposes or for no purpose; what does it mean to say that *K*, as against *M*, *N*, etc., is the class of the "analytic" statements of L_0?

By saying what statements are analytic for L_0 we explain 'analytic-for-L_0' but not 'analytic', not 'analytic for'. We do not begin to explain the idiom '*S* is analytic for *L*' with variable '*S*' and '*L*', even though we be content to limit the range of '*L*' to the realm of artificial languages.

Actually we do know enough about the intended significance of 'analytic' to know that analytic statements are supposed to be true. Let us then turn to a second form of semantical rule, which says not that such and such statements are analytic but simply that such and such statements are included among the truths. Such a rule is not subject to the criticism of containing the un-understood word 'analytic'; and we may grant for the sake of argument that there is no difficulty over the broader term 'true'. A semantical rule of this second type, a rule of truth, is not supposed to specify all the truths of the language; it merely stipulates, recursively or otherwise, a certain multitude of statements which, along with others unspecified, are to count as true. Such a rule may be conceded to be quite clear. Derivatively, afterward, analyticity can be demarcated thus: a statement is analytic if it is (not merely true but) true according to the semantical rule.

Still there is really no progress. Instead of appealing to an unexplained word 'analytic', we are now appealing to an unexplained phrase 'semantical rule'. Not every true statement which says that the statements of some class are true can count as a semantical rule—otherwise *all* truths would be "analytic" in the sense of being true according to semantical rules. Semantical rules are distinguishable, apparently, only by the fact of appearing on a page under the heading "Semantical Rules"; and this heading is itself then meaningless.

We can say indeed that a statement is *analytic-for-*L_0 if and only if it is true according to such and such specifically appended "semantical rules," but then we find ourselves back at essentially the same case which was originally discussed: "*S* is analytic-for-L_0 if and only if. . . ." Once we seek to explain '*S* is analytic for *L*' generally for variable '*L*' (even allowing limitation of '*L*' to artificial languages), the explanation 'true according to the semantical rules of *L*' is unavailing; for the relative term 'semantical rule of' is as much in need of clarification, at least, as 'analytic for'.

It might conceivably be protested that an artificial language *L* (unlike a natural one) is a language in the ordinary sense *plus* a set of explicit semantical rules—the whole constituting, let us say, an ordered pair; and that the semantical rules of *L* then are specifiable simply as the second component of the pair *L*. But, by the same token and more simply, we might construe an artificial language *L* outright as an ordered pair whose second component is the class of its analytic statements; and then the analytic statements of *L* become specifiable simply as the statements in the second component of *L*. Or better still, we might just stop tugging at our bootstraps altogether.

Not all the explanations of analyticity known to Carnap and his readers have been covered explicitly in the above considerations, but the extension to other forms is not hard to see. Just one additional factor should be mentioned which sometimes enters: sometimes the semantical rules are in effect rules of translation into ordinary language, in which case the analytic statements of the artificial language are in effect recognized as such from the analyticity of their specified translations in ordinary language. Here certainly there can be no thought of an illumination of the problem of analyticity from the side of the artificial language.

From the point of view of the problem of analyticity the notion of an artificial language with semantical rules is a *feu follet par excellence*. Semantical rules determining the analytic statements of an artificial language are of interest only in so far as we already understand the notion of analyticity; they are of no help in gaining this understanding.

Appeal to hypothetical languages of an artificially simple kind could conceivably be useful in clarifying analyticity, if the mental or behavioral or cultural factors relevant to analyticity—whatever they may be—were somehow sketched into the simplified model. But a model which takes analyticity merely as in irreducible character is unlikely to throw light on the problem of explicating analyticity.

It is obvious that truth in general depends on both language and extralinguistic fact. The statement 'Brutus killed Caesar' would be false if the world had been different in certain ways, but it would also be false if the word 'killed' happened rather to have the sense of 'begat'. Hence the temptation to suppose in general that the truth of a statement is somehow analyzable into a linguistic component and a factual component. Given this supposition, it next seems reasonable that in some statements the factual component should be null; and these are the analytic statements. But, for all its a priori reasonableness, a boundary between analytic and synthetic statements simply has not been drawn. That there is such a distinction to be drawn at all is an unempirical dogma of empiricists, a metaphysical article of faith.

Further Readings

GENERAL

Chisholm, Roderick, *Perceiving: A Philosophical Study*, Cornell University Press, Ithaca, N.Y., 1957.

Hirst, R. J. (ed.), *Perception and the External World*, Macmillan, New York, 1965.

Merleau-Ponty, M., *Phenomenology of Perception*, Routledge & Kegan Paul, London, 1962.

Plato, *Theatetus* (in F. M. Cornford, *Plato's Theory of Knowledge*, Routledge & Kegan Paul, London, 1935).

REALISM

Brain, W. R., *Mind, Perception and Science*, Blackwell, Oxford, 1951.
Chisholm, Roderick M., *Realism and the Background of Phenomenology*, Free Press, New York, 1960.
Grice, H. P., "The Causal Theory of Perception," *Proceedings of the Aristotelian Society: Supplementary Volumes, 35* (1961).
Hirst, R. J., *The Problems of Perception*, Allen & Unwin, London, 1959.
Lovejoy, A. O., *The Revolt Against Dualism*, Open Court, La Salle, Ill., 1930.
Montague, William P., *The Ways of Knowing*, Macmillan, New York, 1925.
Perry, R. B., E. B. Holt, *et al.*, *The New Realism*, Macmillan, New York, 1912.
Russell, Bertrand, *Our Knowledge of the External World*, Norton, New York, 1929.
Russell, Bertrand, *Philosophy*, Norton, New York, 1927, chaps. 12 and 13.
Santayana, George, *Scepticism and Animal Faith*, Scribner's, New York, 1923, chaps. 18–22.
Smythies, J. R., *Analysis of Perception*, Routledge & Kegan Paul, London, 1956.
Stace, W. T., "The Refutation of Realism," *Mind, 43* (1934).

IDEALISM

Berkeley, George, *Three Dialogues Between Hylas and Philonous*, (1713). Scribner's selections, N.Y., 1929.
Ducasse, C. J., "Moore's Refutation of Idealism," in P. A. Schilpp (ed.), *The Philosophy of G. E. Moore*, Northwestern University Press, Evanston, Ill., 1942.
Ewing, A. C., *Idealism*, Methuen, London, 1934.
Ewing, A. C. (ed.), *The Idealist Tradition from Berkeley to Blanshard*, Free Press, New York, 1957.
Moore, G. E., "The Refutation of Idealism," in *Philosophical Studies*, Routledge & Kegan Paul, 1922.
Warnock, G. J., *Berkeley*, Penguin, Baltimore, 1953.

SENSE DATA AND PHENOMENALISM

Austin, J. L., *Sense and Sensibilia*, Oxford University Press, London, 1962.
Ayer, A. J., *The Foundations of Empirical Knowledge*. Macmillan, New York, 1940.
Ayer, A. J., "Perception," in C. A. Mace (ed.), *British Philosophy in the Mid-Century*. Allen & Unwin, London, 1957.
Ayer, A. J., "Phenomenalism," *Proceedings of the Aristotelian Society, 46* (1946–1947).
Barnes, W. H. F., "The Myth of Sense-Data," *Proceedings of the Aristotelian Society, 45* (1944–1945).
Broad, C. D., *The Mind and Its Place in Nature*, Routledge & Kegan Paul, London, 1951, chap. 4.
Broad, C. D., *Scientific Thought*, Routledge & Kegan Paul, London, 1927.
Chisholm, Roderick, "The Theory of Appearing," in Max Black (ed.), *Philosophical Analysis*. Cornell University Press, Ithaca, N.Y., 1950.
Firth, Roderick, "Radical Empiricism and Perceptual Relativity," *Philosophical Review, 59* (1950).
Hume, David, *A Treatise of Human Nature*, 1739–1740, Book I, Scribner Selections, 1927.
Lean, Martin, *Sense-Perception and Matter*, Routledge & Kegan Paul, London, 1953.
Lewis, C. I., *An Analysis of Knowledge and Valuation*, Open Court, La Salle, Ill., 1947.
Lewis, C. I., *An Analysis of Knowledge* Scribner's, New York, 1929.
Mach, Ernst, *Contributions Toward the Analysis of Sensations*, Open Court, La Salle, Ill., 1897.
Marhenke, Paul, "Phenomenalism," in Max Black (ed.), *Philosophical Analysis*, Cornell University Press, Ithaca, N.Y., 1950.
Mill, John Stuart, *An Examination of Sir William Hamilton's Philosophy*, Longmans. London, 1872.
Moore, G. E., *Some Main Problems of Philosophy*, Macmillan, New York, 1953, chap. 2.
Paul, G. A., "Is There a Problem About Sense-Data?" *Proceedings of the Aristotelian Society: Supplementary Volumes, 15* (1936).
Pearson, Karl, *The Grammar of Science*, Dutton, New York, 1937, chaps. 2–5.
Price, H. H., *Perception*, Methuen, London, 1932.
Prichard, H. A., "The Sense-Datum Fallacy," *Proceedings of the Aristotelian Society: Supplementary Volumes, 17* (1938).

Stace, W. T., *The Theory of Knowledge and Existence,* Oxford University Press, Fair Lawn, N.J., 1932.

Whiteley, C. H., *An Introduction to Metaphysics,* Methuen, London, 1950.

NECESSARY TRUTH

Aristotle, Metaphysica, Book IV, in *Basic Works of Aristotle,* Richard McKeon (ed.), Random House, New York, 1941.

Ayer, A. J., *Language, Truth and Logic,* Dover, New York, 1950, chap. 4.

Benacerraf, P., and H. Putnam (eds.), *Philosophy of Mathematics,* Prentice-Hall, Englewood Cliffs, N.J., 1964.

Blanshard, Brand, *Reason and Analysis,* Allen & Unwin, London, 1962, chap. 10.

Carnap, Rudolf, "Meaning and Synonymy in Natural Languages," *Philosophical Studies, 6* (1955), also in Rudolph Carnap, *Meaning and Necessity,* 2nd ed., University of Chicago Press, Chicago, 1956.

Ewing, A. C., *The Fundamental Problems of Philosophy,* Macmillan, New York, 1951, chap. II.

Frege, Gottlob, *The Foundations of Arithmetic,* trans. J. L. Austin, Harper & Row, New York, 1953, chaps. 1 and 5.

Gasking, Douglas, "Mathematics and the World," in A. Flew (ed.), *Logic and Language, Second Series,* Blackwell, Oxford, 1953, also in Benacerraf and Putnam.

Grice, H. P., and P. F. Strawson, "In Defense of a Dogma," *Philosophical Review, 65* (1956).

Hempel, Carl G., "Geometry and Empirical Science," in Feigl and Sellars (eds.), *Readings in Philosophical Analysis,* Appleton-Century-Crofts, New York, 1949.

Hempel, Carl G., "On the Nature of Mathematical Truth," in Feigl and Sellars (eds.), *Readings in Philosophical Analysis,* Appleton-Century-Crofts, New York, 1949, also in Benacerraf and Putnam.

Kemeny, J. G., "Analyticity versus Fuzziness," *Synthese,* 1963.

Leibniz, G. W., "On the Supersensible Element in Knowledge, and on the Immaterial in Nature," in P. P. Wiener (ed.), *Leibniz-Selections* Scribner's, New York, 1951.

Lewis, C. I., *Mind and the World Order,* Scribner's, New York, 1929, chaps. 7, 8, and 9.

Locke, John, *An Essay Concerning Human Understanding,* especially bk. IV, chaps. 7 and 8, Dover, N.Y., 1959.

Malcolm, Norman, "Are Necessary Propositions Really Verbal?" *Mind, 49* (1940).

Nagel, Ernest, "Logic Without Ontology," in Feigl and Sellars (eds.), *Readings in Philosophical Analysis,* Appleton-Century-Crofts, New York, 1949, also in Benacerraf and Putnam.

Plato, *Meno.* Liberal Arts Press, New York, 1949.

Putnam, Hilary, "The Analytic and Synthetic," in Feigl and Maxwell (eds.), *Minnesota Studies in the Philosophy of Science,* University of Minnesota Press, Minneapolis, 1962, vol. III.

Quine, W. V., "Carnap and Logical Truth," in Quine, *The Ways of Paradox,* Random House, New York, 1966.

Quine, W. V., "Necessary Truth," in Quine, *The Ways of Paradox,* Random House, New York, 1966.

Quine, W. V., "Truth by Convention," in Quine, *The Ways of Paradox,* Random House, New York, 1966, also in both Feigl and Sellars, and Benacerraf and Putnam.

Russell, Bertrand, *Introduction to Mathematical Philosophy,* Allen & Unwin, London, 1919, chaps. 1, 2, 13, 14, and 18.

Russell, Bertrand, *The Problems of Philosophy,* Oxford University Press, London, 1912, chaps. 7 and 8.

Schlick, Moritz, "*Is There a Factual a Priori?*" in Feigl and Sellars (eds.), *Readings in Philosophical Analysis,* Appleton-Century-Crofts, New York, 1949.

Waismann, Friedrich, "Analytic-Synthetic," *Analysis,* 1949–1952.

White, Morton, "The Analytic and the Synthetic: An Untenable Dualism," in L. Linsky (ed.), *Semantics and the Philosophy of Language,* University of Illinois Press, Urbana, Ill., 1952.

White, Morton, *Toward Reunion in Philosophy,* Harvard University Press, Cambridge, Mass., 1956, chaps. 7, 8, and 9.

Wittgenstein, Ludwig, *Remarks on the Foundations of Mathematics,* Macmillan, New York, 1956 (selections reprinted in Benacerraf and Putnam).

VIII

LANGUAGE AND MEANING

LL OF US will see immediately that there is a difference between "table" and "bfflf." An obvious difference is that the former can be pronounced more easily than the latter. But this difference is not very interesting from the philosopher's point of view. The important difference can be put in more than one way. We understand "table," but not "bfflf," we know what "table" means, but not what "bfflf" means; we know what a table is, but not what a bfflf is, or what it is to bfflf—the point is that we do not really know what bfflf says.

Philosophers who are interested in language consider this to be one of the central questions in the philosophy of language: What is it that distinguishes a word from a set of meaningless marks or a string of meaningless noises? This is sometimes put into the form: What is it for a word to have meaning? There has been a range of answers to this question. Two of the most important are that a word has meaning because it stands in a certain relation to a thing and that a word has meaning because it has a use in a language.

Before looking at these two different answers let us note that there is a certain danger in discussing questions about language, since the discussion must be carried on within language. Consider the sentence "This sentence is false." Grammatically it is correct; but once we think about it we realize that it leads to a strange and undesirable result. Presumably, the sentence is either true or false. Let us assume that it is true. Then, since what it says is that it is false, it must be false. So if it is true, it is false. If, however, it is false, then the opposite of what it says must be the case. And since the opposite of being false is being true, then it must be true. So if it is false, it is true. This leaves us with the unhappy result that we have a sentence which is true if and only if it is false, and this is a clear contradiction.

All of this goes to show that any discussion of language must proceed with caution. The dangers of paradox are less acute when we are talking about meaning than when we are talking about truth. It is important to realize, however, that discussions about language draw conclusions about some bit of language, and these conclusions must be applicable to the language in which the conclusions are drawn.

It is worthwhile to see that, while questions of meaning are of interest in themselves, they are also of relevance to other problems in philosophy, among them necessary truth. For example, if an analytic statement is characterized as true by virtue of the meanings of its terms, it is obvious that some account of meaning is needed to understand this characterization. (On this matter see Quine, "One Dogma of Empiricism," in Section VII, "Knowledge, Perception, and Necessary Truth.")

Word-Thing Theory

According to one version of the word-thing theory, the meaning of a word is whatever the word refers to, that is, the meaning and the referent of a word are the same. According to the other version, the meaning is not what the word refers to, but certain attributes of the thing to which it refers. The meaning and the referent are distinguished, but the meaning is still a thing; viz., a set of attributes. Philosophers who hold a form of this theory sometimes point out that the word "meaning" may be used in contexts other than linguistic contexts. For example, we say that the expression on his face means that he is pleased and that the green traffic light means go. In cases such as these it is natural to say that there are two things involved: the sign and that of which it is the sign.

When "meaning" is used in linguistic contexts (e.g., we say "a word has meaning," "one understands the meaning," "these words have the same meaning"), the tendency is to assume that here too there are two things: there is the word, on the one hand, and its meaning, on the other. The task of the philosopher, then, is to find something that will serve as the meaning of a word.

John Locke said that words stand for our ideas. The meaning of "horse" is the idea that the word calls up in each of us. This view does justice to the fact that while different people use the same words, it does not follow that each word means exactly the same thing to each person. This is because each person associates an idea, his own idea, with each word, and it may well be that two people have different ideas associated with the same word.

On the other hand, Locke's theory of ideas also provides an account of what makes speech intelligent and of how men can understand the speech of others. To speak intelligently is to use words with which the speaker has associated some of his own ideas; were one to have no ideas associated with the words he uses, his speech would be of no more worth than that of a parrot. To understand the speech of another is to have the speaker's words call up in your mind the ideas which he associates with the words he uses. According to Locke, then, words refer to their associated ideas and these ideas are the meanings of the words. (See Locke, "On the Signification of Words," in this section.)

Another form of the word-thing theory is put forward by John Stuart Mill. Mill distinguishes different kinds of things to which a word may be related. For Mill, a word refers to the things to which the word can be applied. For example, "cow" refers to each cow. This is expressed by saying the one word *denotes* each cow. The name "Lyndon Johnson" denotes the man who was elected President of the United States in 1964.

On the other hand, many words have what Mill calls a *connotation.* When we call something a horse, it is so called because it has certain attributes—four legs, a tail, a certain kind of hoof; these attributes are the connotation of the word. The connotation of a word is the set of attributes which we require a thing to have before we will call it by that word. (See Mill, "On Naming," in this section.)

The above theories agree that the meaning of a word is some thing with which the word is associated. There are difficulties with such theories, however. First, it appears that not all words are, in fact, associated with things. For example, words like "of," "and," "by," seem not to stand for, denote, or connote anything at all (even Locke and Mill realized this). This casts doubt on the applicability of the word-thing theory to all cases.

A second difficulty is that it is extremely hard to give a coherent account of what the *things* in question are supposed to be. Ideas, for example, are very elusive. How does one differentiate them? How does one decide how many ideas one has in his mind over a five-minute period? There are similar difficulties with the notion of attribute. Where are attributes? How do we tell one attribute from another?

A third difficulty is that, for many of the terms in a language, there seems to be no common set of attributes possessed by all of those things to which we apply the term. For example, not all tables have one thing in common (except for the fact that they are all called "tables"). It seems, therefore, as if there may not be any one set of attributes or one idea associated with a word.

In addition to these problems with word-thing theories, a deeper dissatisfaction with them has been expressed by Ludwig Wittgenstein. He felt that there was something basically wrong with the very attempt to find a *thing* that was the meaning of a word. He argued that even if such a thing were found, it would not answer the question to which we are addressing ourselves, "What is the meaning of a word?" or "What is it for a word to have meaning?" The problem at hand is to give an account of what it is that gives a sign, or word, life. In itself, it is a dead thing. If we accept some form of the word-thing theory, we are left with the same problem. Instead of having one dead thing, the word, we have two dead things, the word and the thing with which it is associated. Many philosophers in the twentieth century have come to agree that the search for the thing which is the meaning of a word is misguided, and that the life of a word is its *use* in the language. (See Ryle, "The Theory of Meaning," in this section.)

One early form of the use theory is that held by Moritz Schlick. He talks about the meaning of a sentence, rather than the meaning of a word, and says that to know the meaning of a sentence one must know the circumstances that would have to obtain in order for the sentence to be true. That is, one must know how to tell whether the sentence is true or false—how to verify or falsify it. This was expressed by saying that "the meaning of a proposition is the method of its verification," and the particular theory is called the verification theory of meaning.

Verificationists were careful to distinguish actual from possible verification, and to say that for a proposition to have meaning it was sufficient that it be possible to verify it. Otherwise, a proposition like "Brutus killed Caesar" would be meaningless because we cannot go back in time, as we would have to, in order actually to verify it. It is sufficient that we know what would verify it for it to have meaning, for example, the eyewitness report of someone living at the time of the assassination. Verificationists also stressed that by "possible" they meant "logically possible," not "empirically possible." For example, at the present stage of our mastery of space travel and observation, it is not empirically possible to verify "There are mountains on Pluto." There is, however, nothing impossible in principle about being able to verify it—as there is about being able to verify "Time is unreal." (For further uses of the verifiability thesis see the selection entitled "Elimination of Metaphysics" in Section X.)

Other philosophers who hold the use theory are not so concerned with what would count as the verification of a proposition as with what it is to know the meaning of a word. They note that to say of a person that he knows what a word means is to say that he knows how to use the word, that is, he can make statements, ask questions, give commands with it. This suggests that to learn the meaning of a word is not to acquire some piece of knowledge of the form "This refers to that," or "An X is whatever has these attributes"; it is to master a set of skills, as one does when he learns how to play a game; it is a case of coming to know how to do something, rather than of coming to know that such and such is the case.

The game analogy goes further than this. In many ways, a word is like a piece in a chess game. Both a word and a chess piece have uses: it is not sufficient merely to be able to point to a piece of wood; one must be able to move the chess piece in a game before he can be said to know the piece. Similarly to know what a word means is to be able to use the word in playing what Wittgenstein called "language-games." Ryle in "The Theory of Meaning" gives a clear statement of the game analogy.

Philosophers who defend the use theory do not deny that some words stand for things, but they point out that words stand for things only because they are used in certain ways. Its use in the language determines what, if anything, a word stands for—the standing for does not come first.

Early proponents of the use theory were not very systematic, but they did note that words are used in many ways—in telling jokes, asking questions, issuing commands, and pronouncing verdicts. More recently some philosophers have attempted to classify such uses systematically. An especially interesting use of language, considered in detail by J. L. Austin, is the *performative*—the use of words to perform an action. When a person says "I promise," he has, in uttering those words, actually promised. He did not *say* that he promised; he *promised;* in saying "I promise" he performs an action, just as one who kicks a football performs an action. (See Austin, "Performative Utterances.") Austin later gave an even more detailed classification of the different kinds of actions performed with the use of words: a *locutionary act* is the act of uttering any words at all; an *illocutionary act* is performed *in* uttering certain words; a *perlocutionary act* is performed *by* uttering the words; e.g., "I promise." *By* saying "I promise," I got him to stop bothering me. *By* yelling "Fire!" I got the people to leave the theater. These are perlocutions. Sometimes we perform all three of these kinds of acts at once. For example, when, while standing at the altar, I uttered the words "I will," I performed a locutionary act. *In* saying these words, I got married and *by* saying them I, hopefully, made a certain woman very happy. That is, I performed illocutionary and perlocutionary acts as well.

Many contemporary philosophers have shown that language is a far more complex tool than it was previously thought to be. Just as the word-thing theory was said to have presented an oversimplified picture of what it is for a word to have meaning, so, some philosophers now contend, many theories of language have oversimplified the facts of language by supposing that every statement made within language is either true or false. Consider the following performative utterances. "I promise to help you tomorrow," and "I christen thee the good ship 'Hope,'" are both perfectly fine English sentences; but how would one decide whether they were true or false? Indeed, what would it mean to say they were true or false? There are, it has been pointed out, ways in which they might go wrong. For example, I might not intend to keep my promise, or I might not in fact keep my promise, or I might not be in the legal position to perform a christening. Yet none of these ways of failing is a matter of being false, or of falsity.

The selections that follow discuss in greater detail many of the theories of meaning that we have just considered.

OF THE SIGNIFICATION OF WORDS

JOHN LOCKE

1. Man, though he have great variety of thoughts, and such from which others as well as himself might receive profit and delight; yet they are all within his own breast, invisible and hidden from others, nor can of themselves be made to appear. The comfort and advantage of society not

From *An Essay Concerning Human Understanding* (1690), Book III, Chapter 2.

being to be had without communication of thoughts, it was necessary that man should find out some external sensible signs, whereof those invisible ideas, which his thoughts are made up of, might be made known to others. For this purpose nothing was so fit, either for plenty or quickness, as those articulate sounds, which with so much ease and variety he found himself able to make. Thus we may conceive how *words*, which were by nature so well adapted to that purpose, came to be made use of by men as the signs of their ideas; not by any natural connexion that there is between particular articulate sounds and certain ideas, for then there would be but one language amongst all men; but by a voluntary imposition, whereby such a word is made arbitrarily the mark of such an idea. The use, then, of words, is to be sensible marks of ideas; and the ideas they stand for are their proper and immediate signification.

2. The use men have of these marks being either to record their own thoughts, for the assistance of their own memory; or, as it were, to bring out their ideas, and lay them before the view of others: words, in their primary or immediate signification, stand for nothing but *the ideas in the mind of him that uses them*, how imperfectly soever or carelessly those ideas are collected from the things which they are supposed to represent. When a man speaks to another, it is that he may be understood: and the end of speech is, that those sounds, as marks, may make known his ideas to the hearer. That then which words are the marks of are the ideas of the speaker: nor can any one apply them as marks, immediately, to anything else but the ideas that he himself hath: for this would be to make them signs of his own conceptions, and yet apply them to other ideas; which would be to make them signs and not signs of his ideas at the same time; and so in effect to have no signification at all. Words being voluntary signs, they cannot be voluntary signs imposed by him on things he knows not. That would be to make them signs of nothing, sounds without signification. A man cannot make his words the signs either of qualities in things, or of conceptions in the mind of another, whereof he has none in his own. Till he has some ideas of his own, he cannot suppose them to correspond with the conceptions of another man; nor can he use any signs for them: for thus they would be the signs of he knows not what, which is in truth to be the signs of nothing. But when he represents to himself other men's ideas by some of his own, if he consent to give them the same names that other men do, it is still to his own ideas; to ideas that he has, and not to ideas that he has not.

3. This is so necessary in the use of language, that in this respect the knowing and the ignorant, the learned and the unlearned, use the words they speak (with any meaning) all alike. They, in every man's mouth, stand for the ideas he has, and which he would express by them. A child having taken notice of nothing in the metal he hears called *gold*, but the bright shining yellow colour, he applies the word gold only to his own idea of that colour, and nothing else; and therefore calls the same colour in a peacock's tail gold. Another that hath better observed, adds to shining yellow great weight: and then the sound gold, when he uses it,

stands for a complex idea of a shining yellow and a very weighty substance. Another adds to those qualities fusibility: and then the word gold signifies to him a body, bright, yellow, fusible, and very heavy. Another adds malleability. Each of these uses equally the word gold, when they have occasion to express the idea which they have applied it to: but it is evident that each can apply it only to his own idea; nor can he make it stand as a sign of such a complex idea as he has not.

4. But though words, as they are used by men, can properly and immediately signify nothing but the ideas that are in the mind of the speaker; yet they in their thoughts give them a secret reference to two other things.

First, *They suppose their words to be marks of the ideas in the minds also of other men, with whom they communicate:* for else they should talk in vain, and could not be understood, if the sounds they applied to one idea were such as by the hearer were applied to another, which is to speak two languages. But in this men stand not usually to examine, whether the idea they, and those they discourse with have in their minds be the same: but think it enough that they use the word, as they imagine, in the common acceptation of that language; in which they suppose that the idea they make it a sign of is precisely the same to which the understanding men of that country apply that name.

5. Secondly, Because men would not be thought to talk barely of their own imagination, but of things as really they are; therefore they often suppose the *words to stand also for the reality of things.* But this relating more particularly to substances and their names, as perhaps the former does to simple ideas and modes, we shall speak of these two different ways of applying words more at large, when we come to treat of the names of mixed modes and substances in particular: though give me leave here to say, that it is a perverting the use of words, and brings unavoidable obscurity and confusion into their signification, whenever we make them stand for anything but those ideas we have in our own minds.

6. Concerning words, also, it is further to be considered:

First, that they being immediately the signs of men's ideas, and by that means the instruments whereby men communicate their conceptions, and express to one another those thoughts and imaginations they have within their own breasts; there comes, by constant use, to be such a connexion between certain sounds and the ideas they stand for, that the names heard, almost as readily excite certain ideas as if the objects themselves, which are apt to produce them, did actually affect the senses. Which is manifestly so in all obvious sensible qualities, and in all substances that frequently and familiarly occur to us.

7. Secondly, That though the proper and immediate signification of words are ideas in the mind of the speaker, yet, because by familiar use from our cradles, we come to learn certain articulate sounds very perfectly, and have them readily on our tongues, and always at hand in our memories, but yet are not always careful to examine or settle their significations perfectly; it often happens that men, even when they would

apply themselves to an attentive consideration, do set their thoughts more on words than things. Nay, because words are many of them learned before the ideas are known for which they stand: therefore some, not only children but men, speak several words no otherwise than parrots do, only because they have learned them, and have been accustomed to those sounds. But so far as words are of use and signification, so far is there a constant connexion between the sound and the idea, and a designation that the one stands for the other; without which application of them, they are nothing but so much insignificant noise.

8. Words, by long and familiar use, as has been said, come to excite in men certain ideas so constantly and readily, that they are apt to suppose a natural connexion between them. But that they signify only men's peculiar ideas, and that *by a perfect arbitrary imposition*, is evident, in that they often fail to excite in others (even that use the same language) the same ideas we take them to be signs of: and every man has so inviolable a liberty to make words stand for what ideas he pleases, that no one hath the power to make others have the same ideas in their minds that he has, when they use the same words that he does. And therefore the great Augustus himself, in the possession of that power which ruled the world, acknowledged he could not make a new Latin word: which was as much as to say, that he could not arbitrarily apppoint what idea any sound should be a sign of, in the mouths and common language of his subjects. It is true, common use, by a tacit consent, appropriates certain sounds to certain ideas in all languages, which so far limits the signification of that sound, that unless a man applies it to the same idea, he does not speak properly: and let me add, that unless a man's words excite the same ideas in the hearer which he makes them stand for in speaking, he does not speak intelligibly. But whatever be the consequence of any man's using of words differently, either from their general meaning, or the particular sense of the person to whom he addresses them; this is certain, their signification, in his use of them, is limited to his ideas, and they can be signs of nothing else.

ON NAMING

JOHN STUART MILL

"A name," says Hobbes, "is a word taken at pleasure to serve for a mark which may raise in our mind a thought like to some thought we had before, and which being pronounced to others, may be to them a sign of what thought the speaker had before in his mind." This simple definition

From *A System of Logic,* 10th ed. (first published in 1843), Book I, Chapters 1 and 2, Longmans, Green & Co., London, 1879.

of a name, as a word (or set of words) serving the double purpose of a mark to recall to ourselves the likeness of a former thought, and a sign to make it known to others, appears unexceptionable. Names, indeed, do much more than this; but whatever else they do, grows out of, and is the result of this: as will appear in its proper place.

Are names more properly said to be the names of things, or of our ideas of things? The first is the expression in common use; the last is that of some metaphysicians, who conceived that in adopting it they were introducing a highly important distinction. The eminent thinker, just quoted, seems to countenance the latter opinion. "But seeing," he continues, "names ordered in speech (as is defined) are signs of our conceptions, it is manifest they are not signs of the things themselves; for that the sound of this word *stone* should be the sign of a stone, cannot be understood in any sense but this, that he that hears it collects that he that pronounces it thinks of a stone."

If it be merely meant that the conception alone, and not the thing itself, is recalled by the name, or imparted to the hearer, this of course cannot be denied. Nevertheless, there seems good reason for adhering to the common usage, and calling (as indeed Hobbes himself does in other places) the word *sun* the name of the sun, and not the name of our idea of the sun. For names are not intended only to make the hearer conceive what we conceive, but also to inform him what we believe. Now, when I use a name for the purpose of expressing a belief, it is a belief concerning the thing itself, not concerning my idea of it. When I say, "the sun is the cause of day," I do not mean that my idea of the sun causes or excites in me the idea of day: or in other words, that thinking of the sun makes me think of day. I mean, that a certain physical fact, which is called the sun's presence (and which, in the ultimate analysis, resolves itself into sensations, not ideas) causes another physical fact, which is called day. It seems proper to consider a word as the *name* of that which we intend to be understood by it when we use it; of that which any fact that we assert of it is to be understood of; that, in short, concerning which, when we employ the word, we intend to give information. Names, therefore, shall always be spoken of in this work as the names of things themselves, and not merely of our ideas of things.

. . .

All names are names of something, real or imaginary; but all things have not names appropriated to them individually. For some individual objects we require, and consequently have, separate distinguishing names; there is a name for every person, and for every remarkable place. Other objects, of which we have not occasion to speak so frequently, we do not designate by a name of their own; but when the necessity arises for naming them, we do so by putting together several words, each of which, by itself, might be and is used for an indefinite number of other objects; as when I say, *this stone:* "this" and "stone" being, each of them, names that may be used of many other objects besides the particular one meant, though the only object of which they can both be used at the given moment, consistently with their signification, may be the one of which I wish to speak.

Were this the sole purpose for which names, that are common to more things than one, could be employed; if they only served, by mutually limiting each other, to afford a designation for such individual objects as have no names of their own: they could only be ranked among contrivances for economizing the use of language. But it is evident that this is not their sole function. It is by their means that we are enabled to assert *general* propositions; to affirm or deny any predicate of an indefinite number of things at once. The distinction, therefore, between *general* names, and *individual* or *singular* names, is fundamental; and may be considered as the first grand division of names.

A general name is familiarly defined, a name which is capable of being truly affirmed, in the same sense, of each of an indefinite number of things. An individual or singular name is a name which is only capable of being truly affirmed, in the same sense, of one thing.

Thus, *man* is capable of being truly affirmed of John, George, Mary, and other persons without assignable limit; and it is affirmed of all of them in the same sense; for the word man expresses certain qualities, and when we predicate it of those persons, we assert that they all possess those qualities. But *John* is only capable of being truly affirmed of one single person, at least in the same sense. For, though there are many persons who bear that name, it is not conferred upon them to indicate any qualities, or anything which belongs to them in common; and cannot be said to be affirmed of them in any *sense* at all, consequently not in the same sense. "The king who succeeded William the Conqueror," is also an individual name. For, that there cannot be more than one person of whom it can be truly affirmed, is implied in the meaning of the words. Even "*the* king," when the occasion or the context defines the individual of whom it is to be understood, may justly be regarded as an individual name.

It is not unusual, by way of explaining what is meant by a general name, to say that it is the name of a *class*. But this, though a convenient mode of expression for some purposes, is objectionable as a definition, since it explains the clearer of two things by the more obscure. It would be more logical to reverse the proposition, and turn it into a definition of the word *class:* "A class is the indefinite multitude of individuals denoted by a general name."

. . .

The second general division of names is into *concrete* and *abstract*. A concrete name is a name which stands for a thing; an abstract name is a name which stands for an attribute of a thing. Thus *John, the sea, this table*, are names of things. *White*, also, is the name of a thing, or rather of things. Whiteness, again, is the name of a quality or attribute of those things. Man is a name of many things; humanity is a name of an attribute of those things. *Old* is a name of things; *old age* is a name of one of their attributes.

I have used the words concrete and abstract in the sense annexed to them by the schoolmen, who, notwithstanding the imperfections of their philosophy, were unrivalled in the construction of technical language, and whose definitions, in logic at least, though they never went more than a little way into the subject, have seldom, I think, been altered but to be spoiled. A practice, however, has grown up in more modern times, which, if not introduced by Locke, has gained currency chiefly from his example, of applying the expression "abstract name" to all names which are the result of abstraction or generalization, and consequently to all general names, instead of confining it to the names of attributes. The metaphysicians of the Condillac school,—whose admiration of Locke, passing over the profoundest speculations of that truly original genius, usually fastens with peculiar eagerness upon his weakest points,—have gone on imitating him in this abuse of language, until there is now some difficulty in restoring the word to its original signification. A more wanton alteration in the meaning of a word is rarely to be met with; for the expression *general name*, the exact equivalent of which exists in all languages I am acquainted with, was already available for the purpose to which *abstract* has been misappropriated, while the misappropriation leaves that important class of words, the names of attributes, without any compact distinctive appellation. The old acceptation, however, has not gone so completely out of use, as to deprive those who still adhere to it of all chance of being understood. By *abstract*, then, I shall always, in Logic proper, mean the opposite of *concrete;* by an abstract name, the name of an attribute; by a concrete name, the name of an object.

Do abstract names belong to the class of general, or to that of singular names? Some of them are certainly general. I mean those which are names not of one single and definite attribute, but of a class of attributes. Such is the word *colour*, which is a name common to whiteness, redness, &c. Such is even the word whiteness, in respect of the different shades of whiteness to which it is applied in common: the word magnitude, in respect of the various degrees of magnitude and the various dimensions of space; the word weight, in respect of the various degrees of weight. Such also is the word *attribute* itself, the common name of all particular attributes. But when only one attribute, neither variable in degree nor in kind, is designated by the name; as visibleness; tangibleness; equality; squareness; milkwhiteness; then the name can hardly be considered general; for though it denotes an attribute of many different objects, the attribute itself is always conceived as one, not many. To avoid needless logomachies, the best course would probably be to consider these names as neither general nor individual, and to place them in a class apart.

It may be objected to our definition of an abstract name, that not only the names which we have called abstract, but adjectives, which we have placed in the concrete class, are names of attributes; that *white*, for example, is as much the name of the colour as *whiteness* is. But (as before remarked) a word ought to be considered as the name of that which we intend to be understood by it when we put it to its principal use, that is, when we employ it in predication. When we say snow is white, milk is white, linen is white, we do not mean it to be understood that snow, or linen, or milk, is a colour. We mean that they are things having the colour. The reverse is the case with the word whiteness; what we affirm to *be* whiteness is not snow, but the colour of snow. Whiteness, therefore, is the name of the colour exclusively: white is a name of all things whatever having the colour; a name, not of the quality of whiteness, but of every white object. It is true, this name was given to all those various objects on account of the quality; and we may therefore say, without impropriety, that the quality forms part of its signification; but a name can only be said to stand for, or to be a name of, the things of which it can be predicated. We shall presently see that all names which can be said to have any signification, all names by applying which to an individual we give any information respecting that individual, may be said to *imply* an attribute of some sort; but they are not names of the attribute; it has its own proper abstract name.

This leads to the consideration of a third great division of names, into *connotative* and *non-connotative*, the latter sometimes, but improperly, called *absolute*. This is one of the most important distinctions which we shall have occasion to point out, and one of those which go deepest into the nature of language.

A non-connotative term is one which signifies a subject only, or an attribute only. A connotative term is one which denotes a subject, and implies an attribute. By a subject is here meant anything which possesses attributes. Thus John, or London, or England, are names which signify a subject only. Whiteness, length, virtue, signify an attribute only. None of these names, therefore, are connotative. But *white*, *long*, *virtuous*, are connotative. The word white, denotes all white things, as snow, paper, the foam of the sea, &c., and implies, or in the language of the schoolmen, *connotes*, the attribute *whiteness*. The word white is not predicated of the attribute, but of the subjects, snow, &c.; but when we predicate it of them, we convey the meaning that the attribute whiteness belongs to them. The same may be said of the other words above cited. Virtuous, for example, is the name of a class, which includes Socrates, Howard, the Man of Ross, and an undefinable number of other individuals, past, present, and to come. These individuals, collectively and severally, can alone be said with propriety to be denoted by the word: of them alone can it properly be said to be a name. But it is a name applied to all of them in consequence of an attribute which they are supposed to possess in common, the attribute which has received the name of virtue. It is applied to all beings that are considered to possess this attribute; and to none which are not so considered.

All concrete general names are connotative. The word *man*, for example, denotes Peter, Jane, John, and an indefinite number of other individuals, of whom, taken as a class, it is the name. But it is applied to them, because they possess, and to signify that they possess, certain attributes. These seem to be, corporeity, animal life, rationality, and a certain external form, which for distinction we call the human. Every existing thing, which possessed all these attributes, would be called a man; and anything which possessed none of them, or only one, or two, or even three of them without the fourth, would not be so called. For example, if in the interior of Africa there were to be discovered a race of animals possessing reason equal to that of human beings, but with the form of an elephant, they would not be called men. Swift's Houyhnhnms would not be so called. Or if such newly-discovered beings possessed the form of man without any vestige of reason, it is probable that some other name than that of man would be found for them. How it happens that there can be any doubt about the matter, will appear hereafter. The word *man*, therefore, signifies all these attributes, and all subjects which possess these attributes. But it can be predicated only of the subjects. What we call men, are the subjects, the individual Stiles and Nokes; not the qualities by which their humanity is constituted. The name, therefore, is said to signify the subjects *directly*, the attributes *indirectly;* it *denotes* the subjects, and implies, or involves, or indicates, or as we shall say henceforth *connotes*, the attributes. It is a connotative name.

. . .

It has been seen that all concrete general names are connotative. Even abstract names, though the names only of attributes, may in some instances be justly considered as connotative; for attributes themselves may have attributes ascribed to them; and a word which denotes attributes may connote an attribute of those attributes. Of this description, for example, is such a word as *fault;* equivalent to *bad* or *hurtful quality*. This word is a name common to many attributes, and connotes hurtfulness, an attribute of those various attributes. When, for example, we say that slowness, in a horse, is a fault, we do not mean that the slow movement, the actual change of place of the slow horse, is a bad thing, but that the property or peculiarity of the horse, from which it derives that name, the quality of being a slow mover, is an undesirable peculiarity.

In regard to those concrete names which are not general but individual, a distinction must be made.

Proper names are not connotative: they denote the individuals who are called by them; but they do not indicate or imply any attributes as belonging to those individuals. When we name a child by the name of Paul, or a dog by the name Caesar, these names are simply marks used to enable those individuals to be made subjects of discourse. It may be said, indeed, that we must have had some reason for giving them those names rather than any others; and this is true; but the name, once given, is independent of the reason. A man may have been named John, because that was the name of his father; a town may have been named Dartmouth, because it is situated at the mouth of the Dart. But it is no part of the signification of the word John, that the father of the person so called bore the same name; nor even of the word Dartmouth, to be situated at the mouth of the Dart. If sand should choke up the mouth of the river, or an earthquake change its course, and remove it to a distance from the town, the name of the town would not necessarily be changed. That fact, therefore, can form no part of the signification of the word; for otherwise, when the fact confessedly ceased to be true, no one would any longer think of applying the name. Proper names are attached to the objects themselves, and are not dependent on the continuance of any attribute of the object.

But there is another kind of names, which, although they are individual names, that is, predicable only of one object, are really connotative. For, though we may give to an individual a name utterly unmeaning, which we call a proper name—a word which answers the purpose of showing what thing it is we are talking about, but not of telling anything about it; yet a name peculiar to an individual is not necessarily of this description. It may be significant of some attribute, or some union of attributes, which, being possessed by no object but one, determines the name exclusively to that individual. "The sun" is a name of this description; "God," when used by a monotheist, is another. These, however, are scarcely examples of what we are now attempting to illustrate, being, in strictness of language, general, not individual names: for, however they may be *in fact* predicable only of one object, there is nothing in the meaning of the words themselves which implies this: and, accordingly, when we are imagining and not affirming, we may speak of many suns; and the majority of mankind have believed, and still believe, that there are many gods. But it is easy to produce words which are real instances of connotative individual names. It may be part of the meaning of the connotative name itself, that there can exist but one individual possessing the attribute which it connotes: as for instance, "the *only* son of John Stiles;" "the *first* emperor of Rome." Or the attribute connoted may be a connexion with some determinate event, and the connexion may be of such a kind as only one individual could have; or may at least be such as only one individual actually had; and this may be implied in the form of the expression. "The father of Socrates" is an example of the one kind (since Socrates could not have had two fathers); "the author of the *Iliad*," "the murderer of Henri Quatre," of the second. For, though it is conceivable that more persons than one might have participated in the authorship of the *Iliad*, or in the murder of Henri Quatre, the employment of the article *the* implies that, in fact, this was not the case. What is here done by the word *the*, is done in other cases by the context: thus, "Caesar's army" is an individual name, if it appears from the context that the army meant is that which Caesar commanded in a particular battle. . . .

From the preceding observations it will easily be collected, that whenever the names given to objects convey any information, that is, whenever they have properly any meaning, the meaning resides not in what they *denote*, but in what they *connote*. The only names of objects which connote nothing are *proper* names; and these have, strictly speaking, no signification.

If, like the robber in the Arabian Nights, we make a mark with chalk on a house to enable us to know it again, the mark has a purpose, but it has not properly any meaning. The chalk does not declare anything about the house; it does not mean, This is such a person's house, or This is a house which contains booty. The object of making the mark is merely distinction. I say to myself, All these houses are so nearly alike that if I lose sight of them I shall not again be able to distinguish that which I am now looking at, from any of the others; I must therefore contrive to make the appearance of this one house unlike that of the others, that I may hereafter know when I see the mark—not indeed any attribute of the house—but simply that it is the same house which I am now looking at. Morgiana chalked all the other houses in a similar manner, and defeated the scheme: how? simply by obliterating the difference of appearance between that house and the others. The chalk was still there, but it no longer served the purpose of a distinctive mark.

When we impose a proper name, we perform an operation in some degree analogous to what the robber intended in chalking the house. We put a mark, not indeed upon the object itself, but, so to speak, upon the idea of the object. A proper name is but an unmeaning mark which we connect in our minds with the idea of the object, in order that whenever the mark meets our eyes or occurs to our thoughts, we may think of that individual object. Not being attached to the thing itself, it does not, like the chalk, enable us to distinguish the object when we see it; but it enables us to distinguish it when it is spoken of, either in the records of our own experience, or in the discourse of others; to know that what we find asserted in any proposition of which it is the subject, is asserted of the individual thing with which we were previously acquainted.

When we predicate of anything its proper name; when we say, pointing to a man, this is Brown or Smith, or pointing to a city, that it is York, we do not, merely by so doing, convey to the reader any information about them, except that those are their names. By enabling him to identify the individuals, we may connect them with information previously possessed by him; by saying, This is York, we may tell him that it contains the Minster. But this is in virtue of what he has previously heard concerning York; not by anything implied in the name. It is otherwise when objects are spoken of by connotative names. When we say, The town is built of marble, we give the hearer what may be entirely new information, and this merely by the signification of the many-worded connotative name, "built of marble." Such names are not signs of the mere objects, invented because we have occasion to think and speak of those objects individually; but signs which accompany an attribute: a kind of livery in which the attribute clothes all objects which are recognised as possessing it. They are not mere marks, but more, that is to say, significant marks; and the connotation is what constitutes their significance.

As a proper name is said to be the name of the one individual which it is predicated of, so (as well from the importance of adhering to analogy, as for the other reasons formerly assigned) a connotative name ought to be considered a name of all the various individuals which it is predicable of, or in other words *denotes*, and not of what it connotes. But by learning what things it is a name of, we do not learn the meaning of the name: for to the same thing we may, with equal propriety, apply many names, not equivalent in meaning. Thus, I call a certain man by the name Sophroniscus: I call him by another name, The father of Socrates. Both these are names of the same individual, but their meaning is altogether different; they are applied to that individual for two different purposes: the one, merely to distinguish him from other persons who are spoken of; the other to indicate a fact relating to him, the fact that Socrates was his son. I further apply to him these other expressions: a man, a Greek, an Athenian, a sculptor, an old man, an honest man, a brave man. All these are, or may be, names of Sophroniscus, not indeed of him alone, but of him and each of an indefinite number of other human beings. Each of these names is applied to Sophroniscus for a different reason, and by each whoever understands its meaning is apprised of a distinct fact or number of facts concerning him; but those who knew nothing about the names except that they were applicable to Sophroniscus, would be altogether ignorant of their meaning. It is even possible that I might know every single individual of whom a given name could be with truth affirmed, and yet could not be said to know the meaning of the name. A child knows who are its brothers and sisters, long before it has any definite conception of the nature of the facts which are involved in the signification of those words.

In some cases it is not easy to decide precisely how much a particular word does or does not connote; that is, we do not exactly know (the case not having arisen) what degree of difference in the object would occasion a difference in the name. Thus, it is clear that the word man, besides animal life and rationality, connotes also a certain external form; but it would be impossible to say precisely what form; that is, to decide how great a deviation from the form ordinarily found in the beings whom we are accustomed to call men, would suffice in a newly-discovered race to make us refuse them the name of man. Rationality, also, being a quality which admits of degrees, it has never been settled what is the lowest degree of that quality which would entitle any creature to be considered a human being. In all such cases, the meaning of the general name is so far unsettled and vague; mankind have not come to any positive agreement about the matter. When we come to treat of Classification, we shall have occasion to show under what conditions this vagueness may exist without practical inconvenience; and cases will appear in which the ends of language are better promoted by it than by complete precision; in order that, in natural history for instance, individuals or species of no very marked character may be ranged with those more strongly characterized individuals or species, to which, in all their properties taken together, they bear the nearest resemblance.

MEANING AND VERIFICATION

MORITZ SCHLICK

I

Philosophical questions, as compared with ordinary scientific problems, are always strangely paradoxical. But it seems to be an especially strange paradox that the question concerning the meaning of a proposition should constitute a serious philosophical difficulty. For is it not the very nature and purpose of every proposition to express its own meaning? In fact, when we are confronted with a proposition (in a language familiar to us) we usually know its meaning immediately. If we do not, we can have it explained to us, but the explanation will consist of a new proposition; and if the new one is capable of expressing the meaning, why should not the original one be capable of it? So that a snippy person when asked what he meant by a certain statement might be perfectly justified in saying, 'I meant exactly what I said!'.

It is logically legitimate and actually the normal way in ordinary life and even in science to answer a question concerning the meaning of a proposition by simply repeating it either more distinctly or in slightly different words. Under what circumstances, then, can there be any sense in asking for the meaning of a statement which is well before our eyes or ears?

Evidently the only possibility is that we have not *understood* it. And in this case what is actually before our eyes or ears is nothing but a series of words which we are unable to handle; we do not know how to use it, how to 'apply it to reality'. Such a series of words is for us simply a complex of signs 'without meaning', a mere sequel of sounds or a mere row of marks on paper, and we have no right to call it 'a proposition' at all; we may perhaps speak of it as 'a sentence'.

If we adopt this terminology we can now easily get rid of our paradox by saying that we cannot inquire after the meaning of a proposition, but can ask about the meaning of a sentence, and that this amounts to asking, 'What proposition does the sentence stand for?'. And this question is answered either by a proposition in a language with which we are already perfectly familiar; or by indicating the logical rules which will make a proposition out of the sentence, *i.e.*, will tell us exactly in what circumstances the sentence is to be *used*. These two methods do not actually

Reprinted from *The Philosophical Review*, 45, 1936, by permission of the editors.

differ in principle; both of them give meaning to the sentence (transform it into a proposition) by locating it, as it were, within the system of a definite language; the first method making use of a language which is already in our possession, the second one building it up for us. The first method represents the simplest kind of ordinary 'translation'; the second one affords a deeper insight into the nature of meaning, and will have to be used in order to overcome philosophical difficulties connected with the understanding of sentences.

The source of these difficulties is to be found in the fact that very often we do not know how to handle our own words; we speak or write without having first agreed upon a definite logical grammar which will constitute the signification of our terms. We commit the mistake of thinking that we know the meaning of a sentence (*i.e.*, understand it as a proposition) if we are familiar with all the words occurring in it. But this is not sufficient. It will not lead to confusion or error as long as we remain in the domain of everyday life by which our words have been formed and to which they are adapted, but it will become fatal the moment we try to think about abstract problems by means of the same terms without carefully fixing their signification for the new purpose. For every word has a definite signification only within a definite context into which it has been fitted; in any other context it will have no meaning unless we provide new rules for the use of the word in the new case, and this may be done, at least in principle, quite arbitrarily.

Let us consider an example. If a friend should say to me, 'Take me to a country where the sky is three times as blue as in England!' I should not know how to fulfill his wish; his phrase would appear nonsensical to me, because the word 'blue' is used in a way which is not provided for by the rules of our language. The combination of a numeral and the name of a color does not occur in it; therefore my friend's sentence has no meaning, although its exterior linquistic form is that of a command or a wish. But he can, of course, give it a meaning. If I ask him, 'What do you mean by "three times as blue"?', he can arbitrarily indicate certain definite physical circumstances concerning the serenity of the sky which he wants his phrase to be the description of. And then, perhaps, I shall be able to follow his directions; his wish will have become meaningful for me.

Thus, whenever we ask about a sentence, 'What does it mean?', what we expect is instruction as to the circumstances in which the sentence is to be used; we want a description of the conditions under which the sentence will form a *true* proposition, and of those which will make it *false*. The meaning of a word or a combination of words is, in this way, determined by a set of rules which regulate their use and which, following Wittgenstein, we may call the rules of their *grammar*, taking this word in its widest sense.

(If the preceding remarks about meaning are as correct as I am convinced they are, this will, to a large measure, be due to conversations with Wittgenstein which have greatly influenced my own views about these matters. I can hardly exaggerate my indebtedness to this philosopher. I do not wish to impute to him any responsibility for the contents of this article, but I have reason to hope that he will agree with the main substance of it.)

Stating the meaning of a sentence amounts to stating the rules according to which the sentence is to be used, and this is the same as stating the way in which it can be verified (or falsified). The meaning of a proposition is the method of its verification.

The 'grammatical' rules will partly consist of ordinary definitions, *i.e.*, explanations of words by means of other words, partly of what are called 'ostensive' definitions, *i.e.*, explanations by means of a procedure which puts the words to actual use. The simplest form of an ostensive definition is a pointing gesture combined with the pronouncing of the word, as when we teach a child the signfication of the sound 'blue' by showing a blue object. But in most cases the ostensive definition is of a more complicated form; we cannot point to an object corresponding to words like 'because', 'immediate', 'chance', 'again', etc. In these cases we require the presence of certain complex situations, and the meaning of the words is defined by the way we use them in these different situations.

It is clear that in order to understand a verbal definition we must know the signification of the explaining words beforehand, and that the only explanation which can work without any previous knowledge is the ostensive definition. We conclude that there is no way of understanding any meaning without ultimate reference to ostensive definitions, and this means, in an obvious sense, reference to 'experience' or 'possibility of verification'.

This is the situation, and nothing seems to me simpler or less questionable. It is this situation and nothing else that we describe when we affirm that the meaning of a proposition can be given only by giving the rules of its verification in experience. (The addition, 'in experience', is really superfluous, as no other kind of verification has been defined.)

This view has been called the "experimental theory of meaning"; but it certainly is no theory at all, for the term 'theory' is used for a set of hypotheses about a certain subject-matter, and there are no hypotheses involved in our view, which proposes to be nothing but a simple statement of the way in which meaning is *actually* assigned to propositions, both in everyday life and in science. There has never been any other way, and it would be a grave error to suppose that we believe we have discovered a new conception of meaning which is contrary to common opinion and which we want to introduce into philosophy. On the contrary, our conception is not only entirely in agreement with, but even derived from, common sense and scientific procedure. Although our criterion of meaning has always been employed in practice, it has very rarely been formulated in the past, and this is perhaps the only excuse for the attempts of so many philosophers to deny its feasibility.

The most famous case of an explicit formulation of our criterion is Einstein's answer to the question, What do we mean when we speak of two events at distant places happening simultaneously? This answer consisted in a description of an experimental method by which the simultaneity of such events was actually ascertained. Einstein's philosophical opponents maintained—and some of them still maintain—that they knew the meaning of the above question independently of any method of verification. All I am trying to do is to stick consistently to Einstein's position and to admit no exceptions from it. (Professor Bridgman's book on *The Logic of Modern Physics* is an admirable attempt to carry out this program for all concepts of physics.) I am not writing for those who think that Einstein's philosophical opponents were right.

III

Verifiability means possibility of verification. Professor Lewis justly remarks that to "omit all examination of the wide range of significance which could attach to 'possible verification', would be to leave the whole conception rather obscure".* For our purpose it suffices to distinguish between two of the many ways in which the word 'possibility' is used. We shall call them 'empirical possibility' and 'logical possibility'. Professor Lewis describes two meanings of 'verifiability' which correspond exactly to this difference; he is fully aware of it, and there is hardly anything left for me to do but carefully to work out the distinction and show its bearing upon our issue.

I propose to call 'empirically possible' anything that does not contradict the laws of nature. This is, I think, the largest sense in which we may speak of empirical possibility; we do not restrict the term to happenings which are not only in accordance with the laws of nature but also with the actual state of the universe (where 'actual' might refer to the present moment of our own lives, or to the condition of human beings on this planet, and so forth). If we chose the latter definition (which seems to have been in Professor Lewis's mind when he spoke of "possible experience as conditioned by the actual", *loc. cit.* 141) we should not get the sharp boundaries we need for our present purpose. So 'empirical possibility' is to mean 'compatibility with natural laws'.

Now, since we cannot boast of a complete and sure knowledge of nature's laws, it is evident that we can never assert with certainty the empirical possibility of any fact, and here we may be permitted to speak of *degrees* of possibility. Is it possible for me to lift this book? Surely!—This table? I think so!—This billiard table? I don't think so!—This automobile? Certainly not!—It is clear that in these cases the answer is given by *experience*, as the result of experiments performed in the past. Any judgment about empirical possibility is based on experience and will

* C. I. Lewis, "Experience and Meaning", *Philosophical Review*, 1934, p. 137.

often be rather uncertain; there will be no sharp boundary between possibility and impossibility.

Is the possibility of verification which we insist upon of this empirical sort? In that case there would be different degrees of verifiability, the question of meaning would be a matter of more or less, not a matter of yes or no. In many disputes concerning our issue it is the empirical possibility of verification which is discussed; the various examples of verifiability given by Professor Lewis, *e.g.*, are instances of different empirical circumstances in which the verification is carried out or prevented from being carried out. Many of those who refuse to accept our criterion of meaning seem to imagine that the procedure of its application in a special case is somewhat like this: A proposition is presented to us ready made, and in order to discover its meaning we have to try various methods of verifying or falsifying it, and if one of these methods works we have found the meaning of the proposition; but if not, we say it has no meaning. If we really had to proceed in this way, it is clear that the determination of meaning would be entirely a matter of experience, and that in many cases no sharp and ultimate decision could be obtained. How could we ever know that we had tried long enough, if none of our methods were successful? Might not future efforts disclose a meaning which we were unable to find before?

This whole conception is, of course, entirely erroneous. It speaks of meaning as if it were a kind of entity inherent in a sentence and hidden in it like a nut in its shell, so that the philosopher would have to crack the shell or sentence in order to reveal the nut or meaning. We know from our considerations in section I that a proposition cannot be given 'ready made'; that meaning does not inhere in a sentence where it might be discovered, but that it must be bestowed upon it. And this is done by applying to the sentence the rules of the logical grammar of our language, as explained in section I. These rules are not facts of nature which could be 'discovered', but they are prescriptions stipulated by acts of definition. And these definitions have to be known to those who pronounce the sentence in question and to those who hear or read it. Otherwise they are not confronted with any proposition at all, and there is nothing they could try to verify, because you can't verify or falsify a mere row of words. You cannot even start verifying before you know the meaning, *i.e.*, before you have established the possibility of verification.

In other words, the possibility of verification which is relevant to meaning cannot be of the empirical sort; it cannot be established *post festum*. You have to be sure of it before you can consider the empirical circumstances and investigate whether or no or under what conditions they will permit of verification. The empirical circumstances are all-important when you want to know if a proposition is *true* (which is the concern of the scientist), but they can have no influence on the *meaning* of the proposition (which is the concern of the philosopher). Professor Lewis has seen and expressed this very clearly (*loc. cit.*, 142, first six lines), and our Vienna positivism, as far as I can answer for it, is in complete agreement with him on this point. It must be emphasized that when we speak of verifiability we mean *logical* possibility of verification, and nothing but this.

I call a fact or a process 'logically possible' if it can be *described, i.e.*, if the sentence which is supposed to describe it obeys the rules of grammar we have stipulated for our language. (I am expressing myself rather incorrectly. A fact which could not be described would, of course, not be any fact at all; *any* fact is logically possible. But I think my meaning will be understood.) Take some examples. The sentences, 'My friend died the day after tomorrow'; 'The lady wore a dark red dress which was bright green'; 'The campanile is 100 feet and 150 feet high'; 'The child was naked, but wore a long white nightgown', obviously violate the rules which, in ordinary English, govern the use of the words occurring in the sentences. They do not describe any facts at all; they are meaningless, because they represent *logical* impossibilities.

It is of the greatest importance (not only for our present issue but for philosophical problems in general) to see that whenever we speak of logical impossibility we are referring to a discrepancy between the definitions of our terms and the way in which we use them. We must avoid the severe mistake committed by some of the former Empiricists like Mill and Spencer, who regarded logical principles (*e.g.*, the Law of Contradiction) as laws of nature governing the psychological process of thinking. The nonsensical statements alluded to above do not correspond to thoughts which, by a sort of psychological experiment, we find ourselves unable to think; they do not correspond to any thoughts at all. When we hear the words, 'A tower which is both 100 feet and 150 feet high', the image of two towers of different heights may be in our mind, and we may find it psychologically (empirically) impossible to combine the two pictures into one image, but it is not this fact which is denoted by the words 'logical impossibility'. The height of a tower cannot be 100 feet and 150 feet at the same time; a child cannot be naked and dressed at the same time—not because we are unable to imagine it, but because our definitions of 'height', of the numerals, of the terms 'naked' and 'dressed', are not compatible with the particular combinations of those words in our examples. 'They are not compatible with such combinations' means that the rules of our language have not provided any use for such combinations; they do not describe any fact. We could change these rules, of course, and thereby arrange a meaning for the terms 'both red and green', 'both naked and dressed'; but if we decide to stick to the ordinary definitions (which reveal themselves in the way we actually use our words) we have decided to regard those combined terms as meaningless, *i.e.*, not to use them as the description of *any* fact. Whatever fact we may or may not imagine, if the word 'naked' (or 'red') occurs in its description we have decided that the word 'dressed' (or 'green') cannot be put in its place in the same description. If we do not follow this rule it means that we want to introduce a new definition of the words, or that we don't mind using words without meaning and like to indulge in nonsense. (I am far from condemning this attitude under all circumstances; on certain occasions—as in *Alice in Wonderland*—it may be the only sensible attitude and far more delightful than any treatise on Logic. But in such a treatise we have a right to expect a different attitude.)

The result of our considerations is this: Verifiability, which is the sufficient and necessary condition of meaning, is a possibility of the logical order; it is created by constructing the sentence in accordance with the rules by which its terms are defined. The only case in which verification is (logically) impossible is the case where you have *made* it impossible by not setting any rules for its verification. Grammatical rules are not found anywhere in nature, but are made by man and are, in principle, arbitrary; so you cannot give meaning to a sentence by *discovering* a method of verifying it, but only by *stipulating* how it *shall* be done. Thus logical possibility or impossibility of verification is always *self-imposed*. If we utter a sentence without meaning it is always *our own fault*.

The tremendous philosophic importance of this last remark will be realized when we consider that what we said about the meaning of *assertions* applies also to the meaning of *questions*. There are, of course, many questions which can never be answered by human beings. But the impossibility of finding the answer may be of two different kinds. If it is merely empirical in the sense defined, if it is due to the chance circumstances to which our human existence is confined, there may be reason to lament our fate and the weakness of our physical and mental powers, but the problem could never be said to be absolutely insoluble, and there would always be some hope, at least for future generations. For the empirical circumstances may alter, human facilities may develop, and even the laws of nature may change (perhaps even suddenly and in such a way that the universe would be thrown open to much more extended investigation). A problem of this kind might be called practically unanswerable or technically unanswerable, and might cause the scientists great trouble, but the philosopher, who is concerned with general principles only, would not feel terribly excited about it.

But what about those questions for which it is *logically* impossible to find an answer? Such problems would remain insoluble under all imaginable circumstances; they would confront us with a definite hopeless *Ignorabimus;* and it is of the greatest importance for the philosopher to know whether there are any such issues. Now it is easy to see from what has been said before that this calamity could happen only if the question itself had no meaning. It would not be a genuine question at all, but a mere row of words with a question-mark at the end. We must say that a question is meaningful, if we can *understand* it, *i.e.*, if we are able to decide for any given proposition whether, if true, it would be an answer to our question. And if this is so, the actual decision could only be prevented by empirical circumstances, which means that it would not be *logically* impossible. Hence no meaningful problem can be insoluble in *principle*. If in any case we find an answer to be logically impossible we know that we really have not been asking anything, that what sounded like a question was actually a nonsensical combination of words. A genuine question is one for which an answer is logically possible. This is one of the most characteristic results of our empiricism. It means that in principle there are no limits to our knowledge. The boundaries which must be acknowledged are of an empirical nature and, therefore, never ultimate; they can be pushed back further and further; there is no unfathomable mystery in the world.

The dividing line between logical possibility and impossibility of verification is absolutely sharp and distinct; there is no gradual transition between meaning and nonsense. For either you have given the grammatical rules for verification, or you have not; *tertium non datur*.

Empirical possibility is determined by the laws of nature, but meaning and verifiability are entirely independent of them. Everything that I can describe or define is logically possible—and definitions are in no way bound up with natural laws. The proposition 'Rivers flow uphill' is meaningful, but happens to be false because the fact it describes is *physically* impossible. It will not deprive a proposition of its meaning if the conditions which I stipulate for its verification are incompatible with the laws of nature; I may prescribe conditions, for instance, which could be fulfilled only if the velocity of light were greater than it actually is, or if the Law of Conservation of Energy did not hold, and so forth.

An opponent of our view might find a dangerous paradox or even a contradiction in the preceding explanations, because on the one hand we insisted so strongly on what has been called the "*empirical*-meaning requirement", and on the other hand we assert most emphatically that meaning and verifiability do not depend on any empirical conditions whatever, but are determined by purely logical possibilities. The opponent will object: if meaning is a matter of experience, how can it be a matter of definition and logic?

In reality there is no contradiction or difficulty. The word 'experience' is ambiguous. Firstly, it may be a name for any so-called 'immediate data'—which is a comparatively modern use of the word—and secondly we can use it in the sense in which we speak, *e.g.*, of an 'experienced traveler', meaning a man who has not only seen a great deal but also knows how to profit from it for his actions. It is in this second sense (by the way, the sense the word has in Hume's and Kant's philosophy) that verifiability must be declared to be independent of experience. The possibility of verification does not rest on any 'experiential truth', on a law of nature or any other true general proposition, but is determined solely by our definitions, by the rules which have been fixed for our language, or which we can fix arbitrarily at any moment. All of these rules ultimately point to ostensive definitions, as we have explained, and through them verifiability is linked to *experience* in the *first* sense of the word. No rule of expression presupposes any law or regularity in the world (which is the condition of 'experience' as Hume and Kant use the word), but it does presuppose data and situations, to which names can be attached. The rules of language are rules of the application of language; so there must be something to which it can be applied. Expressibility and verifiability are one and the same thing. There is no antagonism between logic and experience. Not only can the logician be an empiricist at the same time; he *must* be one if he wants to understand what he himself is doing.

IV

Let us glance at some examples in order to illustrate the consequences of our attitude in regard to certain issues of traditional philosophy. Take the famous case of the reality of the other side of the moon (which is also one of Professor Lewis's examples). None of us, I think, would be willing to accept a view according to which it would be nonsense to speak of the averted face of our satellite. Can there be the slightest doubt that, according to our explanations, the conditions of meaning are amply satisfied in this case?

I think there can be no doubt. For the question, 'What is the other side of the moon like?' could be answered, for instance, by a description of what would be seen or touched by a person located somewhere behind the moon. The question whether it be physically possible for a human being—or indeed any other living being—to travel around the moon does not even have to be raised here; it is entirely irrelevant. Even if it could be shown that a journey to another celestial body were absolutely incompatible with the known laws of nature, a proposition about the other side of the moon would still be meaningful. Since our sentence speaks of certain places in space as being filled with matter (for that is what the words 'side of the moon' stand for), it will have meaning if we indicate under what circumstances a proposition of the form, 'this place is filled with matter', shall be called true or false. The concept 'physical substance at a certain place' is defined by our language in physics and geometry. Geometry itself is the grammar of our propositions about 'spatial' relations, and it is not very difficult to see how assertions about physical properties and spatial relations are connected with 'sense-data' by ostensive definitions. This connection, by the way, is *not* such as to entitle us to say that physical substance is 'a mere construction put upon sense-data', or that a physical body is 'a complex of sense-data'—unless we interpret these phrases as rather inadequate abbreviations of the assertion that all propositions containing the term 'physical body' require for their verification the presence of sense-data. And this is certainly an exceedingly trivial statement.

In the case of the moon we might perhaps say that the meaning-requirement is fulfilled if we are able to 'imagine' (picture mentally) situations which would verify our proposition. But if we should say in general that verifiability of an assertion implies possibility of 'imagining' the asserted fact, this would be true only in a restricted sense. It would not be true in so far as the possibility is of the empirical kind, i.e., implying specific human capacities. I do not think, for instance, that we can be accused of talking nonsense if we speak of a universe of ten dimensions, or of beings possessing sense-organs and having perceptions entirely different from ours; and yet it does not seem right to say that we are able to 'imagine' such beings and such perceptions, or a ten-dimensional world. But we *must* be able to say under what *observable* circumstances we should assert the existence of the beings or sense-organs just referred to. It is clear that I can speak meaningfully of the sound of a friend's voice without being able actually to recall it in my imagination.— This is not the place to discuss the logical grammar of the word 'to imagine'; these few remarks may caution us against accepting too readily a *psychological* explanation of verifiability.

We must not identify meaning with any of the psychological data which form the material of a mental sentence (or 'thought') in the same sense in which articulated sounds form the material of a spoken sentence, or black marks on paper the material of a written sentence. When you are doing a calculation in arithmetic it is quite irrelevant whether you have before your mind the images of black numbers or of red numbers, or no visual picture at all. And even if it were empirically impossible for you to do any calculation without imagining black numbers at the same time, the mental pictures of those black marks could, of course, in no way be considered as constituting the meaning, or part of the meaning, of the calculation.

Carnap is right in putting great stress upon the fact (always emphasized by the critics of 'psychologism') that the question of meaning has nothing to do with the psychological question as to the mental processes of which an act of thought may consist. But I am not sure that he has seen with equal clarity that reference to ostensive definitions (which we postulate for meaning) does *not* involve the error of a confusion of the two questions. In order to understand a sentence containing, *e.g.*, the words 'red flag', it is indispensable that I should be able to indicate a situation where I could point to an object which I should call a 'flag', and whose color I could recognize as 'red' as distinguished from other colors. But in order to do this it is *not* necessary that I should actually call up the image of a red flag. It is of the utmost importance to see that these two things have nothing in common. At this moment I am trying in vain to imagine the shape of a capital G in German print; nevertheless I can speak about it without talking nonsense, and I know I should recognize it if I saw the letter. Imagining a red patch is utterly different from referring to an ostensive definition of 'red'. Verifiability has nothing to do with any images that may be associated with the words of the sentence in question.

No more difficulty than in the case of the other side of the moon will be found in discussing, as another significant example, the question of 'immortality', which Professor Lewis calls, and which is usually called, a *metaphysical* problem. I take it for granted that 'immortality' is not supposed to signify never-ending life (for that might possibly be meaningless on account of infinity being involved), but that we are concerned with the question of survival after 'death'. I think we may agree with Professor Lewis when he says about this hypothesis: "Our understanding of what would verify it has no lack of clarity." In fact, I can easily imagine, *e.g.*, witnessing the funeral of my own body and continuing to exist without a body, for nothing is easier than to describe a world which differs from our ordinary world only in the complete absence of all data which I would call parts of my own body.

We must conclude that immortality, in the sense defined, should not be regarded as a 'metaphysical problem', but is an empirical hypothesis, because it possesses logical verifiability. It could be verified by following the prescription: 'Wait until you die!' Professor Lewis seems to hold that this method is not satisfactory from the point of view of science. He says:

> The hypothesis of immortality is unverifiable in an obvious sense. . . . If it be maintained that only what is scientifically verifiable has meaning, then this conception is a case in point. It could hardly be verified by science; and there is no observation or experiment which science could make, the negative result of which would disprove it.*

I fancy that in these sentences the private method of verification is rejected as being unscientific because it would apply only to the individual case of the experiencing person himself, whereas a scientific statement should be capable of a *general* proof, open to any careful observer. But I see no reason why even this should be declared to be impossible. On the contrary, it is easy to describe experiences such that the hypothesis of an invisible existence of human beings after their bodily death would be the most acceptable explanation of the phenomena observed. These phenomena, it is true, would have to be of a much more convincing nature than the ridiculous happenings alleged to have occurred in meetings of the occultists—but I think there cannot be the slightest doubt as to the possibility (in the logical sense) of phenomena which would form a scientific justification of the hypothesis of survival after death, and would permit an investigation by scientific methods of that form of life. To be sure, the hypothesis could never be established as absolutely true, but it shares this fate with all hypotheses. If it should be urged that the souls of the deceased might inhabit some supercelestial space where they would not be accessible to our perception, and that therefore the truth or falsity of the assertion could never be tested, the reply would be that if the words "supercelestial space" are to have any meaning at all, that space must be defined in such a way that the impossibility of reaching it or of perceiving anything in it would be merely empirical, so that some means of overcoming the difficulties could at least

* *Loc. cit.*, 143.

be described, although it might be beyond human power to put them into use.

Thus our conclusion stands. The hypothesis of immortality is an empirical statement which owes its meaning to its verifiability, and it has no meaning beyond the possibility of verification. If it must be admitted that science could make no experiment the negative result of which would disprove it, this is true only in the same sense in which it is true for many other hypotheses of similar structure—especially those that have sprung up from other motives than the knowledge of a great many facts of experience which must be regarded as giving a high probability to the hypothesis.

THE THEORY OF MEANING

GILBERT RYLE

We can all use the notion of *meaning*. From the moment we begin to learn to translate English into French and French into English, we realize that one expression does or does not mean the same as another. But we use the notion of meaning even earlier than that. When we read or hear something in our own language which we do not understand, we wonder what it means and ask to have its meaning explained to us. The ideas of understanding, misunderstanding and failing to understand what is said already contain the notion of expressions having and lacking specifiable meanings.

It is, however, one thing to ask, as a child might ask, What, if anything, is meant by 'vitamin', or 'abracadabra' or '$(a + b)^2 = a^2 + b^2 + 2ab$'? It is quite another sort of thing to ask What are meanings? It is, in the same way, one thing to ask, as a child might ask, What can I buy for this shilling?, and quite another sort of thing to ask What is purchasing-power? or What are exchange-values?

Now answers to this highly abstract question, What are meanings? have, in recent decades, bulked large in philosophical and logical discussions. Preoccupation with the theory of meaning could be described as the occupational disease of twentieth-century Anglo-Saxon and Austrian philosophy. We need not worry whether or not it is a disease. But it might be useful to survey the motives and the major results of this preoccupation.

Incidentally it is worth noticing that many of these issues were explicitly canvassed—and some of them conclusively settled—in certain

Reprinted from *British Philosophy in the Mid-Century*, 1957, pp. 239–264, by permission of the author and Allen & Unwin, Ltd., London.

of Plato's later Dialogues, and in the logical and other works of Aristotle. Some of them, again, were dominant issues in the late Middle Ages and later still with Hobbes; and some of them, thickly or thinly veiled in the psychological terminology of 'ideas', stirred uneasily inside British epistemology between Locke and John Stuart Mill. But I shall not, save for one or two back-references, discuss the early history of these issues.

The shopkeeper, the customer, the banker and the merchant are ordinarily under no intellectual pressure to answer or even ask the abstract questions What is purchasing-power? and What are exchange-values? They are interested in the prices of things, but not yet in the abstract question What is the real nature of that which is common to two articles of the same price? Similarly, the child who tries to follow a conversation on an unfamiliar topic, and the translator who tries to render Thucydides into English are interested in what certain expressions mean. But they are not necessarily interested in the abstract questions What is it for an expression to have a meaning? or What is the nature and status of that which an expression and its translation or paraphrase are both the vehicles? From what sort of interests, then, do we come to ask this sort of question? Doubtless there are many answers. I shall concentrate on two of them which I shall call 'the Theory of Logic' and 'the Theory of Philosophy'. I shall spend a good long time on the first; not so long on the second.

(1) *THE THEORY OF LOGIC*

The logician, in studying the rules of inference has to talk of the components of arguments, namely their premisses and conclusions and to talk of them in perfectly general terms. Even when he adduces concrete premisses and conclusions, he does so only to illustrate the generalities which are his proper concern. In the same way, he has to discuss the types of separable components or the types of distinguishable features of these premiss-types and conclusion-types, since it is sometimes on such components or features of premisses and conclusions that the inferences from and to them pivot.

Now the same argument may be expressed in English or in French or in any other language; and if it is expressed in English, there may still be hosts of different ways of wording it. What the logician is exploring is intended to be indifferent to these differences of wording. He is concerned with what is said by a premiss-sentence or a conclusion-sentence, not with how it is worded.

So, if not in the prosecution of his inquiry, at least in his explanations of what he is doing, he has to declare that his subject-matter consist not of the sentences and their ingredient words in which arguments are expressed, but of the propositions or judgments and their constituent terms, ideas or concepts of which the sentences and words are the vehicles.

Sometimes he may say that his subject-matter consists of sentence-meanings and their constituent word-meanings or phrase-meanings, though this idiom is interestingly repellent. Why it is repellent we shall, I hope, see later on. So in giving this sort of explanation of his business, he is talking *about* meanings, where in the prosecution of that business he is just operating *upon* them.

For our purposes it is near enough true to say that the first influential discussion of the notion of meaning given by a modern logician was that with which John Stuart Mill opens his *System of Logic* (1843). He acknowledges debts both to Hobbes and to the Schoolmen, but we need not trace these borrowings in detail.

Mill's contributions to Formal or Symbolic Logic were negligible. It was not he but his exact contemporaries, Boole and de Morgan, and his immediate successors, Jevons, Venn, Carroll, McColl and Peirce who, in the English-speaking world, paved the way for Russell. On the other hand, it is difficult to exaggerate the influence which he exercised, for good and for ill, upon British and Continental philosophers; and we must include among these philosophers the Symbolic Logicians as well, in so far as they have philosophized about their technical business. In particular, Mill's theory of meaning set the questions, and in large measure, determined their answers for thinkers as different as Brentano, in Austria; Meinong and Husserl, who were pupils of Brentano; Bradley, Jevons, Venn, Frege, James, Peirce, Moore and Russell. This extraordinary achievement was due chiefly to the fact that Mill was original in producing a doctrine of meaning at all. The doctrine that he produced was immediately influential, partly because a doctrine was needed and partly because its inconsistencies were transparent. Nearly all of the thinkers whom I have listed were in vehement opposition to certain parts of Mill's doctrine, and it was the other parts of it from which they often drew their most effective weapons.

Mill, following Hobbes's lead, starts off his account of the notion of meaning by considering single words. As we have to learn the alphabet before we can begin to spell, so it seemed natural to suppose that the meanings of sentences are compounds of the components, which are the meanings of their ingredient words. Word-meanings are atoms, sentence-meanings are molecules. I say that it seemed natural, but I hope soon to satisfy you that it was a tragically false start. Next Mill, again following Hobbes's lead, takes it for granted that all words, or nearly all words, are names, and this, at first, sounds very tempting. We know what it is for 'Fido' to be the name of a particular dog, and for 'London' to be the name of a particular town. There, in front of us, is the dog or the town which has the name, so here, one feels, there is no mystery. We have just the familiar relation between a thing and its name. The assimilation of all or most other single words to names gives us, accordingly, a cosy feeling. We fancy that we know where we are. The dog in front of us is what the word 'Fido' stands for, the town we visited yesterday is what the word 'London' stands for. So the classification of all or most single words as names makes us feel that what a word means is in all cases some manageable thing that that word is the name of. Meanings, at least word-meanings, are nothing abstruse or remote, they are, *prima facie*, ordinary things and happenings like dogs and towns and battles.

Mill goes further. Sometimes the grammatical subject of a sentence is not a single word but a many-worded phrase, like 'the present Prime Minister' or 'the first man to stand on the summit of Mt. Everest'. Mill has no qualms in classifying complex expressions like these also as names, what he calls 'many-worded names'. There do not exist proper names for everything we want to talk about; and sometimes we want to talk about something or somebody whose proper name, though it exists, is unknown to us. So descriptive phrases are coined by us to do duty for proper names. But they are still, according to Mill, names, though the tempting and in fact prevailing interpretation of this assertion differs importantly from what Mill usually wanted to convey. For, when Mill calls a word or phrase a 'name', he is using 'name' not, or not always, quite in the ordinary way. Sometimes he says that for an expression to be a name it must be able to be used as the subject or the predicate of a subject-predicate sentence—which lets in, e.g. adjectives as names. Sometimes his requirements are more stringent. A name is an expression which can be the subject of a subject-predicate sentence—which leaves only nouns, pronouns and substantival phrases. 'Name', for him, does not mean merely 'proper name'. He often resisted temptations to which he subjected his successors.

Before going any further, I want to make you at least suspect that this initially congenial equation of words and descriptive phrases with names is from the outset a monstrous howler—if, like some of Mill's successors, though unlike Mill himself, we do systematically construe 'name' on the model of 'proper name'. The assumption of the truth of this equation has been responsible for a large number of radical absurdities in philosophy in general and the philosophy of logic in particular. It was a fetter round the ankles of Meinong, from which he never freed himself. It was a fetter round the ankles of Frege, Moore and Russell, who all, sooner or later, saw that without some big emendations, the assumption led inevitably to fatal impasses. It was, as he himself says in his new book, a fetter round the ankles of Wittgenstein in the *Tractatus*, though in that same book he had found not only the need but the way to cut himself partially loose from it.

I am still not quite sure why it seems so natural to assume that all words are names, and even that every possible grammatical subject of a sentence, one-worded or many-worded, stands to something as the proper name 'Fido' stands to the dog Fido, and, what is a further point, that the thing it stands for is what the expression means. Even Plato had had to fight his way out of the same assumption. But he at least had a special excuse. The Greek language had only the one word ὄνομα where we have the three words 'word', 'name' and 'noun'. It was hard in Greek even to say that the Greek counterpart to our verb 'is' was a word but not a noun. Greek provided Plato with no label for verbs, or for adverbs, conjunctions etc. That 'is' is a word, but is not a name or even a noun was a tricky thing to say in Greek where ὄνομα did duty both for our word 'word', for our word 'name' and, eventually, for our word 'noun'. But even without this excuse people still find it natural to assimilate all words to names, and the meanings of words to the bearers of those alleged names. Yet the assumption is easy to demolish.

First, if every single word were a name, then a sentence composed of five words, say 'three is a prime number' would be a list of the five objects named by those five words. But a list, like 'Plato, Aristotle, Aquinas, Locke, Berkeley' is not a sentence. It says nothing, true or false. A sentence, on the contrary, may say something–some one thing–which is true or false. So the words combined into a sentence at least do something jointly which is different from their severally naming the several things that they name if they do name any things. What a sentence means is not decomposable into the set of things which the words in it stand for, if they do stand for things. So the notion of *having meaning* is at least partly different from the notion of *standing for*.

More than this. I can use the two descriptive phrases 'the Morning Star' and 'the Evening Star', as different ways of referring to Venus. But it is quite clear that the two phrases are different in meaning. It would be incorrect to translate into French the phrase 'the Morning Star' by 'l'Étoile du Soir'. But if the two phrases have different meanings, then Venus, the planet which we describe by these two different descriptions, cannot be what these descriptive phrases mean. For she, Venus, is one and the same, but what the two phrases signify are different. As we shall see in a moment Mill candidly acknowledges this point and makes an important allowance for it.

Moreover it is easy to coin descriptive phrases to which nothing at all answers. The phrase 'the third man to stand on the top of Mt. Everest' cannot, at present, be used to refer to anybody. There exists as yet no one whom it fits and perhaps there never will. Yet it is certainly a significant phrase, and could be translated into French or German. We know, we have to know, what it means when we say that it fits no living mountaineer. It means *something*, but it does not designate *somebody*. What it means cannot, therefore, be equated with a particular mountaineer. Nor can the meaning conveyed by the phrase 'the first person to stand on the top of Mt. Everest' be equated with Hillary, though, we gather, it fits him and does not fit anyone else. We can understand the question, and even entertain Nepalese doubts about the answer to the question 'Is Hillary the first person to conquer Mt. Everest?' where we could not understand the question 'Is Hillary Hillary?'

We could reach the same conclusion even more directly. If Hillary was, *per impossibile*, identified with what is meant by the phrase 'the first man to stand on the top of Mt. Everest', it would follow that the meaning of at least one phrase was born in New Zealand, has breathed through an oxygen-mask and has been decorated by Her Majesty. But this is patent nonsense. Meanings of phrases are not New Zealand citizens; what is expressed by a particular English phrase, as well as by any paraphrase or translation of it, is not something with lungs, a surname, long legs and a sunburnt face. People are born and die and sometimes wear boots; meanings are not born and do not die and they never wear boots—or go barefoot either. The Queen does not decorate meanings. The phrase 'the first man to stand on the top of Mt. Everest' will not lose its meaning when Hillary dies. Nor was it meaningless before he reached the summit.

Finally, we should notice that most words are not nouns; they are, e.g. adverbs, or verbs, or adjectives or prepositions or conjunctions or pronouns. But to classify as a name a word which is not even a noun strikes one as intolerable the moment one considers the point. How could 'ran' or 'often' or 'and' or 'pretty' be the name of anything? It could not even be the grammatical subject of a sentence. I may ask what a certain economic condition, moral quality or day of the week is called and get the answer 'inflation', 'punctiliousness' or 'Saturday'. We do use the word 'name' for what something is called, whether it be what a person or river is called, or what a species, a quality, an action or a condition is called. But the answer to the question 'What is it called?' must be a noun or have the grammar of a noun. No such question could be answered by giving the tense of a verb, an adverb, a conjunction or an adjective.

Mill himself allowed that some words like 'is', 'often', 'not', 'of', and 'the' are not names, even in his hospitable use of 'name'. They cannot by themselves function as the grammatical subjects of sentences. Their function, as he erroneously described it, is to subserve, in one way or another, the construction of many-worded names. They do not name extra things but are ancillaries to the multi-verbal naming of things. Yet they certainly have meanings. 'And' and 'or' have different meanings, and 'or' and the Latin 'aut' have the same meaning. Mill realized that it is not always the case that for a word to mean something, it must denote somebody or some thing. But most of his successors did not notice how important this point was.

Even more to Mill's credit was the fact that he noticed and did partial justice to the point, which I made a little while back, that two different descriptive phrases may both fit the same thing or person, so that the thing or person which they both fit or which, in his unhappy parlance, they both name is not to be equated with either (or of course both) of the significations of the two descriptions. The two phrases 'the previous Prime Minister' and 'the father of Randolph Churchill' both fit Sir Winston Churchill, and fit only him; but they do not have the same meaning. A French translation of the one would not be a translation of the other. One might know or believe that the one description fitted Sir Winston Churchill while still questioning whether the other did so too. From just knowing that Sir Winston was Prime Minister one could not infer that Randolph Churchill is his son, or *vice versa*. Either might have been true without the other being true. The two phrases cannot, therefore, carry the same information.

Mill, in effect, met this point with his famous theory of denotation and connotation. Most words and descriptive phrases, according to him, do two things at once. They *denote* the things or persons that they are, as he unhappily puts it, all the names of. But they also *connote* or signify the simple or complex attributes by possessing which the thing or person denoted is fitted by the description. Mill's word 'connote' was a very unhappily chosen word and has misled not only Mill's successors but Mill himself. His word 'denote' was used by him in a far from uniform way, which left him uncommitted to consequences from which some of his successors, who used it less equivocally, could not extricate themselves. For Mill, proper names denote their bearers, but predicate-expressions also denote what they are truly predicable of. Fido is denoted by 'Fido' and by 'dog' and by 'four-legged'.

So to ask for the function of an expression is, on Mill's showing, to ask a double question. It is to ask Which person or persons, thing or things the expression denotes? in one or other of Mill's uses of this verb—Sir Winston Churchill, perhaps—; but it is also to ask What are the properties or characteristics by which the thing or person is described?—say that of having begotten Randolph Churchill. As a thing or person can be described in various ways, the various descriptions given will differ in connotation, while still being identical in denotation. They characterize in different ways, even though their denotation is identical. They carry different bits of information or misinformation about the same thing, person or event.

Mill himself virtually says that according to our ordinary natural notion of meaning, it would not be proper to say that, e.g. Sir Winston Churchill is the meaning of a word or phrase. We ordinarily understand by 'meaning' not the thing denoted but only what is connoted. That is, Mill virtually reaches the correct conclusions that the meaning of an expression is never the thing or person referred to by means of it; and that descriptive phrases and, with one exception, single words are never names, in the sense of 'proper names'. The exception is just those relatively few words which really are proper names, i.e. words like 'Fido', and 'London', the words which do not appear in dictionaries.

Mill got a further important point right about these genuine proper names. He said that while most words and descriptive phrases both denote or name and connote, proper names only denote and do not connote. A dog may be called 'Fido', but the word 'Fido' conveys no information or misinformation about the dog's qualities, career or whereabouts, etc. There is, to enlarge this point, no question of the word 'Fido' being paraphrased, or correctly or incorrectly translated into French. Dictionaries do not tell us what proper names mean—for the simple reason that they do not mean anything. The word 'Fido' names or denotes a particular dog, since it is what he is called. But there is no room for anyone who hears the word 'Fido' to understand it or misunderstand it or fail to understand it. There is nothing for which he can require an elucidation or a definition. From the information that Sir Winston

Churchill was Prime Minister, a number of consequences follow, such as that he was the leader of the majority party in Parliament. But from the fact that yonder dog is Fido, no other truth about him follows at all. No information is provided for anything to follow from. Using a proper name is not committing oneself to any further assertions whatsoever. Proper names are appellations and not descriptions; and descriptions are descriptions and not appellations. Sir Winston Churchill *is* the father of Randolph Churchill. He is not *called* and was not christened 'the father of Randolph Churchill'. He is called 'Winston Churchill'. The Lady Mayoress of Liverpool can give the name *Mauretania* to a ship which thenceforward has that name. But if she called Sir Winston Churchill 'the father of Sir Herbert Morrison' this would be a funny sort of christening, but it would not make it true that Morrison is the son of Sir Winston Churchill. Descriptions carry truths or falsehoods and are not just arbitrary bestowals. Proper names are arbitrary bestowals, and convey nothing true and nothing false, for they convey nothing at all.

Chinese astronomers give the planets, stars and constellations names quite different from those we give. But it does not follow that a single proposition of Western astronomy is rejected by them, or that a single astronomical proposition rejected by us is accepted by them. Stellar nomenclature carries with it no astronomical truths or falsehoods. Calling a star by a certain name is not saying anything about it, and saying something true or false about a star is not naming it. Saying is not naming and naming is not saying.

This brings out a most important fact. Considering the meaning (or Mill's 'connotation') of an expression is considering what can be said with it, i.e. said truly or said falsely, as well as asked, commanded, advised or any other sort of saying. In this, which is the normal sense of 'meaning', the meaning of a sub-expression like a word or phrase, is a functional factor of a range of possible assertions, questions, commands and the rest. It is tributary to sayings. It is a distinguishable common locus of a range of possible tellings, askings, advisings, etc. This precisely inverts the natural assumption with which, as I said earlier, Mill and most of us start, the assumption namely that the meanings of words and phrases can be learned, discussed and classified before consideration begins of entire sayings, such as sentences. Word-meanings do not stand to sentence-meanings as atoms to molecules or as letters of the alphabet to the spellings of words, but more nearly as the tennis-racket stands to the strokes which are or may be made with it. This point, which Mill's successors and predecessors half-recognized to hold for such little words as 'if', 'or', 'all', 'the' and 'not', holds good for all significant words alike. Their significances are their rôles inside actual and possible sayings. Mill's two-way doctrine, that nearly all words and phrases both denote, or are names, and connote, i.e. have significance, was therefore, in effect, though unwittingly, a coalition between an atomistic and a functionalist view of words. By the irony of fate, it was his atomistic view which was, in most quarters, accepted as gospel truth for the next fifty or seventy years.

Indeed, it was more than accepted, it was accepted without the important safeguard which Mill himself provided when he said that the thing or person denoted by a name was not to be identified with what that name meant. Mill said that to mean is to connote. His successors said that to mean is to denote, or, more rarely, both to denote and to connote. Frege was for a long time alone in seeing the crucial importance of Mill's argument that two or more descriptive phrases with different senses may apply to the same planet or person. This person or planet is not, therefore, what those phrases mean. Their different senses are not their comon denotation. Russell early realized the point which Mill did not very explicitly make, though Plato had made it, that a sentence is not a list. It says one thing; it is not just an inventory of a lot of things. But only much later, if at all, did Russell see the full implications of this.

I surmise that the reason why Mill's doctrine of denotation, without its safeguards, caught on, while his truths about connotation failed to do so, were two. First, the word 'connote' naturally suggests what we express by 'imply', which is not what is wanted. What the phrase 'the previous Prime Minister of the United Kingdom' signifies is not to be equated with any or all of the consequences which can be inferred from the statement that Churchill is the previous Prime Minister. Deducing is not translating. But more important was the fact that Mill himself rapidly diluted his doctrine of connotation with such a mass of irrelevant and false sensationalist and associationist psychology, that his successors felt forced to ignore the doctrine in order to keep clear of its accretions.

Let me briefly mention some of the consequences which successors of Mill actually drew from the view, which was not Mill's, that to mean is to denote, in the toughest sense, namely that all significant expressions are proper names, and what they are the names of are what the expressions signify.

First, it is obvious that the vast majority of words are unlike the words 'Fido' and 'London' in this respect, namely, that they are general. 'Fido' stands for a particular dog, but the noun 'dog' covers this dog Fido, and all other dogs past, present and future, dogs in novels, dogs in dog breeders' plans for the future, and so on indefinitely. So the word 'dog', if assumed to denote in the way in which 'Fido' denotes Fido, must denote something which we do not hear barking, namely either the set or class of all actual and imaginable dogs, or the set of canine properties which they all share. Either would be a very out-of-the-way sort of entity. Next, most words are not even nouns, but adjectives, verbs, prepositions, conjunctions and so on. If these are assumed to denote in the way in which 'Fido' denotes Fido, we shall have a still larger and queerer set of nominees or *denotata* on our hands, namely nominees whose names could not even function as the grammatical subjects of sentences. (Incidentally it is not true even that all ordinary general nouns can function by themselves as subjects of sentences. I can talk about *this* dog, or *a* dog, or *the* dog which . . . ; or about *dogs, all* dogs, or *most* dogs, and so on. But I cannot make the singular noun 'dog' by itself the grammatical subject of a sentence, save inside quotes, though I can do this with nouns like 'grass', 'hydrogen' and 'Man'.) Finally, since complexes of words, like descriptive and other phrases, and entire clauses and sentences have unitary meanings, then these too will have to be construed as denoting complex entities of very surprising sorts. Now Meinong in Austria and Frege in Germany, as well as Moore and Russell in this country, in their early days, accepted some or most of these consequences. Consistently with the assumed equation of signifying with naming, they maintained the objective existence or being of all sorts of abstract and fictional *entia rationis*.

Whenever we construct a sentence, in which we can distinguish a grammatical subject and a verb, the grammatical subject, be it a single word or a more or less complex phrase, must be significant if the sentence is to say something true or false. But if this nominative word or phrase is significant, it must, according to the assumption, denote something which is there to be named. So not only Fido and London, but also centaurs, round squares, the present King of France, the class of albino Cypriots, the first moment of time, and the non-existence of a first moment of time must all be credited with some sort of reality. They must *be*, else we could not say true or false things of them. We could not truly say that round squares do not exist, unless in some sense of 'exist' there exist round squares for us, in another sense, to deny existence of. Sentences can begin with abstract nouns like 'equality' or 'justice' or 'murder' so all Plato's Forms or Universals must be accepted as entities. Sentences can contain mentions of creatures of fiction, like centaurs and Mr. Pickwick, so all conceivable creatures of fiction must be genuine entities too. Next, we can say that propositions are true or false, or that they entail or are incompatible with other propositions, so any significant 'that'-clause, like 'that three is a prime number' or 'that four is a prime number', must also denote existent or subsistent objects. It was accordingly, for a time, supposed that if I know or believe that three is a prime number, my knowing or believing this is a special relation holding between me on the one hand and the truth or fact, on the other, denoted by the sentence 'three is a prime number'. If I weave or follow a romance, my imagining centaurs or Mr. Pickwick is a special relation holding between me and these centaurs or that portly old gentleman. I could not imagine him unless he had enough being to stand as the correlate-term in this postulated relation of being imagined by me.

Lastly, to consider briefly what turned out, unexpectedly, to be a crucial case, there must exist or subsist classes, namely appropriate *denotata* for such collectively employed plural descriptive phrases as 'the elephants in Burma', or 'the men in the moon'. It is just of such classes or sets that we say that they number 3000, say, in the one case, and 0 in the other. For the results of counting to be true or false, there must be entities submitting to numerical predicates; and for the propositions of arithmetic to be true or false there must exist or subsist an infinite range of such classes.

At the very beginning of this century Russell was detecting some local unplausibilities in the full-fledged doctrine that to every significant grammatical subject there must correspond an appropriate *denotatum* in the way in which Fido answers to the name "Fido". The true proposition 'round squares do not exist' surely cannot require us to assert that there really do subsist round squares. The proposition that it is false that four is a prime number is a true one, but its truth surely cannot force us to fill the Universe up with an endless population of objectively existing falsehoods.

But it was classes that first engendered not mere unplausibilities but seemingly disastrous logical contradictions–not merely peripheral logical contradictions but contradictions at the heart of the very principles on which Russell and Frege had taken mathematics to depend. We can collect into classes not only ordinary objects like playing-cards and bachelors, but also such things as classes themselves. I can ask how many shoes there are in a room and also how many pairs of shoes, and a pair of shoes is already a class. So now suppose I construct a class of all the classes that are not, as anyhow most classes are not, members of themselves. Will this class be one of its own members or not? If it embraces itself, this disqualifies it from being one of the things it is characterized as embracing; if it is not one of the things it embraces, this is just what qualifies it to be one among its own members.

So simple logic itself forbids certain ostensibly denoting expressions to denote. It is at least unplausible to say that there exist objects denoted by the phrase 'round squares'; there is self-contradiction in saying that there exists a class which is a member of itself on condition that it is not, and *vice versa*.

Russell had already found himself forced to say of some expressions which had previously been supposed to name or denote, that they had to be given exceptional treatment. They were not names but what he called 'incomplete symbols', expressions, that is, which have no meaning, in the sense of denotation, by themselves; their business was to be auxiliary to expressions which do, as a whole, denote. (This was what Mill had said of the syncategorematic words.) The very treatment which had since the Middle Ages been given to such little words as 'and', 'not', 'the', 'some' and 'is' was now given to some other kinds of expressions as well. In effect, though not explicitly, Russell was saying that, e.g. descriptive phrases were as syncategorematic as 'not', 'and' and 'is' had always been allowed to be. Here Russell was on the brink of allowing that the meanings or significations of many kinds of expressions are matters not of *naming* things, but of *saying* things. But he was, I think, still held up by the idea that saying is itself just another variety of naming, i.e. naming a complex or an 'objective' or a proposition or a fact–some sort of postulated *Fido rationis*.

He took a new and most important further step to cope with the paradoxes, like that of the class of classes that are not members of themselves. For he now wielded a distinction, which Mill had seen but left inert, the distinction between sentences which are either true or false on the one hand, and on the other hand sentences which, though proper in vocabulary and syntax, are none the less nonsensical, meaningless or absurd; and therefore neither true nor false. To assert them and to deny them are to assert and deny nothing. For reasons of a sort which are the proper concern of logic, certain sorts of concatenations of words and phrases into sentences produce things which cannot be significantly said. For example, the very question Is the class of all classes which are not members of themselves a member of itself or not? has no answer. Russell's famous 'Theory of Types' was an attempt to formulate the reasons of logic which make it an improper question. We need not consider whether he was successful. What matters for us, and what made the big difference to subsequent philosophy, is the fact that at long last the notion of meaning was realized to be, at least in certain crucial contexts, the obverse of the notion of the nonsensical—what can be said, truly or falsely, is at last contrasted with what cannot be significantly said. The notion of meaning had been, at long last, partly detached from the notion of naming and reattached to the notion of saying. It was recognized to belong to, or even to constitute the domain which had always been the province of logic; and as it is at least part of the official business of logic to establish and codify rules, the notion of meaning came now to be seen as somehow compact of rules. To know what an expression means involves knowing what can (logically) be said with it and what cannot (logically) be said with it. It involves knowing a set of bans, fiats and obligations, or, in a word, it is to know the rules of the employment of that expression.

It was, however, not Russell but Wittgenstein who first generalized or half-generalized this crucial point. In the *Tractatus Logico-Philosophicus*, which could be described as the first book to be written on the philosophy of logic, Wittgenstein still had one foot in the denotationist camp, but his other foot was already free. He saw and said, not only what had been said before, that the little words, the so-called logical constants, 'not', 'is', 'and' and the rest do not stand for objects, but also, what Plato had also said before, that sentences are not names. Saying is not naming. He realized, as Frege had done, that logicians' questions are not questions about the properties or relations of the *denotata*, if any, of the expressions which enter into the sentences whose logic is under examination. He saw, too, that all the words and phrases that can enter into sentences are governed by the rules of what he called, slightly metaphorically, 'logical syntax' or 'logical grammar'. These rules are what are broken by such concatenations of words and phrases as result in nonsense. Logic is or includes the study of these rules. Husserl had at the beginning of the century employed much the same notion of 'logical grammar.'

It was only later still that Wittgenstein consciously and deliberately withdrew his remaining foot from the denotationist camp. When he said 'Don't ask for the meaning, ask for the use', he was imparting a lesson which he had had to teach to himself after he had finished with the *Tractatus*. The use of an expression, or the concept it expresses, is the rôle it is employed to perform, not any thing or person or event for which it might be supposed to stand. Nor is the purchasing power of a coin to be equated with this book or that car-ride which might be bought with it. The purchasing power of a coin has not got pages or a terminus. Even more instructive is the analogy which Wittgenstein now came to draw between significant expressions and the pieces with which are played games like chess. The significance of an expression and the powers or functions in chess of a pawn, a knight or the queen have much in common. To know what the knight can and cannot do, one must know the rules of chess, as well as be familiar with various kinds of chess-situations which may arise. What the knight may do cannot be read out of the material or shape of the piece of ivory or boxwood or tin of which this knight may be made. Similarly to know what an expression means is to know how it may and may not be employed, and the rules governing its employment can be the same for expressions of very different physical compositions. The word 'horse' is not a bit like the word 'cheval'; but the way of wielding them is the same. They have the same rôle, the same sense. Each is a translation of the other. Certainly the rules of the uses of expressions are unlike the rules of games in some important respects. We can be taught the rules of chess up to a point before we begin to play. There are manuals of chess, where there are not manuals of significance. The rules of chess, again, are completely definite and inelastic. Questions of whether a rule has been broken or not are decidable without debate. Moreover we opt to play chess and can stop when we like, where we do not opt to talk and think and cannot opt to break off. Chess is a diversion. Speech and thought are not only diversions. But still the partial assimilation of the meanings of expressions to the powers or the values of the pieces with which a game is played is enormously revealing. There is no temptation to suppose that a knight is proxy for anything, or that learning what a knight may or may not do is learning that it is a deputy for some ulterior entity. We could not learn to play the knight correctly without having learned to play the other pieces, nor can we learn to play a word by itself, but only in combination with other words and phrases.

Besides this, there is a further point which the assimilation brings out. There are six different kinds of chess-pieces, with their six different kinds of rôles in the game. We can imagine more complex games involving twenty or two hundred kinds of pieces. So it is with languages. In contrast with the denotationist assumption that almost all words, all phrases and even all sentences are alike in having the one rôle of naming, the assimilation of language to chess reminds us of what we knew *ambulando* all along, the fact that there are indefinitely many kinds of words, kinds of phrases, and kinds of sentences—that there is an indefinitely large variety of kinds of rôles performed by the expressions we use in saying things. Adjectives do not do what adverbs do, nor do all adjectives do the same sort of thing as one another. Some nouns are proper names, but most are not. The sorts of things that we do with sentences are different from the sorts of things that we do with most single words—and some sorts of things that we can significantly do with some sorts of sentences, we cannot significantly do with others. And so on.

There is not one basic mould, such as the 'Fido'-Fido mould, into which all significant expressions are to be forced. On the contrary, there is an endless variety of categories of sense or meaning. Even the *prima facie* simple notion of naming or denoting itself turns out on examination to be full of internal variegations. Pronouns are used to denote people and things, but not in the way in which proper names do so. No one is *called* 'he' or 'she'. 'Saturday' is a proper name, but not in the same way as 'Fido' is a proper name—and neither is used in the way in which the fictional proper name 'Mr. Pickwick' is used. The notion of denotation, so far from providing the final explanation of the notion of meaning, turns out itself to be just one special branch or twig on the tree of signification. Expressions do not mean because they denote things; some expressions denote things, in one or another of several different manners, because they are significant. Meanings are not things, not even very queer things. Learning the meaning of an expression is more like learning a piece of drill than like coming across a previously unencountered object. It is learning to operate correctly with an expression and with any other expression equivalent to it.

(2) *THE THEORY OF PHILOSOPHY*

I now want to trace, rather more cursorily, the other main motive from which thinkers have posed the abstract question What are meanings? or What is it for an expression to have a certain sense?

Until fairly recently philosophers have not often stepped back from their easels to consider what philosophy is, or how doing philosophy differs from doing science, or doing theology, or doing mathematics. Kant was the first modern thinker to see or try to answer this question—and a very good beginning of an answer he gave; but I shall not expound his answer here.

This question did not begin seriously to worry the general run of philosophers until maybe sixty years ago. It began to become obsessive only after the publication of the *Tractatus*. Why did the philosophy of philosophy start so late, and how did it come to start when and as it did?

It is often not realized that the words 'philosophy' and 'philosopher' and their equivalents in French and German had for a long time much less specific meanings than they now possess. During the seventeenth, the eighteenth and most of the nineteenth centuries a 'philosopher' was almost any sort of a *savant*. Astronomers, chemists and botanists were called 'philosophers' just as much as were Locke, Berkeley or Hume. Descartes's philosophy covered his contributions to optics just as much as his contributions to epistemology. In English there existed for a long time no special word for the people we now call 'scientists'. This noun was deliberately coined only in 1840, and even then it took some time to catch on. His contemporaries could not call Newton a 'scientist', since there was no such word. When a distinction had to be made, it was made by distinguishing 'natural philosophy' from 'moral' and 'metaphysical philosophy'. As late as 1887, Conan Doyle, within two or three pages of one story, describes Sherlock Holmes as being totally ignorant of philosophy, as we use the word now, and yet as having his room full of philosophical, i.e. scientific, instruments, like test-tubes, retorts and balances. A not very ancient Oxford Chair of Physics still retains its old label, the Chair of Experimental Philosophy.

Different from this quite important piece of etymological history is the fact that both in Scotland and in England there existed from perhaps the time of Hartley to that of Sidgwick and Bradley a strong tendency to suppose that the distinction between natural philosophy, i.e. physical and biological science on the one hand and metaphysical and moral philosophy, perhaps including logic, on the other, was that the latter were concerned with internal, mental phenomena, where the former were concerned with external, physical phenomena. Much of what we now label 'philosophy', *sans phrase*, was for a long time and by many thinkers confidently, but quite wrongly equated with what we now call 'psychology'. John Stuart Mill sometimes, but not always, uses even the grand word 'metaphysics' for the empirical study of the workings of men's minds. Protests were made against this equation particularly on behalf of philosophical theology, but for a long time the anti-theologians had it their own way. A philosopher, *sans phrase*, was a Mental and Moral Scientist—a scientist who was exempted from working in the laboratory or the observatory only because his specimens were collected at home by introspection. Even Mansel, himself a philosophical theologian with a good Kantian equipment, maintained that the science of mental phenomena, what we call 'psychology', was the real basis of even ontological or theological speculations.

So not only did the wide coverage of the word 'philosophy' encourage people not to look for any important differences between what scientists, as we now call them, do and what philosophers, as we now call them, do; but even when such differences were looked for, they were apt to be found in the differences between the investigation of physical phenomena by the laboratory scientist and the investigation of psychological phenomena by the introspecting psychologist.

As I see it, three influences were chiefly responsible for the collapse of the assumption that doing philosophy, in our sense, is of a piece with doing natural science or at least of a piece with doing mental science or psychology.

First, champions of mathematics like Frege, Husserl and Russell had to save mathematics from the combined empiricism and psychologism of the school of John Stuart Mill. Mathematical truths are not mere psychological generalizations; equations are not mere records of deeply rutted associations of ideas; the objects of geometry are not of the stuff of which mental images are made. Pure mathematics is a non-inductive and a non-introspective science. Its proofs are rigorous, its terms are exact, and its theorems are universal and not merely highly general truths. The proofs and the theorems of Formal or Symbolic Logic share these dignities with the proofs and theorems of mathematics. So, as logic was certainly a part of philosophy, not all of philosophy could be ranked as 'mental science'. There must, then, be a field or realm besides those of the material and the mental; and at least part of philosophy is concerned with this third realm, the realm of non-material and also non-mental 'logical objects'—such objects as concepts, truths, falsehoods, classes, numbers and implications.

Next, armchair mental science or introspective psychology itself began to yield ground to experimental, laboratory psychology. Psychologists like James began to put themselves to school under the physiologists and the statisticians. Scientific psychology began first to rival and then to oust both *a priori* and introspective psychology, and the tacit claim of epistemologists, moral philosophers and logicians to be mental scientists had to be surrendered to those who used the methods and the tools of the reputable sciences. So the question raised its head What then were the objects of the inquiries of epistemologists, moral philosophers and logicians, if they were not, as had been supposed, psychological states and processes? It is only in our own days that, anyhow in most British Universities, psychologists have established a Faculty of their own separate from the Faculty of Philosophy.

Thirdly, Brentano, reinforcing from medieval sources a point made and swiftly forgotten by Mill, maintained as an *a priori* principle of psychology itself, that it is of the essence of mental states and processes that they are *of* objects or contents. Somewhat as in grammar a transitive verb requires an accusative, so in the field of ideas, thoughts and feelings, acts of consciousness are directed upon their own metaphorical accusatives. To see is to see something, to regret is to regret something, to conclude or suppose is to conclude or suppose that something is the case. Imagining is one thing, the thing imagined, a centaur, say, is another. The centaur has the body of a horse and does not exist. An act of imagining a centaur does exist and does not have the body of a horse. Your act of supposing that Napoleon defeated Wellington is different from my act of supposing it; but what we suppose is the same and is what is expressed by our common expression 'that Napoleon defeated Wellington'. What is true of mental acts is, in general, false of their accusatives or 'intentional objects', and *vice versa*.

Brentano's two pupils, Meinong and Husserl, happened, for different reasons, to be especially, though not exclusively, interested in applying this principle of intentionality or transitivity to the intellectual, as distinct from the sensitive, volitional or affective acts of consciousness. They set out, that is, to rectify the Locke-Hume-Mill accounts of abstraction, conception, memory, judgment, supposal, inference and the rest, by distinguishing in each case, the various private, momentary and repeatable acts of conceiving, remembering, judging, supposing and inferring from their public, non-momentary accusatives, namely, the concepts, the propositions and the implications which constituted their objective correlates. Where Frege attacked psychologistic accounts of thinking from the outside, they attacked them from the inside. Where Frege argued, for instance, that numbers have nothing psychological or, of course, physical about them, Husserl and Meinong argued that for the mental processes of counting and calculating to be what they are, they must have accusatives or objects numerically and qualitatively other than those processes themselves. Frege said that Mill's account of mathematical entities was false because psychological; Husserl and Meinong, in effect, said that the psychology itself was false because non-'intentional' psychology. The upshot, however, was much the same. With different axes to grind, all three came to what I may crudely dub 'Platonistic' conclusions. All three maintained the doctrine of a third realm of non-physical, non-psychological entities, in which realm dwelled such things as concepts, numbers, classes and propositions.

Husserl and Meinong were both ready to lump together all these accusatives of thinking alike under the comprehensive title of Meanings (*Bedeutungen*), since what I think is what is conveyed by the words, phrases or sentences in which I express what I think. The 'accusatives' of my ideas and my judgings are the meanings of my words and my sentences. It easily followed from this that both Husserl and Meinong, proud of their newly segregated third realm, found that it was this realm which provided a desiderated subject-matter peculiar to logic and philosophy and necessarily ignored by the natural sciences, physical and psychological. Mental acts and states are the subject-matter of psychology. Physical objects and events are the subject-matter of the physical and biological sciences. It is left to philosophy to be the science of this third domain which consists largely, though not entirely, of thought-objects or Meanings—the novel and impressive entities which had been newly isolated for separate investigation by the application of Brentano's principle of intentionality to the specifically intellectual or cognitive acts of consciousness.

Thus, by the first decade of this century it was dawning upon philosophers and logicians that their business was not that of one science among others, e.g. that of psychology; and even that it was not an inductive, experimental or observational business of any sort. It was intimately concerned with, among other things, the fundamental concepts and principles of mathematics; and it seemed to have to do with a special domain which was not bespoken by any other discipline, namely the so-called third realm of logical objects or Meanings. At the same time, and in some degree affected by these influences, Moore consistently and Russell spasmodically were prosecuting their obviously philosophical and logical inquiries with a special *modus operandi*. They, and not they alone, were deliberately and explicitly trying to give analyses of concepts and propositions—asking What does it really mean to say, for example, that this is good? or that that is true? or that centaurs do not exist? or that I see an inkpot? or What are the differences between the distinguishable senses of the verb 'to know' and the verb 'to be'? Moore's regular practice and Russell's frequent practice seemed to exemplify beautifully what, for example, Husserl and Meinong had declared in general terms to be the peculiar business of philosophy and logic, namely to explore the third realm of Meanings. Thus philosophy had acquired a right to live its own life, neither as a discredited pretender to the status of the science of mind, nor yet as a superannuated handmaiden of *démodé* theology. It was responsible for a special field of facts, facts of impressively Platonized kinds.

Before the first world war discussions of the status and rôle of philosophy *vis-à-vis* the mathematical and empirical sciences were generally cursory and incidental to discussions of other matters. Wittgenstein's *Tractatus* was a complete treatise dedicated to fixing the position mainly of Formal Logic but also, as a necessary corollary, the position of general philosophy. It was this book which made dominant issues of the theory of logic and the theory of philosophy. In Vienna some of its teachings were applied polemically, namely to demolishing the pretensions of philosophy to be the science of transcendent realities. In England, on the whole, others of its teachings were applied more constructively, namely to stating the positive functions which philosophical propositions perform, and scientific propositions do not perform. In England, on the whole, interest was concentrated on Wittgenstein's description of philosophy as an activity of clarifying or elucidating the meanings of the expressions used, e.g. by scientists; that is, on the medicinal virtues of his account of the nonsensical. In Vienna, on the whole, interest was concentrated on the lethal potentialities of Wittgenstein's account of nonsense. In both places, it was realized that the criteria between the significant and the nonsensical needed to be systematically surveyed, and that it was for the philosopher and not the scientist to survey them.

At this point, the collapse of the denotationist theory of meaning began to influence the theory of philosophy as the science of Platonized Meanings. If the meaning of an expression is not an entity denoted by it, but a style of operation performed with it, not a nominee but a rôle, then it is not only repellent but positively misleading to speak as if there existed a Third Realm whose denizens are Meanings. We can distinguish this knight, as a piece of ivory, from the part it or any proxy for it may play in a game of chess; but the part it may play is not an extra entity, made of some mysterious non-ivory. There is not one box housing the ivory chessmen and another queerer box housing their functions in chess games. Similarly we can distinguish an expression as a set of syllables from its employment. A quite different set of syllables may have the same employment. But its use or sense is not an additional substance or subject of predication. It is not a non-physical, non-mental object—but not because it is either a physical or a mental object, but because it is not an object. As it is not an object, it is not a denizen of a Platonic realm of objects. To say, therefore, that philosophy is the science of Meanings, though not altogether wrong, is liable to mislead in the same way as it might mislead to say that economics is the science of exchange-values. This, too, is true enough, but to word this truth in this way is liable to make people suppose that the Universe houses, under different roofs, commodities and coins here and exchange-values over there.

Hence, following Wittgenstein's lead, it has become customary to say, instead, that philosophical problems are linguistic problems—only linguistic problems quite unlike any of the problems of philology, grammar, phonetics, rhetoric, prosody, etc., since they are problems about the logic of the functionings of expressions. Such problems are so widely different from, e.g. philological problems, that speaking of them as linguistic problems is, at the moment, as Wittgenstein foresaw, misleading people as far in one direction, as speaking of them as problems about Meanings or Concepts or Propositions had been misleading in the other direction. The difficulty is to steer between the Scylla of a Platonistic and the Charybdis of a lexicographical account of the business of philosophy and logic.

There has been and perhaps still is something of a vogue for saying that doing philosophy consists in analysing meanings, or analysing the employments of expressions. Indeed, from Transatlantic journals I gather that at this very moment British philosophy is dominated by some people called 'linguistic analysts'. The word 'analysis' has, indeed, a good laboratory or Scotland Yard ring about it; it contrasts well with such expressions as 'speculation', 'hypothesis', 'system-building' and even 'preaching' and 'writing poetry'. On the other hand it is a hopelessly misleading word in some important respects. It falsely suggests, for one thing, that any sort of careful elucidation of any sorts of complex or subtle ideas will be a piece of philosophizing; as if the judge, in explaining to the members of the jury the differences between manslaughter and murder, was helping them out of a philosophical quandary. But, even worse, it suggests that philosophical problems are like the chemist's or the detective's problems in this respect, namely that they can and should be tackled piecemeal. Finish problem A this morning, file the answer, and go on to problem B this afternoon. This suggestion does violence to the vital fact that philosophical problems inevitably interlock in all sorts of ways. It would be patently absurd to tell someone to finish the problem of the nature of truth this morning, file the answer and go on this afternoon to solve the problem of the relations between naming and saying, holding over until tomorrow problems about the concepts of existence and non-existence. This is, I think, why at the present moment philosophers are far more inclined to liken their task to that of the cartographer than to that of the chemist or the detective. It is the foreign relations, not the domestic constitutions of sayables that engender logical troubles and demand logical arbitration.

PERFORMATIVE UTTERANCES

J. L. AUSTIN

I

You are more than entitled not to know what the word 'performative' means. It is a new word and an ugly word, and perhaps it does not mean anything very much. But at any rate there is one thing in its favour, it is not a profound word. I remember once when I had been talking on this subject that somebody afterwards said: 'You know, I haven't the least idea what he means, unless it could be that he simply means what he says'. Well, that is what I should like to mean.

Let us consider first how this affair arises. We have not got to go very far back in the history of philosophy to find philosophers assuming more or less as a matter of course that the sole business, the sole interesting business, of any utterance—that is, of anything we say—is to be true or at least false. Of course they had always known that there are other kinds of things which we say—things like imperatives, the expressions of wishes, and exclamations—some of which had even been classified by grammarians, though it wasn't perhaps too easy to tell always which was which. But still philosophers have assumed that the only things that they are interested in are utterances which report facts or which describe situations truly or falsely. In recent times this kind of approach has been questioned—in two stages, I think. First of all people began to say: 'Well, if these things are true or false it ought to be possible to decide which they are, and if we can't decide which they are they aren't any good but are, in short, nonsense'. And this new approach did a great deal of good; a great many things which probably are nonsense were found to be such. It is not the case, I think, that all kinds of nonsense have been adequately classified yet, and perhaps some things have been dismissed as nonsense which really are not; but still this movement, the verification movement, was, in its way, excellent.

However, we then come to the second stage. After all, we set some limits to the amount of nonsense that we talk, or at least the amount of nonsense that we are prepared to admit we talk; and so people began to ask whether after all some of those things which, treated as statements, were in danger of being dismissed as nonsense did after all really set out to be statements at all. Mightn't they perhaps be intended not to report

Reprinted from John Austin, *Philosophical Papers,* 1961, by permission of the Clarendon Press, Oxford.

facts but to influence people in this way or that, or to let off steam in this way or that? Or perhaps at any rate some elements in these utterances performed such functions, or, for example, drew attention in some way (without actually reporting it) to some important feature of the circumstances in which the utterance was being made. On these lines people have now adopted a new slogan, the slogan of the 'different uses of language'. The old approach, the old statemental approach, is sometimes called even a fallacy, the descriptive fallacy.

Certainly there are a great many uses of language. It's rather a pity that people are apt to invoke a new use of language whenever they feel so inclined, to help them out of this, that, or the other well-known philosophical tangle; we need more of a framework in which to discuss these uses of language; and also I think we should not despair too easily and talk, as people are apt to do, about the *infinite* uses of language. Philosophers will do this when they have listed as many, let us say, as seventeen; but even if there were something like ten thousand uses of language, surely we could list them all in time. This, after all, is no larger than the number of species of beetle that entomologists have taken the pains to list. But whatever the defects of either of these movements—the 'verification' movement or the 'use of language' movement—at any rate they have effected, nobody could deny, a great revolution in philosophy and, many would say, the most salutary in its history. (Not, if you come to think of it, a very immodest claim.)

Now it is one such sort of use of language that I want to examine here. I want to discuss a kind of utterance which looks like a statement and grammatically, I suppose, would be classed as a statement, which is not nonsensical, and yet is not true or false. These are not going to be utterances which contain curious verbs like 'could' or 'might', or curious words like 'good', which many philosophers regard nowadays simply as danger signals. They will be perfectly straightforward utterances, with ordinary verbs in the first person singular present indicative active, and yet we shall see at once that they couldn't possibly be true or false. Furthermore, if a person makes an utterance of this sort we should say that he is *doing* something rather than merely *saying* something. This may sound a little odd, but the examples I shall give will in fact not be odd at all, and may even seem decidedly dull. Here are three or four. Suppose, for example, that in the course of a marriage ceremony I say, as people will, 'I do'—(sc. take this woman to be my lawful wedded wife). Or again, suppose that I tread on your toe and say 'I apologize'. Or again, suppose that I have the bottle of champagne in my hand and say 'I name this ship the *Queen Elizabeth*'. Or suppose I say 'I bet you sixpence it will rain tomorrow'. In all these cases it would be absurd to regard the thing that I say as a report of the performance of the action which is undoubtedly done—the action of betting, or christening, or apologizing. We should say rather that, in saying what I do, I actually perform that action. When I say 'I name this ship the *Queen Elizabeth*' I do not describe the christening ceremony, I actually perform the christening; and when I say

'I do' (sc. take this woman to be my lawful wedded wife), I am not reporting on a marriage, I am indulging in it.

Now these kinds of utterance are the ones that we call *performative* utterances. This is rather an ugly word, and a new word, but there seems to be no word already in existence to do the job. The nearest approach that I can think of is the word 'operative', as used by lawyers. Lawyers when talking about legal instruments will distinguish between the preamble, which recites the circumstances in which a transaction is effected, and on the other hand the operative part—the part of it which actually performs the legal act which it is the purpose of the instrument to perform. So the word 'operative' is very near to what we want. 'I give and bequeath my watch to my brother' would be an operative clause and is a performative utterance. However, the word 'operative' has other uses, and it seems preferable to have a word specially designed for the use we want.

Now at this point one might protest, perhaps even with some alarm, that I seem to be suggesting that marrying is simply saying a few words, that just saying a few words *is* marrying. Well, that certainly is not the case. The words have to be said in the appropriate circumstances, and this is a matter that will come up again later. But the one thing we must not suppose is that what is needed in addition to the saying of the words in such cases is the performance of some internal spiritual act, of which the words then are to be the report. It's very easy to slip into this view at least in difficult, portentous cases, though perhaps not so easy in simple cases like apologizing. In the case of promising—for example, 'I promise to be there tomorrow'—it's very easy to think that the utterance is simply the outward and visible (that is, verbal) sign of the performance of some inward spiritual act of promising, and this view has certainly been expressed in many classic places. There is the case of Euripides' Hippolytus, who said 'My tongue swore to, but my heart did not'—perhaps it should be 'mind' or 'spirit' rather than 'heart', but at any rate some kind of backstage artiste. Now it is clear from this sort of example that, if we slip into thinking that such utterances are reports, true or false, of the performance of inward and spiritual acts, we open a loophole to perjurers and welshers and bigamists and so on, so that there are disadvantages in being excessively solemn in this way. It is better, perhaps, to stick to the old saying that our word is our bond.

However, although these utterances do not themselves report facts and are not themselves true or false, saying these things does very often *imply* that certain things are true and not false, in some sense at least of that rather woolly word 'imply'. For example, when I say 'I do take this woman to be my lawful wedded wife', or some other formula in the marriage ceremony, I do imply that I'm not already married, with wife living, sane, undivorced, and the rest of it. But still it is very important to realize that to imply that something or other is true, is not at all the same as saying something which is true itself.

These performative utterances are not true or false, then. But they do suffer from certain disabilities of their own. They can fail to come off in special ways, and that is what I want to consider next. The various ways in which a performative utterance may be unsatisfactory we call, for the sake of a name, the infelicities; and an infelicity arises—that is to say, the utterance is unhappy—if certain rules, transparently simple rules, are broken. I will mention some of these rules and then give examples of some infringements.

First of all, it is obvious that the conventional procedure which by our utterance we are purporting to use must actually exist. In the examples given here this procedure will be a verbal one, a verbal procedure for marrying or giving or whatever it may be; but it should be borne in mind that there are many non-verbal procedures by which we can perform exactly the same acts as we perform by these verbal means. It's worth remembering too that a great many of the things we do are at least in part of this conventional kind. Philosophers at least are too apt to assume that an action is always in the last resort the making of a physical movement, whereas it's usually, at least in part, a matter of convention.

The first rule is, then, that the convention invoked must exist and be accepted. And the second rule, also a very obvious one, is that the circumstances in which we purport to invoke this procedure must be appropriate for its invocation. If this is not observed, then the act that we purport to perform would not come off—it will be, one might say, a misfire. This will also be the case if, for example, we do not carry through the procedure—whatever it may be—correctly and completely, without a flaw and without a hitch. If any of these rules are not observed, we say that the act which we purported to perform is void, without effect. If, for example, the purported act was an act of marrying, then we should say that we 'went through a form' of marriage, but we did not actually succeed in marrying.

Here are some examples of this kind of misfire. Suppose that, living in a country like our own, we wish to divorce our wife. We may try standing her in front of us squarely in the room and saying, in a voice loud enough for all to hear, 'I divorce you'. Now this procedure is not accepted. We shall not thereby have succeeded in divorcing our wife, at least in this country and others like it. This is a case where the convention, we should say, does not exist or is not accepted. Again, suppose that, picking sides at a children's party, I say 'I pick George'. But George turns red in the face and says 'Not playing'. In that case I plainly, for some reason or another, have not picked George—whether because there is no convention that you can pick people who aren't playing, or because George in the circumstances is an inappropriate object for the procedure of picking. Or consider the case in which I say 'I appoint you Consul', and it turns out that you have been appointed already—or perhaps it may even transpire that you are a horse; here again we have the infelicity of inappropriate circumstances, inappropriate objects, or what not. Examples of flaws and hitches are perhaps scarcely necessary—one party in the marriage ceremony says 'I will', the other says 'I won't'; I say 'I bet sixpence', but nobody says 'Done', nobody takes up the offer. In all these and other such cases, the act which we purport to perform, or set out to perform, is not achieved.

But there is another and a rather different way in which this kind of utterance may go wrong. A good many of these verbal procedures are designed for use by people who hold certain beliefs or have certain feelings or intentions. And if you use one of these formulae when you do not have the requisite thoughts or feelings or intentions then there is an abuse of the procedure, there is insincerity. Take, for example, the expression, 'I congratulate you'. This is designed for use by people who are glad that the person addressed has achieved a certain feat, believe that he was personally responsible for the success, and so on. If I say 'I congratulate you' when I'm not pleased or when I don't believe that the credit was yours, then there is insincerity. Likewise if I say I promise to do something, without having the least intention of doing it or without believing it feasible. In these cases there is something wrong certainly, but it is not like a misfire. We should not say that I didn't in fact promise, but rather that I did promise but promised insincerely; I did congratulate you but the congratulations were hollow. And there may be an infelicity of a somewhat similar kind when the performative utterance commits the speaker to future conduct of a certain description and then in the future he does not in fact behave in the expected way. This is very obvious, of course, if I promise to do something and then break my promise, but there are many kinds of commitment of a rather less tangible form than that in the case of promising. For instance, I may say 'I welcome you', bidding you welcome to my home or wherever it may be, but then I proceed to treat you as though you were exceedingly unwelcome. In this case the procedure of saying 'I welcome you' has been abused in a way rather different from that of simple insincerity.

Now we might ask whether this list of infelicities is complete, whether the kinds of infelicity are mutually exclusive, and so forth. Well, it is not complete, and they are not mutually exclusive; they never are. Suppose that you are just about to name the ship, you have been appointed to name it, and you are just about to bang the bottle against the stem; but at that very moment some low type comes up, snatches the bottle out of your hand, breaks it on the stem, shouts out 'I name this ship the *Generalissimo Stalin*', and then for good measure kicks away the chocks. Well, we agree of course on several things. We agree that the ship certainly isn't now named the *Generalissimo Stalin*, and we agree that it's an infernal shame and so on and so forth. But we may not agree as to how we should classify the particular infelicity in this case. We might say that here is a case of a perfectly legitimate and agreed procedure which, however, has been invoked in the wrong circumstances, namely by the wrong person, this low type instead of the person appointed to do it. But on the other hand we might look at it differently and say that this is a case where the procedure has not as a whole been gone through correctly, because part of the procedure for naming a ship is that you should first of all get yourself appointed as the person to do the naming and that's what this fellow did not do. Thus the way we should classify infelicities in different cases will be perhaps rather a difficult matter, and may even in the last resort be a bit arbitrary. But of course lawyers, who have to deal very much with this kind of thing, have invented all kinds of technical terms and have made numerous rules about different kinds of cases, which enable them to classify fairly rapidly what in particular is wrong in any given case.

As for whether this list is complete, it certainly is not. One further way in which things may go wrong is, for example, through what in general may be called misunderstanding. You may not hear what I say, or you may understand me to refer to something different from what I intended to refer to, and so on. And apart from further additions which we might make to the list, there is the general over-riding consideration that, as we are performing an act when we issue these performative utterances, we may of course be doing so under duress or in some other circumstances which make us not entirely responsible for doing what we are doing. That would certainly be an unhappiness of a kind—any kind of non-responsibility might be called an unhappiness; but of course it is a quite different kind of thing from what we have been talking about. And I might mention that, quite differently again, we could be issuing any of these utterances, as we can issue an utterance of any kind whatsoever, in the course, for example, of acting a play or making a joke or writing a poem—in which case of course it would not be seriously meant and we shall not be able to say that we seriously performed the act concerned. If the poet says 'Go and catch a falling star' or whatever it may be, he doesn't seriously issue an order. Considerations of this kind apply to any utterance at all, not merely to performatives.

That, then, is perhaps enough to be going on with. We have discussed the performative utterance and its infelicities. That equips us, we may suppose, with two shining new tools to crack the crib of reality maybe. It also equips us—it always does—with two shining new skids under our metaphysical feet. The question is how we use them.

II

So far we have been going firmly ahead, feeling the firm ground of prejudice glide away beneath our feet which is always rather exhilarating, but what next? You will be waiting for the bit when we bog down, the bit where we take it all back, and sure enough that's going to come but it will take time. First of all let us ask a rather simple question. How can we be sure, how can we tell, whether any utterance is to be classed as a performative or not? Surely, we feel, we ought to be able to do that. And we should obviously very much like to be able to say that there is a grammatical criterion for this, some grammatical means of deciding whether an utterance is performative. All the examples I have given hitherto do in fact have the same grammatical form; they all of them begin with the verb in the first person singular present indicative active—not just any kind of verb of course, but still they all are in fact of that form. Furthermore, with these verbs that I have used there is a typical asymmetry between the use of this person and tense of the verb and the use of the same verb in other persons and other tenses, and this asymmetry is rather an important clue.

For example, when we say 'I promise that . . .', the case is very different from when we say 'He promises that . . .', or in the past tense 'I promised that . . .'. For when we say 'I promise that . . .' we do perform an act of promising—we give a promise. What we do *not* do is to report on somebody's performing an act of promising—in particular, we do not report on somebody's use of the expression 'I promise'. We actually do use it and do the promising. But if I say 'He promises', or in the past tense 'I promised', I precisely do report on an act of promising, that is to say an act of using this formula 'I promise'—I report on a present act of promising by him, or on a past act of my own. There is thus a clear difference between our first person singular present indicative active, and other persons and tenses. This is brought out by the typical incident of little Willie whose uncle says he'll give him half-a-crown if he promises never to smoke till he's 55. Little Willie's anxious parent will say 'Of course he promises, don't you, Willie?' giving him a nudge, and little Willie just doesn't vouchsafe. The point here is that he must do the promising himself by saying 'I promise', and his parent is going too fast in saying he promises.

That, then, is a bit of a test for whether an utterance is performative or not, but it would not do to suppose that every performative utterance has to take this standard form. There is at least one other standard form, every bit as common as this one, where the verb is in the passive voice and in the second or third person, not in the first. The sort of case I mean is that of a notice inscribed 'Passengers are warned to cross the line by the bridge only', or of a document reading 'You are hereby authorized' to do so-and-so. These are undoubtedly performative, and in fact a signature is often required in order to show who it is that is doing the act of warning, or authorizing, or whatever it may be. Very typical of this kind of performative—especially liable to occur in written documents of course—is that the little word 'hereby' either actually occurs or might naturally be inserted.

Unfortunately, however, we still can't possibly suggest that every utterance which is to be classed as a performative has to take one or another of these two, as we might call them, standard forms. After all it would be a very typical performative utterance to say 'I order you to shut the door'. This satisfies all the criteria. It is performing the act of ordering you to shut the door, and it is not true or false. But in the appropriate circumstances surely we could perform exactly the same act by simply saying 'Shut the door', in the imperative. Or again, suppose that somebody sticks up a notice 'This bull is dangerous', or simply 'Dangerous bull', or simply 'Bull'. Does this necessarily differ from sticking up a notice, appropriately signed, saying 'You are hereby warned that this bull is dangerous'? It seems that the simple notice 'Bull' can do just the same job as the more elaborate formula. Of course the difference is that if we just stick up 'Bull' it would not be quite clear that it is a warning; it might be there just for interest or information, like 'Wallaby' on the cage at the zoo, or 'Ancient Monument'. No doubt we should know from the nature of the case that it was a warning, but it would not be explicit.

Well, in view of this break-down of grammatical criteria, what we should like to suppose—and there is a good deal in this—is that any utterance which is performative could be reduced or expanded or analysed into one of these two standard forms beginning 'I . . .' so and so or beginning 'You (or he) hereby . . .' so and so. If there was any justification for this hope, as to some extent there is, then we might hope to make a list of all the verbs which can appear in these standard forms, and then we might classify the kinds of acts that can be performed by performative utterances. We might do this with the aid of a dictionary, using such a test as that already mentioned—whether there is the characteristic asymmetry between the first person singular present indicative active and the other persons and tenses—in order to decide whether a verb is to go into our list or not. Now if we make such a list of verbs we do in fact find that they fall into certain fairly well-marked classes. There is the class of cases where we deliver verdicts and make estimates and appraisals of various kinds. There is the class where we give undertakings, commit ourselves in various ways by saying something. There is the class where by saying something we exercise various rights and powers, such as appointing and voting and so on. And there are one or two other fairly well-marked classes.

Suppose this task accomplished. Then we could call these verbs in our list explicit performative verbs, and any utterance that was reduced to one or the other of our standard forms we could call an explicit performative utterance. 'I order you to shut the door' would be an explicit performative utterance, whereas 'Shut the door' would not—that is simply a 'primary' performative utterance or whatever we like to call it. In using the imperative we may be ordering you to shut the door, but it just isn't made clear whether we are ordering you or entreating you or imploring you or beseeching you or inciting you or tempting you, or one or another of many other subtly different acts which, in an unsophisticated primitive language, are very likely not yet discriminated. But we need not overestimate the unsophistication of primitive languages. There are a great many devices that can be used for making clear, even at the primitive level, what act it is we are performing when we say something—the tone of voice, cadence, gesture—and above all we can rely upon the nature of the circumstances, the context in which the utterance is issued. This very often makes it quite unmistakable whether it is an order that is being given or whether, say, I am simply urging you or entreating you. We may, for instance, say something like this: 'Coming from him I was bound to take it as an order'. Still, in spite of all these devices, there is an unfortunate amount of ambiguity and lack of discrimination in default of our explicit performative verbs. If I say something like 'I shall be there', it may not be certain whether it is a promise, or an expression of intention, or perhaps even a forecast of my future behaviour, of what is going to happen to me; and it may matter a good deal, at least in developed societies, precisely which of these things it is. And that is why the explicit performative verb is evolved—to make clear exactly which it is, how far it commits me and in what way, and so forth.

This is just one way in which language develops in tune with the society of which it is the language. The social habits of the society may considerably affect the question of which performative verbs are evolved and which, sometimes for rather irrelevant reasons, are not. For example, if I say 'You are a poltroon', it might be that I am censuring you or it might be that I am insulting you. Now since apparently society approves of censuring or reprimanding, we have here evolved a formula 'I reprimand you', or 'I censure you', which enables us expeditiously to get this desirable business over. But on the other hand, since apparently we don't approve of insulting, we have not evolved a simple formula 'I insult you', which might have done just as well.

By means of these explicit performative verbs and some other devices, then, we make explicit what precise act it is that we are performing when we issue our utterance. But here I would like to put in a word of warning. We must distinguish between the function of making explicit what act it is we are performing, and the quite different matter of *stating* what act it is we are performing. In issuing an explicit performative utterance we are not stating what act it is, we are showing or making explicit what act it is. We can draw a helpful parallel here with another case in which the act, the conventional act that we perform, is not a speech-act but a physical performance. Suppose I appear before you one day and bow deeply from the waist. Well, this is ambiguous. I may be simply observing the local flora, tying my shoe-lace, something of that kind; on the other hand, conceivably I might be doing obeisance to you. Well, to clear up this ambiguity we have some device such as raising the hat, saying 'Salaam', or something of that kind, to make it quite plain that the act being performed is the conventional one of doing obeisance rather than some other act. Now nobody would want to say that lifting your hat was stating that you were performing an act of obesiance; it certainly is not, but it does make it quite plain that you are. And so in the same way to say 'I warn you that . . .' or 'I order you to . . .' or 'I promise that . . .' is not to state that you are doing something, but makes it plain that you are—it does constitute your verbal performance, a performance of a particular kind.

So far we have been going along as though there was a quite clear difference between our performative utterances and what we have contrasted them with, statements or reports or descriptions. But now we begin to find that this distinction is not as clear as it might be. It's now that we begin to sink in a little. In the first place, of course, we may feel doubts as to how widely our performatives extend. If we think up some odd kinds of expression we use in odd cases, we might very well wonder whether or not they satisfy our rather vague criteria for being performative utterances. Suppose, for example, somebody says 'Hurrah'. Well, not true or false; he is performing the act of cheering. Does that make it a performative utterance in our sense or not? Or suppose he says 'Damn'; he is performing the act of swearing, and it is not true or false. Does that make it performative? We feel that in a way it does and yet it's rather different. Again, consider cases of 'suiting the action to the words'; these too may make us wonder whether perhaps the utterance should be classed as performative. Or sometimes, if somebody says 'I am sorry', we wonder whether this is just the same as 'I apologize'—in which case of course we have said it's a performative utterance—or whether perhaps it's to be taken as a description, true or false, of the state of his feelings. If he had said 'I feel perfectly awful about it', then we should think it must be meant to be a description of the state of his feelings. If he had said 'I apologize', we should feel this was clearly a performative utterance, going through the ritual of apologizing. But if he says 'I am sorry' there is an unfortunate hovering between the two. This phenomenon is quite common. We often find cases in which there is an obvious pure performative utterance and obvious other utterances connected with it which are not performative but descriptive, but on the other hand a good many in between where we're not quite sure which they are. On some occasions of course they are obviously used the one way, on some occasions the other way, but on some occasions they seem positively to revel in ambiguity.

Again, consider the case of the umpire when he says 'Out' or 'Over', or the jury's utterance when they say that they find the prisoner guilty. Of course, we say, these are cases of giving verdicts, performing the act of appraising and so forth, but still in a way they have some connexion with the facts. They seem to have something like the duty to be true or false, and seem not to be so very remote from statements. If the umpire says 'Over', this surely has at least something to do with six balls in fact having been delivered rather than seven, and so on. In fact in general we may remind ourselves that 'I state that . . .' does not look so very different from 'I warn you that . . .' or 'I promise to . . .'. It makes clear surely that the act that we are performing is an act of stating, and so functions just like 'I warn' or 'I order'. So isn't 'I state that . . .' a performative utterance? But then one may feel that utterances beginning 'I state that . . .' do have to be true or false, that they *are* statements.

Considerations of this sort, then, may well make us feel pretty unhappy. If we look back for a moment at our contrast between statements and performative utterances, we realize that we were taking statements very much on trust from, as we said, the traditional treatment. Statements, we had it, were to be true or false; performative utterances on the other hand were to be felicitous or infelicitous. They were the doing of something, whereas for all we said making statements was not doing something. Now this contrast surely, if we look back at it, is unsatisfactory. Of course statements are liable to be assessed in this matter of their correspondence or failure to correspond with the facts, that is, being true or false. But they are also liable to infelicity every bit as much as are performative utterances. In fact some troubles that have arisen in the study of statements recently can be shown to be simply troubles of infelicity. For example, it has been pointed out that there is something very odd about saying something like this: 'The cat is on the mat but I don't believe it is'. Now this is an outrageous thing to say, but it is not self-contradictory. There is no reason why the cat shouldn't be on the mat without my believing that it is. So how are we to classify what's wrong with this peculiar statement? If we remember now the doctrine of infelicity we shall see that the person who makes this remark about the cat is in much the same position as somebody who says something like this: 'I promise that I shall be there, but I haven't the least intention of being there'. Once again you can of course perfectly well promise to be there without having the least intention of being there, but there is something outrageous about saying it, about actually avowing the insincerity of the promise you give. In the same way there is insincerity in the case of the person who says 'The cat is on the mat but I don't believe it is', and he is actually avowing that insincerity—which makes a peculiar kind of nonsense.

A second case that has come to light is the one about John's children—the case where somebody is supposed to say 'All John's children are bald but John hasn't got any children'. Or perhaps somebody says 'All John's children are bald', when as a matter of fact—he doesn't say so—John has no children. Now those who study statements have worried about this; ought they to say that the statement 'All John's children are bald' is meaningless in this case? Well, if it is, it is not a bit like a great many other more standard kinds of meaninglessness; and we see, if we look back at our list of infelicities, that what is going wrong here is much the same as what goes wrong in, say, the case of a contract for the sale of a piece of land when the piece of land referred to does not exist. Now what we say in the case of this sale of land, which of course would be effected by a performative utterance, is that the sale is void—void for lack of reference or ambiguity of reference; and so we can see that the statement about all John's children is likewise void for lack of reference. And if the man actually says that John has no children in the same breath as saying they're all bald, he is making the same kind of outrageous utterance as the man who says 'The cat is on the mat and I don't believe it is', or the man who says 'I promise to but I don't intend to'.

In this way, then, ills that have been found to afflict statements can be precisely paralleled with ills that are characteristic of performative utterances. And after all when we state something or describe something or report something, we do perform an act which is every bit as much an act as an act of ordering or warning. There seems no good reason why stating should be given a specially unique position. Of course philosophers have been wont to talk as though you or I or anybody could just go round stating anything about anything and that would be perfectly in order, only there's just a little question: is it true or false? But besides the little question, is it true or false, there is surely the question: *is* it in order? Can you go round just making statements about anything? Suppose for example you say to me 'I'm feeling pretty mouldy this morning'. Well, I say to you 'You're not'; and you say 'What the devil do you mean, I'm not?' I say 'Oh nothing—I'm just stating you're not, is it true or false?' And you say 'Wait a bit about whether it's true or false, the question is what did you mean by making statements about somebody else's feeling? I told you I'm feeling pretty mouldy. You're just not in a position to say, to state that I'm not'. This brings out that you can't just make statements about other people's feelings (though you can make guesses if you like); and there are very many things which, having no knowledge of, not being in a position to pronounce about, you just can't state. What we need to do for the case of stating, and by the same token describing and reporting, is to take them a bit off their pedestal, to realize that they are speech-acts no less than all these other speech-acts that we have been mentioning and talking about as performative.

Then let us look for a moment at our original contrast between the performative and the statement from the other side. In handling performatives we have been putting it all the time as though the only thing that a performative utterance had to do was to be felicitous, to come off, not to be a misfire, not to be an abuse. Yes, but that's not the end of the matter. At least in the case of many utterances which, on what we have said, we should have to class as performative—cases where we say 'I warn you to . . .', 'I advise you to . . .' and so on—there will be other questions besides simply: was it in order, was it all right, as a piece of advice or a warning, did it come off? After that surely there will be the question: was it good or sound advice? Was it a justified warning? Or in the case, let us say, of a verdict or an estimate: was it a good estimate, or a sound verdict? And these are questions that can only be decided by considering how the content of the verdict or estimate is related in some way to fact, or to evidence available about the facts. This is to say that we do require to assess at least a great many performative utterances in a general dimension of correspondence with fact. It may still be said, of course, that this does not make them *very* like statements because still they are not true or false, and that's a little black and white speciality that distinguishes statements as a class apart. But actually—though it would take too long to go on about this—the more you think about truth and falsity the more you find that very few statements that we ever utter are just true or just false. Usually there is the question are they fair or are they not fair, are they adequate or not adequate, are they exaggerated or not exaggerated? Are they too rough, or are they perfectly precise, accurate, and so on? 'True' and 'false' are just general labels for a whole dimension of different appraisals which have something or other to do with the relation between what we say and the facts. If, then, we loosen up our ideas of truth and falsity we shall see that statements, when assessed in relation to the facts, are not so very different after all from pieces of advice, warnings, verdicts, and so on.

We see then that stating something is performing an act just as much as is giving an order or giving a warning; and we see, on the other hand, that, when we give an order or a warning or a piece of advice, there is a question about how this is related to fact which is not perhaps so very different from the kind of question that arises when we discuss how a statement is related to fact. Well, this seems to mean that in its original form our distinction between the performative and the statement is considerably weakened, and indeed breaks down. I will just make a suggestion as to how to handle this matter. We need to go very much farther back, to consider all the ways and senses in which saying anything at all is doing this or that—because of course it is always doing a good many different things. And one thing that emerges when we do do this is that, besides the question that has been very much studied in the past as to what a certain utterance *means*, there is a further question distinct from this as to what was the *force*, as we may call it, of the utterance. We may be quite clear what 'Shut the door' means, but not yet at all clear on the further point as to whether as uttered at a certain time it was an order, an entreaty or whatnot. What we need besides the old doctrine about meanings is a new doctrine about all the possible forces of utterances, towards the discovery of which our proposed list of explicit performative verbs would be a very great help; and then, going on from there, an investigation of the various terms of appraisal that we use in discussing speech-acts of this, that, or the other precise kind—orders, warnings, and the like.

The notions that we have considered then, are the performative, the infelicity, the explicit performative, and lastly, rather hurriedly, the notion of the forces of utterances. I dare say that all this seems a little unremunerative, a little complicated. Well, I suppose in some ways it is unremunerative, and I suppose it ought to be remunerative. At least, though, I think that if we pay attention to these matters we can clear up some mistakes in philosophy; and after all philosophy is used as a scape-goat, it parades mistakes which are really the mistakes of everybody. We might even clear up some mistakes in grammar, which perhaps is a little more respectable.

And is it complicated? Well, it is complicated a bit; but life and truth and things do tend to be complicated. It's not things, it's philosophers that are simple. You will have heard it said, I expect, that over-simplification is the occupational disease of philosophers, and in a way one might agree with that. But for a sneaking suspicion that it's their occupation.

Further Readings

LANGUAGE AND MEANING

Alston, William P., "Meaning and Use," *Philosophical Quarterly*, 1963.

Alston, William P., *Philosophy of Language*, Prentice Hall, Englewood Cliffs, N.J., 1964.

Austin, J. L., *How to Do Things with Words*, Oxford University Press, London, 1962.

Ayer, A. J., *Language, Truth, and Logic*, Gollancz, London, 1936.

Ayer, A. J., "Philosophy and Language," Oxford University Press, London, 1960, also in *The Concept of a Person and Other Essays*, Macmillan, London, 1963.

Brentano, Franz, "Genuine and Fictitious Objects," in R. M. Chisholm (ed.), *Realism and the Background of Phenomenology*, Free Press, New York, 1960.

Caton, C. (ed.), *Philosophy and Ordinary Language*, University of Illinois Press, Urbana, 1963.

Chappell, Vere (ed.), *Ordinary Language: Essays in Philosophical Method*, Prentice-Hall, Englewood Cliffs, N.J., 1964.

Chomsky, Noam, "A Review of B. F. Skinner's *Verbal Behavior*," *Language*, *35* (1959).

Chomsky, Noam, *Syntactic Structures*, Monton, Hague, 1957.

Fodor, J. A. and Katz, J. J., *The Structure of Language*, Prentice-Hall, Englewood Cliffs, N.J., 1965.

Frankena, W., "Some Aspects of Language," in Paul Henle (ed.), *Language, Thought, and Culture*, University of Michigan Press, Ann Arbor, 1958.

Frege, Gottlob, "On Sense and Reference," in Peter Geach and Max Black (eds.), *Philosophical Writings*, Blackwells, Oxford, 1952.

Grice, H. P., "Meaning," *Philosophical Review*, *66* (1957).

Hempel, C. G., "Problems and Changes in the Empiricist Criterion of Meaning," *Revue Internationale de Philosophie*, *4* (1950), also in Linsky (ed.), *Semantics and Philosophy of Language.*

Henle, Paul (ed.), *Language, Thought and Culture*, University of Michigan Press, Ann Arbor, 1958.

Katz, Jerrold J., *The Philosophy of Language*, Harper & Row, New York, 1966.

Lewis, C. I., "Modes of Meaning," *Philosophy and Phenomenological Research*, *4* (1944), also in Linsky.

Linsky, L. (ed.), *Semantics and the Philosophy of Language*, University of Illinois Press, Urbana, 1952.

Marhenke, Paul, "The Criterion of Significance," *Proceedings and Addresses of the American Philosophical Association*, 1950, also in Linsky.

Moore, G. E., "Wittgenstein's Lectures in 1930–1933," *Mind* (1954 and 1955), also in Moore's *Philosophical Papers*, Allen and Unwin, London, 1959.

Ogden, C. K. and I. A. Richards, *The Meaning of Meaning*, Harcourt, Brace, & World, New York, 1938.

Quine, W. V., *Word and Object*, Wiley, New York, 1960.

Searle, J. R., "Meaning and Speech Acts," *Philosophical Review*, (1962).

Skinner, B. F., *Verbal Behavior*, Appleton-Century-Crofts, New York, 1957.

Urmson, J. O., *Philosophical Analysis*, Clarendon Press, Oxford, 1956.

Warnock, J., "Verification and Use of Language," *Revue Internationale de Philosophie*, 1951.

Wittgenstein, L., *The Blue and Brown Books*, Blackwell, Oxford, 1958, pp. 1–44.

Wittgenstein, L., *Philosophical Investigations*, Blackwell, Oxford, 1953, Part I, pars. 1–132.

Ziff, Paul, *Semantic Analysis*, Cornell University Press, Ithaca, 1960.

TRUTH

Austin, J. L., "Truth," *Proceedings of the Aristotelian Society*, suppl. vol. 24 (1950), also in Pitcher.

Ayer, A. J., "Truth," *The Concept of a Person and Other Essays*, Macmillan, London, 1963.

Blanshard, Brand, *The Nature of Thought*, Vol. II, Macmillan, New York, 1940.

Bradley, F. H., *Appearance and Reality: A Metaphysical Essay*, 2nd ed, Clarendon Press, Oxford, 1897, Chapters 15 and 24.

Bradley, F. H., "On Truth and Practice," *Mind*, *51* (1904).

James, William, *Pragmatism*, Lectures 2 and 6, Makay, New York, 1907.

Joachim, H. H., *The Nature of Truth*, Clarendon Press, Oxford, 1906.

Moore, G. E., "William James's Pragmatism," *Philosophical Studies*, Routledge & Kegan Paul, London, 1922.

Pitcher, George (ed.), *Truth*, Prentice-Hall, Englewood Cliffs, N.J., 1964, see bibliography.

Russell, Bertrand, *The Problems of Philosophy*, Oxford University Press, London, 1912, see chap. 12.

Strawson, P. F., "Truth," *Analysis, 9* (1949), also in M. MacDonald Blackwell (ed.), *Philosophy and Analysis*, Oxford, Fair Lawn, N.J., 1954.

Strawson, P. F., "Truth," *Proceedings of the Aristotelian Society*, suppl. vol. 24 (1950), also in Pitcher.

Tarski, A., "The Semantic Conception of Truth," *Philosophy and Phenomenological Research*, *4* (1944).

Woozley, A. D., *Theory of Knowledge: An Introduction*, Hutchinson, London, 1949, chaps. 6 and 7.

IX

GOD AND RELIGIOUS BELIEF

Where did the universe come from? For what reason, if any, is it in existence? What is the purpose, if any, of human existence? How is man similar to and how is he different from other things in the universe? Is man a part of nature, or is he separate from nature?

These are questions many people try to answer at some time. Often they uncritically accept the beliefs of their society or immediate family or friends. Those who, on the other hand, have reflected seriously on these questions have put forward a variety of answers. Among the most important views are those which make reference to a God and are based on the teachings of a religion.

Let us describe in outline a typical, but far from universal, religious conception of man and of his relation to the world: Everything, including man, was created by an Infinite Being, God. Man, however, is special, for God gave man a soul. This makes it possible for man to engage in activities and realize potentialities that make up the distinctively human side of his nature. After man's body dies, his soul continues to live forever.

God is also the source and foundation of all moral values. Knowledge of His will, therefore, provides man with the understanding of how to live his life. Man is, in fact, under an obligation to God, and the fulfillment of this obligation is necessary for the supreme joy that God promises to man. One of the most important obligations man has is to love his fellow man and to treat him with respect.

In light of this outline, we see that the notion of God provides a way to answer each of our initial questions. Because of this, philosophers have been deeply interested in questions concerning God's existence and nature.

1

With respect to God's existence, some affirm it (theism), others deny it (atheism), others confess ignorance (agnosticism), and still others claim the question has no meaning.

Those who affirm His existence sometimes present evidence or proofs.

Traditionally there have been two kinds of proof offered for God's existence.

Some believe that a person can know that God exists without inferring it from facts we come to learn about through observing the world. Such proofs are called *a priori.* The most famous of these is St. Anselm's ontological argument. St. Anselm claims that one can infer that God exists simply from the very notion or concept of God. (See the selection by Anselm entitled "The Ontological Proof" included in this section.)

Others maintain that *a posteriori* arguments are required. These are arguments based on facts about the world learned through observation. The most famous of these are the five proofs given by St. Thomas Aquinas. One of the most interesting of these is the teleological argument (the fifth), which is based on the design and harmony we discover in the world. (See the selection entitled "Five Proofs for the Existence of God" included in this section.)

If a person rejects these arguments for God's existence, he may accept atheism or agnosticism and try to formulate his basic beliefs and attitudes independently of religion. (See Section XI, "World Views and Philosophical Commitment.") Or he may accept theism and yet admit that he has no grounds for his belief. (See the selection by Kierkegaard entitled "Subjective Truth" included in this section.) The term "faith" is sometimes used to characterize this posture. Some philosophers are highly critical of this position, because they feel it is not rational to hold an important belief without any evidence for its truth.

The concept of faith is discussed by Paul Tillich. Tillich's thought represents a recent stage in the development of the existentialist movement within the philosophy of religion. The conception of faith he presents is in line with his general de-emphasis of the cognitive side of religion (religion as a set of beliefs or dogmas for which one provides evidence or proofs). Existentialist philosophers of religion see religion as a deeply personal affair in which the person commits his whole self, not just his mind. They say that the truly religious person cannot assume an objective, scientific stance with respect to God. But this is just what people who try to prove His existence do. They do not see that God is not to be dissected logically, but to be loved. (See the selection by Tillich entitled "Faith and Religious Symbols" included in this section.)

The existentialist movement receives impetus from the development of science. As science develops, it often advances theories that conflict with some traditional religious beliefs. Often, these beliefs give way to the claims of science. Some advocates of religion praise it for its flexibility in adapting its doctrines to accommodate scientific advancements. Others, however, say that religions have no right to concern themselves at all with factual claims about the world—this is the province of science, not religion. Just as religion should desist from entering the province of science, it should also desist from using the methods of science, viz., the methods of proof and evidence. Religious existentialism, then, is a movement which tries to retain what it takes to be a deeply important mode of man's existence, that is, the religious mode, but it strips it of its cognitive pretensions.

Even if a person accepts theism, it is not clear what he has accepted until one has some conception of God's nature, of what He is. The properties assigned to God by western religions typically make Him a highly personal Being. He loves man, is concerned about him, will listen to his supplications, imposes obligations upon him, and punishes him. Some religions, however, do not conceive God in personal terms. In fact, some religions seem to dispense with the concept of a God altogether. Since the word "God" suggests to many a personal Being, other terms such as "the Absolute" or "Ultimate Reality" may be used. Often these religions are monistic in that they think of all "things" as being basically one, as partaking of a common reality. The Absolute is all there is, although from our finite perspective, it appears that all things are separate, and not one. This pantheistic tendency is de-emphasized in personal western religions.

II

The magnification of God, e.g., calling Him infinite, creates serious problems. We shall mention three:

1. If God is all-powerful, then He can eliminate the evil that exists in the world if He wants to. Since He is all-good, He presumably wants to. Why, then, is there evil? The problem of evil has plagued many believers, some of whom have concluded that if God exists, He cannot be both omnipotent and all-good. They believe, in other words, that one can prove that the traditional notion of God contains a contradiction and therefore that no such God exists.

2. One way of dealing with the problem of evil is to say that the moral evil is not God's fault, but man's. God could have prevented man from committing evil deeds, but only at the expense of taking away the precious gift of freedom. It is better for man to have the power to choose between good and evil, even if he occasionally chooses evil, than not to have this power at all.

Regardless of the merits of this approach to one kind of evil (there is still the problem of natural evil—sickness, natural catastrophes, death), it presupposes that man is free. But another attribute of God is omniscience. He, therefore, knows how we will choose before we actually do choose. Are we, then, really free? If God is so powerful, does He not really make us do *all* that we do, as well as make us choose as we do? The second problem, then, is whether or not it is possible for man to retain even limited freedom and dignity if God is infinite in all respects. (See Augustine, "Foreknowledge and Free Will," Section III.)

3. If God is personal, He has attributes that are similar to human attributes, such as goodness. But He is also infinite. It is said, therefore, that His goodness is infinite or perfect. But what is infinite goodness? Is it goodness in the same sense as Jones' goodness, except a great deal more?

If so, then we at least have a rough idea of what we are ascribing to God. But some claim that it demeans God to say that His goodness is of the same kind as Jones'. He must be good in a different sense of "good." But if the term "good" as applied to God has a different sense, what does it mean? Surely, we understand the term because we understand what it means when it is applied to Jones. To say that it has a different sense when applied to God suggests to some that it means nothing at all. The use of the term is, at least, misleading unless its meaning is the same as it is in the human context. And this is apparently precluded by the qualifier "infinite." Some have concluded that talk about God is meaningless. We cannot give a sense to the terms we use to characterize Him.

Others draw similar conclusions on similar grounds. Some say that if sentences about God make sense, it ought to be possible to decribe conditions under which one can verify or falsify these sentences. (See Antony Flew "Theology and Falsification.") But religious thinkers do not state these conditions, or they see everything that happens as the manifestation of God or God's will. Since they refuse to say under what conditions they would grant that something was *not* a manifestation of God, it is said that their claim is vacuous or meaningless.

III

Of the various proofs of God's existence, one of the most interesting is the argument from religious experience. Some men claim that God exists because they have had a unique experience of Him. The experience is called "mystical" and is said to be so different from ordinary experience that it is or borders on the ineffable. Mystics have, nonetheless, tried to describe the experience. They often claim that through it they are in touch with or are absorbed into the Divine. But the description of the Divine varies from mystic to mystic. Some see it as a personal God and others as impersonal ultimate reality.

Some conclude that the mystic's experience is not cognitive. It is not an experience which warrants a knowledge claim about the world, that is, a claim to the effect that there is a God. They argue that the fact that mystics' interpretations of the experience vary shows that each is introducing into the experience beliefs and conceptions drawn from his own distinctive cultural background. The experience, like any other, is of scientific interest only insofar as it would be valuable to ascertain the conditions under which such experiences occur.

But others, like Stace, are more sympathetic. Stace tries to see just how far one can accept the *common* claim of mystics, granting that some differences among mystics can be culturally explained.

The following selections reflect the deep concern which philosophers have had and still have about the phenomenon of religious belief.

THE ONTOLOGICAL PROOF

ST. ANSELM

PREFACE

Some time ago, at the urgent request of some of my brethren, I published a brief work,* as an example of meditation on the grounds of faith. I wrote it in the role of one who seeks, by silent reasoning with himself, to learn what he does not know. But when I reflected on this little book, and saw that it was put together as a long chain of arguments, I began to ask myself whether *one* argument might possibly be found, resting on no other argument for its proof, but sufficient in itself to prove that God truly exists, and that he is the supreme good, needing nothing outside himself, but needful for the being and well-being of all things. I often turned my earnest attention to this problem, and at times I believed that I could put my finger on what I was looking for, but at other times it completely escaped my mind's eye, until finally, in despair, I decided to give up searching for something that seemed impossible to find. But when I tried to put the whole question out of my mind, so as to avoid crowding out other matters, with which I might make some progress, by this useless preoccupation, then, despite my unwillingness and resistance, it began to force itself on me more persistently than ever. Then, one day, when I was worn out by my vigorous resistance to the obsession, the solution I had ceased to hope for presented itself to me, in the very turmoil of my thoughts, so that I enthusiastically embraced the idea which, in my disquiet, I had spurned.

I thought that the proof I was so glad to find would please some readers if it were written down. Consequently, I have written the little work that follows, dealing with this and one or two other matters, in the role of one who strives to raise his mind to the contemplation of God and seeks to understand what he believes. Neither this essay nor the other one I have already mentioned really seemed to me to deserve to be called a book or to bear an author's name; at the same time, I felt that they could not be published without some title that might encourage anyone into whose hands they fell to read them, and so I gave each of them a title. The first I

Reprinted from *A Scholastic Miscellany*, Vol. X, LCC, ed. and tr. by E. R. Fairweather, 1956, by permission of the Westminster Press, Philadelphia, and the SCM Press, London.

* The *Monologion*, probably Anselm's first work, was written at Bec in the second half of 1076. (Translator's note.)

called *An Example of Meditation on the Grounds of Faith*, and the second *Faith Seeking Understanding*.

But when both of them had been copied under these titles by a number of people, I was urged by many people—and especially by Hugh, the reverend archbishop of Lyons, apostolic legate in Gaul, who ordered this with apostolic authority—to attach my name to them. In order to do this more fittingly, I have named the first *Monologion* (or *Soliloquy*), and the second *Proslogion* (or *Address*).

GOD TRULY IS

And so, O Lord, since thou givest understanding to faith, give me to understand—as far as thou knowest it to be good for me—that thou dost exist, as we believe, and that thou art what we believe thee to be. Now we believe that thou art a being than which none greater can be thought. Or can it be that there is no such being, since "the fool hath said in his heart, 'There is no God' "? But when this same fool hears what I am saying—"A being than which none greater can be thought"—he understands what he hears, and what he understands is in his understanding, even if he does not understand that it exists. For it is one thing for an object to be in the understanding, and another thing to understand that it exists. When a painter considers beforehand what he is going to paint, he has it in his understanding, but he does not suppose that what he has not yet painted already exists. But when he has painted it, he both has it in his understanding and understands that what he has now produced exists. Even the fool, then, must be convinced that a being than which none greater can be thought exists at least in his understanding, since when he hears this he understands it, and whatever is understood is in the understanding. But clearly that than which a greater cannot be thought cannot exist in the understanding alone. For if it is actually in the understanding alone, it can be thought of as existing also in reality, and this is greater. Therefore, if that than which a greater cannot be thought is in the understanding alone, this same thing than which a greater cannot be thought is that than which a greater can be thought. But obviously this is impossible. Without doubt, therefore, there exists, both in the understanding and in reality, something than which a greater cannot be thought.

GOD CANNOT BE THOUGHT OF AS NONEXISTENT

And certainly it exists so truly that it cannot be thought of as nonexistent. For something can be thought of as existing, which cannot be thought of as not existing, and this is greater than that which *can* be thought of as not existing. Thus, if that than which a greater cannot be thought can be thought of as not existing, this very thing than which a greater cannot be thought is *not* that than which a greater cannot be thought. But this is contradictory. So, then, there truly is a being than which a greater cannot be thought—so truly that it cannot even be thought of as not existing.

And *thou* art this being, O Lord our God. Thou so truly are, then, O Lord my God, that thou canst not even be thought of as not existing. And this is right. For if some mind could think of something better than thou, the creature would rise above the Creator and judge its Creator; but this is altogether absurd. And indeed, whatever is, except thyself alone, can be thought of as not existing. Thou alone, therefore, of all beings, has being in the truest and highest sense, since no other being so truly exists, and thus every other being has less being. Why, then, has "the fool said in his heart, 'There is no God,'" when it is so obvious to the rational mind that, of all beings, thou dost exist supremely? Why indeed, unless it is that he is a stupid fool?

HOW THE FOOL HAS SAID IN HIS HEART WHAT CANNOT BE THOUGHT

But how did he manage to say in his heart what he could not think? Or how is it that he was unable to think what he said in his heart? After all, to say in one's heart and to think are the same thing. Now if it is true—or, rather, since it is true—that he thought it, because he said it in his heart, but did not say it in his heart, since he could not think it, it is clear that something can be said in one's heart or thought in more than one way. For we think of a thing, in one sense, when we think of the word that signifies it, and in another sense, when we understand the very thing itself. Thus, in the first sense God can be thought of as nonexistent, but in the second sense this is quite impossible. For no one who understands what God is can think that God does not exist, even though he says these words in his heart—perhaps without any meaning, perhaps with some quite extraneous meaning. For God is that than which a greater cannot be thought, and whoever understands this rightly must understand that he exists in such a way that he cannot be nonexistent even in thought. He, therefore, who understands that God thus exists cannot think of him as nonexistent.

Thanks be to thee, good Lord, thanks be to thee, because I now understand by thy light what I formerly believed by thy gift, so that even if I were to refuse to believe in thy existence, I could not fail to understand its truth.

REPLY TO THE CRITICISMS OF GAUNILO

. . . But, you say, suppose that someone imagined an island in the ocean, surpassing all lands in its fertility. Because of the difficulty, or rather the impossibility, of finding something that does not exist, it might well be called "Lost Island." By reasoning like yours, he might then say that we cannot doubt that it truly exists in reality, because anyone can easily conceive it from a verbal description.* I state confidently that if anyone discovers something for me, other than that "than which a greater cannot be thought," existing either in reality or in thought alone, to which the logic of my argument can be applied, I shall find his lost island and give it to him, never to be lost again. But it now seems obvious that this being than which a greater cannot be thought cannot be thought of as nonexistent, because it exists by such a sure reason of truth. For otherwise it would not exist at all. In short, if anyone says that he thinks it does not exist, I say that when he thinks this, he either thinks of something than which a greater cannot be thought or he does not think. If he does not think, he does not think of what he is not thinking of as nonexistent. But if he does think, then he thinks of something which cannot be thought of as nonexistent. For if it could be thought of as nonexistent, it could be thought of as having a beginning and an end. But this is impossible. Therefore, if anyone thinks of it, he thinks of something that cannot even be thought of as nonexistent. But he who thinks of this does not think that it does not exist; if he did, he would think what cannot be thought. Therefore, that than which a greater cannot be thought cannot be thought of as nonexistent.

You say, moreover, that when it is said that the highest reality cannot be *thought of* as nonexistent, it would perhaps be better to say that it cannot be *understood* as nonexistent, or even as possibly nonexistent. But it is more correct to say, as I said, that it cannot be thought. For if I had said that the reality itself cannot be understood not to exist, perhaps you yourself, who say that according to the very definition of the term what is false cannot be understood, would object that nothing that is can be understood as nonexistent. For it is false to say that what exists does not exist. Therefore it would not be peculiar to God to be unable to be understood as nonexistent. But if some one of the things that most certainly are can be understood as nonexistent, other certain things can similarly be understood as nonexistent. But this objection cannot be applied to "thinking," if it is rightly considered. For although none of the things that exist can be understood not to exist, still they can all be thought of as nonexistent, except that which most fully is. For all those things—and only those—which have a beginning or end or are composed of parts can be thought of as nonexistent, along with anything that does

* Cf. Gaunilo, *Pro insipiente*, 6.

not exist as a whole anywhere or at any time (as I have already said). But the only being that cannot be thought of as nonexistent is that in which no thought finds beginning or end or composition of parts, but which any thought finds as a whole, always and everywhere.

You must realize, then, that you can think of yourself as nonexistent, even while you know most certainly that you exist. I am surprised that you said you did not know this. For we think of many things as nonexistent when we know that they exist, and of many things as existent when we know that they do not exist—all this not by a real judgment, but by imagining that what we think is so. And indeed, we can think of something as nonexistent, even while we know that it exists, because we are able at the same time to think the one and know the other. And yet we cannot think of it as nonexistent, while we know that it exists, because we cannot think of something as at once existent and nonexistent. Therefore, if anyone distinguishes these two senses of the statement in this way, he will understand that nothing, as long as it is known to exist, can be thought of as nonexistent, and that whatever exists, except that than which a greater cannot be thought, can be thought of as nonexistent, even when it is known to exist. So, then, it is peculiar to God to be unable to be thought of as nonexistent, and nevertheless many things, as long as they exist, cannot be thought of as nonexistent. I think that the way in which it can still be said that God is thought of as nonexistent is stated adequately in the little book itself.*

FIVE PROOFS FOR THE EXISTENCE OF GOD

ST. THOMAS AQUINAS

. . . *I answer that,* The existence of God can be proved in five ways.

The first and more manifest way is the argument from motion. It is certain, and evident to our senses, that in the world some things are in motion. Now whatever is moved is moved by another, for nothing can be moved except it is in potentiality to that towards which it is moved whereas a thing moves inasmuch as it is in act. For motion is nothing else than the reduction of something from potentiality to actuality. But nothing can be reduced from potentiality to actuality, except by something in a state of actuality. Thus that which is actually hot, as fire, makes

* Cf. *Proslogion,* Chapter IV. (See p. 392 above.)

wood, which is potentially hot, to be actually hot, and thereby moves and changes it. Now it is not possible that the same thing should be at once in actuality and potentiality in the same respect, but only in different respects. For what is actually hot cannot simultaneously be potentially hot; but it is simultaneously potentially cold. It is therefore impossible that in the same respect and in the same way a thing should be both mover and moved, i.e., that it should move itself. Therefore, whatever is moved must be moved by another. If that by which it is moved be itself moved, then this also must needs be moved by another, and that by another again. But this cannot go on to infinity, because then there would be no first mover, and, consequently, no other mover, seeing that subsequent movers move only inasmuch as they are moved by the first mover, as the staff moves only because it is moved by the hand. Therefore, it is necessary to arrive at a first mover, moved by no other; and this everyone understands to be God.

The second way is from the nature of efficient cause. In the world of sensible things we find there is an order of efficient causes. There is no case known (neither is it, indeed, possible) in which a thing is found to be the efficient cause of itself; for so it would be prior to itself, which is impossible. Now in efficient causes it is not possible to go on to infinity, because in all efficient causes following in order, the first is the cause of the intermediate cause, and the intermediate is the cause of the ultimate cause, whether the intermediate cause be several, or one only. Now to take away the cause is to take away the effect. Therefore, if there be no first cause among efficient causes, there will be no ultimate, nor any intermediate, cause. But if in efficient causes it is possible to go on to infinity, there will be no first efficient cause, neither will there be an ultimate effect, nor any intermediate efficient causes; all of which is plainly false. Therefore it is necessary to admit a first efficient cause, to which everyone gives the name of God.

The third way is taken from possibility and necessity, and runs thus. We find in nature things that are possible to be and not to be, since they are found to be generated, and to be corrupted, and consequently, it is possible for them to be and not to be. But it is impossible for these always to exist, for that which can not-be at some time is not. Therefore, if everything can not-be, then at one time there was nothing in existence. Now if this were true, even now there would be nothing in existence, because that which does not exist begins to exist only through something already existing. Therefore, if at one time nothing was in existence, it would have been impossible for anything to have begun to exist; and thus even now nothing would be in existence—which is absurd. Therefore, not all beings are merely possible, but there must exist something the existence of which is necessary. But every necessary thing either has its necessity caused by another, or not. Now it is impossible to go on to infinity in necessary things which have their necessity caused by another, as has been already proved in regard to efficient causes. Therefore we cannot but admit the existence of some being having of itself its own necessity, and not receiving it from another, but rather causing in others their necessity. This all men speak of as God.

The fourth way is taken from the gradation to be found in things. Among beings there are some more and some less good, true, noble, and the like. But *more* and *less* are predicated of different things according as they resemble in their different ways something which is the maximum, as a thing is said to be hotter according as it more nearly resembles that which is hottest; so that there is something which is truest, something best, something noblest, and, consequently, something which is most being, for those things that are greatest in truth are greatest in being, as it is written in *Metaph.* II (*Metaph.* Ia, 1 993b30). Now the maximum in any genus is the cause of all in that genus, as fire, which is the maximum of heat, is the cause of all hot things, as is said in the same book (993b25). Therefore there must also be something which is to all beings the cause of their being, goodness, and every other perfection; and this we call God.

The fifth way is taken from the governance of the world. We see that things which lack knowledge, such as natural bodies, act for an end, and this is evident from their acting always, or nearly always in the same way, so as to obtain the best result. Hence it is plain that they achieve their end, not fortuitously, but designedly. Now whatever lacks knowledge cannot move towards an end, unless it be directed by some being endowed with knowledge and intelligence; as the arrow is directed by the archer. Therefore some intelligent being exists by whom all natural things are directed to their end; and this being we call God.

THE EXISTENCE OF GOD

J. J. C. SMART

This lecture is not to discuss whether God exists. It is to discuss reasons which philosophers have given for saying that God exists. That is, to discuss certain arguments.

First of all it may be as well to say what we may hope to get out of this. Of course, if we found that any of the traditional arguments for the existence of God were sound, we should get out of our one hour this Sunday afternoon something of inestimable value, such as one never got out of any hour's work in our lives before. For we should have got out of one hour's work the answer to that question about which, above all, we want to know the answer. (This is assuming for the moment that the

Reprinted with permission of The Macmillan Company from *New Essays in Philosophical Theology* by A. Flew and A. C. Macintyre (eds.). First published in the *Church Quarterly Review*, London, 1955.

question 'Does God exist?' is a proper question. The fact that a question is all right as far as the rules of ordinary grammar are concerned does not ensure that it has a sense. For example, 'Does virtue run faster than length?' is certainly all right as far as ordinary grammar is concerned, but it is obviously not a meaningful question. Again, 'How fast does time flow?' is all right as far as ordinary grammar is concerned, but it has no clear meaning. Now some philosophers would ask whether the question 'Does God exist?' is a proper question. The greatest danger to theism at the present moment does not come from people who deny the validity of the arguments for the existence of God, for many Christian theologians do not believe that the existence of God can be proved, and certainly nowhere in the Old or New Testaments do we find any evidence of people's religion having a metaphysical basis. The main danger to theism today comes from people who want to say that 'God exists' and 'God does not exist' are equally absurd. The concept of God, they would say, is a nonsensical one. Now I myself shall later give grounds for thinking that the question 'Does God exist?' is not, in the full sense, a proper question, but I shall also give grounds for believing that to admit this is not necessarily to endanger theology.)

However, let us assume for the moment that the question 'Does God exist?' is a proper question. We now ask: Can a study of the traditional proofs of the existence of God enable us to give an affirmative answer to this question? I contend that it can not. I shall point out what seem to me to be fallacies in the main traditional arguments for the existence of God. Does proving that the arguments are invalid prove that God does not exist? Not at all. For to say that an argument is invalid is by no means the same thing as to say that its conclusion is false. Still, if we do find that the arguments we consider are all fallacious, what do we *gain* out of our investigation? Well, one thing we gain is a juster (if more austere) view of what philosophical argument can do for us. But, more important, we get a deeper insight into the logical nature of certain concepts, in particular, of course, the concepts of deity and existence. Furthermore we shall get some hints as to whether philosophy can be of any service to theologians, and if can be of service, some hints as to how it can be of service. I think that it can be, but I must warn you that many, indeed perhaps the majority, of philosophers today would not entirely agree with me here. . . .

One very noteworthy feature which must strike anyone who first looks at the usual arguments for the existence of God is the extreme brevity of these arguments. They range from a few lines to a few pages. St. Thomas Aquinas presents five arguments in three pages! Would it not be rather extraordinary if such a great conclusion should be got so easily? Before going on to discuss any of the traditional arguments in detail I want to give general grounds for suspecting anyone who claims to settle a controversial question by means of a short snappy argument.

My reason for doubting whether a short snappy argument can ever settle any controversial question is as follows: *any argument can be reversed*. Let me explain this. A question of elementary logic is involved.

Let us consider an argument from two premisses, p, q, to a conclusion r:

$$\frac{\begin{matrix} p \\ q \end{matrix}}{r}$$

If the argument is valid, that is, if r really does follow from p and q, the argument will lead to agreement about r provided that there already is agreement about p and q. For example, if we have the premisses

p All A, B and C grade cricketers are entitled to a free pass to the Adelaide Oval for Test matches, Sheffield Shield matches, etc. (quite uncontroversial, it can be got from the rules of the South Australian Cricket Association).

q John Wilkin is an A, B or C grade cricketer. (Quite uncontroversial, everyone knows it.)

we may conclude

r John Wilkin is entitled to a free pass to the Adelaide Oval for Test matches, Sheffield Shield matches, etc.

But we now consider this argument*:

p Nothing can come into existence except through the activity of some previously existing thing or being.

q The world had a beginning in time.

therefore

r The world came into existence through the activity of some previously existing thing or being.

If this argument is valid (as it certainly is) then it is equally the case that

(not-r) The world did not come into existence through the activity of some previously existing thing or being

implies that either

(not-p) Something *can* come into existence otherwise than through the activity of a previously existing thing or being

or

(not-q) The world had no beginning in time.

That is, if $\frac{\begin{matrix} p \\ q \end{matrix}}{r}$ is valid $\frac{\begin{matrix} \text{not-}r \\ q \end{matrix}}{\text{not-}p}$ and $\frac{\begin{matrix} \text{not-}r \\ p \end{matrix}}{\text{not-}q}$ must be equally valid.

Now it is possible that a person might think that we have *fewer* reasons for believing r than we have for believing (not-p) or (not-q). In which case the argument $\frac{\begin{matrix} p \\ q \end{matrix}}{r}$ though perfectly valid

* I owe this illustration, and the whole application to the idea of "reversing the argument", to Prof. D. A. T. Gasking of Melbourne.

will not convince him. For he will be inclined to argue in the opposite direction, that is, from the falsity of r to the falsity of either p or q.

This last example is perhaps itself a—not very good—argument for the existence of God, but I have given it purely as an example to show *one* of the things to look out for when criticizing more serious arguments. The other thing to look out for, of course, is whether the argument is *valid*. It is my belief that in the case of any metaphysical argument it will be found that if the premisses are uncontroversial the argument is unfortunately not valid, and that if the argument is valid the premisses will unfortunately be just as doubtful as the conclusion they are meant to support.

With these warnings in mind let us proceed to the discussion of the three most famous arguments for the existence of God. These are:

(1) The Ontological Argument.
(2) The Cosmological Argument.
(3) The Teleological Argument.

The first argument—the ontological argument—really has no premisses at all. It tries to show that there would be a contradiction in denying that God exists. It was first formulated by St. Anselm and was later used by Descartes. It is not a convincing argument to modern ears, and St. Thomas Aquinas gave essentially the right reasons for rejecting it. However, it is important to discuss it, as an understanding of what is wrong with it is necessary for evaluating the second argument, that is, the cosmological argument. This argument does have a premiss, but not at all a controversial one. It is that something exists. We should all, I think, agree to that. The teleological argument is less austere in manner than the other two. It tries to argue to the existence of God not purely *a priori* and not from the mere fact of *something* existing, but from the actual features we observe in nature, namely those which seem to be evidence of design or purpose.

We shall discuss these three arguments in order. I do not say that they are the only arguments which have been propounded for the existence of God, but they are, I think, the most important ones. For example, of St. Thomas Aquinas' celebrated 'Five Ways' the first three are variants of the cosmological argument, and the fifth is a form of the teleological argument.

The Ontological Argument. This, as I remarked, contains no factual premiss. It is a *reductio-ad-absurdum* of the supposition that God does not exist. Now *reductio-ad-absurdum* proofs are to be suspected whenever there is doubt as to whether the statement to be proved is *significant*. For example, it is quite easy, as anyone who is familiar with the so-called Logical Paradoxes will know, to produce a not *obviously* nonsensical statement, such that both it *and* its denial imply a contradiction. So unless we are sure of the significance of a statement we cannot regard a *reductio-ad-absurdum* of its contradictory as proving its truth. This point of view is well known to those versed in the philosophy of mathematics; there is a well-known school of mathematicians, led by Brouwer, who refuse in certain circumstances to employ *reductio-ad-absurdum* proofs. However, I shall not press this criticism of the ontological argument, for this criticism is somewhat abstruse (though it has been foreshadowed by Catholic philosophers, who object to the ontological argument by saying that it does not first show that the concept of an infinitely perfect being is a *possible* one). We are at present assuming that 'Does God exist?' is a proper question, and if it is a proper question there is no objection so far to answering it by means of a *reductio-ad-absurdum* proof. We shall content ourselves with the more usual criticisms of the ontological argument.

The ontological argument was made famous by Descartes. It is to be found at the beginning of his Fifth Meditation. As I remarked earlier it was originally put forward by Anselm, though I am sorry to say that to read Descartes you would never suspect that fact! Descartes points out that in mathematics we can deduce various things purely *a priori*, 'as for example', he says, 'when I imagine a triangle, although there is not and perhaps never was in any place . . . one such figure, it remains true nevertheless that this figure possesses a certain determinate nature, form, or essence, which is . . . not framed by me, nor in any degree dependent on my thought; as appears from the circumstance, that diverse properties of the triangle may be demonstrated, for example that its three angles are equal to two right, that its greatest side is subtended by its greatest angle, and the like'. Descartes now goes on to suggest that just as having the sum of its angles equal to two right angles is involved in the idea of a triangle, so *existence* is involved in the very idea of an infinitely perfect being, and that it would therefore be as much of a contradiction to assert that an infinitely perfect being does not exist as it is to assert that the three angles of a triangle do not add up to two right angles or that two of its sides are not together greater than the third side. We may then, says Descartes, assert that an infinitely perfect being *necessarily* exists, just as we may say that two sides of a triangle are together *necessarily* greater than the third side.

This argument is highly fallacious. To say that a so-and-so exists is not in the least like saying that a so-and-so has such-and-such a property. It is not to amplify a concept but to say that a concept applies to something, and whether or not a concept applies to something can not be seen from an examination of the concept itself. Existence is not a property. 'Growling' is a property of tigers, and to say that 'tame tigers growl' is to say something about tame tigers, but to say 'tame tigers exist' is not to say something about tame tigers but to say that there are tame tigers. Prof. G. E. Moore once brought out the difference between existence and a property such as that of being tame, or being a tiger, or being a growler, by reminding us that though the sentence 'some tame tigers do not *growl*' makes perfect sense, the sentence 'some tame tigers do not *exist*' has no clear meaning. The fundamental mistake in the ontological argument, then, is that it treats 'exists' in 'an infinitely perfect being exists' as if it ascribed a property existence to an infinitely perfect being, just as 'is loving' in 'an infinitely perfect being is loving' ascribes a property, or as 'growl' in 'tame tigers growl' ascribes a property: the verb 'to exist' in 'an infinitely perfect being exists' does not ascribe a property to something already conceived of as existing but says that the concept of an infinitely perfect being applies to something. The verb 'to exist' here takes us right out of the purely conceptual world. This being so, there can never be any *logical contradiction* in denying that God exists. It is worth mentioning that we are less likely to make the sort of mistake that the ontological argument makes if we use the expression 'there is a so-and-so' instead of the more misleading form of words 'a so-and-so exists'.

I should like to mention another interesting, though less crucial, objection to Descartes' argument. He talks as though you can deduce further properties of, say, a triangle, by considering its definition. It is worth pointing out that from the definition of a triangle as a figure bounded by three straight lines you can only deduce trivialities, such as that it is bounded by more than one straight line, for example. It is not at all a contradiction to say that the two sides of a triangle are together not greater than the third side, or that its angles do not add up to two right angles. To get a contradiction you have to bring in the specific axioms of Euclidean geometry. (Remember school geometry, how you used to prove that the angles of a triangle add up to two right angles. Through the vertex *C* of the triangle *ABC* you drew a line parallel to *BA*, and so you assumed the axiom of parallels for a start. Definitions, by themselves, are not deductively potent. Descartes, though a very great mathematician himself, was profoundly mistaken as to the nature of mathematics. However, we can interpret him as saying that from the definition of a triangle, *together with the axions of Euclidean geometry*, you can deduce various things, such as that the angles of a triangle add up to two right angles. But this just shows how pure mathematics is a sort of game with symbols; you start with a set of axioms, and operate on them in accordance with certain rules of inference. All the mathematician requires is that the axiom set should be *consistent*. Whether or not it has application to reality lies outside pure mathematics. Geometry is no fit model for a proof of real existence.

We turn now to the *Cosmological Argument*. This argument does at least seem more promising than the ontological argument. It does start with a factual premiss, namely that something exists. The premiss that something exists is indeed a very abstract one, but nevertheless it *is* factual, it does give us a foothold in the real world of things, it does go beyond the consideration of mere concepts. The argument has been put forward in various forms, but for present purposes it may be put as follows:

Everything in the world around us is *contingent*. That is, with regard to any particular thing, it is quite conceivable that it might not have existed. For example, if you were asked why you existed, you could say that it was because of your parents, and if asked why they existed you could go still further back, but however far you go back you have not, so it is argued, made the fact of your existence really intelligible. For however far back you go in such a series you only get back to something which itself might not have existed. For a really satisfying explanation of why anything contingent (such as you or me or this table) exists you must eventually begin with something which is not itself contingent, that is, with something of which we cannot say that it might not have existed, that is we must begin with a necessary being. So the first part of the argument boils down to this. *If anything exists an absolutely necessary being must exist. Something exists. Therefore an absolutely necessary being must exist.*

The second part of the argument is to prove that a necessarily existing being must be an infinitely perfect being, that is, God. Kant* contended that this second stage of the argument is just the ontological argument over again, and of course if this were so the cosmological argument would plainly be a fraud; it begins happily enough with an existential premiss ('something exists') but this would only be a cover for the subsequent employment of the ontological argument. This criticism of Kant's has been generally accepted but I think that certain Thomist philosophers have been right in attributing to Kant's own criticism a mistake in elementary logic. Let us look at Kant's criticism. Kant says, correctly enough, that the conclusion of the second stage of the cosmological argument is 'All necessarily existing beings are infinitely perfect beings'. This, he says, implies that 'Some infinitely perfect beings are necessarily existing beings'. Since, however, there could be only one infinitely perfect, unlimited, being, we may replace the proposition 'Some infinitely perfect beings are necessarily existing beings' by the proposition 'All infinitely perfect beings are necessarily existing beings'. (To make this last point clearer let me take an analogous example. If it is true that some men who are Prime Minister of Australia are Liberals and if it is also true that there is only one Prime Minister of Australia, then we can equally well say that all men who are Prime Minister of Australia are Liberals. For 'some' means 'at least one', and if there is only one Prime Minister, then 'at least one' is equivalent to 'one', which in this case is 'all'.) So the conclusion of the second stage of the cosmological argument is that 'all infinitely perfect beings are necessarily existing beings'. This, however, is the principle of the ontological argument, which we have already criticized, and which, for that matter, proponents of the cosmological argument like Thomas Aquinas themselves reject.

Kant has, however, made a very simple mistake. He has forgotten that the existence of a necessary being has already been proved (or thought to have been proved) in the first part of the argument. He changes 'All necessary beings are infinitely perfect beings' round to 'Some infinitely perfect beings are necessary beings'. If this change round is to be valid the existence of a necessary being is already presupposed. Kant has been

* *Critique of Pure Reason*, A 603.

misled by an ambiguity in 'all'. 'All X's are Y's' may take it for granted that there are some X's or it may not. For example if I say, 'All the people in this room are interested in Philosophy', it is already agreed that there are some people in this room. So we can infer that 'Some of the people interested in Philosophy are people in this room'. So 'All the people in this room are interested in Philosophy' says more than 'If anyone were in this room he would be interested in Philosophy', for this would be true even if there were in fact no people in this room. (As I wrote this lecture I was quite sure that *if* anyone came he would be interested in Philosophy, and I could have been quite sure of this even if I had doubted whether anyone would come.) Now sometimes 'All X's are Y's' does mean only 'If anything is an X it is a Y'. Take the sentence 'All trespassers will be prosecuted'. This does not imply that some prosecuted people will be trespassers, for it does not imply that there are or will be any trespassers. Indeed the object of putting it on a notice is to make it more likely that there won't be any trespassers. All that 'All trespassers will be prosecuted' says is, 'If anyone is a trespasser then he will be prosecuted'. So Kant's criticism won't do. He has taken himself and other people in by using 'all' sometimes in the one way and sometimes in the other.

While agreeing thus far with Thomist critics of Kant* I still want to assert that the cosmological argument is radically unsound. The trouble comes much earlier than where Kant locates it. The trouble comes in the *first* stage of the argument. For the first stage of the argument purports to argue to the existence of a necessary being. And by 'a necessary being' the cosmological argument means 'a *logically* necessary being', i.e. 'a being whose non-existence is inconceivable in the sort of way that a triangle's having four sides is inconceivable'. The trouble is, however, that the concept of a logically necessary being is a self-contradictory concept, like the concept of a round square. For in the first place 'necessary' is a predicate of *propositions*, not of things. That is, we can contrast *necessary* propositions such as '$3 + 2 = 5$', 'a thing cannot be red and green all over', 'either it is raining or it is not raining', with *contingent* propositions, such as 'Mr. Menzies is Prime Minister of Australia', 'the earth is slightly flattened at the poles', and 'sugar is soluble in water'. The propositions in the first class are guaranteed solely by the rules for the use of the symbols they contain. In the case of the propositions of the second class a genuine possibility of agreeing or not agreeing with reality is left open; whether they are true or false depends not on the conventions of our language but on reality. (Compare the contrast between 'the equator is 90 degrees from the pole', which tells us nothing about geography but only about our map-making conventions, and 'Adelaide is 55 degrees from the pole', which does tell us a geographical fact.) So no informative proposition can be logically necessary. Now since 'necessary' is a word

* See, for example, Fr. T. A. Johnston, *Australasian Journal of Philosophy*, Vol. XXI, pp. 14–15, or D. J. B. Hawkins, *Essentials of Theism*, pp. 67–70, and the review of Fr. Hawkins' book by A. Donagan, *Australasian Journal of Philosophy*, Vol. XXVIII, especially p. 129.

which applies primarily to propositions, we shall have to interpret 'God is a necessary being' as 'The proposition 'God exists' is logically necessary.' But this *is* the principle of the ontological argument, and there is no way of getting round it this time in the way that we got out of Kant's criticism. No existential proposition can be logically necessary, for we saw that the truth of a logically necessary proposition depends only on our symbolism, or to put the same thing in another way, on the relationship of concepts. We saw, however, in discussing the ontological argument, that an existential proposition does not say that one concept is involved in another, but that a concept applies to something. An existential proposition must be very different from any logically necessary one, such as a mathematical one, for example, for the conventions of our symbolism clearly leave it open for us either to affirm or deny an existential proposition; it is not our symbolism but reality which decides whether or not we must affirm it or deny it.

The demand that the existence of God should be *logically* necessary is thus a self-contradictory one. When we see this and go back to look at the first stage of the cosmological argument it no longer seems compelling, indeed it now seems to contain an absurdity. If we cast our minds back, we recall that the argument was as follows: that if we explain why something exists and is what it is, we must explain it by reference to something else, and we must explain that thing's being what it is by reference to yet another thing, and so on, back and back. It is then suggested that unless we can go back to a logically necessary first cause we shall remain intellectually unsatisfied. We should otherwise only get back to something which might have been otherwise, and with reference to which the same questions can again be asked. This is the argument, but we now see that in asking for a logically necessary first cause we are doing something worse than asking for the moon. It is only *physically* impossible for us to get the moon; if I were a few million times bigger I could reach out for it and give it to you. That is, I know what it would be *like* to give you the moon, though I cannot *in fact* do it. A logically necessary first cause, however, is not impossible in the way that giving you the moon is impossible; no, it is *logically* impossible. 'Logically necessary being' is a self-contradictory expression like 'round square'. It is not any good saying that we would only be intellectually satisfied with a logically necessary cause, that nothing else would do. We can easily have an absurd wish. We should all like to be able to eat our cake and have it, but that does not alter the fact that our wish is an absurd and self-contradictory one. We reject the cosmological argument, then, because it rests on a thorough absurdity.

Having reached this conclusion I should like to make one or two remarks about the necessity of God. First of all, I think that it is undeniable that if worship is to be what religion takes it to be, then God must be a necessary being in some sense or other of 'necessary'. He must not be just one of the things in the world, however big. To concede that he was just one of the things in the world, even a big one, would reduce religion to something near idolatry. All I wish to point out is that God can not be a *logically* necessary being, for the very supposition that he is is self-contradictory. (Hence, of course, to say that God is not logically necessary is not to place any limitations on him. It is not a limitation on your walking ability that you cannot go out of the room and not go out. To say that someone cannot do something self-contradictory is not to say that he is in any way impotent, it is to say that the sentence 'he did such and such and did not do it' is not a possible description of anything.) Theological necessity cannot be logical necessity. In the second place, I think I can see roughly what sort of necessity theological necessity might be. Let me give an analogy from physics. It is not a *logical* necessity that the velocity of light in a vacuum should be constant. It would, however, upset physical theory considerably if we denied it. Similarly it is not a logical necessity that God exists. But it would clearly upset the structure of our religious attitudes in the most violent way if we denied it or even entertained the possibility of its falsehood. So if we say that it is a *physical* necessity that the velocity of light *in vacuo* should be constant—(deny it and prevailing physical theory would have to be scrapped or at any rate drastically modified)—similarly we can say that it is a *religious* necessity that God exists. That is, we believe in the necessity of God's existence because we are Christians; we are not Christians because we believe in the necessity of God's existence. There are no short cuts to God. I draw your attention to the language of religion itself, where we talk of *conversion*, not of *proof*. In my opinion religion can stand on its own feet, but to found it on a metaphysical argument *a priori* is to found it on absurdity born of ignorance of the logic of our language. I am reminded of what was said about the Boyle lectures in the eighteenth century: that no one doubted that God existed until the Boyle lecturers started to prove it.

Perhaps now is the time to say why I suggested at the beginning of the lecture that 'Does God exist?' is not a proper question. Once again I make use of an analogy from science. 'Do electrons exist?' (asked just like that) is not a proper question. In order to acquire the concept of an electron we must find out about experiments with cathode-ray tubes, the Wilson cloud chamber, about spectra and so on. We then find the concept of the electron a useful one, one which plays a part in a mass of physical theory. When we reach this stage the question 'Do electrons exist?' no longer arises. Before we reached this stage the question 'Do electrons exist?' had no clear meaning. Similarly, I suggest, the question 'Does God exist?' has no clear meaning for the unconverted. But for the converted the question no longer arises. The word 'God' gets its meaning from the part it plays in religious speech and literature, and in religious speech and literature the question of existence does not arise. A theological professor at Glasgow once said to me: 'Religion is "O God, if you exist, save my soul if it exists!"' This of course was a joke. It clearly is just *not* what religion is. So within religion the question 'Does God exist?' does not arise, any more than the question 'Do electrons exist?' arises within physics. Outside religion the question 'Does God exist?' has as little meaning as the question 'Do electrons exist?' as asked by the scientifically ignorant. Thus I suggest that it is possible to hold that the question 'Does God exist?' is not a proper question without necessarily also holding that religion and theology are nonsensical.

The cosmological argument, we saw, failed because it made use of the absurd conception of a *logically* necessary being. We now pass to the third argument which I propose to consider. This is the *Teleological Argument*. It is also called 'the Argument from Design'. It would be better called the argument *to* design, as Kemp Smith does call it, for clearly that the universe has been designed by a great architect is to assume a great part of the conclusion to be proved. Or we could call it 'the argument from apparent design'. The argument is very fully discussed in Hume's *Dialogues Concerning Natural Religion*, to which I should like to draw your attention. In these dialogues the argument is presented as follows: 'Look round the world: Contemplate the whole and every part of it: You will find it to be nothing but one great machine, subdivided into an infinite number of lesser machines. . . . The curious adapting of means to ends, throughout all nature, resembles exactly, though it much exceeds, the productions of human contrivance. . . . Since therefore the effects resemble each other, we are led to infer, by all the rules of analogy, that the causes also resemble; and that the Author of nature is somewhat similar to the mind of man; though possessed of much larger faculties, proportioned to the grandeur of the work which he has executed.'

This argument may at once be criticized in two ways: (1) We may question whether the analogy between the universe and artificial things like houses, ships, furniture, and machines (which admittedly are designed) is very close. Now in any ordinary sense of language, it is true to say that plants and animals have *not* been designed. If we press the analogy of the universe to a plant, instead of to a machine, we get to a very different conclusion. And why should the one analogy be regarded as any better or worse than the other? (2) Even if the analogy were close, it would only go to suggest that the universe was designed by a *very great* (not infinite) architect, and note, an *architect*, not a *creator*. For if we take the analogy seriously we must notice that we do not create the materials from which we make houses, machines and so on, but only *arrange* the materials.

This, in bare outline, is the general objection to the argument from design, and will apply to any form of it. In the form in which the argument was put forward by such theologians as Paley, the argument is, of course, still more open to objection. For Paley laid special stress on such things as the eye of an animal, which he thought must have been contrived by a wise Creator for the special benefit of the animal. It seemed to him inconceivable how otherwise such a complex organ, so well suited to the needs of the animal, should have arisen. Or listen to Henry More: 'For why have we three joints in our legs and arms, as also in our fingers, but that it was much better than having two or four? And why are our fore-teeth sharp like chisels to cut, but our inward teeth broad to grind [instead of] the fore-teeth broad and the other sharp? But we might have made a hard shift to have lived through in that worser condition. Again, why are the teeth so luckily placed, or rather, why are there not teeth in other bones as well as in the jaw-bones? for they might have been as capable as these. But the reason is, nothing is done foolishly or in vain; that is, there is a divine Providence that orders all things.' This type of argument has lost its persuasiveness, for the theory of Evolution explains why our teeth are so luckily placed in our jaw-bones, why we have the most convenient number of joints in our fingers, and so on. Species which did not possess advantageous features would not survive in competition with those which did.

The sort of argument Paley and Henry More used is thus quite unconvincing. Let us return to the broader conception, that of the universe as a whole, which seems to show the mark of a benevolent and intelligent Designer. Bacon expressed this belief forcibly: 'I had rather beleave all the Fables in the Legend and the Talmud and the Alcoran than that this Universal Frame is without a Minde.' So, in some moods, does the universe strike us. But sometimes, when we are in other moods, we see it very differently. To quote Hume's dialogues again: 'Look around this Universe. What an immense profusion of beings, animated and organized, sensible and active! You admire this prodigious variety and fecundity. But inspect a little more narrowly these living existences, the only beings worth regarding. How hostile and destructive to each other! How insufficient all of them for their own happiness! . . . the whole presents nothing but the idea of a blind Nature, impregnated by a great vivifying principle, and pouring forth from her lap, without discernment or parental care, her maimed and abortive children!' There is indeed a great deal of suffering, some part of which is no doubt attributable to the moral choices of men, and to save us from which would conflict with what many people would regard as the greater good of moral freedom, but there is still an immense residue of apparently needless suffering, that is, needless in the sense that it could be prevented by an omnipotent being. The difficulty is that of reconciling the presence of evil and suffering with the assertion that God is both omnipotent and benevolent. If we *already* believe in an omnipotent and benevolent God, then some attempt may be made to solve the problem of evil by arguing that the values in the world form a sort of organic unity, and that making any *part* of the world better would perhaps nevertheless reduce the value of the whole. Paradoxical though this thesis may appear at first sight, it is perhaps not theoretically absurd. If, however, evil presents a *difficulty* to the believing mind, it presents an *insuperable* difficulty to one who wishes to argue rationally from the world as we find it to the existence of an omnipotent and benevolent God. As Hume puts it: 'Is the world considered in general, and as it appears to us in this life, different from what a man . . . would *beforehand* expect from a very powerful, wise and benevolent Deity? It must be a strange prejudice to assert the contrary. And from thence I conclude, that, however consistent the world may be, allowing certain suppositions and conjectures, with the idea of such a Deity, it can never afford us an inference concerning his existence.'

The teleological argument is thus extremely shaky, and in any case, even if it were sound, it would only go to prove the existence of a very great architect, not of an omnipotent and benevolent Creator.

Nevertheless, the argument has a fascination for us that reason can not easily dispel. Hume, in his twelfth dialogue, and after pulling the argument from design to pieces in the previous eleven dialogues, nevertheless speaks as follows: 'A purpose, an intention, a design strikes everywhere the most careless, the most stupid thinker; and no man can be so hardened in absurd systems as at all times to reject it . . . all the sciences almost lead us insensibly to acknowledge a first Author.' Similarly Kant, before going on to exhibit the fallaciousness of the argument, nevertheless says of it: 'This proof always deserves to be mentioned with respect. It is the oldest, the clearest and the most accordant with the common reason of mankind. It enlivens the study of nature, just as it itself derives its existence and gains ever new vigour from that source. It suggests ends and purposes, where our observation would not have detected them by itself, and extends our knowledge of nature by means of the guiding-concept of a special unity, the principle of which is outside nature. This knowledge . . . so strengthens the belief in a supreme Author of nature that the belief acquires the force of an irresistible conviction.' It is somewhat of a paradox that an invalid argument should command so much respect even from those who have demonstrated its invalidity. The solution of the paradox is perhaps somewhat as follows*: The argument from design is no good as an argument. But in those who have the seeds of a genuinely religious attitude already within them the facts to which the argument from design draws attention, facts showing the grandeur and majesty of the universe, facts that are evident to anyone who looks upwards on a starry night, and which are enormously multiplied for us by the advance of theoretical science, these facts have a powerful effect. But they only have this effect on the already religious mind, on the mind which has the capability of feeling the religious type of awe. That is, the argument from design is in reality no argument, or if it is regarded as an argument it is feeble, but it is a potent instrument in heightening religious emotions.

Something similar might even be said of the cosmological argument. As an argument it cannot pass muster at all; indeed it is completely absurd, as employing the notion of a logically necessary being. Nevertheless it does appeal to something deep seated in our natures. It takes its stand on the fact that the existence of you or me or this table is not logically necessary. Logic tells us that this fact is not a fact at all, but is a truism, like the 'fact' that a circle is not a square. Again, the cosmological argument tries

* See also N. Kemp Smith's Henrietta Hertz Lecture, "Is Divine Existence Credible?", *Proceedings of the British Academy*, 1931.

to base the existence of you or me or this table on the existence of a logically necessary being, and hence commits a rank absurdity, the notion of a logically necessary being being self-contradictory. So the only rational thing to say if someone asks "Why does this table exist?' is some such thing as that such and such a carpenter made it. We can go back and back in such a series, but we must not entertain the absurd idea of getting back to something logically necessary. However, now let us ask, 'Why should anything exist at all?' Logic seems to tell us that the only answer which is not absurd is to say, 'Why shouldn't it?' Nevertheless, though I know how any answer on the lines of the cosmological argument can be pulled to pieces by a correct logic, I still feel I want to go on asking the question. Indeed, though logic has taught me to look at such a question with the gravest suspicion, my mind often seems to reel under the immense significance it seems to have for me. That anything should exist at all does seem to me a matter for the deepest awe. But whether other people feel this sort of awe, and whether they or I ought to is another question. I think we ought to. If so, the question arises: If 'Why should anything exist at all?' cannot be interpreted after the manner of the cosmological argument, that is, as an absurd request for the nonsensical postulation of a logically necessary being, what sort of question is it? What sort of question is this question 'Why should anything exist at all?' All I can say is, that I do not yet know.

SUBJECTIVE TRUTH

SOREN KIERKEGAARD

THE RELEVANCE OF PROOFS FOR THE EXISTENCE OF GOD

But what is this unknown something with which the Reason collides when inspired by its paradoxical passion, with the result of unsettling even man's knowledge of himself? It is the Unknown. It is not a human being, in so far as we know what man is; nor is it any other known thing. So let us call this unknown something: *God*. It is nothing more than a name we assign to it. The idea of demonstrating that this unknown something (God) exists, could scarcely suggest itself to the Reason. For if God does not exist it would of course be impossible to prove it; and if he does exist it would be folly to attempt it. For at the very outset, in

Reprinted from *Philosophical Fragments*, pp. 31–35, and *Concluding Unscientific Postscript*, pp. 173–189, translated by David F. Swenson, by permission of the publishers, Princeton University Press, 1944.

beginning my proof, I will have presupposed it, not as doubtful but as certain (a presupposition is never doubtful, for the very reason that it is a presupposition), since otherwise I would not begin, readily understanding that the whole would be impossible if he did not exist. But if when I speak of proving God's existence I mean that I propose to prove that the Unknown, which exists, is God, then I express myself unfortunately. For in that case I do not prove anything, least of all an existence, but merely develop the content of a conception. Generally speaking, it is a difficult matter to prove that anything exists; and what is still worse for the intrepid souls who undertake the venture, the difficulty is such that fame scarcely awaits those who concern themselves with it. The entire demonstration always turns into something very different from what it assumes to be, and becomes an additional development of the consequences that flow from my having assumed that the object in question exists. Thus I always reason from existence, not toward existence, whether I move in the sphere of palpable sensible fact or in the realm of thought. I do not for example prove that a stone exists, but that some existing thing is a stone. The procedure in a court of justice does not prove that a criminal exists, but that the accused, whose existence is given, is a criminal. Whether we call existence an *accessorium* or the eternal *prius*, it is never subject to demonstration. Let us take ample time for consideration. We have no such reason for haste as have those who from concern for themselves or for God or for some other thing, must make haste to get its existence demonstrated. Under such circumstances there may indeed be need for haste, especially if the prover sincerely seeks to appreciate the danger that he himself, or the thing in question, may be non-existent unless the proof is finished; and does not surreptitiously entertain the thought that it exists whether he succeeds in proving it or not.

If it were proposed to prove Napoleon's existence from Napoleon's deeds, would it not be a most curious proceeding? His existence does indeed explain his deeds, but the deeds do not prove *his* existence, unless I have already understood the word "his" so as thereby to have assumed his existence. But Napoleon is only an individual, and in so far there exists no absolute relationship between him and his deeds; some other person might have performed the same deeds. Perhaps this is the reason why I cannot pass from the deeds to existence. If I call these deeds the deeds of Napoleon the proof becomes superfluous, since I have already named him; if I ignore this, I can never prove from the deeds that they are Napoleon's, but only in a purely ideal manner that such deeds are the deeds of a great general, and so forth. But between God and his works there exists an absolute relationship; God is not a name but a concept. Is this perhaps the reason that his *essentia involvit existentiam?** The works

* So Spinoza, who probes the depths of the God-idea in order to bring existence out of it by way of thought, but not it should be noted as if existence were an accidental circumstance, but rather as if it constituted an essential determination of content. Here lies Spinoza's profundity, but let us examine his reasoning. In *principia philosophiae Cartesianae, pars I, propositio VII, lemma I,* he says: "*quo res sua natura*

of God are such that only God can perform them. Just so, but where then are the works of God? The works from which I would deduce his existence are not immediately given. The wisdom of God in nature, his goodness, his wisdom in the governance of the world—are all these manifest, perhaps, upon the very face of things? Are we not here confronted with the most terrible temptations to doubt, and is it not impossible finally to dispose of all these doubts? But from such an order of things I will surely not attempt to prove God's existence; and even if I began I would never finish, and would in addition have to live constantly in suspense, lest something so terrible should suddenly happen that my bit of proof would be demolished. From what works then do I propose to derive the proof? From the works as apprehended through an ideal interpretation, i.e., such as they do not immediately reveal themselves. But in that case it is not from the works that I prove God's existence. I merely develop the ideality I have presupposed, and because of my confidence in *this* I make so bold as to defy all objections, even those that have not yet been made. In beginning my proof I presuppose the ideal interpretation, and also that I will be successful in carrying it through; but what else is this but to presuppose that God exists, so that I really begin by virtue of confidence in him?

And how does God's existence emerge from the proof? Does it follow straightway, without any breach of continuity? Or have we not here an analogy to the behaviour of these toys, the little Cartesian dolls? As soon

---

perfectior est, eo majorem existentiam et magis necessariam involvit; et contra, quo magis necessarian existentiam res sua natura involvit, eo perfectior." The more perfect therefore a thing is, the more being it has; the more being it has, the more perfect it is. This is however a tautology, which becomes still more evident in a note, *nota II:* "*quod hic non loquimur de pulchritudine et aliis perfectionibus, quas homines ex superstitione et ignorantia perfectiones vocare voluerunt. Sed per perfectionem intelligo tantum realitatem sive esse.*" He explains *perfectio* by *realitas, esse;* so that the more perfect a thing is, the more it is; but its perfection consists in having more *esse* in itself; that is to say, the more a thing is, the more it is. So much for the tautology, but now further. What is lacking here is a distinction between factual being and ideal being. The terminology which permits us to speak of more or less of being, and consequently of degrees of reality or being, is in itself lacking in clearness, and becomes still more confusing when the above distinction is neglected; when, in other words, Spinoza does indeed speak profoundly, but fails first to consider the difficulty. In the case of factual existence it is meaningless to speak of more or less of being. A fly, when it exists, has as much being as God; the stupid remark I here set down has as much factual existence as Spinoza's profundity; for factual existence is subject to the dialectic of Hamlet: to be or not to be. Factual existence is wholly indifferent to any and all variations in essence, and everything that exists participates without petty jealousy in being, and participates in the same degree. Ideally to be sure, the case is quite different. *But the moment I speak of being in the ideal sense I no longer speak of being, but of essence.* Highest ideality has this necessity and therefore it is. But this its being is identical with its essence; such being does not involve it dialectically in the determinations of factual existence, since it is; nor can it be said to have more or less of being in relation to other things. In the old days this used to be expressed, if somewhat imperfectly, by saying that if God is possible, he is *eo ipso* necessary (Leibniz). Spinoza's principle is thus quite correct and his tautology in order; but it is also certain that he altogether evades the difficulty. For the difficulty is to lay hold of God's factual existence, and to introduce God's ideal essence dialectically into the sphere of factual existence.

as I let go of the doll it stands on its head. As soon as I let it go—I must therefore let it go. So also with the proof for God's existence. As long as I keep my hold on the proof, i.e., continue to demonstrate, the existence does not come out, if for no other reason than that I am engaged in proving it; but when I let the proof go, the existence is there. But this act of letting go is surely also something; it is indeed a contribution of mine. Must not this also be taken into the account, this little moment, brief as it may be—it need not be long, for it is a *leap*. However brief this moment, if only an instantaneous now, this "now" must be included in the reckoning. If anyone wishes to have it ignored, I will use it to tell a little anecdote, in order to show that it really does exist. Chrysippus was experimenting with a sorites to see if he could not bring about a break in its quality, either progressively or retrogressively. But Carneades could not get it in his head when the new quality actually emerged. Then Chrysippus told him to try making a little pause in the reckoning, and so—so it would be easier to understand. Carneades replied: With the greatest pleasure, please do not hesitate on my account; you may not only pause, but even lie down to sleep, and it will help you just as little; for when you awake we will begin again where you left off. Just so; it boots as little to try to get rid of something by sleeping as to try to come into the possession of something in the same manner.

Whoever therefore attempts to demonstrate the existence of God (except in the sense of clarifying the concept, and without the *reservatio finalis* noted above, that the existence emerges from the demonstration by a leap) proves in lieu thereof something else, something which at times perhaps does not need a proof, and in any case needs none better; for the fool says in his heart that there is no God, but whoever says in his heart or to men: Wait just a little and I will prove it—what a rare man of wisdom is he!* If in the moment of beginning his proof it is not absolutely undetermined whether God exists or not, he does not prove it; and if it is thus undetermined in the beginning he will never come to begin, partly from fear of failure, since God perhaps does not exist, and partly because he has nothing with which to begin.—A project of this kind would scarcely have been undertaken by the ancients. Socrates at least, who is credited with having put forth the physico-teleological proof for God's existence, did not go about it in any such manner. He always presupposes God's existence, and under this presupposition seeks to interpenetrate nature with the idea of purpose. Had he been asked why he pursued this method, he would doubtless have explained that he lacked the courage to venture out upon so perilous a voyage of discovery without having made sure of God's existence behind him. At the word of God he casts his net as if to catch the idea of purpose; for nature herself finds many means of frightening the inquirer, and distracts him by many a digression.

. . .

* What an excellent subject for a comedy of the higher lunacy!

TRUTH AS SUBJECTIVITY

The way of objective reflection makes the subject accidental, and thereby transforms existence into something indifferent, something vanishing. Away from the subject the objective way of reflection leads to the objective truth, and while the subject and his subjectivity become indifferent, the truth also becomes indifferent, and this indifference is precisely its objective validity; for all interest, like all decisiveness, is rooted in subjectivity. The way of objective reflection leads to abstract thought, to mathematics, to historical knowledge of different kinds; and always it leads away from the subject, whose existence or non-existence, and from the objective point of view quite rightly, becomes infinitely indifferent. Quite rightly, since as Hamlet says, existence and non-existence have only subject significance. At its maximum this way will arrive at a contradiction, and in so far as the subject does not become wholly indifferent to himself, this merely constitutes a sign that his objective striving is not objective enough. At its maximum this way will lead to the contradiction that only the objective has come into being, while the subjective has gone out; that is to say, the existing subjectivity has vanished, in that it has made an attempt to become what in the abstract sense is called subjectivity, the mere abstract form of an abstract objectivity. And yet, the objectivity which has thus come into being is, from the subjective point of view at the most, either an hypothesis or an approximation, because all eternal decisiveness is rooted in subjectivity.

. . .

In an attempt to make clear the difference of way that exists between an objective and a subjective reflection, I shall now proceed to show how a subjective reflection makes its way inwardly in inwardness. Inwardness in an existing subject culminates in passion; corresponding to passion in the subject the truth becomes a paradox; and the fact that the truth becomes a paradox is rooted precisely in its having a relationship to an existing subject. Thus the one corresponds to the other. By forgetting that one is an existing subject, passion goes by the board and the truth is no longer a paradox; the knowing subject becomes a fantastic entity rather than a human being, and the truth becomes a fantastic object for the knowledge of this fantastic entity.

When the question of truth is raised in an objective manner, reflection is directed objectively to the truth, as an object to which the knower is related. Reflection is not focussed upon the relationship, however, but upon the question of whether it is the truth to which the knower is related. If only the object to which he is related is the truth, the subject is accounted to be in the truth. When the question of the truth is raised *subjectively, reflection is directed subjectively to the nature of the individual's relationship; if only the mode of this relationship is in the truth, the individual is in the truth even if he should happen to be thus related to what is not true.** Let us take as an example the knowledge of God. Objectively, reflection is directed to the problem of whether this object is the true God; subjectively, reflection is directed to the question whether the individual is related to a something *in such a manner* that his relationship is in truth a God-relationship. On which side is the truth now to be found? Ah, may we not here resort to a mediation, and say: It is on neither side, but in the mediation of both? Excellently well said, provided we might have it explained how an existing individual manages to be in a state of mediation. For to be in a state of mediation is to be finished, while to exist is to become. Nor can an existing individual be in two places at the same time—he cannot be an identity of subject and object. When he is nearest to being in two places at the same time he is in passion; but passion is momentary, and passion is also the highest expression of subjectivity.

The existing individual who chooses to pursue the objective way enters upon the entire approximation-process by which it is proposed to bring God to light objectively. But this is in all eternity impossible, because God is a subject, and therefore exists only for subjectivity in inwardness. The existing individual who chooses the subjective way apprehends instantly the entire dialectical difficulty involved in having to use some time, perhaps a long time, in finding God objectively; and he feels this dialectical difficulty in all its painfulness, because every moment is wasted in which he does not have God.** That very instant he has God, not by virtue of any objective deliberation, but by virtue of the infinite passion of inwardness. The objective inquirer, on the other hand, is not embarrassed by such dialectical difficulties as are involved in devoting an entire period of investigation to finding God—since it is possible that the inquirer may die tomorrow; and if he lives he can scarcely regard God as something to be taken along if convenient, since God is precisely that which one takes *a tout prix*, which in the understanding of passion constitutes the true inward relationship to God.

It is at this point, so difficult dialectically, that the way swings off for everyone who knows what it means to think, and to think existentially; which is something very different from sitting at a desk and writing about what one has never done, something very different from writing *de*

* The reader will observe that the question here is about essential truth, or about the truth which is essentially related to existence, and that it is precisely for the sake of clarifying it as inwardness or as subjectivity that this contrast is drawn.

** In this manner God certainly becomes a postulate, but not in the otiose manner in which this word is commonly understood. It becomes clear rather that the only way in which an existing individual comes into relation with God, is when the dialectical contradiction brings his passion to the point of despair, and helps him to embrace God with the "category of despair" (faith). Then the postulate is so far from being arbitrary that it is precisely a life-necessity. It is then not so much that God is a postulate, as that the existing individual's postulation of God is a necessity.

omnibus dubitandum and at the same time being as credulous existentially as the most sensuous of men. Here is where the way swings off, and the change is marked by the fact that while objective knowledge rambles comfortably on by way of the long road of approximation without being impelled by the urge of passion, subjective knowledge counts every delay a deadly peril, and the decision so infinitely important and so instantly pressing that it is as if the opportunity had already passed.

Now when the problem is to reckon up on which side there is most truth, whether on the side of one who seeks the true God objectively, and pursues the approximate truth of the God-idea; or on the side of one who, driven by the infinite passion of his need of God, feels an infinite concern for his own relationship to God in truth (and to be at one and the same time on both sides equally, is as we have noted not possible for an existing individual, but is merely the happy delusion of an imaginary I-am-I): the answer cannot be in doubt for anyone who has not been demoralized with the aid of science. If one who lives in the midst of Christendom goes up to the house of God, the house of the true God, with the true conception of God in his knowledge, and prays, but prays in a false spirit; and one who lives in an idolatrous community prays with the entire passion of the infinite, although his eyes rest upon the image of an idol: where is there most truth? The one prays in truth to God though he worships an idol; the other prays falsely to the true God, and hence worships in fact an idol.

When one man investigates objectively the problem of immortality, and another embraces an uncertainty with the passion of the infinite: where is there most truth, and who has the greater certainty? The one has entered upon a never-ending approximation, for the certainty of immortality lies precisely in the subjectivity of the individual; the other is immortal, and fights for his immortality by struggling with the uncertainty. Let us consider Socrates. Nowadays everyone dabbles in a few proofs; some have several such proofs, others fewer. But Socrates! He puts the question objectively in a problematic manner: *if* there is an immortality. He must therefore be accounted a doubter in comparison with one of our modern thinkers with the three proofs? By no means. On this "if" he risks his entire life, he has the courage to meet death, and he has with the passion of the infinite so determined the pattern of his life that it must be found acceptable—*if* there is an immortality. Is any better proof capable of being given for the immortality of the soul? But those who have the three proofs do not at all determine their lives in conformity therewith; if there is an immortality it must feel disgust over their manner of life: can any better refutation be given of the three proofs? The bit of uncertainty that Socrates had, helped him because he himself contributed the passion of the infinite; the three proofs that the others have do not profit them at all, because they are dead to spirit and enthusiasm, and their three proofs, in lieu of proving anything else, prove just this. A young girl may enjoy all the sweetness of love on the basis of what is merely a weak hope that she is beloved, because she rests everything on this weak hope; but many a wedded matron more than once subjected to the strongest expressions of love, has in so far indeed had proofs, but strangely enough has not enjoyed *quod erat demonstrandum.* The Socratic ignorance, which Socrates held fast with the entire passion of his inwardness, was thus an expression for the principle that the eternal truth is related to an existing individual, and that this truth must therefore be a paradox for him as long as he exists; and yet it is possible that there was more truth in the Socratic ignorance as it was in him, than in the entire objective truth of the System, which flirts with what the times demand and accommodates itself to *Privatdocents.*

The objective accent falls on WHAT is said, the subjective accent on HOW it is said. This distinction holds even in the aesthetic realm, and receives definite expression in the principle that what is in itself true may in the mouth of such and such a person become untrue. In these times this distinction is particularly worthy of notice, for if we wish to express in a single sentence the difference between ancient times and our own, we should doubtless have to say: "In ancient times only an individual here and there knew the truth; now all know it, except that the inwardness of its appropriation stands in an inverse relationship to the extent of its dissemination.* Aesthetically the contradiction that truth becomes untruth in this or that person's mouth, is best construed comically: In the ethico-religious sphere, accent is again on the "how." But this is not to be understood as referring to demeanor, expression, or the like; rather it refers to the relationship sustained by the existing individual, in his own existence, to the content of his utterance. Objectively the interest is focussed merely on the thought-content, subjectively on the inwardness. At its maximum this inward "how" is the passion of the infinite, and the passion of the infinite is the truth. But the passion of the infinite is precisely subjectivity, and thus subjectivity becomes the truth. Objectively there is no infinite decisiveness, and hence it is objectively in order to annul the difference between good and evil, together with the principle of contradiction, and therewith also the infinite difference between the true and the false. Only in subjectivity is there decisiveness, to seek objectivity is to be in error. It is the passion of the infinite that is the

* *Stages on Life's Way,* Note on p. 426. Though ordinarily not wishing an expression of opinion on the part of reviewers, I might at this point almost desire it, provided such opinions, so far from flattering me, amounted to an assertion of the daring truth that what I say is something that everybody knows, even every child, and that the cultured know infinitely much better. If it only stands fast that everyone knows it, my standpoint is in order, and I shall doubtless make shift to manage with the unity of the comic and the tragic. If there were anyone who did not know it I might perhaps be in danger of being dislodged from my position of equilibrium by the thought that I might be in a position to communicate to someone the needful preliminary knowledge. It is just this which engages my interest so much, this that the cultured are accustomed to say: that everyone knows what the highest is. This was not the case in paganism, nor in Judaism, nor in the seventeen centuries of Christianity. Hail to the nineteenth century! Everyone knows it. What progress has been made since the time when only a few knew it. To make up for this, perhaps, we must assume that no one nowadays does it.

decisive factor and not its content, for its content is precisely itself. In this manner subjectivity and the subjective "how" constitute the truth.

But the "how" which is thus subjectively accentuated precisely because the subject is an existing individual, is also subject to a dialectic with respect to time. In the passionate moment of decision, where the road swings away from objective knowledge, it seems as if the infinite decision were thereby realized. But in the same moment the existing individual finds himself in the temporal order, and the subjective "how" is transformed into a striving, a striving which receives indeed its impulse and a repeated renewal from the decisive passion of the infinite, but is nevertheless a striving.

When subjectivity is the truth, the conceptual determination of the truth must include an expression for the antithesis to objectivity, a momento of the fork in the road where the way swings off; this expression will at the same time serve as an indication of the tension of the subjective inwardness. Here is such a definition of truth: *An objective uncertainty held fast in an appropriation-process of the most passionate inwardness is the truth*, the highest truth attainable for an *existing* individual. At the point where the way swings off (and where this is cannot be specified objectively, since it is a matter of subjectivity), there objective knowledge is placed in abeyance. Thus the subject merely has, objectively, the uncertainty; but it is this which precisely increases the tension of that infinite passion which constitutes his inwardness. The truth is precisely the venture which chooses an objective uncertainty with the passion of the infinite. I contemplate the order of nature in the hope of finding God, and I see omnipotence and wisdom; but I also see much else that disturbs my mind and excites anxiety. The sum of all this is an objective uncertainty. But it is for this very reason that the inwardness becomes as intense as it is, for it embraces this objective uncertainty with the entire passion of the infinite. In the case of a mathematical proposition the objectivity is given, but for this reason the truth of such a proposition is also an indifferent truth.

But the above definition of truth is an equivalent expression for faith. Without risk there is no faith. Faith is precisely the contradiction between the infinite passion of the individual's inwardness and the objective uncertainty. If I am capable of grasping God objectively, I do not believe, but precisely because I cannot do this I must believe. If I wish to preserve myself in faith I must constantly be intent upon holding fast the objective uncertainty, so as to remain out upon the deep, over seventy thousand fathoms of water, still preserving my faith.

In the principle that subjectivity, inwardness, is the truth, there is comprehended the Socratic wisdom, whose everlasting merit it was to have become aware of the essential significance of existence, of the fact that the knower is an existing individual. For this reason Socrates was in the truth by virtue of his ignorance, in the highest sense in which this was possible within paganism. To attain to an understanding of this, to comprehend that the misfortune of speculative philosophy is again and again to have forgotten that the knower is an existing individual, is in our objective age difficult enough. "But to have made an advance upon Socrates without even having understood what he understood, is at any rate not "Socratic." Compare the "Moral" of the *Fragments.*

Let us now start from this point, and as was attempted in the *Fragments*, seek a determination of thought which will really carry us further. I have nothing here to do with the question of whether this proposed thought-determination is true or not, since I am merely experimenting; but it must at any rate be clearly manifest that the Socratic thought is understood within the new proposal, so that at least I do not come out behind Socrates.

When subjectivity, inwardness, is the truth, the truth becomes objectively a paradox; and the fact that the truth is objectively a paradox shows in its turn that subjectivity is the truth. For the objective situation is repellent; and the expression for the objective repulsion constitutes the tension and the measure of the corresponding inwardness. The paradoxical character of the truth is its objective uncertainty; this uncertainty is an expression for the passionate inwardness, and this passion is precisely the truth. So far the Socratic principle. The eternal and essential truth, the truth which has an essential relationship to an existing individual because it pertains essentially to existence (all other knowledge being from the Socratic point of view accidental, its scope and degree a matter of indifference), is a paradox. But the eternal essential truth is by no means in itself a paradox; but it becomes paradoxical by virtue of its relationship to an existing individual. The Socratic ignorance gives expression to the objective uncertainty attaching to the truth, while his inwardness in existing is the truth. To anticipate here what will be developed later, let me make the following remark. The Socratic ignorance is an analogue to the category of the absurd, only that there is still less of objective certainty in the absurd, and in the repellent effect that the absurd exercises. It is certain only that it is absurd, and precisely on that account it incites to an infinitely greater tension in the corresponding inwardness. The Socratic inwardness in existing is an analogue to faith; only that the inwardness of faith, corresponding as it does, not to the repulsion of the Socratic ignorance, but to the repulsion exerted by the absurd, is infinitely more profound.

Socratically the eternal essential truth is by no means in its own nature paradoxical, but only in its relationship to an existing individual. This finds expression in another Socratic proposition, namely, that all knowledge is recollection. This proposition is not for Socrates a cue to the speculative enterprise, and hence he does not follow it up; essentially it becomes a Platonic principle. Here the way swings off; Socrates concentrates essentially upon accentuating existence, while Plato forgets this and loses himself in speculation. Socrates' infinite merit is to have been an *existing* thinker, not a speculative philosopher who forgets what it means to exist. For Socrates therefore the principle that all knowledge is recollection has at the moment of his leave-taking and as the constantly rejected possibility of engaging in speculation, the following two-fold significance: (1) that the knower is essentially *integer*, and that with respect to the knowledge of the eternal truth he is confronted with no other difficulty than the circumstance that he exists; which difficulty, however, is so essential and decisive for him that it means that existing, the process of transformation to inwardness in and by existing, is the truth; (2) that existence in time does not have any decisive significance, because the possibility of taking oneself back into eternity through recollection is always there, though this possibility is constantly nullified by utilizing the time, not for speculation, but for the transformation to inwardness in existing.*

The infinite merit of the Socratic position was precisely to accentuate the fact that the knower is an existing individual, and that the task of existing is his essential task. Making an advance upon Socrates by failing

* This will perhaps be the proper place to offer an explanation with respect to a difficulty in the plan of the *Fragments*, which had its ground in the fact that I did not wish at once to make the case as difficult dialectically as it is, because in our age terminologies and the like are turned so topsy-turvy that it is almost impossible to secure oneself against confusion. In order if possible clearly to exhibit the difference between the Socratic position (which was supposed to be the philosophical, the pagan-philosophical position) and the experimentally evoked thought-determination which really makes an advance beyond the Socratic, I carried the Socratic back to the principle that all knowledge is recollection. This is, in a way, commonly assumed, and only one who with a specialized interest concerns himself with the Socratic, returning again and again to the sources, only for him would it be of importance on this point to distinguish between Socrates and Plato. The proposition does indeed belong to both, only that Socrates is always departing from it, in order to exist. By holding Socrates down to the proposition that all knowledge is recollection, he becomes a speculative philosopher instead of an existential thinker, for whom existence is the essential thing. The recollection-principle belongs to speculative philosophy, and recollection is immanence, and speculatively and eternally there is no paradox. But the difficulty is that no human being is speculative philosophy; the speculative philosopher himself is an existing individual, subject to the claims that existence makes upon him. There is no merit in forgetting this, but a great merit in holding it fast, and this is precisely what Socrates did. To accentuate existence, which also involves the qualification of inwardness, is the Socratic position; the Platonic tendency, on the other hand, is to pursue the lure of recollection and immanence. This puts Socrates fundamentally in advance of speculative philosophy; he does not have a fantastic beginning, in which the speculative philosopher first disguises himself, and then goes on and on to speculate, forgetting the most important thing of all, which is to exist. But precisely because Socrates is thus in advance of speculation, he presents, when properly delineated, a certain analogous resemblance to that which the experiment described as in truth going beyond the Socratic. The truth as paradox in the Socratic sense becomes analogous to the paradox *sensu eminentiori*, the passion of inwardness in existing becomes an analogue to faith *sensu eminentiori*. That the difference is none the less infinite, that the characterization which the *Fragments* made of that which in truth goes beyond the Socratic remains unchanged, it will be easy to show; but by using at once apparently the same determinations, or at any rate the same words, about these two different things, I feared to cause a misunderstanding. Now I think there can be no objection to speaking of the paradoxical and of faith in reference to Socrates, since it is quite correct to do so when properly understood. Besides, the old Greeks also used the word πιστις, though not by any means in the sense of the experiment; and they used it in such a manner that, especially with reference to a work of Aristotle where the term is employed, it would be possible to set forth some very enlightening considerations bearing upon its difference from faith *sensu eminentiori*.

to understand this, is quite a mediocre achievement. This Socratic principle we must therefore bear in mind, and then inquire whether the formula may not be so altered as really to make an advance beyond the Socratic position.

Subjectivity, inwardness, has been posited as the truth; can any expression for the truth be found which has a still higher degree of inwardness? Aye, there is such an expression, provided the principle that subjectivity or inwardness is the truth begins by positing the opposite principle: that subjectivity is untruth. Let us not at this point succumb to such haste as to fail in making the necessary distinctions. Speculative philosophy also says that subjectivity is untruth, but says it in order to stimulate a movement in precisely the opposite direction, namely, in the direction of the principle that objectivity is the truth. Speculative philosophy determines subjectivity negatively as tending toward objectivity. This second determination of ours, however, places a hindrance in its own way while proposing to begin, which has the effect of making the inwardness far more intensive. Socratically speaking, subjectivity is untruth if it refuses to understand that subjectivity is truth, but, for example, desires to become objective. Here, on the other hand, subjectivity in beginning upon the task of becoming the truth through a subjectifying process, is in the difficulty that it is already untruth. Thus, the labor of the task is thrust backward, backward, that is, in inwardness. So far is it from being the case that the way tends in the direction of objectivity,
of the task is thrust backward, backward, that is, in inwardness. So far is
that the beginning merely lies still deeper in subjectivity.

But the subject cannot be untruth eternally, or eternally be presupposed as having been untruth; it must have been brought to this condition in time, or here become untruth in time. The Socratic paradox consisted in the fact that the eternal was related to an existing individual, but now existence has stamped itself upon the existing individual a second time. There has taken place so essential an alteration in him that he cannot now possibly take himself back into the eternal by way of recollection. To do this is to speculate; to be able to do this, but to reject the possibility by apprehending the task of life as a realization of inwardness in existing, is the Socratic position. But now the difficulty is that what followed Socrates on his way as a rejected possibility, has become an impossibility. If engaging in speculation was a dubious merit even from the point of view of the Socratic, it is now neither more nor less than confusion.

The paradox emerges when the eternal truth and existence are placed in juxtaposition with one another; each time the stamp of existence is brought to bear, the paradox becomes more clearly evident. Viewed Socratically the knower was simply an existing individual, but now the existing individual bears the stamp of having been essentially altered by existence.

Let us now call the untruth of the individual *Sin*. Viewed eternally he cannot be sin, nor can he be eternally presupposed as having been in sin. By coming into existence therefore (for the beginning was that subjectivity is untruth), he becomes a sinner. He is not born as a sinner in the sense that he is presupposed as being a sinner before he is born, but he is born in sin and as a sinner. This we might call *Original Sin*. But if existence has in this manner acquired a power over him, he is prevented from taking himself back into the eternal by way of recollection. If it was paradoxical to posit the eternal truth in relationship to an existing individual, it is now absolutely paradoxical to posit it in relationship to such an individual as we have here defined. But the more difficult it is made for him to take himself out of existence by way of recollection, the more profound is the inwardness that his existence may have in existence; and when it is made impossible for him, when he is held so fast in existence that the back door of recollection is forever closed to him, then his inwardness will be the most profound possible. But let us never forget that the Socratic merit was to stress the fact that the knower is an existing individual; for the more difficult the matter becomes, the greater the temptation to hasten along the easy road of speculation, away from fearful dangers and crucial decisions, to the winning of renown and honors and property, and so forth. If even Socrates understood the dubiety of taking himself speculatively out of existence back into the eternal, although no other difficulty confronted the existing individual except that he existed, and that existing was his essential task, now it is impossible. Forward he must, backward he cannot go.

Subjectivity is the truth. By virtue of the relationship subsisting between the eternal truth and the existing individual, the paradox came into being. Let us now go further, let us suppose that the eternal essential truth is itself a paradox. How does the paradox come into being? By putting the eternal essential truth into juxtaposition with existence. Hence when we posit such a conjunction within the truth itself, the truth becomes a paradox. The eternal truth has come into being in time: this is the paradox. If in accordance with the determinations just posited, the subject is prevented by sin from taking himself back into the eternal, now he need not trouble himself about this; for now the eternal essential truth is not behind him but in front of him, through its being in existence or having existed, so that if the individual does not existentially and in existence lay hold of the truth, he will never lay hold of it.

Existence can never be more sharply accentuated than by means of these determinations. The evasion by which speculative philosophy attempts to recollect itself out of existence has been made impossible. With reference to this, there is nothing for speculation to do except to arrive at an understanding of this impossibility; every speculative attempt which insists on being speculative shows *eo ipso* that it has not understood it. The individual may thrust all this away from him, and take refuge in speculation; but it is impossible first to accept it, and then to revoke it by means of speculation, since it is definitely calculated to prevent speculation.

When the eternal truth is related to an existing individual it becomes a paradox. The paradox repels in the inwardness of the existing individual, through the objective uncertainty and the corresponding Socratic ignorance. But since the paradox is not in the first instance itself paradoxical (but only in its relationship to the existing individual), it does not repel with a sufficient intensive inwardness. For without risk there is no faith, and the greater the risk the greater the faith; the more objective security the less inwardness (for inwardness is precisely subjectivity), and the less objective security the more profound the possible inwardness. When the paradox is paradoxical in itself, it repels the individual by virtue of its absurdity, and the corresponding passion of inwardness is faith. But subjectivity, inwardness, is the truth; for otherwise we have forgotten what the merit of the Socratic position is. But there can be no stronger expression for inwardness than when the retreat out of existence into the eternal by way of recollection is impossible; and when, with truth confronting the individual as a paradox, gripped in the anguish and pain of sin, facing the tremendous risk of the objective insecurity, the individual believes. But without risk no faith, not even the Socratic form of faith, much less the form of which we here speak.

When Socrates believed that there was a God, he held fast to the objective uncertainty with the whole passion of his inwardness, and it is precisely in this contradiction and in this risk, that faith is rooted. Now it is otherwise. Instead of the objective uncertainty, there is here a certainty, namely, that objectively it is absurd; and this absurdity, held fast in the passion of inwardness, is faith. The Socratic ignorance is as a witty jest in comparison with the earnestness of facing the absurd; and the Socratic existential inwardness is as Greek light-mindedness in comparison with the grave strenuosity of faith.

What now is the absurd? The absurd is—that the eternal truth has come into being in time, that God has come into being, has been born, has grown up, and so forth, precisely like any other individual human being, quite indistinguishable from other individuals. For every assumption of immediate recognizability is pre-Socratic paganism, and from the Jewish point of view, idolatry; and every determination of what really makes an advance beyond the Socratic must essentially bear the stamp of having a relationship to God's having come into being; for faith *sensu strictissimo*, as was developed in the *Fragments*, refers to becoming. When Socrates believed that there was a God, he saw very well that where the way swings off there is also an objective way of approximation, for example by the contemplation of nature and human history, and so forth. His merit was precisely to shun this way, where the quantitative siren song enchants the mind and deceives the existing individual.

In relation to the absurd, the objective approximation-process is like the comedy, *Misunderstanding upon Misunderstanding*, which is generally played by *Privatdocents* and speculative philosophers. The absurd is precisely by its objective repulsion the measure of the intensity of faith in inwardness. Suppose a man who wishes to acquire faith; let the comedy begin. He wishes to have faith, but he wishes also to safeguard himself by means of an objective inquiry and its approximation-process. What happens? With the help of the approximation-process the absurd becomes something different; it becomes probable, it becomes increasingly probable, it becomes extremely and emphatically probable. Now he is ready to believe it, and he ventures to claim for himself that he does not believe as shoemakers and tailors and simple folk believe, but only after long deliberation. Now he is ready to believe it; and lo, now it has become precisely impossible to believe it. Anything that is almost probable, or probable, or extremely and emphatically probable, is something he can almost know, or as good as know, or extremely and emphatically almost *know*—but it is impossible to *believe*. For the absurd is the object of faith, and the only object that can be believed.

FAITH AND RELIGIOUS SYMBOLS

PAUL TILLICH

WHAT FAITH IS

FAITH AS ULTIMATE CONCERN

Faith is the state of being ultimately concerned: the dynamics of faith are the dynamics of man's ultimate concern. Man, like every living being, is concerned about many things, above all about those which condition his very existence, such as food and shelter. But man, in contrast to other living beings, has spiritual concerns—cognitive, aesthetic, social, political. Some of them are urgent, often extremely urgent, and each of them as well as the vital concerns can claim ultimacy for a human life or the life of a social group. If it claims ultimacy it demands the total surrender of him who accepts this claim, and it promises total fulfillment even if all other claims have to be subjected to it or rejected in its name. If a national group makes the life and growth of the nation its ultimate concern, it demands that all other concerns, economic well-being, health and life, family, aesthetic and cognitive truth, justice and humanity, be sacrificed. The extreme nationalisms of our century are laboratories for the study of what ultimate concern means in all aspects of human existence, including the smallest concern of one's daily life. Everything is centered in the only god, the nation—a god who certainly proves to be a demon, but who shows clearly the unconditional character of an ultimate concern.

But it is not only the unconditional demand made by that which is one's

Reprinted, with deletions, from *Dynamics of Faith*, Harper & Row, New York, 1957, by permission of the publishers.

ultimate concern, it is also the promise of ultimate fulfillment which is accepted in the act of faith. The content of this promise is not necessarily defined. It can be expressed in indefinite symbols or in concrete symbols which cannot be taken literally, like the "greatness" of one's nation in which one participates even if one has died for it, or the conquest of mankind by the "saving race," etc. In each of these cases it is "ultimate fulfillment" that is promised, and it is exclusion from such fulfillment which is threatened if the unconditional demand is not obeyed.

An example—and more than an example—is the faith manifest in the religion of the Old Testament. It also has the character of ultimate concern in demand, threat and promise. The content of this concern is not the nation—although Jewish nationalism has sometimes tried to distort it into that—but the content is the God of justice, who, because he represents justice for everybody and every nation, is called the universal God, the God of the universe. He is the ultimate concern of every pious Jew, and therefore in his name the great commandment is given: "You shall love the Lord your God with all your heart, and with all your soul, and with all your might" (Deut 6:5). This is what ultimate concern means and from these words the term "ultimate concern" is derived. They state unambiguously the character of genuine faith, the demand of total surrender to the subject of ultimate concern. The Old Testament is full of commands which make the nature of this surrender concrete, and it is full of promises and threats in relation to it. Here also are the promises of symbolic indefiniteness, although they center around fulfillment of the national and individual life, and the threat is the exclusion from such fulfillment through national extinction and individual catastrophe. Faith, for the men of the Old Testament, is the state of being ultimately and unconditionally concerned about Jahweh and about what he represents in demand, threat and promise.

Another example—almost a counter-example, yet nevertheless equally revealing—is the ultimate concern with "success" and with social standing and economic power. It is the god of many people in the highly competitive Western culture and it does what every ultimate concern must do: it demands unconditional surrender to its laws even if the price is the sacrifice of genuine human relations, personal conviction, and creative *eros*. Its threat is social and economic defeat, and its promise—indefinite as all such promises—the fulfillment of one's being. It is the breakdown of this kind of faith which characterizes and makes religiously important most contemporary literature. Not false calculations but a misplaced faith is revealed in novels like *Point of No Return*. When fulfilled, the promise of this faith proves to be empty.

Faith is the state of being ultimately concerned. The content matters infinitely for the life of the believer, but it does not matter for the formal definition of faith. And this is the first step we have to make in order to understand the dynamics of faith.

FAITH AS A CENTERED ACT

Faith as ultimate concern is an act of the total personality. It happens in the center of the personal life and includes all its elements. Faith is the most centered act of the human mind. It is not a movement of a special section or a special function of man's total being. They all are united in the act of faith. But faith is not the sum total of their impacts. It transcends every special impact as well as the totality of them and it has itself a decisive impact on each of them.

. . .

THE SOURCE OF FAITH

We have described the act of faith and its relation to the dynamics of personality. Faith is a total and centered act of the personal self, the act of unconditional, infinite and ultimate concern. The question now arises: what is the source of this all-embracing and all-transcending concern? The word "concern" points to two sides of a relationship, the relation between the one who is concerned and his concern. In both respects we have to imagine man's situation in itself and in his world. The reality of man's ultimate concern reveals something about his being, namely, that he is able to transcend the flux of relative and transitory experiences of his ordinary life. Man's experiences, feelings, thoughts are conditioned and finite. They not only come and go, but their content is of finite and conditional concern—unless they are elevated to unconditional validity. But this presupposes the general possibility of doing so; it presupposes the element of infinity in man. Man is able to understand in an immediate personal and central act the meaning of the ultimate, the unconditional, the absolute, the infinite. This alone makes faith a human potentiality.

Human potentialities are powers that drive toward actualization. Man is driven toward faith by his awareness of the infinite to which he belongs, but which he does not own like a possession. This is in abstract terms what concretely appears as the "restlessness of the heart" within the flux of life.

The unconditional concern which is faith is the concern about the unconditional. The infinite passion, as faith has been described, is the passion for the infinite. Or, to use our first term, the ultimate concern is concern about what is experienced as ultimate. In this way we have turned from the subjective meaning of faith as a centered act of the personality to its objective meaning, to what is meant in the act of faith. It would not help at this point of our analysis to call that which is meant in the act of faith "God" or "a god." For at this step we ask: What in the idea of God constitutes divinity? The answer is: It is the element of the unconditional and of ultimacy. This carries the quality of divinity. If this is seen, one can understand why almost every thing "in heaven and on earth" has received ultimacy in the history of human religion. But we also can understand that a critical principle was and is at work in man's religious consciousness, namely, that which is really ultimate over against what claims to be ultimate but is only preliminary, transitory, finite.

The term "ultimate concern" unites the subjective and the objective side of the act of faith—the *fides qua creditur* (the Faith through which one believes) and the *fides quae creditur* (the faith which is believed). The first is the classical term for the centered act of the personality, the ultimate concern. The second is the classical term for that toward which this act is directed, the ultimate itself, expressed in symbols of the divine. This distinction is very important, but not ultimately so, for the one side cannot be without the other. There is no faith without a content toward which it is directed. There is always something meant in the act of faith. And there is no way of having the content of faith except in the act of faith. All speaking about divine matters which is not done in the state of ultimate concern is meaningless. Because that which is meant in the act of faith cannot be approached in any other way than through an act of faith.

In terms like ultimate, unconditional, infinite, absolute, the difference between subjectivity and objectivity is overcome. The ultimate of the act of faith and the ultimate that is meant in the act of faith are one and the same. This is symbolically expressed by the mystics when they say that their knowledge of God is the knowledge God has of himself; and it is expressed by Paul when he says (I Cor. 13) that he will know as he is known, namely, by God. God never can be object without being at the same time subject. Even a successful prayer is, according to Paul (Rom. 8), not possible without God as Spirit praying within us. The same experience expressed in abstract language is the disappearance of the ordinary subject-object scheme in the experience of the ultimate, the unconditional. In the act of faith that which is the source of this act is present beyond the cleavage of subject and object. It is present as both and beyond both.

This character of faith gives an additional criterion for distinguishing true and false ultimacy. The finite which claims infinity without having it (as, e.g., a nation or success) is not able to transcend the subject-object scheme. It remains an object which the believer looks at as a subject. He can approach it with ordinary knowledge and subject it to ordinary handling. There are, of course, many degrees in the endless realm of false ultimacies. The nation is nearer to true ultimacy than is success. Nationalistic ecstasy can produce a state in which the subject is almost swallowed by the object. But after a period the subject emerges again, disappointed radically and totally, and by looking at the nation in a skeptical and calculating way does injustice even to its justified claims. The more idolatrous a faith the less it is able to overcome the cleavage between subject and object. For that is the difference between true and idolatrous faith. In true faith the ultimate concern is a concern about the truly ultimate; while in idolatrous faith preliminary, finite realities are elevated to the rank of ultimacy. The inescapable consequence of idolatrous faith is "existential disappointment," a disappointment which penetrates into the very existence of man! This is the dynamics of idolatrous faith: that it is faith, and as such, the centered act of a personality; that the centering point is something which is more or less on to the periphery; and that, therefore, the act of faith leads to the loss of the center and to a disruption of the personality. The ecstatic character of even an idolatrous faith can hide this consequence only for a certain time. But finally it breaks into the open.

. . .

SYMBOLS OF FAITH

THE MEANING OF SYMBOL

Man's ultimate concern must be expressed symbolically, because symbolic language alone is able to express the ultimate. This statement demands explanation in several respects. In spite of the manifold research about the meaning and function of symbols which is going on in contemporary philosophy, every writer who uses the term "symbol" must explain his understanding of it.

Symbols have one characteristic in common with signs; they point beyond themselves to something else. The red sign at the street corner points to the order to stop the movements of cars at certain intervals. A red light and the stopping of cars have essentially no relation to each other, but conventionally they are united as long as the convention lasts. The same is true of letters and numbers and partly even words. They point beyond themselves to sounds and meanings. They are given this special function by convention within a nation or by international conventions, as the mathematical signs. Sometimes such signs are called symbols; but this is unfortunate because it makes the distinction between signs and symbols more difficult. Decisive is the fact that signs do not participate in the reality of that to which they point, while symbols do. Therefore, signs can be replaced for reasons of expediency or convention, while symbols cannot.

This leads to the second characteristic of the symbol: It participates in that to which it points: the flag participates in the power and dignity of the nation for which it stands. Therefore, it cannot be replaced except after an historic catastrophe that changes the reality of the nation which it symbolizes. An attack on the flag is felt as an attack on the majesty of the group in which it is acknowledged. Such an attack is considered blasphemy.

The third characteristic of a symbol is that it opens up levels of reality which otherwise are closed for us. All arts create symbols for a level of reality which cannot be reached in any other way. A picture and a poem reveal elements of reality which cannot be approached scientifically. In the creative work of art we encounter reality in a dimension which is closed for us without such works. The symbol's fourth characteristic not only opens up dimensions and elements of reality which otherwise would remain unapproachable but also unlocks dimensions and elements of our soul which correspond to the dimensions and elements of reality. A great play gives us not only a new vision of the human scene, but it opens up hidden depths of our own being. Thus we are able to receive what the play reveals to us in reality. There are within us dimensions of which we cannot become aware except through symbols, as melodies and rhythms in music.

Symbols cannot be produced intentionally—this is the fifth characteristic. They grow out of the individual or collective unconscious and cannot function without being accepted by the unconscious dimension of our being. Symbols which have an especially social function, as political and religious symbols, are created or at least accepted by the collective unconscious of the group in which they appear.

The sixth and last characteristics of the symbol is a consequence of the fact that symbols cannot be invented. Like living beings, they grow and they die. They grow when the situation is ripe for them, and they die when the situation changes. The symbol of the "king" grew in a special period of history, and it died in most parts of the world in our period. Symbols do not grow because people are longing for them, and they do not die because of scientific or practical criticism. They die because they can no longer produce response in the group where they originally found expression.

These are the main characteristics of every symbol. Genuine symbols are created in several spheres of man's cultural creativity. We have mentioned already the political and the artistic realm. We could add history and, above all, religion, whose symbols will be our particular concern.

RELIGIOUS SYMBOLS

We have discussed the meaning of symbols generally because, as we said, man's ultimate concern must be expressed symbolically! One may ask: Why can it not be expressed directly and properly? If money, success or the nation is someone's ultimate concern, can this not be said in a direct way without symbolic language? Is it not only in those cases in which the content of the ultimate concern is called "God" that we are in the realm of symbols? The answer is that everything which is a matter of unconditional concern is made into a god. If the nation is someone's ultimate concern, the name of the nation becomes a sacred name and the nation receives divine qualities which far surpass the reality of the being and functioning of the nation. The nation then stands for and symbolizes the true ultimate, but in an idolatrous way. Success as ultimate concern is not the national desire of actualizing potentialities, but is readiness to sacrifice all other values of life for the sake of a position of power and social predominance. The anxiety about not being a success is an idolatrous form of the anxiety about divine condemnation. Success is grace; lack of success, ultimate judgment. In this way concepts designating ordinary realities become idolatrous symbols of ultimate concern.

The reason for this transformation of concepts into symbols is the character of ultimacy and the nature of faith. That which is the true ultimate transcends the realm of finite reality infinitely. Therefore, no finite reality can express it directly and properly. Religiously speaking, God transcends his own name. This is why the use of his name easily becomes an abuse or a blasphemy. Whatever we say about that which concerns us ultimately, whether or not we call it God, has a symbolic meaning. It points beyond itself while participating in that to which it points. In no other way can faith express itself adequately. The language of faith is the language of symbols. If faith were what we have shown that it is not, such an assertion could not be made. But faith, understood as the state of being ultimately concerned, has no language other than symbols. When saying this I always expect the question: Only a symbol? He who asks this question shows that he has not understood the difference between signs and symbols nor the power of symbolic language, which surpasses in quality and strength the power of any nonsymbolic language. One should never say "only a symbol," but one should say "not less than a symbol." With this in mind we can now describe the different kinds of symbols of faith.

The fundamental symbol of our ultimate concern is God. It is always present in any act of faith, even if the act of faith includes the denial of God. Where there is ultimate concern, God can be denied only in the name of God. One God can deny the other one. Ultimate concern cannot deny its own character as ultimate. Therefore, it affirms what is meant by the word "God." Atheism, consequently, can only mean the attempt to remove any ultimate concern—to remain unconcerned about the meaning of one's existence. Indifference toward the ultimate question is the only imaginable form of atheism. Whether it is possible is a problem which must remain unsolved at this point. In any case, he who denies God as a matter of ultimate concern affirms God, because he affirms ultimacy in his concern. God is the fundamental symbol for what concerns us ultimately. Again it would be completely wrong to ask: So God is nothing but a symbol? Because the next question has to be: A symbol for what? And then the answer would be: For God! God is symbol for God. This means that in the notion of God we must distinguish two elements: the element of ultimacy, which is a matter of immediate experience and not symbolic in itself, and the element of concreteness, which is taken from our ordinary experience and symbolically applied to God. The man whose ultimate concern is a sacred tree has both the ultimacy of concern and the concreteness of the tree which symbolizes his relation to the ultimate. The man who adores Apollo is ultimately concerned, but not in an abstract way. His ultimate concern is symbolized in the divine figure of

Apollo. The man who glorifies Jahweh, the God of the Old Testament, has both an ultimate concern and a concrete image of what concerns him ultimately. This is the meaning of the seemingly cryptic statement that God is the symbol of God. In this qualified sense God is the fundamental and universal content of faith.

It is obvious that such an understanding of the meaning of God makes the discussions about the existence or non-existence of God meaningless. It is meaningless to question the ultimacy of an ultimate concern. This element in the idea of God is in itself certain. The symbolic expression of this element varies endlessly through the whole history of mankind. Here again it would be meaningless to ask whether one or another of the figures in which an ultimate concern is symbolized does "exist." If "existence" refers to something which can be found within the whole of reality, no divine being exists. The question is not this, but: which of the innumerable symbols of faith is most adequate to the meaning of faith? In other words, which symbol of ultimacy expresses the ultimate without idolatrous elements? This is the problem, and not the so-called "existence of God"—which is in itself an impossible combination of words. God as the ultimate in man's ultimate concern is more certain than any other certainty, even that of oneself. God as symbolized in a divine figure is a matter of daring faith, of courage and risk.

God is the basic symbol of faith, but not the only one. All the qualities we attribute to him, power, love, justice, are taken from finite experiences and applied symbolically to that which is beyond finitude and infinity. If faith calls God "almighty," it uses the human experience of power in order to symbolize the content of its infinite concern, but it does not describe a highest being who can do as he pleases. So it is with all the other qualities and with all the actions, past, present and future, which men attribute to God. They are symbols taken from our daily experience, and not information about what God did once upon a time or will do sometime in the future. Faith is not the belief in such stories, but it is the acceptance of symbols that express our ultimate concern in terms of divine actions.

Another group of symbols of faith are manifestations of the divine in things and events, in persons and communities, in words and documents. This whole realm of sacred objects is a treasure of symbols. Holy things are not holy in themselves, but they point beyond themselves to the source of all holiness, that which is of ultimate concern.

. . .

The way to a universal faith is the old way of the prophets, the way of calling idolatry idolatry and rejecting it for the sake of that which is really ultimate. Such faith may never be able to express itself in *one* concrete symbol, although it is the hope of every great religion that it will provide the all-embracing symbol in which the faith of man universally will express itself. Such a hope is only justified if a religion remains aware of the conditional and non-ultimate character of its own symbols. Christianity expresses this awareness on the symbol of the "cross of the Christ"—even if the Christ in churches neglect the meaning of this symbol by attributing ultimacy to their own particular expression of ultimacy. The radical self-criticism of Christianity makes it most capable of universality—so long as it maintains this self-criticism as a power in its own life.

THE PROBLEM OF EVIL

JOHN LAIRD

On the whole it seems appropriate to begin this discussion of God's common grace by enquiring into the positive evidence in favour of that conception. By doing so we shall supplement a part of the argument in the last lecture. In that lecture we say that if certain things could be shown, for example the propitiousness of physical nature to certain finite spirits, then a theist would be confronted with sundry possible interpretations. We are now asking whether such things can be shown.

In discussing this worn-out tenacious theme, I shall deal, rather narrowly, with man and his place in the cosmos. This restricted treatment may indeed be parochial, but unless our standards of value have no general significance (in which case the question falls) we are bound to test our general theories in the instance in which the issue seems plainest, and that is with reference to man. For I believe man is the bearer of the highest values with which we have any empirical acquaintance. Again, since the human parish is so very wide, it seems better, because it seems sufficient for present purposes, to limit the discussion to two features of the problem of evil (as it is called) and to discuss, on the one hand, suffering, and on the other hand, sin. There are other "problems" of human evil, such as the "problems" of human transcience, ignorance, ugliness, weakness and poverty of opportunity. Some questions may be begged and some answers stolen when the problem is restricted in the way in which I intend to restrict it now, but its general outlines, I think, should not be appreciably dimmed.

What, then, is the theological "problem" of suffering? What bearing has our suffering upon providential and upon antiprovidential arguments?

There is no problem if the last word on the subject must be simply that suffering occurs, and there is no problem if suffering be not an evil.

Reprinted from *Mind and Deity*, chapter entitled "Providence," Philosophical Library, New York, 1941, by permission of the publishers. The original title of this section is "Do Suffering and Sin Constitute Evidence Against a Providential God?"

Again, there is no problem if God be altogether omnipotent and also wholly good, for in that case the existence of any pain whatever (if pain be evil) entails a plain contradiction. Such a God could always bestow the palm without the dust. On the other hand there is a problem for those theists who admit that some at least of the suffering that exists is a genuine evil, and do not renounce every possibility of talking sense about the question by committing themselves to a childish interpretation of "omnipotence."

Philosophers with a Stoical bent have often argued that pain is not an evil. So said Seneca—among other things. According to him* the genuine recipients of divine favour were stalwarts like Mucius who kept his hand in the flames, Regulus who preferred Punic torture to un-Roman bad faith, Cato re-opening the self-inflicted wound that had failed to bring him the honourable release of a vanquished patriot. This grim picture would seem to present Seneca with an insoluble "problem of pleasure." For pleasure also exists. According to Seneca it is the base coin with which the high gods repay base natures, giving unworthy mortals something that they desire but also giving them something that, unlike pain, is an evil.

It is needless, however, to pursue the point. Whether or not pleasure is an unworthy thing, suffering is an evil, for all Seneca's moral rhetoric. It is evil unmitigated unless it is necessary for an ulterior good that swamps or annuls its evil. If, using anthropomorphic language, we were to say that God was indifferent to suffering as such, we should be saying that God was callous. If he applauded the suffering, like the saints in heaven who have sometimes been thought to applaud the sufferings of the damned in hell, he would be cruel.

Accordingly we are usually told in the theodicies that pain is not purposeless, but is a salutary warning in matters of health and is our schoolmaster in matters of moral education. The doctrine is still pretty grim, but it might be true for all that, and it is consistent with the belief in a non-omnipotent providence. The implication, however, would be that no suffering is purposeless, and it is hard to suppose that such is the truth. In the case of animal suffering, for instance (where the moral discipline of the sufferers cannot be a relevant consideration), it is difficult to believe that the suffering of slaughtered animals before humane killing became general was justified in terms of this argument, and also that the diminution of animal suffering after humane killing was generally practised is likewise justified. In the case of human beings the same difficulty would arise in connection with advances in our knowledge and use of anaesthetics. We all know of the arguments that have been raised about the use of anaesthetics in childbirth. More generally, there would be a similar problem regarding the moral effects of a rise in the standard of comfortable living.

Obviously, however, it would be unreasonable to expect that every instance of pain that could be cited conveyed a clearly intelligible benefit

* In *De Providentia.*

either to the sufferer or to some other being, or else had to be adjudged to be an instance of finally unjustifiable evil. "Nothing would be more alarming in reality," von Hugel said, "than to find that religion, when pressed, could give us nothing but just what we want."* If the line of argument mentioned above supplied the rudiments of an answer to the question set it would have done a great deal; for the argument itself has the widest ramifications. If, however, it be assumed, as is not unreasonable, that what appear to be close factual connections should be held to be metaphysically stubborn if not even indissoluble, the above type of argument has strength and soundness. I have spoken of the palm without the dust, but no one seriously supposes that it is possible to win a race without running it, or to run it without a quickened pulse and bursting lungs. That should be clear as a matter of course, and the argument may be persuasively extended in the way that is commonly done. We are told that the conquest of perils and the overcoming of obstacles imply the reality of the perils and of the obstacles. In a psychological way, perhaps indissoluble, it may be said to imply the reality of fears, and doubts, and depression, and actual anguish, if not inevitably, at least generally in the course of nature. In this sense there are joys of earth that would have no place in a sheltered heaven, and some of these, say the explorer's zest or the romantic lover's or even the struggles of an ambitious author, may be sweeter and keener because of the risk and because of the painful struggle. It might further be argued that there would be no risk if there were not, sometimes, an actual disaster.

Such arguments, then, must be accorded a certain weight, but although they are empirical they are also rather high-handed in what they say of empirical fact. We find empirically that some (perhaps much) suffering has a beneficial function, and we are entitled to surmise that frequently, when this beneficial function is not apparent, it may nevertheless occur. On the other hand, it would also be legitimate to surmise that some of the apparent benefits of suffering are illusory; and in any case we should be flying a very speculative kite if we maintained that all suffering must be beneficial because we know that some of it is.

That would have to be said even if we admitted that the very audacity of a hypothesis may be one of its better motives to credence. It may, for instance, be more plausible to explain the hurly-burly of our sensations by supposing that permanent physical objects exist and act than by making suppositions that keep closer to the whirling impermanence of our actual sensory experience. Such ideas outstrip the evidence of our senses (according to many interpretations of that evidence) by a mile; but we are all accustomed to make them. So here. The bolder flights of theistic optimism may seem safer and better credible than a more timid resort to whatever gods there may be. The boldness of these flights, however, should not take the form of suppressing or of denying the anti-providential arguments. Courage of that kind is neither hardheaded nor empirical.

An equally familiar objection to the providential hypothesis is that

* *The Reality of God*, p. 15.

even if all suffering had some beneficial office, it would still be impossible to defend the amount of suffering that exists. Cancer may give an occasion for fortitude and for a certain melancholy dignity, but, in its case, anodynes are better than dignity and most of the suffering is sheer waste.

In the instance of cancer, this argument may be very forcible, but it relies on a general principle that seems to be exceedingly dubious. How can anyone who told that the existence of some (and of much) suffering is consistent with the government of a benign providence take it upon himself to say how much suffering there ought to be? With what measure does such an one compute the permissible quota of suffering? How, for that matter, does he compute the amount of suffering that exists, how could he determine whether or not this computed quantum of suffering (with or without taking its relation to joy into account) either demanded or was opposed to an explanation in terms of a beneficent providence? It seems to me, as I have suggested in an earlier lecture,* that the problem is quite indeterminate, and that, because it is indeterminate, we have no business to speak with confidence either about the need for inferring the existence of a providence on these grounds or about the success of the antiprovidentialists in maintaining the opposite opinion. That, I think, is the decisive feature of this affair.

It is not impressive, I allow, to argue that the pain in the world is of small account. The well-known Epicurean tag that pain is brief if it is severe, and tolerable if it is prolonged, is not very accurate and is not very profound. Agony need not be very brief. If it is brief it may recur. Years of dull misery, seldom alleviated, have often to be borne. Similarly it is difficult to have patience with the shallow view that there are always compensations for the most shocking events, and that the compensations really do compensate. If that argument were pressed to its extremities, the conclusion would be that it is all one whether cancer is conquered like leprosy and smallpox, whether women are widowed in war or raped in peace, whether torture and flogging persist in a judicial system, whether poison gas is or is not to be used. There is a great deal of pain in the world, and much of it is peculiarly revolting, but I do not see how we are able to conjecture whether there is more of it, or less, than a divine regimen would permit.

In the large, I believe, it is reasonable to hold that there has been and that there is a favourable balance of pleasure over pain on this planet. I think it is true, speaking broadly, that life is sweet and that while there is life there is hope. If the latter statement is true, the former could not easily be false. For hope is glad. If some Miserrimus Doleful tells us that we are the dupes of hope, that, looking back on our lives, we should always say "Never again" if we were candid, that the sight of a healthy little child should always make us sad, thinking of what the poor little mite will have to go through, the answer is clearly that hope is not the less pleasant because it is illusory. The hopefulness of our vitality may not

* Lecture LX in the First Series.

be very creditable to our intelligence, but it is very comforting to the heart.

That, I think, is what we should say on the whole, however true it may be that we are often tempted to think like the Chorus in Murder in the Cathedral:

> O, late, late, late!, late is the time, late too late, and rotten the year;
> Evil the wind, and bitter the sea, and the sky, grey, grey, grey.

So far as I can see, however, this argument is just another illustration of the impossibility of arguing with precision to or against the existence of a benevolent providence from the credit-balance of happiness over suffering. Let it be held that the positive correlation between vitality and hopefulness is something inevitable and in the long run preponderant. It follows that wherever there is life there will be hope, and so that there is some reason for expecting a favourable balance of joy over pain. But life exists. Therefore, by hypothesis, this favourable balance exists whether we are to say of our sorrows, with Seneca, "veniunt non incident," or, contrariwise, "incident non veniunt."* The assertion is that a preponderance of happiness is an inevitable characteristic of life as such. That assertion, however, is not evidence that a providence must have contrived the favourable balance that exists in fact, and it is not evidence against that view. The inference to a providential cause of the favourable balance is neither helped nor hindered.

Let us now pass from the problem of physical evil (i.e. of suffering) to the problem of moral evil (i.e. of sin).

The problem of sin is more intricate and more difficult for a theist than the problem of pain, but rather similar arguments are frequently employed in both cases.

Very few theists suggest that sin, if and where it exists, is not an evil. In this respect the Stoics contrasted vice with pain, for they said that depravity and dishonour were genuine evils although mere pain was not. Again, if anyone were disposed to doubt that sin is an evil, he might be reminded that even the illusion of sinfulness is itself an unworthy thing. A hypersensitive conviction of sin is not so good as sinlessness. Apart from that, many sins are plainly most foul. Moreover sin seems often to be a sort of rebellion against the right and the good, and so, in a host of ways, to be thoroughly anomalous in a supposedly moral universe.

Notwithstanding these special features of the problem, however (and notwithstanding many other special features that I shall here neglect) the writers of theodicies are usually disposed to attempt a solution of the problem of moral evil on the same lines as they try to follow in the case of the problem of suffering. Sin is implied, at least indirectly, they say, if high moral character is to be won. There must be a certain liberty to sin (and, therefore, sometimes the actuality of sinning) if moral achievement

* [(Ed. Trans.) "They are coming; they will not fall by chance. They will fall by chance; they are not coming."]

be genuine. Providence would not be gracious to man if he denied man such opportunities. There must be moral evil if there is to be moral good.

Such an apology for actual sinning seems to be rather weak. In the first place it raises difficulties concerning some of the moral virtues. For example, it seems to involve a theory definitely inconsistent with what we usually believe to be true concerning the virtue of purity. Granting that a man may be pure if his heart is cleansed, it is not at all apparent why a garment that is cleansed should be whiter than a garment that has never been stained. Again, even if there ought to be a certain liberty to make mistakes it surely does not follow that there ought to be any liberty to become thoroughly vicious and depraved. Consider, once again, what we commonly hold when a man has been victorious in some terrible moral struggle. We praise his resolution and respect the toughness of his moral fibre, but we do not usually regard him as an ideal man, any more than we think that the conquest of some physical disadvantage is better than physical fitness that had no such disadvantages to overcome. Indeed, I think we might say generally that the struggle with evil tendencies is not a necessary prerequisite of saintliness. That is what Christians have to maintain when they accept the dogma of the Master's sinlessness. They are asserting dogmatically (whether or not the Gospels* expressly assert Christ's sinlessness) that the highest moral character does not imply a struggle with vicious tendencies. Passing to lighter instances, I should say that there is a certain plausibility in Plato's suggestion** that the best doctors are those who are themselves rather delicate but that there is nothing like a metaphysical necessity about the circumstance.

These comments refer to the peculiar characteristics of many sins and to the heinousness of certain sins rather than to the simple fact of sin's existence. Therefore they lead to the second point in the parallel between misery and wickedness, namely whether, allowing that there may or must be some sinning in a righteously ordered universe, there is any sufficient reason for believing that, in such a universe, there could be as many sins and as revolting sins as there are in this universe. As in the case of suffering it seems to me that the problem put is quite indeterminate and does not admit of an answer. How can we pretend to say how much sin there would be if God's common grace abounds, but does not always bring good out of evil? If we cannot say whether the actual universe favours human morality more than a secular universe would do, how could we say that a providence either should or should not be supposed?

* John viii. 46 is obviously not decisive. Outside the Gospels, Hebrews iv. 15 is evidence only of the writer's theology, and similarly of Hebrews vii. 26. The same should be said of Paul in 2 Corinthians v. 21, and of John in 1 John iii. 5. It should be noted that Matthew v. 28 forbids us from holding that serious temptation without actual sin is possible.

** Rep. 408. d.

THEOLOGY AND FALSIFICATION

ANTONY FLEW

Let us begin with a parable. It is a parable developed from a tale told by John Wisdom in his haunting and revelatory article "Gods."* Once upon a time two explorers came upon a clearing in the jungle. In the clearing were growing many flowers and many weeds. One explorer says, "Some gardener must tend this plot." The other disagrees, "There is no gardener." So they pitch their tents and set a watch. No gardener is ever seen. "But perhaps he is an invisible gardener." So they set up a barbed-wire fence. They electrify it. They patrol with bloodhounds. (For they remember how H. G. Well's *The Invisible Man* could be both smelt and touched though he could not be seen.) But no shrieks ever suggest that some intruder has received a shock. No movements of the wire ever betray an invisible climber. The bloodhounds never give cry. Yet still the Believer is not convinced. "But there is a gardener, invisible, intangible, insensible to electric shocks, a gardener who has no scent and makes no sound, a gardener who comes secretly to look after the garden which he loves." At last the Sceptic despairs, "But what remains of your original assertion? Just how does what you call an invisible, intangible, eternally elusive gardener differ from an imaginary gardener or even from no gardener at all?"

In this parable we can see how what starts as an assertion, that something exists or that there is some analogy between certain complexes of phenomena, may be reduced step by step to an altogether different status, to an expression perhaps of a "picture preference."** The Sceptic says there is no gardener. The Believer says there is a gardener (but invisible, etc.). One man talks about sexual behaviour. Another man prefers to talk of Aphrodite (but knows that there is not really a superhuman person additional to, and somehow responsible for, all sexual phenomena).† The

Reprinted from *New Essays in Philosophical Theology*, SCM Press, London, and Macmillan, New York, 1955, pp. 96–99, by permission of the publishers and the author.

* *P.A.S.*, 1944–5, reprinted as Ch. X of *Logic and Language*, Vol I (Blackwell, 1951), and in his *Philosophy and Psychoanalysis* (Blackwell, 1953).

** Cf. J. Wisdom, "Other Minds", *Mind*, 1940; reprinted in his *Other Minds* (Blackwell, 1952).

† Cf. Lucretius, *De Rerum Natura*, II, 655–60,

> Hic siquis mare Neptumum Cereremque vocare
> Constituet fruges et Bacchi nomine abuti
> Mavolat quam laticis proprium proferre vocamen
> Concedamus ut hic terrarum dictitet orbem
> Esse deum matrem dum vera re tamen ipse
> Religione animum turpi contingere parcat.

process of qualification may be checked at any point before the original assertion is completely withdrawn and something of that first assertion will remain (Tautology). Mr. Wells's invisible man could not, admittedly, be seen, but in all other respects he was a man like the rest of us. But though the process of qualification may be, and of course usually is, checked in time, it is not always judiciously so halted. Someone may dissipate his assertion completely without noticing that he has done so. A fine brash hypothesis may thus be killed by inches, the death by a thousand qualifications.

And in this, it seems to me, lies the peculiar danger, the endemic evil, of theological utterance. Take such utterances as "God has a plan," "God created the world," "God loves us as a father loves his children". They look at first sight very much like assertions, vast cosmological assertions. Of course, this is no sure sign that they either are, or are intended to be, assertions. But let us confine ourselves to the cases where those who utter such sentences intend them to express assertions. (Merely remarking parenthetically that those who intend or interpret such utterances as crypto-commands, expressions of wishes, disguised ejaculations, concealed ethics, or as anything else but assertions, are unlikely to succeed in making them either properly orthodox or practically effective).

Now to assert that such and such is the case is necessarily equivalent to denying that such and such is not the case.* Suppose then that we are in doubt as to what someone who gives vent to an utterance is asserting, or suppose that, more radically, we are sceptical as to whether he is really asserting anything at all, one way of trying to understand (or perhaps it will be to expose) his utterance is to attempt to find what he would regard as counting against, or as being incompatible with, its truth. For if the utterance is indeed an assertion, it will necessarily be equivalent to a denial of the negation of that assertion. And anything which would count against the assertion, or which would induce the speaker to withdraw it and to admit that it had been mistaken, must be part of (or the whole of) the meaning of the negation of that assertion. And to know the meaning of the negation of an assertion, is as near as makes no matter, to know the meaning of that assertion.** And if there is nothing which a putative assertion denies then there is nothing which it asserts either: and so it is not really an assertion. When the Sceptic in the parable asked the Believer, "Just how does what you call an invisible, intangible, eternally elusive gardener differ from an imaginary gardener or even from no gardener at all?" he was suggesting that the Believer's earlier statement had been so eroded by qualification that it was no longer an assertion at all.

Now it often seems to people who are not religious as if there was no conceivable event or series of events the occurrence of which would be admitted by sophisticated religious people to be a sufficient reason for

* For those who prefer symbolism: $p \equiv \sim\sim p$.
** For by simply negating $\sim p$ we get $p{:}\sim\sim p \equiv p$.

conceding "There wasn't a God after all" or "God does not really love us then." Someone tells us that God loves us as a father loves his children. We are reassured. But then we see a child dying of inoperable cancer of the throat. His earthly father is driven frantic in his efforts to help, but his Heavenly Father reveals no obvious sign of concern. Some qualification is made—God's love is "not a merely human love" or it is "an inscrutable love", perhaps—and we realize that such sufferings are quite compatible with the truth of the assertion that "God loves us as a father (but, of course, . . .)". We are reassured again. But then perhaps we ask: what is this assurance of God's (appropriately qualified) love worth, what is this apparent guarantee really a guarantee against? Just what would have to happen not merely (morally and wrongly) to tempt but also (logically and rightly) to entitle us to say "God does not love us" or even "God does not exist"? I therefore put to the succeeding symposiasts the simple central questions, "What would have to occur or to have occurred to constitute for you a disproof of the love of, or of the existence of, God?"

TRUTH IN MYSTICAL EXPERIENCE

W. T. STACE

. . . The argument and the counterargument appear to have reached a deadlock. It is quite certain that mere agreement or unanimity as regards experiences is not enough to establish objectivity since many illusions, such as double vision or the yellow appearance of objects to one who has swallowed santonin, are quite universal. This was the argument by which the sceptic sought to defeat the case for mystical objectivity. And it is plainly a valid objection. But the sceptic in pointing it out seems also to have defeated himself if it is a part of his claim that universal verifiability is sufficient to prove the objectivity of a sense experience. For he has shown that there are many illusions which are universally verifiable.

But the conclusion which we ought to draw is not difficult to see. It is that unanimity, even universal agreement of experiences, though it may be a *part* of what constitutes objectivity, is not the *whole* of what constitutes it, either in the case of mystical experience or in that of sense experience. There must be some other condition, some x, which is required, as well as universality, to make an experience objective. Therefore if we wish to enquire whether the claim to mystical objectivity is

Reprinted with minor deletions, from "The Problem of Objective Reference," *Mysticism and Philosophy*, by W. T. Stace. Published by J. B. Lippincott Company.

valid there are two steps which we must take. We must first discover what x is. And then we must enquire whether x is possessed by mystical experience. For the argument of the last few paragraphs, in which we expounded the reply which the proponent of mystical objectivity could give to the criticism of the sceptic, has shown satisfactorily, I think, that mystical experience does possess the requisite kind and degree of universality. The case for mystical objectivity therefore now wholly depends on whether x is a characteristic of it or not.

The view which I advocate is that x is *order*. An experience is objective when it is orderly both in its internal and its external relations. An experience is subjective when it is disorderly either in its internal or its external relations.* Being public is *one* of the characteristics of being orderly, whereas being private is *one* of the marks of the disorderly. Publicity is therefore *part* of the definition of objectivity. But objectivity can only be completely and satisfactorily defined in terms of the much wider concept of order.

By order I mean law, that is to say, regularity of succession, repetition of pattern, "constant conjunction" of specifiable items. Order is thus a quite general concept of which what we call nature or the natural order of our daily world is a particular instance. Strictly speaking, objectivity is to be defined in terms of the general concept of order and not in terms of our particular world order. It is possible to conceive that there is somewhere a systematic order of events of which the laws would be quite different from those with which we are familiar. There might be a universe in which universal gravitation would be replaced by universal mutual repulsion of objects, in which heat invariably produced the solidification of water and cold invariably produced boiling. This could be an instance of order. An experience in such a universe which was orderly in terms of that kind of order would be objective in that order.

But, if we confine ourselves to speaking here only of the world of our daily experience, we may observe that the objectively real world is what we call the order of nature, i.e., the system of orderly events stretching in a time series into a past to which there is no discernible beginning and which, it is presumed, will extend indefinitely into the future. Those of our experiences which are orderly in terms of this world order are called objective. Those which are disorderly in the sense that, either internally or externally, they infringe the laws of this world order are called subjective and are labeled dreams or hallucinations. (There is of course a distinction between dreams and hallucinations, but the nature of this distinction does not concern us because both are in the same sense

* This view is also at least implicit in what Professor Broad says about the snakes and rats seen by the drunkard (see p. 136 above). For he points out that we brand these creatures as hallucinatory because they do not produce the effects which are always produced by such animals if they are real. If they were real, we should expect fox terriers or mongooses to show traces of excitement, cheese to be nibbled, corn to disappear from bins, and so on. We find that no such effects are observed in the bedrooms of persons suffering from delirium tremens. (Broad, *op. cit.*, p. 195.) In short, the rat and snake experience is disorderly in its external relations.

subjective, i.e., in the sense just explained.) It must be recognized that the concept of a world order is not and could not be the product of a single mind and could not be erected on the basis of a single individual's experience. It is a product of all human experiences stretching back into a remote past. That is why publicity, the capacity to be shared by all persons, the possibility of being publicly verified, is a part, but only a part, of the criterion of objectivity. This will have to be more fully explained.

Hallucinations and dreams are always disorderly; that is, they infringe the laws of nature, in one or both of two ways. What happens in a dream may *in itself* be a breach of natural law. Thus a real, objective kettle put on the fire always boils. But a dream-kettle put on the fire might freeze. We say "anything might happen in a dream," meaning that a dream does not have to obey natural laws while an objective experience does. If someone asserted he had seen a kettle of water freeze when it was put on the fire, we might say "you must have been dreaming." This is an example of an experience which is condemned as subjective because it is disorderly in its internal relations or within its own borders.

But sometimes a dream may be perfectly orderly within itself and commit no breaches of natural law. But in that case it will be found that a breach of natural law occurs in the external relations of the dream experience with the other areas of experience which immediately surround it and in the matrix of which it is embedded. The breach occurs at the edges of the dream, so to speak, at the boundaries between dreaming and waking. For instance, I go to bed in my house in the United States. I dream that I am walking down a familiar London street and that I meet my brother and converse with him. Then I wake up and find myself once more in my bed in America. Nothing within the dream was in any way disorderly. The street, the walking, the conversation with my brother—all could have happened and were perfectly natural. But what could *not* have happened, and would if it did happen involve breaches of natural law, is that I should pass from my bed in America to a London street without crossing the intervening distance and then come back again in the same supernatural way. Of course it might be possible to explain otherwise than by the hypothesis of dream some experience—though hardly the whole dream experience just mentioned—in which I seemed to myself to pass suddenly from my bed in America to London. I might have fallen asleep in America, gone into a cataleptic trance, been transported unconscious across the Atlantic, and awakened in London, and then in another cataleptic trance have been brought back to America! But when we say that this did not happen, but that I had a dream, part of our *meaning* is that what seemed to happen was not actually explained by any such series of natural and orderly events.

To complete the theory it is necessary only to show the role which publicity, or universal agreement of experiences, plays in it and why such agreement, though it is a part of the criterion of objectivity, is not by itself sufficient to ensure it. According to our view, to say that an experience is objective means that it is orderly, and it can only be this if it is part of the systematic order of the world. Any other experience will be found to be disorderly either internally or in its external relations or both. Now the world order, since it is a series of events extending from the indefinite past into the indefinite future, transcends the experiences of any single mind. The evidence of it is the evidence of the whole human race. There is only one world order (so far as we know), namely, that in the experiencing of which all normal human beings participate—that on which, so to speak, all windows open. There are not a multitude of orderly systems of events, one for each individual. Therefore an experience which is merely private is not objective, not because it is private, but because, being private, it will always be found to be disorderly.

What we have, however, especially to explain is why the mere fact that all men agree in their accounts of an experience is insufficient to establish its objectivity. This was the defect which we found in the argument from unanimity in its application to mystical experience. We pointed out that an experience might be universal and publicly accessible and yet subjective. And we gave the examples of mirages, santonin experiences, and double vision. What our theory has to show is that these experiences are subjective not because they are private—since in fact they are not private—but because they are disorderly. Let us take the case of double vision. It is not disorderly that a man whose eyes are crossed should *see* things double. But it is disorderly that the crossing of the eyes should produce the actual objective duplication of objects. For there is no law of nature under which this could be subsumed and explained. On the contrary, according to all known causal laws, the crossing of a man's eyes produces no effect on the objects which he is seeing. Therefore what he is experiencing, viz., the appearance of duplication, is in conflict with natural law, is disorderly, and is for that reason subjective.

Since orderliness is the criterion of objectivity, we have now to apply it to mystical states of consciousness to ascertain whether they are objective. Are mystical experiences orderly in the sense required? The definition of order is the constant conjunction of repeatable items of experience. The definition makes no mention of sense experience and is quite independent of it. It will apply to any kind of experience. The orderliness and objectivity of sense contents will mean the constant conjunction of specifiable items of sense experience. The orderliness and objectivity of nonsensuous contents will mean the constant conjunction of specifiable items of nonsensuous experience. We have simply to ask therefore whether mystical experiences are orderly in this sense.

We will take first the introvertive type of mystical experience. It is nonsensuous, since all sensations and images are specifically excluded from it. Does it consist of constant conjunctions of items of nonsensuous experiences? The answer is obviously that it does not. For this would require that there should be within the introvertive experience a multiplicity of particular items of experience. But the very essence of the experience is that it is undifferentiated, distinctionless, and destitute of all multiplicity. There are no distinguishable items or events among which repeatable patterns or regular sequences could be traced. With this the claim of introvertive experience to objectivity collapses. It cannot be objective. But the sceptic should not at this point prematurely claim a victory. For we shall find that, although the experience is not objective, neither is it subjective. We have indeed a long way still to go before we can determine its status.

To see this we must now apply to the experience the criterion of subjectivity as we previously applied the criterion of objectivity. To be subjective in the sense in which an hallucination or a dream is subjective an experience must exhibit positive infringements of natural law, either internally or externally. It must be *dis*orderly. It is not enough to establish the merely negative conclusion that it lacks order—which is all we have shown so far. Mystical experiences are of course parts of the natural order in the same sense in which dreams and hallucinations are so. They have their causes and effects, and it is an objective fact that this man at this time and at this place has a dream or an hallucination or a mystical experience. But to discover whether an experience of any kind is subjective in the sense in which a dream is subjective, or objective in the sense in which a veridical sense perception is objective, we have to look at the internal content of the experience to see whether, either in itself or in its relations to what lies outside its boundaries, it is orderly or disorderly. Now if we apply this test to the introvertive mystical experience we find that it cannot be subjective for precisely the same reason which shows that it cannot be objective. It cannot be disorderly within its own boundaries as would be a dream of a kettle of water freezing when put on the fire. For there are no distinguishable items within it to constitute sequences which are contrary to the constant conjunctions in the world order. For the same reason it cannot conflict with the natural order in its external relations, for this too requires that specifiable items within the experience should conflict with items outside it—as for instance being in London in my dream conflicts with being in bed in America without traversing the intervening distance. But there are no items within the introvertive experience which could conflict with anything outside it. It follows from these considerations that it is not subjective.

There is really nothing new in the conclusion which we have reached. We shall find that the proposition that mystical experience is neither subjective nor objective is itself a mystical doctrine which is explicitly put forward by all the more philosophical mystics. They have not reached it by a process of reasoning as we have done in this section. They have simply felt intuitively that it is the natural and proper interpretation of their experience. It is true that this seems to conflict with our finding in the last chapter that a sense of objectivity is one of the common characteristics of all mystical experience. But "sense of objectivity" is in reality a very unsophisticated phrase, though it was a convenient one to use at a certain stage of thinking. The fact is that the mystic feels an intense and burning conviction that his experience is not a mere dream—a something which is shut up entirely inside his own consciousness. He feels that it transcends his own petty personality, that it is vastly greater than himself, that it in some sense passes out beyond his individuality into the infinite. This he expresses—for lack of better words—by saying that it is "real," that it is the "true and only reality," and so on. It is natural to pass on from this to saying that it "exists" outside himself, that it is objective, etc. We shall have to do our best to illuminate all this in the sequel. Our immediate concern is only to show that there is no real contradiction between the earlier expression "sense of objectivity" and the more accurate statement that mystical experience is neither subjective nor objective.

Do the same arguments and conclusions apply to the extrovertive type of experience? At first sight it would seem that the case is quite different here because in this experience there does exist a multiplicity of distinguishable items, and these items are in space even if they do not exhibit any temporal flux. The extrovertive mystic perceives with his physical senses the blades of grass, the wood, the stone, but he perceives them as "all one." He perceives them as both distinct and identical. In so far as he perceives them as distinct, they are of course the sort of distinguishable items which exhibit orderliness. The grass, the wood, and the stone are simply objective parts of the natural order.

But it seems to me that although the grass, the wood, and the stone are thus objective, their oneness is not. The multiplicity in the experience is not as such a mystical perception. Only the oneness is. But the oneness as such has no multiplicity and no distinguishable items in it. Indeed it is, in the mystic's view, the very same oneness as is perceived in the introvertive experience. There is the unity outside and the unity inside. But these are not two unities, but one and the same. This is certainly the mystical claim. At any rate the exterior oneness, like the interior oneness, has in it no multiplicity of items or events. Hence the same arguments apply to it as to the introvertive experience, and the same conclusion must be drawn. It is neither objective nor subjective.

TRANSSUBJECTIVITY

Although the argument from unanimity does not show that the experiences of the mystic are objective—as was claimed by Bucke, William James, and a large number of other writers, including Professor C. D. Broad—yet it does yield one very important conclusion. It is strong evidence that the mystics have not in any fundamental way misreported their experiences. The sceptic may maintain that, although the mystic may believe that he has suppressed all sensations, images, and conceptual thoughts, this cannot in fact be so. To this it must be answered that, if we had only one report of a person who claimed that he had reached a wholly distinctionless and undifferentiated experience, we should be right to regard such a report with grave suspicion. We should suppose that he must have made some mistake. But if we have a very large number of such reports from independent sources all of which confirm the first report, our scepticism ought to abate somewhat. And if we find such independent reports coming from many diverse cultures, times, and countries of the world—from the ancient Hindus, from the medieval Christians, from Persians and Arabians, from Buddhist China, Japan, Burma, and Siam, from modern European and American intellectuals—this profoundly impressive agreement amounts to very strong evidence that the experiences were not misreported but were actually just what the mystics say they were.

If, this being accepted, we consider again the introvertive experience, we find that—at least in the major mystical traditions—the experience is reported to be a self-transcending one. The individual, having suppressed all empirical mental content, arrives at a pure unity, a pure consciousness, which is also the pure ego. It might be supposed that what he thus reaches is his own individual pure ego. But he reports the further fact that this self, which seems at first to be his own private self, experiences itself as at once becoming one with or becoming dissolved in an infinite and universal self. The boundary walls of the separate self fade away, and the individual finds himself passing beyond himself and becoming merged in a boundless and universal consciousness. This aspect of the mystical experience was emphasized in the section on the dissolution of individuality in the last chapter. The conclusion which the mystic draws—not however by way of a reasoned conclusion, but as something immediately experienced—is that what he has reached is not merely his individual pure ego but the pure ego of the universe; or, otherwise put, that his individual self and the universal self are somehow identical. This is the conclusion explicitly drawn in the Upanishads, but it is objected to by the theologians of the theistic religions on the ground that it involves the heresy of pantheism. But for reasons which we have discussed, the universal ego cannot be regarded as objective, although since it transcends the individual it cannot be regarded as subjective either.

We all, mystics and nonmystics alike, have been conditioned to regard the distinction between subjective and objective as absolute in such a way that any third alternative is excluded. Hence the mystic, who feels that he has been in touch with what is outside and beyond himself, is likely enough to express this by using phrases which imply that the universal self is an objective reality. I am here maintaining that, although the mystic may be justified in his belief in a transcendent and universal self, yet there is a certain error in his way of speaking if he maintains that it has an objective existence. We must for the present rest content with the conclusion that its status is transsubjective. Whether anything more definite and satisfying can be said will be discussed in later sections of this chapter.

The critical reader may very well say that he cannot, as the above remarks assume, accept as convincing the mystic's statement that his experience *itself* is transsubjective. Suppose the reader has reluctantly agreed that the unanimous and independent evidence of the mystics in many diverse cultures and ages and places shows that they have not misdescribed their experiences, yet this was agreed to on the assumption that the experience was merely being thought of as a psychological fact within the subjectivity of the mystic's mind. But now the reader is being asked to agree that the experience itself goes beyond itself into non-subjectivity. He will no doubt object that it would be much easier and better to see whether the dissolution of his own individuality which the mystic says he feels cannot be explained by some interpretational hypothesis which would not involve the enormous leap of postulating a cosmic pure ego. For instance, is it not a fact that in quite ordinary experiences we often lose all consciousness of individuality—we forget ourselves and lose ourselves momentarily because we are absorbed in some very engrossing pursuit? And may not the mystic's feeling of the loss of individuality be quite simply explained in a similar way?

This objection would undoubtedly carry great weight if it were not for one further consideration which I have not yet disclosed. There is a line of reasoning which, so far as I know, no mystic or anyone else has ever urged or even been conscious of, but which, on the condition that we accept its premiss, decisively supports the view of the mystic against that of the sceptic. The premiss of the argument is that the mystic has in fact eliminated all the empirical contents of his consciousness and is left with the pure consciousness which is his own individual pure ego. This premiss does not go beyond his own subjectivity. But once this is admitted, we shall find that it is logically impossible to stop there and that we are compelled to postulate that the pure individual ego is in reality not merely individual but is universal and cosmic. The reasoning is as follows:

Suppose that two persons *A* and *B* each suppresses in himself all specific mental content, and that therefore each attains the mystical consciousness of his own pure ego. Would it then be the case that *A* has reached *A*'s private pure ego, and that *B* has reached *B*'s private pure ego, so that what we have here in this situation is two distinct and separate pure egos? The natural answer to expect would of course be, Yes. But if so, then there must be something which separates *A*'s ego from *B*'s ego, some principle of division or individuation which makes them two distinct entities. What is the principle of individuation?

Let us first ask what is the principle of individuation which separates two minds in ordinary life, two minds which have not sought or attained any mystical consciousness but are operating at the level of everyday experience. What, for example, makes the mind of the writer of this book a different psychical entity from the mind of the reader? If this question were asked, not about the minds, but about the physical bodies of the writer and the reader, the answer would be very simple. The basic principle of individuation here would be space. An interval of space separates our two bodies and makes them two distinct entities. This is no doubt oversimple. Where two persons live at different periods, time will separate them as well as space. Also different physical qualities may enter into the differentiation. The writer's hair may be white, the reader's brown. But we can ignore these complications and concentrate only on the basic principle of differentiation which in this case is space.

But we are here asking what the principle of division is as between two minds, not two bodies. Perhaps the preliminary objection will be raised that we cannot ask such a question without assuming a mind-body dualism, and that to make such an assumption is objectionable. This is a misunderstanding. The question assumes no theory at all, either dualistic or monistic, as to the relation between mind and body. It only assumes that it is possible to speak and think intelligibly in "mentalistic" or introspective terms as well as in physical terms. It assumes that it is not meaningless to talk of one's inner thoughts and feelings and that statements about them are not simply statements about the body, although there is no doubt some very intimate connection between them. Our question does not involve any theory at all, or the denial of any theory. It does not move on the level of theory but on the level of experience. It is a plain statement of experienced fact that a man can talk sensibly about his ideas, feelings, intentions, wishes, etc., and that when he does so he is not talking about his stomach, legs, or brain. We may now therefore return to our queston and ask what is the principle of individuation which distinguishes two minds which are both operating at the level of everyday experience.

If we thus abstract from bodily differences, it seems clear to me that there is only one circumstance which distinguishes one mind from another, namely that each has a different stream of consciousness or, what amounts to the same thing, a different stream of experiences. Over any given period of time the sensations, images, emotions, and thoughts which constitute *A*'s inner biography will be different from those which constitute *B*'s inner biography. We need not trouble ourselves about the puzzle whether, when *A* and *B* are said in common speech to be looking at the "same" material object, they are actually having one identical sensation or two private but similar sensations. For whether there is at such a point of time an actual intersection of the two streams of consciousness or only a similarity, the fact remains that by and large *A*'s stream of mental contents is during most of its duration entirely distinct from *B*'s. And this, so far as I can see, is the *only* thing which distinguishes any one mind from any other. In other words, minds are distinguished from one another by their empirical contents and by nothing else. It follows that if *A* and *B* have suppressed within themselves all empirical contents then there is left nothing whatever which can distinguish them and make them two; and if *A* and *B* have thereby reached the mystical consciousness of their pure egos, then there is nothing to distinguish them or make them two pure egos.

If we make use of the philosopher's distinction between the pure ego and the empirical ego, then what follows from this argument is that there exists a multiplicity of empirical egos in the universe, but that there can be only one pure ego. Hence the mystic who has reached what seems at first to be his own private pure ego has in fact reached the pure ego of the universe, the pure cosmic ego.

This explains and agrees with the experience of self-transcendence which the mystic always reports. Both the experience of the mystic and the wholly independent speculative reasoning of the philosopher just outlined converge on the same conclusion and support each other. If it were not for the speculative reasoning, the sceptic might well explain away the experienced feeling of self-transcendence, the fading away of personal identity into "boundless being" reported by Tennyson, the disappearance of the "I" and its dissolution in the "universal pool" reported by Koestler, the same experiences reported by Christian mystics and Sufis in their own theological language, and by Hindus and Buddhists in terms appropriate to their special cultures and theories—the sceptic might explain all this away by an appeal to the self-forgetfulness of a person absorbed in some all-engrossing object of attention. Such an obvious commonplace of everyday psychological fact would in any case seem—at least to the present writer—utterly insufficient to bear the weight of explaining the entirely unusual and uncommonplace and indeed extraordinary experiences of the mystics. But it is better to rely on the reasoned argument which has been discovered and set forth in this section.

There *is* therefore a universal cosmic self with which the mystic makes contact and with which he becomes identified. But the difficulty about this is the meaning of the word "is" in the last sentence. It cannot be taken to mean "exist," since this would make it objective. But we must rest for the moment at least with the conclusion that it is transsubjective though not objective, leaving our final accounting with the difficulties which it involves to a later section.

DO DRUGS HAVE RELIGIOUS IMPORT?

HUSTON SMITH

DRUGS AND RELIGION VIEWED PHENOMENOLOGICALLY

Phenomenology attempts a careful description of human experience. The question the drugs pose for the phenomenology of religion, therefore, is whether the experiences they induce differ from religious experiences reached naturally, and if so how.

Reprinted, with deletions, from *The Journal of Philosophy* (Vol. LXI, No. 18, October 1, 1964) by permission of the editors and author.

Even the Bible notes that chemically induced psychic states bear *some* resemblance to religious ones. Peter had to appeal to a circumstantial criterion—the early hour of the day—to defend those who were caught up in the Pentecostal experience against the charge that they were merely drunk: "These men are not drunk, as you suppose, since it is only the third hour of the day" (Acts 2:15); and Paul initiates the comparison when he admonishes the Ephesians not to "get drunk with wine . . . but [to] be filled with the spirit" (Ephesians 5:18). Are such comparisons, paralleled in the accounts of virtually every religion, superficial? How far can they be pushed?

Not all the way, students of religion have thus far insisted. With respect to the new drugs, Prof. R. C. Zaehner has drawn the line emphatically. "The importance of Huxley's *Doors of Perception*," he writes, "is that in it the author clearly makes the claim that what he experienced under the influence of mescalin is closely comparable to a genuine mystical experience. If he is right, . . . the conclusions . . . are alarming."* Zaehner thinks that Huxley is not right, but I fear that it is Zaehner who is mistaken.

There are, of course, innumerable drug experiences that have no religious feature; they can be sensual as readily as spiritual, trivial as readily as transforming, capricious as readily as sacramental. If there is one point about which every student of the drugs agrees, it is that there is no such thing as the drug experience *per se*—no experience that the drugs, as it were, merely secrete. Every experience is a mix of three ingredients: drug, set (the psychological make-up of the individual), and setting (the social and physical environment in which it is taken). But given the right set and setting, the drugs can induce religious experiences indistinguishable from experiences that occur spontaneously. Nor need set and setting be exceptional. The way the statistics are currently running, it looks as if from one-fourth to one-third of the general population will have religious experiences if they take the drugs under naturalistic conditions, meaning by this conditions in which the researcher supports the subject but does not try to influence the direction his experience will take. Among subjects who have strong religious inclinations to begin with, the proportion of those having religious experiences jumps to three-fourths. If they take the drugs in settings that are religious too, the ratio soars to nine in ten.

How do we know that the experiences these people have really are religious? We can begin with the fact that they say they are. The "one-fourth to one-third of the general population" figure is drawn from two sources. Ten months after they had had their experiences, 24 per cent of the 194 subjects in a study by the California psychiatrist Oscar Janiger characterized their experiences as having been religious.** Thirty-two

* *Mysticism, Sacred and Profane* (New York: Oxford, 1961), p. 12.

** Quoted in William H. McGlothlin, "Long-lasting Effects of LSD on Certain Attitudes in Normals," printed for private distribution by the RAND Corporation, May, 1962, p. 16.

per cent of the 74 subjects in Ditman and Hayman's study reported, looking back on their LSD experience, that it looked as if it had been "very much" or "quite a bit" a religious experience; 42 per cent checked as true the statement that they "were left with a greater awareness of God, or a higher power, or ultimate reality."* The statement that three-fourths of subjects having religious "sets" will have religious experiences comes from the reports of sixty-nine religious professionals who took the drugs while the Harvard project was in progress.**

In the absence of (a) a single definition of religious experience acceptable to psychologists of religion generally and (b) foolproof ways of ascertaining whether actual experiences exemplify any definition, I am not sure there is any better way of telling whether the experiences of the 333 men and women involved in the above studies were religious than by noting whether they seemed so to them. But if more rigorous methods are preferred, they exist; they have been utilized, and they confirm the conviction of the man in the street that drug experiences can indeed be religious. In his doctoral study at Harvard University, Walter Pahnke worked out a typology of religious experience (in this instance of the mystical variety) based on the classic cases of mystical experiences as summarized in Walter Stace's *Mysticism and Philosophy*. He then administered psilocybin to ten theology students and professors in the setting of a Good Friday service. The drug was given "double-blind," meaning that neither Dr. Pahnke nor his subjects knew which ten were getting psilocybin and which ten placebos to constitute a control group. Subsequently the reports the subjects wrote of their experiences were laid successively before three college-graduate housewives who, without being informed about the nature of the study, were asked to rate each statement as to the degree (strong, moderate, slight, or none) to which it exemplified each of the nine traits of mystical experience enumerated in the typology of mysticism worked out in advance. When the test of significance was applied to their statistics, it showed that "those subjects who received psilocybin experienced phenomena which were indistinguishable from, if not identical with . . . the categories defined by our typology of mysticism."†

With the thought that the reader might like to test his own powers of discernment on the question being considered, I insert here a simple test I gave to a group of Princeton students following a recent discussion sponsored by the Woodrow Wilson Society:

Below are accounts of two religious experiences. One occurred under the influence of drugs, one without their influence. Check the one you think *was* drug-induced.

* *Ibid.*, pp. 45, 46.

** Timothy Leary, "The Religious Experience: Its Production and Interpretation," *The Psychedelic Review*, 1, 3 (1964): 325.

† "Drugs and Mysticism: An Analysis of the Relationship between Psychedelic Drugs and the Mystical Consciousness," a thesis presented to the Committee on Higher Degrees in History and Philosophy of Religion, Harvard University, June 1963.

I

Suddenly I burst into a vast, new, indescribably wonderful universe. Although I am writing this over a year later, the thrill of the surprise and amazement, the awesomeness of the revelation, the engulfment in an overwhelming feeling-wave of gratitude and blessed wonderment, are as fresh, and the memory of the experience is as vivid, as if it had happened five minutes ago. And yet to concoct anything by way of description that would even hint at the magnitude, the sense of ultimate reality . . . this seems such an impossible task. The knowledge which has infused and affected every aspect of my life came instantaneously and with such complete force of certainty that it was impossible, then or since, to doubt its validity.

II

All at once, without warning of any kind, I found myself wrapped in a flame-colored cloud. For an instant I thought of fire . . . the next, I knew that the fire was within myself. Directly afterward there came upon me a sense of exultation, of immense joyousness accompanied or immediately followed by an intellectual illumination impossible to describe. Among other things, I did not merely come to believe, but I saw that the universe is not composed of dead matter, but is, on the contrary, a living Presence; I became conscious in myself of eternal life. . . . I saw that all men are immortal: that the cosmic order is such that without any preadventure all things work together for the good of each and all; that the foundation principle of the world . . . is what we call love, and that the happiness of each and all is in the long run absolutely certain.

On the occasion referred to, twice as many students (46) answered incorrectly as answered correctly (23). I bury the correct answer in a footnote to preserve the reader's opportunity to test himself.*

• • •

DRUGS AND RELIGION VIEWED PHILOSOPHICALLY

Why do people reject evidence? Because they find it threatening, we may suppose. Theologians are not the only professionals to utilize this mode of defense. In his *Personal Knowledge*,** Michael Polanyi recounts the way the medical profession ignored such palpable facts as the painless amputation of human limbs, performed before their own eyes in hundreds of successive cases, concluding that the subjects were imposters who were either deluding their physicians or colluding with them. One physician, Esdaile, carried out about 300 major operations painlessly under mesmeric

* The first account is quoted anonymously in "The Issue of the Consciousness-expanding Drugs," *Main Currents in Modern Thought*, **20**, 1 (September–October, 1963): 10–11. The second experience was that of Dr. R. M. Bucke, the author of *Cosmic Consciousness*, as quoted in William James, *The Varieties of Religious Experience* (New York: Modern Library, 1902), pp. 390–391. The former experience occurred under the influence of drugs; the latter did not.

** Chicago: Univ. of Chicago Press, 1958.

trance in India, but neither in India nor in Great Britain could he get medical journals to print accounts of his work. Polanyi attributes this closed-mindedness to "lack of a conceptual framework in which their discoveries could be separated from specious and untenable admixtures."

The "untenable admixture" in the fact that psychotomimetic drugs can induce religious experience is its apparent implicate: that religious disclosures are no more veridical than psychotic ones. For religious skeptics, this conclusion is obviously not untenable at all; it fits in beautifully with their thesis that *all* religion is at heart an escape from reality. Psychotics avoid reality by retiring into dream worlds of make-believe; what better evidence that religious visionaries do the same than the fact that identical changes in brain chemistry produce both states of mind? Had not Marx already warned us that religion is the "opiate" of the people?—apparently he was more literally accurate than he supposed. Freud was likewise too mild. He "never doubted that religious phenomena are to be understood only on the model of the neurotic symptoms of the individual."* He should have said "psychotic symptoms."

So the religious skeptic is likely to reason. What about the religious believer? Convinced that religious experiences are not fundamentally delusory, can he admit that psychotomimetic drugs can occasion them? To do so he needs (to return to Polanyi's words) "a conceptual framework in which [the discoveries can] be separated from specious and untenable admixtures," the "untenable admixture" being in this case the conclusion that religious experiences are in general delusory.

One way to effect the separation would be to argue that, despite phenomenological similarities between natural and drug-induced religious experiences, they are separated by a crucial *ontological* difference. Such an argument would follow the pattern of theologians who argue for the "real presence" of Christ's body and blood in the bread and wine of the Eucharist despite their admission that chemical analysis, confined as it is to the level of "accidents" rather than "essences," would not disclose this presence. But this distinction will not appeal to many today, for it turns on an essence-accident metaphysics which is not widely accepted. Instead of fighting a rear-guard action by insisting that if drug and non-drug religious experiences cannot be distinguished empirically there must be some transempirical factor that distinguishes them and renders the drug experience profane, I wish to explore the possibility of accepting drug-induced experiences as religious without relinquishing confidence in the truth-claims of religious experience generally.

To begin with the weakest of all arguments, the argument from authority: William James did not discount *his* insights that occurred while his brain chemistry was altered. The paragraph in which he retrospectively evaluates his nitrous oxide experiences has become classic, but it is so pertinent to the present discussion that it merits quoting once again.

* *Totem and Taboo*, Sigmund Freud, (New York: Modern Library, 1938)

> One conclusion was forced upon my mind at that time, and my impression of its truth has ever since remained unshaken. It is that our normal waking consciousness, rational consciousness as we call it, is but one special type of consciousness, whilst all about it, parted from it by the filmiest of screens, there lie potential forms of consciousness entirely different. We may go through life without suspecting their existence; but apply the requisite stimulus, and at a touch they are there in all their completeness, definite types of mentality which probably somewhere have their field of application and adaptation. No account of the universe in its totality can be final which leaves these other forms of consciousness quite disregarded. How to regard them is the question—for they are so discontinuous with ordinary consciousness. Yet they may determine attitudes though they cannot furnish formulas, and open a region though they fail to give a map. At any rate, they forbid a premature closing of our accounts with reality. Looking back on my own experiences, they all converge toward a kind of insight to which I cannot help ascribing some metaphysical significance (*op. cit.*, 378–379).

To this argument from authority, I add two arguments that try to provide something by way of reasons. Drug experiences that assume a religious cast tend to have fearful and/or beatific features, and each of my hypotheses relates to one of these aspects of the experience.

Beginning with the ominous, "fear of the Lord," awe-ful features, Gordon Wasson, the New York banker-turned-mycologist, describes these as he encountered them in his psilocybin experience as follows: "Ecstasy! In common parlance . . . ecstasy is fun. . . . But ecstasy is not fun. Your very soul is seized and shaken until it tingles. After all, who will choose to feel undiluted awe? . . . The unknowing vulgar abuse the word; we must recapture its full and terrifying sense."* Emotionally the drug experience can be like having forty-foot waves crash over you for several hours while you cling desperately to a life-raft which may be swept from under you at any minute. It seems quite possible that such an ordeal, like any experience of a close call, could awaken rather fundamental sentiments respecting life and death and destiny and trigger the "no atheists in foxholes" effect. Similarly, as the subject emerges from the trauma and realizes that he is not going to be insane as he had feared, there may come over him an intensified appreciation like that frequently reported by patients recovering from critical illness. "It happened on the day when my bed was pushed out of doors to the open gallery of the hospital," reads one such report:

> I cannot now recall whether the revelation came suddenly or gradually; I only remember finding myself in the very midst of those wonderful moments, beholding life for the first time in all its young intoxication of loveliness, in its unspeakable joy, beauty, and importance. I cannot say exactly what the mysterious change was. I saw no new thing, but I saw all the usual things in a miraculous new light—in what I believe is their true light. I saw for the first time how wildly beautiful and joyous, beyond any words of mine to describe, is the whole of life. Every human being moving across that porch, every

* "The Hallucinogenic Fungi of Mexico: An Inquiry into the Origins of the Religious Idea among Primitive Peoples," *Harvard Botanical Museum Leaflets*, **19**, 7 (1961).

sparrow that flew, every branch tossing in the wind, was caught in and was a part of the whole mad ecstasy of loveliness, of joy, of importance, of intoxication of life.*

If we do not discount religious intuitions because they are prompted by battlefields and *physical* crises; if we regard the latter as "calling us to our senses" more often than they seduce us into delusions, need comparable intuitions be discounted simply because the crises that trigger them are of an inner, *psychic* variety?

Turning from the hellish to the heavenly aspects of the drug experience, *some* of the latter may be explainable by the hypothesis just stated; that is, they may be occasioned by the relief that attends the sense of escape from high danger. But this hypothesis cannot possibly account for *all* the beatific episodes, for the simple reason that the positive episodes often come first, or to persons who experience no negative episodes whatever. Dr. Sanford Unger of the National Institute of Mental Health reports that among his subjects "50 to 60% will not manifest any real disturbance worthy of discussion," yet "around 75% will have at least one episode in which exaltation, rapture, and joy are the key descriptions."** How are we to account for the drug's capacity to induce peak experiences, such as the following, which are *not* preceded by fear?

A feeling of great peace and contentment seemed to flow through my entire body. All sound ceased and I seemed to be floating in a great, very very still void or hemisphere. It is impossible to describe the overpowering feeling of peace, contentment, and being a part of goodness itself that I felt. I could feel my body dissolving and actually becoming a part of the goodness and peace that was all around me. Words can't describe this. I feel an awe and wonder that such a feeling could have occurred to me.†

Consider the following line of argument. Like every other form of life, man's nature has become distinctive through specialization. Man has specialized in developing a cerebral cortex. The analytic powers of this instrument are a standing wonder, but the instrument seems less able to provide man with the sense that he is meaningfully related to his environment: to life, the world, and history in their wholeness. As Albert Camus describes the situation, "If I were . . . a cat among animals, this life would have a meaning, or rather this problem would not arise, for I should belong to this world. I would *be* this world to which I am now opposed by my whole consciousness."‡ Note that it is Camus' consciousness that opposes him to his world. The drugs do not knock this

* Margaret Prescott Montague, *Twenty Minutes of Reality* (St. Paul, Minn.: Macalester Park, 1947), pp. 15, 17.

** "The Current Scientific Status of Psychedelic Drug Research," read at the Conference on Methods in Philosophy and the Sciences, New School for Social Research, May 3, 1964, and scheduled for publication in David Solomon, ed., *The Conscious Expanders* (New York: Putnam, fall of 1964).

† Quoted by Dr. Unger in the paper just mentioned.

‡ *The Myth of Sisyphus* (New York: Vintage, 1955), p. 38.

consciousness out, but while they leave it operative they also activate areas of the brain that normally lie below its threshold of awareness. One of the clearest objective signs that the drugs are taking effect is the dilation they produce in the pupils of the eyes, and one of the most predictable subjective signs is the intensification of visual perception. Both of these responses are controlled by portions of the brain that lie deep, further to the rear than the mechanisms that govern consciousness. Meanwhile we know that the human organism is interlaced with its world in innumerable ways it normally cannot sense—through gravitational fields, body respiration, and the like: the list could be multiplied until man's skin began to seem more like a thoroughfare than a boundary. Perhaps the deeper regions of the brain which evolved earlier and are more like those of the lower animals—"If I were . . . a cat . . . I should belong to this world"—can sense this relatedness better than can the cerebral cortex which now dominates our awareness. If so, when the drugs rearrange the neurohumors that chemically transmit impulses across synapses between neurons, man's consciousness and his submerged, intuitive, ecological awareness might for a spell become interlaced. This is, of course, no more than a hypothesis, but how else are we to account for the extraordinary incidence under the drugs of that kind of insight the keynote of which James described as "invariably a reconciliation"? "It is as if the opposites of the world, whose contradictoriness and conflict make all our difficulties and troubles, were melted into one and the same genus, but *one of the species*, the nobler and better one, *is itself the genus, and so soaks up and absorbs its opposites into itself*" (*op. cit.*, 379).

THE DRUGS AND RELIGION VIEWED "RELIGIOUSLY"

Suppose that drugs can induce experiences indistinguishable from religious experiences and that we can respect their reports. Do they shed any light, not (we now ask) on life, but on the nature of the religious life?

One thing they may do is throw religious experience itself into perspective by clarifying its relation to the religious life as a whole. Drugs appear able to induce religious experiences; it is less evident that they can produce religious lives. It follows that religion is more than religious experiences. This is hardly news, but it may be a useful reminder, especially to those who incline toward "the religion of religious experience"; which is to say toward lives bent on the acquisition of desired states of experience irrespective of their relation to life's other demands and components.

Further Readings

GENERAL

Books of General Interest

Aquinas, St. Thomas, *Summa Contra Gentiles*, trans. Anton C. Pegis, Doubleday, Garden City, N.Y., 1955.

Burtt, E. A., *Man Seeks the Divine*, 2d ed., Harper & Row, New York, 1964.

Ducasse, C. J., *A Philosophical Scrutiny of Religion*, Ronald Press, New York, 1953.

Kaufmann, Walter, *Critique of Religion and Philosophy*, Harper & Row, New York, 1958.

Martin, C. B., *Religious Belief*, Cornell University Press, Ithaca, N.Y., 1959.

McTaggart, J. M. E., *Some Dogmas of Religion*, E. Arnold, London, 1906.

Noss, John B., *Man's Religions*, 3d ed., Macmillan, New York, 1962.

Santayana, George, *Reason in Religion*, Scribner's, New York, 1906.

Tennant, F. R., *Philosophical Theology*, Cambridge University Press, New York, 1928.

Anthologies

Abernathy, G. L., and T. A. Langford, (eds.), *Philosophy of Religion*, Macmillan, New York, 1962.

Alston, William P. (ed.), *Religious Belief and Philosophic Thought*, Harcourt, Brace & World, New York, 1963.

Bronstein, D. J. and H. M. Schulweis, (eds.), *Approaches to the Philosophy of Religion*, Prentice-Hall, Englewood Cliffs, N.J., 1954.

Flew, Antony and Alasdair MacIntyre, (eds.), *New Essays in Philosophical Theology*, Macmillan, New York, 1955.

Hartshorne, Charles and W. L. Rease, (eds.), *Philosophers Speak of God*, University of Chicago Press, Chicago, 1953.

Hook, Sidney (ed.), *Religious Experience and Truth*, New York University Press, New York, 1961.

Mourant, J. A. (ed.), *Readings in the Philosophy of Religion*, Crowell, New York, 1959.

Smart, Ninian (ed.), *Historical Selections in the Philosophy of Religion*, Harper & Row, New York, 1962.

THE EXISTENCE OF GOD

Descartes, Rene, *Meditations*, trans. Laurence Lafleur, Liberal Arts, New York, 1951, bks. III and V.

Hick, John, *The Philosophy of Religion*, Prentice-Hall, Englewood Cliffs, N.J., 1963.

Hick, John (ed.), *The Existence of God*, Macmillan, New York, 1964.

Hume, David, *Dialogues Concerning Natural Religion*, Hafner, New York, 1948.

Hume, David, *An Inquiry Concerning Human Understanding*, Liberal Arts, New York, 1955, chaps. 10 and 11.

Kant, Immanuel. *The Critique of Practical Reason*, trans. Lewis White Beck, Liberal Arts, New York, 1956.

Lewis, C. S., *Miracles: A Preliminary Study*, Macmillan, New York, 1947.

Malcolm, Norman, "Anselm's Ontological Arguments," *Philosophical Review*, *69* (1960).

Paley, William, *Evidences of the Existence and Attributes of the Deity*, London.

Pascal, Blaise, *Pensees*, ed. H. F. Stewart, London, 1950.

Taylor, A. E., *Does God Exist?* Macmillan, New York, 1945.

Wisdom, John, "Gods," in *Philosophy and Psycho-analysis*, Philosophical Library, New York, 1953.

MYSTICISM AND RELIGIOUS EXPERIENCE

Broad, C. D., *Religion, Philosophy and Psychical Research*, Harcourt, Brace & World, New York, 1953.

Buber, Martin, *I and Thou*, trans. R. S. Smith, T. & T. Clark, Edinburgh, 1937.

James, William, *Varieties of Religious Experience*, Longmans, New York, 1902.

Leuba, J. H., *The Psychology of Religious Mysticism*, Harcourt, Brace & World, New York, 1925.
Otto, Rudolf, *The Idea of the Holy*, 2d ed., trans. J. W. Harvey, Oxford University Press, Fair Lawn, N.J., 1958.
Pratt, James B., *The Religious Consciousness*, Macmillan, New York, 1920.
Stace, W. T., *Time and Eternity*, Princeton University Press, Princeton, N.J., 1952.
Stace, W. T., (ed.), *The Teachings of the Mystics*, New American Library, New York, 1960.

THE PROBLEM OF EVIL

St. Augustine, *Enchiridion*, trans. A. C. Outler, Westminster, Philadelphia, 1955.
Leibniz, G. W., *Theodicy*, trans. E. M. Huggard, Routledge & Kegan Paul, London, 1951.
Lewis, C. S., *The Problem of Pain*, Macmillan, New York, 1950.
Mill, John Stuart, *Three Essays on Religion*, London, 1874.
Smart, Ninian, "Omnipotence, Evil and Supermen," *Philosophy, 36* (1961).
Wisdom, John, "God and Evil," *Mind, 44* (1935).

IMMORTALITY

Broad, C. D., "Human Personality and the Possibility of its Survival," University of California Press, Berkeley, Calif., 1955.
Butler, Joseph, *Analogy of Religion*, 1736, Oxford, London, 1896, chap. 1.
Ducasse, C. J., *Nature, Mind, and Death*, Open Court, La Salle, Ill., 1951, pt. IV.
James, William, *Human Immortality*, Houghton Mifflin, Boston, 1898.
Royce, Josiah, *The Conception of Immortality*, Houghton Mifflin, Boston, 1900.

X

WORLD VIEWS AND PHILOSOPHICAL COMMITMENT

PHILOSOPHY does not always come in disconnected fragments called problems; problems are related to other problems, concepts to other concepts. Any answer, even a partial one, to one question has consequences for a whole range of other questions. Whatever answer we give to the question "Is man free or not?" has immediate consequences for our conception of criminal responsibility and moral praise and blame; like an Alexander Calder mobile an adjustment in one part of the structure calls for adjustment throughout the entire system.

Hopefully, a more or less complete picture of the interconnections could come at the end of philosophic inquiry. Few thinkers, however, have had the patience to wait until all the pieces could be brought together into some most general scheme. These philosophers have a passion to see things whole; the search for a most general system of concepts is of first importance. (See Whitehead, "Speculative Philosophy," and Bradley, "Objections to Metaphysics.")

Other philosophers are suspicious about this most pretentious side of philosophy. They are doubtful that a general scheme is in close enough contact with concrete experience to contribute anything to knowledge. (See Ayer, "Elimination of Metaphysics" and Wisdom, "Philosophy and Psychoanalysis.")

Still others are impatient with the intellectual play of categories or the concern with objective knowledge; they feel themselves plunged into life, faced with crucial practical problems too pressing for detached speculation. Their questions are "What should I do?" "How should I choose?" "Is there anything other than myself to which I could give my final allegiance?" (See Sartre, "Existentialism and Human Decision.")

Each of the following selections attempts to articulate one of these attitudes toward philosophy.

SPECULATIVE PHILOSOPHY

ALFRED NORTH WHITEHEAD

SECTION I

This course of lectures is designed as an essay in Speculative Philosophy. Its first task must be to define "speculative philosophy," and to defend it as a method productive of important knowledge.

Speculative Philosophy is the endeavour to frame a coherent, logical, necessary system of general ideas in terms of which every element of our experience can be interpreted. By this notion of "interpretation" I mean that everything of which we are conscious, as enjoyed, perceived, willed, or thought, shall have the character of a particular instance of the general scheme. Thus the philosophical scheme should be coherent, logical, and, in respect to its interpretation, applicable and adequate. Here "applicable" means that some items of experience are thus interpretable, and "adequate" means that there are no items incapable of such interpretation.

"Coherence," as here employed, means that the fundamental ideas, in terms of which the scheme is developed, presuppose each other so that in isolation they are meaningless. This requirement does not mean that they are definable in terms of each other; it means that what is indefinable in one such notion cannot be abstracted from its relevance to the other notions. It is the ideal of speculative philosophy that its fundamental notions shall not seem capable of abstraction from each other. In other words, it is presupposed that no entity can be conceived in complete abstraction from the system of the universe, and that it is the business of speculative philosophy to exhibit this truth. This character is its coherence.

The term "logical" has its ordinary meaning, including "logical" consistency, or lack of contradiction, the definition of constructs in logical terms, the exemplification of general logical notions in specific instances, and the principles of inference. It will be observed that logical notions must themselves find their places in the scheme of philosophic notions.

It will also be noticed that this ideal of speculative philosophy has its rational side and its empirical side. The rational side is expressed by the terms "coherent" and "logical." The empirical side is expressed by the terms "applicable" and "adequate." But the two sides are bound together by clearing away an ambiguity which remains in the previous explanation of the term "adequate." The adequacy of the scheme over every item does not mean adequacy over such items as happen to have been considered. It means that the texture of observed experience, as illustrating the philosophic scheme, is such that all related experience must exhibit the same texture. Thus the philosophic scheme should be "necessary," in the sense of bearing in itself its own warrant of universality throughout all experience, provided that we confine ourselves to that which communicates with immediate matter of fact. But what does not so communicate is unknowable, and the unknowable is unknown;* and so this universality defined by "communication" can suffice.

This doctrine of necessity in universality means that there is an essence to the universe which forbids relationships beyond itself, as a violation of its rationality. Speculative philosophy seeks that essence.

SECTION II

Philosophers can never hope finally to formulate these metaphysical first principles. Weakness of insight and deficiencies of language stand in the way inexorably. Words and phrases must be stretched towards a generality foreign to their ordinary usage; and however such elements of language be stabilized as technicalities, they remain metaphors mutely appealing for an imaginative leap.

There is no first principle which is in itself unknowable, not to be captured by a flash of insight. But, putting aside the difficulties of language, deficiency in imaginative penetration forbids progress in any form other than that of an asymptotic approach to a scheme of principles, only definable in terms of the ideal which they should satisfy.

The difficulty has its seat in the empirical side of philosophy. Our datum is the actual world, including ourselves; and this actual world spreads itself for observation in the guise of the topic of our immediate experience. The elucidation of immediate experience is the sole justification for any thought; and the starting point for thought is the analytic observation of components of this experience. But we are not conscious of any clear-cut complete analysis of immediate experience, in terms of the various details which comprise its definiteness. We habitually observe by the method of difference. Sometimes we see an elephant, and sometimes we do not. The result is that an elephant, when present, is noticed. Facility of observation depends on the fact that the object observed is important when present, and sometimes is absent.

The metaphysical first principles can never fail of exemplification. We can never catch the actual world taking a holiday from their sway. Thus, for the discovery of metaphysics, the method of pinning down thought to the strict systematization of detailed discrimination, already effected

* This doctrine is a paradox. Indulging in a species of false modesty, "cautious" philosophers undertake its definition.

by antecedent observation, breaks down. This collapse of the method of rigid empiricism is not confined to metaphysics. It occurs whenever we seek the larger generalities. In natural science this rigid method is the Baconian method of induction, a method which, if consistently pursued, would have left science where it found it. What Bacon omitted was the play of a free imagination, controlled by the requirements of coherence and logic. The true method of discovery is like the flight of an aeroplane. It starts from the ground of particular observation; it makes a flight in the thin air of imaginative generalization; and it again lands for renewed observation rendered acute by rational interpretation. The reason for the success of this method of imaginative rationalization is that, when the method of difference fails, factors which are constantly present may yet be observed under the influence of imaginative thought. Such thought supplies the differences which the direct observation lacks. It can even play with inconsistency; and can thus throw light on the consistent, and persistent, elements in experience by comparison with what in imagination is inconsistent with them. The negative judgment is the peak of mentality. But the conditions for the success of imaginative construction must be rigidly adhered to. In the first place, this construction must have its origin in the generalization of particular factors discerned in particular topics of human interest; for example, in physics, or in physiology, or in psychology, or in aesthetics, or in ethical beliefs, or in sociology, or in languages conceived as storehouses of human experience. In this way the prime requisite, that anyhow there shall be some important application, is secured. The success of the imaginative experiment is always to be tested by the applicability of its results beyond the restricted locus from which it originated. In default of such extended application, a generalization started from physics, for example, remains merely an alternative expression of notions applicable to physics. The partially successful philosophic generalization will, if derived from physics, find applications in fields of experience beyond physics. It will enlighten observation in those remote fields, so that general principles can be discerned as in process of illustration, which in the absence of the imaginative generalization are obscured by their persistent exemplification.

Thus the first requisite is to proceed by the method of generalization so that certainly there is some application; and the test of some success is application beyond the immediate origin. In other words, some synoptic vision has been gained.

In this description of philosophic method, the term "philosophic generalization" has meant "the utilization of specific notions, applying to a restricted group of facts, for the divination of the generic notions which apply to all facts."

In its use of this method natural science has shown a curious mixture of rationalism and irrationalism. Its prevalent tone of thought has been ardently rationalistic within its own borders, and dogmatically irrational beyond those borders. In practice such an attitude tends to become a dogmatic denial that there are any factors in the world not fully expressible in terms of its own primary notions devoid of further generalization. Such a denial is the self-denial of thought.

The second condition for the success of imaginative construction is unflinching pursuit of the two rationalistic ideals, coherence and logical perfection.

Logical perfection does not here require any detailed explanation. An example of its importance is afforded by the rôle of mathematics in the restricted field of natural science. The history of mathematics exhibits the generalization of special notions observed in particular instances. In any branches of mathematics, the notions presuppose each other. It is a remarkable characteristic of the history of thought that branches of mathematics developed under the pure imaginative impulse, thus controlled, finally receive their important application. Time may be wanted. Conic sections had to wait for eighteen hundred years. In more recent years, the theory of probability, the theory of tensors, the theory of matrices are cases in point.

The requirement of coherence is the great preservative of rationalistic sanity. But the validity of its criticism is not always admitted. If we consider philosophical controversies, we shall find that disputants tend to require coherence from their adversaries, and to grant dispensations to themselves. It has been remarked that a system of philosophy is never refuted; it is only abandoned. The reason is that logical contradictions, except as temporary slips of the mind—plentiful, though temporary—are the most gratuitous of errors; and usually they are trivial. Thus, after criticism, systems do not exhibit mere illogicalities. They suffer from inadequacy and incoherence. Failure to include some obvious elements of experience in the scope of the system is met by boldly denying the facts. Also while a philosophical system retains any charm of novelty, it enjoys a plenary indulgence for its failures in coherence. But after a system has acquired orthodoxy, and is taught with authority, it receives a sharper criticism. Its denials and its incoherences are found intolerable, and a reaction sets in.

Incoherence is the arbitrary disconnection of first principles. In modern philosophy Descartes' two kinds of substance, corporeal and mental, illustrate incoherence. There is, in Descartes' philosophy, no reason why there should not be a one-substance world, only corporeal, or a one-substance world, only mental. According to Descartes, a substantial individual "requires nothing but itself in order to exist." Thus this system makes a virtue of its incoherence. But on the other hand, the facts seem connected, while Descartes' system does not; for example, in the treatment of the body-mind problem. The Cartesian system obviously says something that is true. But its notions are too abstract to penetrate into the nature of things.

SECTION III

In its turn every philosophy will suffer a deposition. But the bundle of philosophic systems expresses a variety of general truths about the universe, awaiting co-ordination and assignment of their various spheres of validity. Such progress in co-ordination is provided by the advance of philosophy; and in this sense philosophy has advanced from Plato onwards. According to this account of the achievement of rationalism, the chief error in philosophy is overstatement. The aim at generalization is sound, but the estimate of success is exaggerated. There are two main forms of such overstatement. One form is what I have termed elsewhere* the "fallacy of misplaced concreteness." This fallacy consists in neglecting the degree of abstraction involved when an actual entity is considered merely so far as it exemplifies certain categories of thought. There are aspects of actualities which are simply ignored so long as we restrict thought to these categories. Thus the success of a philosophy is to be measured by its comparative avoidance of this fallacy, when thought is restricted within its categories.

The other form of overstatement consists in a false estimate of logical procedure in respect to certainty, and in respect to premises. Philosophy has been haunted by the unfortunate notion that its method is dogmatically to indicate premises which are severally clear, distinct, and certain; and to erect upon those premises a deductive system of thought.

But the accurate expression of the final generalities is the goal of discussion and not its origin. Philosophy has been misled by the example of mathematics; and even in mathematics the statement of the ultimate logical principles is beset with difficulties, as yet insuperable.** The verification of a rationalistic scheme is to be sought in its general success, and not in the peculiar certainty, or initial clarity, of its first principles. In this connection the misuse of the *ex absurdo* argument has to be noted; much philosophical reasoning is vitiated by it. The only logical conclusion to be drawn, when a contradiction issues from a train of reasoning, is that at least one of the premises involved in the inference is false. It is rashly assumed without further question that the peccant premise can at once be located. In mathematics this assumption is often justified, and philosophers have been thereby misled. But in the absence of a well-defined categoreal scheme of entities, issuing in a satisfactory metaphysical system, every premise in a philosophical argument is under suspicion.

Philosophy will not regain its proper status until the gradual elaboration of categoreal schemes, definitely stated at each stage of progress, is

* Cf. *Science and the Modern World*, Ch. III.

** Cf. *Principia Mathematica*, by Bertrand Russell and A. N. Whitehead, Vol. I, Introduction and Introduction to the Second Edition. These introductory discussions are practically due to Russell, and in the second edition wholly so.

recognized as its proper objective. There may be rival schemes, inconsistent among themselves; each with its own merits and its own failures. It will then be the purpose of research to conciliate the differences. Metaphysical categories are not dogmatic statements of the obvious; they are tentative formulations of the ultimate generalities.

If we consider any scheme of philosophic categories as one complex assertion, and apply to it the logician's alternative, true or false, the answer must be that the scheme is false. The same answer must be given to a like question respecting the existing formulated principles of any science.

The scheme is true with unformulated qualifications, exceptions, limitations, and new interpretations in terms of more general notions. We do not yet know how to recast the scheme into a logical truth. But the scheme is a matrix from which true propositions applicable to particular circumstances can be derived. We can at present only trust our trained instincts as to the discrimination of the circumstances in respect to which the scheme is valid.

The use of such a matrix is to argue from it boldly and with rigid logic. The scheme should therefore be stated with the utmost precision and definiteness, to allow of such argumentation. The conclusion of the argument should then be confronted with circumstances to which it should apply.

The primary advantage thus gained is that experience is not interrogated with the benumbing repression of common sense. The observation acquires an enhanced penetration by reason of the expectation evoked by the conclusion of the argument. The outcome from this procedure takes one of three forms: (i) the conclusion may agree with the observed facts; (ii) the conclusion may exhibit general agreement, with disagreement in detail; (iii) the conclusion may be in complete disagreement with the facts.

In the first case, the facts are known with more adequacy and the applicability of the system to the world has been elucidated. In the second case, criticisms of the observation of the facts and of the details of the scheme are both required. The history of thought shows that false interpretations of observed facts enter into the records of their observation. Thus both theory, and received notions as to fact, are in doubt. In the third case a fundamental reorganization of theory is required either by way of limiting it to some special province, or by way of entire abandonment of its main categories of thought.

SECTION IV

The field of a special science is confined to one genus of facts, in the sense that no statements are made respecting facts which lie outside that genus. The very circumstance that a science has naturally arisen concerning a set of facts secures that facts of that type have definite relations among themselves which are very obvious to all mankind. The common obviousness of things arises when their explicit apprehension carries immediate importance for purposes of survival, or of enjoyment—that is to say, for purposes of "being" and of "well-being." Elements in human experience, singled out in this way, are those elements concerning which language is copious and, within its limits, precise. The special sciences, therefore, deal with topics which lie open to easy inspection and are readily expressed by words.

The study of philosophy is a voyage towards the larger generalities. For this reason in the infancy of science, when the main stress lay in the discovery of the most general ideas usefully applicable to the subject-matter in question, philosophy was not sharply distinguished from science. To this day, a new science with any substantial novelty in its notions is considered to be in some way peculiarly philosophical. In their later stages, apart from occasional disturbances, most sciences accept without question the general notions in terms of which they develop. The main stress is laid on the adjustment and the direct verification of more special statements. In such periods scientists repudiate philosophy; Newton, justly satisfied with his physical principles, disclaimed metaphysics.

The fate of Newtonian physics warns us that there is a development in scientific first principles, and that their original forms can only be saved by interpretations of meaning and limitations of their field of application—interpretations and limitations unsuspected during the first period of successful employment. One chapter in the history of culture is concerned with the growth of generalities. In such a chapter it is seen that the older generalities, like the older hills, are worn down and diminished in height, surpassed by younger rivals.

Thus one aim of philosophy is to challenge the half-truths constituting the scientific first principles. The systematization of knowledge cannot be conducted in watertight compartments. All general truths condition each other; and the limits of their application cannot be adequately defined apart from their correlation by yet wider generalities. The criticism of principles must chiefly take the form of determining the proper meanings to be assigned to the fundamental notions of the various sciences, when these notions are considered in respect to their status relatively to each other. The determination of this status requires a generality transcending any special subject-matter.

. . .

SECTION V

Every science must devise its own instruments. The tool required for philosophy is language. Thus philosophy redesigns language in the same way that, in a physical science, pre-existing appliances are redesigned. It is exactly at this point that the appeal to facts is a difficult operation. This appeal is not solely to the expression of the facts in current verbal statements. The adequacy of such sentences is the main question at issue. It is true that the general agreement of mankind as to experienced facts is best expressed in language. But the language of literature breaks down precisely at the task of expressing in explicit form the larger generalities—the very generalities which metaphysics seeks to express.

The point is that every proposition refers to a universe exhibiting some general systematic metaphysical character. Apart from this background, the separate entities which go to form the proposition, and the proposition as a whole, are without determinate character. Nothing has been defined, because every definite entity requires a systematic universe to supply its requisite status. Thus every proposition proposing a fact must, in its complete analysis, propose the general character of the universe required for that fact. There are no self-sustained facts, floating in nonentity. This doctrine, of the impossibility of tearing a proposition from its systematic context in the actual world, is a direct consequence of the fourth and the twentieth of the fundamental categoreal explanations which we shall be engaged in expanding and illustrating. A proposition can embody partial truth because it only demands a certain type of systematic environment, which is presupposed in its meaning. It does not refer to the universe in all its detail.

One practical aim of metaphysics is the accurate analysis of propositions; not merely of metaphysical propositions, but of quite ordinary propositions such as "There is beef for dinner today," and "Socrates is mortal." The one genus of facts which constitutes the field of some special science requires some common metaphysical presupposition respecting the universe. It is merely credulous to accept verbal phrases as adequate statements of propositions. The distinction between verbal phrases and complete propositions is one of the reasons why the logicians' rigid alternative, "true or false," is so largely irrelevant for the pursuit of knowledge.

. . .

For example, the word "Socrates," referring to the philosopher, in one sentence may stand for an entity presupposing a more closely defined background than the word "Socrates," with the same reference, in another sentence. The word "mortal" affords an analogous possibility. A precise language must await a completed metaphysical knowledge.

The technical language of philosophy represents attempts of various schools of thought to obtain explicit expression of general ideas presupposed by the facts of experience. It follows that any novelty in metaphysical doctrines exhibits some measure of disagreement with statements of the facts to be found in current philosophical literature. The extent of disagreement measures the extent of metaphysical divergence. It is, therefore, no valid criticism of one metaphysical school to point out that its doctrines do not follow from the verbal expression of the facts accepted by another school. The whole contention is that the doctrines in question supply a closer approach to fully expressed propositions.

SECTION VI

It has been an objection to speculative philosophy that it is overambitious. Rationalism, it is admitted, is the method by which advance is made within the limits of particular sciences. It is, however, held that this limited success must not encourage attempts to frame ambitious schemes expressive of the general nature of things.

One alleged justification of this criticism is ill-success: European thought is represented as littered with metaphysical systems, abandoned and unreconciled.

. . .

But the main objection, dating from the sixteenth century and receiving final expression from Francis Bacon, is the uselessness of philosophic speculation. The position taken by this objection is that we ought to describe detailed matter of fact, and elicit the laws with a generality strictly limited to the systematization of these described details. General interpretation, it is held, has no bearing upon this procedure; and thus any system of general interpretation, be it true or false, remains intrinsically barren. Unfortunately for this objection, there are no brute, self-contained matters of fact, capable of being understood apart from interpretation as an element in a system. Whenever we attempt to express the matter of immediate experience, we find that its understanding leads us beyond itself, to its contemporaries, to its past, to its future, and to the universals in terms of which its definiteness is exhibited. But such universals, by their very character of universality, embody the potentiality of other facts with variant types of definiteness. Thus the understanding of the immediate brute fact requires its metaphysical interpretation as an item in a world with some systematic relation to it. When thought comes upon the scene, it finds the interpretations as matters of practice. Philosophy does not initiate interpretations. Its search for a rationalistic scheme is the search for more adequate criticism, and for more adequate justification, of the interpretations which we perforce employ. Our habitual experience is a complex of failure and success in the enterprise of interpretation. If we desire a record of uninterpreted experience, we must ask a stone to record its autobiography. Every scientific memoir in its record of the "facts" is shot through and through with interpretation. The methodology of rational interpretation is the product of the fitful vagueness of consciousness. Elements which shine with immediate distinctness, in some circumstances, retire into penumbral shadow in other circumstanses, and into black darkness on other occasions. And yet all occasions proclaim themselves as actualities within the flux of a solid world, demanding a unity of interpretation.

Philosophy frees itself from the taint of ineffectiveness by its close relations with religion and with science, natural and sociological. It attains its chief importance by fusing the two, namely, religion and science, into one rational scheme of thought. Religion should connect the rational generality of philosophy with the emotions and purposes springing out of existence in a particular society, in a particular epoch, and conditioned by particular antecedents. Religion is the translation of general ideas into particular thoughts, particular emotions, and particular purposes; it is directed to the end of stretching individual interest beyond its self-defeating particularity. Philosophy finds religion, and modifies it; and conversely religion is among the data of experience which philosophy must weave into its own scheme. Religion is an ultimate craving to infuse into the insistent particularity of emotion that non-temporal generality which primarily belongs to conceptual thought alone. In the higher organisms the differences of tempo between the mere emotions and the conceptual experiences produce a life-tedium, unless this supreme fusion has been effected. The two sides of the organism require a reconciliation in which emotional experiences illustrate a conceptual justification, and conceptual experiences find an emotional illustration.

OBJECTIONS TO METAPHYSICS

F. H. BRADLEY

The writer on metaphysics has a great deal against him. Engaged on a subject which more than others demands peace of spirit, even before he enters on the controversies of his own field, he finds himself involved in a sort of warfare. He is confronted by prejudices hostile to his study, and he is tempted to lean upon those prejudices, within him and around him, which seem contrary to the first. It is on the preconceptions adverse to metaphysics in general that I am going to make some remarks by way of introduction.

We may agree, perhaps, to understand by metaphysics an attempt to know reality as against mere appearance, or the study of first principles or ultimate truths, or again the effort to comprehend the universe, not simply piecemeal or by fragments, but somehow as a whole. Any such

Reprinted from *Appearance and Reality*, pp. 1–6, by permission of The Clarendon Press, Oxford.

pursuit will encounter a number of objections. It will have to hear that the knowledge which it desires to obtain is impossible altogether; or, if possible in some degree, is yet practically useless; or that, at all events, we can want nothing beyond the old philosophies. And I will say a few words on these arguments in their order.

(a) The man who is ready to prove that metaphysical knowledge is wholly impossible has no right here to any answer. He must be referred for conviction to the body of this treatise. And he can hardly refuse to go there, since he himself has, perhaps unknowingly, entered the arena. He is a brother metaphysician with a rival theory of first principles. And this is so plain that I must excuse myself from dwelling on the point. To say that reality is such that our knowledge cannot reach it, is a claim to know reality; to urge that our knowledge is of a kind which must fail to transcend appearance, itself implies that transcendence. For, if we had no idea of a beyond, we should assuredly not know how to talk about failure or success. And the test, by which we distinguish them, must obviously be some acquaintance with the nature of the goal. Nay, the would-be sceptic, who presses on us the contradictions of our thoughts, himself asserts dogmatically. For these contradictions might be ultimate and absolute truth, if the nature of the reality were not known to be otherwise. But this introduction is not the place to discuss a class of objections which are themselves, however unwillingly, metaphysical views, and which a little acquaintance with the subject commonly serves to dispel. So far as is necessary, they will be dealt with in their proper place; and I will therefore pass to the second main argument against metaphysics.

(b) It would be idle to deny that this possesses great force. "Metaphysical knowledge," it insists, "may be possible theoretically, and even actual, if you please, to a certain degree; but, for all that, it is practically no knowledge worth the name." And this objection may be rested on various grounds. I will state some of these, and will make the answers which appear to me to be sufficient.

The first reason for refusing to enter on our field is an appeal to the confusion and barrenness which prevail there. "The same problems," we hear it often, "the same disputes, the same sheer failure. Why not abandon it and come out? Is there nothing else more worth your labour?" To this I shall reply more fully soon, but will at present deny entirely that the problems have not altered. The assertion is about as true and about as false as would be a statement that human nature has not changed. And it seems indefensible when we consider that in history metaphysics has not only been acted on by the general development, but has also reacted. But, apart from historical questions, which are here not in place, I am inclined to take my stand on the admitted possibility. If the object is not impossible, and the adventure suits us—what then? Others far better than ourselves have wholly failed—so you say. But the man who succeeds is not apparently always the man of most merit, and even in philosophy's cold world perhaps some fortunes go by favour. One never knows until one tries.

But to the question, if seriously I expect to succeed, I must, of course, answer, No. I do not suppose, that is, that satisfactory knowledge is possible. How much we can ascertain about reality will be discussed in this book; but I may say at once that I expect a very partial satisfaction. I am so bold as to believe that we have a knowledge of the Absolute, certain and real, though I am sure that our comprehension is miserably incomplete. But I dissent emphatically from the conclusion that, because imperfect, it is worthless. And I must suggest to the objector that he should open his eyes and should consider human nature. Is it possible to abstain from thought about the universe? I do not mean merely that to every one the whole body of things must come in the gross, whether consciously or unconsciously, in a certain way. I mean that, by various causes, even the average man is compelled to wonder and to reflect. To him the world, and his share in it, is a natural object of thought, and seems likely to remain one. And so, when poetry, art, and religion have ceased wholly to interest, or when they show no longer any tendency to struggle with ultimate problems and to come to an understanding with them; when the sense of mystery and enchantment no longer draws the mind to wander aimlessly and to live it knows not what; when, in short, twilight has no charm—then metaphysics will be worthless. For the question (as things are now) is not whether we are to reflect and ponder on ultimate truth—for perhaps most of us do that, and are not likely to cease. The question is merely as to the way in which this should be done. And the claim of metaphysics is surely not unreasonable. Metaphysics takes its stand on this side of human nature, this desire to think about and comprehend reality. And it merely asserts that, if the attempt is to be made, it should be done as thoroughly as our nature permits. There is no claim on its part to supersede other functions of the human mind; but it protests that, if we are to think, we should sometimes try to think properly. And the opponent of metaphysics, it appears to me, is driven to a dilemma. He must either condemn all reflection on the essence of things,—and, if so, he breaks, or, rather, tries to break, with part of the highest side of human nature,—or else he allows us to think, but not to think strictly. He permits, that is to say, the exercise of thought so long as it is entangled with other functions of our being; but as soon as it attempts a pure development of its own, guided by the principles of its own distinctive working, he prohibits it forthwith. And this appears to be a paradox, since it seems equivalent to saying, You may satisfy your instinctive longing to reflect, so long as you do it in a way which is unsatisfactory. If your character is such that in you thought is satisfied by what does not, and cannot, pretend to be thought proper, that is quite legitimate. But if you are constituted otherwise, and if in you a more strict thinking is a want of your nature, that is by all means to be crushed out. And, speaking for myself, I must regard this as at once dogmatic and absurd.

But the reader, perhaps, may press me with a different objection. Admitting, he may say, that thought about reality is lawful, I still do not understand why, the results being what they are, you should judge it to be desirable. And I will try to answer this frankly. I certainly do not suppose that it would be good for every one to study metaphysics, and I cannot express any opinion as to the number of persons who should do so. But I think it quite necessary, even on the view that this study can produce no positive results, that it should still be pursued. There is, so far as I can see, no other certain way of protecting ourselves against dogmatic superstition. Our orthodox theology on the one side, and our commonplace materialism on the other side (it is natural to take these as prominent instances), vanish like ghosts before the daylight of free sceptical enquiry. I do not mean, of course, to condemn wholly either of these beliefs; but I am sure that either, when taken seriously, is the mutilation of our nature. Neither, as experience has amply shown, can now survive in the mind which has thought sincerely on first principles; and it seems desirable that there should be such a refuge for the man who burns to think consistently, and yet is too good to become a slave, either to stupid fanaticism or dishonest sophistry. That is one reason why I think that metaphysics, even if it end in total scepticism, should be studied by a certain number of persons.

And there is a further reason which, with myself perhaps, has even more weight. All of us, I presume, more or less, are led beyond the region of ordinary facts. Some in one way and some in others, we seem to touch and have communion with what is beyond the visible world. In various manners we find something higher, which both supports and humbles, both chastens and transports us. And, with certain persons, the intellectual effort to understand the universe is a principal way of thus experiencing the Deity. No one, probably, who has not felt this, however differently he might describe it, has ever cared much for metaphysics. And, wherever it has been felt strongly, it has been its own justification. The man whose nature is such that by one path alone his chief desire will reach consummation, will try to find it on that path, whatever it may be, and whatever the world thinks of it; and, if he does not, he is contemptible. Self-sacrifice is too often the "great sacrifice" of trade, the giving cheap what is worth nothing. To know what one wants, and to scruple at no means that will get it, may be a harder self-surrender. And this appears to be another reason for some persons pursuing the study of ultimate truth.

(c) And that is why, lastly, existing philosophies cannot answer the purpose. For whether there is progress or not, at all events there is change; and the changed minds of each generation will require a difference in what has to satisfy their intellect. Hence there seems as much reason for new philosophy as there is for new poetry. In each case the fresh production is usually much inferior to something already in existence; and yet it answers a purpose if it appeals more personally to the reader. What is really worse may serve better to promote, in certain respects and in a certain generation, the exercise of our best functions. And that is why, so long as we alter, we shall always want, and shall always have new metaphysics.

I will end this introduction with a word of warning. I have been obliged to speak of philosophy as a satisfaction of what may be called the mystical side of our nature—a satisfaction which, by certain persons, cannot be as well procured otherwise. And I may have given the impression that I take the metaphysician to be initiated into something far higher than what the common herd possesses. Such a doctrine would rest on a most deplorable error, the superstition that the mere intellect is the highest side of our nature, and the false idea that in the intellectual world work done on higher subjects is for that reason higher work. Certainly the life of one man, in comparison with that of another, may be fuller of the Divine, or, again, may realize it with an intenser consciousness; but there is no calling or pursuit which is a private road to the Deity. And assuredly the way through speculation upon ultimate truths, though distinct and legitimate, is not superior to others. There is no sin, however prone to it the philosopher may be, which philosophy can justify so little as spiritual pride.

ELIMINATION OF METAPHYSICS

A. J. AYER

The traditional disputes of philosophers are, for the most part, as unwarranted as they are unfruitful. The surest way to end them is to establish beyond question what should be the purpose and method of a philosophical enquiry. And this is by no means so difficult a task as the history of philosophy would lead one to suppose. For if there are any questions which science leaves it to philosophy to answer, a straightforward process of elimination must lead to their discovery.

We may begin by criticising the metaphysical thesis that philosophy affords us knowledge of a reality transcending the world of science and common sense. Later on, when we come to define metaphysics and account for its existence, we shall find that it is possible to be a metaphysician without believing in a transcendent reality; for we shall see that many metaphysical utterances are due to the commission of logical errors, rather than to a conscious desire on the part of their authors to go beyond the limits of experience. But it is convenient for us to take the case of those who believe that it is possible to have knowledge of a transcendent reality as a starting-point for our discussion. The arguments which we use to refute them will subsequently be found to apply to the whole of metaphysics.

One way of attacking a metaphysician who claimed to have knowledge

From A. J. Ayer: *Language, Truth, and Logic,* Dover Publications, Inc., New York, 1946, and Victor Gollancz, Ltd., London. Reprinted through the permission of the publishers.

of a reality which transcended the phenomenal world would be to enquire from what premises his propositions were deduced. Must he not begin, as other men do, with the evidence of his senses? And if so, what valid process of reasoning can possibly lead him to the conception of a transcendent reality? Surely from empirical premises nothing whatsoever concerning the properties, or even the existence, of anything super-empirical can legitimately be inferred. But this objection would be met by a denial on the part of the metaphysician that his assertions were ultimately based on the evidence of his senses. He would say that he was endowed with a faculty of intellectual intuition which enabled him to know facts that could not be known through sense-experience. And even if it could be shown that he was relying on empirical premises, and that his venture into a non-empirical world was therefore logically unjustified, it would not follow that the assertions which he made concerning this non-empirical world could not be true. For the fact that a conclusion does not follow from its putative premise is not sufficient to show that it is false. Consequently one cannot overthrow a system of transcendent metaphysics merely by criticising the way in which it comes into being. What is required is rather a criticism of the nature of the actual statements which comprise it. And this is the line of argument which we shall, in fact, pursue. For we shall maintain that no statement which refers to a "reality" transcending the limits of all possible sense-experience can possibly have any literal significance; from which it must follow that the labours of those who have striven to describe such a reality have all been devoted to the production of nonsense.

It may be suggested that this is a proposition which has already been proved by Kant. But although Kant also condemned transcendent metaphysics, he did so on different grounds. For he said that the human understanding was so constituted that it lost itself in contradictions when it ventured out beyond the limits of possible experience and attempted to deal with things in themselves. And thus he made the impossibility of a transcendent metaphysic not, as we do, a matter of logic, but a matter of fact. He asserted, not that our minds could not conceivably have had the power of penetrating beyond the phenomenal world, but merely that they were in fact devoid of it. And this leads the critic to ask how, if it is possible to know only what lies within the bounds of sense-experience, the author can be justified in asserting that real things do exist beyond, and how he can tell what are the boundaries beyond which the human understanding may not venture, unless he succeeds in passing them himself. As Wittgenstein says, "in order to draw a limit to thinking, we should have to think both sides of this limit,"* a truth to which Bradley gives a special twist in maintaining that the man who is ready to prove that metaphysics is impossible is a brother metaphysician with a rival theory of his own.**

* *Tractatus Logico-Philosophicus*, Preface.
** Bradley, *Appearance and Reality*, 2d ed., p. 1.

Whatever force these objections may have against the Kantian doctrine, they have none whatsoever against the thesis that I am about to set forth. It cannot here be said that the author is himself overstepping the barrier he maintains to be impassable. For the fruitlessness of attempting to transcend the limits of possible sense-experience will be deduced, not from a psychological hypothesis concerning the actual constitution of the human mind, but from the rule which determines the literal significance of language. Our charge against the metaphysician is not that he attempts to employ the understanding in a field where it cannot profitably venture, but that he produces sentences which fail to conform to the conditions under which alone a sentence can be literally significant. Nor are we ourselves obliged to talk nonsense in order to show that all sentences of a certain type are necessarily devoid of literal significance. We need only formulate the criterion which enables us to test whether a sentence expresses a genuine proposition about a matter of fact, and then point out that the sentences under consideration fail to satisfy it. And this we shall now proceed to do. We shall first of all formulate the criterion in somewhat vague terms, and then give the explanations which are necessary to render it precise.

The criterion which we use to test the genuineness of apparent statements of fact is the criterion of verifiability. We say that a sentence is factually significant to any given person, if and only if, he knows how to verify the proposition which it purports to express—that is, if he knows what observations would lead him, under certain conditions, to accept the proposition as being true, or reject it as being false. If, on the other hand, the putative proposition is of such a character that the assumption of its truth, or falsehood, is consistent with any assumption whatsoever concerning the nature of his future experience, then, as far as he is concerned, it is, if not a tautology, a mere pseudo-proposition. The sentence expressing it may be emotionally significant to him; but it is not literally significant. And with regard to questions the procedure is the same. We enquire in every case what observations would lead us to answer the question, one way or the other; and, if none can be discovered, we must conclude that the sentence under consideration does not, as far as we are concerned, express a genuine question, however strongly its grammatical appearance may suggest that it does.

As the adoption of this procedure is an essential factor in the argument of this book, it needs to be examined in detail.

In the first place, it is necessary to draw a distinction between practical verifiability, and verifiability in principle. Plainly we all understand, in many cases believe, propositions which we have not in fact taken steps to verify. Many of these are propositions which we could verify if we took enough trouble. But there remain a number of significant propositions, concerning matters of fact, which we could not verify even if we chose; simply because we lack the practical means of placing ourselves in the situation where the relevant observations could be made. A simple and familiar example of such a proposition is the proposition that there are mountains on the farther side of the moon.* No rocket has yet been invented which would enable me to go and look at the farther side of the moon, so I am unable to decide the matter by actual observation. But I do know what observations would decide it for me, if, as is theoretically conceivable, I were once in a position to make them. And therefore I say that the proposition is verifiable in principle, if not in practice, and is accordingly significant. On the other hand, such a metaphysical pseudo-proposition as "the Absolute enters into, but is itself incapable of, evolution and progress,"** is not even in principle verifiable. For one cannot conceive of an observation which would enable one to determine whether the Absolute did, or did not, enter into evolution and progress. Of course it is possible that the author of such a remark is using English words in a way in which they are not commonly used by English-speaking people, and that he does, in fact, intend to assert something which could be empirically verified. But until he makes us understand how the proposition that he wishes to express would be verified, he fails to communicate anything to us. And if he admits, as I think the author of the remark in question would have admitted, that his words were not intended to express either a tautology or a proposition which was capable, at least in principle, of being verified, then it follows that he has made an utterance which has no literal significance even for himself.

A further distinction which we must make is the distinction between the "strong" and the "weak" sense of the term "verifiable." A proposition is said to be verifiable, in the strong sense of the term, if, and only if, its truth could be conclusively established in experience. But it is verifiable, in the weak sense, if it is possible for experience to render it probable. In which sense are we using the term when we say that a putative proposition is genuine only if it is verifiable?

It seems to me that if we adopt conclusive verifiability as our criterion of significance, as some positivists have proposed,† our argument will prove too much. Consider, for example, the case of general propositions of law—such propositions, namely, as "arsenic is poisonous"; "all men are mortal"; "a body tends to expand when it is heated." It is of the very nature of these propositions that their truth cannot be established with certainty by any finite series of observations. But if it is recognised that such general propositions of law are designed to cover an infinite number of cases, then it must be admitted that they cannot, even in principle, be verified conclusively. And then, if we adopt conclusive verifiability as our criterion of significance, we are logically obliged to treat these general propositions of law in the same fashion as we treat the statements of the metaphysician.

* This example has been used by Professor Schlick to illustrate the same point.

** A remark taken at random from *Appearance and Reality*, by F. H. Bradley.

† E.g., M. Schlick, "Positivismus und Realismus," *Erkenntnis*, vol. 1, 1930. F. Waismann, "Logische Analyse des Warscheinlichkeitsbegriffs," *Erkenntnis*, vol. I, 1930.

In face of this difficulty, some positivists* have adopted the heroic course of saying that these general propositions are indeed pieces of nonsense, albeit an essentially important type of nonsense. But here the introduction of the term "important" is simply an attempt to hedge. It serves only to mark the authors' recognition that their view is somewhat too paradoxical, without in any way removing the paradox. Besides, the difficulty is not confined to the case of general propositions of law, though it is there revealed most plainly. It is hardly less obvious in the case of propositions about the remote past. For it must surely be admitted that, however strong the evidence in favour of historical statements may be, their truth can never become more than highly probable. And to maintain that they also constituted an important, or unimportant, type of nonsense would be unplausible, to say the very least. Indeed, it will be our contention that no proposition, other than a tautology, can possibly be anything more than a probable hypothesis. And if this is correct, the principle that a sentence can be factually significant only if it expresses what is conclusively verifiable is self-stultifying as a criterion of significance. For it leads to the conclusion that it is impossible to make a significant statement of fact at all.

Nor can we accept the suggestion that a sentence should be allowed to be factually significant if, and only if, it expresses something which is definitely confutable by experience.** Those who adopt this course assume that, although no finite series of observations is ever sufficient to establish the truth of a hypothesis beyond all possibility of doubt, there are crucial cases in which a single observation, or series of observations, can definitely confute it. But, as we shall show later on, this assumption is false. A hypothesis cannot be conclusively confuted any more than it can be conclusively verified. For when we take the occurrence of certain observations as proof that a given hypothesis is false, we presuppose the existence of certain conditions. And though, in any given case, it may be extremely improbable that this assumption is false, it is not logically impossible. We shall see that there need be no self-contradiction in holding that some of the relevant circumstances are other than we have taken them to be, and consequently that the hypothesis has not really broken down. And if it is not the case that any hypothesis can be definitely confuted, we cannot hold that the genuineness of a proposition depends on the possibility of its definite confutation.

Accordingly, we fall back on the weaker sense of verification. We say that the question that must be asked about any putative statement of fact is not, Would any observations make its truth or falsehood logically certain? but simply, Would any observations be relevant to the determination of its truth or falsehood? And it is only if a negative answer is given to this second question that we conclude that the statement under consideration is nonsensical.

* E.g., M. Schlick, "Die Kausalität in der gegenwärtigen Physik," *Naturwissenschaft*, vol. 19, 1931.

** This has been proposed by Karl Popper in his *Logik der Forschung*.

To make our position clearer, we may formulate it in another way. Let us call a proposition which records an actual or possible observation an experiential proposition. Then we may say that it is the mark of a genuine factual proposition, not that it should be equivalent to an experiential proposition, or any finite number of experiential propositions, but simply that some experiential propositions can be deduced from it in conjunction with certain other premises without being deducible from those other premises alone.*

This criterion seems liberal enough. In contrast to the principle of conclusive verifiability, it clearly does not deny significance to general propositions or to propositions about the past. Let us see what kinds of assertion it rules out.

A good example of the kind of utterance that is condemned by our criterion as being not even false but nonsensical would be the assertion that the world of sense-experience was altogether unreal. It must, of course, be admitted that our senses do sometimes deceive us. We may, as the result of having certain sensations, expect certain other sensations to be obtainable which are, in fact, not obtainable. But, in all such cases, it is further sense-experience that informs us of the mistakes that arise out of sense-experience. We say that the senses sometimes deceive us, just because the expectations to which our sense-experiences give rise do not always accord with what we subsequently experience. That is, we rely on our senses to substantiate or confute the judgements which are based on our sensations. And therefore the fact that our perceptual judgements are sometimes found to be erroneous has not the slightest tendency to show that the world of sense-experience is unreal. And, indeed, it is plain that no conceivable observation, or series of observations, could have any tendency to show that the world revealed to us by sense-experience was unreal. Consequently, anyone who condemns the sensible world as a world of mere appearance, as opposed to reality, is saying something which, according to our criterion of significance, is literally nonsensical.

An example of a controversy which the application of our criterion obliges us to condemn as fictitious is provided by those who dispute concerning the number of substances that there are in the world. For it is admitted both by monists, who maintain that reality is one substance, and by pluralists, who maintain that reality is many, that it is impossible to imagine any empirical situation which would be relevant to the solution of their dispute. But if we are told that no possible observation could give any probability either to the assertion that reality was one substance or to the assertion that it was many, then we must conclude that neither assertion is significant. We shall see later on that there are genuine logical and empirical questions involved in the dispute between monists and pluralists. But the metaphysical question concerning "substance" is ruled out by our criterion as spurious.

A similar treatment must be accorded to the controversy between

* This is an over-simplified statement, which is not literally correct. I give what I believe to be the correct formulation in the Introduction.

realists and idealists, in its metaphysical aspect. A simple illustration, which I have made use of in a similar argument elsewhere,* will help to demonstrate this. Let us suppose that a picture is discovered and the suggestion made that it was painted by Goya. There is a definite procedure for dealing with such a question. The experts examine the picture to see in what way it resembles the accredited works of Goya, and to see if it bears any marks which are characteristic of a forgery; they look up contemporary records for evidence of the existence of such a picture, and so on. In the end, they may still disagree, but each one knows what empirical evidence would go to confirm or discredit his opinion. Suppose, now, that these men have studied philosophy, and some of them proceed to maintain that this picture is a set of ideas in the perceiver's mind, or in God's mind, others that it is objectively real. What possible experience could any of them have which would be relevant to the solution of this dispute one way or the other? In the ordinary sense of the term "real," in which it is opposed to "illusory," the reality of the picture is not in doubt. The disputants have satisfied themselves that the picture is real, in this sense, by obtaining a correlated series of sensations of sight and sensations of touch. Is there any similar process by which they could discover whether the picture was real, in the sense in which the term "real" is opposed to "ideal"? Clearly there is none. But, if that is so, the problem is fictitious according to our criterion. This does not mean that the realist-idealist controversy may be dismissed without further ado. For it can legitimately be regarded as a dispute concerning the analysis of existential propositions, and so as involving a logical problem which can be definitively solved. What we have just shown is that the question at issue between idealists and realists becomes fictitious when, as is often the case, it is given a metaphysical interpretation.

There is no need for us to give further examples of the operation of our criterion of significance. For our object is merely to show that philosophy, as a genuine branch of knowledge, must be distinguished from metaphysics. We are not now concerned with the historical question how much of what has traditionally passed for philosophy is actually metaphysical. We shall, however, point out later on that the majority of the "great philosophers" of the past were not essentially metaphysicians, and thus reassure those who would otherwise be prevented from adopting our criterion by considerations of piety.

As to the validity of the verification principle, in the form in which we have stated it, a demonstration will be given in the course of this book. For it will be shown that all propositions which have factual content are empirical hypotheses; and that the function of an empirical hypothesis is to provide a rule for the anticipation of experience. And this means that every empirical hypothesis must be relevant to some actual, or possible, experience, so that a statement which is not relevant to any experience is not an empirical hypothesis, and accordingly has no factual content. But this is precisely what the principle of verifiability asserts.

* Vide "Demonstration of the Impossibility of Metaphysics," *Mind*, 1934, p. 339.

It should be mentioned here that the fact that the utterances of the metaphysician are nonsensical does not follow simply from the fact that they are devoid of factual content. It follows from that fact, together with the fact that they are not *a priori* propositions. And in assuming that they are not *a priori* propositions, we are once again anticipating the conclusions of a later chapter in this book. For it will be shown there that *a priori* propositions, which have always been attractive to philosophers on account of their certainty, owe this certainty to the fact that they are tautologies. We may accordingly define a metaphysical sentence as a sentence which purports to express a genuine proposition, but does, in fact, express neither a tautology nor an empirical hypothesis. And as tautologies and empirical hypotheses form the entire class of significant propositions, we are justified in concluding that all metaphysical assertions are nonsensical. Our next task is to show how they come to be made.

The use of the term "substance," to which we have already referred, provides us with a good example of the way in which metaphysics mostly comes to be written. It happens to be the case that we cannot, in our language, refer to the sensible properties of a thing without introducing a word or phrase which appears to stand for the thing itself as opposed to anything which may be said about it. And, as a result of this, those who are infected by the primitive superstition that to every name a single real entity must correspond assume that it is necessary to distinguish logically between the thing itself and any, or all, of its sensible properties. And so they employ the term "substance" to refer to the thing itself. But from the fact that we happen to employ a single word to refer to a thing, and make that word the grammatical subject of the sentences in which we refer to the sensible appearances of the thing, it does not by any means follow that the thing itself is a "simple entity," or that it cannot be defined in terms of the totality of its appearances. It is true that in talking of "its" appearances we appear to distinguish the thing from the appearances, but that is simply an accident of linguistic usage. Logical analysis shows that what makes these "appearances" the "appearances of" the same thing is not their relationship to an entity other than themselves, but their relationship to one another. The metaphysician fails to see this because he is misled by a superficial grammatical feature of his language.

A simpler and clearer instance of the way in which a consideration of grammar leads to metaphysics is the case of the metaphysical concept of Being. The origin of our temptation to raise questions about Being, which no conceivable experience would enable us to answer, lies in the fact that, in our language, sentences which express existential propositions and sentences which express attributive propositions may be of the same grammatical form. For instance, the sentences "Martyrs exist" and "Martyrs suffer" both consist of a noun followed by an intransitive verb, and the fact that they have grammatically the same appearance leads one to assume that they are of the same logical type. It is seen that in the proposition "Martyrs suffer," the members of a certain species are credited with a certain attribute, and it is sometimes assumed that the same thing is true of such a proposition as "Martyrs exist." If this were actually the case, it would, indeed, be as legitimate to speculate about the Being of martyrs as it is to speculate about their suffering. But, as Kant pointed out,* existence is not an attribute. For, when we ascribe an attribute to a thing, we covertly assert that it exists: so that if existence were itself an attribute, it would follow that all positive existential propositions were tautologies, and all negative existential propositions self-contradictory; and this is not the case.** So that those who raise questions about Being which are based on the assumption that existence is an attribute are guilty of following grammar beyond the boundaries of sense.

A similar mistake has been made in connection with such propositions as "Unicorns are fictitious." Here again the fact that there is a superficial grammatical resemblance between the English sentences "Dogs are faithful" and "Unicorns are fictitious," and between the corresponding sentences in other languages, creates the assumption that they are of the same logical type. Dogs must exist in order to have the property of being faithful, and so it is held that unless unicorns in some way existed they could not have the property of being fictitious. But, as it is plainly self-contradictory to say that fictitious objects exist, the device is adopted of saying that they are real in some non-empirical sense—that they have a mode of real being which is different from the mode of being of existent things. But since there is no way of testing whether an object is real in this sense, as there is for testing whether it is real in the ordinary sense the assertion that fictitious objects have a special non-empirical mode of real being is devoid of all literal significance. It comes to be made as a result of the assumption that being fictitious is an attribute. And this is a fallacy of the same order as the fallacy of supposing that existence is an attribute, and it can be exposed in the same way.

In general, the postulation of real non-existent entities results from the superstition, just now referred to, that, to every word or phrase that can be the grammatical subject of a sentence, there must somewhere be a real entity corresponding. For as there is no place in the empirical world for many of these "entities," a special non-empirical world is invoked to house them. To this error must be attributed, not only the utterances of a Heidegger, who bases his metaphysics on the assumption that "Nothing" is a name which is used to denote something peculiarly mysterious,† but also the prevalence of such problems as those concerning the reality of propositions and universals whose senselessness, though less obvious, is no less complete.

* Vide *The Critique of Pure Reason,* "Transcendental Dialectic," Book II, chap. iii, section 4.

** This argument is well stated by John Wisdom, *Interpretation and Analysis,* pp. 62, 63.

† Vide *Was ist Metaphysik,* by Heidegger: criticised by Rudolf Carnap in his "Überwindung der Metaphysik durch logische Analyse der Sprache," *Erkenntnis,* vol. II, 1932.

These few examples afford a sufficient indication of the way in which most metaphysical assertions come to be formulated. They show how easy it is to write sentences which are literally nonsensical without seeing that they are nonsensical. And thus we see that the view that a number of the traditional "problems of philosophy" are metaphysical, and consequently fictitious, does not involve any incredible assumptions about the psychology of philosophers.

Among those who recognize that if philosophy is to be accounted a genuine branch of knowledge it must be defined in such a way as to distinguish it from metaphysics, it is fashionable to speak of the metaphysician as a kind of misplaced poet. As his statements have no literal meaning, they are not subject to any criteria of truth or falsehood: but they may still serve to express, or arouse, emotion, and thus be subject to ethical or æsthetic standards. And it is suggested that they may have considerable value, as means of moral inspiration, or even as works of art. In this way, an attempt is made to compensate the metaphysician for his extrusion from philosophy.*

PHILOSOPHY AND PSYCHOANALYSIS

JOHN WISDOM

I. PHILOSOPHICAL CONFLICT

Wittgenstein once said that he "holds no opinions in philosophy" and, again that he tries to remove "a feeling of puzzlement, to cure a sort of mental cramp." This emphasizes much more what evil philosophy removes than what good it brings. Nevertheless, all who have felt the old philosophical puzzles know the cramp Wittgenstein refers to. Indeed if one thinks of a philosopher one thinks of a man who talks like this, for example:

> We fancy we sometimes know what other creatures are thinking and how they are feeling. But all we really know is how they nod and smile at this, bark and frown at that. No reasoning from such information will justify a conclusion about how they think and feel; it won't even tell us that they think and feel at all, much less will it tell us what goes on in the souls behind their faces. True we can infer from the faces of clocks what goes on within. But that is different. For some of us have sometimes noted a clock's face and quickly

* For a discussion of this point, see also C. A. Mace, "Representation and Expression," *Analysis*, vol. I, no. 3; and "Metaphysics and Emotive Language," *Analysis*, vol. II, nos. 1 and 2.

Reprinted from *Philosophy and Psycho-analysis*, 1953, by permission of Basil Blackwell, Ltd.

looked within. None of us has ever noted a friend's face and then quickly looked within. Maybe we have looked within his body and found a decayed tooth or other sand in the transmission. But not in the happiest days have we ever viewed the landscapes he alone can view. And yet though it seems we *can't* know how others think and feel surely we often *do* know.

The trouble spreads. The philosopher soon finds himself saying:

Not only do I not know how or whether anything else thinks or feels but also I cannot really know what is happening in any place hidden from me, in the inside of a clock, for example, or beyond the horizon. I can open some clocks quickly but none quickly enough. On Tuesday at 2 P.M., I know only what is happening near me, within the walls of my room, in my own little ark. For what is happening far away on the waste of waters or in the roaring Strand, I am obliged to rely on doves and telephones. However fast I hurry to the place I'm always late. The dove brings a leaf perhaps, but by the time I reach the distant Spring the leaves are turning or it's full Summer. For, if not, it wasn't Spring but still Winter when I started. Finding fallen leaves in November I may say I was right when in April, in Germany, I thought it was Spring in England. But the fallen leaves are not the Spring of which I dreamed in April. That is now for ever in the past. Even that I don't really know, obliged as I am to rely for all knowledge of the past upon dead leaves, bones, stones, documents and the faded photos in the family album and my memory. Nor do I know the future. For even if I knew what had happened this wouldn't guarantee what will happen.

And now if I know nothing of the past and nothing of the future then all I seem to see and hear may have no more substance than a dream. For just as a phoenix is not a phoenix unless it renews itself in its own ashes so bread that comes down from Heaven isn't bread but manna, and a dagger that vanishes is not a dagger but an image.

Further, even if I knew the future and could with perfect propriety predict to all eternity the pattern of my sensations, would this give substance to the shadows in a mirror that mirrors nothing?

And yet, surely, I do know these things it seems I can't know? I do know that where there's smoke there's fire, that the stone I kick is real, that the friend who speaks with me is not a talking doll.

So spreads and swings the philosophic hesitation. Driven by a caricature of curiosity which is kept for ever hungry by an inexorable desire to be logically perfect and factually infallible the philosopher diminishes his claims to knowledge; agnosticism about the minds of others becomes agnosticism about all things but his own thought as he thinks it—in other words Solipsism. And Solipsism soon becomes Scepticism, the "claim" that we know nothing. For when the philosopher become Solipsist fancies himself about to reap the reward of his logical purity in perfect knowledge, limited indeed but invulnerable, just then the statement he had hoped to make dwindles to the senseless whimper of an elderly infant in the mansions of the dead.* I don't mean, of course, that all philosophers in the end become Sceptics and find peace in death. On the contrary, no philosopher becomes really a Sceptic; because if a man really feels what

* With apologies to Paul Nash. For fuller treatment see *Other Minds*, VII, John Wisdom.

the Sceptic says he feels then he is said to have "a sense of unreality" and is removed to a home. In fact the sceptical philosopher never succeeds in killing his primitive credulities which, as Hume says, reassert themselves the moment he takes up the affairs of life and ceases to murmur the incantations which generate his philosophic doubt. More than that, most philosophers refuse to be Sceptics even in their philosophic moments; these travellers on the road to Nothing mostly look back and would return whence they have come, but cannot. In this sad case, some talk of trans-sensual spheres glimpsed by a trans-sensual awareness, an apprehension of Reality mediated by, but not limited to, the sights and sounds, the headaches and the heartaches to which we seem confined; others, the Realists, pretend that nothing's happened, that everything's all right, that fine-spun argument can never shake the common sense they had and hold; others, the Phenomenalists, say that everything's all right because the ideal of knowledge of reality beyond appearance is only unattainable because it's unintelligible; others hurry agitatedly from one cult to another; others stand poised "betwixt a world destroyed and world restored," paralysed in the cramp of conflict.

We have come upon these people before—in other difficulties; indeed they are ourselves. And none of them is at ease. This comes out plainly in those who say they are not. But even those who have erected a temple for tranquility have often a hidden fear of its falling about their ears. The Transcendentalist must constantly defend himself against the Sceptic and even against the Realist, who are the more menacing because they are not only outside him but also within. The realist must keep forgetting the philosophic qualms which though crammed down into Tartarus are not dead—the confidence he professes is never what it was before he ate of the forbidden tree. The phenomenalist protests too much that there was no baby in the bath water he threw away. None of them is easy—or if he is, he shouldn't be. This last qualification reminds us of the incompleteness in the description of the proper philosopher as one who tries to cure uneasiness. He may set himself to disturb complacency. So may a psychoanalyst. We may recognize this without forgetting how much philosophy and analytic work by patient and analyst is conflict and the cure of it.

II. PHILOSOPHICAL AND OBSESSIONAL DOUBT

I have used words with a clinical flavour in the sketch of philosophers which I have just given because I want to bring out likenesses, connections, between states of philosophical stress and other states of stress arising from internal sources as opposed to states of stress arising from external sources. A general or a business man who has to decide what to do in a complicated situation may go over the many relevant considerations carefully and may do so many times. A judge considers carefully, even anxiously, the arguments of contending counsel. But the general, the business man and the judge may consider their problems very patiently and still be very different from the neurotic. The neurotic may discuss his problems—he may indeed—but he never means business; the discussion is not a means to action, to something other than itself; on the contrary, after a while we get the impression that in spite of his evident unhappiness and desire to come from hesitation to decision he also desires the discussion never to end and dreads its ending. Have you not quite often had this impression with philosophers?—philosophers other than ourselves, for we, of course, are never neurotic. I once discussed with a man in a mental hospital whether he should continue to starve himself and study the Scriptures or take more nourishment and lend a hand at home. He put the matter well and with an admirable impartiality, but some months later I learned that he had died in the hospital, still, I believe, unable to settle the issue. And we have all read of the man who cannot be sure that he has turned off the tap or the light. He must go again to make sure, and then perhaps he must go again because though he knows the light's turned off he yet can't *feel* sure. He is obsessed by a chronic doubt. Has he done what he ought about the light or the tap? Perhaps his doubt is less limited, perhaps he is constantly questioning himself as to whether he has done what he ought. Such a man will often want rules of life to save him from continual conflict. Or again, his doubt may be less a matter of whether he has done this or that, or what he ought, and more a doubt as to what is happening where he can't see. He has slammed his front door, he hasn't much time to catch his train, but still he turns back because he wants to feel perfectly sure that things are all right behind the door—to which fortunately he has a key. At least he has a key until, like a philosopher, he wishes to see behind the door without opening it. Instantly it becomes "a veil past which I cannot see" and in the darkness of the cave one cannot tell whether She smiles or frowns. If we are watching shadows on a wall and want to know whether the shadows are telling the truth about what is going on behind our backs we can turn our heads and look; we aren't like an infant who, helpless in his cradle, cannot turn his head and cries when his mother goes out of sight; nor like philosophers who perpetually feel they don't know what's going on behind their backs, and who, still like the child, dread to know, cling to their ignorance. God or the gods know what really is so, what goes on among "objective realities," but we know only what goes on among our own toys, copies of real things. The gods know but they never tell us anything, as James Forsyte continually complained when age now instead of youth confined him to his bed. The gods know but they tell us nothing—a conspiracy of silence among the arch-deceivers.

Yesterday a man just beginning philosophy told me that he had said to a friend: "Some philosophers don't believe in material things and I am now not sure that I do." His friend said, taking hold of the table, "You don't believe there's a table here? You're mad."

I said:

Your friend's right. There is something very odd about the situation when a philosopher says "I don't believe there's a table here" or "I doubt whether there's a table here." It's not that his question is odd, I mean it's not simply his uttering these words "I'm not sure whether there's a table here" which strikes us as odd. If when you are seeking water in the desert someone gazes at what looks like water in the distance and says "I doubt whether there's really water there," you don't think him absurd. But the philosopher says "I am not sure" while he's drinking the water; he says it when no one would, or when no one but a madman would, or when no one but a madman or a philosopher would. And then also he is queer in that he doesn't act, doesn't feel, doesn't anticipate the future in the way his words suggest. In this he is at once more and less queer than a madman. The madman says, perhaps, "I shouldn't open that door" and his eyes widen in almost furious terror. You say "Why not?" and continue to walk towards the door. He clutches your arm and says, softly, "There's a tiger in there." You say "Nonsense, I've only just been in the room. You don't suppose a furniture firm has just driven up outside, erected a ladder, and slipped a tiger in through the window, do you?" "Ah!" the madman says, "He hides" or "You can't see him."

This is the psychotic and he is different from the neurotic who says that he must make sure that he hasn't left the lights on but that, of course, it's all nonsense and that he really knows he has turned them off, or that he must make quite sure that his hands are quite clean although it is true he has only just washed them. The neurotic, we might say, doesn't believe what he says. Still he does go back at the risk of losing his train to make sure that the lights are off. The philosopher doesn't. His acts and feelings are even less in accordance with his words than are the acts and feelings of the neurotic. He, even more than the neurotic and much more than the psychotic, doesn't believe what he says, doesn't doubt when he says he's not sure. (Compare wishes when he says he doesn't, i.e. unconsciously wishes.) But if we say that the philosopher doesn't believe what he says, that he's only pretending to doubt, then we must remember that he's very different from someone who, wishing to deceive us, pretends. The philosopher isn't one who merely makes it seem to others that he is in doubt; he also seems to himself to doubt. In other words, although many of his acts and feelings are unsuitable to his words, some are suitable and, in particular, as he speaks he has much of the feeling characteristic of doubt. When he says "Perhaps it's all in my mind," he feels something of the relief or disappointment of one who fearing this, hoping that, says "Maybe it's all a dream."

But now what is it that makes philosophers go on in the way they do?

III. THE PHILOSOPHER IS DIFFERENT

There is a big difference between the philosopher and both the psychotic and the obsessional neurotic. It lies in the flow of justificatory talk, of rationalization, which the philosopher produces when asked why he takes the extraordinary line he does. It is true that both the psychotic and neurotic listen to reason and defend themselves. The philosopher defends himself more elaborately. But this is not the point. The point is, aren't his rationalizations reasons?

When we call justifying talk "rationalization" we hint that we are not impressed by it and do not expect others to be. But we are impressed by the philosopher's talk, it has a universal effect, reluctantly we are impressed by it. The trouble is that it doesn't impress us quite enough to make us satisfied with his conclusions while yet it impresses us; the reasons seem not quite good enough and not quite bad enough and—connected fact—it seems the same with the reasons for opposing conclusions. At the same time the position is not what it is in science or crime where some evidence lends probability to one hypothesis and other evidence lends probability to another and we may contentedly wait for more evidence to tip the scales. For the philosopher's proofs profess to be *proofs* or nothing. And yet, too, we cannot, as in mathematics or logic, bring the conflict to an end by finding the slip in one of the calculations which purport to demonstrate the conflicting conclusions. There's something queer about philosophical reasons and the reasoning goes on too long.

IV. FIRST AS TO THE QUEERNESS OF PHILOSOPHICAL REASONS AND CONFLICT

Contrast a logical conflict. Lately it was reported in the Press that a railway official upon being asked the cause of a recent run of accidents replied, "Well, the men are tired, the rolling stock a little the worse for wear, but it's not so much that as the working out of the law of averages." This explanation is based on the logical doctrine that the longer a die has been thrown without a six the more probable is a six on the next throw, and we may imagine someone who argues for this as follows: when a die is about to be thrown 100 times the probability of at least one six being thrown is very great, namely .999999988 approximately. It may happen, however, that no six has appeared in the first 25 throws. In such a case unless a six appears in the next 75 throws there will have been 100 throws without a six and this, as we have seen, is improbable to the degree .000000012. Therefore it is improbable to the degree .000000012 that no six will appear in the next 75 throws. Again, if it should happen that no six appears in the first 99 throws then unless a six appears in the next throw there will have been 100 throws without a six and this is improbable to the degree .000000012. Therefore it is then improbable to the degree .000000012 that there will not be a six on the next throw, while before the throws started this was not improbable but probable to the degree 5/6.

This reasoning may temporarily impress us but we soon reply: the probability of a six after a long run of anything but sixes is still one in six if we assume that the die is not loaded, while if we do not assume this the probability of a six, so far from having increased as you suggest, has decreased, for the long run of throws without a six suggests that there is something about the die which prevents its falling six uppermost. Your reasoning in favour of the increasing probability of a six is tempting but it's fallacious. When you say "It may happen that no six has appeared in the first 25 throws—in such a case, unless a six appears in the next 75 throws there will have been 100 throws without a six and this, as we have seen, is improbable to the degree .000000012"—do you mean that we have seen that given only that a die is about to be thrown 100 times then it is improbable to a degree .000000012 that there will be no sixes? or do you mean that we have seen that given that a die has been thrown 25 times without a six and that it will be thrown another 75 times, then it is improbable to a degree .000000012 that at the end there will have been no six thrown? The former is true, the latter is false. For given that a die has been thrown 25 times without a six and that it will be thrown another 75 times, the improbability that at the end of the 100 throws no six will have been thrown is the improbability of throwing a six in the next 75 throws, that is $1 - (\frac{5}{6})^{75}$.* And when 99 throws have been made and another is about to be made, the improbability of this series of 100 throws not including a six, is the improbability of not throwing a six in the next throw, that is 5/6.

Here the difficulty is cleared up; one proof is definitely mistaken and the mistake is found; the other proof is sound and the matter is settled. So much for the Monte Carlo fallacy.

It may seem a pity that philosophy cannot be conducted on these lines. But it cannot. A philosophical conflict is like a logical or arithmetical conflict. But it's different too. The peculiarity of philosophical conflicts has only lately been grasped. Philosophical theories such as "Matter (or Mind) does not exist" are neither theories nor theorems; they are what they sound like—paradoxes; and philosophical questions are not questions (scientific) nor problems (logic)—but are more like riddles such as

> Can one man do what another does? Surely he can. And yet surely it can't be that he can. For suppose A scratches his head. Then if B scratches his head he doesn't do what A does since it's not B's head but A's that A scratches. But if B scratches A's head then again he doesn't do what A does since A scratches his own head and B scratches someone else's.

But here drinks are served all round. For now nobody cares whether we say "No man can do what another man does," or say "If a man, A, scratches his head and a man, B, also scratches his, B's, head then each does what the other does," or say "If a man, A, scratches his head and a man, B, also scratches A's head then each does what the other does." And

* Neglecting the fact that the 25 throws without a six suggest slightly that the die is loaded. This, negligible in a small number of throws, is not negligible in a large number of throws. It is this, I think, and not the explanation offered in Keynes's *Probability*, p. 316, which is the main source of the Petersbourg Paradox.

now that nobody cares, the original paradox "No man can do what another does" cannot be mistaken for a theory about human powers like "No man can play billiards like Lindrum." And, what is more, now that everybody understands, now that everybody has explained his reasons, the doctrine "No man can do what another does" can no longer be mistaken for a theorem like "No man can draw isosceles triangles with the angles at the base unequal." In fact the paradox now appears as a paradox though in doing so it ceases to be one. For it now appears that one who says "No man can do what another does" cuts a caper and encourages us to do likewise, not pointlessly but in order to reveal a concealed curiosity, namely that one man does what another does only when he does something different. One who says "No man can do what another does" introduces a new logic to show up a hidden feature of the old, uses language oddly in order to show up an oddity in our usual use. And one who says "No man can know the mind of another as he does his own" or "No one can really know the mind of another" does the same sort of thing. His statement doesn't come out of experience in the way "No one can know what a Red man feels" comes out of experience; and it doesn't come out of ordinary language in the way "No one can know what a good poker player is thinking" or "No one can marry his widow's sister" does. It is not a statement of fact nor of logic. It comes out of language and out of experience—but in its own way—like "Tyger, tyger! burning bright." It comes from extraordinary experience of the ordinary calling for extraordinary use of ordinary language. And to burst this way the bonds of habitual modes of projection is no more extraordinary than a caricature, or a picture that is not a photograph.

The consequence is that paradoxes are not established by experiment and statistics and cannot be proved by conclusive-deductive reasoning. They can be supported by inconclusive-deductive reasoning. The reasoning cannot be conclusive for, if it were, then the opposite of the paradox could not also be supported, and if its opposite could not be supported it would not be a paradox. And the reasoning will not be effective unless it leads to or comes from a new apprehension of the familiar—without that it will be dead words, for after all tigers don't burn even in forests at night.

A paradox is a flag which declares a discovery—not a new continent nor a cure for pneumonia but a discovery in the familiar—but often it is also the Blue Peter of a new voyage. For often we don't properly understand a paradox until, beginning by regarding it literally, we have noted objections to it and held to it because of the reasons for it, and again noted objections and again held to it, and have come by this route to a state where we are no longer driven to assert it or to deny it. There's no short cut to this; for if *before* treating a paradox and its denial as incompatible and arguing for a win we say "No doubt there's much in both" this leaves us entirely vague as to what is in either. No—the journey to the new freedom is mostly long and arduous, the work of bringing to light and setting in order with respect to one another what drives us to accept, and what forces us to deny, a paradox, what makes it so fascinating, so attractive and so repugnant, may fairly take a long time. But it can take too long.

V. PHILOSOPHICAL DISPUTE CAN GO ON TOO LONG

It may fairly take a woman a long time to decide which of two men is the right one for her to marry and it may take a man a long time to decide which of two professions is the right one for him to take up. But again in each case it may take too long. At first as we review with our friend the many considerations that bear on the issue we accompany him with interest, later with patience, but at last with irritation. For in time we feel that the difficulty is no longer a matter of coming to know his own mind, but of making up his mind. He still represents himself as ignorant of what would suit him and in this way conceals his incapacity to choose. "Win or a place, win or a place" shout those who quote the possible investments, but still he hesitates. And why can't he decide? Not merely because the considerations are so balanced. There's often nothing to choose on looks, form, breeding, and price between one horse and another, but this doesn't prevent people deciding before the flags go down which one to back. No, his chronic indecision, whether it takes the form of enthusiastic oscillation or melancholy inactivity, is due to the fact that besides the reasons revealed in the course of talking the matter over there are others which remain hidden. Family disputes are often very interminable and often have an unpleasant sweetness because they are conducted wholly in terms of what is "right" or "reasonable" while each disputant knows that forces quite other than those mentioned are at work and often knows the other knows. It is not that the things mentioned, the things brought up in the discussion, are not at work but that other things unmentioned and unmentionable are also at work and being unmentioned do not work themselves out, so the disputes get their character—unpleasantly sweet and interminable.

The man I mentioned earlier who died in hospital discussing with himself an issue between altruism and the development of the true self, analysed himself in vain. Had he overweighted this? Had he neglected that? We struggle to pass from conflict into harmony, to find, as Aristotle said, the proper point between opposites. But unlike Aristotle we cannot face the prospect of choices without end and feel we must have rules to live by. To represent a difficult choice as ignorance of our duty in the situation we are in enables us to escape from facing the hidden sources of our hesitation. How much more can we escape into the wider inquiries of what acts, in general, are right and what, in general, makes good things good. Here we may wander for ever and when darkness begins to fall still build an altar to an unknown god.

When earlier I introduced the Monte Carlo fallacy I did so because I thought of it as one which arises purely from linguistic sources, as one which can be removed by turning the light on to linguistic confusion. And it is true that this trouble is more completely curable by linguistic treatment than are more philosophical troubles where the relevant facts of language form such a labyrinth that pressed in one quarter one may always take cover in another. But now it strikes me how very persistent and how very prevalent is even the simple Monte Carlo fallacy. One constantly hears people say "Ah! that was too good to last" or "When we were having all the fine weather I thought we should have to pay for it" or again, after a run of misadventures, "Something will turn up. The luck must turn." Of course, to expect specially bad weather after specially good is not irrational if records show that regularly soon after specially good weather specially bad weather comes. But so far as I know there are no such records and so far as the people who use this argument know there are no such records. What they rely upon is "the laws of chance working themselves out"; what they rely upon is their feeling that though they don't know what card Fate will next deal them they do know what pack she holds so that if till now there have been no aces there'll be a lot of them soon to make up. True, there are people who when all has gone well for a long time feel more confident than ever; *they* feel that this just shows that Fate is with them. But there are others who begin to feel that they've had more than they deserve and that Fate will soon remind them that they are mortals, Polycrates and Amasis. And this last feeling finds expression, "justification," rationalization, in talk about the laws of chance—confused talk because without the confusion it wouldn't express the way they feel. It's the same when things go badly; some fall into despair, others feel that they have been punished enough and that even the most implacable Fate will now be prepared to "give them a break." So it appears how even this very purely logical paradox is not purely logical. It is true that the reasoning which leads to it, though fallacious, is plausible, it impresses us, and it does so partly because we have not a very firm and adequate understanding of the use of our linguistic tools in many discussions about probabilities; *but it does so also because the resulting paradox suits many people and suits something in most of us.* Gambling has a peculiar and half-secret fascination for many people; so also for many has the most theoretical talk about probability and chance. I submit that though the logical or linguistic explanation of the Monte Carlo fallacy is very adequate we would have a still more adequate explanation were we able to bring out not only the features of language that make for the committing of that fallacy but also other causes hidden beneath the flow of talk. And *if this is true of the Monte Carlo fallacy it is much more true of the philosophical paradoxes.*

Chance and Necessity, Freedom and Deity, Mind and Matter, Space and Time—these words have in them the detachment of the intellect but also echoes from the heart, and the fascination of them is not confined to professional philosophers. I remember how years ago one night in the "Elephant" a gentleman who, it was plain, had already been there some time took me aside in order to explain to me something of the connection between Mind and Matter. The big words of metaphysics have an appeal which is wide and deep and old and we cannot fully understand and resolve the riddles they present without understanding that appeal. In this sketch of philosophers I have been hinting at this. I have been hinting at connections with what psycho-analysts try to bring into the light. True, philosophy has never been merely a psychogenic disorder nor is the new philosophical technique merely a therapy. There's a difference. Philosophers reason for and against their doctrines and in doing so show us not new things but old things anew. Nevertheless, having recognized how different is philosophy from therapy it is worth noticing the connections: (*a*) how philosophical discussion is the bringing out of latent opposing forces like arriving at a decision and not like learning what is behind a closed door or whether $235 \times 6 = 1420$; (*b*) how, often, when the reasoning is done we find that besides the latent linguistic sources there are others non-linguistic and much more hidden which subtly co-operate with the features of language to produce philosophies; (*c*) how, in consequence, a purely linguistic treatment of philosophical conflicts is often inadequate; (*d*) how the non-linguistic sources are the same as those that trouble us elsewhere in our lives so that the riddles written on the veil of appearance are indeed riddles of the Sphinx.

EXISTENTIALISM AND HUMAN DECISION

JEAN-PAUL SARTRE

. . . What is meant by the term *existentialism?*

Most people who use the word would be rather embarrassed if they had to explain it, since, now that the word is all the rage, even the work of a musician or painter is being called existentialist. A gossip columnist in *Clartés* signs himself *The Existentialist*, so that by this time the word has been so stretched and has taken on so broad a meaning, that it no longer means anything at all. It seems that for want of an advance-guard doctrine analogous to surrealism, the kind of people who are eager for scandal and flurry turn to this philosophy which in other respects does not at all serve their purposes in this sphere.

Actually, it is the least scandalous, the most austere of doctrines. It is intended strictly for specialists and philosophers. Yet it can be defined easily. What complicates matters is that there are two kinds of existen-

Reprinted from Sartre's *Existentialism and Human Emotions*, 1957, pp. 12–33, by permission of Philosophical Library, New York.

tialist; first, those who are Christian, among whom I would include Jaspers and Gabriel Marcel, both Catholic; and on the other hand the atheistic existentialists, among whom I class Heidegger, and then the French existentialists and myself. What they have in common is that they think that existence precedes essence, or, if you prefer, that subjectivity must be the starting point.

Just what does that mean? Let us consider some object that is manufactured, for example, a book or a paper-cutter: here is an object which has been made by an artisan whose inspiration came from a concept. He referred to the concept of what a paper-cutter is and likewise to a known method of production, which is part of the concept, something which is, by and large, a routine. Thus, the paper-cutter is at once an object produced in a certain way and, on the other hand, one having a specific use; and one can not postulate a man who produces a paper-cutter but does not know what it is used for. Therefore, let us say that, for the paper-cutter, essence—that is, the ensemble of both the production routines and the properties which enable it to be both produced and defined—precedes existence. Thus, the presence of the paper-cutter or book in front of me is determined. Therefore, we have here a technical view of the world whereby it can be said that production precedes existence.

When we conceive God as the Creator, He is generally thought of as a superior sort of artisan. Whatever doctrine we may be considering, whether one like that of Descartes or that of Leibnitz, we always grant that will more or less follows understanding or, at the very least, accompanies it, and that when God creates He knows exactly what He is creating. Thus, the concept of man in the mind of God is comparable to the concept of paper-cutter in the mind of the manufacturer, and, following certain techniques and a conception, God produces man, just as the artisan, following a definition and a technique, makes a paper-cutter. Thus, the individual man is the realization of a certain concept in the divine intelligence.

In the eighteenth century, the atheism of the *philosophes* discarded the idea of God, but not so much for the notion that essence precedes existence. To a certain extent, this idea is found everywhere; we find it in Diderot, in Voltaire, and even in Kant. Man has a human nature; this human nature, which is the concept of the human, is found in all men, which means that each man is a particular example of a universal concept, man. In Kant, the result of this universality is that the wild-man, the natural man, as well as the bourgeois, are circumscribed by the same definition and have the same basic qualities. Thus, here too the essence of man precedes the historical existence that we find in nature.

Atheistic existentialism, which I represent, is more coherent. It states that if God does not exist, there is at least one being in whom existence precedes essence, a being who exists before he can be defined by any concept, and that this being is man, or, as Heidegger says, human reality. What is meant here by saying that existence precedes essence? It means that, first of all, man exists, turns up, appears on the scene, and, only afterwards, defines himself. If man, as the existentialist conceives him, is indefinable, it is because at first he is nothing. Only afterward will he be something, and he himself will have made what he will be. Thus, there is no human nature, since there is no God to conceive it. Not only is man what he conceives himself to be, but he is also only what he wills himself to be after this thrust toward existence.

Man is nothing else but what he makes of himself. Such is the first principle of existentialism. It is also what is called subjectivity, the name we are labeled with when charges are brought against us. But what do we mean by this, if not that man has a greater dignity than a stone or table? For we mean that man first exists, that is, that man first of all is the being who hurls himself toward a future and who is conscious of imagining himself as being in the future. Man is at the start a plan which is aware of itself, rather than a patch of moss, a piece of garbage, or a cauliflower; nothing exists prior to this plan; there is nothing in heaven; man will be what he will have planned to be. Not what he will want to be. Because by the word "will" we generally mean a conscious decision, which is subsequent to what we have already made of ourselves. I may want to belong to a political party, write a book, get married; but all that is only a manifestation of an earlier, more spontaneous choice that is called "will." But if existence really does precede essence, man is responsible for what he is. Thus, existentialism's first move is to make every man aware of what he is and to make the full responsibility of his existence rest on him. And when we say that a man is responsible for himself, we do not only mean that he is responsible for his own individuality, but that he is responsible for all men.

The word subjectivism has two meanings, and our opponents play on the two. Subjectivism means, on the one hand, that an individual chooses and makes himself; and, on the other, that it is impossible for man to transcend human subjectivity. The second of these is the essential meaning of existentialism. When we say that man chooses his own self, we mean that every one of us does likewise; but we also mean by that that in making this choice he also chooses all men. In fact, in creating the man that we want to be, there is not a single one of our acts which does not at the same time create an image of man as we think he ought to be. To choose to be this or that is to affirm at the same time the value of what we choose, because we can never choose evil. We always choose the good, and nothing can be good for us without being good for all.

If, on the other hand, existence precedes essence, and if we grant that we exist and fashion our image at one and the same time, the image is valid for everybody and for our whole age. Thus, our responsibility is much greater than we might have supposed, because it involves all mankind. If I am a workingman and choose to join a Christian trade-union rather than be a communist, and if by being a member I want to show that the best thing for man is resignation, that the kingdom of man is not of this world, I am not only involving my own case—I want to be resigned for everyone. As a result, my action has involved all humanity. To take a more individual matter, if I want to marry, to have children; even if this marriage depends solely on my own circumstances or passion or wish, I am involving all humanity in monogamy and not merely myself. Therefore, I am responsible for myself and for everyone else. I am creating a certain image of man of my own choosing. In choosing myself, I choose man.

This helps us understand what the actual content is of such rather grandiloquent words as anguish, forlornness, despair. As you will see, it's all quite simple.

First, what is meant by anguish? The existentialists say at once that man is anguish. What that means is this: the man who involves himself and who realizes that he is not only the person he chooses to be, but also a lawmaker who is, at the same time, choosing all mankind as well as himself, can not help escape the feeling of his total and deep responsibility. Of course, there are many people who are not anxious; but we claim that they are hiding their anxiety, that they are fleeing from it. Certainly, many people believe that when they do something, they themselves are the only ones involved, and when someone says to them, "What if everyone acted that way?" they shrug their shoulders and answer, "Everyone doesn't act that way." But really, one should always ask himself, "What would happen if everybody looked at things that way?" There is no escaping this disturbing thought except by a kind of double-dealing. A man who lies and makes excuses for himself by saying "not everybody does that," is someone with an uneasy conscience, because the act of lying implies that a universal value is conferred upon the lie.

Anguish is evident even when it conceals itself. This is the anguish that Kierkegaard called the anguish of Abraham. You know the story: an angel has ordered Abraham to sacrifice his son; if it really were an angel who has come and said, "You are Abraham, you shall sacrifice your son," everything would be all right. But everyone might first wonder, "Is it really an angel, and am I really Abraham? What proof do I have?"

There was a madwoman who had hallucinations; someone used to speak to her on the telephone and give her orders. Her doctor asked her, "Who is it who talks to you?" She answered, "He says it's God." What proof did she really have that it was God? If an angel comes to me, what proof is there that it's an angel? And if I hear voices, what proof is there that they come from heaven and not from hell, or from the subconscious, or a pathological condition? What proves that they are addressed to me? What proof is there that I have been appointed to impose my choice and my conception of man on humanity? I'll never find any proof or sign to convince me of that. If a voice addresses me, it is always for me to decide that this is the angel's voice; if I consider that such an act is a good one, it is I who will choose to say that it is good rather than bad.

Now, I'm not being singled out as an Abraham, and yet at every moment I'm obliged to perform exemplary acts. For every man, everything happens as if all mankind had its eyes fixed on him and were guiding itself by what he does. And every man ought to say to himself, "Am I really the kind of man who has the right to act in such a way that humanity might guide itself by my actions?" And if he does not say that to himself, he is masking his anguish.

There is no question here of the kind of anguish which would lead to quietism, to inaction. It is a matter of a simple sort of anguish that anybody who has had responsibilities is familiar with. For example, when a military officer takes the responsibility for an attack and sends a certain number of men to death, he chooses to do so, and in the main he alone makes the choice. Doubtless, orders come from above, but they are too broad; he interprets them, and on this interpretation depend the lives of ten or fourteen or twenty men. In making a decision he can not help having a certain anguish. All leaders know this anguish. That doesn't keep them from acting; on the contrary, it is the very condition of their action. For it implies that they envisage a number of possibilities, and when they choose one, they realize that it has value only because it is chosen. We shall see that this kind of anguish, which is the kind that existentialism describes, is explained, in addition, by a direct responsibility to the other men whom it involves. It is not a curtain separating us from action, but is part of action itself.

When we speak of forlornness, a term Heidegger was fond of, we mean only that God does not exist and that we have to face all the consequences of this. The existentialist is strongly opposed to a certain kind of secular ethics which would like to abolish God with the least possible expense. About 1880, some French teachers tried to set up a secular ethics which went something like this: God is a useless and costly hypothesis; we are discarding it; but, meanwhile, in order for there to be an ethics, a society, a civilization, it is essential that certain values be taken seriously and that they be considered as having an *a priori* existence. It must be obligatory, *a priori*, to be honest, not to lie, not to beat your wife, to have children, etc., etc. So we're going to try a little device which will make it possible to show that values exist all the same, inscribed in a heaven of ideas, though otherwise God does not exist. In other words—and this, I believe, is the tendency of everything called reformism in France—nothing will be changed if God does not exist. We shall find ourselves with the same norms of honesty, progress, and humanism, and we shall have made of God an outdated hypothesis which will peacefully die off by itself.

The existentialist, on the contrary, thinks it very distressing that God does not exist, because all possibility of finding values in a heaven of ideas disappears along with Him; there can no longer be an *a priori* Good, since there is no infinite and perfect consciousness to think it. Nowhere is it written that the Good exists, that we must be honest, that we must not lie; because the fact is we are on a plane where there are only men. Dostoievsky said, "If God didn't exist, everything would be possible." That is the very starting point of existentialism. Indeed, everything is permissible if God does not exist, and as a result man is forlorn, because neither within him nor without does he find anything to cling to. He can't start making excuses for himself.

If existence really does precede essence, there is no explaining things away by reference to a fixed and given human nature. In other words, there is no determinism, man is free, man is freedom. On the other hand, if God does not exist, we find no values or commands to turn to which legitimize our conduct. So, in the bright realm of values, we have no excuse behind us, nor justification before us. We are alone, with no excuses.

That is the idea I shall try to convey when I say that man is condemned to be free. Condemned, because he did not create himself, yet, in other respects is free; because, once thrown into the world, he is responsible for everything he does. The existentialist does not believe in the power of passion. He will never agree that a sweeping passion is a ravaging torrent which fatally leads a man to certain acts and is therefore an excuse. He thinks that man is responsible for his passion.

The existentialist does not think that man is going to help himself by finding in the world some omen by which to orient himself. Because he thinks that man will interpret the omen to suit himself. Therefore, he thinks that man, with no support and no aid, is condemned every moment to invent man. Ponge, in a very fine article, has said, "Man is the future of man." That's exactly it. But if it is taken to mean that this future is recorded in heaven, that God sees it, then it is false, because it would really no longer be a future. If it is taken to mean that, whatever a man may be, there is a future to be forged, a virgin future before him, then this remark is sound. But then we are forlorn.

To give you an example which will enable you to understand forlornness better, I shall cite the case of one of my students who came to see me under the following circumstances: his father was on bad terms with his mother, and, moreover, was inclined to be a collaborationist; his older brother had been killed in the German offensive of 1940, and the young man, with somewhat immature but generous feelings, wanted to avenge him. His mother lived alone with him, very much upset by the half-treason of her husband and the death of her older son; the boy was her only consolation.

The boy was faced with the choice of leaving for England and joining the Free French Forces—that is, leaving his mother behind—or remaining with his mother and helping her to carry on. He was fully aware that the woman lived only for him and that his going-off—and perhaps his death—would plunge her into despair. He was also aware that every act that he did for his mother's sake was a sure thing, in the sense that it was helping her to carry on, whereas every effort he made toward going off and fighting was an uncertain move which might run aground and prove completely useless; for example, on his way to England he might, while passing through Spain, be detained indefinitely in a Spanish camp; he might reach England or Algiers and be stuck in an office at a desk job. As a result, he was faced with two very different kinds of action: one, concrete, immediate, but concerning only one individual; the other concerned an incomparably vaster group, a national collectivity, but for that very reason was dubious, and might be interrupted en route. And, at the same time, he was wavering between two kinds of ethics. On the one hand, an ethics of sympathy, of personal devotion; on the other, a broader ethics, but one whose efficacy was more dubious. He had to choose between the two.

Who could help him choose? Christian doctrine? No. Christian doctrine says, "Be charitable, love your neighbor, take the more rugged path, etc., etc." But which is the more rugged path? Whom should he love as a brother? The fighting man or his mother? Which does the greater good, the vague act of fighting in a group, or the concrete one of helping a particular human being to go on living? Who can decide *a priori?* Nobody. No book of ethics can tell him. The Kantian ethics says, "Never treat any person as a means, but as an end." Very well, if I stay with my mother, I'll treat her as an end and not as a means; but by virtue of this very fact, I'm running the risk of treating the people around me who are fighting, as means; and, conversely, if I go to join those who are fighting, I'll be treating them as an end, and, by doing that, I run the risk of treating my mother as a means.

If values are vague, and if they are always too broad for the concrete and specific case that we are considering, the only thing left for us is to trust our instincts. That's what this young man tried to do; and when I saw him, he said, "In the end, feeling is what counts. I ought to choose whichever pushes me in one direction. If I feel that I love my mother enough to sacrifice everything else for her—my desire for vengeance, for action, for adventure—then I'll stay with her. If, on the contrary, I feel that my love for my mother isn't enough, I'll leave."

But how is the value of a feeling determined? What gives his feeling for his mother value? Precisely the fact that he remained with her. I may say that I like so-and-so well enough to sacrifice a certain amount of money for him, but I may say so only if I've done it. I may say "I love my mother well enough to remain with her" if I have remained with her. The only way to determine the value of this affection is, precisely, to perform an act which confirms and defines it. But, since I require this affection to justify my act, I find myself caught in a vicious circle.

On the other hand, Gide has well said that a mock feeling and a true feeling are almost indistinguishable; to decide that I love my mother and will remain with her, or to remain with her by putting on an act, amount somewhat to the same thing. In other words, the feeling is formed by the acts one performs; so, I can not refer to it in order to act upon it. Which means that I can neither seek within myself the true condition which will impel me to act, nor apply to a system of ethics for concepts which will permit me to act. You will say, "At least, he did go to a teacher for advice." But if you seek advice from a priest, for example, you have chosen this priest; you already knew, more or less, just about what advice he was going to give you. In other words, choosing your adviser is involving yourself. The proof of this is that if you are a Christian, you will say, "Consult a priest." But some priests are collaborating, some are just marking time, some are resisting. Which to choose? If the young man chooses a priest who is resisting or collaborating, he has already decided on the kind of advice he's going to get. Therefore, in coming to see me he knew the answer I was going to give him, and I had only one answer to give: "You're free, choose, that is, invent." No general ethics can show you what is to be done; there are no omens in the world. The Catholics will reply, "But there are." Granted—but, in any case, I myself choose the meaning they have.

When I was a prisoner, I knew a rather remarkable young man who was a Jesuit. He had entered the Jesuit order in the following way: he had had a number of very bad breaks; in childhood, his father died, leaving him in poverty, and he was a scholarship student at a religious institution where he was constantly made to feel that he was being kept out of charity; then, he failed to get any of the honors and distinctions that children like; later on, at about eighteen, he bungled a love affair; finally at twenty-two, he failed in military training, a childish enough matter, but it was the last straw.

This young fellow might well have felt that he had botched everything. It was a sign of something, but of what? He might have taken refuge in bitterness or despair. But he very wisely looked upon all this as a sign that he was not made for secular triumphs, and that only the triumphs of religion, holiness, and faith were open to him. He saw the hand of God in all this, and so he entered the order. Who can help seeing that he alone decided what the sign meant?

Some other interpretation might have been drawn from this series of setbacks; for example, that he might have done better to turn carpenter or revolutionist. Therefore, he is fully responsible for the interpretation. Forlornness implies that we ourselves choose our being. Forlornness and anguish go together.

As for despair, the term has a very simple meaning. It means that we shall confine ourselves to reckoning only with what depends upon our will, or on the ensemble of probabilities which make our action possible. When we want something, we always have to reckon with probabilities. I may be counting on the arrival of a friend. The friend is coming by rail or street-car; this supposes that the train will arrive on schedule, or that the street-car will not jump the track. I am left in the realm of possibility; but possibilities are to be reckoned with only to the point where my action comports with the ensemble of these possibilities, and no further. The moment the possibilities I am considering are not rigorously involved by my action, I ought to disengage myself from them, because no God, no scheme, can adapt the world and its possibilities to my will. When Descartes said, "Conquer yourself rather than the world," he meant essentially the same thing.

The Marxists to whom I have spoken reply, "You can rely on the support of others in your action, which obviously has certain limits because you're not going to live forever. That means: rely on both what others are doing elsewhere to help you, in China, in Russia, and what they will do later on, after your death, to carry on the action and lead it to its fulfillment, which will be the revolution. You even *have* to rely upon that, otherwise you're immoral." I reply at once that I will always rely on fellow-fighters insofar as these comrades are involved with me in a common struggle, in the unity of a party or a group in which I can more or less make my weight felt; that is, one whose ranks I am in as a fighter and whose movements I am aware of at every moment. In such a situation, relying on the unity and will of the party is exactly like counting on the fact that the train will arrive on time or that the car won't jump the track. But, given that man is free and that there is no human nature for me to depend on, I can not count on men whom I do not know by relying on human goodness or man's concern for the good of society. I don't know what will become of the Russian revolution; I may make an example of it to the extent that at the present time it is apparent that the proletariat plays a part in Russia that it plays in no other nation. But I can't swear that this will inevitably lead to a triumph of the proletariat. I've got to limit myself to what I see.

Given that men are free and that tomorrow they will freely decide what man will be, I can not be sure that, after my death, fellow-fighters will carry on my work to bring it to its maximum perfection. Tomorrow, after my death, some men may decide to set up Fascism, and the others may be cowardly and muddled enough to let them do it. Fascism will then be the human reality, so much the worse for us.

Actually, things will be as man will have decided they are to be. Does that mean that I should abandon myself to quietism? No. First, I should involve myself; then, act on the old saw, "Nothing ventured, nothing gained." Nor does it mean that I shouldn't belong to a party, but rather that I shall have no illusions and shall do what I can. For example, suppose I ask myself, "Will socialization, as such, ever come about?" I know nothing about it. All I know is that I'm going to do everything in my power to bring it about. Beyond that, I can't count on anything. Quietism is the attitude of people who say, "Let others do what I can't do." The doctrine I am presenting is the very opposite of quietism, since it declares, "There is no reality except in action." Moreover, it goes further, since it adds, "Man is nothing else than his plan; he exists only to the extent that he fulfills himself; he is therefore nothing else than the ensemble of his acts, nothing else than his life."

According to this, we can understand why our doctrine horrifies certain people. Because often the only way they can bear their wretchedness is to think, "Circumstances have been against me. What I've been and done doesn't show my true worth. To be sure, I've had no great love, no great friendship, but that's because I haven't met a man or woman who was worthy. The books I've written haven't been very good because I haven't had the proper leisure. I haven't had children to devote myself to because I didn't find a man with whom I could have spent my life. So there remains within me, unused and quite viable, a host of propensities, inclinations, possibilities, that one wouldn't guess from the mere series of things I've done."

Now, for the existentialist there is really no love other than one which manifests itself in a person's being in love. There is no genius other than one which is expressed in works of art; the genius of Proust is the sum of Proust's works; the genius of Racine is his series of tragedies. Outside of that, there is nothing. Why say that Racine could have written another tragedy, when he didn't write it? A man is involved in life, leaves his impress on it, and outside of that there is nothing. To be sure, this may seem a harsh thought to someone whose life hasn't been a success. But, on the other hand, it prompts people to understand that reality alone is what counts, that dreams, expectations, and hopes warrant no more than to define a man as a disappointed dream, as miscarried hopes, as vain expectations. In other words, to define him negatively and not positively. However, when we say, "You are nothing else than your life," that does not imply that the artist will be judged solely on the basis of his works of art; a thousand other things will contribute toward summing him up. What we mean is that a man is nothing else than a series of undertakings, that he is the sum, the organization, the ensemble of the relationships which make up these undertakings.

Further Readings

Ayer, A. J., *The Concept of a Person and Other Essays,* Macmillan, London, 1963.

Ayer, A. J., "Demonstration of the Impossibility of Metaphysics," *Mind, 43* (1934).

Bergson, Henri, *An Introduction to Metaphysics,* Liberal Arts, New York, 1949.

Blanshard, Brand, *The Nature of Thought,* Macmillan, New York, 1940.

Blanshard, Brand, *Reason and Analysis,* Open Court, La Salle, Ill., 1962.

Bradley, F. H., *Appearance and Reality: A Metaphysical Essay,* Clarendon Press, Oxford, 1951.

Broad, C. D., "Critical and Speculative Philosophy," in J. H. Muirhead (ed.), *Contemporary British Philosophy,* Macmillan, New York, 1924.

Campbell, C. A., *On Selfhood and Godhood,* Allen & Unwin, London, 1957.

Carnap, Rudolf, "The Elimination of Metaphysics Through Logical Analysis of Language," in Ayer, *Logical Positivism,* Free Press, New York, 1959.

Carnap, Rudolf, *Philosophy and Logical Syntax,* Routledge & Kegan Paul, London, 1935.

Collingwood, R. G., *An Essay on Metaphysics,* Clarendon Press, Oxford, 1940.

De George, Richard T., *Classical and Contemporary Metaphysics,* Holt, Rinehart and Winston, New York, 1962.

Dewey, John, "The Subject Matter of Metaphysics," *Journal of Philosophy, 12* (1915).

Hampshire, S., *Thought and Action,* Chatto and Windus, London, 1959.

Heidegger, Martin, *Being and Time,* trans. J. Macquarrie and E. Robinson, Harper & Row, New York, 1962.

Heidegger, Martin, "What Is Metaphysics," *Existence and Being,* ed. W. Brock, Regnery, Chicago, 1949.

Husserl, Edmund, *The Idea of Phenomenology,* Martinus Nijhoff, Hague, 1964.

Husserl, Edmund, *The Paris Lectures,* Martinus Nijhoff, Hague, 1964.

Kant, Immanuel, *Prolegomena to Any Future Metaphysics,* trans. L. W. Beck, Bobbs-Merrill, New York, 1951.

Kennick, W. E., and M. Lazerowitz, (eds.), *Metaphysics: Readings and Reappraisals,* Prentice-Hall, Englewood Cliffs, N.J., 1966, see section 8, "The Nature of Metaphysics."

Lazerowitz, M., *The Structure of Metaphysics,* Routledge & Kegan Paul, London, 1955.

Maritain, Jacques, *A Preface to Metaphysics,* Sheed, London, 1948.

Passmore, J., *Philosophical Reasoning,* Scribner, New York, 1961.

Pears, D. F. (ed.), *The Nature of Metaphysics,* Macmillan, London, 1957.

Plantinga, Alvin, "An Existentialist's Ethics," *Review of Metaphysics, 12* (1958).

Ryle, G., *Philosophical Arguments,* Clarendon Press, Oxford, 1945.

Sartre, Jean-Paul, *Being and Nothingness,* Philosophical Library, New York, 1956.

Strawson, P. F., *Individuals: An Essay in Descriptive Metaphysics,* Methuen, London, 1959.

Taylor, Richard, *Metaphysics,* Prentice-Hall, Englewood Cliffs, N.J., 1963.

Waismann, F., "How I See Philosophy," *Contemporary British Philosophy,* ed. H. D. Lewis, 3rd series, Allen & Unwin, London, 1956.

Williams, B. A. O., "Metaphysical Argument," in Pears (ed.), *Nature of Metaphysics,* Macmillan, London, 1957.

Wisdom, John, "Metaphysics and Verification," *Mind, 47* (1938).

ALTERNATIVE TOPICS

1. DUALISMS

2. ANTI-DUALISMS

3. MATERIALISM AND IDEALISM

4. PHENOMENOLOGY AND EXISTENTIALISM

5. POSITIVISM AND LOGICAL EMPIRICISM

6. LANGUAGE AND PHILOSOPHY

7. PHILOSOPHIC METHOD

8. PHILOSOPHIC PROOFS

9. SCIENCE AND PHILOSOPHY

10. RELEVANCE OF SCIENCE TO SPECIAL PROBLEMS IN PHILOSOPHY

11. PHILOSOPHY OF HISTORY

12. VALUE AND OBLIGATION

13. EXPERIENCE

14. CONSCIOUSNESS

See Section II, "Personal Identity and Knowledge of Other Minds"

15. KNOWLEDGE

See Section II, "Personal Identity and Knowledge of Other Minds," and Section IV, "Explanation and Human Action"

16. SKEPTICISM

17. ANSWERS TO SKEPTICISM

18. RATIONALITY AND REASON

19. SUBSTANCE

20. EXISTENCE

21. CAUSALITY

22. FREEDOM

23. IMMORTALITY

24. GOD

INDEX